Bayou St. John
IN COLONIAL LOUISIANA

1699-1803

By: Edna B. Freiberg

Illustrations By: John Chase

First Printing
June, 1980

Library of Congress Cataloging in Publication Data

Freiberg, Edna B. 1917-
Bayou St. John in Colonial Louisiana, 1699-1803.

Bibliography

Includes index

SUMMARY: Traces the early history of Bayou St. John, which developed into an important transportation route and drainage facility for New Orleans and surrounding areas.

1. Saint John Bayou, La.—History. 2. New Orleans—History. 3. Louisiana—History-To 1803. (1. Saint John Bayou, La.—History. 2. New Orleans—History. 3. Louisiana—History-to 1803) I. Chase, John Churchill. II. Title.
F379.N56S333 976.3'35 80-13370

Printed by Harvey Press
3632 Desire Parkway, New Orleans, Louisiana 70126

Designed by Rose Leonhard

DEDICATION

To my mother,
Alma Moe Bottolfson
Deronda, Wisconsin
(1887-1969)

and

To my husband,
Harry A. Freiberg, Jr.
New Orleans, Louisiana

God's greatest gifts to me.

INTRODUCTION

Where is Bayou St. John? a visitor to the city might ask. A mile and a half northwest of where the Mississippi fronts the French Quarter one is abruptly introduced to the butt-end of the main body of the bayou—near Mercy Hospital, at the juncture of North Jefferson Davis Parkway and Lafitte Avenue.

From this point the stream—intermittently spanned by one railroad and ten roadway bridges, one dam-waterfall and a foot-bridge—winds east and north for three and a half miles to its mouth at Lake Pontchartrain.

Driving east from the city-end of Bayou St. John, North Jefferson Davis Parkway leads directly into Moss Street on the lakeside of Orleans Avenue. Curving with the bayou's west bank, Moss Street soon intersects with Carrollton Avenue—site of the ancient village of the Acolapissas. These Indians lived in Latania-thatched huts in this vicinity prior to the coming of the French in 1699.

Shortly after the arrival of the French, the Biloxi Indians occupied the abandoned huts for a period of years; and during early French occupation, several of the first settlers, entering the region through Bayou St. Jean, lived in the empty habitations temporarily until they could build on their assigned concessions.

Looking to the right on Carrollton Avenue, the Esplanade Avenue bridge may be seen within a block and a half, and across the street from the bridge is the entrance to City Park.

Lakeside of Esplanade, Carrollton Avenue curves northerly into Wisner Boulevard, which traces the west bank of Bayou St. John to Robert E. Lee Boulevard. Driving along Wisner Boulevard, the vast stretches of greenery and golf courses to the left constitute the fourteen-hundred-plus acreage of City Park—one of the largest municipal parks in this country. The history of this property alone would easily fill a volume.

North of Robert E. Lee Boulevard, Wisner Boulevard continues on as Beauregard Avenue to Lake Pontchartrain; and although the bayou is still to the right, one is not aware of it behind the high, wooded levee.

A short distance north of Robert E. Lee Boulevard, a visitor may be tempted to stop for a moment to inspect the old brick ruins of Fort St. John which had its beginnings in the early 1700's. An additional reward awaits those who climb the levee and stroll along its top to where the bayou meets the lake.

Returning to the original point of departure, near Mercy Hospital, there is an interesting alternative to the first leg of the bayou drive. Turning right, across the bridge at Orleans Avenue and North Jefferson Davis Parkway, another Moss Street will be encountered on the east bank of the bayou. Following the windings of the ancient stream on this side, many lovely, and some of the oldest, homes of this area may be seen between Orleans and Esplanade Avenues. *The earliest inhabitants of this region settled their plantation-concessions on this bend of Bayou St. Jean in 1708—ten years before New Orleans was founded.* The handsome dwellings at 924, 1300 and 1440 Moss Street date from the Spanish colonial period.

Near Bell Street on the bayou's east bank marks the beginning of the old Indian Portage Trail (later Bayou Road) by which the first travelers of this area reached the Mississippi River; and it was in this immediate vicinity that the Village and the Port of Bayou St. Jean were established during the first two decades of the 1700's.

Crossing Esplanade Avenue, one will be close to the old village of the Houma Indians southeast of the bridge. From 1706-1720 the neighborhood in the vicinity of Bayou Road and Gentilly Road, near today's St. Louis Cemetery III, was their home.

Continuing up to the next major cross street—DeSaix Boulevard—the impressive Louisiana State University Dental Hospital may be seen to the right. The road ends at this point. Turning left, over the DeSaix Boulevard bridge, will bring the driver back to Wisner Boulevard which continues, as before, to the lake.

Up to the end of Louisiana's colonial period (1803), the bayou had several branches. Four main water fingers converged on its city terminus from every sector of the Mississippi Crescent, draining their waters into the stream; and along both sides of its course to the lake, other bayous, streams, rivulets and coulees drained into Bayou St. John, inducing a kind of current or surface motion and a much clearer water content than what is observed today.

From 1795—in Spanish times—(when it was built) until the mid-1920s (when it was filled in), the Carondelet or Old Basin Canal connected the city-end of the bayou with the ramparts of the original town (French Quarter today) near Toulouse and Basin Streets. This canal ran along the approximate site of present-day Lafitte Avenue.

The spelling "bayou" didn't become popular until the beginning of the nineteenth century. According to an authority on place names of Indian origin, the word is not a corruption of the French "boyau," as has often been thought, but is rather an adaptation of the Choctaw or Mobilian "bayuk" or "bayouk."

The bayou has had many names. When the French were first introduced to it in 1699, the Indians called it Choupithatcha or Soupitcatcha from the Choctaw "shupik," (a garlike fish called a mudfish or grindle) and "hacha" (river). Another Indian variation was Bayouk Choupic or

Shupic, because these fish were found in its sluggish waters.

When the Village of New Orleans—now the Vieux Carré (Old Square) or French Quarter—was established on the Mississippi Crescent in 1718, the bayou was called Rivière d'Orleans by the settlers because of its proximity to the new settlement, despite the fact that eighteen year old French-Canadian Jean Baptiste LeMoyne, Sieur de Bienville (founder of New Orleans) had in 1699 named it Grand Bayou de St. Jean. Some say he named the bayou for himself; others maintain the stream was named in honor of his patron Saint Jean the Baptist. St. Jean is also the patron Saint of French Canada (Quebec), home of Bienville and Iberville—the LeMoyne brothers; and every June 24th, St. John's Day is celebrated there with bonfires and merrymaking.

From 1762 to 1802, when Louisiana was a province of Spain, the stream was labeled Bayu San Juan or Bayu del San Juan on their maps and charts. When the United States acquired Louisiana in 1803, the American stream became Bayou St. John.

Why a history about this bayou? During the earliest exploration of this region, boats or feet were the only means of transportation. The English who had established colonies on the east coast of the continent, made sporadic forays into this area via buffalo trails and Indian paths; but the French, who sought to settle their water-soaked-and-surrounded bailiwick, soon recognized the necessity of the other mode of travel. From the very beginning they realized the importance of the five and a half mile water-shortcut between the Mississippi River and the lake to the north called Pontchartrain.

Prior to 1699, it was through the lake route, the bayou, and over the portage that Canadian trappers, traders and adventurers commuted to continue their journey up the Mississippi—to other French colonies on the upper reaches of the river and to Canada. The Bayouk Shupic route (The Old Route) to the river was preferred to the one farther north—through the lakes and Bayouk Manchac (fourteen miles south of today's Baton Rouge)—which was navigable only during months of high flood waters in the Mississippi River.

For small oared boats, flatboats and schooners, the voyage from the earlier Gulf settlements of Biloxi and Mobile—through the Mississippi Sound, Lakes Borgne and Pontchartrain and up Bayou St. Jean—was much easier and shorter by seventy five miles, than sailing up the formidable Mississippi. There were small floating islands in the approaches to the river mouth which menaced vessels, and the various passes into the river kept filling up with mud, trees and refuse which hurtled down the tumultuous "Father of Waters." A courageous captain, tacking back and forth across the river, found the ascent, against the prevailing northern currents and winds, slow and laborious. From the mouth of the Mississippi, it could take up to thirty days to reach the site of New Orleans.

For one hundred and twenty five years—until the era of the steamboat in the 1820's—Bayou St. John was the welcome last leg of the lake route, by which people and things were transported to the crescent shores of the Mississippi to build the great City of New Orleans on the most elevated site in the immediate area. *The most important reason for founding New Orleans in its present location was the proximity of the settlement to Bayou St. Jean and the lake route.*

From the building of New Orleans' first habitations, Bayou St. Jean—in addition to its importance as a transportation route—has played a continuing role in the drainage of the city, and has provided the means for boating, fishing and swimming in a region where fun-loving folk have always diluted life's difficulties with active pleasure.

For those who like to live on water—from the Indian huts of prehistoric days to some of New Orleans' poshest residences today—the bayou has provided a beautiful water view. Strange as it may seem, in this waterlogged city (most of it below sea level), it is only on Bayou St. John that New Orleanians can enjoy a natural front-yard water scene.

This volume attempts to bring to the reader a feeling for life, as it was lived from day to day, during the colonial period—the kind of information one might glean from a daily newspaper today—the weather, what folks were raising on their arpents, inflation and the high cost of living, the racial situation (Black-White, Red-White, and Red, White and Black), the local warring and what foreign nations were up to that affected the colony. And life has never been complete without a little gossip—who was buying and selling, who was being born, married or passing from the scene, and who was fighting who in the courts of the time. Everything that happened to anybody was of vital interest to the citizens of early Louisiana, because of the limited entertainment, communication and travel opportunities of that era. There was no newspaper until 1794, but there was little need for one, since most of the limited citizenry could neither read nor write.

It might be thought by some that this history is unsympathetic because of its emphasis on the unhappy side of life in early Louisiana. Unfortunately, historians cannot report what isn't in the records. When the colonial governors wrote their superiors in Europe it wasn't to report how well everything was going—how pleasant, industrious and content the colonists were. Those weren't problems that demanded solving. Their letters detailed the difficulties, the obstacles to what the leaders were trying to achieve. Like publications of today, the good life wasn't newsworthy. A colonist got into the records of the time (court, etc.) if he disobeyed the authorities or engaged in some mischief. Luckily for those who are interested in finding out what life was like way back then, other details of every-day existence were sometimes included in these reports.

So often the tendency is to think of olden-times and the people of long ago as being superior to those of today. Human nature has changed very little over thousands of years; only the circumstances in which people operate are different. In fact, those who emigrated to Louisiane (and colonies all over the United States) were usually those who were seeking a better situation than the one from which they sought escape in the old country (Europe). In a few instances, old records mention that some of the first settlers of Louisiane were the very dregs of society. Dregs or not, it is amazing to the author, apprized of the difficult circumstances with which the settlers had to cope, that the colony survived at all. There must have been a good many decent, believing, honest, right-intentioned folk who cared enough to struggle through the impossible and who worked unbelievably hard to make colonial Louisiana a better place in which to live.

Edna B. Freiberg

ACKNOWLEDGMENTS

It all began in 1966 when Manolita (Mrs. Nathaniel J.) Chesnut invited me to speak on the History of Bayou St. John before the Louisiana Landmarks Society of which she was program chairman. A preparatory six-month skim (at Tulane University) on the history of the bayou, where we'd built our home in 1965, whetted my appetite for finding out everything I possibly could about the historic stream and its environs.

But where to begin? The New Orleans Public Library, of course, where City Librarian M. Eugene E. Wright and his staff assisted me in every way they could. Librarian Jean Jones was one of many who, with kindness and dedication, steered me through the delightful intricacies of the Louisiana Department.

The late A. Watson Chapman of the former Rare Books Department (now Special Collections) of Tulane University was one of those rare individuals who not only had discovered his natural niche, but loved to share what he had found with other seekers. How fortunate I am to have known him.

Mrs. Aline H. Morris, capable woman-in-charge of the Louisiana State Museum Library, and hard-working Rose Lambert introduced me to the translations of the colonial records and the many other treasures of the past enclosed in that quiet atmosphere.

For the theory of how the bayou began, my thanks to Dr. Ervin Otvos, who during our research relationship—by telephone and letter—held the position of Assistant Professor in the Earth Sciences Department of LSU-NO, and is now applying his considerable knowledge at the Gulf Coast Research Laboratory, Ocean Springs, Mississippi.

To my bayou neighbor Edmond E. Himel, Jr., my sincere thanks for steering me to various sources of information.

I am indebted to Judge Charles L. Rivet, who thoughtfully took the time to introduce me to the cooperative personnel of the Law Library of Louisiana and the Chief Clerk's Office of the Supreme Court of Louisiana.

For their encouragement in this work, I wish to thank the Honorable Joe W. Sanders, former Chief Justice of the Supreme Court of Louisiana and former Chief Justice Walter B. Hamlin. And for their cooperation—in an already overcrowded schedule—I am indebted to Harold A. Moise, former Chief Clerk, and Andrew J. Falcon, formerly with the Chief Clerk's office, for seeing that I procured the records I needed. And for Johnny's good black coffee (when I could still indulge), which he thoughtfully slipped onto my working area when the digging got heavy, a twinkle of appreciation.

I wish to thank Miss Harriet Lemann, head of the Law Library of Louisiana, and her warm kind assistant, Mrs. Michelena Panzeca (retired), who always enthusiastically searched out the slightest request for information.

In addition to the staffs of the Conveyance Office, the Notarial Archives, the Offices of City Park and the Orleans Levee Board, there are those away from New Orleans who deserve special thanks. Mrs. Joy Davis Eaton, Lands Administrator in the Land Office at Baton Rouge, was helpful in suggesting sources other than those I had gone there to study specifically.

Mr. Richard W. Stephenson, Head of the Reference and Bibliography Section of the Library of Congress, Washington, D. C. went beyond the usual bounds to assist me in finding what was personally interesting and useful in that vast body of accumulated knowledge.

To Mr. John Hebert of the Map Division of the Library of Congress, Alexandria, Virginia, my special thanks for his patience and resourcefulness in pulling out of the archives hundreds of maps of the Louisiana area. And for the same service in the Cartographic Archives of the National Archives, Washington, D. C., I appreciate the good will and energy of Messrs. Gary L. Morgan and Ronald E. Grimm.

And to my friend John Chase, I wish to express my sincere appreciation for his careful and interested collaboration over the past year in the preparation of the illustrations for this volume.

Since the researching and writing of this volume has coincided with my struggle against cancer, I would be less than grateful not to acknowledge the considerable effort expended by the following physicians who have kept me in working condition over the past several years: Dr. Allan M. Goldman, Clinical Professor of Medicine, Tulane Medical School; Irving A. Levin, M. D., Colon and Rectal Surgeon, New Orleans; Ernest Cohen, M.D., Surgeon, New Orleans; and George Richard Blumenschein, Associate Director, Education, Chief Breast Service, Associate Professor of Medicine, U.T., and the very able staff of the M. D. Anderson Hospital and Tumor Institute, Texas Medical Center of Houston, Texas.

A special warm thank-you to Mary Louise Devezin and Louise Moore, whose good care of our home over the past fourteen years has given me the time to research and write; and to artistic creator of coiffures, Gail Petrie, who every Tuesday morning lifted my enthusiasm, as well as my tresses, by listening with unflagging interest to the unfolding saga of Bayou St. John, my continuing friendship.

Of course, I wouldn't be telling the story except for the infinitely patient and loving support of my husband Harry A. Freiberg, Jr., who over the many years not only has kept my spirit from wavering disastrously, but who cheerfully assumed the dreary task of toting typewriters, dictating machines and other writing materials—by auto or airplane—to wherever I needed them, and assisted in the proof-reading of the final printed pages. Without his constant cooperation and encouragement it couldn't have happened.

I do not consider this to be the definitive history of Bayou St. John. Rather I look upon it as the beginning of a task that will go on and on. When private collections of past records become more available and when the Superior Council and Cabildo records and the Notarial Archives and Conveyance records are further translated by those knowledgeable in old French and Spanish, many additional facts will be uncovered, and information, now accepted on the limited basis of what we know, will be corrected and changed. May the search go on, and may future seekers derive as much satisfaction as I have from this initial effort.

Finally I wish to express my admiration for the thousands of hard-working women volunteers in New Orleans. Having, in pre-research days, spent twenty years as a volunteer with the Great Books Program, the Lyceum-Tulane Association, the Brandeis University Women's Auxiliary (especially the Study Groups), the Women's Committee of the New Orleans Philharmonic Symphony Orchestra and the Women's Volunteer Committee of the New Orleans Museum of Art, I know first hand the kind of dedication expended by these workers. For this reason, I would prefer that BAYOU ST. JOHN IN COLONIAL LOUISIANA be sold through women's organizations, with all profits from the book going to the various non-discriminating medical, cultural, charitable and church organizations of New Orleans—a city I love and in which I have so much enjoyed living.

Edna B. Freiberg

CONTENTS

Contents *(continued)*

Grand Bayou de St. Jean
IN FRENCH LOUISIANE
1699-1769

(Although Louisiane had legally become a Spanish province in 1762, it was not until 1769 that the Spanish authorities took over.)

Bayou St. John in Colonial Louisiana

Chapter I

THE BEGINNING OF BAYOU ST. JOHN

What is a bayou? Is it different from a river, creek or stream? Bayou St. John has been labeled all of these, but there is a difference. A bayou is a finger of a larger body of water, but, unlike a river, flows from, not into, the connecting waterbody. Bayous have little current of their own except that induced by connecting streams, heavy rainfall, wind or flooding; their waters rise, fall and flow back and forth according to the condition of the parent body.

Explorers have considered these fingers to be remnants of once independent streams, which through shifting strata or volcanic action became connected to larger bodies of water.[1] However, since there has been no volcanic action in the northern gulf region for the last sixty million years, and the fault theory has been depreciated by knowledgeable earth scientists, the beginnings of Bayou St. John must be sought elsewhere.[2]

Four to six hundred years ago, the bayou known as St. John evolved naturally in an area with a fascinating geological history, so a brief survey of the gradual building up of this region will add significantly to the reader's appreciation of the history of this important waterway.

Sixty million years ago the waters of the Gulf of Mexico licked the shores of Illinois, and earth scientists today refer to that ancient mid-continental water indentation as the "Mississippi Embayment." Large streams flowed into it, carrying silt, sand and clay which gradually filled the embayment with new land and pushed the waters of the gulf further and further south to about its present location.

Several thousand years ago, when the seas of the world flooded continental shores after the last glacial period, the gulf waters inundated coastal Louisiana, forming a broad bay that extended north from the gulf, and stretched from the north shore of Lake Pontchartrain to the high ground north and west of Lake Maurepas. Geologists today call this the "Pontchartrain Embayment."

Then about 3400 to 2500 B.C. a series of underwater sandbars formed along the southern part of the embayment, between today's city of Kenner, Louisiana and the southwestern corner of Mississippi, and as some of the bars slowly grew above sea level, they merged into a fifty-mile chain of shoals and low, narrow sand islands—similar to those offshore Mississippi and Alabama today. Open spaces in the chain allowed for easy exchange of water between the embayment and the gulf to the south; and around 2500 B.C. —when a delta of the ancient Mississippi began to intrude into the area of present-day New Orleans —silt, clay and branches of trees were swept by the river waters around and through the barrier-shoal chain, gradually raising the seafloor into a floodplain covered by lakes, marshes, swamps and occasional river channels.

Father Charlevoix, a French Catholic Priest who traveled early Louisiana, described this sedimentation process: "One tree coming down the river, roots or branches catching, stops a thousand others. Mud coming downstream acts as a cement and covers them by degrees. Every inundation brings a new layer. In ten years, at most, reeds and shrubs begin to grow on them."[3] In 1937 it was estimated that as many as 400,000 tons of silt were carried to the gulf annually by the Mississippi, enough to build an eight-square-mile area thirty feet high in one year.[4]

The layers of sediment compacted and the new land subsided, burying most of the previous sand ridges and islands under the river deposits. However, evidence of that ancient island chain is still to be seen north-northeast of Michoud (Little Oak, Big Oak and Pine "Islands"), at the Rigolets, and in southern Hancock County, Mississippi.

But as new delta land formed south of the Barrier Islands, former water connections between the Pontchartrain Embayment and the gulf were almost cut off, allowing less salt water and more fresh river water to reach the almost completely landlocked embayment, resulting in the formation of the lake we know as Pontchartrain about 800 B.C.

Then the Mississippi River changed channels, as it has done from time to time in the past, whenever its waters found an easier path to the gulf, and the sediment formerly brought downstream was greatly reduced. The river returned twice to the same area, however, leaving behind at each departure many additional feet of earth deposit which raised the surrounding land. Each flood over the riverbanks left a new carpet of sand, silt and clay, but the stretches immediately flanking the river channel retained most of the sediment overflow and slowly built up higher than the surrounding floodplains. These natural levees in southeastern Louisiana sometimes reached a width of over six miles and elevations of from ten to fifteen feet above sea level. It was on these natural levees that Indians traversed our region and built habitations prior to 1700. New Orleans itself started out on the wide east bank natural levee of our present Mississippi River, the channel of which is 1300 to 1800 years old. As late as a half century ago, almost all settlements, highways, plantations and farms of the Mississippi Delta Plain were located on these higher, dryer grounds.

Between approximately 600 B.C. and 1000 A.D. the last important distributary to cross our region cut off from the present Mississippi channel near today's Kenner. The winding outline of present main east-west highways in Metairie and Gentilly mark its original course: Metairie Road, City Park Avenue, and across Bayou St. John to the vicinity of Grand Route St. John, Gentilly Boulevard, Gentilly Road, Old Gentilly Road and Old Gentilly Highway. This distributary was only a fifth to a fourth as wide as that of the present Mississippi channel in New Orleans, and only in a few places did its natural levee reach a height of five to ten feet above sea level.

Between 1100 and 1400 A.D. substantial flow from the Mississippi into the distributary had almost ceased, at which time its levees had reached their maximum height and were the only east-west dry land route in the surrounding swamplands between the Mississippi River to the south and the low beaches of Lake Pontchartrain to the north. As active flow from the Mississippi slowed down, the distributary began to fill up with silt and sand, and gradually deteriorated into a stagnant bayou.

To the earliest inhabitants of this area the westerly portion of it was known as Bayou Chapitoulas (sometimes spelled Tchoupitoulas), because prior to 1700 an Indian tribe of that name had lived near the stream's confluence with the Mississippi. In the early 1700's, the bayou was renamed Metairie, because the stream and the trail flanking it ran from the metairie (farm) of French settlers, who established plantations at the Chapitoulas, to Bayou St. John. The remnants of Bayou Metairie either dried up or were filled in as the city expanded in the nineteenth century, but traces of the original bayou may still be found in Metairie Cemetery on the north side of City Park Avenue; and it has been theorized by some that the southwest segment of Bayou St. John—from Esplanade Avenue to North Jefferson Davis Parkway and Lafitte Avenue —may have originally been an extension of Bayou Chapitoulas.

The other part of the original distributary flowed east from Bayou St. John, and at its terminus split into a number of minor distributaries—

some flowing toward Lake Pontchartrain, others discharging into Lake Borgne in the southeast. As the flow of water decreased, the major portion of this part of the system came to be known as Bayou Sauvage. (The French word "sauvage," meaning savage, wild, untamed, was used by early French travelers when they referred to the Indian natives; therefore, Bayou Sauvage can be loosely translated, according to the intent of the time, as Bayou of the Indians or Indian Bayou as it was also called.) About 1718 the stream was renamed Bayou Gentilly commemorating the Paris suburban home of the Dreux brothers, early settlers along the waterway.

Maps of the late 1700's and early 1800's show that Bayou Metairie (or its extension called Bayou St. Jean) and Bayou Gentilly were connected by a short channel curving between the west side of today's Grand Route St. John and 1222 Moss Street.[5] The early, more primitive maps of the French period (circa 1730) show Bayou Laurier as a straight little stream between the Dugué and LaVigne plantations, whereas the more sophisticated maps of the later Spanish period show the little connecting bayou entirely on the Dugué plantation, curving from its eastern boundary and running contiguous to Bayou Road as it approached Gentilly Bayou. This connecting waterlink, called Bayou Laurier (Laureal) either dried up or was filled in during the nineteenth century.

The natural levees that built up on both sides of the flooding Metairie-Gentilly distributary came to be known in colonial times as the Metairie-Gentilly Ridge, on which the Village of Bayou St. Jean (as the French spelled it) and the suburb of Gentilly—earliest habitations and plantations of this region—were established.

Bayou St. John in its present form came into being four to six hundred years ago, after active flow into the Metairie-Gentilly distributary had stopped. There are various theories as to how it formed. The bayou proper may have begun as a continuation of Bayou Metairie. During that stream's active period, its floodwaters could have overtopped or cut into a low weak section of its own natural levee, and in their tumultuous northerly rush to Lake Pontchartrain carved the initial depression of Bayou St. John. Repetitive flooding through the breach would have deepened the initial trench into a sizable channel, and occasional tropical storm currents, surging south from Lake Pontchartrain, would have contributed to its further enlargement.

Or the bayou may have begun as a result of flooding from the Mississippi River. A thousand to thirteen hundred years ago—after the present Mississippi channel had become established—the river frequently over-

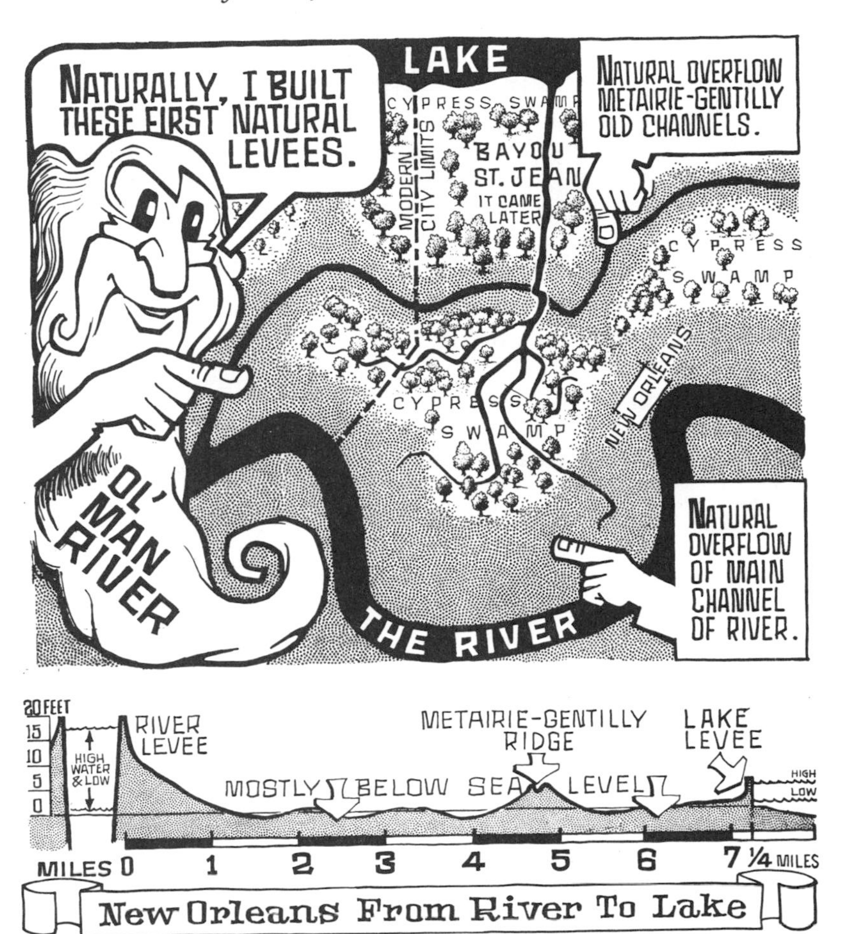

The two shaded areas indicate the natural levees built up by the Mississippi River overflow, and the Metairie-Gentilly Ridge built up by the overflow from the Metairie-Gentilly distributary. The smaller sketch at the bottom shows the land elevations between the Mississippi River and Lake Pontchartrain. The midway rise represents the Metairie-Gentilly Ridge which slowed the drainage flow from the river (the highest land) to the lake.

flowed, filling the low swampland between its own natural levee and the Metairie Ridge with huge, temporary, seasonal lakes.

The lake Bienville discovered in earliest French times, ballooning from one of the branches of Bayou St. John in today's Broadmoor area (Broadway to Toledano and Freret to a point where all the various tracts come to a point near Washington Avenue) was probably a remnant of those periodic bowlfuls that in earlier times stagnated between the

Mississippi and Metairie Ridge. Before improvement of the New Orleans drainage system in the early twentieth century, this twelve-square-block low-lying area flooded deeply during every heavy rainfall.[6]

In prehistoric times, an exceptionally high flood from the Mississippi could have overtopped a relatively low spot in the natural levee of Metairie Bayou near today's Museum of Art in City Park. As the Mississippi floodwaters swept northward to the lake, the low spot in the levee would have deepened with each subsequent flood, the waters cutting away at the breach until the breakthrough was gradually worn down to sea level. At this point the established channel of Bayou St. John would have begun carrying all the water it received north to the lake, even during lower water stages.

If the initial channel had already been established by a breakthrough of Bayou Metairie waters, the flooding Mississippi assisted in the deepening and enlarging of it; and as the crevasse wore down, the waters of the swampland between Bayou Metairie and the Mississippi levee began

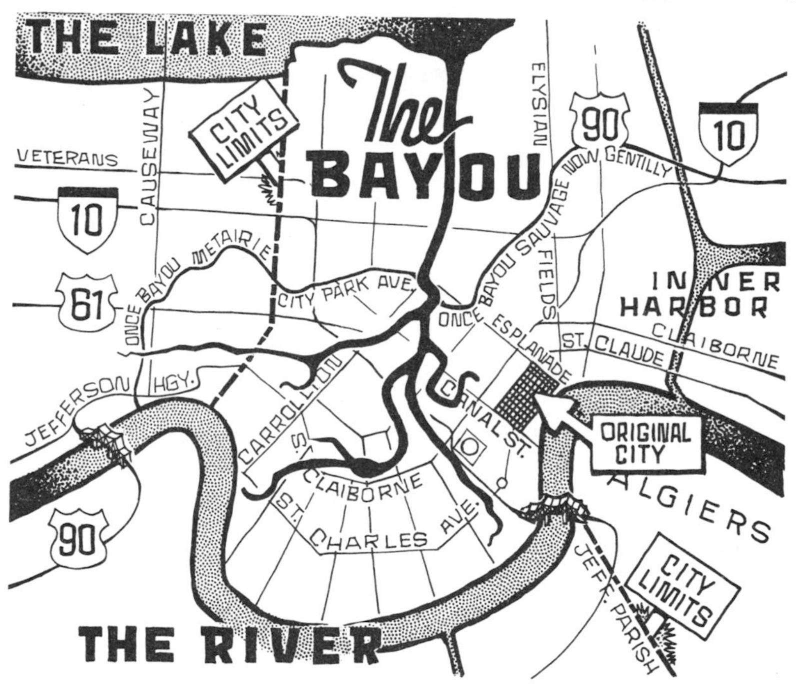

Four branches of Bayou St. Jean drew drainage from today's French Quarter, Uptown and the Carrollton areas to the main body of the bayou which began at today's North Jefferson Davis Parkway and Lafitte Avenue.

to drain toward this outlet into the original bed of Bayou St. John and on to the lake—not only during heavy floods, but also in times of lesser inundation. The surrounding lands remained swampy, but excessive water began to drain off much faster than it had before, eliminating the lakes that had once formed in the lowland bowl between the Mississippi and Metairie; and as these waters drained toward the Metairie crevasse, via the lowest lying land, they began to scour out the southwestern segment of today's Bayou St. John between Esplanade Avenue and Jefferson Davis Parkway and Lafitte Avenue. Minor tributaries and the four branches of Bayou St. John, seen on eighteenth century maps,[7] drew waters from today's French Quarter, Uptown and Carrollton into the developing continuation of the bayou, and over a number of years deepened and enlarged this segment of the stream to its present dimensions.

As the space-gobbling city expanded during the nineteenth century, the four minor branches of Bayou St. John, as well as the network of other small streams and rivulets lacing the area, either dried up or were filled in during the improvement of the New Orleans drainage system.

The theory of the geological origin of Bayou St. John is based on research by Dr. Ervin Otvos, former Assistant Professor in the Earth Sciences Department of Louisiana State University at New Orleans, now head of the Geological Division of the Gulf Coast Research Laboratory at Ocean Springs, Mississippi. Dr. Otvos is at present working on the geological evolution of the New Orleans-Southern Mississippi area, including the barrier ridges, and reminds the reader that radiocarbon dating, used by geologists, is correct only to within one hundred to four hundred years when dealing with periods of hundreds of years. As the time spans increase, so does the margin of error.

Chapter II

DISCOVERY OF THE BAYOU PORTAGE—1699

Long before the white man ever set foot on the soil of Louisiana, the Indian inhabitants had recognized the importance of Bayou St. John as the last leg of the shortest and safest route from the Gulf to the Mississippi River—the two main bodies of water in this area. In early times boats were the main way of getting around this water-logged region to make war, hunt or establish new habitations with better food and living conditions; and the Indians built light canoes of bark, covered with yellow pine pitch, which were strong and easily carried over the land connections between the various bodies of water.

Entering the mouth of the Mississippi and paddling upriver was probably rare in those days, because of the Indians' light craft. Certainly they didn't attempt it during the flood season when trees and other

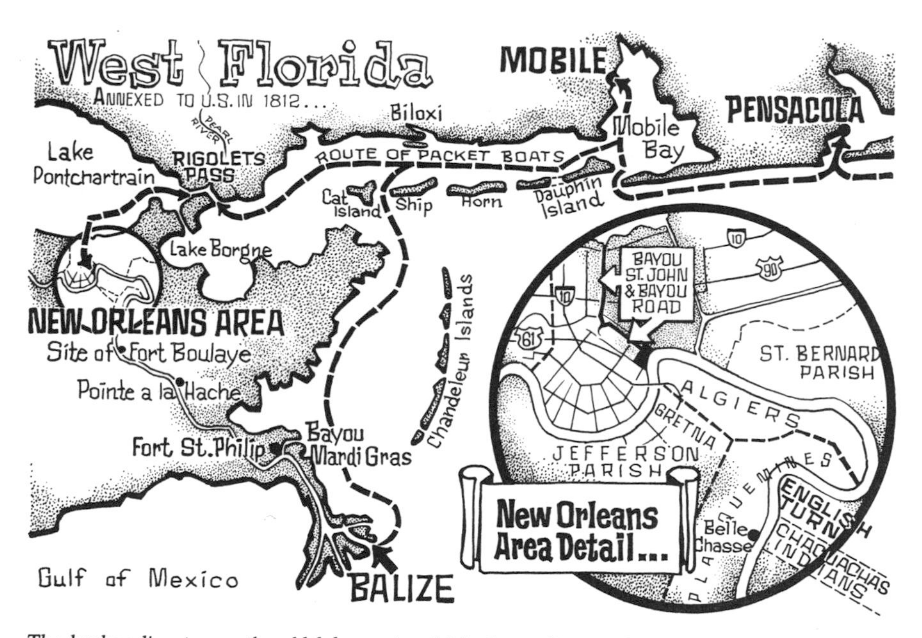

The broken line traces the old lake route which the earliest settlers traveled from Pensacola, Mobile and the Gulf Coast, through the lakes to Bayou St. Jean. A short portage (later Bayou Road) from Bayou St. Jean to the Mississippi completed the shortest and easiest way from the Gulf to the River.

refuse hurtled down the tumultuous Father of Waters. Against prevailing currents and winds from the north, ascent of the stream was slow, laborious, and seventy five miles longer than by the lake-bayou route.[1]

Traveling from places known today as Mobile and Biloxi on the Mississippi Gulf Coast, these early travelers went by way of the Mississippi Sound into Lake Borgne, from whence a channel called the Rigolets brought them into Lake Pontchartrain called "Okwata" (wide water) by the Redman. Skirting the southern coast of that lake, they entered Bayouk Choupic* or Shupik (Bayou Mudfish), and after five and a half miles of paddling that waterway they connected with a trail which they walked to the Michisipy (great river).

Bayou St. John was also called Choupithatcha or Soupitcatcha—a combination of the Choctaw "shupik" (the garlike mudfish) and "hacha" (river), and was so named from the mudfish the Indians enjoyed catching in the sluggish waters.[2]

Recorded history of our state began with the Spanish who made twenty five expeditions into the lower Mississippi Valley between 1513 and 1698, including water exploration of our gulf coast in 1519,[3] Hernando DeSoto's trek across the state in the early 1540s,[4] and Luis de Moscoso's trip down the Mississippi in 1543[5], past the river edge of the bayou portage where New Orleans would be built 175 years later. The Spanish, however, decided that Louisiana was no Peru, her resources not being negotiable on terms attractive to the telescoped desires and life spans of treasure-hungry soldier-adventurers, so the land was left to the Indians for another century and a half.

On April 9, 1682 French Robert Cavelier, Sieur de LaSalle descended the Mississippi from Quebec, (at which time the great stream was called the Colbert in honor of his King's minister), and claimed it and all the lands it drained for France. LaSalle's death on his second trip to the river in 1684-86, plus interminable foreign and domestic turmoil in France, delayed a French follow-up for sixteen years. However, news of Louisiana's virtues had gotten around, and many trapping, trading Frenchmen from Canada ventured down the Colbert, staying for short periods along its shores, near the river's mouth and along the gulf coast, but not being able to secure the necessities of life, the everchanging white population remained inconsequential.[6]

One of these early trader-explorers was M. de Remonville, who returning to the region from a trip to Illinois in 1697, seems to have been

---

*Bayou St. John wasn't the only stream called Bayouk Choupic. Apparently the Indians attached the name to other bayous in which the mudfish was found.

the recorded first to realize the value of establishing a trading post in the lake-bayou-portage area.[7] Remonville would continue to push the advantages of a post or settlement in this general location until the first work began on the settlement of New Orleans in 1718.

Meanwhile the Spanish, who were established in what we know as Mexico and South America, were watchfully aware of what was going on. If the French were to establish a trade route that would link their West Indies colony of St. Domingue with Canada, Spanish control of the Gulf would be split, and piratical raids on Spanish possessions could be expected; so on October 15, 1698 Spanish expeditions from Vera Cruz and Havana founded the colony of Pensacola.[8] Their worries were warranted, for by now King Louis XIV of France had solved some of his most pressing problems and had begun to think about the new world LaSalle had so glowingly represented at court some years before. The economic prospects of connecting his Canadian colony with St. Domingue, via the great river that flowed through the connecting continent into the Gulf of Mexico, were considerable; development of this territory might provide the means of paying his past-due bills and supporting his extravagant way of life.

And no better man could be found to start the ball a-rolling than French-Canadian Pierre LeMoyne, Sieur d'Iberville, the capable seaman-soldier who'd never been defeated in repeated encounters with the English on Hudson Bay. In 1698 he was chosen to head a party of French and Canadians, whose mission it was to find, identify and explore LaSalle's great river to the west, the control of which would decide who would dominate that vast unsettled central territory south of French Canada. Additionally, it was Iberville's responsibility to prevent ever-aggressive England (with established colonies on the east American coast) and Spain (with large holdings east, south and west of the Gulf of Mexico) from effecting a foothold in the middle Gulf region from which they could attack and destroy France's trade route to St. Domingue—trade that would within the next hundred years represent two-thirds of the entire commercial interest of France.[9]

Now according to traditional Orleanians, begins the real history of New Orleans and the bayou known as St. John—history engrained in the genes, and passed on from generation to generation of Creoles and their descendants.

Having landed on the Mississippi Gulf coast at a place they called Biloxi, (present-day Ocean Springs Beach Drive) Iberville took possession in the name of the King;[10] and after building a few rude huts on Ship

Island and observing preliminary protocol with the Indians in an effort to orient himself with respect to his objectives, he departed with fifty men in two packet boats on February 21, 1699 to seek the great river to the west. After a hazardous approach to the river's mouth, through wind, rain, thunder and the almost invisible island tufts dotting the ocean's surface, they passed through today's Breton Sound and entered North Pass, one of the several dangerous, tree-mud-cemented mouths of the Mississippi. To Iberville the entrance looked like rocks, no doubt accounting for the Indians' name for it—Malbouche (bad mouth).

A little upstream they camped for the night and baptized the bayou emptying into the Mississippi at that point "Pointe du Mardi Gras,"[11] thus celebrating the first of what was to become New Orleans' greatest holiday. An interested observer of the naming of the first place on future maps of the state of Louisiana was Iberville's younger brother, Jean Baptiste LeMoyne, Sieur de Bienville, whose life for better—but perhaps more often for worse—would be inextricably entwined with the region he was entering for the rest of his active life.

A few days upstream, on the river they had not as yet identified, the French sought information of their whereabouts from a party of Indians they espied along the riverbank. Fascinated by the white man's wares—beads, knives, awls, axes, looking glasses, small bells—beauty and utility beyond their wildest dreams—one of them, a Bayougoula, was persuaded by a gift of a hatchet to accompany them upstream to his settlement, where Iberville hoped to find evidence of LaSalle's visit which would confirm that this was the river he sought.[12]

Laboriously urging their boats upstream, on March 9, 1699 the expedition stopped for the night about thirty five leagues from the river's mouth. (According to various sources, a league of that time measured anywhere from 2.4 to 3 miles.) Iberville used this time to explore the surrounding countryside, and his Indian Guide led him six leagues above the camp site where he pointed out the river end of a portage path which he said led back to where the French had anchored their ships (Ship Island). In his journal Iberville noted that the Indians dragged their canoes over a fairly good path at this point, and that he saw several pieces of baggage belonging to people going both ways on the trail.[13]

It is questionable whether the Indians simply pointed out the trail and explained where it went, or whether Iberville traveled the trail to the bayou. Romantic historian Grace King has the small party carrying a package via pirogue on Bayou St. John to the lake, from whence they could see their ships in the distance.[14]

Whatever the extent of their introduction, this was the first time Iberville and Bienville saw the portage that led from the Mississippi to Bayou Choupic of the Indians—the bayou that in French times would be called St. Jean.

If one-way streets are favorable, that same route can be traveled today, from the river to the bayou. Beginning at Governor Nicholls and Decatur Street, near the Mississippi River, the ancient trail—traveled by Indians since time unknown, and by Canadian trappers and traders long before Iberville arrived—leads one down Governor Nicholls toward the lake. Through the French Quarter to North Claiborne (where Governor Nicholls becomes Bayou Road) the street then angles northeasterly, crossing Esplanade Avenue at North Miro, and a few blocks further on, Bayou Road intersects with Grand Route St. John. A sharp turn to the left on that street will, within three-quarters of a mile, bring the traveler to the shores of Bayou St. John at 1300 Moss Street.

The route of this old Indian portage trail, called Bayou Road in French times, has varied through the years. The original trail curved around trees and other natural obstacles, and the stretch leading away from the bayou, began west of today's Grand Route St. John—probably halfway between DeSoto and Bell Streets, as early French maps and American conveyance records of the area would indicate—and in 1777 the road was shifted northeasterly by twenty feet at the request of a bayou plantation owner who wanted his neighbor, across Bayou Road, to contribute half the road's width. The route leading away from the bayou today (Grand Route St. John) was no doubt established about 1810, when a new bridge was built two hundred yards lakeside of the previous structure, and when Daniel Clark developed Faubourg St. John in the first decade of the 1800s.[15]

The portion of the road running through the French Quarter was in French times located on St. Anne Street. Other maps fix the route on Dumaine Street; and a 1728 map in the Library of Congress makes them both right, because it shows Bayou Road branching at Bourbon Street—then the back of the settlement of New Orleans—and continuing on both St. Anne and Dumaine Streets to what would today be Rampart Street, where the branches again joined and continued on as Bayou road.[16]

In Spanish times, as the original city (today's French Quarter) stretched toward the esplanade, Hospital Street became the city segment of Bayou Road; and in the nineteenth century, after the War Between the States, Hospital was renamed Governor Nicholls, in honor of an outstanding Louisiana governor of that era.

Contemporary needs no longer require the water route afforded by Bayou St. John to Lake Pontchartrain. Several low-spanning bridges and a dam at Robert E. Lee Boulevard, near the lake, would today require too many short portages for comfortable pirogue passage. But proceeding from Lake Pontchartrain, the old lake route continues as before—easterly through the Rigolets or Chef Menteur to Lake Borgne, through the Mississippi Sound (between the Gulf coastline and Cat, Ship, Horn and Dauphin Islands) to the coastal communities of Bay St. Louis, Biloxi, Mobile and Pensacola.

If such ponderous perusal of a historic path is not to the reader's interest, a stroll down Decatur Street on the river edge of the French Quarter, will bring him to a historic plaque between St. Ann and St. Peter Streets which reads "New Orleans—sighted by Iberville and Bienville as Indian Portage* to lake and gulf, 1699."[17]

---

*As this book goes to print, researcher Benjamin F. Erlanger has discovered Lafon's Plan du Faubourg St. Jean, 1809, at the New Orleans Public Library (Louisiana Division). The map clearly marks the location of the new bridge (1809-1810) at Grand Route St. John, and that of the old bridge (from the 1750s) opposite Bell Street. This indicates that Bayou Road (the portage) of earlier times ran along the site of Bell Street. The question is when? Was the segment of Bayou Road leading away from Bayou St. Jean in this location from the earliest times? From the 1750s when the road was staked out by Sieurs DeMorand and Latil? From 1777 when Bayou Road was moved easterly by twenty feet at the request of Joseph Chalon? The author's conclusion is that pior to 1809 Bayou Road was located very near or on Bell Street, rather than between Bell and DeSoto Streets as indicated elsewhere in this volume.

Chapter III

BAYOU ST. JEAN RECEIVES ITS NAME—1699

Having verified that the Mississippi was the great stream he sought, having visited the various Indian nations along the Mississippi as far north as the Red River, and having discovered an alternative short-cut from the Mississippi to the Gulf (Bayou Manchac, which he called River Iberville), Iberville supervised the quick construction of Fort Biloxi, and departed for France in early May, 1699, leaving eighty men and their officers including his younger brother Bienville, to look after things until he returned.[1]

From this temporary main French settlement (Old Biloxi) in the new colony, nineteen year old Bienville and a few companions set off one day in May to take another look at the Mississippi-lake portage they'd discovered on their first trip up the river with Iberville; they left at an early hour to avoid the stinging of little flies or gnats the Indians called maringouins (a South American Indian word for mosquito). Later, a Jesuit Father of early French times was to observe in his diary that in the short time the French had been on the Mississippi the little pest had caused more cursing than the world had heard up to that time.[2]

Retracing the lakes and channels to which Iberville had given names, the little party in the longboat entered Lake Borgne (incomplete, like a man with one eye, because the body of water wasn't completely landlocked—it was later called Blind Lake,)[3] and advanced through the connecting channel called the Rigolets. They passed Pointe-aux-Coquille (The Shells), a narrow thrust of land to their immediate left, as they entered Lake Pontchartrain (named for France's Minister of Marine). From there they sailed across open water to Pointe-aux-Herbes, a generous round of land that jutted into Lake Pontchartrain from its southern shore. Hugging the coast of the choppy lake, they oared southwesterly, searching for some meaningful variation in the marginal morass, gaping and pointing at the more than occasional alligator that slithered in and out of the watery canes and grasses that stretched endlessly away from the cypress-studded lakeshore.

Three leagues beyond Pointe-aux-Herbes, the Indians in the party pointed out a variation in the sameness caused by the waters of a bayouk joining those of the lake. By means of this bayouk, they explained, the

Mississippi could be reached easily and quickly.[4] (Historian Marcel Giraud intimates that Bayou St. John was explored between Iberville's first and second visits to Louisiana in 1699.)[5] It must have been difficult for the young adventurers not to enter Bayouk Choupic from its lake end—not to go all the way on this water short-cut of which they'd now seen both ends and which had been described to them by the Indians. But eager to probe other possibilities the lake had to offer, careful exploration of Bayouk Choupic was left for another day.

At the suggestion of their guides, familiar with a less ardous travel trail, they pushed west to another bayouk, where some of them waded through the swamp to the Mississippi River. This could have been Bayou LaBarre, which as late as 1868 remained a major bayou, ten feet deep and navigable by pirogues as far inland as Bayou Metairie.[6] In 1699 it was undoubtedly a well known, long-time water and land passage of the Indians. Having spent the night on the banks of the Michisipy, not far upstream from the Choupithatcha portage, they returned to their boats at the lake the next day to delight their companions with stories of the wild turkeys perched in the trees under which they'd slept. It had been easy to kill as many as they wanted to eat, because unaccustomed to the sound of a gun, the birds hadn't been frightened away.[7]

Circumnavigating Lake Pontchartrain's twenty-eight-league rim (it measured seven across) the young men noted the many streams running into it, as well as Pass Manchac that connected Lake Pontchartrain with smaller Lake Maurepas (named for the son of France's Minister of Marine). Returning to Fort Biloxi the way they'd come, they killed buffalo and deer along the way. Buffalo were found in great numbers east and west of the Mississippi when Louisiane (so-called, so-spelled by the French) was first explored and settled, but as coastal areas became inhabited, the animals tended to retreat inland.[8]

Between Iberville's initial departure in May of 1699 and his return on December 7, 1699, Bienville and his friends visited the bayou many times, and it was on one of these journeys that Bayouk Choupic of the Indians was renamed Bayou St. Jean by the young explorer. A little imagination easily dictates the occasion.

The bayou and the country bordering it, observed by Bienville, was a far cry from the neat, deep, wide, cement-walled stream that fronts contiguous residential sections today. Entering the bayou from the lake, the bottoms of their canoes scraped the sandbar where the waters met those of the lake. Hardly a foot deep, lake currents promoted this shoal condition at the mouth of all the bayous that joined Pontchartrain's waters. Immediately on entering they noted the elevated mound to their right, the only high ground in sight. Paddling past it, they saw that a small stream from the west connected with the bayou, and looking back noticed that the stream curved northerly, connecting with Lake Pontchartrain a little to the west. The elevated ground was an island, on which Fort St. Jean would be established in the next few years.[9]

A short way inland, they swerved their canoes to the right to avoid the build-up of silt from the stream that joined the bayou from the east (approximately Robert E. Lee Boulevard today). The youthful troop soon learned that from both banks of its entire length, coolies, rivulets and streams poured their contents into the bayou, and it was necessary to look ahead—to anticipate the swirl of water—so their canoes wouldn't run aground on the build-up of sand, silt and refuse these streams brought with them.

Huge cypress trees studded the bayou's course, as they paddled down the soft brown, multi-islanded waters that wound over and through the growing things that pushed up from its soft, unsettled mud bottom—nowhere more than three to four feet below them. One of the Indians explained that the waters weren't as big now as they were during the wet season, when it was hard to make out the banks of the bayouk, because they were overflowed on both sides as far as the eye could see.

Pushing aside the long lank streams of grey moss straggling down from the trees to the undergrowth of dwarf trees, shrubs, reeds and grasses that needled through the swamp[10] to right and left as far as they could see, Bienville thought it desolate country—a fitting haunt for the weird sisters to brew their infernal potions. (A hundred and fifty years later the Voodoos would assume that prerogative along the banks of Bayou St. John.)

Careful not to gouge the bottom of his canoe on the large tree trunks, roots and branches, barely submerged beneath the surface, Bienville eyed with interest the bayou spilling in from the right. (The remnants of Bayou Noir still thread through the lake end of City Park south of Robert E. Lee Boulevard.)[11]

A short way down the bayou—on the same side—a few huts huddled along the bank. An Indian in the party explained that nobody lived there permanently—that it was a camp used by Redmen traveling this route during the dry summer months. Pulling up to the bank for a better look, Bienville saw the shelters were supported by slender poles of swamp oak covered with leaves of Latania.[12]

Absorbed with the abandoned camp (near today's Kennedy High School) Bienville almost missed the two-pronged stream that ruffled the bayou's surface on the opposite bank. Between the two water-outlets, an island projected into the middle of the bayou—an island that would appear on an early map as "Ile aux Baptime."[13] On today's bayou, this island would be near the Vista Shores Country Club located a couple squares south of Robert E. Lee Boulevard on the bayou's east bank.[14]

Several hundred yards further on, Bayouk Choupic curved sharply to the left, behind yet another island that hove into view. About the middle of the curve an angry little stream entered from the east, tossing branches and other refuse into "his bayou." This was the most action the party had seen thus far and deserved a little looking into. Besides, it was time to eat, and the island—the driest place in sight—seemed a safe enough place to stop. Neither the island nor the entering bayou are in existence today, but on nineteenth century maps they both bore the name "Bienville," because, as legend has it, this was where Bienville had his first meal on Bayou St. Jean.[15] On today's map Bayou L'Ille Bienville would enter Bayou St. John at Park Island Drive. Of course, Park Island wasn't there in those days.

As they oared away an hour later, it was almost impossible to find a water-path deep enough to get out of the sharp curve. Constantly filling up with sand, branches and refuse brought in by Bayou Bienville, this spot would be well-named "Devil's Elbow" or "Devil's Slough" by frustrated navigators of the 1800s.[16]

The narrower channel on the east side of Park Island today is the original bed of the bayou which Bienville passed with such difficulty. Today's Park Island was created when land to the west of it was excavated in the mid-1800s, making a deeper channel than the original bayou had to offer.

From that point on, only the larger connecting streams were of interest to the travelers of 1699. A mile beyond Isle de Bienville, they swerved their canoes sharply to avoid the build-up of sand that spewed halfway across the stream from the east, leaving bare breadth and depth to paddle through. Later this connecting stream would become a mill race of plantation owners and would continue to drain into the bayou until the first levees were built north of the mill race in the early 1890s. A remnant of that filled-in canal can be observed today near Florida Avenue, east of Wisner Overpass.

The visitors noted that the land on either side seemed to be getting higher. A girdle of palmetto divided the cypress swamp from the lower slopes of a ridge that rose gradually ahead of them. Pulling over to the side of the stream Bienville's discerning eye picked out some of the best trees he'd seen—oak, persimmon, liriodendron, pecan, wild cherry, acacia and sweet gum.[17] The ground continued high, above the bayou waters. Soil permitting, this was land on which settlers could build and plant. And so they would. The Metairie-Gentilly ridge was to be the first and best agricultural area of this region.

Just around the next big bend Bienville noticed an Indian trail tracing the water's edge on his right;[18] and he found himself listening for the woodland call of a communicating Redman echoing through the lonely stretches. Or might it be a blood-chilling warwhoop? prefacing a violent exchange of hunting grounds.

Preoccupation butted reality in the form of another bayou—as big as Bayouk Choupic—flowing in from the northwest. On its further side an Indian trail intersected with the one along Bayouk Choupic, and a huge felled log bridged the juncture of the two streams. In years ahead this connecting waterway would be known by the various names of Chapitoulas, Cypress or Metairie Bayou.[19] Along both banks of the stream was a sprinkling of swamp dwellings, more permanent in appearance than those they'd seen before. A few of the structures were close to Bayouk Choupic, and others—it was impossible to determine how many—extended back along the other bayou. Deserted now, Bienville's guide explained that these were the former habitations of the Acolapissa Indians (The Nation Who Hear and See) who had recently moved to the north shore of Lake Pontchartrain to escape the continuing raids of the Chickasaws. Within a year the huts would be occupied by the Biloxi Indians who had begun to move from their original home on the Gulf Coast to Bayouk Choupic. Some of the Indians would be invited to occupy the land of Louis Juchereau de St. Denis in 1708;[20] and some of the abandoned dwellings—from Bayouk Choupic back along Bayouk Chapitoulas—would provide temporary shelter for many a newly-arrived French settler in the years ahead.

Directly across the stream—on the east bank—the obviously rich, high land would within nine years be conceded to Antoine Rivard de LaVigne and a handful of other French and Canadian colonists—the earliest landowners of this region.[21] On today's map their concessions would stretch approximately from Grand Route St. John to a point beyond Esplanade Avenue.

Near the joining of the bayous, tales tell us, Bienville first set foot on historic Bayou bend. Gazing about the quiet wilderness, infringed only by soft swamp sounds, he and one of the Indians sauntered down the trail alongside Bayouk Choupic. A few yards further on, the stream took a sharp turn around a bosky bend to the right. If he had left the trail and followed that bank southwesterly, Bienville would soon have reached the end of Bayouk Choupic, which within three-fourths of a mile branched into several small streamlets that fingered into the various corners of the surrounding swamplands. However, the trees and undergrowth, spilling into the water along the bank, were too formidable for easy penetration. That part of the stream would have to wait for another time. Besides, the path lay straight ahead—across Bayouk Choupic on another treetrunk bridge—to the beginning of a trail on the far bank—the portage trail that led to the River St. Louis. (Iberville had rechristened the "Colbert"—Rivière St. Louis—in honor of his King.) The bayou end of the portage trail began somewhat west of today's Grand Route St. John, near 1222 Moss Street.

Teetering on the primitive bridge, Bienville almost toppled in as he leaned sideways to see what looked like another bayou connecting with Bayouk Choupic's east bank a short distance to the left of the portage trail. The short stretch of water, called Laurier or Laureal by the French, linked Bayous St. Jean and Gentilly during the eighteenth and early nineteenth centuries.

Over the log bridge, Bienville and his companion continued up the portage trail for three-fourths of a mile and paused where the path divided. One trail continued in a southwesterly direction toward the River St. Louis, while the other well-traveled route forked off to the northeast along the large bayou with which the small waterway Laurier connected.

The early French called the larger waterway Bayou Sauvage or Indian Bayou, and later it would be renamed Bayou Gentilly. Near the junction of the two trails Indians camped for many years to come. Nearly two hundred years later their presence would still be felt when their burial grounds dampened the enthusiasm of prospective purchasers of home sites near the location.[22]

Historian Giraud says Bienville named the Bayou for himself,[23] because he used it so much. Others say the stream was named in honor of his patron Saint, John the Baptist. Historian Grace King can't quite make up her mind. In one book she says it was named for the man, and in another she opts for the Saint.[24] Struggling for identity under such a resourceful older brother, who had named everything else, it may have been of the essence for Bienville to identify with a place he thought of as his own—his private room as it were. Whatever his motivation, from that time on Grand Bayou de St. Jean of French times, Bayu San Juan of the Spanish, or the American Bayou St. John has always, in the hearts of history lovers, been incontrovertibly linked with Jean Baptiste LeMoyne, Sieur de Bienville.

In September of 1699 Bienville and five companions had again come to the Mississippi via the lakes, Bayou St. Jean and the portage trail, and were paddling down the river in two canoes when they encountered an English ship on that captious curve about eighteen miles below New Orleans, which can be best appreciated from an airplane. Ship's Captain Bond informed Bienville of his intention to settle his shipload of French Huguenots on the lower reaches of the big river, whereupon Bienville informed him in no uncertain terms that the French were already well established and protected upstream, and ordered the English ship out of the river. Having crossed swords with Iberville in Hudson Bay waters not long before, and remembering young Bienville, who had been with his brother on that occasion, Bond apparently decided that the presumption of the young man must be solidly backed up, so he didn't press his point. But more than miffed, and threatening to return, he turned the corvette about, retracing Detour a l'Anglais ("where the English were encountered,") or English Turn as the curve was to be called thereafter.

The Captain had left homeport about the same time Iberville left Brest, France—on October 24, 1698—but dreading the wilds of a strange land during the winter, he had spent the cold months in British territory on the eastern seaboard,[25] and missed, by a nerve's breadth, the opportunity of colonizing Louisiane. As for Bienville, it wasn't the first, nor would it be the last time when a bit of boldness and bluff claimed the day. Sure that the English were on their way out of the river, Bienville and party paddled back up the Mississippi to the portage on which they cut across to Bayou St. Jean, Lake Pontchartrain and home to Biloxi.[26]

Chapter IV

THE PORTAGE AND THE INDIANS OF BAYOU ST. JEAN—1700-1705

After repeated visits to the bayou portage, Bienville confirmed the opinions of Remonville and other Canadian travelers that the ideal spot for a post was where the portage trail met the Mississippi; so when Iberville returned to Louisiane on December 7, 1699,[1] his younger brother no doubt pressed him to relocate the colony's main settlement from the sandy beaches of Biloxi to the crescent of the River St. Louis, where conditions for growing food and developing trade were far superior. But like any good shirt-sleeved executive, Iberville wanted to see for himself, and in January of 1700 reconnoitered the Lake-Bayou route with Bienville, Father Paul DuRu and others.

Setting off through the lakes, and arriving at the mouth of Bayouk Choupic (for years many would continue to call the stream by its Indian name), it was obvious that the sluggish waterway would not accommodate larger craft, so the barges were left in Lake Pontchartrain, and the party proceeded by pirogue.[2]

At the river end of the bayou they found the half-league portage tough going in January. A part of it was all woods and water, reaching well up on the leg, and on the rest of it they had to push through canebrake and woods.[3] But the tough topography didn't stop them from exploring contiguous territory. On this visit Iberville planted some sugarcane seeds he'd brought with him from St. Domingue in the watery soil of the deserted Quinipissa Village on the Mississippi, a league below the portage. It was a futile attempt, because the seeds were spoiled and didn't grow.[4]

One of Iberville's objectives on his second trip to the colony was to build a fort near the mouth of the Mississippi to protect France's new possession from the Spaniards and Indians.[5] On the advice of a friendly Bayougoula, who claimed to know flood conditions, Bienville selected a site thirty miles below the Bayou St. Jean portage,[6] near today's town of Phoenix. According to Father DuRu's journal, Fort de la Boulaye (also called Fort Mississippi) was built in two weeks;[7] and after dedicating it on February 14, 1700, DuRu again headed for the portage with Iberville, who wished to renew relations with the Indians along the Mississippi River.[8] Going was even tougher this time wading through the portage in water to their waists and mud to their knees.[9]

At the portage, geologist-explorer LeSueur, on his way to search for minerals on the upper Mississippi, met Tonty—a long-time traveler who probably knew the river better than any of his contemporaries. The likable Tonty had come once again to see if he could be of help to his compatriots, but the trail between the bayou and the river was obliterated by winter rains, and LeSueur's porters became hopelessly lost in the cypress swamp. Two of them spent the night in the woods and froze their feet, whereupon the portage came to be called "Portage des Egares," (Portage of the Lost). As late as 1735 a map represented it as such.[10]

Some called it Portage des Bilochis or Billochy (Biloxis), because the Indians first encountered by the French on the Gulf Coast in 1699, traveled it so often.[11]

Others referred to it as the portage of the Fish River, which was misleading, because Fish River was located halfway between Bayou St. Jean and Bayou Manchac seventy miles upriver.

More often it was called the Portage of Lake Pontchartrain, of Bayouk Choupic or Choupithatcha.[12] And later—as repetition became habit—the original road of our region came to be known as the Portage of Bayou St. Jean, or Bayou Road.

Father DuRu refers to the portage as "the rendezvous where LeSueur had visited,"[13] indicating that as early as 1700 the portage was well known to travelers—a place where they got together. It was a crossroads from whence one could take off in many directions: upriver to Illinois Country and Canada, downriver to new Fort de la Boulaye and the mouth of the river; at the bayou-end of the portage the ancient trail bordering Bayou Chapitoulas led to the River St. Louis upstream (near Kenner today), and northerly—through Bayou St. Jean and Lake Pontchartrain—the lake route continued through the Rigolets and Lake Borgne back to Biloxi on the Gulf Coast.

It was only good sense that the French would erect some kind of fortification to protect the bayou entrance to the island between Lake Pontchartrain and the River St. Louis. This immediate area was indeed an island, surrounded by the waters of the gulf on the south, the Mississippi on the west, and a chain of lakes from Borgne to Maurepas and Bayou Manchac (River Iberville) on the north and east. At least for three months of the year it was an island, when the River St. Louis flooded its banks and flowed through the "Iberville gut" as it was called. During the remaining months, the Manchac route had to be traveled with portages. This area would remain a quasi-island for over a hundred years—until

1814, when General Jackson ordered the partial filling of Bayou Manchac as a precaution against English invasion of New Orleans from the north.[14]

Because of the defensive importance of the bayou's mouth, Historians Waring and Cable inform us that a small loghouse with a surrounding stockade was erected in 1701 atop the elevated mound on the west bank of Bayou St. Jean where it met the lake. Armed with a couple pieces of light artillery,[15] this was the beginning of Fort St. Jean, which through varying fate and fortune would guard the mouth of the bayou and the Isle of Orleans for over a hundred years.

Remonville, true believer in the superiority of a portage post, seems also to have been the first to propose that Fort de la Boulaye be abandoned. On August 6, 1702 he suggested that the fort be transferred eleven leagues further up the river, and a half mile inland from it—near Bayou St. Jean—which was much easier to reach than coming through the mouth of the Mississippi. In August the portage was no doubt dry, and Remonville believed that a post in this location would also be very useful as a warehouse for projected Fort Rosalie at Natchez, for which Iberville had drawn plans on his trip upriver in February of 1700.[16]

Apparently the Bayougoula had selected the site of Fort de la Boulaye for the protection of his nation against other Indians rather than for the best interests of the French.[17] Besides flooding badly, Iberville couldn't afford to station several of his limited citizenry at that isolated location for guard duty only. After 1707 the fort was abandoned, and in 1708 Remonville again stressed the importance of establishing Louisiane's principal establishment on high ground dominating Lake Pontchartrain.[18] But it would take ten long bitter years of self-interested infighting and the loss of many colonial lives before Bienville's persistence realized Remonville's vision.

Many Indian nations traveled the crossroads between the river and the lake, by trail or down Bayou St. Jean, in canoes and pirogues. The two main Indian groups of the gulf region were the Chickasaws and Choctaws and their several subtribes. The Chickasaws lived for the most part in what is now northeastern Mississippi and have been described as goodlooking, well-shaped, prideful and highspirited, while Choctaw subtribes inhabited the New Orleans area. The Choctaws were described by Historian DuPratz as the only ugly Indians in Louisiane, due to the fat with which they rubbed their skins and standing in the smoke of their firwood fires to protect themselves from the mosquitoes.[19] From earliest colonial times a loose Choctaw-French versus Chickasaw-

English alignment seemed to prevail, the white nations competing with each other—in the form of gifts to the Indian tribes—to secure their fighting support. Fortunately for the French, these two major Indian groups were extremely antipathetic, for had they combined their forces, sixteen thousand strong, the tiny white minority wouldn't have had a chance.[20]

Very few of the Indian nations actually lived on Bayou St. Jean. Prior to 1699 the Acolapissas (from Aquelou-Pissas) had lived near the intersection of Bayous St. Jean and Chapitoulas (Metairie), and westerly along the banks of the latter; but just before the arrival of the French, three hundred of them had moved to the north shore of Lake Pontchartrain, across from the mouth of Bayou St. Jean, near today's Mandeville and Fontainebleau, because of continuing Chickasaw raids on their bayou village.[21]

By 1700 many Biloxi Indians, whose numbers had been dwindling from malnutrition and long-time swamp living, had moved to Bayou St. Jean, between Lake Pontchartrain and the Mississippi. Occupying the deserted huts of the Acolapissas, the Biloxis also built habitations along and in the vicinity of the portage trail. If it was dryness they sought, their move was ironic, for during the spring flood months, when the Mississippi overflowed its banks, the whole region—from the Mississippi to Lake Pontchartrain—could often be navigated by pirogue.[22]

The only other nation to live on Bayou St. Jean during French times was that of the Houmas who chose for their village a site in the vicinity of the intersection of the portage road and the trail that led east along Bayou Sauvage—near present day St. Louis Cemetery III on Esplanade Avenue.[23]

The name of this tribe is derived from "shakchi humma" (Chakchiuma or Saktce-Homa) which means red crawfish.[24] It is believed that the crawfish was the Houmas' war emblem and may in ancient times have been the totemic symbol of that nation—that is, the sacred creature to which they felt related and from which they believed they had descended. In 1699 a reddish pole (istrouma or iti ouma) to which heads of fish and bear were attached as sacrifices, marked the boundary between the hunting grounds of the Bayougoulas and the Houmas on the Mississippi near today's Baton Rouge—the French translation of iti ouma.[25] The University-lake suburb of Baton Rouge is today called *Istrouma*.

Iberville and Bienville first visited the tribe in March of 1699 where 350 families lived in simple huts of wooden frames covered with palmetto leaves. The French noticed with interest their worship of chickens. Their village was over-run with the feathered creatures, but they never killed them, and wouldn't eat them, even if they were accidently destroyed. The French could purchase them only if they refrained from mentioning their true intentions toward the fowl.[26]

A few years later, an Englishman who was trading with the Tunicas (a tribe living farther upriver) had been forcefully relieved by them of some of his wares. Returning to the Carolinas, he prevailed upon "his Indians" to assist him in revenge. The Tunicas, finding themselves too weak to resist the return invasion, fled south and sought refuge with their neighbors the Houmas. But reluctant to play the grateful role, the guests arose during the night and either murdered or captured most of their benefactors. The Houma hosts who escaped made their way to Bayou St. Jean where the early French found their settlement about 1706. (Other sources give the date as 1702 or 1708.)[27] The village was still in existence as late as 1720,[28] but by then the Houmas were gradually moving on. Perhaps the continuous coming of the white man made them uncomfortable or boded ill for their way of life. After a long unfortunate odyssey down through the years, about two thousand of them still live in Terrebonne and LaFourche parishes, trapping, fishing and tending gardens along the bayous.

Enroute to their present location, they were driven out of Houma (a city named for them,) by the white inhabitants; and ironically their original home, in the northeastern part of the state, is named Tunica Hills, for their ancient enemies.[29]

Chapter V

THE FIRST SETTLERS OF BAYOU ST. JEAN—1706-1715

Bienville was having his problems. The garrison at Biloxi was hungry, because the sandy shores weren't conducive to agriculture, and supply ships from France were few and far between. In 1706 he had no alternative except to let several of his men go hunting and live as best they could 'mongst the various Indian nations they'd come to know.[1] Bienville's young friend Penicaut (carpenter and Indian interpreter) and a few of his companions went to live with the Acolapissa Indians on the north shore of Lake Pontchartrain, with whom they spent a pleasant year.

Penicaut lived in high style with the Indian Chief, dining on buffalo, bear, snow and blue geese and ducks which they hunted, peaches, plums and grapes when they were in season, and various dishes made of corn— the basic food of early Louisiane. Farina froide was the favorite of the French. Parboiled, dried and pounded, the corn became a versatile meal, which mixed with milk and French sugar or chocolate, was very tasty, healthful and easy for travelers to carry.

Evening parties were the rule during their stay with the Indians, with the French playing the violin and dancing with each other and with the Indians who tried to imitate the minuet. After one of these soirees, Penicaut enjoyed a late breakfast of fish, fricasseed in bear fat, and bread made of cornmeal mixed with flour and small beans, served by the Chief himself. And to top it all off, there was a huge tray of wild strawberries, gathered in the woods by the Chief's daughter who was receiving French lessons from Penicaut.[2]

Back at Biloxi, Bienville wasn't faring nearly so well. Not only had he lost his older brother Iberville, who had died of yellow fever enroute to Louisiane for the fourth time in 1706, he had a minor revolution on his hands. In 1704 the Bishop of Quebec had sent twenty three young ladies from Canada to Mobile (capitol of Louisiane since 1702) to become wives of the early colonists, who welcomed them with open arms. However, their new home didn't measure up to expectations. Certainly the food didn't. Although the men had become used to eating corn, these young brides, accustomed to wheat bread, blamed the Bishop of Quebec for sending them to this "land of honey" under false pretexts.[3] Perhaps homesickness, the difficulty of primitive living conditions, and certainly an awareness of their privileged minority status gave them the courage to revolt, and at fury's apex they threatened to leave the colony enmasse if the situation didn't improve.

No less a practical diplomat with the ladies than with the Indians, Bienville turned the matter over to his efficient housekeeper, French-Canadian Madame Langlois, a cousin of Bienville's mother, and an accomplished adaptable cook, who administered to the culinary needs of Bienville and Father Davion, the colony's spiritual adviser. Immediately upon arrival she'd recognized the limitations of her larder and requested recipes from friendly Indian squaws on how to prepare the available local groceries. So taking the young women under her wing, she imparted to them the secrets of grinding corn for bread, which served with honey was not a bad substitute for wheat, and in informal cooking classes her students learned how to make hominy and grits with homemade lye, and Indian succotash from green corn and butterbeans. Having joined the original Club of Creole Cookery, her pupils soon forgot about their "petticoat rebellion."[4]

The arrival of a ship of supplies from France in 1707 relieved the situation somewhat—at least to the extent that Bienville sent word to his visiting forces to return to home base. Penicaut and his friends were as loath to leave their fun and games as were the Indians to lose their newfound friends. But there was one compensation that Frenchmen, above all, would understand. The incoming ship brought wine, which Penicaut remarks "consoled us for the loss of the favors of their girls."[5]

However, the foundering attempt at colonization resulted in loss of confidence on the part of the early colonists, and it was bruited about that the limited government supplies in the warehouse on Dauphin Island, used only for supporting the garrison and official trading purposes, were being sold at six times their cost by those in command, for their own profit.[6] Martin d'Artaguette was sent from France with the title of Commissary General of Louisiane to investigate the situation, and Bienville was fired. But the official who was to take his place died enroute to Louisiane, so Bienville got his job back. But Commissary d'Artaguette stayed on to see that affairs were properly conducted.[7]

No doubt agitating Parisian palates, as well as the nagging agricultural predicament, accounted for the establishment of the first plantations of this region on Bayou St. Jean, on which wheat was to be the principal crop. Following orders from Count de Pontchartrain in Paris, Commissary d'Artaguette persuaded eight colonists to come from Mobile to the banks of the bayou to develop small acreages conceded to them by the

French Colonial government at Mobile. These first concessions had narrow water frontages of 2½ to 3 arpents each,* and early maps show them as long narrow land ribbons extending from Bayou St. Jean to Bayou Gentilly,[8] and beyond for a total of forty arpents depth.

The Commissary was delighted with the preliminary planting. He'd never seen finer grain anywhere. Anticipating a bumper crop, the original concessions were extended, and Bienville and d'Artaguette promised the concessionaires a mill. Unfortunately, the wheat that grew wonderfully in stem and ear burned in the springtime heat of the coast; and d'Artaguette, in a reluctant report, explained that "ten days before it was to mature, some fogs came up that made it completely wither away." Instead of the hundred-plus bushels anticipated, about seven were harvested.[9]

---

*A linear arpent= 191.835 feet; a square arpent is approximately 85% of an English acre.

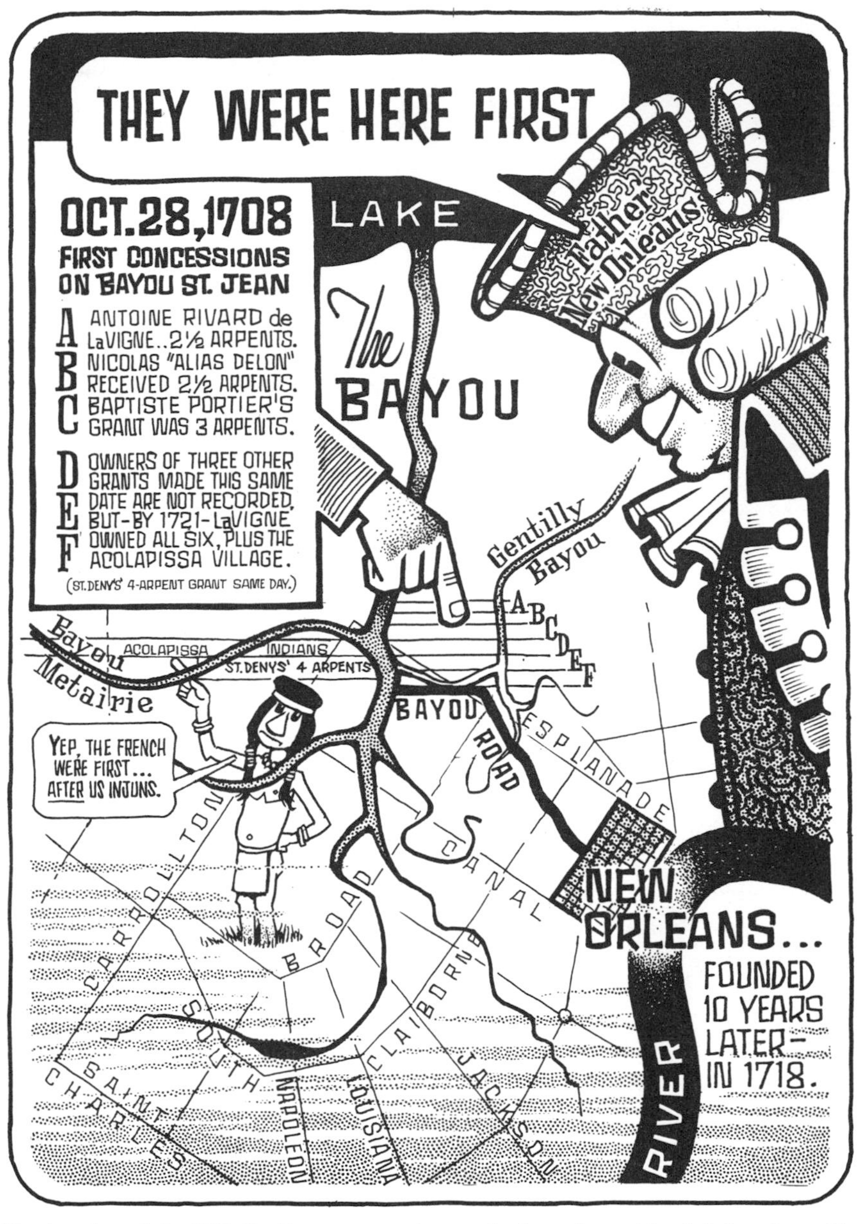

The location of the 1708 St. Denys concession on the bayou's west bank is based on Allou d'Hémécourt's map of 1853 at the Louisiana State Museum Library. On February 10, 1722 this property was acquired by Joseph Girardy.

The original eight settlers quickly dwindled to six, no doubt due to failure of the crop, and maps available to us reveal only three: Baptiste Portier, who is believed to have been the warehouseman of the King of Mobile, Nicolas alias Delon and Antoine Rivard de LaVigne.[10]

Antoine Rivard de LaVigne, twenty five to thirty years old when he settled his bayou plantation in 1708, had been listed—with a wife and one child—on the "Census of Families and Inhabitants of Louisiane" recorded by Nicolas de LaSalle in Mobile on August 1, 1706.[11] A native of Ile Dauphine, Canada, he had married Marie Briard (Briar, Driar), one of the twenty three Canadian girls sent to Mobile in 1704 by the Bishop of Quebec. From this marriage six children would be born. Mrs. LaVigne must have traveled a great deal with her husband, for two of their daughters were born at Ile Dauphine, Canada, and their son Francois Antoine Rivard de LaVigne was born at the Natchez post. After Marie Briar's death, LaVigne would marry Antoinette Fourrier, widow of Henri Martin de Mirebaize, Sieur de Villemont, by whom he had no issue.

Some of the original bayou settlers stayed only a short time, did not fulfill the legal obligations required of concessionaires, and left when they were so inclined. But a few stuck it out, and in 1713 were growing corn near the portage trail.[12]

Of these first bayou settlers, Antoine Rivard de LaVigne (referred to in the records also as Rivard or Rivart) was the only one who stayed on permanently. By 1718 he had purchased the ancient village of the Acolapissas across the bayou from his plantation; and by 1721 he had enlarged his original holdings by purchasing the adjoining concessions of those who had left. An additional three-arpent frontage, granted him by Bienville on February 5, 1721—together with what he already owned— established him as the earliest large-property-owner on Bayou St. Jean, with seventeen arpents front.[13] Today's landmarks would extend the LaVigne plantation approximately from Grand Route St. John northerly to the vicinity of the National Guard property lakeside of Esplanade Avenue.

The inability to grow wheat along the coast of Louisiane was the beginning of the thinking trend, if not the actual trek, toward Natchez, where soil, clime and elevation promised better crops. However, in 1708 there weren't enough people to cultivate land away from the main gulf settlements or soldiers to guard them from the Indians.[14]

Another early land-owner on the bayou was Louis Juchereau de St. Denys (Denis), who had been the first Commandant of Fort de la Boulaye on the lower Mississippi until 1704.[15] A Knight of St. Louis, he received on October 28, 1708 a grant of four arpents front on the west bank of Bayou St. Jean, near today's Carrollton and Moss Streets; the acreage stretched westerly for forty arpents, the usual depth of concessions in those days. An early one-worlder, St. Denys encouraged some friendly Biloxi Indians, who had occupied the portage since 1700, to settle on his plantation with him. Intrigued, however, with the prospect of opening trade relations with the Spaniards to the west (Texas), from 1710-1715 he blazed the Old Spanish Trail across Texas in an attempt to establish trade between the French on the Gulf Coast and the Spanish in Mexico.

St. Denys sold his bayou holdings in 1713 to one Desboumes and Jean Baptiste Beaudreau, alias Graveline, of Pascagoula, a wheeler-dealer of early Louisiane, who throughout the French era would deal with the inhabitants and buy and sell properties at Bayou St. Jean. Although the Spanish trading venture came to naught, St. Denys founded the post of Natchitoches, Louisiana in 1714, where considerable underground trade between the Spanish and the French continued to thrive, and where St. Denys lived until his death in 1744.

About 1715 he established one of the first typical Creole families by marrying Emanuela Sanchez y Navarro, a high-born Spanish lady of Mexico.[16]

Despite the seemingly insuperable impediments to the establishment of a self-sustaining community, the territory continued to be traveled. The lake route had by now become the established passage, infinitely preferred to the trip up the Mississippi, which difficult enough in reality, became even more so in the imaginations of inexperienced, uninformed and fear-prejudiced travelers. M. de Mandeville wrote in 1709 that it was easy to go from Fort Mobile to Lake Pontchartrain, through Bayou St. Jean, and to take the one-league portage to the Mississippi, compared to going through the passes of the Mississippi, seven feet deep at most, and through oft-flooded country full of alligators, snakes and other venimous beasts. The Mississippi, he reported, did nothing but twist, going the rounds of the compass every three leagues; for six months it was a torrent, and for the rest of the year a pirogue could scarcely pass in places.[17]

In a rare moment, when the King of France wasn't warring or nettled by necessities of state, it occurred to him to turn this hopeless colonial project over to a wealthy Parisian merchant. On September 14, 1712 Sieur H. Antoine Crozat, anticipating rich returns from gold and silver in the untouched territory, and trade with the thriving Spanish provinces to the west, accepted a fifteen year monopoly on Louisiane trading rights.[18]

Antoine de la Mothe Cadillac, Colonial governor during Crozat's proprietorship, who arrived in the summer of 1713, displayed nothing but contempt for his contemporary's investment. "Bad country, bad people," he observed immediately upon arrival. "I saw three seedling pear trees, three apple trees, and a little plum tree three feet high with seven sorry plums—about thirty vine plants bearing nine bunches of grapes—each bunch rotted or dried up."

Perhaps Bienville's refusal of his daughter's hand in marriage contributed to his bile. Surely it caused Cadillac little anguish to send Bienville to avenge the death of four Frenchmen in Indian-hostile Natchez in 1715 and to erect Fort Rosalie.[19]

Change of colony management may have renewed the optimism of Remonville and LeSueur, who in 1715 again pressed for a portage post on a stretch of high ground, twelve leagues long and a league and a half wide, which began a quarter of a league in from the river (Metairie-Gentilly Ridge). Remonville pointed out that the site could never flood and that the Biloxis had transported their village to that point on the banks of a stream named the St. Jean River which flowed into Lake Pontchartrain. He again stressed the importance of a warehouse at this point to supply the Natchez Post which was established that year.

Unfortunately for the first promoter of Bayou St. Jean and the portage, Remonville hadn't paid as much attention to his personal affairs as to those of Louisiane. His commercial ventures failed completely, and creditors seized his possessions, whereupon he requested a government position which he believed to be his due, but which was denied him. Remonville wasn't the first to conclude that he'd struggled in vain, nor would he be the last.[20]

Chapter VI

THE BEGINNING OF NEW ORLEANS AND THE VILLAGE AND PORT OF BAYOU ST. JEAN—1716-1719

In January of 1716 the colony was in desperate straits. There remained at Biloxi and Mobile on the Gulf Coast only a hundred and twenty starved troops and sixty colonists and officials, who were being driven into the ground by English-instigated Choctaw and Natchez Indian raids. Practically abandoned by France for the past several years, the colonial council wearily observed that Louisiane had survived only by a miracle.[1]

Considering that an annual investment of 250,000 livres (the livre was the forerunner of the franc and of the same value) had netted him no precious metals, and that the Spanish to the west (Texas) had closed their ports to French ships on his first attempt to trade with them, Crozat asked Royal permission to pull out. Realizing that the development of the colony was too great an undertaking for an individual, the government in Paris granted his request on January 12, 1717.[2]

After the death of King Louis XIV in 1715, Regent Philippe, Duke of Orleans, took over the responsibility of governing until his five year old cousin Louis XV, great grandson of the former king, became old enough to rule.

Frustrated by the pecuniary predicament in which France was steeped because of the wars and extravagant habits of the former king, and desperately seeking means of avoiding complete economic disaster, the Duke of Orleans was easily taken in by a Scottish financial operator-speculator named John Law. Authorized by the crown, Law founded a French private bank in 1716 which became so successful that by December 4, 1718 it had evolved, with Royal blessing, into the Bank of France.

Meanwhile Crozat's Louisiane disaster sparked in the wily Law the idea of selling stock to the French public based on the potential of the new-world colony. So on September 6, 1717 he established the Company of the West with a capital of one hundred million livres to exploit the Mississippi Valley. Receiving a charter from the Crown, granting to it twenty five years of trade monopoly in Louisiane, the Company contracted to settle six thousand white settlers and three thousand slaves in the young colony within ten years.

Immediately people became fascinated with the intriguing new way of getting-rich-quick from the much-touted gold, silver, copper and lead mines of Louisiane, and everybody wanted a share in the bonanza. As inflated rumors of the wealth-to-be-had spread like wildfire, the price of shares climbed higher and higher, and those in the know bought and sold at a profit.[3] With John Law as head of the Company of the West, Directors were appointed on September 12, 1717, and one of the first decisions of the Board was to found New Orleans. (Bienville and Jean Michelle Seigneur de L'Epinet, in their report of May, 1717, on "new posts to be established," had named the projected main settlement "New Orleans.") A town named for his Royal Highness, The Duke of Orleans, would help immeasurably to attract new stockholders. Three days later the Marine Board appointed one Bonnaud as storekeeper and cashier, and in December M. d'Avril was named Major of the new post of New Orleans—an establishment with no location and which existed only in the imagination of a self-interested few.[4]

Meanwhile Jean Michelle Seigneur de L'Epinet, who had come to Mobile as Commandant General to replace Cadillac, was so inefficient he was recalled on September 20, 1717, and Bienville had again resumed command.[5]

Of course, a change in the main establishment of Louisiane had been considered for many years, because Biloxi hadn't worked out; and a site along the Mississippi—connecting Canada with the Gulf—was the logical choice, but the location had to meet several requirements: 1) water communication between it and the earlier posts of Biloxi, Mobile and Dauphin Island, and present and future posts upriver, had to be convenient, 2) the location had to be as floodproof as possible, 3) proximity to good soil, to insure sustenance on the local level, was essential, and 4) it had to be established where ascent of the Mississippi by enemy ships could be prevented.[6]

A naval officer promoted English Turn in 1717, because its cove would provide an excellent port, and its location was prime for intercepting hostile interlopers. Natchez was highly favored because its flood-free rich soil would supply the daily bread of the settlers as well as exports to France. Geographer-Missionary Francois Le Maire opined that the new counter should be located on Lake Pontchartrain at the mouth of Bayou St. Jean. But Manchac, between the Mississippi and Lake Maurepas—seventy miles upriver from the crescent site—seemed to be the preferred spot for the main establishment of Louisiane. Via the River Iberville (Bayou Manchac), which Parisians then believed to be navigable the year around, communication with the gulf coast was convenient. One could proceed up the Mississippi to the Illinois country and Canada. It wasn't too far from the Red River and Yazoo country where wheat plantations were in the planning stage, and hunting could provide interim subsistence. The air was healthy, and the location was higher and dryer than the Bayou St. Jean portage. The only disadvantage was its distance from the sea—sixty five leagues; but this objection was shrugged off, because ships didn't come every day, and the plusses of the place could be enjoyed year-round.

The establishment at Biloxi and Mobile didn't want to move at all and spread rumors that the rivermouth was impassable, that the Mississippi River up to the Bayou St. Jean portage wasn't navigable, and they stirred up Biloxi tradesmen and lake route boatmen whose livelihood might be threatened should traffic up the Mississippi increase.[7]

There was much to be said for the advantages of the lake route. The distance to the Bayou St.Jean portage from Biloxi was seventy five miles further going up the Mississippi than through the lakes and Bayou St. Jean. Weather conditions along the lake-bayou route were much more favorable. Frequent storms along the Chandeleur Islands in the Gulf, and wind-induced choppy water, made the advance—through a series of low islands swimming even with the surface—extremely hazardous at the river approach. They couldn't be seen until a vessel was practically on top of them. The river's numerous passes into the ocean kept filling up with silt, branches and trees whirled downstream during the flood season, and a navigator could never be sure, from one voyage to the next, how deep, shallow or open his chosen channel might be. The tree trunks, logs and assorted wreckage spewing through the river mouth—if not physically damaging to boats—were certainly less than conducive to the ease of new-world hopefuls. If the wind was from the north, as it so often was, a ship had to tackle the current by tacking back and forth against the stream; and since the Mississippi wound like a serpent below New Orleans, the prevailing breeze might propel a sailing vessel forward along one side of a curve, only to leave the navigator waiting for a wind change in order to go any further. How many wind shifts were required for the circumnavigation of English Turn? Sometimes it took up to thirty days to ascend the Mississippi to the Portage of Bayou St. Jean.[8]

Only one knew for sure where New Orleans was going to be. In his special scheme of things it was already there. From 1699, when the Indian guide had pointed out the portage to that young man of nineteen on his first venture up the river with his older brother Iberville, through countless excursions back to the bayou that bore his name, over the Indian trail to the river, in his detailed recommendation of the location to Paris from 1708 on, Bienville's determination had never wavered. It was that elevated tract of land in the surrounding flats and marshes—ten feet above the Mississippi it fronted—where the river crescent swept closest to the lake. Only five miles separated the two waters at this point, and that distance was abbreviated by Bayou St. Jean and the short portage path that continued the lake route to the natural levee of the river to which people and products could easily be transported to build the principal establishment of Louisiane.

The site was close enough to the river's mouth to check the approach of curious, incursive visitors. Wind, current and English Turn would provide time to investigate an intruder before he came too far. Lagniappe was provided in that vessels of a thousand ton could lay their sides close to the shore, needing at most a small bridge in low water to load or unload barrels and bales without exhausting the ship's crew. Employee morale, as Bienville had already learned, was as important then as now.

The site was high enough and far enough away from the four meandering branches of Bayou St. Jean and other small bayous and streams that crept into every corner of the adjacent region; and a league back—at the other end of the portage path—on the banks of Bayous St. Jean, Sauvage and Chapitoulas—the high rich land of the ridge could provide more than enough food for the colony. The river crescent was without a doubt the place for New Orleans.[9] When ships arrived at Dauphin Island on March 9, 1718, with Bienville's appointment as Commandant-General and the Cross of Chevalier de St. Louis, by which his good services were recognized by His Majesty, this man of action swept aside all opposition, chose the site thirty leagues from the sea and left fifty men to clear the ground and construct some houses.

Though historians have differed as to the founding date of the city, in New Orleans it is generally accepted (based on the careful considerations of Historians Baron Marc de Villiers du Terrage and Jean Baptiste Benard de la Harpe) that the first work was done on New Orleans between March 15th and April 15th, 1718. A marker at Founder's Park on Decatur, between St. Ann and St. Peter Streets, identifies the location where Bienville and his men began to clear the ground of trees and brush and to build the first rude shelters of the city.[10]

Bienville, the Company's colonial administrator, must have arbitrarily assumed the task of site-selection, for his employers knew noththing of his choice. On April 14, 1718 instructions delivered by the

Company of the West to Chief Engineer Perrier, who was to come to Louisiane to help build the principal establishment, stated that where New Orleans was to be built was unknown, but Manchac was recommended as the most desirable spot. Perhaps Perrier's death enroute to his new job was a kinder fate than having to face the determination of Bienville;[11] and if that gentleman believed his site selection problems were over with the clearing of the location, it was only because his tenacity outweighed his foresight.

And then there was Marc Antoine Hubert (Commissary General of Louisiane from November 12, 1716 to September 15, 1720), who on March 14, 1718 was appointed Director General of the New Orleans counter, to work with (and check on) Bienville. He came to New Orleans from Mobile in the fall of 1718 by way of Lake Pontchartrain and Rivière d'Orléans, as Bayou St. Jean was sometimes called because of its nearness to the new settlement. He chose for his home a concession of land where Petit Bayou crossed the portage path which was to be called Bayou Road by the French. (Today Hubert's concession would be below the juncture of Esplanade Avenue and Grand Route St. John.) The new Director-General wasn't impressed with his new post which boasted only one palmetto-thatched hut Bienville had built for himself, and which his assistant M. de Pailloux (Paillous) used as living quarters when Bienville was absent. Seeing little future in the place, Hubert asked for, and soon received, a concession at Natchez, where there was plenty of farm land; and from that moment on, he applied all the pressure he could to make Natchez the main settlement of the colony, and aggressively urged all newcomers to follow his lead.[12]

Hubert's disdain for New Orleans was equalled by Geographer Le Maire's confusion as to where it was; or perhaps his description of May 13, 1718 anticipated the far-flung dimensions of today's Orleans Parish, so bewildering to the city's first-time visitor: "Since the last ships came, there is talk of the establishment to be made at New Orleans . . . the name recently given to the space enclosed between the Mississippi and Fish River, and Lakes Pontchartrain and Maurepas . . . I should have liked to mark the place where the fort is planned, but the place is not yet decided upon." He went on to say that the location was excellent provided the Mississippi could be made to empty into Lake Pontchartrain. Bayou St. Jean would have provided the major part of this water link which never came about. (The complete Lake Pontchartrain—Mississippi River connection wouldn't be realized for over two hundred years —not until the Industrial Canal was completed in 1922.)

LeMaire wasn't the only one worrying about New Orleans' drainage. A couple months earlier, in March of 1718, Benard de la Harpe reported that a canal, joining the Mississippi with the lake, had been planned, which would be most useful, even if New Orleans served only as a warehouse for the principal establishment at Natchez.

Bienville himself, who had previously proposed a channel of this kind, urged again in a dispatch of June 6, 1718 that a canal be built between the Mississippi and Lake Pontchartrain for purposes of sanitation. But not allowing his misgivings about drainage to deter him from his main objective, four days later he was complaining to the home office that he was working on New Orleans as diligently as the dearth of workmen permitted. He had stayed on the job for ten days to speed things up, but was grieved to have so few people working on a task that required a labor force a hundred times larger.[13]

If it was Bienville's intent to push the project to the point of no return, he must have been relieved to hear that in October of 1718 the Company of the West had approved the positioning of the borough thirty leagues above the mouth of the Mississippi and the stationing there of a storekeeper-cashier.

Even Geographer LeMaire, who had always insisted that New Orleans should be on Lake Pontchartrain, finally conceded at the end of 1718 that orders had come to transfer the principal spot to the banks of the Mississippi; but six months later, the Grand Vicar of the Bishop of Quebec—reflecting general opinion on the subject—wrote that the precise bearings of New Orleans, in relation to Lake Pontchartrain, were unknown to him.

During the last months of 1718 the sparsely-hutted rectangle on the river-rim served merely as a stop-over for parties going up river.[14]

Nor was nature an ally of the incipient settlement. In the spring of 1719 the Mississippi rose to an unprecedented height (according to the Indians) and flooded the entire town. Immediately conceding the myopia that up to now they had been loth to admit about the placement of the post, the Company's second sight resulted in desertion of the crescent curve for almost three years. Even Bienville had real doubts this time. Admitting that it might be difficult to maintain a town at New Orleans, he reported that the site was drowned under a half foot of water, and that the only remedy was to build levees and dig a canal from the Mississippi to Lake Pontchartrain, which would require only a half league of digging—from the river to Bayou St. Jean.[15] (It would take seventy five years for this task to be partially accomplished.)

New Orleans drainage was unique in that it flowed away from—not into—the Mississippi. The excessive waters drained away from the highest land in the vicinity—the natural levees along the river—back through a multitude of creeks, rivulets and branches of Bayou St. Jean to the main body of the bayou, and from there to Lake Pontchartrain. But the gradual land decline toward the bayou and the rise of the Metairie-Gentilly Ridge, representing a quasi-dam between the river and the lake, slowed the process to a trickle. Since most of the area was below sea level, the situation was critical in times of heavy rainfall and springtime floods.

The need for improving the natural drainage system was all too evident from the very beginning, and provided the weight that again tipped the scale in favor of another location for the principal settlement of Louisiane. Not one to ignore such an advantage, Hubert immediately pumped for Natchez, where the lands lay higher and the climate was cooler, and he peremptorily transferred to that place most of the supplies warehoused at New Orleans, leaving behind little more than a garrison and a few clerks. Perhaps the decision of the Company on April 23, 1719 to send a clerk to New Orleans to sell wine at four reales per pint helped sustain the morale of the bereft.[16]

The flood had little effect on the higher land at Bayou St. Jean; and the vital Pellerin, camping on the banks of the bayou in April of 1719, found a place he liked and asked for a concession on the stream. During his sojourn on the bayou, he reported seeing three Canadian houses and a warehouse which belong to the Company[17]—the beginning of the Village of Bayou St. Jean. Today these earliest structures would be located between Esplanade Avenue and Dumaine Street, along Moss Street on both sides of Bayou St. John.

As construction began on New Orleans, it was necessary to protect the supplies brought from Biloxi via the lake route until they were used. This need was met with the building of a warehouse in 1719-1720 on the west side of the portage road at Bayou St. Jean. It was a logical location, since it was to this spot—the early Port of Bayou St. Jean—that flatboats and other small, shallow-draught vessels came from Lake Pontchartrain. Here water transports were unloaded and supplies transferred to carts which trundled them over Bayou Road to the river rim, for use at that prospective settlement or for reloading on vessels bound for French settlements upstream. During the waiting time—between unloading and carting—the materials were stored in the King's warehouse ("magasin du roi" on early maps) to protect them from the weather.[18]

Pellerin didn't stay on the bayou for very long. By hook or by crook Hubert soon talked him out of it, and he, too, was off to Natchez.

Chapter VII

THE FIRST PERMANENT SETTLERS ON BAYOU ST. JEAN—1717-1721

In response to the propaganda of the Company of the West, colonists were on their way to the promised land of Louisiane. Many would die enroute, some would pass through to other posts, others would stay for a while 'til greener pastures beckoned, but a few would settle down and make their homes in New Orleans and on Bayou St. Jean.

The passenger list of the ship *Union* that left Chef de Baye May 28, 1717 included Jean Lavergne and Jacques Lorreins (Tarascon). In early Spanish times a Jean Lavergne would own land adjoining Fort St. Jean at the mouth of the bayou, and a succession of Lorreins would be active, outstanding citizens of Bayou St. Jean during French, Spanish and American times.[1]

In 1718 the Dreux brothers—Mathurin and Pierre—received from the Company of the West a choice forested acreage along Bayou Sauvage, in return—it is said—for their assistance in laying out New Orleans. Their ridge concession was high, impervious to river, lake and bayou overflow, and the two brothers would cut timber, make bricks and raise cattle on their land—a place they called Gentilly (the celebrated Condé estate just outside Paris, from whence they came). These respected genial gentlemen would come to be known as the Sieurs of Gentilly; and the waterway on which their land was located would thenceforth be known as Bayou Gentilly.[2]

On April 23, 1718 the Company of the West sent to the new establishment—which, as yet, hadn't received official recognition—twelve pioneer citizens and their families, a total of sixty eight people. Ordered by the Company to live within the limits of New Orleans, they were told to raise gardens only, and that larger concessions near New Orleans would be granted them as they demonstrated their ability to develop the land. Among these hopefuls were Bivard, a surgeon, Mircou, a wigmaker, Dufour (forefather of contemporary Historian Charles Dufour) and Antoine LePage DuPratz, a twenty three year old Dutchman who would live on Bayou St. Jean and elsewhere in Louisiana for sixteen years. His History of Louisiana, published in France in 1758, deals in fascinating detail with his varied experiences in the colony.

Landing at Dauphin Island on August 25, 1718, DuPratz didn't arrive in the New Orleans area until January of 1719. Arriving by the lake route, he noted with keen curiosity the many rivulets running into Lake Pontchartrain, making the lake almost fresh, although it was connected to the sea. Fresh and salt water fish in the same body of water sparked his interest, as well as carp which in France would have been considered monstrous.

Entering Bayou Choupic, named for a fish (the Indian name for Bayou St. Jean was still being used), they passed the redoubt and its guard at the bayou's entrance and continued up the stream to the site of the former village of the Acolapissas, near the juncture of Bayou St. Jean and Bayou Chapitoulas. The village—now the property of Sieur LaVigne— served as a temporary home for DuPratz and his entourage until he selected a permanent residence on the east bank of the bayou near LaVigne's plantation. He liked his new location, because it was only a short distance from where the capital was being founded, to which he could transport his crops via Bayou Road.

Representing the Company of the West, M. Paillous, Bienville's assistant, put DuPratz in possession of his land; and he and his party built a hut and lodging forty yards from the creek of St. Jean. From a neighbor the new Bayou citizen purchased a Chetimache slave to cook for them. She couldn't speak French, but they communicated by signs. A cooking fire, carefully built at a distance from the combustible hut, attracted and hypnotized a five foot alligator. (The bayou abounded with the creatures in early times.) The Indian girl called DuPratz's attention to the visitor, and he ran for his gun; but when he came back she'd already run the monster off by beating it on the nose with a stick. It was a game with the children of her tribe, she teased; the little ones chased and killed them for fun, as their elders cheered them on.

In the history DuPratz would write later from memory he revealed that some of the banks from Lake St. Louis (Pontchartrain) to the town (Village of Bayou St. Jean) were inhabited by planters in 1719, as were the banks of a nearby creek called Gentilly. He soon learned to cope with the mosquitoes by burning a little brimstone morning and evening. The smoke not only killed them, the smell of the pesticide kept the peskies away for days; and only an hour after applying this primitive pest control, the decontaminated hut could again be safely entered.

DuPratz was pleased with his bayou plantation. He found the soil good, and everything grew vigorously. The peachstones he planted in the spring soon had shoots four feet tall "with branches to match," and having taken good care of the seeds he brought with him, he was the only one to have salad plants, which the neighbors—as they perenially will—came to borrow.

DuPratz lived on Bayou St. Jean for only two years. Becoming friendly with Hubert, the inevitable happened, and the two of them moved to Natchez about the same time. He took with him a male and a female slave he'd purchased from the Company of the West for 1,320 livres (about $250.00) as well as his Chetimache cook. When her father heard that DuPratz was planning to leave, he came to buy his daughter back, but she wanted none of it. Explaining to her father that she had relatives among the Natchez who would help them out, and that it was fine country where one lived to a ripe old age, her father capitulated, and performed a ceremony of "the placing of hands" whereby he transferred her to the white man as a ward.[3]

The Company of the West was now fulfilling its contract by importing slaves into Louisiane to work in the fields of the expanding colony. The plantations of the West Indies had been developed only by the use of black labor, since the consensus of that day was that they were fitter than white men for working the land, and it was believed Louisiane would never prosper without a sufficient number of slaves.

Bienville had imported two slaves from the West Indies as early as 1708, but prior to Crozat's grant of 1712, there had been only a handful of Negroes in Louisiane, who had no doubt come with travelers from St. Domingue. Although Crozat's contract had allowed him to bring a boatload a year from the Guinea Coast, he evidently never exercised the privilege. The first large shipment of 250 slaves arrived in 1719, and for the next years they continued to come regularly until by 1731 the Company would have imported more than six thousand Blacks—a hundred percent more than its contract demanded.

These unfortunates (largely prisoners of war taken in fighting between the various African tribes and disposed of by the victor) came from as far away as the upper reaches of the Congo, were sold to slave-traders by Africans, herded together on the coast of Guinea and brought in cargo lots to Louisiane. The first shipments came to Pensacola, Mobile and Biloxi, and then to New Orleans as that settlement began to grow. The assemblage of these "barbarous hordes" close to the village of New Orleans was feared by the limited populace, so they were assigned to a place across the river (Algiers today), euphemistically called "The Plantation of the Company," which was established between 1720 and 1724. The site was taken out of land Bienville had ceded to himself in 1719, and the slaves were kept there—hopefully engaged in some productive work—until they could be sold and claimed by their new owners. The average price of a slave sold by the Company in 1721 was fixed at six hundred livres—about $120.00, payable in one, two or three years.[4]

Enterprising Claude Joseph Villars Dubreuil (also called DuBreuil Villars or de Villars) of Bayou St. Jean, Chapitoulas and Louisiane at large was the initial moving force in improving the local drainage system. A native of Dijon, France, he arrived on the *Comte de Toulouse* in March of 1719 at the age of thirty. One of the few strong enough to withstand Hubert's anti-New Orleans crusade, he immediately took over two concessions located away from the village—one below today's Esplanade Ave. and the other at the Chapitoulas, a short distance upriver. The plantation below Esplanade fronted for 7 arpents, 18 toises* on the Mississippi, extending from the upper corner of Barracks Street to what would later be the upper corner of D'Enghein Street, and angled lakeward to Gentilly and Bayou St. Jean. The Bayou frontage of this plantation stretched approximately from a point south of today's DeSaix Boulevard to the vicinity of Wisner Overpass.

In 1720 Dubreuil no doubt superintended the building of the New Orleans dikes by slaves of the Company of the West, for his memoirs inform us that in the beginning the Mississippi at flood stage put two feet of disease and death-causing waters in all the houses. When desperate Company directors asked for his help, he immediately took over, building two-thirds of the levees at his own expense, which should have made him the most popular man in town. A hardworking, intelligent mechanic, and man of many trades, he was the first to dig deep ditches to drain the waters from his land, setting an example that was followed by others. Records of early times reveal Dubreuil's continuing involvement in matters of personal importance to the bayou settlers as well as community projects of vaster scope. Reaping rich rewards in his long-lived career, he eventually owned up to five hundred slaves and had the reputation of being the wealthiest planter in French Louisiane.

The location of New Orleans and its drainage problems continued to trouble the settlers. In a report of 1720 Jean Baptiste Benard de la Harpe, one of the major leaders in the development of the colony, stated that "the land is flooded, impractical, unhealthy, unfit for the cultivation of rice, communication with the Mississippi is by Lake Pontchartrain via the creek of St. Jean, which is short—one-half league long, and along level banks. Much of this could be alleviated by inexpensive drainage."

* A toise = 6.39 English feet

Advocating the building of a canal from the Mississippi to Lake Pontchartrain, following Bayou St. Jean, in 1720 he aided in the preparation of a map showing such a canal.[5]

In 1719 Chartier de Baulne (M. Cartier DeBeame or Beaune) brought his family and thirty other persons to Bayou St. Jean where they settled down in the old Village of the Acolapissas. He and his entourage seem to have been the only semi-permanent tenants of that place. The 1721 census listed him as the sole resident of the ancient village, and he lived there until 1724 when his twelve arpent frontage near Bayou Chapitoulas was purchased by his neighbors, the Chauvin brothers—Louis Beaulieu and Nicholas de LaFrénière. Another Chauvin brother, Joseph Delery, had settled there first in 1719. They were friends of early Bayou St. Jean settler St. Denis, who had no doubt encouraged them to settle at the Chapitoulas—a location easily reached via Bayou St. Jean, Bayou Chapitoulas and the Indian trail that ran along it.

The Chauvin plantations produced rice, potatoes, beans and indigo, and were at that time the finest and best cultivated lands in Louisiane, replete with mills, forges and a hundred Negroes to work the land. They were really up-to-date on their equipment, because forges and plows had been used in the lower Mississippi Valley for only two years at that time.

Various early descriptions of places mention the Acolapissas on the west bank of Bayou St. Jean; so their village must have extended from the bayou westerly along Bayou Chapitoulas for a considerable distance. DeBaulne had settled in the most westerly portion at the Chapitoulas.

Lord de Baulne came to Louisiane with the title of Procureur General du Roi (King's Attorney) to serve on the Superior Council of Louisiane, the governing body of the colony. Created in 1712, and reorganized by the Edict of 1719, the Council was a working court of five to seven members—two lawyers and the others laymen—which officials could be reduced or enlarged by the council itself or by the King's decree. Unfortunately, DeBaulne's conduct and violation of Company policies lost him his job in 1722, at which time Francois Fleuriau became Attorney General.[6]

On May 27, 1719 family-minded Joseph Girardy was the recipient of five arpents front on the west bank of Bayou St. Jean, in the area between Dumaine and Carrollton on today's Moss Street. His land extended back toward today's Canal Street for forty arpents. (This was the same general area in which Louis Juchereau de St. Denis had received a concession in 1708; Denis had in 1713 sold his four arpents to DesBoumes and Graveline.) A DuMont Montigny map of 1722 in the New Orleans Public Library locates the Girardy residence immediately riverside of the Indian trail along Bayou Chapitoulas.

Two maps of the early French period (circa 1730) in the Library of Congress show the main Girardy residence on different sides of Chemin Chapitoulas, the road that led from upstream Mississippi to Bayou St. Jean.[7] However, the road was fixed on the lakeside of the residence when Marie Louise Girardy received eight arpents of land (lower City Park today) from Louis Turpin in 1734 and lived on the acreage with her husband Charles Lorreins (Tarascon) later on. The arpents of the Tarascons also included a number of slave cabins, and would be the site over which a lengthy family court battle would be waged in 1752.

Girardy was to father many daughters—Angelique, by the Indian Francoise, and four others by his wife Jeanne Henry (Héry)—most of whom would marry and settle down on the west bank of the bayou close to home. Of all the early settlers on Bayou St. Jean, Girardy would live there the longest—until his death in 1759.

In 1720 Francois Dugué (Duguay) and Etienne Stephen Langlois received concessions on the east bank of Bayou St. Jean, to the southwest of LaVigne's plantation. These two land grants were settled about the same time, but since Langlois' title described his acreage as "adjoining the Francois property," twenty year old bachelor Dugué must have gotten there a little ahead of him. Dugué (no doubt a relative of baker Etienne Duguay on the December 1699 Census at Fort Biloxi) received a 2½ arpent frontage on the bayou that stretched from the southern border of LaVigne's plantation to the lakeside of Bayou Road. An early map, pencil-marked circa 1723, also shows Francois Dugué claiming the tract on the west bank of Bayou St. Jean that reached north from Bayou Chapitoulas (Metairie) toward the lake, making him a very early claimant of what is known today as lower City Park.[8]

With only the old portage trail separating their properties, Etienne Langlois became Dugué's neighbor on September 21, 1720 when he acquired his 3½ arpent frontage which stretched westerly from Bayou Road. A few months later Jean Baptiste Provenche (Provenchez) settled his three-arpent bayou frontage to the immediate west of Langlois on April 21, 1721, but held on to it for only three years. On September 17, 1724 he sold his land to his neighbor, and the combined acreage of the two grants was known from that time on as the Langlois concession, which would today extend approximately from a point between DeSoto and Bell Streets westerly to the vicinity of Orleans Street, with the usual depth of forty arpents. Etienne Langlois (a quiet man who evidently didn't become involved, for he isn't mentioned in the early court records) and his wife Marie Catherine Beaudreau, would have several children during a rather short married life.

Although the original titles of Langlois and Provenche added up to only six and a half arpents front, conveyances of that property from 1752 on would record it as eight arpents.[9] Irregular measurement of early concessions was the rule rather than the exception. In thickly wooded swampy terrain the most skillful surveyor made errors, and trying to measure swampland was like measuring a grainfield. There really were no dependable landmarks. When a sturdy tree was designated as such, it could be felled in the next storm. But since there was more land than hands to work it in those days, these mistakes were of little immediate consequence. It was only later—when subsequent owners of the land began to check original titles—that legal disputation over boundaries arose. This—plus the difficulty of translating French measurements into Spanish and English-American distances—makes it necessary for the location of these early properties on today's maps to be approximate, for it is impossible to know the exact boundaries of most of the original concessions on Bayou St. Jean.

The map marked 1723 (which should be 1724 or later since it doesn't designate the property of Provenche) shows a considerable concession on the bayou's west bank, located obliquely across the stream from Langlois' plantation, claimed by Bonnaud. This was no doubt Arnaud Bonnaud, Storekeeper-Warehouse Guard, first appointee of the Company of the West in 1717. Since he first worked in the Company warehouse at the foot of Bayou Road, what would have been more logical than to acquire property right across the bayou from his job?

To the immediate west of the Bonnaud claim, another strip of land—between Bayou St. Jean and Bayou Chapitoulas—was claimed by Francois Trudeau, an early colonist. Some of these concessionaires didn't follow through on their legal obligations and forfeited their grants which then reverted to the Company and were ceded to somebody else. This could have happened in this instance, or the property may have been sold. Eventually much of the land would belong to Joseph Girardy.

The map of 1723 also reveals two ribbon concessions farther lakeside on Bayou St. Jean, angling southeasterly from Bayou St. Jean to Bayou Gentilly. The one closest to New Orleans was claimed by Sr. Jean Saubagne (Soubagne, Soubaignie), a litigious early settler of Gentilly. Since the Bayou St. Jean end of his grant (near today's Park Island) was overflowed most of the year, Saubagne built his home on the higher Gentilly Ridge. The records reveal nothing of Sieur le Cheuve, who claimed the adjoining strip of land.[10]

And then there was Charlotte, heroine of a romantic old tale of Bayou St. Jean. Legend has it that the Duke of Brunswick-Wolfembuttel had arranged the marriage of his beautiful and virtuous daughter to the Czarevitch Alexis, son of Peter the Great of Russia—but only after she'd fallen in love with the Chevalier d'Aubant, an officer of her father's household. On the day of the marriage d'Aubant was presented with a passport and "permission" to leave the country. Where he went nobody knew, but in 1718 he turned up in Louisiane as a captain of the colonial troops. Beyond the ordinary discharge of his duties he sought no diversion with fellow-officers, preferring his lonely retreat on the banks of Bayou St. Jean close to a small village of friendly Indians, (the park end of Esplanade Avenue). The only objet d'art in his rude retreat was a full length portrait of a beautiful lady who gazed with intense melancholy on a heart crushed by a heavy crown placed on an adjacent table. The seldom visitor, 'though tempted to ask, intuited that this was forbidden territory.

Meanwhile, back at the palace, Charlotte's imperial existence left much to be desired. A womanizing lush, her husband had struck her in a rage and left her for dead. Recovering from her swoon, she connived with a soul-sister to escape her continuing misery by re-enacting Juliet's feigned death-scene. The funeral took place, and no one was the wiser, but with the German emigrants of 1721 came one of regal beauty and manner, who immediately asked about Chevalier d'Aubant, to whom, she said she'd been recommended. Informed that he'd be sent for, she preferred to be conducted to his bayou lodging.

Needless to say, they were married, but didn't live happily ever after. Having attracted attention, as the unusual few are apt to do, they went back to Paris to avoid further publicity. But there Charlotte was recognized by an old acquaintance and had to flee to escape the inevitable results of detection. Her military spouse departed for the Island of Bourbon on a lengthy assignment, and after his death in 1754, it is said Charlotte and a daughter returned to Paris where she lived until 1781 and died destitute.

Over the years many would-be-Sherlocks have debunked this fascinating tale, the most stunning put-down being that Catherine II supposedly revealed that the body of the Czarevitch's wife had been embalmed and exposed to the public for several days after her death.

Nor does the story stand up to local research. There is no record in the 1720-1723 St. Louis Cathedral Marriage Records of a d'Aubant nor does any other colonial document reveal such a person. LaVigne, Dugué, Langlois and Girardy are listed in the yearly Census, from 1721 to 1728, as permanent residents of Bayou St. Jean, but there is no d'Aubant. Only two leaf-locked trees stood for many years near today's Esplanade Avenue bridge, pointing to the dwelling place of the lovers, but they, too, are long gone.[11]

Chapter VIII

BAYOU ST. JEAN DECIDES THE LOCATION OF NEW ORLEANS 1721-1722

The "ladies" who came to Ship Island on January 8, 1721 filled a woeful discrepancy in the man-molded colony, but Bienville wasn't impressed with the eighty eight who arrived on *La Baleine,* nor with sour Sister Gertrude, one of three nuns in whose custody they were sent to insure the piety, good conduct, duty and purity of Louisiane's future mothers. The destitute girls, who had worked in the Salpetrière Hospital of Paris, and whose fortunes could go nowhere but up, were no doubt attracted by the dower offered each—two pair of coats, two shirts and undershirts, six head-dresses and other furnishings—so they might marry as soon as possible.

The Captain of *La Baleine* had paid no more attention to his cargo than had the sisters. During those weeks at sea, romance had blossomed ahead of schedule, and on June 25th Bienville reported that many of the girls, who could scarcely be offered to good residents, had been married off to sailors who had insistently asked for them. But as Historian Penicaut nonchalantly remarks, "so great was the want of the country, this merchandise was soon disposed of."[1]

The location of the principal settlement of Louisiane had been the continuing topic of discussion for years, but now the time had come to resolve the thorny problem once and for all. The places reflected on before were thoroughly rehashed, in addition to which Natchitoches was an added possibility. Pensacola had been considered for a short time, despite the fact that this easternmost location would have required four transfers when merchandise was being transported from the Illinois country to France. The clumsy shipping situation notwithstanding, Engineer-in-Chief Le Blond de la Tour was commanded to establish the settlement. Then a sudden order of August 20, 1720 (one of several during the alternating French-Spanish ownership of Pensacola from 1719 to 1722) restored the place to the Spanish, and the Company's attention veered in the opposite direction.

In his report of 1720 Jean Baptiste Benard de la Harpe laid down a shrewd plan for seizure of Texas from the Spanish, pointing out the relationship of the western frontier, trade with the Indians and the proposed settlement at St. Bernard Bay on the shores of Texas, showing, how all this would fit into a grand strategy for seizing Texas, and even Mexico.

Despite Bienville's opposition, la Harpe was a member of the abortive expeditions of 1720 and 1721 that sailed to occupy Matagorda Beach (near Indianola, Texas) which France claimed because La Salle had landed there on his second expedition in 1685.

In September of 1720, the Company of the Indies (formerly Company of the West) had issued instructions to establish a post at the mouth of Bayou Manchac, with which everybody seemed to agree—everybody except the Mobile-Biloxi establishment, including some members of the Company Board, who up to now had gone along with Manchac only to divert interest from New Orleans. But with preponderant support for the site, the Company decided on Manchac, then rapidly reverted to indecision, for on November 8, 1720 Assistant Engineer de Pauger was ordered to go to New Orleans to examine the site of that town, and *if necessary,* transfer the settlement to a location that didn't flood so badly.[2]

Some of the neglect and confusion about starting the new settlement may well be attributed to the unfortunate situation in Paris. John Law had united two rival companies, Des Indes Orientales and De Chine to his Company of the West, and called the united association La Compagnie Des Indes. Monopolizing all of France's foreign trade, his company nevertheless was in February of 1720 in serious trouble due to out-of-sight inflation. There was a kind of madness in the nation, and shares sky-rocketed to forty times their nominal price. Men sold everything to speculate; foreigners and scavengers flooded into Paris with their own and stolen funds, and everybody seemed to be getting rich. But were they? The issue of shares at extreme market price, valued at 12,000,000,000 livres, required 600,000,000 livres annually to pay a five-percent dividend, and Law's Company didn't have the profits to pay. Shares began to fall in value, as people began selling them. For over two years Law had manipulated everybody, including the rulers of the kingdom, which in any era is no mean feat; but finally in December, 1720—having become the object of public hatred—he secretly fled the country penniless, to be consigned to the realm of the ignored, which for one who has inhaled the heights must be the meanest stroke of all.[3]

After Law's finale, it could have been weariness with the whole thing, anxiety about unforeseen drawbacks in another, untried location, the cost of starting a new establishment, or perhaps it was just Bienville's belief in the place; for when he got around to implementing the Company's orders of the previous November, he send de Pauger to the crescent site in March of 1721, and there seemed to be no doubt in the mind of the Assistant Engineer that "this was it," as he set about preparing a plan of New Orleans. De Pauger was surprised to see that this highly-touted-and-attacked establishment consisted of only a few cabins among bushes and clumps of trees which made alignment of the streets impossible. But no man to be poletrapped by a few problems, de Pauger applied himself vigorously with the aid of a handful of convicts who soon deserted. Rejuvenating his work force with an officer and ten soldiers, at an additional cost of a gill of brandy per man per day, enough clearing was done in twelve days so that all the streets could be projected.[4]

Recorders of history may give varying reasons why the crescent site was chosen for the principal settlement of Louisiane, but all of them—without exception—agree that *New Orleans was built where it is because Bayou St. Jean and the short portage–connecting Lake Pontchartrain and the Mississippi River–provided a vitally needed, safe transportation route by which all the coastal settlements could be reached by boat*: and most of them agreed with Historian Baron Marc de Villiers that "in spite of the swampy soil, exposed to flood when the river rose, the choice of site was good, and the vision of Bienville was clear."

Bienville's vision was also self-interested for on March 27, 1719 he had conceded to himself an eight mile river-front tract, which extended from the upper edge of the settlement to the Chapitoulas, and reached from the Mississippi back to the coulées of Bayou St. Jean. (From today's Bienville Street in the Quarter to Southport, above Carrollton, with a width to Claiborne Avenue.) He also claimed a 112-arpent-length of land (by three miles wide) on the opposite side of the river, including today's Algiers. Although these transactions were not to prove popular with the local citizens, it was all perfectly legal, confirmed by the Company of the Indies on February 6, 1720.[5]

Despite the attention that focused on the building of New Orleans, the main deterrent to effecting a self-sustaining colony was the lack of stable settlers—colonists content to foster and protect their arpents. On October 20, 1719 Bienville had complained bitterly to Paris: "It's most disagreeable for an officer charged with the defence of a colony to have but a band of deserters, smugglers and scoundrels who would not only abandon him, but would turn against him." As an antidote to these ills, the Company of the Indies recruited Germans to settle the land; and in June and July of 1721—unaware of the fugitive status of John Law—120 German men, women and children, having arrived in Biloxi, headed for Law's concession in Arkansas. To reach their destination, some of them came the old route—from Biloxi through the Mississippi Sound, Lake Pontchartrain and Bayou St. Jean, wading over the swampy portage to New Orleans, where they embarked in thirty boats to go upriver.

The newer route was through Lakes Pontchartrain, Maurepas and Bayou Manchac to the Mississippi, but it was probably used very little, for a report of 1721 states that the Iberville River (Bayou Manchac) was dry for half the year, so most of the boats had to pass through Bayou St. Jean. A memoir of that period, in the archives of Paris, revealed that Bayou St. Jean had three and a half feet of water and that boats could go up its two-league length to where several French planters lived and where a store was located. After merchandise was landed there, it was carted three-fourths of a league to New Orleans.

To facilitate travel and commerce at the little Port of Bayou St. Jean, no doubt the old log bridge of the Indians at this point had been replaced with a safer, more useable wooden structure (similar to the one constructed in Gentilly in the early 1720s) by the early Bayou St. Jean dwellers.[6]

The following year, between December 15th and January 31st, three hundred and thirty more German men and women traveled Bayou St. Jean and Bayou Road (the old route) to the Mississippi, went upriver and settled down twenty five miles above New Orleans at La Côte des Allemands (The German Coast). In 1725, some of the Germans who'd arrived in 1721, and who'd survived the hardships of Arkansas, came downriver to settle near their compatriots.[7]

On September 5, 1721 the Company of the Indies defined the districts of Louisiane as Biloxi, Mobile, Alabama, Natchez, Yazoo, Red River, Arkansas, Illinois and New Orleans. The last was designated as the first district where the Commandant General was to make his residence. However, it was not until December 23, 1721 that the Company officials signed the order transferring the general management to New Orleans, making it the capitol of Louisiane.[8]

The same order included instructions to build a fort and store at the Balize (buoy, beacon), known today as Pilot Town, where ascent of the river by incoming vessels, or transfer of goods to other boats, could be arranged. Since 1717 the French had been promoting navigation up the river by trying to improve conditions at the mouth of the Mississippi and dispelling rumors about the dangerous passes.[9]

More than twenty years after the French first came to Louisiane and injudiciously settled on the sandy acres at Dauphin Island and Biloxi, the colony finally began to look up agriculturally. After almost complete

Langlois, Dugúe, LaVigne and Girardy were the first permanent settlers of the Village of Bayou St. Jean in the early 1720s, at the time New Orleans was being built (1718-1722). The brickyard on Bayou Road, just outside New Orleans, is indicated on a circa 1730 French map of early New Orleans.

dependence on France, Vera Cruz and Havana for their provisions (in the vicinity of some of the richest soil of the country) the Company of the Indies was now beginning to grant more concessions of productive land near New Orleans, improving prospects of feeding the colony at the local level.

The Census of 1721 included an enthusiastic report to the home office that the land at New Orleans and surrounding areas was very good, producing rice, cotton, corn, vegetables of all kinds and abundant tobacco—the richest crop on the market. It was believed Louisiane would be able to supply all the tobacco France could use. Leaf or twist, it was purchased from growers at the Company warehouse for 25 livres per one hundred pounds, rice brought 12 livres per quintal, and peltries and furs were bought at a fixed price. Indigo, which had just begun to grow, promised to do well; it was believed that two, maybe three good crops a year might be anticipated in the future.[10]

The Census revealed that the Bayou St. Jean settlers were better off than the average:

The Village of Bayou St. Jean, one league from New Orleans:

	Men	*Women*	*Children*	*French Servants*	*Negro Slaves*	*Indian Slaves*	*Cattle*	*Horses*
Rivard or LaVigne	1	1	6		11	2	30	4
Francois Dugué	1				3	3	7	
Langlois	1	1	1		8	1	4	
Joseph Girardy	1	1	2		10	2	15	
The Ancient Village des Colapissas:								
M. de Beame (Baulne) Procurer-General	1	1	2	3	9		5	2

In 1721 LaVigne was the wealthiest with eleven Negro and two Indian slaves to work his land and tend his thirty cattle. On the west bank of the bayou, Girardy ran a close second with ten Negroes, two Indian slaves and fifteen cattle. Langlois and Dugué weren't far behind, nor was De Baulne, at the Village of the Acolapissas, with nine Negro slaves and three French servants.

And when it came to horses, LaVigne's four, de Baulne's two and the Gentilly Dreux brothers' five constituted a goodly percentage of the total of twenty eight in the entire colony at that time. Most early equines were brought to New Orleans by Indians who captured them in skirmishes with the Spanish west of Natchitoches, which source would continue to supply transportation for New Orleans throughout the French domination of Louisiane.[11]

There was another LaVigne, listed as a Gentilly settler, with "a wife, one child and one French servant." This could have been the family of Jean Baptiste LaVigne, an old settler, mentioned in the records of 1720, or some other relative of Antoine Rivard de LaVigne of Bayou St. Jean.[12]

1721 had been a telling year. From a combination military post, sales counter and camping ground, New Orleans had become a small town. An État de la Louisiane of that year concluded that "the store which serves as a warehouse for New Orleans at the St. Jean brook is indispensible. It could be done away with only after the Manchac brook has been cleared." And since Bayou Manchac never did become navigable, the warehouse at the foot of Bayou Road—built in 1719-20—continued to be a useful fixture of French Louisiane.[13]

French goods were available at the warehouse. Wine sold at 120 livres the barrique. At Biloxi, Mobile and New Orleans all merchandise was sold by the Company at five percent over the invoice price of France. As distances increased, the price went up—seventy percent over invoice price at Natchez, eighty percent at Arkansas, and at the Illinois the price doubled. This kind of trade attracted the coureur des bois—half peddler, half hunter, with a little broker mixed in. He was the first middleman of Louisiane, bringing products of France to the Indians and settlers away from the Gulf coast, and exchanging them for products of the country. Local tradespeople also anticipated sales to the Spanish near Natchitoches and on the upper Arkansas River who were too far away from Mexico to get their requirements from that source.[14] Many residents of Bayou St. Jean pursued this kind of trade as a part time involvement.

Father Pierre Francois Xavier de Charlevoix visited New Orleans in January of 1722, and his fascinating travel account describes his introduction to the region. "In the afternoon we crossed Lake Pontchartrain for seven, eight leagues. Those who had navigated this lake (previously) found it so full of caiman (alligators) they could scarcely give a stroke of the oar without hitting one. They are at present very scarce, and we only saw some traces of them at our encamping, for the animals lay their eggs on land." Charlevoix noted the military post (Fort St. Jean), defended by a battery of six guns, at the mouth of Bayou St. Jean as they entered that stream.

Despite the gains of 1721, the good father wasn't impressed with the settlement of New Orleans. Commenting that its environs were not remarkable and that the place wasn't as well situated as he'd been told, he added: "Others are not of the same opinion, one of their reasons being that a league from hence, inclined to the northeast, they have found a little river which they have called Bayou St. Jean, which at the end of two leagues discharges itself into Lake Pontchartrain which communicates with the sea. By this means, they say, they are able to keep up a certain commerce between the capitol and la Maubile, Biloxi and other posts we possess near the sea."

Charlevoix assessed New Orleans as being far from the eight hundred fine houses and five parishes reported in French papers two years before. He found only a hundred barracks, badly arranged, a big storehouse built of wood, two or three houses that would be no ornament to a French village, and half a sorry warehouse. He especially deplored the fact that the Lord's services were being carried on in a place that also served as a mundane establishment.

However, not without hope, he opined that the day might not be too far off when "this wild and desert place, which the reeds and trees do yet almost wholly cover, will be an opulent city and the metropolis of a great and rich colony."[15]

When the order of the previous December—to locate the seat of government at New Orleans—arrived at Biloxi on May 26, 1722, all layers of opposition magically melted. It seemed that everybody had always realized the potential of the place and had suggestions for improving it. Even Hubert ate crow. Having moved away from New Orleans in 1720, he had put up a corn mill, planted wheat and oats on his vast Natchez holdings, and for a time thrived as one of fate's favorites—until the Indians (instigated, some said, by his enemies) killed some of his livestock and harrassed him in other ways. Discouraged, he sold his plantation and was ordered back to France.

Bienville, among others, must have been surprised to hear that Hubert viewed with pleasure the transfer of the principal settlement to New Orleans, and his observation that he, Hubert, would have brought all the ships into the river had it not been for the opposition of LeGac, the second Councillor of the Colony. No period has an edge on hindsighters, and Hubert was making sounds like a man who needed a job.[16] Chief Engineer Louis Pierre Le Blond de la Tour, leader of the malcontents since his arrival in 1720, immediately endorsed de Pauger's plan of building two jetties at the river mouth so the enforced rush of water through the narrowed channel would deepen the river bed by pushing out the deposits and refuse. De Pauger's method wouldn't be completely effected for another hundred and fifty years— when Captain Eads, in 1879, would make the system work.

Borrowing from de Pauger seemed to be a habit with de la Tour, who didn't much care for his own plan of New Orleans—a sketch of a few squares back from the river, probably on the banks of Bayou St. Jean. Adopting the lay-out of his assistant, de la Tour went to work with a vigor to match his previous reluctance, despite the tremendous drawbacks under which the workers had to labor. Cypress was their main material— the only wood that would stand up to New Orleans weather— and it had to be hauled from Bayou St. Jean to the river crescent by strong arms and *one* cart—the only equipment available.

A report of an assistant engineer in the national archives of France described the process: "The first step was to give it (New Orleans) air by breaking the ground and cutting the trees, thick as the hair on a man's head. We lost no time about it, exposing ourselves to the ardour of the sun and the onslaught of insects from daybreak until nightfall. In less than three months, we had cleared a square representing a good quarter of a league of forest. After which, (in order) that the town might take shape, we urged the inhabitants to erect houses on the sites we marked for them. Each one vied with the rest to finish his house first, so that in a very short time everybody had shelter, and the company's goods were under cover in two fine stores, the framework for one having been brought from Biloxi. The plan, as arranged, is handsome. The streets are perfectly aligned and of convenient width. In the center of the town, facing the square (today's Jackson Square) are all the public buildings. At the end is the church, with the Director's house on one side and the stores on the other. The architecture of all the buildings is of the same model, very simple. There is only one story, raised a foot above the level of the ground, resting on carefully placed foundations and covered with bark or boards. Each block or ile is divided into five parts, so that each private citizen may be comfortably lodged and may have a yard or garden. This city was founded by the Company of the Indies in 1722."[17]

New Orleans was on its way—four years after Bienville and his handful of workers had begun the first clearing.

Chapter IX

GROWING PAINS OF NEW ORLEANS AND THE BAYOU SETTLEMENT 1722-1725

One of the earliest social events on Bayou St. Jean was the May 12, 1722 marriage of Antoine Rivard de LaVigne's daughter Marie to Joseph Lamy, whose Canadian parents lived in Illinois.[1]

Lucky was the choice of a spring wedding, for a few months later Mother Nature presented her own spectacular on September 11, 1722 when a fierce hurricane raged against the settlement for fifteen hours, injuring hospitalized patients and destroying thirty four huts, including those serving as church and rectory. The entire fleet of small vessels on the Mississippi was put out of commission, and some larger ships and flatboats, loaded with grain, fowl and produce, ran aground. Bayou St. Jean rose three feet, the Mississippi nearly eight; and the gunpowder was saved just in time when it was moved to a dovecote Bienville had built for his own use.[2]

Labor for rebuilding was impossible to come by, and food supplies were short. De la Tour immediately imposed price controls on items necessary to survival, and with the brash optimism needed to carry a leader through such a calamity, he shrugged off the loss of the huts, saying they were temporary, old and out of alignment and would have had to be torn down anyway.[3]

Unfortunately for the Commandant-General, De la Tour's optimism didn't reflect public opinion. As Bienville's arpents had grown more valuable, and he the wealthier from their produce, envious rumors had begun to circulate that he'd obtained them under false pretenses, saying they were overflowed when, in fact, they were the best lands to be had.

This accusation, smacking of earlier charges against him of having operated for private advantage, capped the complaints that had been accumulating from the beginning of the colony. The barren Biloxi coast had provided no food for the newcomers, and once initial supplies were gone, replacements from France had been practically non-existent. Most of the early arrivals had been unreasonably afraid of coming up the Mississippi through its mouth, and since there were very few small boats in which they could have come by the lake route to Bayou St. Jean, it was only in the past months that some of them had been able to establish homes and raise food in the New Orleans area. More than half the workingmen who'd come to Biloxi had died from hunger, disease and lack of medical attention.

Under Royal orders of December 8, 19 and 30, 1722, Jacques de La Chaise was sent to the colony to find out why the large outlay of money and life—from 1717 to 1722—hadn't resulted in greater profit to Company and King. Arriving on the ship *Venus*, which anchored at Ship Island, he traveled to New Orleans quietly and unobserved. Suspicious of the local government, French officials felt justified in taking these secret, drastic steps to remedy the disease that was paralyzing their project.

Accompanied by fellow commissioner du Sauvoy (Saunoy), Capuchin Father Raphael de Luxembourg and a friar, de La Chaise completed his journey via the lake route. Arriving at the Village of Bayou St. Jean, they spent the night there, and next morning the small party walked into New Orleans to begin house-cleaning the local administration which would result in Bienville's ouster-order on February 16, 1724. De la Tour and Sauvoy died before they could report to Paris on that first Louisiana hayride, but de La Chaise, appointed first councillor of the Superior Council in January of 1724, worked hard and faithfully in New Orleans until his death eight years later.[4]

The streets of New Orleans had been named by November 2, 1722, and 1723 continued to be a very busy time in the colony. The government and the Commandant-General's residence were finally transferred to New Orleans, and Assistant Engineer Franquet de Chaville completed the big store and other buildings, and finished the 500-toise levee on the Mississippi—all this, despite the epidemics that were killing eight or nine people every day. Supplies were as short as ever, but not the humor of the colony commanders in handling their problems. One Villeneuve, a resourceful workman under the Engineers, had killed a number of dogs and cats and sold their meat to the hospital, resulting in a menu of "plenty of roast dog" according to one of the patient-witnesses in a subsequent lawsuit. The unique punishment pronounced by Bienville and the Councillors, was that Villeneuve be paraded up and down and then put on a wooden horse for two hours with a cat draped about his neck (if one was left to be found), sporting a placard inscribed "Eater of Dogs and Cats."[5]

A report to the Company of the Indies of 1724 noted that the Bayou four—LaVigne, Girardy, Langlois and Dugué—were continuing to prosper on a higher level than the average colonist, and were diversifying their endeavors: "This bayou is established by four settlers, the least of whom has eight to ten Negroes, and each has very fine land. Next year these settlers will no doubt raise a quantity of indigo, having had this year a supply of grain; and though their land is only a league back of New Orleans, it is not subject to inundation." The report mentioned widespread flooding of other concessions, and praised Bienville's plantation as having more grain than the others as well as the finest crop of indigo.[6]

April of 1724 saw the beginning of the building of the barracks and completion of the officers' pavillion, which also served as a temporary church for over a year, as work on the Lord's house continued.

Bear oil, deerskins, sassafras, pecans and poultry were traded to the colonists by the Indians; and peltry, lumber and tobacco went to France on ships that brought settlers and French goods to Louisiane. But many necessary items were in short supply. Two women were summoned before the Council for selling eggs at sixteen cents each—double the market price. Condemned to a fine of 100 francs each, fifteen days and expulsion from the city, they were warned that the dungeon awaited in the event they tried it again.[7]

With continued importation of slaves by the Company of the Indies, it was necessary in 1724 for Bienville to activate the Code Noir in the colony. Brutal as it was by today's standards, the Black Code, first established in 1685 to administer slavery conditions in French colonies, permitted privileges denied in the English colonies of North America. Slaves could own personal property under certain circumstances; and masters— though often neglecting their responsibilities—were required by law to provide religious training for their slaves. Throughout the entire French era a slave could complain in the courts against his master, could testify under oath, and received considerate attention to his complaints which were often maintained in legal conflicts. The records of the Superior Council disclose many instances of slave emancipation by 1) wills of their owners, 2) the purchase of their freedom with money earned from their owners, or 3) as a reward for faithful service or an unusual heroism, such as saving a life in the master's family.[8]

However, from the very beginning crime and misdemeanor, on the part of slave or freeman, weren't alien to the bayou sector; and Antoine Rivard de LaVigne, active on all levels of bayou existence, didn't hesitate to use the governing body to keep things running right. Superior Council records of May 24, 1723 disclose his complaint that during the previous five months two run-away slaves, belonging to Gentilly neighbor Coustillas, had been killing and eating a number of cattle near Bayou

Chapitoulas (Metairie) and other places in the vicinity. This was a serious matter, because of the shortage of domesticated animals. The same month Chief Warehouse Guard Arnaud Bonnaud asked the Council to institute proceedings against one LeRoux for shooting one of his cows. He described the loss as personal and public—the latter, because it demoralized order in the colony.

Eight year old witness Francois Trudeau, who had come to the bayou on the feast of Corpus Christi to pick blackberries, had observed the stranger shooting at a black and white cow.[9]

Dugué's place, near the harbor of Bayou St. Jean and the main drag—Bayou Road—attracted many a character who was passing through. In 1723, LaVigne was at Dugué's home when Francois Rillieux paid them a visit. Rillieux would for the next hundred years be a familiar name along Bayou St. Jean; but on this occasion the twenty five year old boatmaster, having just returned from a journey for his concessionaire-employer, brought with him several articles of clothing, slippers, soap, etc. which he'd discovered in the possession of a slave while at sea. Rillieux had ordered the slave bound and beaten in an attempt to find out who the goods belonged to, but the Negro insisted they'd been given to him by a slave of the Company. Returning to the Port of Bayou St. Jean, Rillieux heard that Locksmith Didier had been robbed, and searching about, found him working at Dugué's plantation. On describing the articles he'd lost, Didier's belongings were returned to him.

Apparently workers plied their various trades from one plantation to another, for the Census of 1724 lists Laurent Ritter, the younger, as an occupant of the habitation of Francois Dugué on Bayou St. Jean. And on March 18, 1725 Dugué was having trouble with a botson-edge tool maker, who complained to the Superior Council that he'd ironed the cart of Mr. Francois residing at the bayou for the sum of eighty francs, but had received nothing in return but words of offense. The Council granted him action. Dugué's youth and single status may have accounted for his bad temper. Of the four early residents of the Village of Bayou St. Jean, he was the only bachelor. Or maybe, with two plantations to look after, he'd bitten off more than he could chew. In addition to his east bank bayou property, he was also claiming the tract on the west bank which extended north from Chemin Chapitoulas (Metairie Road).[10]

Dugué's neighbor LaVigne was having trouble of another kind, because he'd barred a road that ran through the Gentilly end of his plantation. Originally, this right-of-way had been an old Indian trail which the Dreux brothers had improved at their own expense in 1720 and on which there was a bridge over a bayou built by several Gentilly settlers.

LaVigne had his reasons. The road ran through his sown fields, and because the fence-gates protecting his planting were often left open by careless travelers, considerable damage was being done to his crops by roving cattle. So he set up an alternative route, not far from the original road, which provided only a log bridge over the bayou.

On March 8, 1725 outraged Jean Saubagne and another neighbor—on behalf of all Gentilly citizens—petitioned the Superior Council to make LaVigne do right. On May 5th LaVigne countered with an offer to furnish a day's worth of Negro labor to build a bridge on the alternate road, if every other Gentilly resident would do the same. Apparently they weren't willing, because on May 14th they were again before the Council asking that LaVigne be called to account for his actions. On May 25th de Pauger, Chief Engineer for the King, ordered examination of the premises and recommended the new road. On June 18th, the court viewers—Attorney General Fleuriau, Councillor Paul Perry and the Recorder—agreed that the new road looked passable, but recommended that a bridge be built. Finally on June 25th a Solomon judgment ended the matter when the Council decreed that LaVigne should furnish a road and bridge, passable by horses and carts, and allow use of the old road until the new bridge was finished. Gentilly residents, however, were to be responsible for the upkeep of the new bridge; but since LaVigne had been the one to start the ruckus, he had to pay all court costs.[11]

LaVigne, however, wasn't so involved with minor frustrations he lost sight of the bigger scene. As New Orleans continued to grow, necessitating importation of supplies and workmen from Biloxi and Mobile, the deficiencies of the local transportation route became obvious.

In 1724 Adrien Gilbert proposed dredging the mouth of the Mississippi as well as the entrance to Bayou St. Jean at Lake Pontchartrain, because it was so difficult for laden flatboats to cross the sandbar at that point. And in 1725, Bienville asked the Company of the Indies to assist LaVigne in the improvement of the stream: "Bayou St. Jean, which is behind the city, is of such great convenience because of the communication which it affords with Lake Pontchartrain, and consequently with the sea, that it cannot be esteemed too highly. In order to facilitate navigation, what would be necessary to clear it out, is to remove from it all the trees that hang over its banks and threaten to fall into it. A good settler on this bayou named Rivart (LaVigne) offers to undertake this work and promises to complete it in three years, because no work can be done on it except when the water is low. For that purpose he asks that we lend him the pulleys, tools and ropes necessary, and that the Company grant him a concession one side of the land of this bayou as far as the lake, which is about three quarters of a league. This land is subject to overflow, which he would drain in order to make pastures. This proposal appears to me to be advantageous and so inexpensive for the company and of such great assistance to New Orleans that I do not think it ought to be rejected."

The alert LaVigne, realizing the potential of bayou property over two hundred years before most of it was developed, had intentions of extending his east bank seventeen-arpent holdings all the way to the lake. The only other mention of this project in the colonial archives at Paris is the reference "Bienville's Project of trusting the work to LaVigne." There is no evidence that the work was done or that any land was allotted to LaVigne in payment. It would be interesting to know how this enterprising citizen of Bayou St. Jean would have proceeded—with limited means—to effect what has taken so many so long to achieve.[12]

On the west bank of the bayou, Joseph Girardy was developing his property, and had commissioned one Cabassier to build an extension to his house south of Chemin Chapitoulas as well as a 28′ x 19′ barn. Having already paid six barrels of rice, a barrel of sweet potatoes, a cow and a calf for the work to be done, Cabassier finished the barn, but forgot about the extension to the house, whereupon Girardy hauled him before the Superior Council. The tribunal decided he had to return the livestock to Girardy because he hadn't fulfilled his contract.[13]

Most transactions of that time represented exchanges of goods or services because of the severe shortage of money. The only coins in early Louisiane were those brought by the colonists or received from sailors paying for provisions. The few piastres that found their way into the colony from Spanish settlements were soon on ships going back to France to buy needed goods. As the colony began to grow, the acute need for small currency was met by French coinage of six and twelve denier pieces for use only in the American colonies. Lasting but a short time, all that remained of the coin was the expression "sol marque," which even today—'mongst old Creoles—means the lowest form of value.[14]

A hopeful beam in the gloomy picture was projected by Capuchin Father Raphael, who in September 1725, established the first school in New Orleans. Father Cecil, a Capuchin monk who knew Latin, mathematics, drawing, singing and whose handwriting was fairly good, was put in charge. A year later Raphael reported that studies were progressing very well, despite the small number of pupils. There were very few young people in the colony, and the majority of the inhabitants, who were in a position to send their children to school, were satisfied if their offspring simply learned how to read and write.

Progress of this preliminary educational attempt was checked because of a misunderstanding and legal entanglement between the Capuchin Fathers and the Company of the Indies as to who should pay for the little building Langlois sold Father Raphael for a schoolhouse in 1727.

It was a small beginning for education in Louisiane, and coincided with Bienville's return to France, where in 1725 he was removed from command of Louisiane and was forbidden to return to the colony. For his years of struggle, he was awarded an annual pension of 3,000 livres.

In 1726 the Company of the Indies assigned to the Jesuits all the Indian missions in the Province of Louisiane, which marked the beginning of a far reaching conflict between the Capuchins and the Jesuits, which affected not only ecclesiastical affairs, but which was to spread to the domestic and political life of the colony, sewing discord in the commercial and military management of Louisiane.[15]

Chapter X

BAYOU PROBLEMS UNDER PÉRIER AND THE NATCHEZ MASSACRE 1726-1731

De Pauger's downhill disillusionment with the frustrated, unforgiving colonists ended when he died of a slow fever on June 5, 1726.[1] On April 11th of the same year twenty arpents of Bienville's concession, immediately uptown from the original village, were leased to the Jesuits who had come to New Orleans the year before. The land, which today covers the heart of the commercial district, was leased by Bienville's agent for $1,600.00 making the ex-Commandant the first subdivider of this region.

On May 1, 1728 Bienville, through his local agent, would lease them the adjoining five arpents, and on December 2, 1743 Ceasar Le Breton des Chapelles would sell them another five arpents on the immediate uptown side of the other properties. The acreage became a plantation with a Jesuit school and church, and would in 1741 be the site of the first sugar planting in New Orleans.[2]

On Bayou St. Jean problems of parenthood were manifesting themselves, even in those days of stricter discipline. Hunter Etienne Beaucour petitioned the Superior Council in 1726 to collect a hundred francs from Bonhomme Visse, father of a young lad who'd pirated a pirogue from the bayou and returned it in a "plight of unfitness for further use."[3]

And the LaVignes were having tutor trouble. Francois Nicolas de Knepper, a live-in teacher, who'd been employed to teach the children reading and writing, appeared before the Superior Council in 1726 claiming that his employers owed him seventy francs plus his clothing which they'd seized, because they maintained he hadn't completed his contract. Despite his intellectual bent, de Knepper was no slouch when it came to practical shrewdness. He'd already collected ten francs of his bill from one of LaVigne's debtors.

LaVigne was nipped by annoyances of all kinds. In June of the same year, Jean Saubagne of Gentilly—the same who'd instigated the earlier complaint about the road—was after him again. This time LaVigne's cattle had broken into the Saubagne plantation, damaging a lot of his growing crop. Only someone with a farm background can realize the ravages of thirty four rampaging cattle, and estimate how little time it would take them to destroy the growing equivalent of eight pecks of peas, a quarter of marsh beans, two quarters of wheat, six barrels of sweet potatoes, two barrels of the same retarded in growth, one peach tree of two years (equivalent to six trees of one year), as well as corn, leeks, pumpkins, melons, onions and figs.

Litigation of this kind provides about the only record of what was growing on the bayou in those days, for which the reader may thank the litigious Saubagne (Soubaigné), but LaVigne wasn't so grateful. Admitting that, despite precautions, some of his cattle had invaded the Saubagne premises, he dispatched estimators to "the troublesome party" to estimate the damage done; but Saubagne, not about to trust LaVigne's proceedings, countered with reports of his own inspectors.

On the basis of the Council findings, LaVigne was ordered to supply 1,450 potato settings, as well as the equivalent of other damaged planting, from the returns of his next crop.[4]

Their differences notwithstanding, LaVigne and Saubagne had a problem in common, with each other and all land-owners of that day. Their help was running away. Twenty year old Sansoucy, an unbaptized Indian slave of LaVigne's, had run away and having been apprehended, the reasons for his unscheduled departure were the subject of inquiry on March 31, 1727. Through an interpreter, who worked for the Company of the Indies, Sansoucy said he hadn't been able to find a stray ox his master had sent him to retrieve, and had been afraid to return without the animal. Having taken refuge in a marooner village called Natanapolle, he'd hidden out for a time with fifteen other males and an Indian woman—all fugitive slaves belonging to Bienville, LaVigne and others. Since records do not indicate he was a repeater, it is probable that the worst punishment he received was a stern remonstrance against repetition of his act.

Saubagne's problem was a bit more complicated. His negro Biron, of the Bambara nation, not only had run away several times, but had on the last occasion given his master quite a chase. Notified of Biron's absence by another of his slaves on July 7, 1728, Saubagne took after him and spied the runaway sitting 'mongst the cane some distance from the city. Calling to him to give up, and firing his gun in the air to frighten him into surrendering, Biron took off at high speed. After a rapid circuit of the woods, Saubagne spotted him, whereupon Biron again began to run, but stumbled over a cane. Pointing his gun at him, Saubagne warned that if he moved he was dead, which convinced Biron to return to the plantation.

Arriving home, another Negro was ordered to put the captive in chains, whereupon Biron grabbed for his master's gun. With the help of the other slaves, Saubagne managed to hold on to his weapon, which, however, was broken in the struggle.

Samba, a Christian Bambara interpreter, was brought into the hearings to speak for Biron as well as to explain to him what was going on. Admitting that he'd seized the gun, the runaway said he'd done so because he feared his master was going to shoot him, and that the gun had broken during the fracas. For his untoward conduct Biron was flogged at the foot of the gallows and returned to his master with a warning that future excursions of this kind would result in graver penalities.[5]

Either the fevers that beset the early colonists, or the difficulties of coping in general must have gotten to Saubagne, for his succession was being sued in February of 1731 for the payment of two Negroes he'd purchased on October 15, 1729. The guardian of the Saubagne minors was ordered by the Superior Council to pay 2,000 francs worth of tobacco to retire the debt, or return the two slaves to the petitioner.[6]

One might think all the furor of establishing the primary settlement of the colony would have focused the eyes of the world on New Orleans, but in 1727 it wasn't even on the map. Marie Madeleine Hachard, one of the six Ursuline sisters who'd arrived on August 6th to take over duties at the hospital and educate the girls of the colony, had a tough time proving to her father in France that the town existed at all. Having purchased two maps on which he found no indication of the new capitol, she assured him that new maps would surely correct the error. However, somebody's zodiac was out of focus, for the third map he bought showed Nouvelle Orleans on the shores of Lake Pontchartrain.[7]

Jean Baptiste Beaudreau (Graveline) of Pascagoula, who in 1713 had purchased west bank Bayou St.Jean property from St. Denis, had invested again along that stream, for when Francois Dugué's small two and one half arpent plantation to the immediate east of Bayou Road was purchased by Luis Brazillier in 1729, Dugué represented Graveline in the transaction, indicating that the latter had either purchased the property or held a mortgage on it.

Graveline was also again interested in west bank bayou property. The arpents he'd purchased there in 1713 from St. Denis were now part of the Girardy plantation, but on April 14, 1730 he claimed to have acquired an eight arpent plantation north of Chemin Chapitoulas (today's Carrollton Avenue and lower City Park) and to have established a dairy on it. (The same land claimed by Dugué in 1723.) However, typical of his quick-silver land-dealing, Graveline soon ceded the arpents to Sr. Derbanne of Natchitoches, who as quickly retroceded them to him on July 4, 1733.[8] The early settlers of Louisiane were no slouches when it came to buying and selling.

The King was also expanding his holdings on the bayou. The warehouse—for temporary storage of merchandise unloaded at the Port of Bayou St. Jean—had been built west of Bayou Road on the banks of the stream in 1719. After Brazillier purchased the Dugué plantation, he transferred twenty toises front on Bayou St. Jean by forty five deep on his land, a short distance east of Bayou Road for the Royal Naval Arsenal,[9] where it remained throughout French and early Spanish times. A map in the Library of Congress, circa 1730 (because it locates the Dugué residence) shows the King's Warehouse (Magasin du Roi) still located west of Bayou Road (west of DeSoto Street today), not far from the Dauterive (Langlois) habitation.

Another Library of Congress map of the same period eliminates the site of the King's Warehouse west of Bayou Road, and shows only an open-sided structure for the protection of travelers at the foot of the road on the stream.

This map also reveals four buildings on Bayou St. Jean, directly in front of the Dugué residence, marked as the place of debarkment for bateaux and pirogues. This is probably the Naval Arsenal site transferred to the French government by Brazillier after his purchase of the plantation in 1729. The small Dugué plantation was not to change hands again for a long time. Luis Brazillier lived to be an old man, and his son Jean Baptiste, who inherited the land from his father, would live there for many years after that, into Spanish times.

Brazillier's neighbors to the northeast had their hands full. Madame Antoine Rivard de LaVigne was having tutor trouble again. Rene Galbee requested the assistance of the Council to collect 376 francs, 15 sous she owed him for service. (Galbee must have been with the LaVigne's for some time, as teachers' salaries were notoriously low. Nine years later reading was being taught for forty cents a month.) There was also the matter of toilet paper and cobblers items the teacher had lent Mrs. LaVigne and which he wanted returned. Their differences were amicably adjusted on August 20th—Galbee and everybody else forgiving Madame LaVigne for any oversights at this time. Large problems loomed on her horizon, for she'd lost her husband on February 11, 1729.[10]

The Library of Congress map showing the site of the Naval Arsenal reveals several interesting aspects of Bayou Road of the early 1730s. Just outside New Orleans, on the west side of the road, is located a sizable building for the manufacture of bricks, and right across the road are eighteen cabins to house the negro brick-workers, (de Morand plantation. See Chapter XI).

Between these cabins and the road that branched east along Bayou Gentilly are located two habitations—for one Boreau and a Captain Mavoir, of whom nothing else is mentioned in the early records. The latter is marked "la fayancerie" on another map of the same period.

On Bayou Road near Chemin Gentilly is Petit Bayou ou Lavoir (small bayou where the laundry was done). This small bayou ballooned into two ponds, one on either side of Bayou Road, located in the approximate area of Broad Street, downtown of Esplanade Street today.

A bit beyond Petit Bayou another small bayou crossed the road, immediately south of the entrance to the Dauterive (Langlois) residence.

It wasn't exactly the age of Aquarius for Etienne de Périer. Overloaded with instructions, responsibility and optimism he had come to the colony in 1727 to succeed Bienville. One of the projects proposed by the Company of the Indies, in typical big-company resolution form, was: "Whereas it is maintained that the diseases which prevail in New Orleans during the summer proceed from the want of air and from the city being smothered by the neighboring woods, which press so close around it, it shall be the care of M. Périer to have them cut down, as far as Lake Pontchartrain." Needless to say, this wasn't accomplished in 1727 or over one hundred years later when the same suggestion was made to the Mayor of New Orleans by a Louisiana Governor.[11]

By November 15, 1727, Périer, with the vigor of a new official, had enlarged upon Chaville's 500 toise effort of 1724, and completed in front of New Orleans a levee 1800 yards long and 18 feet wide at its summit, which—with decreased dimensions—continued eighteen miles above as well as below the city. Although it proved to be a decided deterrent to spring flooding, the river water continued to seep through the porous earthen levee. New Orleans was little more than a would-be-urban swamp, divided into squares, which in turn were divided into lots. Each lot was rimmed by a shallow ditch which drained into larger channels surrounding the squares. In those days what wasn't wanted was simply tossed out the door. The uncovered ditches attracted mosquitoes and snakes, and the colony's animals wandered about at will, adding their refuse to that of their owners. The ditches draining the blocks were laid out in a way to impel their flow into larger main drainage arteries which led to the rear of the town. From there, it was hoped, the excessive waters and their flotsam and jetsam would descend through small rivulets and branches of Bayou St. Jean to the main body of that stream, and thence to Lake Pontchartrain. But the system didn't work very well, because the landslope from the Mississippi to the back of town (then Dauphine Street), and from there to Bayou St. Jean wasn't steep enough to insure a rapid enough flow to flush the conduit content; so the soft soil of the city, and the swamps behind its ramparts, retained the muck and stinking sewerage, providing a perfect breeding ground for mosquitoes and other insects and pests.[12]

Périer apparently had drainage, as well as transportation, in mind when he announced to the Company of the Indies in 1727 that he was about to improve communication with the sea, through the lakes, by cutting a canal from New Orleans to Bayou St. Jean. Attempting to effect what Bienville and his contemporaries had advocated ten years earlier, Périer went so far as to make arrangements with the inhabitants to lend their Negroes to do the work, which was begun, but to which subsequent events put a stop.[13]

The subsequent events were colored red. Knowing nothing of Indian psychology, in which Bienville had excelled, the new Commandant-General had reinstated Sieur de Chopart (Chepart, d'Etcheparre) in his Natchez post, after he'd been dismissed, at the request of the Indians, because of offensive tyrannical behavior. Immediately upon reinstatement Chopart vengefully reduced the price the Natchez received for furs and limited their trading privileges; but the direst blow was demanding of Grand Sun, their leader, the site of their village White Apple so he could build a town to honor the French King. White Apple, the location of which had been confirmed to the Natchez by Bienville, meant more to them than just a place to live. It was the revered spot where their forebears lay buried, and where a perpetual fire burned in their sacred temple, before which the Natchez leaders deliberated the entire night following Chopart's demands. Next day they pleaded with the Commandant for a postponement of their evacuation so they could gather the current crops, or they'd have no food for the coming year. At first Chopart dismissed their request with threats and curses, but he wasn't beyond bribery. His terms became more flexible when Grand Sun's emissary whispered in broken French that a great stack of skins and furs awaited him if he delayed the Natchez departure 'til spring.

This gave the Indians time to plan a suitable revenge, and they invited all the nations to join with them in wiping out the French from the settlement of the Tonicas down to New Orleans. Runners were sent to neighboring villages with bundles of sticks, representing the number of days that would elapse before the day of reckoning. A stick was to be removed every morning, and the day of the last stick was to mark the general attack.

But there was a little fly in the Natchez ointment called Stung Arm, niece of Grand Sun, who cringed at the idea of any harm coming to Father Cosme who had administered so kindly to the needs of the Natchez. Too, she'd become more than fond of a young French subaltern who'd recently arrived at the post from New Orleans. Taking the risk of betraying her tribe (the penalty would have been death had the Natchez found out) she requested an audience with Chopart to whom she confided the entire plot. But rather than gratefully accepting her act of mercy, he accused her of lying and dismissed her with threats of public whipping if he heard more tales.

Braves from far and near carried on nocturnal dances and death chants, striking terror to the hearts of the French who wondered about these unusual proceedings; but Chopart jeered that the Natchez were skunks compared to the Choctaw wolves he'd battled in the wilds of Pontchartrain.

As the sticks in the Natchez bundle dwindled (it is said Stung Arm had surreptitiously removed a couple extra to avert a collusive attack on the French), so did the patience of some of the Chiefs who had heard soldiers were on the way upriver from New Orleans. Fearful that their plans might be thwarted, they urged an immediate attack, and final preparations were hastily concluded. As the pall of night was dissipating, Father Cosme sounded three shrill blasts on his shepherd's horn to call the devout to worship on St. Andrew's Day, November 28, 1729, and the cloud of red destruction descended, aided by some Congo slaves of Natchez colonists, who'd been waiting for the signal of attack. The defenseless settlers fell like chaff before the flailing knives and tomahawks. They were the lucky ones. Others—their ears and noses sliced away—were slowly roasted to death. Most of the women were taken as slaves, but the pregnant ones had their unborn slashed from their flanks, and dying, saw their near-offspring thrown to voracious dogs prowling the scene of the massacre.

Chopart suffered a unique justice planned by Grand Sun, who had decreed him unworthy of death by a warrior's weapon; Little Snake, a mean, deformed Redman, found Chopart cringing in the magazine. Yelling with insane glee, he battered the brain of the sprawling Commandant with a child's wooden tomahawk and tore off a remnant of the shattered scalp to present to his chief. About 250 colonists were slain; and as many women and children, plus two hundred negro slaves, were taken prisoner.

When some of the colonists near Natchez brought the devastating news to New Orleans on December 2nd, a former resident of that hapless settlement no doubt congratulated himself on having returned to New Orleans. Historian LePage DuPratz, former resident of Bayou St. Jean, had come back in 1726 to become Inspector of the Plantation of the Company.[14]

Fearing that the Indians intended to wipe out the entire French population, Périer ordered all the men in town and along the river to remain armed, and Negroes were put to work on an entrenchment around the town. A moat, with a palisade of sharp stakes, wedged closely together, was New Orleans' first attempt at fortification—more psychological than material—for an order was issued four years later to fill up the ditch.

The attack of the Natchez set off Louisiane's only major Indian War.[15] Unaware of the intended complicity of the Choctaws in the massacre, Périer solicited their assistance; enraged at the Natchez for jumping the gun and depriving them of their share of the booty, they responded quickly. On February 12, 1730 fifteen hundred of them joined M. De Loubois and marched on the two Natchez forts at St. Catherine's Creek —a league from the settlement the Natchez had burned after the massacre. After days of negotiation and Grand Sun's release of the women, children and slaves to the Choctaws, Loubois had to pay ransom to his Choctaw allies before they'd turn the slaves over to him. Then as final aspects of the surrender were being settled, the Natchez slipped out of the fort during the night carrying with them all of their war plunder. A disgusted Loubois returned to New Orleans,[16] but obviously this was not the end of the affair.

Almost everybody in New Orleans had lost a relative in the massacre, and the Village of Bayou St. Jean was no exception. Angelique Girardy (daughter of Joseph Girardy and the Indian Francoise) lost her husband Alain Dugué whom she'd married June 25, 1727. And those fortunate families, who had escaped the onslaught, weren't spared its traumatic aftermath. Living with fear became a way of life.

One day a woman from Bayou St. Jean dashed into New Orleans screaming that Indians were raiding the bayou, had massacred all the settlers and were in hot pursuit of her. A general alarm was sounded, men gathered in the square (Jackson Square today), where powder and balls were distributed. Women took refuge in the church and on vessels anchored in the river. The Commandant General sent out a scouting party to establish the defensive-offensive situation; but a cautious two-hour casing of the surrounding area uncovered nothing more deleterious than a couple of hunters in the bayou woods who'd fired two or three shots. It was also evident by this time that the hustler of hysteria had sipped a trifle too much tafia (low grade rum made from sugarcane).[17]

Violence became commonplace in those desperate days. Four captured Natchez, brought to New Orleans by the friendly Tonica Indians, were burned in an elaborate ceremony between the town and the levee—a sporting event for which the entire settlement turned out. In retaliation, the Natchez murdered the Tonica Chief and destroyed most of that nation.

A grain of good in the hysteria was the freeing of the Negroes who'd proved loyal to the French at Natchez, and the Attorney General suggested that a company of these dependable Blacks be organized for instant call against any Indian uprising, but fear-fostered evil became the rule of the day. One plot suggesting another, a faithful Negress informed her owner of a master massacre brewing 'mongst the Blacks, and the chief conspirators were discovered and dealt with. But unable to determine whether or not a coalition existed between the Negroes and the Indians, the French decided to pit one potential enemy against the other. The Negroes were summoned, accused of treason and threatened with hanging because they were in league with the Redmen to exterminate the French. Protesting their innocence, the Negroes begged for mercy and offered to prove their good will by marching on their so-called collaborators. Given hatchets, bayonets and knives, eighty of them set upon the unfortunate Tchaouachas who lived along the banks of the Mississippi below English Turn; seven or eight of them were killed, and their women and children were taken prisoner. When the Tchaouachas came to New Orleans to ask why the attack had taken place, Périer had no answer and released the women and children to accompany their men back to the settlement. However, one thing had been achieved. The enemy was divided. This single expedition made the Negroes and Indians mortal enemies for all time.[18]

A little cheer seeped through the bayou gloom when Francois Antoine Rivard de LaVigne married on February 20, 1730. Young LaVigne was the son of deceased Antoine Rivard de LaVigne by his first marriage to Marie Briard, and the young bride—Jeanne Antoinette de Villemont—was the daughter of LaVigne, Sr.'s second wife Antoinette Fourrier, by her first marriage to Henri Martin Mirbaise Sieur de Villemont. Lieutenant de Villemont had come to Louisiane in 1719 with his wife Antoinette Fourrier and their two daughters Jeanne Antoinette and Marie Anne to settle his concession on the Ouachita River 120 leagues from the capitol.

The marriage was a happy ending to one set of live-in complications brought about by early deaths, which resulted in consecutive marriages for fairly young people. Today's resolution of the ennui of monogamy in the divorce courts, was, it appears, accomplished in a more seemly manner by the fevers of the early 1700s.

Francois Antoine Rivard (LaVigne) and his wife would have three daughters: Jeanne Antoinette, born February 17, 1732, who died the same year; Jeanne Antoinette, born May of 1734, and Marie Francoise, a posthumous child, born in 1735 or 1736.[19]

Not so publicized an affair was the June 26, 1730 marriage of Angelique Girardy, widow of Alain Dugué, killed by the Indians at Natchez, to Widower Jean Baptiste Rejas, called La Prade, native of Quebec and now a resident on the lower Mississippi.[20]

The early 1730s marked the end—in the records—of an early settler of Bayou St. Jean. Etienne Langlois, at that time, either died or moved away from his eight-arpent plantation located to the immediate west of Brazillier's plantation. A map of the early 1730s in the Library of Congress shows no Langlois residence, but marks the house on that property as belonging to Capitaine du St. Derive, no doubt an abbreviation of Renaud d'Hauterive, subsequent owner of the Langlois plantation. Langlois had also been conceded a seven-arpent-front plantation across the river in January, 1725. On September 19, 1733 either he or his succession sold the arpents to DuBreuil, who had other holdings in the area.[21]

The Natchez affair was yet to be settled, so when a ship arrived from France with five hundred soldiers of the Marine, under command of Périer's brother, no time was lost in marching fifteen hundred men to accost the Natchez who had built a French-type fort on the Red River to which they'd fled after the massacre. Louis Billouart Kerlérec—future Governor of Louisiane—was a member of that French force, which in January 1731 burned the Indian fort and took four hundred and eighty four prisoners in five and a half days of fighting.

The Natchez were brought to New Orleans where the men were imprisoned and the women and children were put on the slave plantation until all of them, including Stung Arm, who'd warned the French of the impending disaster, were shipped off to St. Domingue as slaves. The half-wit Little Snake and two of the murdering ravishing negro slaves were broken alive on the wheel in the courtyard of the little fort then located at the juncture of today's Decatur and Barracks Streets.[22]

The Natchez massacre put a heavy load on the limited facilities of the Ursulines, who on arriving in 1727 had taken up quarters in the two story brick Kolly house which was located on the uptown edge of the settlement, diagonally across the way from Bienville's residence, in the square bounded by Royal, Chartres, Bienville and Conti Streets. The sudden influx of orphan girls, which the Ursulines took under wing (in addition to their regular boarding school pupils and Negro and Indian women and girls whom they instructed every day from 1:00 to 2:30) necessitated their move to larger quarters at Ursulines, Old Levee, L'Arcenal and Conde Streets in 1734.[23] The present archiepiscopal residence, built 1748-1750, replacing the 1734 edifice (which was located nearer the river) stands today at 1114 Chartres Street—the oldest building in the Mississippi Valley. Architect-Historian Samuel Wilson believes the staircase in the present structure is from the original 1734 building.

Because of one worthless commander, the Natchez—noblest of the Indian nations according to Historian DuPratz—were ruthlessly rooted out of existence. Hundreds of tried and true tillers of the soil, as the Natchez colonists had proved to be, were gone. A dozen years of the best colonizing was down the drain. And other colonists, living away from the coast, moved back toward garrisoned New Orleans and Mobile where they felt safer.

The unfortunate affair also spelled finis to the Company of the Indies in Louisiane. The Natchez concessionaires, claiming that their contract had been violated because the Commandant, his officers and sergeants had lived outside the fort proper, sued the Company of the Indies for 132,993 livres. Considering the more than twenty million livres the Company had already spent, the cost of this suit, rebuilding and protecting the colony, plus replacing military equipment, was more than their resources could sustain, and they surrendered their charter to the crown in 1731.[24]

Soon after, France sent M. de Salmon, Commissary-General of the Marine and Inspector of Louisiane, to take possession of the colony in the King's name. The plantation of the company became the King's Plantation, DuPratz became the King's Inspector—in which position he'd remain until 1734—and Commandant-General Périer of the Company of the Indies now became Governor Périer under the King of France.[25]

Chapter XI

DEATH OF EARLY SETTLERS--
NEW LANDOWNERS ON BAYOU ST. JEAN
1731-1735

Bachelor Francois Dugué finally took the plunge. Borrowing a hundred francs, he spent twenty of them for a marriage contract and the balance for a mattress at a sale of a fellow colonist. Both purchases were a bit premature, for he didn't marry Marie Bruslé (daughter of Philippe Antoine Bruslé, Agent of the Company of the Indies, and Marthe Fremont) until a year later—on April 2, 1731—after Notary Rossard had gone to court to collect the hundred francs he'd lent the prospective groom. Dugué was probably short on cash because he'd purchased a plantation across the river, which measured eighteen arpents on the Mississippi by forty arpents in depth, on which there was a sawmill, lumber, farm animals and seventeen Negroes and Negresses to work it all.

Marriage isn't for everybody, and in this instance Dugué was "it." He died either that year or early the next, for his widow married Raymond St. Martin Jauriguibery (spelled differently in every record) on November 25, 1732. It took a long time to settle Dugué's estate, because Notary Rossard had omitted a formality in both of Marie Bruslé's marriage contracts, which resulted in their annulment, followed by claims and counter claims. The Company of the Indies (which continued to operate in the colony in a limited capacity) demanded over 10,667 livres for Negroes and merchandise advanced Dugué. Sieur Bruslé sued for the return of his daughter's six-thousand-livre-dowry, plus costs of administering her affairs between husbands. Marie's second husband requested the 3,999 livres he'd paid on Dugué's debts, after marrying the widow, because he had expected her contribution to the marriage to cover that sum.

The Dugué plantation on the other side of the river went up for sale, but there was little demand for a facility of that kind. The sale was advertised to the beat of the drum, cancelled and postponed to a future date three times because the bids received didn't approach the value of the property. On the fourth try, the bid was no higher, but the land was adjudicated to DuBreuil for 500 livres. Then in bewildering succession the property changed hands several times during the next few months and finally ended up in the hands of Sr. Jean Baptiste Raguet, councilor of the local government, who on March 20, 1736 promised to pay 500 livres for the plantation. The estate wasn't settled until May 31, 1737—

hopefully to the interest of someone other than the lawyers and notaries.[1]

In March of 1731 the Superior Council was holding an unusual session at the request of Claude Jousset de La Loire (Loere), son of Jean Baptiste de La Loire and Ann Badean, natives of Montreal and New Rochelle, who had come to Mobile in 1704. Claude Jousset was attempting to prove that he was the first male child born in Louisiane, so he could collect the bounty the French Government offered to the first-born in American French colonies. His application had been filed in 1725, but due to lack of evidence, and more likely the unsettled circumstances surrounding Bienville's removal from office, the case had been postponed. La Loire suggested that Messrs. Bienville, Boisbrant and D'Artaguette—presently in France—could vouch for his claim, even though the original documents had been lost.

In an effort to conclude the matter, the oldest colonists were questioned. Jean Baptiste Beaudreau (Graveline) of Pascagoula, sixty two years of age, testified in support of the claim, saying La Loire was the first male child at Mobile. Fifty five year old Nicolas Chauvin de Lafrénière stated that Claude had been born twenty six years before, his parents having arrived some years prior to that time. Fifty one year old Francois Carrière, settler at English Turn, had been acquainted with Claude's parents at the old Fort of Mobile and knew of nobody else who could challenge La Loire's claim.

After the evidence was in on March 4, 1731 and the notice posted on the door of the church and the council chamber, the Attorney General declared that anyone challenging La Loire's claim must present himself to the Registry of the Council within fifteen days or lose all rights in the matter.

Bureaucratic wheels turned slowly. It was not until November 26, 1747 that the certificate—and we trust, the reward—was presented to Jean Baptiste de La Loire, the father. Perhaps he was the one who deserved it, having survived those early years and having sired a son who lived to pursue the recognition. Claude La Loire would live to be seventy six years old, and remained in Louisiane until his death in 1781.[2]

On May 12, 1731 Charles de Morand (Morant), married to Dame Anne Hay, bought a sizable plot of ground just outside the ramparts of New Orleans, on the west side of Bayou Road, which led from the settlement to Bayou St. Jean. On this property he established a brickyard, and five months later was petitioning the Superior Council for damages, because Sieur Boissere had killed one of his Negroes. On being interrogated, Boissere admitted the deed, but stoutly defended his action on the grounds that de Morand had killed one of his pigs. Five years later, the Company of the Indies would back de Morand in the purchase of Negroes and merchandise for his business, to the extent of 15,314 livres, 15 sols, which he and his wife promised to repay in five equal payments in as many years. De Morand (who more than doubled his holdings in 1756, with a concession from the French Government directly across Bayou Road from his original holdings), and his heirs, proved to be stable, staying citizens, owning the original Bayou Road plantation and other property as late as the 1770s.[3]

An important local social event was the January 12, 1732 wedding of Louis DuBreuil Villars, native of Paris, son of Sieur Claude Joseph DuBreuil Villars, concessioner at Chapitoulas as well as owner of property just below New Orleans that extended from the Mississippi to Bayou St. Jean. The bride was Felicite de La Chaise, native of Nantes, Brittany, daughter of deceased Jacques de La Chaise, (former King's Commissioner and General Director of the Colony), and Marguerite Cailly.[4]

Matrimony was contagious in bayou country, for the Dreux brothers of Gentilly soon followed suit. On November 17, 1732 Mathurin married Claudine Francoise Hugot, and Pierre married Anne Corbin Bachemin on April 28, 1733. They all lived together in the same house, a showplace of the time, with lovely gardens, spacious rooms and galleries. Both of them officers in the provincial militia, the Dreuxs lived quietly and well, never becoming involved politically, and were the kind of folks you could always count on when the chips were down. The records of the time disclose that they were always giving of their time to act as tutors for orphans, arbitrators in times of difficulty and curators in the event of death 'mongst their bayou neighbors.[5]

Meanwhile, in Paris Bienville had been cleared of the charges brought against him, and was asked to again take on the responsibility of Louisiane; so in 1733 he came back to the colony with the title of Governor for the first time. Hardship having humbled him little, he hustled Périer out of his house and set about improving things. On October 1, 1733 he signed emancipation orders for his slaves Jorge and Marie, his wife, for their good and faithful service of twenty six years.[6]

In 1734 the much pondered proposition of connecting Bayou St. Jean with the settlement of New Orleans, by means of a canal, was again the subject of discussion. Because of the LeMoynes' high regard for the order, Bienville no doubt believed that if anybody could do the job it would be the Jesuits. On August 10th, he and Commissary Salmon ceded to the Society of Jesus a triangular tract of land, 339 arps, 200 toises in area—a part of the city commons along the upper boundary of the town—extending from the Mississippi River back to Bayou St. Jean. (Today this would be approximately from Iberville Street in the French Quarter uptown to Common Street.) The grant was made on the specific condition that the canal be dug; if not, the land would revert to the King's domain. But not even the ambition and ability of the good fathers could achieve this, for when all Jesuit property was seized by the French Colonial government in 1763, this tract was not included in the land returned to New Orleans, because it had already reverted to the city.[7]

If there wasn't to be a new canal, at least land transportation was being improved. The times demanded roads for the carriages which had been brought over from Havana in 1730 and the coaches introduced by Bienville in 1733. By 1735 most men of means in New Orleans owned a chaise, two horses, and some even had berlins. So from New Orleans to Gentilly and Bayou St. Jean there was to be a wagon road forty feet wide. Those owning property abutting the road were to keep it, and any bridges on it, in good repair. This didn't work too much of a hardship on the Bayou Road dwellers, as the law was never enforced in its entirety.[8]

Meanwhile, in far off Illinois a land sale of August 21-22, 1731 was finally recorded on February 18, 1734, confirming that Jean Bruent (Bonnet, Bourbonnois) and Jean Olivier had sold Louis Turpin two adjacent lots of land, measuring eight arpents front on Bayou St. Jean by forty deep. Today these arpents would include Carrollton Avenue and extend north into lower City Park and was the same land on which Graveline had established a dairy in 1730. Graveline must have abandoned his project, for in 1734—three months after purchasing it—the new owner, Turpin, donated this land to Marie Louise Girardy, minor daughter of Jeanne Henry (Héry) and her husband Joseph Girardy (their plantation was situated to the immediate south of these arpents) who paid Turpin the token sum of one hundred crowns for the land and accepted it for his daughter.

This gave Joseph Girardy—the only living survivor of the four original permanent land owners at the Village of Bayou St. Jean—control over as much land as his neighbor Francois Antoine de LaVigne across the bayou. Girardy's five-arpent concession of 1719 had by 1734 expanded to nine arpents, as he had acquired the original 1708 concession of Louis Juchereau de St. Denys, as well as the Bayou St. Jean sector of the Village of the Acolapissas which in 1718 had been owned by Antoine Rivard de LaVigne, his father. Girardy's holdings of the 1730s would today extend northerly, along the bayou's west bank, to a point in lower City Park.

Nobody would have dreamed—least of all Joseph Girardy, who above all else appreciated a close family relationship—that twenty years later this innocent land transaction would become the basis of a long family court battle.[9] The Girardys, at the moment, were too involved with marriage plans for their minor daughter Marie Francoise, who was to be a June bride. On June 20, 1734 she married Joseph Milon, son of deceased Pierre Milon and Francoise Dominé. Carpenter Joseph Milon worked with Senior Contractor DuBreuil on many government projects in early Louisiane, and a couple of years after his marriage signed a contract with Commissary Salmon to repair the barracks and four pavillions at Fort Condé near Mobile.[10]

The marriage of Francois Antoine Rivard de LaVigne didn't last very long. Having outlived his father by only six years, he died on September 25, 1735, on which day Judge Salmon, the Procurator and the Clerk of Court were called to the LaVigne home. They came to affix the seals on his possessions, according to legal procedures of the time, in order that the property rights of minor heirs and creditors might be protected. Only the young widow was at home. Her mother had gone to Gentilly, and the body had already been sent to New Orleans for burial.

It is probable that young Rivard, as well as his father, died of smallpox, which took many lives about this time, adding fear of contact to the loneliness of loss. Even if they weren't sure about contagion, government officials, too, must have hesitated to enter the premises of the deceased. Antoinette Fourrier, the young widow's mother, was sent for, and upon arrival declared that nothing had been diverted from the effects of the succession.

The property, inventoried on October 6, 1735, consisted of clothes, the seventeen-arpent plantation, nine slaves, fourteen head of cattle and one lot of ground in New Orleans. Offering to get the papers which were in town, the elder Widow Rivard stated that the furniture belonged to her, having been left to her at the partition of her husband's estate on July 17, 1733. The deceased elder Rivard had also owned a six-arpent-front plantation across the Mississippi which he'd purchased in 1728 and which had been sold by his succession to DuBreuil on September 19, 1733. The Widows Rivard (mother and daughter) jointly acknowledged that they owed the Company of the Indies a thousand francs for a Negro they'd purchased, payable in two semi-annual installments.

Early widowhood was particularly precarious to twenty year old Jeanne Antoinette de Villemont, Widow Rivard; not only did she have an eighteen month old daughter, she was carrying a child and was herself a minor. The Attorney General immediately petitioned a meeting of the family (to elect a tutor and proceed to the appraisement of the property of the deceased) which took place on October 7th. At this family meeting the elder Widow Rivard was elected Tutrix and Gentilly neighbor Mathurin Dreux under-tutor, to guide and look after the interests of the bereaved young family.[11]

Because of the prevalence of fevers and limited medical know-how, it wasn't uncommon for very young children to lose both parents at the same time, so French laws concerning the affairs of minor orphans were quite strict.

The edict of December 15, 1721 provided for the appointment of dual tutors—in France and in the colony—when minors inherited property in both places; and by the 1730s the selection and duties of tutors had become a legal rite, witnessed by all members of the family, and involved pertinent oaths which could be dissolved only by the Superior Council. On October 1, 1741 the French government would update and cover any orphan problems that had been overlooked in the earlier instrument.

Tutors, under jurisdiction of the local judge, supervised the education and revenues of their charges. If a minor wished to marry, he not only required his tutor's consent, but also the approval of family members in meeting (helpful neighbors and friends in the absence of family), and all proceedings were certified by the Judge. An interesting aspect of the earlier edict prohibited a minor from selling an inherited slave until he, the owner, came of age at 25.

When people remarried, marriage contracts guaranteed that any minor children of previous alliances be raised in the Roman Catholic faith, and that their education be paid for out of the joint resources of the new bride and groom. Thus the interests of children, who under new marital arrangements might not have fared so well, were safeguarded.

The subrogé tutor, referred to in some of these cases, was similar to the under-tutor, and was usually appointed when the deceased left debts or when there was a prospect of conflict between the widow or widower and the deceased's minor heirs.[12]

The colony, as a whole, was barely creeping along. There was a desperate shortage of money, and it was now becoming evident that Louisiane would never be economically self-sustaining. Though exempting from duty all merchandise and goods coming from the mother country, France was unwilling to compete with her colonies and placed import restrictions on crops she could grow at home; and rival nations and colonies were obviously less than eager to assist the new colony. There was a substantial exchange of goods and ideas between French St. Domingue (on the route to New Orleans) and Louisiane. This was especially true of seeds, means and methods of plantation agriculture, and accounted for the West Indian architecture of some of the houses built along Bayou St. Jean. Since the bulk of one-crop West Indian produce was raised for export, they were happy to receive beans and rice in exchange, as well as planks and bricks that were made in Louisiane from the earliest times. Tobacco, which the Indians were growing when the French arrived, continued to be raised and exported. The Jesuits and other settlers were now raising indigo. For the first couple of decades corn had been the staple; now there were indications of a change to rice. Deerskins, beaver hides, bear and deer grease and tallow were frequently mentioned in the trade records of the locality. The versatile bear oil was practically a coin of the realm; in addition to being a medium of exchange, it was also used as a lard substitute, lubricant for machinery, dressing for salads, ointment for the body, a softener of leather, oil for lamps and a cosmetic for the hair and beards of those days which rivaled the most hirsuit of today's hippies.

These products hardly supplied the requirements of a people who were building from scratch and needed everything; and the too frequent floods, hurricanes and freezes, a general lack of know-how and implements in a strange climate, and the pressure of Indians and political uncertainty didn't contribute to stable progress.[13]

One might say conditions in 1735 weren't conducive to optimism when Bienville and Commissary Salmon, in a joint dispatch to Paris, reported that the mortality of cattle was frightful, the drought excessive and the heat suffocating. From Christmas to St. John (June 24th) the waters had been so high that many of the levees had broken. The one in front of the city had given way, and everyone was on the verge of abandoning his house and going to live on a boat. Then the drought hit, and the river went down fifteen feet—a circumstance never before experienced; and the lands having been drowned in water, produced little or nothing in the way of crops.

And that not being enough, Louisiane was literally going to the dogs. The colonists could hardly step out of their homes without being bitten. Having increased to an intolerable point, the Royal Commissary ordered that the animals be hunted down on certain days, from five to six in the morning; and Indians and Negroes, prohibited from having dogs, were sentenced to wear an iron collar if they disobeyed.[14]

Chapter XII

BAYOU ST. JEAN AND THE INDIAN WARS 1736-1743

1736 began happily with a marriage in the LaVigne family on Bayou St. Jean. In February Demoiselle Francoise Rivard (minor daughter of the deceased elder LaVigne and Marie Briar of Dauphin Island) married Jean Baptiste Bouché de Montbrun of Quebec, Canada. Her stepmother, the elder Widow LaVigne, stipulated for her; and in July turned over to the newlyweds the bride's share of her father's estate—a Negro, Negress, fourteen cattle and a horse. Francois Rivard, brother of the bride, continued to live on Bayou St. Jean for many years, and didn't collect his part of the estate for nine years which obviously was not to his interest, for when he got around to receiving his share of the Act of Division of July 7, 1736, all he got on January 28, 1745 was one Negro.[1] Perhaps room and board during the intervening years accounted for the difference.

1736 wasn't bright for Bienville. His magic with the Indians was gone; or perhaps the Natchez affair had massacred for all time the pristine good will that had once existed between the red and the white man. An unwritten code for all Indian nations provided that when a tribe, weakened by war or some other debility, sought shelter with another nation who was willing to take them in, pursuit by an enemy to their new home constituted a declaration of war on the host-nation as well as on the pursued. Whether Bienville had forgotten this ancient custom, or in his frustration arbitrarily ignored it, he demanded that the Chickasaws surrender the few Natchez who sought shelter in their camp. The Chickasaws refused, and Bienville prepared for war.

Sending word to Commandant M. D'Artaguette of the Illinois post to meet him in Chickasaw country (area of the upper Talahatchie, Tombigbee and Yazoo Rivers) on May 10th, Bienville took off down Bayou St. Jean in early 1736 to negotiate with the Choctaws at Mobile. They agreed to support the French for a specified amount of goods, a part of which was delivered to them immediately.[2]

Meanwhile, other preparations were going on. For nineteen days in November of 1735 and ten days in January, 1736 St. Montigny and a negro helper at Bayou St. Jean were painting the King's boat and the *Louisiana*, in exchange for thirty quarters of rice Montigny owed the Crown. On February 4, 1736 Louis Joseph DuBreuil Villars agreed to loan Commissary

Salmon the money he needed to prepare for the upcoming conflict in return for a contract covering the dayswork the war would entail.

That same month the little Village of Bayou St. Jean was abristle with the chaos of outfitting and marshalling a small army of 544 white men and 44 Negroes commanded by free Blacks.[3] On March 4th, thirty flat-bottomed barges and a fleet of large pirogues, constructed at the Royal Navy Yards (located on the Brazillier plantation near the Port of Bayou St. Jean), manned by uniformed regulars, leather-skirted militia and Blacks who could be trusted on a mission of this kind, set off through the tall bullrushes, canebrakes and moss-hung cypresses down the bayou. By way of the lakes and the Mississippi Sound, they arrived at Fort Condé near Mobile March 28th, and on April 2nd headed north— the French by boat on the river Mobile, their Choctaw allies marching along the east bank of the stream. Arriving at the Tombigbee depot on April 23rd, they built a fort, and the Choctaws received the rest of their goods. From that point on movement was laboriously slow. On May 26th they reached the Chickasaw Village, and an Indian scout was sent out to contact D'Artaguette, who was nowhere to be found.

D'Artaguette had arrived May 10th—according to plan—with 130 Frenchmen and 366 Indians, but the latter—no more inclined to military than agricultural discipline—didn't want to wait. Frustrated by their fretfulness, D'Artaguette was maneuvered into an unscheduled attack in which he was wounded, whereupon his Indians, in the hard reality of their primitive world, deserted him. D'Artaguette's supplies were confiscated by the Chickasaws, and he and several of his men were captured and held hostage to exact leverage from the French.

Instead of logically proceeding to attack the Natchez Village in the rear of the Chickasaw settlement, Bienville, too, succumbed to the pressure of his Choctaw allies who couldn't wait to lay hands on the Chickasaw possessions.

The enemy had a clear advantage fighting from a substantial fort, as well as from ditches dug stomach deep in the earth. They held their fire until the French were well within musket range and then let them have it. Thirty two of Bienville's men fell dead, and sixty one were wounded. When the French troops fell back, the six hundred Choctaws who'd been hovering at a safe distance—painted and whooping as wildly as the enemy—sprang into action. Immediately twenty two of them were laid low, whereupon they turned tail and scampered off, to the ironic amusement of the white contingent. Simon, commander of the Negro troops, was also chided unmercifully by his white fellow-officers because his men had fled in the thick of danger. To save their reputation and his, he leapt on his horse and dashed out in front of the enemy, inviting shots from all sides. Miraculously he escaped with his life, and black honor was vindicated.

The quartered carcasses of fallen fellows, displayed on the palisade pickets next morning, was no invitation to remain. The French pulled out, and none too soon; arriving back at the river, the water had receded so rapidly that had they dallied two more days it would have been necessary to destroy their boats and return by land. Floating down to Fort Condé, where they left reinforcements, the remaining group was deposited at the Port of Bayou St. Jean the latter part of June—a sick, wounded and discouraged remnant of a short, inglorious campaign in what is now northeastern Mississippi.[4]

A pitiful postscript to this fiasco was the fate of D'Artaguette and forty five of his officers and men, who'd been taken prisoner in May. With the retreat of Bienville, their value as hostages ceased, and they, with Father Senac, Chaplain of the expedition, were led out to a plain, tied four to a stake and burned to death on a slow fire.[5] The death of this honorable officer and his men was another "Natchez" for the colonists, in addition to which Bienville had lost a hundred and twenty men, and the expense of it all was much more than the scanty resources of the colony could sustain.

It was the most "iffy" expedition of French colonial history—if the Indians had been more stable, if the French forces had coordinated their timing and attacks from various vantage points, the results might have been favorable to Bienville. The Governor had his own excuses, complaining to France of the cowardly troops sent him. "Blackguards, these useless beings aren't worth the food bestowed on them. Burdens to the colony, no efficient military service can be expected of them." And to cap it all, he claimed they were very, very short —only four and a half feet tall—and compensated in vice for what they lacked in stature.[6] The situation was untenable, but the next step required preparation.

Meanwhile, personal plans were being made on Bayou St. Jean. A little over a year had now elapsed since the death of Jeanne Antoinette de Villemont, Widow Rivard's husband—a respectable period of mourning— and she was preparing for her second marriage to Jean Francois Huchet, Ecuyer Sieur de Kernion. Born in Quimper, France in 1700, the only child of Pierre Guillaume Huchet and his second wife Thomase Reneé Guesdan de Keravel, young Kernion had come to Louisiane in 1720 as an officer on *La Loire* which brought settlers to the Ste. Reine Concession, one of the largest grants of land made by the Company on the Mississippi above Baton Rouge. The groom, whose family dated back to 1240, had brought his credentials. Genealogy was a matter of great significance in those days; and the practice of tracing the family tree has been passed down to present day descendants of the early Creoles, who, at the tip of a hat, will reel off relatives for generations back.

This marriage of October 4, 1736, was an event of great importance, Governor Bienville and Commissary Salmon being among the socially prominent guests.[7]

Practical considerations, however, preceded the celebration. First—both spouses agreed to provide and care for Jeanne Antoinette and Marie Francoise Rivard, infant children of the bride-to-be and her deceased first husband. Then the future groom assisted with the estate inventory and appraisement of the late Francois Antoine Rivard de LaVigne, Jr.

The same day an inventory was made of Kernion's possessions—slaves and furniture—which he intended to add to the community with his bride.

By the end of the year any differences that may have existed between the new groom and his mother in law had been settled amicably; and six years later—in July of 1742—the younger generation received slaves from her, representing Mrs. Kernion's share in the estate of her father Sr. de Villemont.

Thus Kernion succeeded to the management and eventual ownership of the seventeen arpent LaVigne holdings on Bayou St. Jean, which, during his proprietorship would expand to twenty-two arpents, nineteen fathoms of Bayou frontage.[8] Today his property—at its most extensive —would reach approximately from Grand Route St. John to the vicinity of DeSaix Boulevard on the east bank of the bayou.

Meanwhile, preparations for war went on. In early 1737 Jacques Carriére de Maloze signed a contract to furnish four boats of green oak and cypress to be delivered in first class condition to either the harbor of New Orleans or Bayou St. Jean during the next several months.

And a goodly amount of bread would be needed to feed the additional troops coming from France, so the summer of 1737 found many residents of Bayou St. Jean contracting to supply the government with wheat from Illinois. In August Commissary Salmon signed a contract with Jean Baptiste de Montbrun, husband of Francoise Rivard, who agreed to furnish the King's store in New Orleans 4,493 pounds of Illinois flour at twenty livres per hundred pounds the following spring. Apparently Rene Bouché de Montbrun was going with him, for a couple days later he leased a Negro to take to Illinois, his contract specifying that in the event the "piece d'Inde" was killed by the Indians or drowned, Montbrun would be liable for his value. The owner would bear the loss of the slave only in the event of natural death.

The following day Francois Rivard (LaVigne), brother-in-law of Jean Baptiste de Montbrun, signed a similar contract for the lease of a Negro, for which he agreed to pay 1,500 pounds of Illinois flour.

Evidently many Bayou people went North at the same time, as it was the custom for as many as twenty boats to travel together for mutual protection.

While camping overnight, along the Mississippi, these Bayou St. Jean travelers no doubt used a "ber" to protect themselves from mosquitoes while sleeping. This ingenious device was a frame of canes, stuck in the ground around a mattress; and a linen or muslin cover was thrown over it to protect the sleeper from the peskies.

Louis Langlois, brother of former bayou resident Etienne, had signed a contract with the Commissary two months earlier, agreeing to furnish 8,535 pounds of Illinois flour at 22 livres per hundred pounds. Before leaving, he made legal arrangements with a local merchant to collect a note for him—a kind of insurance taken by many travelers going on lengthy trips in those hazardous times. Langlois had bad luck with his reluctant slave. Despite the irons he was wearing, the Negro escaped somewhere the other side of Natchez, and Langlois was to see nothing of him for eight years, at which time he would return to New Orleans and report his escape to the Superior Council, explaining that he hadn't wanted to go to Illinois.[9]

Awaiting the arrival of troops from France, Bienville spent some time improving his personal finances by putting in a claim for back salary and other monies due him from the Company of the Indies. Fifteen acres of riverfront across the Mississippi (Algiers Point), on which he held good title, had been taken by the Company in the early 1720's to be used as a slave plantation, for which he now collected 228 francs (about $60.00).

Some of his time was spent checking on the progress of the first Charity Hospital of New Orleans, which came into being in 1736. When Jean Louis—builder and seller of boats, and former sailor for the Company of the Indies—died on January 1, 1736, he left his small estate of 10,000 livres (about $2,500) for the relief of suffering humanity. The money was used to establish St. John's Hospital (Hospital of New Orleans, Hospital of the Poor) in the Kolly House on the edge of the settlement which had been vacated by the Ursuline Nuns in 1734. The property was purchased from Contractor DuBreuil Villars who had bought the house from Widow Kolly of the St. Reine Concession, after her husband had been killed in the Natchez Massacre. DuBreuil was paid 1,250 livres for the 20-fathom-front by 40-fathom-deep lot, the house and outbuildings, and also received an additional 2,180 livres for making necessary repairs, building brick walls and clearing the garden of the hospital. The balance of the small legacy went for hospital apparatus, furniture and reserve. A few dollars went a long way in 1737.

Four, five patients receiving treatment there in 1737 establishes St. John's as the oldest charity hospital in the United States; although the French "hôpital" described an almshouse as well as a place for taking care of the sick, it has been reliably established that Jean Louis' hospital administered only to the sick (malades).

The first workers at St. John's were slaves; and on July 15, 1737 Sengalese Francois Tiocou, who had received his freedom for loyalty to the French at Natchez, and his slave wife Marie Aram offered to work for the hospital seven years to buy her freedom. On March 6, 1744 the emancipation papers would be signed by the Governor and the Commissary making Marie Aram a free Black.[10]

In 1737 Luis Brazillier (called Tourangeau)—who had purchased the Dugué property on Bayou St. Jean in 1729—quadrupled his holdings on the bayou by purchasing the adjoining Langlois plantation—eight arpents front by the usual depth—from M. Renaud D'Hauterive. This transaction established Brazillier, with 10½ arpents front, (which today would extend approximately from Grand Route St. John westerly to Orleans Street) as the second largest landowner on the east bank of Bayou St. Jean. The property of Kernion—the largest landowner—was located immediately lakeside of Brazillier's arpents.

It is possible D'Hauterive sold the plantation because of the financial problems he and his bride were having with the estate of her former husband. Sr. Francois Duval, Cashier of the Co. of the Indies from 1731 to 1735, had died owing his employer a large sum. When his widow remarried plantation owner D'Hauterive, the couple assumed the debts of her former husband's estate, and on January 15, 1736 acknowledged that Duval's succession owed the Company of the Indies 191,975 livres. Nothing was done about the debt for over a year—until March 23, 1737—when the D'Hauterives, sensing a superior bargaining situation, suggested to Commissary Salmon that a compromise be effected, by which the D'Hauterives be permitted to settle the debt for 20,000 livres. Though this represented only a small percentage of what they owed, the Company, which was attempting to wind up its affairs in Louisiane, accepted the proposition, provided the whole debt be paid off within two years. The D'Hauterives received their receipt for payment-in-full in September of 1739.[11]

The summer of 1737 seems to have been open season on the Company's former employees. On July 15th, Philippe AntoineИруслé—member of the Superior Council, former Agent of the Company, and father-in law of deceased Bayou resident Francois Dugué—was summoned before the Council by his successor, Agent Jean Baptiste Faucon Dumanoir, who claimed a shortage of 10,543 livres in Brusle's accounts—an amount which had accumulated during his service from 1732 to 1737. Dumanoir asked the council to issue an order for the seizure of five Negroes, and Truslé was then informed by the Sheriff that the Negroes would be imprisoned to insure payment of his debt unless he could furnish a solvent property-owning guardian who would, at his own risk, be responsible for presenting the slaves when and if they were called for. Having anticipated the procedure, Truslé promptly presented Sr. Barthelmy Bimont, a New Orleans resident, who agreed to fulfill the requirements, whereupon the slaves were released.

The trauma of the affair no doubt contributed to Truslé's early demise, for he died October 7, 1738 while his wife and child were visiting France. But the Negroes lived on. Six years later, Truslé's widow, Marthe Fremont, leased six slaves for 1,700 livres to Andre Fabry who wished to use them in trading with the Indians.[12]

Bienville was interested in the barracks which were going up on either side of the Place d'Armes. The first was finished May 4, 1738, but bad weather, which prevented the contractors from working for five months, held up completion of the second building. Most of the oxen, used for hauling carts, had died for lack of pasture during the winter, and although others were procured, the rains made Bayou Road (where the lime ovens were located) so impassable that Negroes had to carry the lime in sacks on their backs to the construction site. Rafters for the roof came from Bayou St. Jean the same way.

While the barracks were going up, the nearby church and presbytery were crumbling to pieces, necessitating an urgent meeting of the colony's inhabitants with Bienville and Salmon. To pay for needed repairs and construction a tax of fifty sols was imposed on each slave, and non-slave owners were assessed according to their means. Bienville donated 9,048 livres to the cause, a sum realized from the sale of *La Maria*, a ship the French had captured on the high seas the year before. (Privateering by the Spanish, French and English in the Gulf of Mexico was not an unexpected occurrence, nor was the practice frowned upon, unless it happened to one's own vessel.) Preparation for the Chickasaw war, however, caused plans for the new Capuchin presbytery to be postponed until 1744, at which time the 1739 deliberations would be reactivated and an additional tax would be imposed on the ovens of the local inhabitants.[13]

On August 28, 1738 Commissary Salmon signed a contract with Jean Baptiste Saucier (Saussier) who would marry the daughter of Bayou St. Jean resident Joseph Girardy at the end of the war. Saucier contracted to furnish fresh meat—beef and deer—but when conditions didn't permit delivery of fresh flesh, salt was to be provided by the Guardian of the King's Store to preserve the protein for the troops. To insure fulfillment of contract, Saucier mortgaged all his movables and immovables.

Most men of property serving in the armed forces of the colony made sure their wills were in good order before the second Indian expedition was launched. One of these was Gentilly resident Jacques Coustillas (Coustilhas), who owned a large plantation (east of *LaBrasserie*, Dreux's Brewery Concession), conceded to him in 1722 and 1724. In addition to running a plantation, Coustillas also used his brig the *Jean Baptiste* to import slaves for the Company of the Indies from the Island of Martinique and the Guinea Coast. To insure that his valuable cargo was handled carefully, Coustillas, on April 24, 1737, contracted to pay the Marine Captain in command of his brig ten livres per head for adult Negroes and 5 livres for those ten to fifteen years of age, who arrived in good shape at New Orleans. For those under ten there was no bounty. The Captain's wage was 130 livres per month, and he was permitted to bring back four Negroes, twelve to eighteen years old, to sell for his own profit. If the Blacks didn't arrive in good condition, he stood the chance of losing not only his salary, but also his slaves.

On August 26, 1738—the evening before he left to establish and command a post in Arkansas—Coustillas dictated his last will and testament, which included freedom for six slaves on his Gentilly plantation in the event of his death. He also made legal arrangements for the management of his indigo plantation, for payment of his bills and investment of funds accruing during his absence.

He died a few months later, in early 1739, after establishing the Arkansas Fort for his Majesty. When the news of his death reached New Orleans, Louis Connard, his wife and four children—slaves of Coustillas—immediately petitioned for their freedom, according to the terms of the will, and their manumission was soon confirmed by Bienville and Salmon. Eight years later Jeanette—one of the freed slaves—was ordered by the Council to sell herself back into slavery, because she'd violated the terms of her manumission by stealing and accumulating debts. The 1,900 livres she received for herself paid what she owed, and the balance was donated to St. John's Hospital. Thirty five piastres were paid to St. Martin de Jaureguibery (husband of deceased Dugué's wife) who lived on Bayou Road, when he proved he'd lent that amount to Jeanette's deceased sister Marguerite. Marguerite, who had died in 1746, had left all her belongings to Jeanette on condition that her sister settle her debts. This was one, among many, she'd failed to meet.

Despite Coustillas' attempt to prepare for the worst, his estate was in a mess. The man who'd served as his plantation administrator had also died, and creditors were suing the succession for what was due them.[14] Neighbor Pierre Dreux petitioned for the loss of a horse he'd once used to haul settlers' goods from Bayou St. Jean to New Orleans. Some time previous to Coustillas' departure for the war, Dreux's horse had wandered onto the plantation of his neighbor who not only ordered his Negroes to kill the animal, but also had Dreux's Negroes beaten for allowing it to stray onto his land. Coustillas had given Dreux a substitute animal, but it had proved worthless for the work, and Dreux had received no further satisfaction. Now he wanted 363 francs for his loss. He also demanded payment for twenty eight pounds of Illinois flour and twenty four pounds of French bread he'd supplied the deceased administrator of the plantation.[15]

Bad luck dogged everyone who had anything to do with the Coustillas plantation. At the end of 1739, Sieur Darby, a neighbor who had subleased a part of the plantation, was extremely upset about Bienville's order to plantation owners to furnish slaves for the war. Many of Coustillas' Negroes had been drafted, leaving only sick ones at home. In order to save the indigo crop of the Coustillas acreage, Darby had diverted slaves from his own land, resulting in a loss of thirty five acres of rice.[16]

The affairs of Sr. Gerard Pery, who subsequently took over and attempted to raise indigo on the land, went from bad to worse. By September of 1743, his wife had sued for separation of community and return of her dowry, and by 1756 Pery wouldn't have a sol to his name.[17]

1739 needed a couple of happy events to counteract all the bad news. Mr. and Mrs. Huchet de Kernion of Bayou St. Jean became the proud parents of a son. René would eventually, like his father, become an officer of the colonial troops by order of the King.[18]

The spring of 1739 saw another marriage in the LaVigne family. Demoiselle Francoise de Villemont (daughter of Antoinette Fourrier, the elder Widow Rivard and Sr. Henry de Mirebaize Squire de Villemont, her first husband) married Sieur Francois Louis Jean Caüe, Guardian of the King's Stores in the Army which was to march against the Chickasaws. Not only was the groom involved with his own business, but marrying into the LaVigne clan, he took upon himself complex family problems that wouldn't be resolved in a lifetime—problems involving tutor obligations, curatorships, and obligations to the Company of the Indies—all complicated to a high degree by the inter-involvement of various individuals.[19]

The 1730's had been good to dynamic DuBreuil, whose plantation below the city backed upon Bayou St. Jean. Contractor of Public works for the King, he continued to improve the drainage system of the region and manufactured bricks. He received a commission of Captain in the Louisiane Militia from Versailles in October of 1736—the same year Commissary Salmon and the French Minister were discussing a model of a sawmill for him. Without a doubt, DuBreuil dug the first canal and built the first sawmill near the juncture of today's Elysian Fields and the Mississippi—facilities that would in the latter years of the 1700s be improved upon by Sieurs St. Maxent and Marigny, subsequent owners of the plantation. In the late 1730's DuBreuil's home just below New Orleans was purchased by the French authorities to be used as a residence for the French governors of Louisiane; and when most of Balise, the receiving station at the mouth of the river, was destroyed by the hurricanes of 1739 and 1740, DuBreuil Villars received the contract to rebuild it, as he was the only man in the colony wealthy enough to handle such an undertaking.[20]

On August 20, 1739 Pierre Dreux of Gentilly sold two lots to DuBreuil, who paid for the land with masonry work on Dreux's townhouse, as well as a promise to do other necessary work in the future.

1739 was a busy year for the Dreuxs. Pierre sued Caparaize Mathieu, who, he charged, had shot a cow and bull of his Grand Havana stock. However, his only witnesses were seven of his own slaves whom Mathieu dismissed as prejudiced, so it isn't likely he collected. In the fall of that year Hubert Harant, merchant of New Orleans, and first cousin of the Dreux brothers died; and the two of them settled the Harant succession, paying debts and turning the balance over to Harant's two sisters. The property included a Negress, three Negro children, three lots on Bayou Road and a half lot in town. The Bayou Road lots were sold to Sieur Piquery, the King's Baker, on October 24, 1739 for 360 livres (about $72.00). A month later he turned them over for the same price.[21]

In September, 1739 old time colony resident—and early owner of property on the west bank of Bayou St. Jean—Sr. Francois Trudeau died; and his son, Jean Baptiste Laveau Trudeau, petitioned the council for his emancipation in order to handle the succession.[22]

And others took advantage of the public preoccupation with preparation for war. In late 1739 one Kimper and four soldiers stationed at the guardhouse at the mouth of Bayou St. Jean, deserted their post, seized six Negroes and made off with them in a dugout. The plunderers were pursued to no avail, and when the dugout was later found, near a decomposed corpse, the case was consigned to the files as another unsolved crime in colonial annals.[23]

Meanwhile Bienville had summoned troops from Illinois and the Canadian provinces to meet him in Chickasaw country in August of 1739. Arriving on time, the northern troops built Fort Assumption three-quarters of a league south of Wolf River (present site of Memphis). The Commander-in-Chief, heading up the Mississippi, was late as usual, and didn't get there until November 12th. Then his huge army of French, Negroes, Iroquois, Hurons, Episingles, Algonquins and other Indian nations, as well as horses, cattle and supplies, remained in camp until the following March of 1740—supposedly resolving problems of selecting flood-free overland routes to the site of battle, and perfecting methods of moving horses and cattle on a lengthy march through strange country. None of these problems explain the delay as much as complete lack of enthusiasm for the whole thing. Some of the Choctaws, for the most part allies of the French, kept changing their minds. One Red Shoe in particular couldn't decide who he was for, and supplies ran so low they had to start eating the horses which were to draw the artillery and ammunition. By the middle of March no more than two-hundred effective white men could be mustered to march with the Indians and Negroes against the Chickasaws. Bienville had little recourse except to retreat; but about March 15th, at the request of Captain M. De Celeron and Lt. M. de St. Laurent, he detached a small company of cadets and the Indians who'd come with them from Canada, to offer the Chickasaws peace if they sued for it. Fate was in their favor, for the Chickasaws, believing them to be the vanguard of a large army to follow, immediately signaled their surrender, and as a gesture of good will, even turned over to the French two English traders who happened to be in their camp. Celeron sent the Indian chiefs after the retreating Bienville to effect a treaty of peace. Then razing Fort Assumption, the army crossed the river to Fort St. Francis, where the northern troops were discharged and returned to Canada, and Bienville went back to New Orleans.[24]

Today—from a psychological point of view—this may seem to have been some kind of victory—peace without loss of life on the battlefield. Not so to Bienville. This humiliating campaign, ending in April of 1740, closed his military career in Louisiane. A statement of June 15, 1740, filed by Bienville and Salmon, showed that the expenses of the Chickasaw War from 1737 to 1740 cost as much per year as the entire budget of the colony. Unable to justify his defeats and expenditures, Bienville, at sixty two years of age, asked to be relieved of his duties.[25]

Complications of the war notwithstanding, it was marrying time on Bayou St. Jean. Joseph Girardy and Jeanne Héry gained two sons-in-law the spring of 1740. On March 12, 1740 their daughter Marie Louise married Louis Langlois, brother of deceased Etienne Langlois, one of the early residents of the Village of Bayou St. Jean. And less than a month later, Marie Rose Girardy and Jean Baptiste Saucier (Saussier)— back from the war—signed a marriage contract on April 6th.[26]

In 1741 colonial friends were surprised to hear of the renunciation by Sr. Jean Jacques de La Chaise of his parents' estate in Louisiane. His father had come to the colony in 1722 to investigate Bienville's administration. Now Captain of the Ships of the Company of the Indies in Paris —a position he no doubt merited from his father's achievement—Jean Jacques apparently decided that what he'd receive from his Louisiane inheritance wasn't worth the trouble of collecting it. His sister followed suit.[27]

After the war Francois Caüe and his wife Francoise de Villemont received 3,000-livres-worth of Negroes from the elder Widow Rivard, representing the young woman's share of her father's estate. And, one good turn begetting another, on October 27, 1740 Caüe arranged with his employers to cancel the contract his new mother-in-law had signed with Sr. Prevost back on August 2, 1731 wherein she acknowledged indebtedness of 12,924 livres to the Company of the Indies by the succession of Sr. Villemont, her first husband. Commissary Salmon, probably through Caüe's intervention, had seen fit to reduce the amount by half, and in place of the original instrument, accepted Caüe's official acknowledgment of his debt to the Company in the amount of 6,462 livres.

The years ahead would reveal interesting items about the Caües. Like most estimable citizens of Bayou St. Jean, he didn't restrict himself to one occupation. In addition to his position with the Company of the

Indies, he also operated as a merchant, and in 1744 contracted with Commissary Salmon to furnish merchandise to be used as presents for the Indians—items such as fifty bolts of Holland galloon for capes and forty pounds of vermillion at five sols per pound; and like any sound businessman of the time, he insisted on payment in silver or notes of exchange on the General Treasury of France.

In 1746 Mr. and Mrs. Caüe would legally oblige themselves to pay J.B. B. Piemont, a wholesale merchant of New Orleans, 2,650 livres within a period of two months—noteworthy only because it revealed that women were permitted to enter into such contracts.

However, in 1742 Francois Louis Jean Caüe was in the thick of family complications. The future emancipation of Jeanne Antoinette Rivard (daughter of deceased Antoine Rivard, Jr. and the present Madame Huchet de Kernion)—Caüe's niece—was being discussed. The situation was extremely sticky, and Mathurin Dreux, who had been her curator for years, submitted his resignation on August 28, 1742. Since Jeanne, upon emancipation, would come into control of her share of her father's estate, and because her mother, Mrs. Kernion, was claiming all the movables and immovables of the Rivard, Jr. estate which were supposed to produce the livres due the young lady from her father's succession, Dreux could see nothing but trouble ahead. Being on good terms with all parties involved, he suggested that Jeanne's maternal uncle, Sr. de Caüe, would be the logical curator. But Dreux didn't get off the hook so easily. Ten years later he would again submit his resignation from the same position, and the inheritance wouldn't be settled for another seven years after that.[28]

Mathurin Dreux wanted to be released, because he had problems of his own. His brother Pierre having died, his widow Anne Corbin requested and received Mathurin's consent to sell the Gentilly Plantation *La Brasserie* below the city, on condition that the land be paid for with current money and that the proceeds be used to pay the legitimate debts of the succession and for the benefit of the heirs. Parts of the original plantation having been sold before, 6½ arpents front by 40 deep were sold to Claude Joseph Villars DuBreuil on July 21, 1743.[29]

Meanwhile, two offspring of bayou residents-in-good-standing had married. Francois Héry, called Duplanty (whose name was the same as his father's) and Madeline Brazillier, daughter of Widower Luis Brazillier (called Tourangeau) signed their marriage contract on October 11, 1741. The Duplantys would be residents of Bayou St. Jean for many, many years.[30]

On July 16, 1743 Bienville freed his Negro Zacarie, son of old Marie who had been freed in 1733. Manumitted for good service, Zacarie promised to continue serving his master—or another named by him—for an additional five years, during which time he'd be treated well in sickness and in health. After thirty five fitful years in Louisiane, Bienville returned to France in 1743, and was retired on a yearly pension of 1,800 livres (about $360.00). After squeezing by for most of his service on an annual salary of 2,000 livres (about $400.00), he had finally gotten a raise—probably as an incentive to return to Louisiane—so during the last eight years of his governorship his salary was a more appropriate 12,000 livres. With what he'd saved from his income and realized from the sale of his lands, slaves and personal property in the colony, he had enough to live in comparative ease to the end of his days.[31]

Chapter XIII

BAYOU BANE AND BOON UNDER THE GRAND MARQUIS—1743-1750

The amiable Pierre Cavagnial de Rigaud, Marquis de Vaudreuil, succeeded Bienville as governor of Louisiane on May 27, 1743. Since the Indian wars of Périer and Bienville had encouraged little lightness of spirit or emigration to the colony, the Grand Marquis and his wife, who gathered about her a small Parisian-type court, were the perfect prescription for happier times. New Orleans society dates from the era of Vaudreuil when gay parties became the order of the day, and the first four-wheeled carriage was imported from France.

The new governor was to be well-housed, for the following year Jean Francois Gautreau (Gauthereau), Guardian of the King's Stores at New Orleans, having fulfilled his stint of duty, sold Vaudreuil his plantation on the other side of the Mississippi, several lodgings and buildings, twenty eight Negroes, oxen, cows, calves and heifers for thirty thousand livres.[1]

Up to now the Charity Hospital of New Orleans had been located in the old Kolly house on the upper limits of New Orleans. In 1743 it was necessary to replace it; and the second St. John's Hospital was built at the rear of the village, on the square bounded by Rampart, Basin, St. Peter and Toulouse Streets, with money provided by individual donations. Fronting on the cemetery (bounded by Rampart, St. Peter, Toulouse and Burgundy—in use since 1725) the government gave the 50 X 100 toise hospital plot on condition that the land could be recalled if it was needed.[2]

Prior to this the better homes of the settlement had been located on the first two streets from the river; now the settlers began to push the village boundaries back a couple blocks—back toward the gate in the palisade wall that opened onto Bayou Road which led to the Village and Port of Bayou St. Jean.

Along Bayou Road in the 1740's rose the wide, red-roofed, severely plain dwellings of the rich. Generally one or one and a half stories high, they were raised on pillars—sometimes fifteen feet from the ground—and were surrounded by wide verandas. Set off by extensive grounds, and shaded by myriad magnolia, live oak and other forest trees, these lovely homes fronted plantations of indigo and myrtle which stretched back from either side of that main suburban thoroughfare of French times.

The fragrant myrtle, called anemiche by the Indians, was being promoted by the government as a possible local industry. The waxtree or candleberry (myrica cerifera) had for some time been used in making candles for the local inhabitants, and research disclosed that it took eight pounds of berries to produce one pound of wax. The matter was pursued for many years, but it never became a major business.[3]

The concessionaires of Bayou St. Jean had continued to do well from the beginning. Their houses were different from those in the city—most of them two-story dwellings, built of brick between posts—"briquette entré poteau" the construction was called. And to match the superiority of their dwellings, the occupants were said to exude an air of aristocratic supremacy. However, by comparison with today's market, some of the Bayou St. Jean real estate of yesteryear seems modest indeed. The records of the time reveal a sale to Etienne de Benac—Major of the troops in New Orleans—of two lots on the bayou, on which was situated a house of posts and bricks, built on the ground, thirty feet in length with shingled roof and dependances—all for 2,700 livres (about $540.00). In the manner of the time, the sale had been "posted and cried three consecutive times with no opposition whatsoever." There were no newspapers in those days, but advertising a sale on the door of the church, the council chambers, or some other frequented location, and calling attention to the proposed auction by beating a drum and having the information called out for most of the folk who couldn't read or write, three Sundays in a row, probably reached more prospective buyers in the limited area of that time than do the cramped ads in the back of today's newspapers.[4]

The French were by now quite accustomed to eating corn. Mathurin Dreux, in 1744, furnished the King's warehouse 217 barrels of it on the cob at 9 livres per barrel. But there were those who were still picky. One Joseph St. Maurice had hired himself to Francois Héry (Duplanty)—husband of Madeline Brazillier—for three months to accompany Duplanty's associate to Arkansas. Soon after, however, he filed a complaint with the Superior Council—no doubt to justify non-fulfillment of his contract. He claimed he'd fallen ill, been insulted by Duplanty and had received bad nourishment—only big hominy and very little rice.[5]

In 1744 bayou residents received the news that Louis Juchereau de St. Denis, commandant at Natchitoches and founder of that post, had died on June 20th. St. Denis had been the earliest owner of a part of the

Girardy property on the west bank of Bayou St. Jean. Grief, however, was shortlived in those fatalistic days. People were too wrapped up in their own every-day involvement with survival.[6]

Joseph Milon too had died, and his widow—Marie Francoise Girardy— requested the Council on January 31, 1744 to apprehend her Negro Yamma who had run away. If he was found, he was no doubt subjected to the usual punishment—flogging at the foot of the gallows and a warning about future running away. Before the year was out, Widow Milon had a husband to attend to such matters. On November 24th she married Sr. Joseph DesRuisseaux, Lord of the Isle of Peraut, Canada; and they— together with her four sons by Joseph Milon—maintained as home base the Girardy residence just cityside of Chemin Chapitoulas (Metairie Road) on the west bank of the bayou.

The Council records of these years disclose several legal instruments by which the DesRuisseauxs rented out their slaves. When help on hand outweighed the work to be done, a common practice of the time was to rent one's Negroes, tantamount to earning interest on one's investment capital today. In late 1744 they rented a Negro, his wife and two children for 650 livres, to serve a man on a year's journey to the other side of the lake. The lessee accepted responsibility for anything that might harm or kill the slaves except natural death. Early the next year the DesRuisseauxs rented two slaves for one year on the same terms for 124 livres.

DesRuisseaux also busied himself in 1745 settling the affairs of his bride's former husband, which included dissolving the partnership that had existed between Joseph Milon and Claude Joseph DuBreuil, Senior Contractor of buildings and fortifications for the King. After toting up the assets and debts of the partnership, the Milon estate gained very little. No scaredy-cats these newly-weds, the DesRuisseauxs bought 5,000-livres-worth of merchandise from Sr. Ancelin and with the four Milon children set off for Illinois where DesRuisseaux had obtained exclusive fur trading rights on the Missouri River from 1746 to 1750.

Before leaving he took care of the Milon children's interests by leasing their twelve-lot-square of ground on the outskirts of New Orleans near the DeMorand brickyard. Mr. LeBreton, the lessee, promised to keep up the grounds, fence it, look after the unfinished house, lumber and other materials on the place "as a good father of the family" and return the property when they wanted it back.[7]

Mrs. DesRuisseaux's parents were having their problems too. Angelique (daughter of Girardy by the Indian Francoise prior to his marriage to Jeanne Héry) had died, and her children needed looking after.

In a Catholic community, with no birth control and early deaths due to fevers and other hazards of colonial times, people often married several times in early life, resulting in very large cumulative families. Angelique Girardy had married three times: 1) to Alain Dugué, who'd been killed at Natchez, 2) to Widower Jean Baptiste Rejas (called LaPrade), and 3) to Laurent Lerable. Now five children needed looking after— four of them LaPrade's offspring, and a son by Lerable. At a family meeting called January 22, 1745, Lerable was elected tutor and grandfather Joseph Girardy undertutor to look after the interests of the minors.

The continuing responsibility of a series of marital connections must have often been almost more than the surviving spouse could bear; but the alternative of living alone was even worse for Lerable, who married twice again, had two more children by Marie Jean Dupuy (Dupré) and remained responsible for his own plus Angelique Girardy's orphaned children until other legal, acceptable arrangements were eventually effected.[8]

Entrepreneur Claude Joseph Villars DuBreuil was improving his real estate portfolio in 1745. From *The Brewery* arpents he'd purchased from the Dreux heirs in 1743, he transferred two and a half of the rear arpents to Councillor Raguet on August 9th in exchange for one precious arpent on the Mississippi which Raguet owned in the middle of DuBreuil's river front.[9]

King George's War was waged by England and France from 1744 to 1748, and although the action was fairly well confined to the New England states and Canada, increased concern by the French government for the problems of that region resulted in shrinking attention to Louisiane. Fearful that the English would attack New Orleans by sea, Vaudreuil fortified Balise and English Turn, and privateering was pursued as a business. In 1745 a number of local "gamblers" invested their labor and livres in a vessel to prey on the English. The *Corsaire*, which the investors anticipated would net them a fortune, was fitted out on Bayou St. Jean, but for a symphony of reasons the project didn't come off; and unbeknownst to most of them, the vessel was surreptitiously sold by two of the major investors. Anticipating TV plots of today, the larger cause was publicly exposed because of a couple of smaller ones—a matter of a missing quadrant and an unpaid bill for caulking—advanced by the minor stockholders who felt they'd gotten the short end of the deal. And, shades of eternal connivance, the bureaucrats involved justified their mischief with a public statement that the vessel had been sold to prevent the expedition.[10]

On January 28, 1746 representatives of the Superior Council were called to the home of Charles Lorreins (Tarascon) on Bayou St. Jean to put seals on the possessions of Durantaye, Tarascon's partner of one year, who had drowned in Lake Pontchartrain on his return from Mobile the week before. Details of the accident weren't revealed, but Tarascon's Negro Pierrot and a twenty five year old Negress, who had been accepted by Durantaye from a Pensacola dealer as a 300-livre-payment on a debt, were in the same boat, and survived. Since Durantaye had many debts, his personal chest and effects, as well as the Negress, were taken to the home of Tarascon to be inventoried.[11]

Early the next month the attention and care of all who knew them were focused on Marie Catherine Beaudreau, former wife of deceased Etienne Langlois, and her eight children. Tutrix of her brood, and widowed for the third time by the death of Urbain Gervais, she empowered Benoit de St. Clair, Marine Captain stationed in Illinois, to sell three arpents of land she owned there, so the money could be invested locally for her minor offspring.

Widow Gervais and Benoit were jointly engaged in the trade of foodstuffs and other merchandise between New Orleans and Illinois—items she handled from her home-shop which was located in a part of the residence of Olivier de Vezin, Surveyor of the King's Highways. A small matter thrust itself upon the larger when, in a chatty letter of March 1746, the energetic, life-loving widow implored Benoit to send her pimento as there was no black pepper in New Orleans. She also complained that of all the hams he'd sent, only two were fit to be eaten, and that a customer whose flour shipment had been short, was demanding a barrel of beer as indemnity. Along with the palatable aspects of existence, the Widow Gervais reported that an epidemic in New Orleans had attacked persons of all ages and sexes, killing many.

She knew her travel schedules. Most of the trade convoys left Illinois beginning in February, when flood waters filled the Mississippi and overflowed the land on both sides, at which time the Indians would go hunting, and the convoys weren't so liable to be attacked by them. Convoys going upstream usually left New Orleans between August and November, and traveling time to the Illinois was eight to ten weeks.

Perhaps the fevers extended into the following year, for in December of 1747 Widow Gervais was on the list of fatalities; and after the beds of her children had been removed from her quarters, seals were attached to each end of the bands of paper that were stretched across the doors and windows of her home-shop, so that, in the interest of her many creditors, none of her possessions would be removed.[12]

Louis Langlois, uncle of his brother Etienne's orphaned children, now had his hands full. An inventory of the succession was made, and an auction held in January of 1748. Then Langlois found himself appearing in a series of lawsuits as creditors sued the estate. There was the matter of disposing of a house and five lots in town, and a plantation with seventeen slaves located four and a half leagues from New Orleans, as well as the land in Illinois. He finally leased the plantation and slaves for three years at 840 livres. As tutor, Langlois had to consider the future of his minor charges, and in March of 1748 represented two of his nephews in apprenticeship contracts. Gerard, who was to learn cabinet-making under Francois Bigeon, (called La Violette), for the next five years, would during that time also be furnished board, lodging and laundry. Auguste was apprenticed to a gunsmith for the same length of time. The contracts were executed before a notary, and in the latter instance both Langlois and the gunsmith admitted they didn't know how to sign their names.

Appearing in court on June 1, 1748 at the request of the husbands of three of the daughters, Langlois rendered an account of his brother's succession, but apparently the continuing litigation was getting to him, because he asked to resign as tutor at a family meeting on June 6, 1748. However, after the meeting he was still tutor, and the work went on. Having distributed a part of the estate in 1749, the major part of the work was yet unfinished when he died.[13]

Imposed on her own grief and the difficulties of looking after her own affairs, the burden of her brother-in-law's succession fell on Louis Langlois' widow Marie Louise Girardy; but the job of estate curator was soon assumed by Michael Forestier, husband of daughter Perrine Langlois; and under his guidance Francois, Louis, August, and Gerard Langlois were emancipated.

Benoit St. Clair, former business associate and one of Widow Gervais' creditors, had a tough time collecting what was due him. Having sent his bill from Illinois in 1749, after much legal turmoil and a move back to New Orleans as Captain of the troops (and resident in the home of Widow Buslé), he finally, on July 12, 1752, collected the 2,900 livres due him by the hardest.[14]

Bayou resident Francois Héry (Duplanty) the elder died on January 28, 1746, and the taking of the inventory and raising of the seals from his effects was done at the home of Charles Lorreins (Tarascon) his bayou neighbor. His son of the same name (husband of Madeline Brazillier) now began to assume many of his father's former responsibilities. On March 6, 1746 he rented four Negroes and two Negresses to Franco Vignon LaCombe, who wanted them to work in his tar business in today's Tammany Parish. By contract, LaCombe agreed to furnish each of the Blacks a blanket coat, a skirt for each of the Negresses, and to nourish and support them all in health and illness, at a cost of 300 livres for each male and 250 livres for each female. LaCombe was to pay 850 livres within six months and the balance at the end of the term. Either the tar business wasn't as lucrative as LaCombe had anticipated or he was taking advantage of an easy creditor, for Duplanty didn't get paid until March 9, 1748.

On March 20, 1746 Duplanty's boat, carrying flour for the government, reached Mobile in rainy weather, and fearing damage to the cargo if it wasn't unloaded quickly, several Negroes were borrowed from various plantation owners to get the job done. Unfortunately, one Mingo, belonging to the succession of Sr. Bernard Diron, lifted too heavily, ruptured himself and after suffering internal injuries died seven days later. A complication of legality, as to who was liable, followed; and finally, DuBreuil Villars, who had gotten himself into a financial bind with a large purchase of slaves in 1739, and who now owed everybody—including his bayou friends and the Diron succession—was ordered to pay Widow Diron's new husband the value of the dead slave.

In 1744 Francois Héry (Duplanty) had entered into a partnership with Louis Giscart, (called Benoit), to trade at the Arkansas Post. However, they'd allowed too much credit, and in 1746, Benoit, using Duplanty's Negroes as rowers, went up to Arkansas to recover what he could, with the understanding that the two of them would share the expenses of the trip. Then Duplanty, probably because of his father's death and local responsibilities, decided he wanted out, and on April 11, 1747 sold all his rights in the business, including tallow wax, to Benoit and Sr. Tixerant, Officer of the Marine troops in New Orleans. But the affair wasn't over. Benoit had incurred expenses Duplanty didn't feel he ought to pay, and there was a misunderstanding about the Negro rowers Duplanty had furnished for the trip. Benoit insisted he'd retained one of them for two years only because he needed him to collect debts due the partnership. The Superior Council agreed with Benoit, and ordered Duplanty to pay 447 livres, 7 sols.

The following year Duplanty exchanged two of his slaves—25 year old Samba and 14 year old Marie—valued at 4,000 livres—for three lots with buildings that belonged to Sr. Bimon of the King's Stores at Illinois. Since the property was worth 5,000 livres, Duplanty on June 19, 1748 legally acknowledged the balance of 1,000 livres as a debt. This marks Duplanty's first real estate deal in the records—an interest in which he was to become heavily involved later on.

There also were family duties to attend to. In August of 1748 he stipulated for his minor brother-in-law, Jean Baptiste Brazillier, only son of Luis Brazillier, who was marrying Pelagia Tarascon, minor daughter of Santiago Lorreins (Tarascon) and Maria Avril (Abril). This was to be one of those rare long, childless marriages, during which the couple would live on Bayou St. Jean for twenty six years.[15]

In 1747, in case there were any doubts about the matter, the Grand Marquis defined the boundaries of the New Orleans district, as beginning at the mouth of the Mississippi (including both banks) and extending up to Les Allemands (the German settlement) about twenty five miles above New Orleans; the district also embraced Bayou St. Jean and that part of the country back of town known as Gentilly.

Unsolvable problems of the colony continued to harass the local leadership. Paper money, which had begun to depreciate in the 1730's, had by the mid-1740s declined to where the ratio of bills of exchange to silver was three to one; and subsequent ordinances set a time limit in which treasury notes could be redeemed or become worthless.

Tempers were running high in the Parish Church of St. Louis. Pewholders, including DuBreuil, were protesting that the Curé and Wardens of the Church (including Srs. Dreux, Rivard, DeMorand, Tixerant and Miss Milon) had sold their seats from under them to others for a higher price. The wardens justified that the recent adjudication had been properly published for three consecutive Sundays; and the Curé prayed the Council to confirm the wardens' action because pew prices had been reduced two years before to the prejudice of the church which was falling in ruins from lack of funds. The Superior Council, however, disagreed with the action, and held that the protestors could keep their pews at the price they'd formerly paid. They also set the date for the next auction of pews as the first Sunday of 1748, at which time the price decided on would remain the same for another three years. The decision was read to the congregation to the beat of the drum after High Mass and inscribed in the Register of Deliberations, which made the proceeding very, very binding.[16]

Indian problems were on the governor's mind when he advised Paris that because of the unsuccessful expeditions from 1736 to 1740, the Indians had gotten the idea that the French couldn't win against them. The only resolution, Vaudreuil suggested, was to wipe out all past failures, or face a continuing crisis.

On April 15, 1747 the Indians struck the farming settlement of Les Allemands killing one white man; and his wife, daughter, three black men and two black women were taken prisoner. Severely jolted by the onslaught, the Germans moved from the well-cleared and cultivated left bank to the other side of the Mississippi where they had to start all over. Many abandoned their homes and brought their Negroes with them to New Orleans, and the only way they'd consider going back was if soldiers went with them. This was a stickler for management who'd never had enough troops to reach around to all emergency sites; and now that France was warring with England in the north, requests to the mother country for additional forces fell on deaf ears. Besides the Germans weren't content with just any soldiers. They wanted Swiss troops whose character and living habits were similar to theirs and who made the kind of husbands they wanted their daughters to marry.

With dismay the local government saw some of these ex-Allemanders setting up liquor shops in New Orleans instead of going back to farming. Licenses for operating the six taverns in New Orleans were auctioned off by the government, each proprietor paying an annual 200 livres to the church and 100 livres to the Hospital of the Poor for the privilege of pursuing his business. The liquor shops closed on holidays, at 9:00 p.m. on regular nights and during hours of worship on Sunday. Since the soldiers had their own supervised canteens, the licensed taverns served only the inhabitants, sick people, seafaring men and travelers. It was strictly forbidden to sell liquor to Indians or Negroes.[17]

The Girardys on Bayou St. Jean had different problems. Jean Baptiste Saucier (Saussier), husband of daughter Rose, had died in Illinois, and on November 17, 1747 the widow petitioned Judge Le Normant to order a family meeting so a tutor and under-tutor could be appointed to look after the interests of her two minor children, the youngest of which was only two years old. It was of the essence that this be accomplished soon, as she was about to marry again. Her new husband was Louis Duvernay (son of deceased Louis Duvernay and Ann Marie Faque) who in January of the following year was getting after neighbor Luis Brazillier, asking him to pay for eight and a half boatloads of shells Saucier had hauled to the Girardy plantation two years earlier for the making of lime. In all the confusion of losing her husband the last thing Rose Girardy had had on her mind was shells, and in April of 1747, neighbor Brazillier—without asking anybody's permission—had taken them to make his own lime, paid ten livres on account, and now refused to pay the balance of 350 livres with interest and costs. Obviously neighbors across the bayou wouldn't allow an affair of so little consequence to come between them. The records reveal no further litigation in the matter.[18]

In June of 1747 one of DuBreuil's slaves hung himself in his cabin; and since suicide was a heinous crime against God and State, the corpse—represented by a legal representative—was tried in court.

In December of the same year Sr. Raymond St. Martin de Jaureguibery (who had married the widow of Francois Dugué) sold his Bayou Road plantation and eleven slaves to Sr. Duhommel for 4,000 piastres of 5 livres each.[19]

On March 20, 1748, Sr. Francois Caüe, son-in-law of the elder Widow LaVigne, wished to take a trip to France, but his financial situation prohibited it. The government kept close tabs on those leaving the colony—especially if they owed money—and Caüe was indebted to the Company for 6,462 livres, 4 sols and 4 deniers—the note he'd given the Company in 1740 to cancel out his mother-in-law's debt. It wasn't as if Caüe hadn't been working. He'd been laboring on one complicated concession since 1737, and hadn't received a sol of the 11,462 livres, 4 sols, and 4 deniers they owed him. In desperation he petitioned Commissary Sebastian Francois Ange Le Normant (successor to Salmon who had died) that his obligation be charged to his client's account, without prejudice to the 5,000 livres they'd still owe him. By March 22nd, the succession had assumed the debt and cleared the way for his departure, and it's fascinating to note how—in good bookkeeping form—it all came out even. Caüe wouldn't collect his additional 5,000 livres for another five years.[20]

In March of 1748 one of the residents of Bayou St. Jean assumed new and auspicious responsibilities in addition to those of running his plantation; Jean Francois , Huchet de Kernion was granted a commission as Councillor Assessor by Governor de Vaudreuil and Commissary Le Normant. But prior to his induction into the Superior Council, a thorough inquiry was made into his life, morals and religion. M. Kernion, Warden of the Parish, and Catholic in good standing for many years, received a ready recommendation.[21]

Sometimes the Negroes of that time colluded with the Indians, involving themselves in the bigger issue of red versus white. On May 18, 1748 Acting Attorney General Raguet disclosed that for the past six weeks settlers all the way up to Les Allemands had been suffering theft of cattle, provisions and poultry, in response to which a detachment commanded by M. de Marigny had been sent out to investigate. An Indian and a Negro were captured, and being interrogated, exposed the affair as well as interesting side issues. Six of the run-aways had stolen a couple of pirogues from DuBreuil and Carriére, as well as pistols, powder, balls and some food, and had taken off down Bayou St. Jean to Lake Pontchartrain, where they supplemented their limited larder by hunting deer and teal ducks before crossing the lake. There some Choctaw Indians, who'd been trailing them through the woods, tried to talk them into joining a strike on the French "as they'd been promised all they'd ask for in return for French scalps." After a brief stay in the Indian camp, the Negro captive—not wishing to become implicated—had managed to escape and had accidentally run into a friendly Indian in the woods, where the two of them lived on blackberries and stayed together for mutual protection until they were apprehended.[22]

That same year the 1739 mystery of the slaves kidnapped from Fort St. Jean was solved. Other slaves had continued to disappear after 1739, until a New Orleans traveler recognized some of the missing Negroes in Havana. Through the French consul and a lawyer in Cuba a couple of the slaves were returned, and the fate of some of the missing came to light. Many of those who'd disappeared—including those abducted from Bayou St. Jean—were now living with new owners in Havana; and 'though married and having children at the time of their forced departure, they had begun a new life and were raising second families. The Blacks had adjusted well to their new circumstances; and one wonders how complicated family situations became for those who were returned.[23]

Other Negroes became legally involved through ne'er-do-well whites. In February of 1749 Alain LeBert, sailor on the King's Galley that operated between the Port of Bayou St. Jean and Mobile, was in trouble with the law for taking some table silver and a couple coffers from the Galley, as well as stealing a gun, a horn of powder, a bag of bullets and two loaves of bread from the King's Store on Bayou St. Jean. After LeBert's quick disappearance, a soldier from Mobile accused him of lifting the fifth and sixth planks of the lower flooring of the Store at the Bayou; and the powder horn, held as evidence at the corps de garde, had been recovered in a pirogue abandoned in the bayou by Judice's Negro, to whom LeBert had given the powder. Sr. Vovaret, Guardian of the King's Store at the bayou, admitted to the Attorney General that being in the King's Service, LeBert had been allowed a place at his table the night before, where Vovaret—on retiring—had left him. LeBert was a quick worker. Taking the keys, he'd helped himself and several Negroes to rum, as well as the other property. With a record of past misdeeds, LeBert, the soldier from Mobile and the Negro were ordered to appear for questioning. If they failed to show, they'd be imprisoned and fined ten livres each. Putting a hand on the King's goods was a serious offense in 1749, and when the authorities caught up with LeBert he was sure to get his comeuppance.[24]

The bigger minority issue continued to worry the French colonists. More and more of the Choctaw allies were being lured away by the English who always managed to have more presents for them. A point had been reached where the Choctaws were fighting a civil war—twelve of their villages who traded with the English were engaging thirty who would not. At this stage of the game the French were in the miserable position of trying to be on good terms with all the Indians who were buffers between themselves and the English. With English ships in the Gulf cutting off all imports coming from France, grain had to be imported from Illinois and munitions from Canada through Indian territory.

Intermittent engagements, which up to now had been carried on away from New Orleans, came as close as Bayou St. Jean in 1749, when a short sharp encounter took place between unfriendly Choctaws and local soldiers. This time the French were lucky, capturing all the ammunition, provisions and boats of their adversaries, as well as prisoners—all except two braves who escaped into the bayou swamps.[25]

The colonial situation notwithstanding, the year ended well for Charles DeMorand, plantation owner on Bayou Road. His first son, Charles, was born to him and his second wife Marie (Catherine) de La Chaise on December 27, 1749. The birth certificate, signed by Father Dagobert, revealed that Charles' Godparents were Mr. DuBreuil and Marguarite Darensbourg wife of Jacques de La Chaise, Keeper of the King's Store.

The 1750's were busy years for Joseph DesRuisseaux. Having returned from the north, he received a six-arpent-grant of land on the west bank of Bayou St. Jean from Governor Vaudreuil on August 10, 1750. His new property was located to the immediate lakeside of the eight arpents given Marie Louise Girardy by Turpin in 1734 (today's Carrollton Ave. and lower City Park); and since his father-in-law was growing old, and no doubt unable to keep up with plantation management, DesRuisseaux purchased from him the nine-arpent bayou front south of Marie Louise's acreage on September 1, 1750. Thus, the Girardy-DesRuisseaux holdings on the west bank of Bayou St. Jean extended approximately from today's Orleans Avenue almost to the Wisner Overpass, exceeding the 22-arpent east-bank-holdings of de Kernion. (See footnote p. 111)

Not only did DesRuisseaux have his own considerable affairs to look after, as tutor to his wife's minor children by her first marriage, he was working out their financial problems as well. On returning to New Orleans from Missouri he had found to his amazement that the land he'd leased LeBreton before leaving had been conceded to Councillor De Membrede by Engineer Broutin, because Lessee LeBreton had failed to maintain the grounds. If properties weren't kept in good condition and developed according to law, they could legally be taken back and given by the government to someone who would. Suing LeBreton for his delinquency, DesRuisseaux demanded that the ground be returned to the Milon heirs. Lamely admitting that a few stakes were missing in the fence, and that the cabins were without a couple doors and windows, LeBreton justified that other people, under similar circumstances, had been given six months to make repairs. The Council wasn't convinced. DeMembrede kept the land, and LeBreton was ordered to pay DesRuisseaux (representing the Milon minors) the value of the property he'd lost through carelessness and mismanagement, or replace it with another site of equal value in New Orleans.[26]

At least one of the colony's problems was solved in 1750. Indian leader Red Shoe, who'd given Bienville so much trouble back in 1740, had been up to old tricks again. Having become leader of the pro-English Choctaw faction in the Tombecbee area, this agitator and his followers were finally subdued in 1750 when Grand Pré, commander at that post, led the French Choctaws against him. After the Grand Pré Treaty, the Choctaws realized that Red Shoe had been the main source of dissension 'mongst their people and executed him. Announcing the termination of the war with the Choctaws on January 12, 1751, Governor Vaudreuil strongly urged that Captain de Grand Pré be given the Cross of St. Louis for his valiant efforts in this campaign.[27]

And then there were the Chickasaws. Intent on making up for all past mistakes, Vaudreuil—at the head of seven hundred regulars and a large body of Indians—marched on these old enemies in 1752, but succeeded in doing little other than setting fire to deserted villages and destroying cattle and crops. Sporadic efforts on the part of the French followed, but they never achieved an all-out defeat of the Chickasaws; in fact, nobody ever really conquered that nation—not DeSoto and his Spanish army in 1541—not Bienville and his French troops and Indian allies in 1736-1740 —not Vaudreuil and his army, nor the Creeks, Cherokees, Shawnees and Choctaws who waged war against them at various times.[28]

Allou d'Hémécourt's map of 1853 at the Louisiana State Museum Library states that the five most southwesterly arpents of the "Girardy" plantation were conceded to Joseph DesRuisseaux August 10, 1750. On September 1, 1750 DesRuisseaux purchased nine arpents from Girardy; the fourteen arpent plantation would be inherited by Elizabeth DesRuisseaux Chalon (later Mrs. Estevan Roquigny).

Chapter XIV

BAYOU PEOPLE AND PROPERTY DURING THE GOVERNORSHIP OF KERLÉREC — 1751-1761

Agriculture and trade in the colony left much to be desired, even considering the concessions France had made. The Royal Ordinance of 1732, exempting from duty all merchandise and goods imported into Louisiane from the mother country, had been renewed in 1741 and was again confirmed on November 30, 1751. This trade advantage would continue in force until 1762;[1] but duty or not, the colonists were in no position to buy much of anything from anybody, and France had no ready market for the few commodities Louisiane was able to export, above and beyond its own needs.

The possibility of raising tobacco had been called into question because of alternating long rains and droughts peculiar to this region. Pitch and tar were being produced, but a market had to be found for them. The inhabitants were inclining toward the production of indigo, which for a time remained a popular industry, resulting in the increased cost of slaves experienced along this line. An indigo maker from St. Domingue sold for 1,420 livres—more than DuPratz of Bayou St. Jean had paid for two slaves in 1719.[2]

The first sugarcane of the area had been grown in 1741 on the plantation that stretched uptown from Canal Street—purchased by the Jesuits from Bienville in 1726; and the first sugarmill in the vicinity was built on DuBreuil's plantation below New Orleans in 1751. But most of the processed sugar turned to syrup, leaking out of the barrels in which some of it was exported to Europe. The little that managed to dry was broken into large brown pieces and sold locally as candy. Some of the early cane was also made into tafia, a low grade rum. In a letter of September 30, 1752 DuBreuil stated "I am working now . . . in an effort to establish the sugar industry in this country," but granulation, bleaching and commercial production were as yet only dreams to be realized in the far away future. However, some plantation owners, beginning to realize the profit potential of sugarcane, began turning away from indigo.[3]

DuBreuil also produced 6,000 pounds of myrtle wax in 1752, an industry that flourished for a time, but gradually declined.

The end of King George's War permitted closer scrutiny of the South, and the spy-system of France's Minister Maurepas revealed a distressing amount of contraband trade. The English were receiving indigo from Louisiane in exchange for Negro slaves, and English ships were being fitted out in Louisiane for use in Carolina. Maurepas demanded that Vaudreuil put an end to these practices. Illegal trade in local logwood, exchanged for silver from the Spanish colonies, constituted yet another wedge in the French economic gap of 1748-1752.[4]

At least some of the younger generation, who looked to farming as an occupation, had a better chance of getting a helpmate, when the last contingent of young women arrived from France in 1751. They married immediately, and soldiers with honorable discharges and good records had first choice as to brides. As an incentive to stay in the colony and promote its small tract agricultural base, a soldier was given a dowry of a plot of land, a cow and a calf, five hens, a gun, axe, hoe and rations for three years—if it took that long to become self supporting.[5]

In July of 1752—twenty five years after the death of his wife Jeanne Tremant—Luis Brazillier (Tourangeau) of Bayou St. Jean was being pressed by his son-in-law, Francois Héry (Duplanty), to inventory the community property of his former marriage. This hadn't been done at the time of Jeanne Tremant's death, and now everything had increased in value.

Brazillier was receptive to the idea, saying he wished to set his house in order before he died, so there'd be no misunderstanding or litigation between his two children—Madeline, wife of Duplanty, and Jean Baptiste, who had married Pelagia Lorreins (Tarascon). The official inventory was recorded on August 10, 1752 by officers appointed for that purpose, who examined and listed everything Brazillier owned, including two plantations on the east bank of Bayou St. Jean. The small property immediately lakeside of Bayou Road measured two and a half arpents front by forty in depth, and had been acquired in 1729 from Francois Dugué, who at that time represented Jean Baptiste Beaudreau (Graveline) of Pascagoula. Brazillier's larger plantation (originally owned by Langlois and Provenche) was separated from the smaller property by Bayou Road, and stretched westerly for eight arpents, with the usual depth. It had been purchased from Renaud D'Hauterive in September of 1737.

On December 28, 1752 Duplanty requested that his father-in-law present an official accounting of his deceased wife's succession, so a division could be made between his wife and her brother who had now come of age and was entitled to enjoy his property.

Duplanty was trying to expedite things because he was attempting to start a plantation and needed the money, to which the elder Brazillier responded the following January, explaining to the Superior Council that it wasn't his intention to delay proceedings—he just needed another month to get the report in proper form.

On April 6, 1753 Duplanty petitioned for homologation of the donation made in the marriage contract between himself and Madeline Brazillier on July 15, 1741, so the donation was finally registered in the Registers of the Registry; and 'though he had to cite Brazillier again in October of 1753 to tie up loose ends, the anxious offspring eventually received their just and legal inheritance.[6]

Luis Brazillier's procrastination was partly due to friends' problems with which he'd become involved in 1752. Jacques Lorreins (Tarascon),* father of the bayou Tarascons, had died; and his widow, Marthe Coussine, whom he'd married in 1744, was up to her neck in legality. As curator of the succession Brazillier had his hands full determining the assets and paying the bills of the estate. Settling the succession debts on the basis of a marc to the livre (the marc was worth 8 sols; the livre, 20 sols), everybody was pressing him for payment. Among them, bayou resident Joseph DesRuisseaux was asking 940 livres for a pirogue appropriated by the son of the deceased, as well as thirteen ox hides left with him to be repaired. Brazillier had made twenty five trips to sell Tarascon's Rivière Aux Poisson plantation. The cattle had been sold, but so far there was no buyer for the land.[7] Implicated as they were with each others' affairs, there was very little the bayou neighbors didn't know about each other.

On August 29, 1752 Brazillier got a new neighbor on the city-end of his holdings when LeBreton received a concession from the French government which extended southerly from Brazillier's Bayou plantation west of Bayou Road to the property line of Charles DeMorand, who lived just outside New Orleans proper.[8]

Jean Baptiste Beaudreau (Graveline) was having marital difficulties. Separations were rare in colonial days, but on August 5, 1752 Marie Catherine Vincennes, Beaudreau's second wife, asked the Superior Council for a legal separation and return of her property after her hus-

*Names are often used interchangeably in the early records, and this Jacques Lorreins (Tarascon) is without doubt the Jacques (dit Tarascon) who came to Louisiane in 1717—the father of Carlos, Santiago and Pellagia Lorreins (Tarascon). His first wife, and mother of his three children, had died, and he had remarried. After 1752, Jacques Lorreins (Tarascon), merchant of New Orleans, is another name for Santiago Lorreins (Tarascon), who in 1771 would move to Bayu San Juan.

band had sold their only remaining Negro, bought a lot of unnecessary merchandise with the money, and run up an additional 1,000 livres of debts in Mobile and New Orleans. She'd kept hoping he'd change his ways, but now she was afraid his extravagant habits would bring ruin on her and the children. Having received considerable property from her deceased mother, she asked that it be returned to her, and that Beaudreau be prohibited from selling their house and lot in town in order that her dower might be protected.

The Council ordered an inquiry into the facts before Jean Baptiste Raguet on August 16th, calling witnesses, who'd be paid for appearing and arrested if they failed to show up. At 8:00 A.M. that day Catholic Daniel Hubert (LaCroix) took the oath, declaring he was neither relative nor servant of the contesting parties. Attesting to the facts presented by Madame Beaudreau, he added that her husband was a very wasteful man, often driving very hard bargains, that he gambled, and that a separation would be in the best interests of everyone concerned. In addition to that, he testified that Beaudreau was a libertine and owed him 300 livres which he refused to pay.

Three other witnesses of good reputation testified, agreeing with LaCroix that Beaudreau was a wastrel, without morals and a debaucher of women. Since the defendant didn't appear before the court, judgment in default was rendered against him on November 11th. It took awhile for Beaudreau to digest the bitter news, but on October 30, 1754 he finally allowed that he wished to settle the matter amicably and return his wife's property. She received fifty four cattle, the household furniture and effects and forty pounds of colonial notes, in return for which she assumed responsibility for the maintenance and education of the children and was allowed to occupy the house in town for three years on a monthly rental.[9]

Another tough guy of French times received his just desert in August of 1752. Louis Tixerant, Officer of the Marine troops in New Orleans, hadn't been paying his bills; and the Council ordered him to pay Du Breuil Villars (who needed every cent he could collect) 4,861 livres—a debt dating back to 1735. Tixerant was also cited for 265 livres, plus costs, he owed Widow Piquery for 1747 purchases of flour and baked goods.[10]

The Council records of this time refer, for the first time, to Sr. Andre (Andres) Jung, who in late French and Spanish times would become an uncommonly active and prosperous property owner on Bayou St. Jean. Son of Canadian Jean Jung and Rose Cousada of Bordeaux, France, Andres Jung was the brother of Ship Chandler Jean Jung of Bordeaux, with whom the colonists of Louisiane had long been doing business; and Andres would for years claim Bordeaux as his official residence. But in 1752 he was in trouble. Sr. Nicolas Delisle Dupare (Dupart) was suing him because he'd violated a contract he signed on September 10, 1750, wherein Jung had leased Dupare's plantation, five Negroes and four Negresses, promising that he'd manage things "as a good father of the family."

Despite a contract clause, prohibiting Jung's use of the slaves away from the plantation (they were needed to keep that place in good running order), he'd rented the Negroes to work at English Turn, whereupon Dupare had to hire another Black to do the necessary work on his property. Besides, one of the Negroes had gotten a splinter in his eye while chopping wood, and instead of immediately returning him to Dupare for treatment, Jung had waited two months, and Dupare refused to take the slave back in his damaged condition. Jung then suggested that the slave be doctored, during which time he would continue to pay the agreed-upon rental; but after treatment of two months, the Negro lost his eye, and Dupare demanded indemnity for the diminished value of his half-blind slave, plus the accrued cost of the extra worker on his plantation. The Superior Council ordered that Jung be cited at the next meeting of that body.

In 1753 Jung exchanged a piece of land he owned for two Negroes, and the following years would find this versatile bachelor continually involved in all kinds of buying, selling and trading—on Bayou St. Jean and throughout the colony.[11]

In 1752 Charles Lorreins (Tarascon) had married Marie Louise Girardy, the widow of Louis Langlois; and in the custom of the Girardy family, the newlyweds settled down near her parents on the west bank of Bayou St.Jean, on the piece of land Marie Louise had received from Louis Turpin back in 1734. These eight arpents, located lakeside of the other Girardy property, and north of Chemin Chapitoulas (Metairie Road), had been cleared by Joseph Girardy, who had also built fences and slave cabins on the land; but from the beginning, the site had been used mostly as a common utility ground and cow pasture by the family and other residents of the neighborhood.

When Marie Louise married, her father gave the couple a plough, a cart and whatever assistance he could to cultivate and develop the small plantation, but they didn't live happily ever after. Perhaps Tarascon wasn't as sociable and outgoing as his father-in-law; and since the eight-arpent-plot had been donated to his wife, he probably figured they had the right to do with it as they wished, and have a little privacy in their newly wedded bliss. Friction mounted until they all landed in court in November of 1752, Joseph Girardy claiming that the land was really his because: 1) the donation to his daughter in 1734 wasn't legal since it hadn't been registered, 2) the 100 crowns he had paid Turpin made the transaction a sale to him rather than a donation to his daughter, and 3) he had the right of ownership as the first occupant, having cleared and cultivated the land for eighteen years. If he hadn't done so, the arpents would have been conceded to somebody else.

Everything had been all right, Girardy complained, until his daughter became a widow and married Tarascon. He, Girardy, had given them a home on his land and helped out with everything he could to make a field; then Tarascon "suddenly became a master" and forbad Girardy's and his neighbors' cattle to roam on the land—even threatened to break the arms of his father-in-law's Negroes if they set foot on the property, though their cabins were located there. Girardy asked the court to order Tarascon to revert to old ways with family and friends, to let the Negroes have their cabins, and to allow the cattle to graze freely in the parks or pay for Girardy's clearing, fencing and building.

Then Tarascon had his day in court, tracing the history of the property back to August 21, 1731 when Jean Olivier and Jean Bonnet (owners after Francois Dugué had claimed the land in the early 1720s), had sold the land to John Bruent (called Bourbonois)—both transactions having been registered in Illinois and signed by the now deceased D'Artaguette. Bourbonois had immediately sold the land to Turpin, who in turn ceded it to Sr. Graveline about the same time. As to the hundred crowns paid for the land, Girardy could produce no receipt, and Tarascon denied threatening the Negroes who he said weren't aware of differences between their masters. He explained he intended to fence the land because he hadn't been able to raise a bean because of roving cattle. And as for Girardy's clearing the land, the job hadn't been that enormous. His father-in-law had failed to mention that the acreage had once been a desert (clearing) of the Indians who used it for a camping ground; and what trees Girardy had cut had been for his own use. In fact, there wasn't enough wood left on the place for kindling, let alone the fences that had to be built to keep the cattle out.

On December 2, 1752 the Superior Council declared Girardy to be non-suited in his demands, and ordered him to remove his slave cabins from the land in dispute. The court also counselled the Tarascons to respect their father and ordered the parties to live together with better understanding. Court costs were divided.

But the litigation had opened another can of worms. Jean Baptiste Beaudreau (Graveline) now came forward suing Tarascon for the return of his property, claiming Turpin had no right to donate land he didn't own. Presenting a letter of April 14, 1730 to prove Turpin had sold the property to him, he claimed he'd occupied the land for several years and had established a dairy on it. According to other documents Graveline presented, he'd ceded the arpents to Sr. Derbanne of Natchitoches, who retroceded the land to him July 4, 1733; and since he'd neither sold nor donated it to anyone after that, he claimed that Turpin's donation to Marie Louise Girardy in 1734 was null and void.

Now Tarascon found himself fighting for the family he'd formerly been against. He stated it was evident that lands acquired by Turpin in August, 1731 couldn't have been sold by him to Graveline in 1730, the date of the letter. Tarascon also maintained that even if Graveline had occupied the acres, he had left them in an abandoned condition twenty years earlier and now wanted the land back—not to cultivate it himself (he was too old for that)—but to give it to an illegitimate son who couldn't legally inherit it anyway. Tarascon also reminded the court that on December 2, 1752 it had recognized that Joseph Girardy had possessed the land for eighteen years, clearing and fencing it at his own expense, that he was entitled to sole ownership by right of prescription, and that the court had also ordered Tarascon to stay on the land free of sufferance. On October 6, 1753 the Superior Council maintained its position of the previous year and dismissed the suit with costs.[12]

While the trial was going on, Tarascon was also involved with the estate of his wife's former husband Louis Langlois, and her minor son by him. Louis Langlois' assets didn't begin to cover his debts; before his death, he'd sold most of his movables to acquit the succession of his deceased sister-in-law. The only property left in his estate was a house and plantation in Illinois for which Tarascon was offered 3,000 livres, but the sale was difficult to handle because the property was so far away. (It is possible Langlois had accepted the Gervais property in Illinois in exchange for his movables.) On October 6, 1753 Tarascon asked the Superior Council to convene a family meeting to discuss the sale and expenditure of the proceeds on debts to the interest of the Langlois minor.[13]

With all these aggravations, and with a living to make, it's no wonder tempers snapped at times. Indeed it's a mystery that some of these marriages survived at all; but this trouble so early in their marriage was no doubt accepted by the bombastic Tarascon as an expected challenge, for he handled this problem, as well as many in the future, in his own inimitable headlong way.

As one situation was settled, details of another were being scrutinized on October 28, 1752. Ursule Trepagnier, wife of Sr. Dubuisson, Guardian of the King's Warehouse on Bayou St. Jean, along with five other co-heirs, was petitioning for her share in the succession of her brother Ignace Trepagnier who had died without issue.[14]

At the other end of the bayou there was labor trouble. Carpenter Doua, who had a plantation near the mouth of Bayou St. Jean, had contracted for the repair and refitting of a schooner, and had hired two other carpenters to work for him—one for seven months, the other for three—at one hundred livres per month. In December of 1752 the schooner was about to sail, but since the men hadn't been paid in full, they petitioned the Superior Council to cite Doua for a thousand livres, less the amount he'd already paid them. Sheriff LeNormand had to travel five miles to deliver the citation to Doua on December 26, 1752.[15]

After an absence of twenty two years (he'd fought the Natchez under Périer in 1731) Louis Billouart de Kerlérec was installed as governor of Louisiane on February 9, 1753, to face the immediate complaint that cattle of the local citizenry were being killed in grazing pastures and woods by Negro hunters and others with firearms. Kerlérec immediately issued an ordinance forbidding Negroes and Mulattoes to bear firearms unless they carried an approving note from their master.[16]

Kerlérec's problems weren't black only. The French and Indian War (overture to the Seven Years' War which would begin in 1756) was being weightily waged along the Ohio Valley frontier against the English. With the possibility that the struggle might expand to Louisiane, the destiny of France in the new world was at stake.[17]

Predicting the course of future events, some of the Governor's first visitors were seven Choctaw Chiefs bearing their tribute of nine Chickasaw scalps, for which they were paid "at the rate and in the manner before agreed upon." After two harangueful days, Kerlérec laid down the law, forbidding them to come to New Orleans whenever the spirit moved them, and promised to make regular trips to Mobile, on which occasions justice would be rendered. The first of these treks took place in June of 1753 when Kerlérec went to Mobile, via Bayou St. Jean and the lakes, to settle the matter of some French deserters who'd been taken prisoner by the Indians and for whose return the Choctaws were demanding ransom. The Governor's attitude toward the Indians was initially sympathetic, and one can hardly accuse them of being anything but shrewd when they informed the new white chief that the French had started all the trouble. "You are the first of the white race we have known who have inspired us with new wants from which we cannot free ourselves, but for satisfaction of which you are often but partially prepared, when not wholly unprovided. The English study our tastes with more care. They have more diversified and richer stock of merchandise. Hence, we are driven to trade with them when our hearts are with you—a matter of necessity, not choice."

The new governor had little choice but to go along with their demands as best he could. Wary of an English attack on the gulf coast, he placed a garrison on Cat Island, and difficult as it was, he tried to keep in touch with European policy that affected his fate. It took more than a year to receive an answer to a letter sent to Quebec; and communication with France was not only slower, it was highly questionable if missiles sent either way were ever delivered. Southerly exportation of food from Illinois was now forbidden in order that French troops garrisoned in Canada be guaranteed maintenance, which forced New Orleans not only to supply her own needs, but to import flour from St. Domingue for reshipment to Arkansas, Natchez and Pointe Coupée.

Kerlérec's confidence in the Choctaws had evaporated by the time he returned to the port of Bayou St. Jean in December of 1754, having reimbursed the Indians for forty Chickasaw scalps and having distributed the little merchandise he'd been able to scrape together. The records reveal his turmoil: "Of all the redmen, the Choctaw are the worst beggars, the most deceitful, the worst liars, and added to all these faults, they are the worst drunkards. For eight days this fete has been going on without my being able to absent myself for a minute. I have had to show myself appreciative and evince great show of confidence in their promises, but on the whole I know them well enough to realize they are a crafty, lying and a very selfish lot, and I always keep myself on guard, although I conceal these facts from them. I have not had a single fifteen minutes respite from the break of dawn until midnight, and I have had the greatest trouble getting rid of them." Kerlérec, however, succeeded in his public relations, for the Indians bestowed upon him the title of "Father of the Choctaws," but for containing his tension he paid the price of falling ill, and it took him a long time to recover.[18]

On December 10, 1754—when invasion by the English was a daily possibility—only 1,276 troops and 178 Swiss mercenaries were divided among the sixteen forts of Louisiane, of which Fort St. Jean had but eight; sixty nine were posted at English Turn, twenty five at Les Allemands, twenty one at La Balise and four-hundred-five at New Orleans.[19]

Meanwhile, Madeline Francoise Claudine Dreux of Gentilly had gotten married. In 1753 Chevalier Guy Soniat de Fossat, a young lieutenant, recently arrived in the colony, had won the hand of Mathurin Dreux's daughter. Intelligent, curious and sensitive, he wrote a small history of Louisiane in which is divulged a first hand knowledge of the habits and beliefs of the Indians. In 1759, Historian Grace King relates, Engineer Soniat (derived from the ancient name Saunhac) was promoted to Captain and sent to Illinois to construct and repair forts. Under his supervision Forts Chartres and the Kaskaskias were put in good order to protect the west for years to come. He would be recalled to New Orleans in 1761, continue in the King's service until 1766, and in 1769 would receive permission from France to enter the service of Spain in Louisiane.[20]

On June 19, 1756 Charles DeMorand, owner of a plantation just outside New Orleans, received a concession from the French government just across Bayou Road from his earlier property.

A week before, Luis Brazillier had sold some of the rear arpents of his large (Langlois) plantation on the bayou. On June 10th, D'Auberville bought from him a lot of land which extended twenty fathoms from the Washerwomen's Bridge (near the junction of Bayou and Gentilly Roads) to the boundary of LeBreton's 1752 concession. D'Auberville held the property for only a short time, for after his death, the land was adjudicated to newly-wed Alexander Latil on June 10, 1757. (Three years later—on September 22, 1760 —Brazillier sold the remaining rear portions of the original Langlois Plantation—contiguous to the land sold D'Auberville—to Sieur Duparc, who would eventually acquire all the rear arpents of that plantation.)[21]

Latil's affairs at this time were inextricably bound up with those of the DeMorand family of Bayou Road. Charles DeMorand, Commandant of the Militia Bourgeoise, who since 1731 had owned a brick factory and plantation just outside the settlement of New Orleans, had first been married to Jeanne Hay. After her death, he had married Marie Rene de LaChaise. He had just been granted a sizable concession on the east side of Bayou Road when he died, and his widow was appointed tutrix to their minor children, assisted by under-tutor Alexander Latil. After a time Widow DeMorand and Latil married on April 16, 1757.[22]

The province lost one of its most versatile and enterprising colonists in 1757 when Claude Joseph DuBreuil Villars, active in Louisiane since 1719, took leave of life. His wife died soon after; and on December 15, 1758 Villars DuBreuil, son of the deceased and subrogé tutor of his minor nephews, sold the plantation below the city that extended from the Mississippi River back to Bayou St. Jean, to Jacques de LaChaise. The main house and some other buildings were located on the New Orleans side of the plantation, while a sawmill, rice mill, sugar mill and brickyard with two furnaces (each containing 90,000 bricks) as well as five large sheds, negro quarters and various other constructions were built elsewhere on the arpents. To avoid any misunderstanding on the part of the purchaser, Villars DuBreuil brought to the auction an order from Commissary de Rochemore, explaining that the main house being sold, as well as other buildings between it and the town, were situated on a 2 arpent, 12 toise strip of land that belonged to the King, on which the deceased DuBreuil had been allowed to build because of his special relationship with the government. (During Spanish and early American times there would be considerable controversy between the government and subsequent owners of this plot of land.) Prior to being placed in possession, de LaChaise bound himself to furnish solvent security, and agreed to move the buildings on the strip in question if asked to do so by the government; and Villars DuBreuil was given two months in which to move his furniture from the dwelling house.

Despite legalities, scrupulously attended to, the debt wasn't paid on time. On July 4, 1760 Jacques de LaChaise officially acknowledged that he still owed 40,000 livres on the plantation, but promised to pay that amount, plus five percent interest, within a year. And since Claude Joseph Villars DuBreuil, Jr. hadn't gotten his money, he couldn't pay his bills either; on the same date he acknowledged that he owed his father's succession 32,729 livres. Hoping to collect from de LaChaise, he promised to pay up within the year. As a result of economic conditions arising during the next few years, when the colony was transferred to Spain, relatives and descendants of Villars DuBreuil, Sr.—who had been one of the richest men in the colony—would be reduced to poverty. Dame Felicite de LaChaise, widow of Louis DuBreuil (son of DuBreuil, Sr.) and her six children got along only with the help of relatives, and at age 72 was compelled to seek shelter at the home of her brother in France.[23]

Luckily, the serious situation was lightened by a few happy occasions in 1757. On October 13th Santiago Lorreins (Tarascon)—brother of bayou residents Charles Lorreins (Tarascon) and Mrs. Jean Baptiste Brazillier—signed a marriage contract with Maria Luisa Baudin. Brother Charles and bayou resident Luis Brazillier witnessed the ceremony; and in early Spanish times Santiago Lorreins would live next door to his brother-in-law when he purchased the Kernion plantation on the east bank of Bayou St. Jean,[24] where another wedding took place in 1757.

Mrs. Kernion's daughter Jeanne Antoinette Rivard, child of her first husband LaVigne, married Sieur Christophe de Glapion, an officer in the French Army; and Jeanne's inheritance from her father, the contemplation and discussion of which had caused Mathurin Dreux to submit his resignation as curator in 1742, could now no longer be postponed. Despite Dreux's earlier attempts to withdraw from the firing line, he had continued to serve as curator up to 1754, and when Mr. and Mrs. Glapion met with Mrs. Kernion, everybody agreed that hard feelings and litigation should be avoided. So Sieur Francois Louis Caüe (son-in-law of the elder Widow Rivard)—now Jeanne's subrogé tutor— and Chevalier Mazan were appointed to estimate the value of the LaVigne succession, including the seventeen-arpent-front plantation on the east bank of Bayou St. Jean where the Kernions now lived.

The bayou plantation was priced at 2,100 livres per arpent front or 35,700 livres (approximately $7,000.00). The lot in town was listed at 10,000 livres, slaves at 15,100 livres, and since all the cattle had died, the total value of the succession amounted to 60,800 livres. After succession debts, paid by de Kernion, and 9,300 livres in cash and slaves given the newly-weds at the time of their marriage, were deducted, it was agreed that the balance of 27,500 livres —Jeanne Antoinette's share of her father's estate—would be paid in installments, 5,000 livres in the current year and 13,200 livres in 1759. After years of misunderstanding, and payments that were a little slow in coming, the story—like fairytales of old—ended happily. Dame Jeanne Antoinette Rivard Glapion was finally emancipated, at which time she signed the succession agreement, and she and her husband received the final payment of her inheritance on August 30, 1760.[25]

Meanwhile, the colonial government was ceding more land to substantial citizens. In the late 1750s Marie Elizabeth de Gauvrit, (wife of Sr. Mouléon, and only child of deceased St. Joachim Gauvrit and Marianne Lesterie, his first wife) and Councillor LeBreton,who had settled the Mouléon succession, both received large grants of land west of Bayou St. Jean.

Louis Cezaire LeBreton acquired his first—a modified triangle of land measuring a little over 1,504 acres—on October 6, 1757. This parcel of land was intended to connect his earlier concessions from the French government—one extending lakeward from the Mississippi for forty arpents, and *La Metairie*, a large grant of 2,888 acres, which reached from Metairie Road to Lake Pontchartrain, bounded on the east by the DesRuisseaux property on Bayou St. Jean and on the west by the lands of Sieurs Chauvin, Beaulieu and Montplasir.

Madame de Mouléon's grant of May 10, 1758 was in the same area as that of LeBreton, covering all the vacant land lying between the Jesuits (vicinity of Canal Street today) and the DesRuisseaux plantation on the west bank of Bayou St. Jean. Incomplete transfers of both these concessions, in Spanish and early American times, would during the mid-1800s result in forty years of bitter legal controversy between subsequent owners of the two properties.

Sr. LeBreton didn't hold *La Metairie* for long. On September 9, 1758, he and his wife Madame Catherine Chauvin de Lafrénière, wishing to return to France, exchanged the plantation, together with all buildings, fences, 100 horned cattle, horses, mares and three slaves for a property located five leagues from Bayonne, France, which was owned by Francois Caminada, a French merchant-officer stationed in New Orleans at that time. In the contract, *La Metairie* was valued at 50,000 livres and the Bayonne property at 68,000 livres, so LeBreton paid the officer the difference before taking off for Europe. Arriving in France, he found to his chagrin that the Bayonne property was worth at most 16,000 livres and was mortgaged for 17,000 livres. Writing his attorney in New Orleans, LeBreton had the contract of exchange annulled, got his 18,000 livres back with interest, and regained possession of *La Metairie*. Acquiring another property in France, he purchased the office of Councillor of the Bureau of Currency in that country.[26]

For Governor Kerlérec there seemed to be no respite from misery. If it wasn't the Indians who were making trouble for him it was his own help—on the highest level. Sr. de Rochemore, who arrived in the colony to fill the position of Intendant-Commissary, not only proved the pattern of his adversary position, he emphasized it. In Rochemore's continuing reports to France, Kerlérec could do no right. One clash between the two heads of the colony involved the Intendant's seizure of a vessel commanded by Diaz Anna, a Jamaican Jew, the Commissary citing as his authority the clause in the Black Code outlawing Jews from the colony. Justice finally prevailed when Kerlérec arrested de Rochemore's secretary who had custody of the seized vessel and returned it to its rightful owner.[27]

Drawing a salary of 12,000 livres and needing 40,000 to keep up with spiraling costs, it is no wonder that the Governor sought escape from a deplorable situation. On September 15, 1758 he requested recall and a pension, explaining that he'd been suffering for a long time from rheumatism of the bowels contracted during the Indian Wars of 1731 as well as a severe case of gravel and scurvy.

Even the Ecclesiastics were acting up—the Capuchins and Jesuits vying with each other for religious control of the colony.[28]

The few ships that managed to get to Balise were having trouble coming up river, because the mouth of the Mississippi had changed completely in the last twenty years. No more than one pass was ever navigable for large ships, and the channel depth varied from day to day.

By September of 1758 the colony was desperate because the English had established a blockade in the Gulf of Mexico and cruised constantly between Cape San Antonio and Yucatan—the route taken by French ships coming to New Orleans from St. Domingue. An English flotilla watched the Florida straits and privateers, under English letters of marque, prevented even the smallest ship from entering the Mississippi, Lake Borgne or Mobile Bay. Louisiane was effectively cut off from France and the West Indies, her sources of supply for certain foods, wines and manufactured articles. There was a lack of everything, and flour sold at 250 livres per barrel.[29]

Seemingly oblivious of the larger problems, the people at Bayou St. Jean pursued their personal affairs. In early 1758 Senior citizen Joseph Girardy was in court about a Negro he'd donated by notarial act to Dame Marie Anne Langlois. (Girardy's daughter Marie Louise—Mrs.Charles Lorreins (Tarascon)—had formerly been married to Louis Langlois.) Something had gone awry, for Dame Langlois had never received the Negro, and the Superior Council decided that Girardy had to pay her 2,000 livres. This was the last litigation in which the elderly Girardy was involved, for he died before the year was out. On November 13, 1758 Jeanne Héry, Widow Girardy, declared before a Notary that her age, and living so far from town, made it impossible for her to deal with the details of her husband's estate, and she wished her son-in-law Charles Lorreins (Tarascon) to represent her in all legal matters until such time as she'd officially discharge him from that position. Apparently all wounds from the legal battle of 1752 between Tarascon and his family-in-law had healed over.

It didn't take the Girardy co-heirs very long to come to an agreement about the division of the estate. Present at the official signing on February 23, 1759 were: Charles Lorreins, representing his wife Marie Louise, and acting as procurator for Widow Marie Jeanne Héry; Paul Barré, Widower of Marie Jeanne Girardy, and Louis Duvernay, husband of Marie Rose Girardy, who also represented Joseph DesRuisseaux, husband of Marie Francoise Girardy. DesRuisseaux, who in 1750 had purchased the 9-arpent-front Girardy plantation for 10,000 livres and some of the Negroes for 3,000 livres, agreed to settle the balance he owed at this time. By the following May everything was in order except the matter of dividing two Negroes belonging to the succession. It was arranged that one of them be left with Widow Girardy; and not being able to divide the other—valued at 2,000 livres—he was turned over to Charles Lorreins (Tarascon) who paid Paul Barré 500 livres and Duvernay 1,000 livres for himself and DesRuisseaux.[30]

A couple years later Paul Barré died; and his succession, together with that of Marie Jeanne Girardy, his deceased wife, was being processed on August 17, 1761. The co-heirs included their son Eugene Barré, who was tutor of Charles and Louise Barré, minor siblings, Cecile Barré (wife of Francois Roquigny) and Charlotte Barré (wife of Bossier, surnamed LeBrun).

Despite the difficulty that any large family living in close proximity goes through, the Girardy togetherness survived all of it. As late as August of 1763 Joseph DesRuisseaux and his family were living and eating at the old family home, and paid Mrs. Girardy 900 livres at that time for a board bill up to the following November.[31]

In the spring of 1759 a marriage of interest to Bayou residents took place on February 17th when Jeanne Dreux (minor daughter of Mathurin Dreux and Claudine Francois Harant) married Major Robert Antoine Robin de Longy (Logny), son of Laurent Robin. The bride brought to the marriage 9,500 livres in cash, a Negress Marguerite valued at 1,000 livres, and twelve arpents of Gentilly land. Of the total amount, two-thirds was to remain the property of the bride and any children she might have, with one-third going to the community. The groom gave his bride a dowry of 6,000 livres, secured by a mortgage on his fixed and movable property. The bride's plantation proved to be profitable, for the de Longys sold it a few years later to New Orleans merchant Petit for 10,000 livres.[32]

Francois Héry (Duplanty) was a man of many parts. In addition to running his bayou plantation, the records reveal he was involved in trading, contracting, real estate and shipping. On January 31, 1759 he collected 4,089 livres, 11 sols and 6 deniers as one-fourth owner of the vessel *L'Esperance*. A few years later he signed on one Paul Agrau as agent-captain of his schooner *La Legre*, which operated between Louisiane, St. Domingue and Cap Francais. When he wasn't directly engaged in shipping, Duplanty was financing the voyages of others, and in this regard seems to have been an astute and careful businessman. On May 2, 1764 he lent a local merchant 8,500 livres in gold and silver which was to be repaid when the vessel *Les Deux Amis* returned from Port-au-Prince in four months. The merchant mortgaged all his property to insure the loan, and to make it doubly safe, trader-merchant Gilbert St. Maxent personally guaranteed payment.

Some of Duplanty's leasing situations were complicated. In 1764 he agreed to pay 500 livres in piastres gourdes (5 livres to the piastre) for each voyage the 50 ton schooner *Le Tigre* made on his behalf.The vessel was to be used in the coasting trade—Bayou St. Jean and the lakes to Mobile and Pensacola—and the price would be paid on the return of the schooner from each voyage. In the event the schooner was confiscated by the English, a bondsman obligated himself to pay Duplanty 5,000 livres. If the schooner was lost on its way to Mobile and Pensacola, Duplanty, the lessee was to stand the loss; if this happened on the return ship, Gerome Matubil, the lessor, would pay Duplanty 2,500 livres, with Duplanty reimbursing him for half of all freight charges. By contract Duplanty furnished all the rigging, sails, and utensils, whereas Matubil paid all operating expenses.[33]

Among others involved in shipping about the same time was trader-merchant St. Maxent, who in the fall of 1763 was having trouble getting the right price for his vessel *L'Entrepreneur*. At the first auction he was offered 2,000 livres, on the second try 3,000 livres; finally Sr. Braud, representing Nicolas Le Duff in Martinique, bid 20,500 livres for the vessel which was acceptable to St. Maxent.[34]

On June 29, 1759 a proces verbal was being executed at the home of Francois Rivard de LaVigne on Bayou St. Jean. Francois (son of deceased LaVigne, Sr. and Marie Briar) had continued to live on Bayou St. Jean after his father's death, and this inquiry was being held because of a tragic accident that involved his young brother-in-law Vincent Rillieux. In years to come Rillieux would become a familiar figure on the bayou, but this visit was one he'd always remember. The day before, he, his brother Francisco and their two sisters had been returning to their plantation on Pearl River—about two and a half miles from the Indian Village of Biloxi—when the boys decided they wanted to kill a deer. Telling their sisters to go on ahead—that they'd all meet a half-mile further on—they sent their Negro René into the wood ahead of them to chase the animal out. He soon shouted that the deer was headed in their direction, whereupon Francisco, who'd been leaning on his gun while he was waiting, jumped up on a fallen tree. His gun slipped from his hand, the trigger became entangled in the grass and the gun went off, killing him instantly.

At LaVigne's home Francisco's body was examined by surgeons from the Royal Hospital, the Attorney General and the Clerk of the Superior Council. Questions were asked, evidence given about the unhappy accident, and the report was completed, stating that death was caused by one gunshot wound of a ball of heavy caliber which entered the jaw on the right side and passed out through the skull. This was not the last time seventeen year old Vincent Rillieux would suffer from this experience; the tragedy would come back to haunt him a dozen years later when he would become legally involved on Bayou St. Jean.[35]

Governor Kerlérec's problems pointed in another direction. There was nothing to give the Indians who were already four presents behind. With optimistic forbearance he stated at Mobile: "It's a great evil to be forced to make these nations certain fixed presents at regular times, which practice they look upon as a definite engagement on our part and as a toll due them. But how are we going to stop it? unless we want to give up a settlement advantageously located and which will some day blossom out into a most prosperous colony." And when an Indian brought him an English scalp, he remarked "I have never been in the mood of gleefully receiving English scalps, although the English demand and are daily receiving some of ours." However, war being what it is, the Indian was paid for his trouble.

With the escalation of depressing minutiae, Kerlérec requested transfer again on December 1, 1759—this time to Martinique.[36] Concerned that the scalping might reach New Orleans, a ditch and palisade encircling the town were completed by July of 1760 to keep the Indians out. The downtown segment of this fortification was built on what is today Esplanade Avenue—the piece of ground on which DuBreuil Villars had formerly built his home—but the effort was little more than a psychological gesture, for the city lacked more effective defense such as cannon, men and munitions of war.[37]

1760 was bad news with another issuance of paper money and the capitulation of Montreal on September 8, 1760, spelling doom to France's last possession in Canada. Things went from bad to worse for Kerlérec. Rochemore's removal in 1761 only made way for a more wretched replacement—the faithless Foucault. No cooperation could be counted on from France, because all French vessels had been captured by the enemy, and Spanish promises of financial aid were passed on to the chafing Indians who would yet have quite a while to wait for their past due presents.

Despite France's insistence that Louisiane was as important strategically to Spain as to France, the Hispanic monarch was probably by now pondering the long-ago arrangement that had gotten his country involved in the Seven Years' War. An agreement called the Treaty of the Family Compact, effected after the War of the Spanish Succession in the early 1700s, (confirming a French Prince as monarch of Madrid), pledged the two countries to mutual aid of various kinds.[38] In 1761 the destiny of Louisiane was hopelessly entwined in international politics, and how it all would end was anybody's guess.

Chapter XV

BAYOU ST. JEAN AT THE END OF THE SEVEN YEARS' WAR 1762-1765

One had been captured, but three French ships finally arrived in New Orleans on April 29, 1762 carrying dispatches, troops, merchandise, and more importantly, hope and relief to the colonists—if only a shred of what was needed. With a single exception, these were the first French ships to enter the Mississippi in four years, but even this smattering of optimism would have quickly curdled had the colonists realized that they were the considered pawn in the prospective settlement of the Seven Years' War that was soon to end. The French first offered the province to England if she'd give Havana back to Spain, but the English weren't buying. They wanted Florida because of its superior strategic location.

Contemplating the losses his reflective ally was sure to sustain, Louis XV, in October of 1762, suggested to his cousin Charles III of Spain "if New Orleans and Louisiane can be of any use to your Majesty . . ., to help compensate for any surrender Spain might make to the enemy, I offer the possession of both." Charles replied "the close community of our kingdoms is more useful to me than Louisiane or any other American possession." However, reconsidering, the Spanish decided it might be to their interest to maintain a buffer between their rich Mexican colony and the avid English who were westward bound, so they reluctantly accepted responsibility for the unruly waif nobody wanted. In a secret treaty at Fontainebleau Louis XV ceded Louisiane to Spain on November 3, 1762, and the document became legal ten days later when a hesitant Charles III signed it. Thus began Louisiane's six-plus orphan years, 'though for the first two she wouldn't be aware of her abandoned status. The New Orleans citizenry wouldn't know they were Spanish subjects until the fall of 1764.[1]

Unmindful of world momentum, time had run out for one of the colony's oldest citizens. Marie Catherine Vincennes became a widow in 1762. For the past several years, it had been a downhill trip for her husband Jean Baptiste Beaudreau (Graveline) who had gone blind in 1758 and was at that time unable to sign the papers whereby he turned forty head of cattle over to Luis Brazillier of Bayou St. Jean to cover a debt of 2,000 livres. All that was left to remind friends and acquaintances of this very mortal man was his namesake; on April 7, 1762, twenty four year old Claude and twenty two year old Louise—minor offspring of the deceased and Marie Vincennes—were emancipated to handle their own affairs; and to supervise them, Sieur Mazurier was elected tutor and Jean Baptiste Beaudreau (offspring of a former marriage or liaison?) their under-tutor.[2]

That same year bachelor Andres Jung began concentrating his operations on the local scene. On March 8, 1762, he sold Sieur Jean Francois Le Dee all the cows, bulls, horses, lands, tools, cabins, pickets, pirogues and what else he owned at Attacapas and Opelousas (except his Negro Celadon, whom he kept). In the notarial act, the details of which Le Dee handled for him, Jung promised to pay the Indians for a part of the land he'd occupied in Attacapas. The entire property was sold for 15,000 livres.

A personality picture of the various bayou people often gradually emerged from their cumulative doings in the records, but this particular transaction typified Jung. Like many a present-day business tycoon, he liked to deal in big figures and large enterprises, was bored by detail and left all the picayune aspects of his multi-dealings to underlings.

Later in 1762 Jung bought a slave for the highest price recorded in colonial records. On November 29, 1762 he laid 17,500 livres on the line for thirty year old Negress Jeanne. The transaction also included 4,000 livres for Jeanne's fourteen year old daughter Marguerite, marked for delivery to the purchaser in two years. Jeanne's price could be an error on the part of the translator. A more logical figure would have been 7,500 livres; but even that was very high when slaves were selling for much less. However, considering Jung's personal habits—to be revealed later in his will—the price was not too high. Jeanne was no doubt possessed of very special talents.[3]

Sr. Alexander Latil's thoughts were of another world when at 2:00 A.M. the morning of November 10, 1762 he called officials and witnesses to his Bayou Road home to witness his last will and testament. The invited found him sitting in his armchair by the fireplace, physically ill, but sound of mind and understanding; declaring "lest death take him by surprise, and not knowing the moment of his call, he wished to settle his temporal affairs," execution of the document began. Latil had lived a lot in the past few years. His wife Marie René de LaChaise, Widow DeMorand, had died on February 17, 1760, less than three years after their marriage, and having been appointed tutor of the minor DeMorand children, he had tended to their affairs, including an inventory of their property; then Latil had married Jeanne Grondel, who was now with child.

As wills often do, this one revealed a great deal about the meticulous Latil. He wished to be buried in the church of the parish beside his wife Marie René de LaChaise, the funeral ceremony to be performed by one priest only. In those days of more elaborate funerals, he apparently preferred that his estate be used for more practical purposes by his survivors. To his present wife, Jeanne Grondel, he left a house in the city on a 60′ x 168′ lot, and the contents of his dressing room and bedroom, except for a table with a marble top and mirror which was to be replaced with a chest of drawers trimmed with engraved silver.

To the child his wife was carrying he left the plantation on Bayou Road, purchased from D'Auberville's estate in 1757, on which was situated a crockery factory and two Negroes. In the event the plantation had to be sold, the usufruct was to be paid to his wife until the child came of age. If the child died, the plantation was to be sold and the proceeds divided between his wife and his sister Madame de Bourville who, in turn, was to give half her portion to third brother Jachinte Latil.

The remainder of his holdings—six building lots (purchased from Sr. Rousillon), each measuring 30′ front by 168′, silverware, furniture, equipment and implements were to be sold at auction to settle the DeMorand tutorship account, as well as to pay several personal debts. If the sale didn't net enough to cover, two Negroes were to be sold to make up the difference.

Real love for his stepchildren is revealed in Latil's disposition of his personal belongings which he asked Jacques de LaChaise to deliver to the minors at a future time when they could be used. To stepson Charles DeMorand he left all his personal linen, a small English gun, a hunting knife with silver trim, a saddle, a saddle-cloth with gold embroidery, an English bridle, a pair of small pistols with silver trim, and a silver sword. Vincent Chevalier DeMorand was to receive a fine musket mounted in silver and an emerald ring set with two diamonds; and to Louis DeMorand he willed a small musket with silver trim, a pair of silver shoebuckles, a pair of silver garters, a pair of gold buttons and a silver desk set.

Lastly, he appealed to Treasurer of the Colony Destrehan to extend protection and counsel to his wife and child until Monsieur Grondel's return; and with the appointment of Sr. Dorville, Captain Aide-Major of the colony, as testamentary executor, the document was signed, which should have given Alexander Latil considerable ease of mind. The legal instrument, however, would not be needed for many years to come. A half year later Latil was collecting (for his stepchildren) a 4,000 livre promissory note from their Uncle Jacques DeMorand, and leased some of his property on Bourbon Street to Jacques Lorreins (Tarascon), merchant of New Orleans, at 600 livres per annum. On November 11, 1763 he stipulated for his stepdaughter Marie Felicite DeMorand when the young lady married Joseph Dauterive de Valier. In April of 1765 he leased a DeMorand estate plantation downriver to a partnership consisting of Andres Jung, Nicholas Forstall, Jean Baptiste Garic and Thimoleon Chataubaudo, for which the quartet agreed to pay 6,250 livres every six months to the minors. After November, the lease was held by three, for Jung withdrew from the partnership and was paid 1,115 livres by the others for his share. On May 7, 1765—still tutor of the DeMorand children—Latil rendered an official accounting of his administration of their succession; and many, many years after that, Spanish times would find Latil still active in other areas and endeavors.[4]

By 1763 old bayou resident Luis Brazillier had died, and daughter Madeline—Mrs. Francois Héry (Duplanty)—had inherited the eight arpent Langlois plantation, while son Jean Baptiste received and lived on the adjoining 2½ arpent Dugué plantation lakeside of Bayou Road, where he followed the family pattern of activity and assumption of responsibility when friends and neighbors were in trouble.

And like all involved folk, he wasn't immune to trouble of his own. In early 1763 he was presented with a promissory note dated September 12, 1748 which stipulated that he deliver a cow to one Thomas Lefevre in exchange for a pirogue. Thomas Lefevre was now dead, but demand for payment was being made by Joseph Bailly who had gotten the note from Raymond Ferbos, husband of Widow Lefevre. Brazillier explained to the Superior Council that shortly after he'd signed the note, Lefevre decided he wanted a musket instead of a cow, but upon receiving the gun couldn't find the note, and later said he'd lost it. Receiving a receipt instead, Brazillier had kept it until his father died, at which time he'd destroyed it with a lot of other old paper. Brazillier explained that if he had owed a cow, it would have been listed in the Lefevre succession inventory and that the Widow would have asked for settlement then, because he'd purchased several of their cattle at Chef Menteur at the time of Lefevre's death. Even if the note was legitimate, the defendant maintained, the time for collecting had run out, as the Custom of Paris fixed the time of prescription at ten years between parties present and twenty years for those absent. Brazillier demanded justice and costs from Bailly, and probably got both.[5]

In July of 1763 Andres Jung accepted the tutorship of Jean, Francois and Gabriel Renaud—minor orphans of the late Renaud (St. Laurent) of Pascagoula—and checked the accounts of their former tutrix. However, Jung was no doubt too involved with his far-flung career to give time to tutorship and soon asked to resign. To a family meeting called on October 15th, Gabriel Renaud summoned Srs. Brazillier, Charles Lorreins (Tarascon)—of Bayou St. Jean—Andres Jung and four other officers and friends of the Renaud minors, for the purpose of selecting a tutor for them. Receiving the appointment, Jean Baptiste Brazillier got right down to business and arranged an auction sale on October 31st at which five adult Negroes and two children were leased for a year at 1,765 livres. The terms of the lease were no doubt standard for this kind of contract, stipulating (1) that the price be paid every six months in piastres, and that the lessee (2) take care of the slaves in sickness or in health, (3) assume all risk that might befall the Negroes except natural death, (4) furnish evidence in the event of slave suicide, (5) accept the risk of slave marooning, (6) assume all taxes that might be imposed on slaves, (7) refrain from working the slaves too hard to the prejudice of their health, and (8) furnish good and sufficient security to cover the price of the lease as well as the value of the slaves.

On November 12, 1763 Brazillier reported that Andres Jung had failed to render account of his former tutorship and administration of the Renaud property, which the Council instructed him to do.

A year later Jung was being sued again for 15,000 livres, the cost of a plantation he'd purchased from the Dulino minors on February 2, 1761. He promised to pay the money from Bordeaux, France, which he still maintained as his official residence.

Brazillier's tutorship was not for long. In early 1765 Gabriel Renaud (St. Laurent) and his brother asked that their property be turned over to them, and upon submitting proof of age to Tutor Brazillier, the revenue from the lease and from the sale of three Negroes—6,265 livres in all—was turned over to the St. Laurents on February 27, 1765, at which time Brazillier was officially discharged from his tutorial obligations.[6]

Meanwhile, minus the power of prescience, the King of France on January 1, 1763 appointed Nicolas Chauvin de Lafrénière to the office of Attorney General, little realizing how that appointment would affect the future of the colony. The new appointee was the son of Nicolas Chauvin (one of the three Chauvin Brothers who had settled the Chapitoulas in

1719-20), who had about 1762 built Elmwood Plantation* (on today's River Road) for his residence.

Fortunately for the French the Treaty of Fontainebleau on November 3, 1762 had been secret, because a few months after signing it, they had to take back some of the land they'd ceded Spain to give to Great Britain in order to meet the terms of the Peace Treaty of Paris that settled the Seven Years' War on February 10, 1763. All territory east of the Mississippi, except the quasi-island of Orleans, was transferred to Great Britain. Spain gave up the Florida Peninsula and Pensacola. France gave up Mobile, Tombecbee Post, Biloxi, Baton Rouge and Natchez; and England extended the boundaries of Florida (later divided into east and west Florida) to the Mississippi River. An important aspect of the Paris Treaty was that navigation of the river be free to subjects of both England and France. Unbeknownst to Orleanians, France had now lost all her possessions on the North American continent. The suspicions of New Orleans officials, however, should have been roused when on March 16, 1763 the King announced there was to be in the settlement only a counting house and four companies of infantry for protection and police duty under the command of Captain Charles Philippe Aubry. But in those days of riddle and rumor, this news was no doubt received as just one more link in the continuing chain of uncertainty.[7]

Kerlérec had few pleasant duties, but assigning concessions to worthy citizens must have ranked high among them. In 1763 he granted Mathurin Dreux 108 arpents front by 20 deep on both banks of Bayou Gentilly—land adjoining his other property. The Dreux family would live there a long time; as late as 1812 this land was occupied by Dreux descendants who were confirmed in their possession by the United States government.[8]

Merchant Gilbert Antoine St. Maxent was equally lucky in 1763 when on March 10th he received a point of land bordered by Lake Pontchartrain on the north and the bayou of Chef Menteur on the east. (This property, now a part of New Orleans East, would in 1812 be successfully claimed by Bartholomew Lafon.) Because of his services to the colony St. Maxent was one of the few to be granted the privilege of trading with the Indians. In 1764 the firm of Maxent, LacClède and Co. was established at the settlement of Pain Court (Shortbread) which would eventually evolve

*The Freiberg Mahogany Company, owned and operated by the author's husband and his family, occupied a part of the Lafrénière plantation, near Elmwood, from 1916 to the late 1950s. Located between the Huey P. Long Bridge and Harahan, on Jefferson Highway, the Freibergs leased and eventually purchased the property from the Illinois Central Railroad Company which had owned the land for a long time.

into the City of St. Louis. Though owning three-fourths of the company, St. Maxent's local commitments kept him in the New Orleans area, and his partner Pierre LacClède managed the firm which enjoyed a monopoly on fur-trading from the Missouri River north to Lake St. Peter—a monopoly that would continue until 1767.[9] The next few years would establish St. Maxent as one of the most influential men in Spanish Luisiana.

It was a hot summer that brought ecclesiastical matters to a climax. By an edict of the King on February 2, 1763, the Jesuits had been expelled from France; but since it took time for the ruling to reach the colony, it wasn't until July that Attorney General Lafrénière executed their expulsion from Louisiane. With the exception of their chapels, schools and religious objects used for worship, their property was sold, and they were put aboard the first ship sailing for France. The order wouldn't return to Louisiana until 1835.[10]

Kerlérec remained active until his recall to France on June 29, 1763. In a parting letter to the minister, he reported that the Superior Council had passed a resolution forbidding the importation of slaves from St. Domingue where "firing squads hadn't been enough to stop the crimes of the Negroes." This new threat of complication hardly subtracted from Kerlérec's eagerness to depart—even to an immediate future in the Bastille because of the treacherous tattling of his commissaries.

It was an awkward time for the French King to bestow titles. M. Jean Jacques Blaise d'Abbadie assumed control with the various appellations of Director of the Factory, Director of the Banking Establishment of New Orleans, Director General of Louisiane and First Judge of the Superior Council, but despite vacillation of time and title, he would perform the functions of Governor of Louisiane from June, 1763 until his death on February 4, 1765, because Spain had not as yet arranged to take over her unwanted stepchild.[11]

On October 24, 1763 d'Abbadie, Captain Charles Philippe Aubry and party embarked on Bayou St. Jean and arrived in Mobile on the 31st to negotiate with the Indians. The agenda included giving them their presents for 1760 and '61, bringing about peace between the Choctaws and the Alibamons who were at each others throats, and explaining to the Indians that their territory had been ceded to the British. The first two were accomplished, but the Indians weren't at all sure about their new landlord, who not only feared, but disliked the red man. Robert Farmar had taken possession of Mobile for Great Britain on October 20, 1763, and under new management old Fort Condé became Fort Charlotte in honor of Britain's young queen, and Fort Rosalie at Natchez became

Fort Panmure. (The fort at Pensacola was to be Fort George, and the establishment to be built at Manchac, would be called Fort Bute.)

During d'Abbadie's lengthy stay, the English took over Fort Tombigbee on November 23, 1763 'midst considerable haggling as to who owned the artillery at Mobile and other posts. Since too many bosses in one territory can be as disastrous as multiple cooks in a kitchen, it was of the essence that negotiations between the French, British and Spanish proceed smoothly in the transfer of territories. The frustration of many French and Spanish subjects, who had to pull up roots and make a new life elsewhere within eighteen months after ratification of the Treaty of Paris, had to be dealt with. The French were impatient to release control, but couldn't until their British replacements were installed on the east bank of the Mississippi, nor could the Spanish take over New Orleans and other parts west of the Mississippi until the French were gone.[12]

In the north, the British were preparing an expedition down the Ohio River to reconquer the valley taken from them by the Indians in the summer of 1763. To accomplish this more effectively, it was decided that a force should come up the Mississippi from the south at the same time, joining the northern troops in the heart of Illinois country.

Hardly had d'Abbadie returned to New Orleans when everything started off on left foot. On January 18, 1764 British Major Loftus of Pensacola—in charge of a bateau containing ten men and three officers—had arrived at Bayou St. Jean via the lakes and had arranged that the bateaux which were to transport his party to Illinois were to be portaged from Bayou St. Jean to the Mississippi. The boats, it turned out, were too heavy to be dragged overland, and would probably have ruined Bayou Road which wasn't in great shape to begin with, but d'Abbadie had to handle this matter carefully for it meant the British had to go all the way back and come up the Mississippi to New Orleans. They finally arrived on January 23, 1764, and after dinner with the Governor, the officers were filled in on what they could expect from the Indians of Illinois. In addition to the usual problems, a prophet called The Master of Life was exciting the Redmen against the British, warning them they'd die of smallpox in English prisons. To avoid such disaster many of them were giving up their worship of nature spirits, drinking and polygamy, had begun reciting prayers and were asking to be baptized. Tales of this sort didn't make the British eager for the trip. Twenty deserted immediately, but the French helped the rest of them prepare for the journey—even stopping the King's work to place more labor at their disposal.

By February 27th Major Loftus and a detachment of the 34th Regiment (which had been reconnoitering at Manchac)—a party of 440, including a few women, children and servants—departed in eleven bateaux and two canoes. A French escort accompanied them as far as Pointe Coupée, but some distance beyond—at Davion's Bluff—Indians fired on two of the advance canoes killing six men and wounding seven. Stunned and fearful that engagement would only worsen their sitting-duck-position, the English didn't return fire, but allowed their boats to drift downriver to Manchac and on to New Orleans where they arrived March 26th.

D'Abbadie immediately forwarded his regrets to the Major who accused the French of ordering the Indian attack. To forestall any further uprisings, the Governor stopped all the boats, scheduled to go up-river, at Bayou St. Jean, and attributed failure of the Illinois mission to the harsh inflexible way in which the British dealt with the Indians. This was later confirmed by a Tunica who said "The English are bad at heart. At Point Coupée I heard them talk of the savages with disdain." So the Redmen had attacked the British after they had left French soil.

Leaving ten men and an officer to take care of the boats he was leaving behind, Major Loftus and the larger part of his troops boarded a brigantine and went back to Pensacola. D'Abbadie warned the two officers and twenty men, who were returning to Mobile via Bayou St. Jean, of the animosity of various small Indian tribes who lived along Lake Pontchartrain, and lent them two swivel guns from the King's Store at the bayou for further protection. Refusing a French escort, the English left Bayou St. Jean March 30, 1764, and traveling the lake route, arrived safely in Mobile.[13]

D'Abbadie faced a steadily deteriorating economy. Three-fourths of the citizens were insolvent, and a scarcity of flour forced the Governor to put his soldiers and civil servants on half-rations of rice. Since it was possible to exist at a minimal level on the natural resources of Louisiane, the inhabitants had become lazy, and as far back as 1737 they had begun to trade, exchange and speculate in money and merchandise rather than pursuing the more tedious task of working the soil. Instead of giving worthy employees bonuses of merchandise with which they might trade, d'Abbadie now specified that they receive money; and to keep a close tab on the King's goods used in trading with the Indians, d'Abbadie granted exclusive privileges to only five or six merchants (of which St. Maxent was one), so he could fix responsibility for any wrongdoing.[14]

The colonial government encouraged the production of sugarcane. After DuBreuil Villars' death, Sr. Mazan had purchased his sugar plant near today's Esplanade Avenue; and in 1760 his cane crop was so fine a few other land owners were encouraged to try. The 1764 crop of Jacques de LaChaise, who had purchased DuBreuil's plantation, "gave out sugar of a very fine grain," which spurred optimism to the point that in November d'Abbadie requested France to send six or eight sugarmills to Louisiane to promote the growth of this crop. D'Abbadie sought markets for local rice and tobacco, but the economy was in such straits that the governor—though acting illegally—not only permitted the English to trade with the colonists, he encouraged them to supply Negroes for the development of agriculture. Slave trade routes, through Lakes Borgne, Pontchartrain, Maurepas, Barrataria Bay and the bayous, which persisted into early American times, were no doubt established at this time, with the authorities looking the other way. Shipped by the lake route, the slaves were able to walk the final portage from Bayou St. Jean or Manchac, when that route was useable. Local merchants and officials, conniving with smugglers and pirates, ballooned this practice to the extent that as early as 1763 illicit business was estimated to represent one-sixth of the total trade of the colony.

The English found a continuing market for their products with French inhabitants up and down the Mississippi, and after June of 1764 the people of New Orleans had only a short way to go for what they needed. British vessels, loaded with goods from their Manchac, Baton Rouge and Natchez warehouses, tied up across the Mississippi River, opposite today's Garden District (roughly between Felicity and Toledano Streets) and people rowed over to trade at "Little Manchac," as the floating warehouses were called. Smuggling and privateering became an accepted method of operating on Bayou St. Jean, the Mississippi and other trade channels. Records of the Superior Council reveal contracts of this type of operation—a lucrative practice for everyone connected with it. Each of the ship's crew received his share of the spoils, but the larger profits were made by agents who collected commissions for selling the merchandise and the vessel itself (when the operation was finished), and those who underwrote the expenses of the ventures.[15]

To stimulate agricultural pursuits, d'Abbadie conceded land to those he deemed capable of promoting these ends to the interest of the colony. One large tract, containing 10,120 Paris arpents—between Lakes Pontchartrain and Maurepas, extending from Seus Ravine to River Manchac and a Cypress Grove on the north—was conceded to Marie Rillieux on July 13, 1764. Four years later she was having trouble with bayou resident Charles Lorreins (Tarascon) who'd taken possession of a Choctaw

Indian village and clearing in the middle of her land and had put cows on it. Marie Rillieux explained to the court that d'Abbadie (then deceased) had promised her the title to the village and clearing when the Indians abandoned it, and complained that Tarascon's occupation cut her holdings in two, making things very inconvenient for her. She asked the court to eject Tarascon or make him fence his property for which she was willing to pay half. The irate Tarascon responded that a promise of a title was not a title, that he had lawfully acquired the village and clearing, and that the marshy character of the land made fencing impossible and unnecessary. Maintaining that Marie Rillieux's claim for servitude of passage on his property was ridiculous, he said the Cypress Grove should be used for that purpose, and the only reason she'd started the whole thing was to force him to buy her grant which was illegal. Although the records do not reveal the outcome of the case, Mrs. Rillieux retained her acreage, for as late as 1812, her children Manon, Emelie and Rosalie Malines applied for and received confirmation of ownership of this tract from the government of the United States.[16]

In August of 1764 a direct water route from the Mississippi to Lake Maurepas, through Bayou Manchac, was again being considered. In a report to Paris, d'Abbadie explained he'd given permission to British Sieur Campbell to take charge of the project in which some English deserters and Frenchmen from the colony—including Duplantis (Duplanty) and Brassilier (Jean Baptiste Brazillier) of Bayou St. Jean—were involved. D'Abbadie wasn't sure anyone knew enough to get good results, but since some of the local citizenry would benefit from the money the English would spend, he had agreed to the enterprise. The Governor's suspicions were correct. On September 3, 1764 an English officer and Duplanty set forth to explore Bayou Manchac and got lost. The waters of the Mississippi were very high, and they got mixed up on their bayous, whereupon d'Abbadie predicted that the project would end disastrously without the aid of the Indians.

In December of 1764 Bayou Manchac was again reconnoitered with the use of a very small pirogue, but the trip required a two-mile portage and took a month; and there was talk of somehow tying Bayou St. Jean into the Manchac scheme, but apparently it was decided that this was impossible, for the idea was quickly abandoned. Hopeless as the project seemed, the route was so important to the English they couldn't just slough it off without giving the project every chance of working. Having received intelligence of the transfer of Louisiane, and believing Spain would soon establish forts along the river, precluding British use of it, the English had no choice but to push this alternate route to the Gulf of Mexico.[17]

1764 was a bad year for the slaves of New Orleans and their owners. The records reveal a rash of running away, and the stealing and killing of farm animals, for which the apprehended miscreants paid dearly with floggings, brandings and execution. To understand these harsh penalties, one must bear in mind that with food shortages and official efforts to develop agriculture crimes of this kind were more serious in the 1700s than they are today. And—more importantly—the reaction of the victims extended far beyond their anxiety about the actual misdoing. The white colonists of that era lived in constant dread that the Blacks would revolt and kill them, so extremely severe penalties were imposed not only to suppress future crimes and misdemeanors, but for the more important purpose of forestalling an uprising.

In July of that unhappy year, Andres Jung's Negro Ceasar was put to the torture in an attempt to solve a series of thefts—chickens, clothes from lines, a pig—and for firing on the night patrol. His legs in torture boots, Ceasar quickly implicated a half dozen others. Especially involved was Negro Louis belonging to Sr. Blevin of Illinois, who had stolen a pig from the Jesuits and shared it with Jung's Ceasar in order to get the animal to Bayou St. Jean where he sold his share to Brazillier's Negro, who then refused to pay for it. The unfortunate Ceasar was whipped, branded on the cheek, had his wrists cut, was broken on the rack and executed.

Found guilty of stealing by day and by night, Louis' punishment was designed as an even greater deterrent to crimes of this kind. Condemned to make public atonement before the door of the Parish Church, he knelt bareheaded in a long shirt, a rope around his neck, holding a two-pound torch, and called out in a loud voice for the pardon of God and the King because of the crimes he'd so wickedly committed. After making penance, he was conducted by the hangman to the square (today's Jackson Square) where his arms, legs, thighs and back were broken on a scaffold, after which he was placed on a wheel, face upturned to heaven, to end his pains. After death, his body was taken by the hangman to Bayou Road and left on the wheel, for all to see, until his flesh disintegrated.

Unbeknownst to the average observer, the Council had relented a bit from this harshest of sentences and decreed that Louis be secretly strangled before the blows were struck.

As for the other slaves involved, Marie Jeanne, who had concealed stolen property, was whipped and branded on her right shoulder; another two slaves, who'd hidden Louis and Ceasar, were ordered to watch the executions, after which they were discharged to their masters. And the slave owners, who'd lost their property by public execution, were reimbursed for the value of their slaves out of a fund created by a tax imposed for that purpose on August 6, 1763.[18]

Romance got a bayou slave in trouble in November of 1764. Many cattle had been killed along Bayou St. Jean and in Gentilly, and those in charge on the various plantations were on the constant lookout for anything unusual. So when Duplanty's Negro Francois was caught at St. Maxent's plantation in Gentilly one night, he was immediately arrested and charged with the cow-killing that had been going on. A Councillor was appointed to examine the accused, who revealed that he'd gone to St. Maxent's to visit a Negress there. He had "borrowed" the horse of his overseer, who'd seen him leave and immediately reported him to Duplanty, who had Francois thrust in jail. The accused declared he'd never been a fugitive, nor had he taken anything; and circumstances being what they were the charges were probably dismissed, for the records reveal nothing more about the case. Valuable as trained slaves were, responsible owners would not press charges when none were justified.[19]

The bayou was buzzing the morning of June 16, 1764 about the accident that had happened the night before. Sr. Rocheblave had hired Jean Louis to haul some merchandise from New Orleans to the port of Bayou St. Jean—goods he intended to take back to Mobile. Having unloaded at the King's Store near Bayou Road on Bayou St. Jean, the merchandise was reloaded on the schooner, and the carter was about to return the wagon when Sr. Rocheblave decided he'd ride along and climbed in, despite Jean Louis' warning that the oxen pulling the cart were touchy, because they were young and unaccustomed to working at night. Responding predictably, the animals ran away, and as one of the wagon wheels went over the pickets of Duplanty's garden (to the west of Bayou Road), the cart turned over, Sieur Rocheblave was thrown out, and his head was crushed as he was run over.

Neighbor Kernion came quickly to the scene, took the keys for the King's Warehouse and personal papers off the body, and at midnight sent a messenger to notify authorities of the accident. Judge Nicholas Denis Foucault, Deputy Attorney General de LaPlace and Council Clerk Garic went immediately to the morgue (in the jail) where the body had been transported and was being examined by a surgeon. With blood streaming from the nose and mouth, the doctor reported that the temple bone on the right side was fractured and caved in, which had resulted in concussion, hemorrhage, and death.

Five o'clock next morning the three officials were at the Port of Bayou St. Jean where they collected the keys and papers from Kernion and inspected the boat on which Rocheblave had been loading merchandise for his return to Mobile the following Monday. Finding nothing on which to place seals, an inventory was made of the boat's contents which consisted mainly of wine and a sword of damascened copper. The schooner and its rigging were also inventoried, and the entire property was placed in the hands of Jean Baptiste Brazillier, whose plantation was located to the east of Bayou Road, and who was to be accountable for the inventoried material.

Next day a trunk containing apparel, as well as papers and notes was presented and inventoried; and all effects, titles and the schooner were placed in the hands of Attorney for Vacant Estates Ducros, thereby discharging Brazillier of his responsibility in the matter. Immediately Ducros was swamped with demands for the merchandise on the boat claimed by New Orleans merchants who had sold it to Rocheblave on credit. Sr. Carriére of Mobile, brother-in-law of Rocheblave, petitioned for the return of the schooner, but it was eventually auctioned off for 1,530 livres in letters of exchange, and by August 6, 1764 the matter was settled.[20]

By the end of 1764 some young residents of the bayou had come into their inheritance. Their father Joseph Milon had died in the early 1740s at which time their mother Marie Francoise Girardy had married Joseph DesRuisseaux, who for many years had handled the Milon succession. Eventually, Jacques—the eldest—was appointed guardian of his minor brothers, requested his stepfather to file an account of his handling of the estate, and personally assumed responsibility for it. On December 12, 1764 Jacques rendered an account of his administration of the succession, and after paying all debts, what remained netted each of the boys 12,103 livres, 8 sols and 2 deniers. A week later Jacques appeared before the court with his brothers—Jean of full age, and emancipated minors Maurice and Henri—and partition was made. Jean took his share in money and Maurice and Henri theirs in slaves, obligating themselves not to dispose of the the Blacks before they—the owners—were twenty five years old, whereupon Jacques was discharged from any further responsibility.[21]

Midst rumors that Spain had changed her mind about taking over the colony, orders came from Versailles to make an inventory of all artillery, storehouses, seagoing vessels, hospitals, etc. for which France would be compensated by the new tenant. D'Abbadie had his hands full trying to effect a reconcilation between the Indians and the English, who after a get-tough policy with the Redmen finally decided that if they were ever going to settle their new territory they had no choice except to imitate the French. Like some dedicated students, they eventually established a more successful system than that of their mentors, which included a French interpreter and lots of food and gifts for a great congress of all Indian Nations south of the Ohio River which convened at Mobile in June of 1764. Correspondence between D'Abbadie and Paris about the menace of 3,000 Indians assembled in Mobile, and the present and future problems this might entail, continued into late 1764—after the Governor had received the official news of Louisiane's transfer to Spain. On September 6, 1764 D'Abbadie was ordered to wind things up and return to France within the month, but like most responsible officials he complained that the time was too short to finish everything he had to do.[22]

Official zeal for protecting New Orleans from the Indians had resulted in the confiscation of considerable land along the ramparts on which the primitive defenses were located. Some of this land belonged to St. John's Charity Hospital, and on October 1, 1764 Sr. Jean Baptiste Prevost and Mathurin Dreux, administrators of St. John's, were explaining to the authorities that of the 50 toise front x 100 toise deep lot on which the hospital had been built, three-fourths of the land had been taken for enclosing and fortifying New Orleans. The garden, poultry yard and some of the out-buildings had been moved away or demolished at hospital expense, and they asked the Council to replace the land taken with a plot between the original lot and the City gate.[23]

It was in October that the governor shared the news of the transfer of the province with the citizens, who railed at this turn of events, refusing to accept their abandonment by a country they loved and felt close to. D'Abbadie's journal ended the last of December when he could no longer write. Suffering from paralysis of the arms, constant vomiting and pains in the head, he continued to send correspondence until the day before he died. It was rumored that lead poisoning caused his death; others believed it to be yellow fever. Whatever the cause, everybody seemed to miss the gentle, hard-working Governor after he died on February 4, 1765.[24]

Meanwhile, the bewildered citizenry, fearful of financial ruin by not being compensated for French-issued money, and of being treated badly by an unfamiliar landlord, sent Jean Milhet, commander of the military and the richest merchant in the settlement, to Paris to petition for cancellation of the act of cession. But even with the assistance of the aged Bienville, Milhet's efforts of almost two years came to naught; he never got to see the King. The Acting Prime Minister, aware of what the colony had already cost France, what would be required to repair the fortifications and buildings of Louisiane, and the sums yet to be expended in recalling outstanding paper money, obviously could not recommend rescinding an order he himself had proposed. Milhet's long absence simply postponed the disillusion of those who waited across the ocean.[25]

Chapter XVI

LAND GRANTS ON BAYOU ST. JEAN 1765-1766

Sr. Louis Cezaire LeBreton had just returned to France when his wife died on February 23, 1759, and he had to come back to Louisiane to settle her succession. On October 4, 1763, having remarried, LeBreton petitioned the Superior Council to convene a family meeting to discuss the various problems concerning his four minor children by his first marriage. At this meeting he was given permission to sell *La Metairie*—the only property he could sell at an advantageous price at that particular time. (The date of February 15, 1764 of LeBreton's *La Metairie* concession on the 1884 Survey Map of Pilie and Grandjean, is no doubt that of his repossession of the property.) And who had the right price for the property but up-and-coming merchant Gilberto Antonio St. Maxent. However, St. Maxent didn't hold the land for long. He had his eye on a plot in Gentilly he liked better—land along the ridge that had been granted to the French Capuchins, along with other acreage, in 1726 and 1734. On January 27, 1765 he exchanged *La Metairie*, measuring forty-five to fifty arpents front on Metairie Road, with a depth to Lake Pontchartrain, for an eighteen arpent front on Bayou Gentilly, extending to Lake Pontchartrain. Five priests, representing the Reverend Father Capuchin of the Province of Champagne, Sr. Gilberto Antonio St. Maxent and his wife Marie Anne LaRoche were present at the official signing of the exchange of properties.[1]

The Girardy family of the west bank of Bayou St. Jean was so large it was only logical that their doings would be in the records right along. When Dame Marie Joseph Daigle died, she left eight little ones to be looked after—five by a first marriage to Sr. Roman and three by a second marriage to Jean Baptiste Eugene Barré, grandson of Widow Joseph Girardy. In April of 1765 Joseph DesRuisseaux, Widow Girardy's son-in-law, was chosen tutor, to look after the interests of the Barré offspring.[2]

In mid 1765 Charles Lorreins (Tarascon) and his wife Marie Louise Girardy were at it again; and this time one of the King's officials was involved, which made for a very touchy situation. It had all started in December of 1764 when DesRuisseaux asked Sr. Olivier de Vezin, Overseer of the King's Highways and Surveyor General of Louisiane for the last twenty two years, to survey the land where his property joined that of his brother-in-law Tarascon, for the purpose of laying out and constructing a road from Bayou St. Jean to the Chapitoulas. Each family had agreed to contribute half the land needed for the road. DesRuisseaux owned the former Girardy property south of the old Indian trail called Chemin des Chapitoulas, and Tarascon occupied the eight arpents to the north of the trail, comprising what is today Carrollton Avenue and the city-side segment of lower City Park—land donated to Marie Louise Girardy in 1734 and over which the 1752 court battle had been waged.

De Vezin looked for the line of a previous survey done by the late Mr. Broutin in 1735; but all boundary marks had been obliterated, and finding only a picket fence, he proceeded to set his own boundaries. No sooner had the initial work begun than the Tarascons protested vigorously against the survey, claiming it was prejudicial to their interests, because in laying out the road de Vezin had taken more of their land than DesRuisseaux's. The incident so annoyed Governor d'Abbadie he immediately issued an order that Sr. Tarascon be punished for his insolence (who questioned the King's officials?), but the governor's death in February of 1765 precluded his pushing the matter to a conclusion.

On June 22, 1765 Dame Lorreins (Tarascon) rekindled the fire with an official protest to the Superior Council that de Vezin had done the survey without consulting neighbors in the area who were familiar with the ground, that he had removed old boundaries and made new ones, and she demanded that the land be resurveyed in the presence of all interested parties.

Not about to stand still for such an attack on his considerable reputation, Sr. Olivier de Vezin wasted no time in filing a petition of defamation of character against the Tarascons, wherein he defended his new survey. He stated he had found no old boundary marks, and his accusers would be hard put to prove otherwise. Suggesting that had d'Abbadie lived, the Lorreins would have had their comeupppance before this, he demanded that an inquiry be held into the grievous slanders uttered against his honesty and integrity, ruination of his reputation, undermining of public confidence in him, and the insinuation that he was a liar and a double-dealer.

On August 2nd the Tarascons countered with a petition to the Council to have the land resurveyed by Sr. Lelande de Feriere, sworn expert of Paris, in order that the correct boundaries be established, and that de Vezin be cited to attend the verification and furnish all data connected with his former operation. They averred that after only a couple hours work, Lelande had found that the former limits of their property—established by the late Saucier, deceased husband of Mrs. Lorreins' sister—were nearer the city than those sanctioned by Joseph DesRuisseaux. They asked that the task be expedited, because the matter had dragged on since last February, and they'd been unable to erect proper enclosures for their cattle.

Neighbors on Bayou St. Jean were called as witnesses—Jean, Jacques and Maurice Milon, Langlois, Rivard and Lefevre. The last—a son or other relative of the deceased Lefevre with whom Brazillier had had dealings in 1748—had lived with the DesRuisseauxs where he'd done some carving in exchange for free board. He also made frequent trips to Mobile and Pensacola in connection with his carving business. So it seemed that most of the witnesses were prejudiced in favor of DesRuisseaux.

On August 10, 1765—after the Attorney General demanded that Mr. and Mrs. Charles Lorreins (Tarascon) and Mr. and Mrs. Le Beau (who lived on Bayou St. Jean near Lake Pontchartrain) be imprisoned for their slanderous accusations—the Superior Council arrived at a final decision. It was declared that the Act of Protest and Opposition to the Operations of Sr. Olivier de Vezin, relative to the division of land in the matter of the road from Bayou St. Jean to Chapitoulas, was to be treated as if it had never happened, and was to be so registered.

And for their truculence, Mr. and Mrs. Charles Lorreins (Tarascon) were fined two hundred livres in letters of exchange, payable to Charity Hospital of New Orleans, and eight hundred livres payable to Olivier de Vezin, all of which was settled August 20, 1765. (De Vezin's surveying bill would not be paid until after the death of DesRuisseaux. On July 8, 1768 a bill would be submitted to his succession for 711 livres, 10 sols, which would be paid in wine and flour by Maurice Milon, stepson of DesRuisseaux and guardian of his estate.)

It had turned out to be a very expensive road for the Tarascons, because they had to pay court costs too; and one can imagine the affair did very little to improve family relations.

Ill will—dating back to the family lawsuit of 1752, and accentuated by the road episode—soon flashed again. In November of 1765 Charles Lorreins (Tarascon) was in the woods, on the dividing line of the DesRuisseaux-Tarascon plantations, with two sailors from the *Lamentin*, which was tied up in New Orleans. Tarascon had promised them a tree from his land, and they were in the process of claiming it when Henri and Jean Milon sauntered up and asked by whose permission the sailors were cutting a tree on their property. Tarascon replied that he'd permitted it, whereupon the young men assailed and insulted him in the vilest manner and challenged him to fight. Tarascon promised to pay for the tree if investigation revealed that it was not on his land; it was left where it had fallen, and everybody went home. But Tarascon didn't leave the matter there. On November 14, 1765 he petitioned the Superior Council to cite his nephews for their behavior, and on November 19th the sailors from the ship told their story, but the Milons didn't show up and were ordered by the Council to appear at a later date for questioning.

It was no doubt at this time that Tarascon and his wife figured their eight arpents had caused them enough grief and they sold them to Francois Héry (Duplanty). Three years later, the property, on which a small house was situated, would be included in the Inventory of Duplanty with a valuation of $1,300.00, which record was notarized by Garic on April 25, 1771.[3]

On January 26, 1765 Jean Lavergne who lived on Bayou St. Jean near Lake Pontchartrain married Widow Louise Roquigny. Lavergne, who was also marrying for the second time, would in a few years receive from the Spanish the triangular grant of land stretching west from Fort St. Jean where the bayou met the lake.

In July the heirs of Jacques Roquigny were settling his succession, Lavergne having received from the tutor of the Roquigny minors an accounting of their finances.[4]

That same month Joseph Chalon, merchant of New Orleans, leased his completely furnished home, including a Negro, his wife and four children, and Cupidon, a Mulatto, to Francois Broutin for five years at 1,500 livres. Broutin agreed to return everything in the same condition he received it, and to treat the slaves kindly, giving them medicine when they were sick. Within a few years Chalon would marry the daughter of Joseph DesRuisseaux and Marie Francoise Girardy and settle down on the old Langlois-Brazillier plantation across Bayou St. Jean from his mother-in-law.[5]

At the end of that busy year Jean Tuon declared to the Superior Council that there had been strange happenings at the mouth of the bayou. In September he'd gone aboard a vessel belonging to Sr. Harley, to pilot it into the bayou and help discharge its cargo; but the tide was low, and the vessel had stuck fast on the sandbar at the entrance to the stream. Returning next day to work on releasing the vessel, Tuon found Captain Harley fishing with a net and arguing with two men. After giving them a couple cuffs, he had them bound with a rope and taken to the guardhouse at the bayou's entrance. Unable to free the boat, Tuon kept on working and listening, and before leaving for the day noticed Harley carrying meat and bread to the two prisoners. Next day, all the men were aboard the ship except the two sailors, and Harley told him the fugitives had taken three guns and a compass. Tuon's statement of what he had seen was certified by a physician who verified that Tuon was too ill to testify and unable to leave the city, for which reason his testimony was being recorded. Another record in another city tells the rest of the tale. Jean Tuon recovered from his illness, for the following year he became a plantation owner on the east bank of Bayou St. Jean, not far from the lake, and no doubt continued to pilot boats over the bar at the mouth of the bayou.[6]

The gentle d'Abbadie's successor was not to be remembered so kindly; but under the circumstances of those trying times, no leader could have gained affection. Captain Charles Philippe Aubry, ranking French officer in Louisiane, responsible for directing colonial affairs until the arrival of an accredited Spanish officer, had no illusions about his position. A week after picking up the reins, he wrote "One is very unfortunate to be the head of a colony like Louisiane. The money is all gone; so is the trade, and the lands have lost their value . . . an inconceivable spirit of insubordination has reigned in the country for the last ten years, and all who cannot pay their bills find safe refuge at Mobile where the English governor, Mr. Johnstone, receives them with open arms and helps them to find good occupations."

A month later Aubry hadn't changed his mind when he reported: "It is almost impossible to give satisfaction to the English, the French or the savages, who are all mixed together here. I would like to maintain peace among all these people, but it is a terrible task and one almost impossible of achievement. Coupled with this, the state of my finances is desperate, what with English officers continually passing through here who must be entertained."

As though this wasn't enough to keep a politician in stitches, the bookkeeping was way behind. Treasurer Destrehan had died the day after d'Abbadie, and the books hadn't been balanced since 1755; and to add misery to mix-up, Commissary Foucault was making things tough for Aubry with whom he was hopelessly at odds.

It wasn't much easier for the English. To demonstrate their good will toward the Redmen, they'd gathered all the corn they could find in the New Orleans area to give to the Indians, which resulted in a food shortage for the French colonists who'd come to depend on the grain as their basic starch; and the ship that came to get the corn brought with it an epidemic of smallpox—all of which contributed very little to British popularity. The merchandise the British sent up the river to conciliate the northern tribes was seized by the Redmen in Illinois and divided 'mongst themselves with no thanks to their benefactors.

Then there was the Manchac route. Duplanty and Brazillier had given up, but one Sieur Duparc (the same who purchased the rear arpents of the Langlois plantation in 1760?) had undertaken the so far futile task of establishing a sailing route from the Mississippi to Lake Maurepas.[7]

The British weren't the only ones who were worried about the Mississippi. With no understanding of military protocol, the firing of the English ships' cannon morning and evening upset the Indians no end. Aubry wrote of their travail: "Although I have already explained to them that it is a custom followed by both the French and English, and that they should not be surprised by it, this noise, to which they are not accustomed, frightens their feeble wits, and they take such umbrage from it I feel they might start hostilities such as those of last year that led to grievous results." Against his better judgment even Aubry got the jitters and observed: "The unusual spectacle of this continuous passage of war vessels and foreign troops in sight of New Orleans—though we are at peace and have nothing to fear—stirs in me a degree of alarm in spite of myself. We have no ships, troops or ammunition to oppose any ill design, should they (the British) have any." After giving the situation some consideration, he decided that protocol, the cause of the situation, might also provide a solution. "It seems to me indecorous not to have any batteries on the river. Consequently, I have had twenty pieces of artillery put on carriages in front of the barracks. In this way we can return the salutes fired at us, and we will also inspire more respect."[8]

Despite obstacles, the English hadn't given up on Illinois, and in the summer of 1765 Aubry reported to his French Superior: "All the English officers have been our guests. It has always been the custom, in going from Mobile to New Orleans, to pass through Lake Pontchartrain, arriving thus at Bayou St. Jean. Some English officers, as well as some of their tradesmen, often use this route, as it is the shortest of all, and they throw some money about the country on the way. As this is of advantage to the colony, both Mr. d'Abbadie and I have never shown any objection to it. Monsieur Farmar, who is going up to the Illinois with three hundred men, has written me to say he expects me to let him use this route with his troops. I answered that I could not consent to that—that I would not let a troop of armed men cross over on our lands (on Bayou Road—from Bayou St. Jean to the Mississippi) saying that should they provoke any disorders the inhabitants would blame me; and I, therefore, requested him to go up from la Balise (through the mouth of the Mississippi) it being the customary way."

Having observed the determination and persistence of the British to get on good terms with the Indians and to settle and defend their newly acquired territory, Aubry realized that they might be the biggest obstacle the Spanish would encounter in taking over Louisiane. Their influence extended to every corner of Louisiane. It was more convenient for French colonists at Pointe Coupée, Natchitoches, Attakapas, Arkansas, Illinois and St. Vincents on the Wabash to get the liquor, drygoods, groceries and articles they needed to trade for Indian peltries, tobacco and bear oil at Manchac, Baton Rouge and Natchez than to travel all the way down to New Orleans. And importing more Negroes than they needed from Africa into Jamaica, the English easily disposed of them along the Mississippi, the lakes and into New Orleans itself via Bayou St. Jean.

In his memoir of August, 1765, to assist the future rulers, Aubry recommended construction of small forts at la Vacherie de Dupart (the cowhouse of Dupart), at Bayou St. Jean and at Mazan's plantation, in order to keep watch on the English at Manchac. (If the bayou site Aubry had in mind was Fort St. Jean at the lake he must have meant rebuilding or strengthening the structure that had always been in this location from earliest French times.) And since the Indians preferred British rule to that of the Spanish—as the lesser of two evils—Aubry advised the Spanish to make friends with the Redmen who didn't like the way their brothers in Mexico had been treated.

Despite constant conciliatory efforts on the part of the British, newly built Fort Bute at Manchac (built during the summer of 1765) was attacked on August 29th by Indians who seized all the merchandise and drank all the brandy. Called on the carpet by the French for their untoward act, the Indians explained that the eau-de-vie ("water of life"—brandy) had made them lose their minds. But with French persuasion they managed to round up some of the stolen goods and give it back to the English.[9]

The worst thing a slave (or anybody else, for that matter) could do was to commit suicide. The law of that day branded self-destruction as a crime against church and state, to be punished by infamy and denial of a Christian burial. Jean Francois Huchet de Kernion of Bayou St. Jean and his colleagues on the Superior Council were confronted with a sad, strange case of this kind in November of 1765. That month an Indian slave of Sieur Robin de Logny (husband of Gentilly settler Mathurin Dreux's daughter) committed suicide by hanging himself on a peach tree in the courtyard of the building in which the Superior Council was housed.

According to the custom of the time, a defender was appointed to plead the cause of the deceased, his owner was interrogated, the body was viewed by some of the Council members, a report was made by the King's Surgeon, witnesses were examined, and the defender "bare-headed and standing" was questioned as to the life and morals of the suicide he represented.

Predictably, the corpse was found guilty and delivered into the hands of the executioner. His memory having been condemned in perpetuity, the corpse was tied to the back of a cart and dragged through the streets of the city face down, to a scaffold from which he was hung head down for twenty four hours, after which he was thrown into the public sewer.

On November 16th the Superior Council had another serious matter on its collective minds. To forestall a problem—perpetually feared by the colonists—the council members extended the interdiction against importation of Negroes from St. Domingue to also include those from Martinique. The number of free people of color was rapidly increasing in New Orleans, and an uprising of angry negro slaves was something Louisiane could do without. The seeds of revolution, which would grow into the black uprising at St. Domingue in the 1790s, were beginning to sprout.[10]

Up to this time bayou activity beyond the Metairie Ridge had been confined largely to Fort St. Jean, the piloting of boats across the bar at the bayou's entrance, and the unloading of merchandise into smaller flat-boats which came up to the Port of Bayou St. Jean when lake tides didn't give the stream enough depth for schooners to navigate. The long stretches of swampland from the ridge to the lake had been for the most part unoccupied. For only a short distance lakeward of today's Esplanade Avenue (on the Metairie-Gentilly Ridge) was the land high and dry enough for building. But in 1765-66 interest in the arpents between the two ends of the bayou was no doubt stimulated by the impending new ownership of the colony. The local French may have had doubts about Spanish concession policy and decided to get land while the getting was good. No doubt they also felt that land was a more or less stable possession which would insure at least a minimal living in the uncertain future. So midst heavy mediating 'twixt the Indians, French and English, Aubry spent an occasional hour dispensing land to various worthy individuals—the legality of which would in some instances be severely challenged up to a hundred and fifty years later when the courts questioned whether Aubry, a French representative, had the right to grant land in Louisiane which by a 1762 treaty had become a province of Spain.

Many of these early concessions, along the bayou and Lake Pontchartrain, would constitute the basis of the vast real estate holdings of millionaire Alexander Milne in early American times. The first of these, granted November 19, 1765 to Monsieur Aubert east of the mouth of Bayou St. Jean, extended easterly from Bayou Cochon, and included the entire acreage between the south shore of Lake Pontchartrain and the lands of Gentilly. In Spanish times Charles de LaChaise would own a considerable part of this grant and would sell segments of his part to others who in turn would sell to Milne. In 1812 Milne would own 2,000 arpents in this location.

Charles de LaChaise (son of Dame Marguerite Darensbourg and Sr. Jacques de LaChaise) had spent his adolescent years on his father's plantation below New Orleans (the Dubreuil plantation of 1719), which reached from the Mississippi River back to Gentilly and to Bayou St. Jean; on February 3, 1766 he married into another land-owning family when he signed a marriage contract with Marie Marguerite de Mouléon, daughter of Sr. Henry de Mouléon and Marie Elizabeth de Gauvrit, who had been granted a huge triangle of land west of Bayou St. Jean in 1758. From 1766 on, the de Mouléon and de LaChaise interests were inextricably entwined. Jacques de LaChaise died in 1768; and after de Mouléon's death in 1771, his widow—having divided her husband's estate with her daughter—bought the Jacques de LaChaise plantation on March 22, 1774. During the upcoming Spanish era, Widow de Mouléon and Mr. and Mrs. Charles de LaChaise would together own huge tracts in the bayou-lake area.[11]

Early 1766 was marrying time for a grandchild of Jeanne Héry Girardy of Bayou St. Jean, when Laurent Lerable, Naval officer of New Orleans and son of St. Laurent, third husband of Angelique Girardy, married Marie Francoise Duroche.[12]

In 1766 the Spanish and an epidemic resembling yellow fever collided with the colony simultaneously; and the terrible storm in which Don Antonio de Ulloa arrived at New Orleans on March 5, 1766 would often be recalled as the perfect prelude to his tempestuous tutelage of Louisiane. Traveler, scientist and author of note, the fifty year old intellectual was not the one to cope with the colony at this stage of the game. A member of the most honored scientific societies of the western world, and noted as the astronomer who had discovered the round hole in the moon called "Ulloa's Circle," his wit and wisdom in small select groups —of which Bayou residents Dreux and Gilberto Antonio de St. Maxent would often be a part—were niceties to which the general populace would never be exposed, nor could they have cared less about an invitation. This scholar immediately stepped forth on left foot by reducing the thirty-five livre salary of the ninety soldiers who'd come with him from Havana to the miserable seven livres per month compensation of the French colonial soldier; so the French refused to extend their terms of service, and many of Ulloa's own men quit. With only seventy-five soldiers, the Spanish Governor decided not to present his credentials to the Superior Council until he could reinforce his military back-up.[13]

While Ulloa sized up his new constituency during the summer of 1766, Aubry busied himself issuing grants of land along Bayou St. Jean. On June 12, 1766 carpenter Bartholomew Robert received a concession on the west bank of the bayou that measured seventeen arpents, twenty toises front. Today this grant would begin near Robert E. Lee Boulevard, and extend toward the city for three-fifths of a mile. Forty arpents deep, Robert's land reached west to the vicinity of today's Milne Boulevard.

The following year Robert's daughter Marie Francoise married Andre Bernard, Navigator of Lille, France; and in 1769 Robert lost his wife Jeanne Bodmont. Since she had been married before to Nicholas Roy, by whom she had two children (Francois and Augustin, both of age), and left six children from her second marriage, Widower Robert decided to straighten out the communities in order to avoid legal complications later on. This necessitated petitioning for and holding a family meeting to elect officials to watch out for the interests of the various offspring, making an inventory of all he and his wife had owned in community, arranging for the sale of the property, and dividing what Jeanne Bodmont had owned. At a family meeting, Bartholomew Robert was appointed tutor of his minor children; and Jean Lavergne, his lakeside neighbor, was appointed under-tutor.

The bayou plantation (listed in the inventory as twenty arpents by forty deep, with three Negro cabins and two pirogues), a house and lot on St. Louis Street, and other movables and immovables were sold by the end of 1769, and the surviving spouse bought back the properties he wanted, including the bayou plantation. After enduring a couple years of red tape Robert was satisfied that the economic interest of his children, as well as that of his wife's sons by her first marriage, was secure.[14]

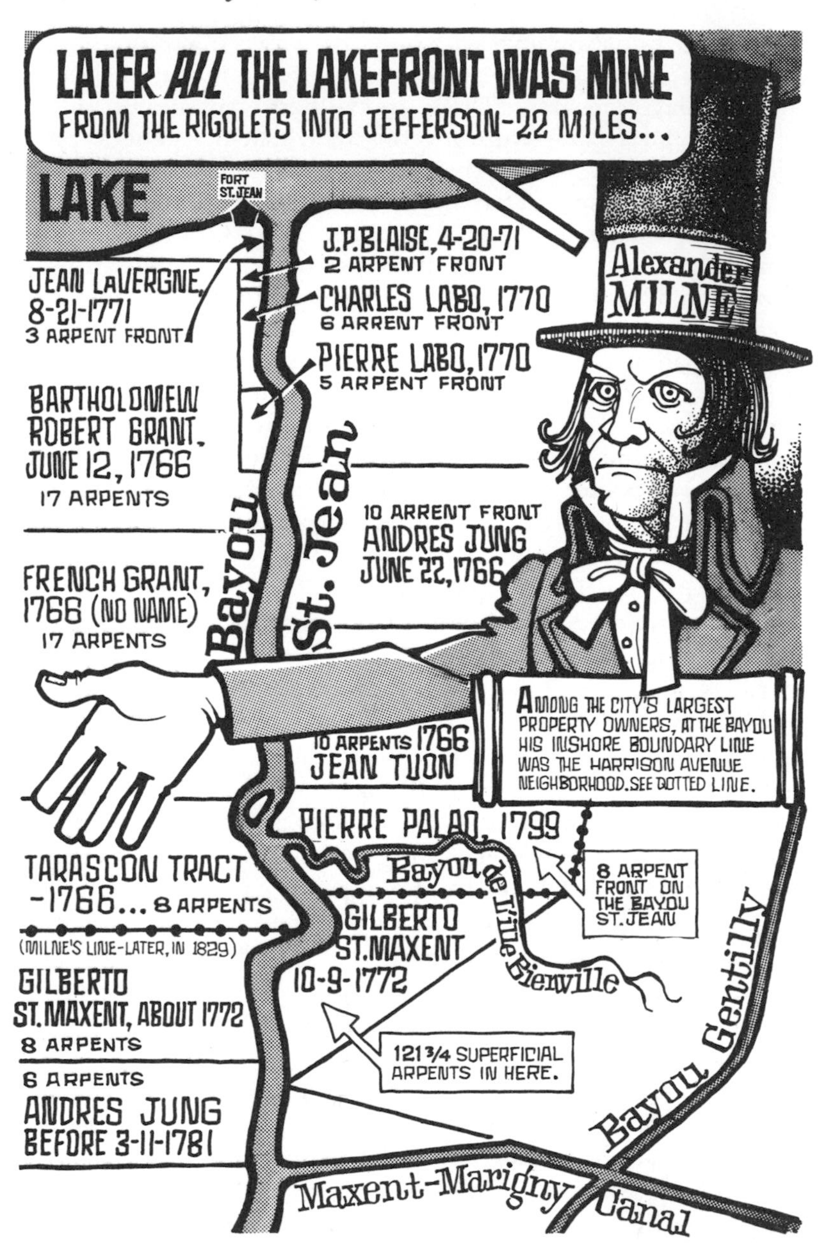

The 1766 concessions on Bayou St. Jean were made by the French during Spanish ownership of Louisiana. Those of later date were Spanish concessions.

A few days after Robert received his succession, a similar sized plot, adjoining his land to the south, was conceded by Aubry on June 17, 1766. The name of the original grantee was not included in the record, but it may have been C. Bartholomew, who seven years later owned property in that location. However, lands changed hands so rapidly in those early years it is possible the plantation had belonged to many in the intervening space of time. The tract extended south from Robert's property for another seventeen arpents, twenty toises, to a point opposite the middle of today's Park Island. Both of these tracts on the Bayou's west bank would belong to Alexander Milne in early American times.[15]

Difficult as it is to believe, the land covered by the above two grants seems to have been conceded twice in the same month, for on June 29, 1766 Bayou residents Jacques Milon and his brothers Jean, Maurice and Henri were granted forty arpents front on the left (west) bank of Bayou St. Jean, their concession bordered by the lands of Lavergne (near Fort St. Jean). One might conclude that the Milon brothers were the original recipients of the claim south of Robert's property, but the dates of the concessions differ, and the number of arpents claimed by the Milons is more than double that of the two other concessions combined. How this complication was eventually solved is one of the mysteries of colonial times. As late as 1832 descendants of the Milons would request confirmation of their title which would be, at that time, recommended by the government of the United States. It is possible Milne settled with the Milon heirs for any rights they may have had in the arpents, for the land was included in the Milne succession inventory of 1839.[16]

The east bank of Bayou St. Jean also saw activity that same summer. Ten arps front, by forty deep, were conceded to entrepreneur Andres Jung on June 22, 1766. Today this plot of land would extend approximately from Fillmore Avenue north to a point near the Vista Shores Club, between Prentiss and Burbank Streets. Jung's neighbor across the bayou —Bartholomew Robert—would purchase this tract from Lavergne (who then owned it) in 1771; and Robert's son's second wife, Marguerite, Widow Durocher, alias Castillion, would sell the property (the Castillion tract) to Alexander Milne in 1805.[17]

A month after Jung received his plantation, a plot of land to the immediate south of his, was conceded to Jean Tuon on July 21, 1766—bayou frontage of ten arpents that would today extend approximately from Mirabeau Avenue to Fillmore Avenue, and east to the vicinity of Paris Avenue.

A year after he got the land, Tuon was having trouble with Jean Baptiste Brazillier, who had promised to buy a boat for him from the Indians. Brazillier, who lived near the Port of Bayou St. Jean, had agreed to make a down payment of trade merchandise to the Indians for Tuon, but when the boat was delivered to him, Brazillier kept it and used it himself. On July 1, 1767, Tuon, through his attorney Doucet, appealed to the authorities to cite Brazillier for his sins, and demanded late delivery of his boat, as well as rental of five livres per day from the time Brazillier received it. Since this is all the records reveal, the litigants— separated by the bayou's length—probably got together, at least on the matter of the boat, which in those days—like a car or truck today—was an absolute operating necessity for one who lived on water. Tuon's property, after intervening sales to other bayou residents, would become Alexander Milne's in 1806.[18]

Charles Lorreins' (Tarascon) proneness to litigation attached itself even to the land he owned, for the eight arpents front, by forty deep plantation, conceded to him in 1766 by Aubry and Foucault, was to become the most controversial of all the properties granted during this interim period. Located considerably lakeside of his former plantation in lower City Park (which he'd sold to Francois Héry Duplanty), the land would today cover the approximate space between the north end of Wisner Overpass and the middle of Park Island on the bayou's west bank, and would reach westerly toward Milne Boulevard.

A hundred and fifty years later—after the land had exchanged hands many times—when records of early concessions had been lost or destroyed, and after official surveys designating it as public land had been made without knowledge of this early grant, the land would be claimed by the public schools of Louisiana as a "sixteenth section," dedicated by various U. S. land grants to the State of Louisiana. U. S. Congressional action of 1806 and 1811 provided that whenever a township was surveyed by the rectangular method, each and every sixteenth section which was found to be public land, and was not covered by a complete or a confirmed grant, went to the State of Louisiana for school purposes. The legal hassle as to who really owned the acres, would remain in the courts for fifteen years during the early 1900s, until the Tarascon grant of 1766 was finally recognized as valid, and the litigant—claiming the land on the basis of that grant—was approved in his ownership, because the concession of 1766 preceded the school land grants of the United States. However, what the schools would accept and receive in exchange for the loss of their sixteenth section would keep the case in court off and on into the 1950s, until the plot of land on Wisner Boulevard, near Robert E. Lee, on which Kennedy High School is built, was finally accepted in exchange for the Tarascon parcel in the middle of City Park near Wisner Overpass.[19] The irritable tenor of the times reflected occasionally in interpersonal relationships. In 1766 Nicolas Perthius was unloading his grievances on the authorities, as he displayed a head wound inflicted by Jacques (Santiago) Lorreins (Tarascon.) Perthius claimed that the injury to his left ear had necessitated cancellation of a trip he had intended to make to Illinois for Antonio St. Maxent, which resulted in the loss of 300 livres salary as well as sums he'd planned to collect, and profit from merchandise he'd intended to sell there. He asked the court for 6,000 livres to cover his losses. The records aren't complete as to how it all happened, but considerable gripe had propelled Perthius to Tarascon's doorstep after he'd retired for the night. Tarascon claimed that Perthius had thrown dirt on his doorstep, overwhelmed him with loud language, called him a rascal and a murderer, accused him of having sold sixty barrels of rum to the Indians, and threatened to run him out of town within twenty four hours. Furthermore, he'd started a fist fight, whereupon Tarascon had laid into him with a stick. Apparently, the Judge learned more about what seemed a justifiable clout, for Perthius won, but not as much as he wanted. On June 7, 1766 Jacques Tarascon was sentenced to pay 200 livres to Charity Hospital and 500 livres to Perthius to make things right.[20]

On July 4, 1766 everybody at the Village of Bayou St. Jean was atwitter over the arrival of the fifty foot schooner *La Catherine,* captained by Andre Serré, alias Grand Nicole. Having presented a questionable passport, the authorities had seized the vessel and its cargo, and the captain and nine sailors who came with him were taken before the Superior Council to explain how they happened to arrive at the Port of Bayou St. Jean.

Bits and pieces of a disconnected tale that didn't add up were disclosed by thirty six year old Venetian Serré. The vessel, he said, was owned by Dominique Monté of the Cape (St. Domingue), who upon reporting to the Governor at Monte Christo had been imprisoned, whereupon the Governor asked Serré to deliver a package to the Governor of Louisiane. He'd been piloted past Ship Island for a hogshead of wine and a case of oil. The authorities weren't convinced, and Serré was jailed until some sense could be made of the situation.

On July 13th the wine and olive oil in the schooner's hold were impounded, the vessel was left in charge of Bailly, a soldier at Bayou St.

Jean, and a slave aboard the schooner was arrested by the Bayou guard for stealing a gun and a hunting knife and trying to escape. Then Serré asked that the schooner be auctioned off, to pay debts (and probably costs of his defense). Sr. Lamothe offered 2,400 livres for the vessel—500 down, the balance to be paid in four months.

Protesting his imprisonment on July 17th, Serré said he had a French commission from the Seamen's Bureau at the Cape, that his passport for the Coast of Santo Domingo had been sent to the Seamen's Bureau of that city, and that his mate had been arrested by the Governor in Monte Christo.

As interrogation continued, various "truths" surfaced. Originally Serré had delivered pigs and oranges from Porte Platte to Port au Prince on his own vessel, and he admitted to having dealt in contraband along the coast of Santo Domingo; but his schooner had been stolen from him in Cuba, and he—in turn—had stolen *La Catherine* and its cargo from Dominique Monté, believing him to be wealthy rather than bankrupt as he turned out to be. Serré had sold most of the cargo to a merchant who still owed him 200 piastres. The sailors supplied the information that the ship had been mounted with four cannon, that police had come aboard her in Havana, that two passengers had been transferred to another vessel in Pensacola, that Captain Serré always had a pistol in one hand and a knife in the other aboardship, and that there was much conjecture as to the status of the Negro aboard.

On August 22nd, after piecing together scraps of information from interminable testimony, an inquiry of accusation was filed, charging Serré with (1) theft of the schooner and cargo, (2) carrying a false passport, and (3) being a pirate. By order of the Council a copy was sent to the Lt. General of the Admiralty at the Cape for his reaction and reply, while Serré was sentenced to remain in prison for a year until the matter could be completely checked out.

In December Lamothe, who had purchased the schooner, refused to pay the balance, to the discomfiture of Joseph Chalon who had guaranteed payment back in July. The case had become hopelessly entangled, as conflicting information came back from distant ports and from witnesses Serré claimed he didn't know. The story continued to evolve, as Serré revealed that the Negro on his ship belonged to a plantation owner who had entrusted him to his care; and he said he'd headed for the Port of Bayou St. Jean, because at some time in the past he'd been captured by an English corsair, and feared that his vessel wasn't sufficiently armed to protect him against many small boats, he believed to be English, that surrounded him.

A year later—in November of 1767—the case was still a lot of question-marks, and as the record ran out, Grand Nicole was still in prison and probably stayed there a long time.[21]

In early September, 1766 the streets of New Orleans resounded to the beat of the drum and the loud proclamation of the first Spanish decree relating to commerce. Studying the records of the colony's French governors, Ulloa had no doubt decided that Louisiane's inhabitants were a bunch of rebellious reprobates, and had determined that the best way of coping with this iniquity was to establish immediate recognition on the part of the governed that Spain was not about to put up with the kind of hanky-panky that had disabled France's administration. Released by Aubry, in the name of Ulloa, the citizenry was informed that future passports must be obtained from the Spanish, that merchants must declare the value of their imports and the price at which they intended to sell them, and that sales of this merchandise must be paid for with money circulating in the colony.

Considering that on May 4, 1766 payment on letters of exchange, drawn from 1763 on, had been suspended, that the paper money in circulation had no value, and that this new decree prohibited all speculation and contraband trading with the Spanish colonies in the Caribbean—a primary source of income for many of the colony's leaders—the response was an immediate protest to the Superior Council.

Perhaps to consider this initial unpopular action away from the clamor, Ulloa took off for quiet Balise, where he had some barracks erected on a small island near the northeast entrance to the river. He named this higher and dryer site St. Carlos, which came to be known as New Balise. His departure may simply have been to await the arrival of the lady from South America whom he was going to marry, but the colonists—preferring to think he was sulking and licking his wounds at the mouth of the river—congratulated themselves on an initial coup and no doubt bypassed the new law whenever they could get away with it.[22]

Meanwhile English General Gage had sent Captain Harry Gordon, Chief Engineer of all British troops in western North America, down the Ohio (the main highway connecting English eastern settlements with their new possessions along the Missisippi) to map the river from Fort Pitt to the Mississippi. After repairing Fort Chartres, Gordon and Assistant Engineer Thomas Hutchins, were to proceed down the Mississippi to New Orleans "noting and scrutinizing all French and Spanish settlements on the west bank." Leaving Fort Chartres on September 18,

1766 Gordon and party quickly slipped down to Natchez, because Lt. Philip Pittman had already charted that section of the stream on his way upriver the previous year. Reviewing Fort Bute and Bayou Manchac— the latter being a possibility with which Hutchins would struggle for years to come— they arrived in New Orleans October 14th and were disappointed with its primitive development. Gordon's observations in the Ottawa Archives bear direct quotation.

"New Orleans is but a small town, not many good houses in it, but in general healthy and the inhabitants well-looked. Its principal staple is their trade for furs and skins from the Illinois; their want of Negroes keeps back the indigo making. They have attempted sugar, and there are now five plantations that produce it, but they do not make it turn out to great account. There is only a stockade around the place, with a large banquet; their dependence for defense is the difficulty of approach. That up the river is tedious and easily opposed, particularly at Detour d'Anglais (English Turn), and there is only twelve feet of water on the bar. The military force of this place is at present small, not above eighty Spaniards remain of those brought with the Governor. He, it was said, expected a thousand men, 300 of which would be sent to the Illinois. Whether that reinforcement was to come from Old Spain or the Havannah, I could not learn with certainty.

"Our boat and baggage being carried to the Bayou St. Jean (over Bayou Road from the Mississippi) for which we paid twenty dollars for the boat alone, and is only two miles distance, we left New Orleans the 15th in the evening and lay that night at the Bayou, (Village of Bayou St. Jean). To this place the trade from Mobile comes and all manner of smuggling. There are three schooners plying between the east side of Lake Pontchartrain and here, employed in bringing tar. There is a good harbor for craft here (Port of Bayou St. Jean). The 16th, in the afternoon, we went along the Bayou, which is two leagues long and twenty five feet wide in many places. It is deep enough, but the windings are so short sometimes that a schooner has difficulty to turn. The grounds on each side were under water except in three or four places where rice had been cut off; and in general the country is overflowed between Lake Pontchartrain and the Mississippi, to within two miles of the last. At dusk we passed the blockhouse at the opening into Lake Pontchartrain, in which was a Sergeant and twelve men—French and Spaniards—and some small cannon mounted. We continued rowing 'til 11:00 o'clock and rested. Next day by noon we were across the lake, the wind in our teeth. That afternoon we went down the Rigolets, which is the communication between the lake and the sea. It is two and a half leagues long, from four to five fathoms deep."[23]

All the interest in real estate along Bayou St. Jean in the mid 1760s, the shared French and Spanish responsibilities in the fort at the mouth of the bayou, the fishermen's village on the east bank south of the fort, and the beginning of a small community to service the fort personnel and to lighter vessels over the sandbar at the bayou's mouth, all no doubt contributed to the general local interest in Lake Pontchartrain as a resort area. It wasn't very far from town. One could come and go by Bayou St. Jean in a day. And the more fashionable Creoles would play and jump about on the smooth bottom of the shallow lake for two, three hours at a time and disport themselves dragging in the nets the fishermen had set earlier in the day. Changing their clothing in the huts of the fishermen, they would then dine on the proceeds of the morning's haul.[24] Thus was set in the mid-1760s an early precedent for an enjoyable resort site at the mouth of Bayou St. Jean—activity that would continue, with lapses of greater or lesser interest, throughout the nineteenth and the early twentieth century.

Chapter XVII

BAYOU DE ST. JEAN BECOMES BAYU SAN JUAN UNDER SPANISH RULE 1766-1768

The indefatigable Girardy family of Bayou St. Jean was engaged as usual. In mid-1766 Jeanne Héry, elderly widow of Joseph Girardy, received 1,000 livres from Joseph DesRuisseaux who was now in charge of the Girardy succession. No mention is made of Charles Lorreins (Tarascon) to whom she'd given power of attorney to handle her affairs at the time of her husband's death. He was busy elsewhere, for in 1766-1767, as curator for Marie Langlois, Widow Simon Grenot, he was proceeding with the inventory of that succession, contesting the validity of the property separation and the protest that Marie Anne had made exhaustive repairs to a house belonging to the succession with no explanation as to why she'd done it or how much it had cost. It is possible that when the Tarascons sold their property (lower City Park) and established a plantation further north on the bayou, it was more convenient for DesRuisseaux, who owned the old Girardy place and lived there, to handle his mother-in-law's affairs.

The responsibility wasn't his for long. On January 28, 1767 DesRuisseaux made his last appearance in the judicial records when his will was recorded. After making the usual Catholic observations, he requested that he be buried among the Christians in the cemetery of the city, details of the funeral to be left to his wife, except that he wished fifty low masses to be celebrated for the repose of his soul.

His will stipulated that the estate he held in indivision for five years, at which time it could be sold to effect partition. (This wise decision prevented rash action on the part of emotional heirs, and later records reveal that the plantation was rented to Duplanty for five years after DesRuisseaux's death.) Perishable property was to be sold immediately to satisfy pressing expenses. He requested that an inventory be made of his estate and that his stepson Etienne Maurice Milon assist his wife, who was to be tutor to their daughter, and that Milon also be appointed Curator ad hoc to Elizabeth, his only child, who would inherit his share of the community.

In the custom of the times he left 1,500 pounds to the almshouse, after debts of the succession were paid; and the son of one Mrs. Betelle was to receive 1,000 pounds. (This name wasn't mentioned in the records before or after DesRuisseaux's death, although it may have been well known to surviving family and friends. To the outsider—200 years later—this bequest constitutes one of those personal mysteries occasionally disclosed in final instruments, as often in our own times as in colonial days.)

Sr. Olivier de Vezin was appointed executor, but in the event he should not accept, Mr. Braquier, Sr. was to be appointed in his stead. The will was completed in DesRuisseaux's room at his home on Bayou St. Jean and signed by him, Notary Garic, Father Dagobert, Sup., Andre le Roux and bayou resident Jean Tuon.

Joseph (Jose) DesRuisseaux, Lord of the Isle of Peraut, Canada, died soon after; for on February 27, 1767 Jeanne Héry received her allotment from Mr. Milon, in charge of Sr. DesRuisseaux's estate. As late as 1771 Maurice Milon, his wife Catherine Guedon and their two children, Charlotte and Maurice, were living in the old Girardy home located to the immediate south of Chemin Chapitoulas (Metairie Road) on the bayou's west bank.

By July of 1767 some of DesRuisseaux's former responsibilities began to fall on the shoulders of his widow Maria Francisca Girardy, who was asked to give an accounting of her late husband's handling of the affairs of the three children of deceased Marie Joseph Daigle and Jean Barré (grandson of Jeanne Héry Girardy). Charles Lorreins (Tarascon) took over this responsibility the following year when the five children of Jacques Roman (first husband of Marie Daigle) requested that the Barré estate (amounting to 30,685 livres, 16 sols) be inventoried and divided.[1]

Another problem nettled Widow DesRuisseaux—what to do about her thirty five year old Creole Catholic slave Kenel, who had taken up with Jean Baptiste, twenty five year old slave of neighbor Jean Baptiste Brazillier. Nobody could keep up with Kenel's comings and goings. While DesRuisseaux was still alive, she had run away to Mobile in a pirogue stolen from the Indians, at which time Brazillier had made extensive inquiries as to whether his slave Jean Baptiste had been seen with her. On being returned to the plantation—after apprehension and imprisonment in Mobile—DesRuisseaux's physician Montegut had been called in the latter part of 1766 to treat Kenel for bad sores on both her legs. After receiving several treatments she had disappeared again with Jean Baptiste, in a boat de la Ronde had rented to Brazillier's tarworks, and this time they'd gone to Brazillier's Chef Menteur plantation where both of them had recently been arrested at midnight abed in a cabin.

Everybody had something to say at the inquiry conducted before Councillor-Judge Louis Piot de Launay. Andres Jung and three others declared they'd seen Widow DesRuisseaux's Negress with Brazillier's Jean Baptiste. Maurice Milon demanded that Jean Baptiste be arrested, but Louis Duvernay (brother-in-law of Widow DesRuisseaux), who lived down the bayou on the DesRuisseaux six-arpent grant, declared that Brazillier had wanted to buy Kenel from Maria Francisca, or that she had wished to purchase Jean Baptiste. Maria Francisca Girardy, Widow DesRuisseaux, said she didn't want to get involved in the matter.

On being interrogated, Jean Baptiste said his master Brazillier—a carter at Bayou St. Jean—had promised to buy Kenel for him, and had given both of them food at his Chef Menteur plantation, where Brazillier kept some poultry and livestock. The slave admitted hiding Kenel in a boat at the plantation, but denied that he'd ever stolen or killed any livestock in the vicinity.

When Brazillier's turn came, he acknowledged that Jean Baptiste was his property and that the slave had previously been a run-away for seven, eight months. However, subsequent to that episode—while he, Brazillier, was out of the city—it was rumored that DesRuisseaux had put a mulatto woman "on his island"* who'd attached herself to his Negro. Brazillier denied trying to take Kenel, saying he'd tried to sell Jean Baptiste to the DesRuisseauxs but was offered such a low price he refused to sell. Finally admitting that Jean Baptiste had remained with de la Ronde for fifty days before coming back, he reluctantly agreed that the Negro should be punished if found guilty.

Kenel identified herself as belonging to the succession of DesRuisseaux of the Bayou where she worked with a hoe in the field. She said she'd been taken away by Jean Baptiste about a year ago in Mr. de la Ronde's boat, at which time they went to the Chef Menteur plantation. She'd never heard that Brazillier was going to buy her, and admitted that this was the second time she'd run away—the first time having been to Mobile where she was arrested and returned to her master.

The reticent Widow DesRuisseaux finally insisted that Kenel had been forced to leave her master's house by Jean Baptiste and had been working in Brazillier's kitchen for the past six months. Judgment was rendered on August 13, 1767 when Kenel was sentenced to be publicly flogged,

*As late as 1817 the heirs of Brazillier claimed—on the basis of ten consecutive years of settlement and cultivation prior to December 20, 1803—a tract of land near Chef Menteur in Lake Pontchartrain known as "Brazillier's Island." Confirmation of the claim—not to exceed 2,000 acres—was recommended by the U. S. Government.

branded on her right shoulder with the fleur de lys and returned to her owner. Jean Baptiste, ordered to witness Kenel's punishment, was to receive sentence later, according to the findings of the court, which the records didn't reveal.

Midst the mourning and litigation, other events lightened the atmosphere. On November 20, 1766 New Orleans merchant Joseph Milhet married Marguerite Wiltz never doubting that many years of wedded bliss lay ahead. The same month Mr. Fazende, Clerk of the Navy, and his wife Charlotte Dreux exchanged properties with Francois Bernoudy, retired officer of the colony. For their thirteen-arpent Gentilly tract, the Fazendes received a twenty-arpent front on the Mississippi nine leagues from New Orleans. Within three months another Dreux married. On February 14, 1767 Pierre Francois, Mathurin's son, tied the knot with Jeanne Hazure of Mobile.[3]

Having finally decided to live in New Orleans, Andres Jung of Bordeaux leased a house in town from Jean Petrete for four years beginning March 15, 1767, at 900 livres silver coin, payable every three months. His contract permitted him to construct any auxiliary buildings he wished on the property. Later in the summer he got around to supplying some of his needs for coastal trading. On June 23, 1767 he gave Sr. Castillion his note for 844 piastres covering purchase of the twenty two ton vessel *St. Jean Baptiste*, including all rigging, sails and utensils.[4]

On March 7, 1767 Jean Baptiste LeMoyne, Sieur de Bienville, founder of New Orleans and true believer in its future greatness, died in Paris at the age of eighty seven. Of passing interest to a handful in that city, the news would not be known for several months to his few relatives and old friends in New Orleans. Having lived so long, those to profit from his last generosity were his servants and nephews, grand nephews and nieces, to whom he left varying amounts, including diamonds. Bienville had managed well in his advanced years and left everything in good order.[5]

Unfortunately, the affairs of the colony weren't tied up so neatly. Aubry, who didn't agree with Ulloa but tried to see things his way, turned Louisiane over to the Spanish claimant ensconced at the mouth of the river on January 27, 1767, and Ulloa's seven month stay at la Balise came to an end in April of that year. Foucault, the ranking French civil servant in New Orleans, couldn't meet the officers' payroll or feed the troops, and received advances from Ulloa, who during that year paid the major part of the colony's expenses.

New Orleans merchant Gilberto Antonio de St. Maxent, who had severed relations with the local anti-Spanish establishment, was helping as much as he could. Since the arrival of *El Volante* on March 5, 1766, St. Maxent had supplied needed provisions, food and ammunition for the Royal frigate, and would continue to do so for another year. He had also established a warm personal relationship with the Spanish, having chosen Ulloa's treasurer as godfather of his infant daughter on March 19, 1766; on July 28, 1767 the Governor himself accepted that honorary responsibility when another daughter was born to the merchant. Why did St. Maxent ally himself with the Spanish when it meant breaking completely with his former colleagues? It wasn't difficult to predict the outcome of inevitable conflict between the forces of Spain and those of the province; or perhaps it was simply for personal gain. Before long St. Maxent would be purchasing twice as many articles for exchange in the Indian fur trade as everybody else in the province put together.[6]

The third generation on Bayou St. Jean was beginning to produce in 1767. On June 19th, Jean René Huchet de Kernion (son of Jean Francois Huchet de Kernion and Jeanne Antoinette Villemont, Widow Rivard, Jr.) married the high and well-born Louise Constance Chauvin de Lery des Islets (Desillest)—daughter of Antoine Chauvin de Lery des Islets and Charlotte Faucon du Manoir. The wedding was a great social event with everybody who was anybody attending.

The next month Marie Rose Saucier (daughter of Marie Rose Girardy and deceased Baptiste Saucier) married Blaise Philipe Joseph Levos on July 21st.[7]

And responsibilities were beginning to ease for a reliable Bayou Road resident. Toward the end of 1767 Marie F. DeMorand (DeMorant) and her husband Joseph D'Hauterive Valier discharged Sr. Alexander Latil, her stepfather, of further obligations as her tutor when she received her share of the DeMorand estate. A couple months later, her brother Charles applied for emancipation (this wouldn't come about until 1771), and petitioned for his share, including a quarter of the silverware listed in the DeMorand inventory.

On December 2, 1767 Jean B. Payen de Noyan, nephew of New Orleans founder Bienville and Captain in the Cavalry, married Catherine Chauvin de Lafrénière, daughter of Attorney General Nicolas Lafrénière. Happy was the bride, with no premonition of events to come that would deprive her of both a husband and a father within the next two years.[8]

The 220 page inventory of all artillery, arms, ammunition and buildings, requested by the French King in 1764, for which France was to be reimbursed by Spain, was finally completed on July 25, 1767 and signed by Foucault, Jean Baptiste Claude Bobé Desclosseaux, Jean de Loyola and Gayarré. Out of a total valuation of 1,062,219 livres for the entire province, the fort at the mouth of Bayou St. Jean was listed as being worth only 3,580 livres; and the modest total would be reduced by Governor-to-be O'Reilly to 761,537 livres, because the cannon weren't worth the cost of transportation, and their value would be deducted from the bottom line.[9]

Jean Milhet's return from Paris at the end of the year severed the colonists' remaining thread of hope for realignment with France, and all the ill will that had been festering against Ulloa slowly swelled to a bilious boil.

To camouflage their resentment at being deprived of the pomp and splendor of a Royal wedding, the colonists claimed their Holy Church and ecclesiastics had been snubbed when Ulloa and the beautiful Marchioness d'Abrado of Peru were married by his personal chaplain at La Balise. To make matters worse, the Governor's new wife didn't seem to notice she was being socially ostracized by the colonial ladies; and when one of her dark-skinned Indian servants from Peru married an officer in Ulloa's home, there was an immediate public clamor of illegal and immoral race-mixing, forbidden by the Code Noir.

The Royal Decree in the spring of 1768, limiting colonial trade to six Spanish ports, in Spanish vessels only, heightened the tension; and every serious concern having its comic aspect, one ridiculous charge followed another. A minor provision of the decree, forbidding importation of French wine, caused the emotional outcry:"We want the wine of Bordeaux, not the poison of Catalonia," and rumor spread that under Spanish rule the colonists would have to subsist on the tortilla—a pancake of pounded corn, cooked on a bed of coals—which at that time was considered food fit only for slaves.[10]

The tenor of the time may have contributed to the prickly postprandial doings near the Port of Bayou St. Jean in May of 1768. Before the Superior Council, wagoner Pierre Phoenard claimed that upon hiring his wagon after a party in Metairie, he'd been set upon by Sieurs Pierre Lacoste, St. Pré, Chalon and Milhet, and assaulted with insults, a cane, a sword and a bar of iron. His injuries had necessitated the abandoning of his wagon and horses and his confinement to bed.

Everyone involved in the fracas had a different story to tell the judge. St. Pré testified that Phoenard and Lacoste had had differences; so the latter administered a few strokes of his cane, whereupon Phoenard advanced, insulted and cursed St. Pré who was trying to make peace. He would have succeeded, St. Pré insisted, if Lacoste hadn't interfered. Then St. Pré—to avoid receiving a horsewhip in the face—threw the enraged Phoenard, flushed with drink, to the ground.

Dominique Milhet, a twenty two year old second captain of the schooner *La Liberte* anchored at the port of Bayou St. Jean, had been visiting the Brazilliers when the noise of the fight attracted him. He saw his captain, Mr. Lacoste, fighting with a wagoner who threatened him with an iron bar. When Lacoste drew a sword, St. Pré took it away from him and slapped the wagoner.

After various versions of the fray were sorted out, the only beneficiary from the vast expenditure of irk was Charity Hospital, which received fifty livres from Lacoste, twenty livres from New Orleans merchant St. Pré, and ten livres from second captain Milhet, Jr.; and the three of them shared costs of court.[11]

July generated another kind of excitement when Maria Isabel (Marie Elizabeth) DesRuisseaux married New Orleans merchant Jose (Joseph) Chalon on July 19, 1768. Four days before the wedding, the marriage contract was drawn up in conformity with the custom of Paris, at Duplanty's home on the bayou (the eight arpent Langlois-Brazillier plantation Magdalena Brazillier Duplanty had inherited from her father). In addition to recording the bridegroom's donation of ten thousand livres to his bride, the instrument specified what each brought to the marriage. Chalon's contribution consisted of a house on a corner lot at St. Philip and Burgundy, adjoining Delahousaye's place. As her dowry, the future wife brought whatever was to come to her from the succession of her late father. The contract spelled out the financial arrangements and alternatives open to the surviving spouse and children in the event of the death of either one. Witnesses for the groom at the marriage contract ceremony were his friends Juan Mercier, Jr., merchant of New Orleans, Thomas de Frant, former Captain of the Troops maintained in the colony, and Francisco Héry (Duplanty). Representing the bride were her mother Maria Francisca Girardy, widow DesRuisseaux, her half brother and surrogate tutor Mauricio Milon, her half brother Santiago Milon and Sr. Francois Braquier, Sr., merchant and friend.

On the plantation next door, Mme. Duplanty's brother, Jean Baptiste Brazillier, was coping with his periodic entanglement with the law. In mid-1768 he was being sued by one Guillaume Le Fresne whom he'd employed for a period of six months at six piastres gourdes per month. In three months Brazillier's work had run out, but he'd promised to continue his employee's salary for the time of the contract. However, Le Fresne, having received but fourteen piastres gourdes, had to petition the authorities to collect the balance.[12]

In the fall of 1768 the colonial boil of resentment burst into suppurating rebellion. Those actively leading the revolt against Spain were Attorney General Nicolas Chauvin de Lafrénière, Commissary Nicolas Denis Foucault, and Jean and Joseph Milhet, Pierre Caresse, Joseph Petit and Pierre Poupet—all merchants of New Orleans; Captain of the Swiss troops in Louisiane Pierre Marquis, naval officer Noyan-Bienville and his brother Jean Baptiste Noyan, retired cavalry officer and planter (both grand-nephews of Bienville), Joseph Roy Villeré, planter and commander of Les Allemands, lawyer Julien Jérôme Doucet, and planters Pierre Hardy de Boisblanc and Balthasar Mazan.

A number of Acadians (French settlers in Acadia since 1604), who'd been expelled from Nova Scotia, Canada by the British in 1755, and who'd arrived in Louisiane ten years later to settle the lands along the bayous, became innocently involved. Having been prior victims of warring European powers and unbelievable hardship on their trek to Louisiane, it isn't hard to understand their apprehension when it was whispered that the Spanish were about to make them slaves. The German settlement up river was also psyched up when it was bruited about what they wouldn't be paid for the provisions they'd supplied to Ulloa. Getting wind of how these anxious elements were being used against him, Ulloa dispatched his friend Antonio St. Maxent to the German coast with funds to quiet their fears. Spies were everywhere, for Lafrénière and Marquis immediately sent Villeré and Andre Verret in hot pursuit, and St. Maxent was arrested at the plantation of Cantrelle, Commander of the Acadians, before he could accomplish his mission. In addition to being roughed up, fifteen hundred piastres were taken from him.

Aubry, who'd consistently protested every phase of the subversion, was asked to take command of the colony; and fearing for Ulloa's life, on October 27, 1768 he saw the Governor, his wife, an officer and twenty men safely aboard *El Volante,* anchored in the harbor.

Three hundred Germans under Villeré, a detachment of Acadians under Noyan, planters from below the city and local citizens—about a thousand in all—gathered in the Plaza de Armas (Jackson Square) in front of the building housing the Superior Council the morning of October 28, 1768, where Lafrénière and others emoted their cause. A petition signed by six hundred, was presented to the Superior Council demanding that Ulloa leave the colony within three days, that freedom of trade be restored and that the privileges and exemptions taken from them by the usurper be restored. Based on the petition, the Council voted Ulloa's expulsion the following day.

Temporary lightness prevailed—an often-aftermath of decisions made and acted upon, regardless of their worth. On All Saints Day, November 1, 1768, a tipsy troop, returning to their homes from a wedding, giddily underestimated the tension of the times and decided to hasten the departure of their oppressor. Cutting the cable of the vessel on which Ulloa and company were temporarily housed, the frigate drifted a distance downstream, where it caught fast and remained until its official release later that day.

Six days after the governor's departure, the Superior Council ordered an inquiry into Ulloa's evils, which was spearheaded by Bayou St. Jean resident Huchet de Kernion and Louis Piot de Launay, Titular Councillors. The inquest resulted in "The Memorial of the Planters and Merchants of Louisiana on the event of October 29, 1768,"—a justification of Ulloa's ouster, published by the official printer Braud on the order of Foucault.[13]

Justification for any revolution is usually advanced after the real reasons—everyday economics and persuasive leaders—have already effected change. Illegal trading had for some time been accepted by the average citizen as a way of getting the necessities of life, and was pursued by colonial leaders, including Lafrénière, to pay their debts and enlarge their fortunes.

There is a great deal to be said for the colonists' concern expressed in this instrument and their evaluation of the predicament in which they found themselves. Colonial exports consisted of lumber, indigo, fur pelts, tobacco, cotton, sugar, clay and pine tar. Fur had no market in Spain where little of it was used. Sugar and lumber from Havana and Peru were preferred to their Louisiane equivalents. Guatemala provided more and better indigo. Peru, Havana and Campeche raised the kind of cotton Spain liked. The Isle of Pines supplied clay and pine tar; and tobacco from Spanish Santo Domingo was superior to that of Louisiane. All of this led the colonists to the indisputable conclusion that their products—not needed or wanted by Spain—would be either unsaleable or would have to be reduced to practically nothing in order to sell. They also wondered how Spain could supply them with what they needed, at a price they could afford, when she had to buy those same items at a high cost.

Then there was the matter of money. From January of 1768 Spain had accepted full responsibility for provisioning New Orleans and other dependencies while Foucault busied himself recalling the rest of the French paper money in the colony. However, after Ulloa's arrival in Havana on December 3, 1768, the only Spanish money to come into Louisiane was for payment of the troops; and even this limited source of currency was nearing its end, for the Spanish garrisons at Manchac and Natchez (to keep an eye on the English in those locations) were dribbling back into New Orleans awaiting the repair of a frigate that would take them back to Havana in May of 1769. Those who were lucky enough to have piastres hid them.

In the ensuing ease of tension following Ulloa's departure, the colonists focused on their individual futures. Unable to be French and unwilling to be Spanish a few went over to the English. For a time there was talk of setting up a republic in Louisiane with the aid of British Governor Elliot of West Florida. The English governor, however, had no intention of promoting difficulties for a power with whom his King was at peace. Nor would action of this kind have set a desirable precedent for the English colonies along the Atlantic seaboard. Too, the basic loyalties of the French colonists weren't so changeable that they could—at the drop of a hat—become subjects of a country toward which they'd been antipathetic for decades. At the same time their common sense dictated that a colony of 12,000—half of them slaves—could hardly oppose the might of Spain for very long; and though they'd willingly followed their leaders in a revolt against oppression, they were reluctant about accepting those same leaders as heads of an independent state of their own. What was going to become of them?[14]

The roiling political picture to the contrary, Maria Francisca Girardy, Widow DesRuisseaux and her daughter Maria Isabel (represented by her husband Jose Chalon) divided the property of the late Jose DesRuisseaux during a peaceful respite in January of 1769.

Widow DesRuisseaux retained twenty five slaves and the two plantations on the west bank of Bayou St. Jean: (1) the fourteen arpent property (the five-arpent DesRuisseaux concession of August 10, 1750 plus the nine arpents he had purchased from Joseph Girardy), evaluated at 18,000 livres, and (2) the six arpent front plantation conceded to DesRuisseaux by the French government on August 10, 1750, valued at six thousand livres. The larger plantation, south of Metairie Road, and the small one to the north of it were separated by the eight arpent frontage—today's Carrollton Avenue and some of lower City Park—sold to Francisco Héry

(Duplanty) by Marie Louise Girardy, Mrs. Charles Lorreins (Tarascon).

Maria Isabel DesRuisseaux Chalon received as her share of the succession twenty three slaves, a 4,000 livres dwelling in the city rented to Sr. Braquier, a 2,000 livres New Orleans house rented to Mr. Gaillard, and five lots of ground near the harbor of the bayou valued at 1,000 livres.

The forty eight slaves in the inventory were valued from a high of 2,500 livres down to 100 livres for an infirm Margarita, the average slave ranging from 1,200 to 1,800 livres; and some of the items divided between the two parties reveal the material values of those days, and the way well-to-do citizens of French Louisiane lived: 120 napkins, 9 tablecloths, 31 sheets, 40 pounds of green candles, 50 pounds of green wax (of the myrtle shrub), 34 pounds of canvas for sails, an indigo cup and related items, 25 pieces of the laurel tree, 450 pounds of maize, 8 barrels of kidney beans, 22 barrels of rice, 28 cows, 15 oxen, 2 bulls, 4 heifer calves, 3 young bulls, 12 bull calves, 36 pieces of real estate on the island, (was this near Brazillier's Island close to Chef Menteur?), 80 sheep, 4 pigs and 4 mother cows.

The land, livestock, buildings and slaves of this considerable estate were appraised at 91,300 livres, and division was made at the plantation on Bayou St. Jean on January 28, 1769.[15]

Across the bayou, DesRuisseaux's neighbor Jean Baptiste Brazillier was in trouble again. In January of 1769 several Gentilly residents petitioned the Superior Council to forbid him and his slaves from hunting cattle on their land. According to the petitioners, the Brazilliers had pastured cattle at Chef Menteur, above Gentilly, some years before, but had long ago transferred them across Lake Pontchartrain. However, on the pretext that he'd left some behind, Brazillier and his Negroes continued to make forays into Gentilly, killing any cattle they came across and transporting them across the lake where the meat was sold as wild oxen instead of French oxen (those belonging to somebody).

Prior to the filing of the charge, two of Dreux's oxen had been killed, and when Brazillier was asked to exhibit skins and heads to check for identifying brands, he replied that his Negroes had eaten and burned the heads; and to cap everything, he threatened to shoot Dreux's cattlekeeper. The cumulative result of Brazillier's incursions had been the reduction of Dreux's former herd of 700-800 head of cattle to fewer than eighty. A certificate was also submitted by St. Maxent, stating that Brazillier had come to his Gentilly plantation three weeks before, claiming that the cattle on the St. Maxent arpents belonged to him, whereupon he'd been ordered off the place. The joint petition to the Council, signed by Fazende, S. Bernoudy, Bernoudy, Dreux, Dreux fils and Dreux Gentilly, demanded that the accused pay a fine to Charity Hospital for his transgressions.

Brazillier could do no right in the spring of 1769; a couple months after being hauled into court by the Gentilly contingent he was being sued by horseshoer Allain Lavergne for 125 livres, 10 sols—payment for work done. All Lavergne had received was 42 livres worth of coal. The case disclosed that Brazillier had originally contracted with Sr. Wilse to do some work on his house for which he was to be paid in coal. However, Wilse left for Barataria and Lavergne had been substituted to complete the job, for which Brazillier offered him old money of the colony. Refusing to accept it, Brazillier had partially paid him in coal. Since the case was discontinued, Brazillier and Lavergne no doubt settled their differences.[16]

1765 through 1769 were busy years for Francisco Héry (Duplanty). Perhaps, without realizing it, he was making the most of the few years left to him. On April 10, 1765 he had to deal with the problems presented by the death of his brother Louis and the calling of a family meeting to discuss the future of Louis' daughter Marie Jeanne Héry.

Pursuing real estate, he had on February 28, 1765 bought a lot and building on Chartres and Conti Streets from Joseph Petit, and on October 12, 1765 Alexandro Latil sold him a lot of land 90′ x 168′ for 21,080 livres.

In December of 1765 the partnership of Héry, Petit and Lamarques had purchased 46,000 livres worth of Negroes. Having paid his part of the obligation, Héry petitioned the authorities on January 12, 1768 to compel his partners to pay their share of the debt.

Héry's company was further involved, having on December 23, 1765 bought several thousand livres worth of merchandise on the installment plan from Jean Baptiste Claude Bobé Desclosseaux, who was attempting to close out personal as well as governmental affairs in the colony. When the first payment came due in August and September of 1766, Duplanty —in lieu of cash—gave Bobé a shipment of calf and doeskin pelts, which Bobé accepted on condition that they were saleable in France at 7 livres, 10 sols each. However, by the first of 1768, Bobé, having been offered but three livres a piece, realized that the pelts had no more value in France than in Louisiane. Before the Superior Council, he demanded the 27,000 livres due him, plus court costs; and if payment wasn't forthcoming, he asked that Duplanty's property be sold to meet the debt. On January 22, 1768 the Sheriff served notice on Duplanty and Co. to pay up, and it is expected they did.

In March of 1768 Duplanty was building a house on Conti Street, and Sr. Charles de Laronde, who lived on the adjoining lot, complained that the chimney on the new one story building, was a fire hazard. Though de Laronde's home had a first story of fireproof brick, the second wooden story was vulnerable to Duplanty's chimney. Duplanty responded that a man was free to build as he liked on his own land, and the court couldn't protest a man's building a chimney providing it was placed sixteen feet from the party wall. De Laronde wasn't satisfied and requested that Duplanty be held responsible for any future damage to his house. Duplanty passed the risk on to somebody else, for the following year he sold a twenty by thirty foot house on a 33′ x 55′ lot on Conti Street for four thousand livres—the entire price to be paid within the year.

He wasn't the only Duplanty buying property. On June 28, 1768 his wife Magdalena Brazillier Duplanty enlarged their real estate holdings by purchasing a huge triangular plantation west of Bayou St. Jean from Madame de Mouléon who'd been granted the arpents in 1758.

While colonial complications rapidly reached their zenith, Duplanty continued his property transactions at breakneck speed. In July of 1769 he bought a lot on Dumaine and Royal and petitioned Foucault's permission to remove old worn-out cabins from the property. He also acquired a house and two and a half arpents of ground on St. Visule Street. About the same time Sr. Balthazar Ricard de Villier and his wife sold him a house and a 60′ x 160′ lot on the corner of Royal and St. Philip, and two months later the new owner was petitioning Foucault's permission to advertise a house for three consecutive Sundays on the door of the church.[17] But larger matters loomed on the horizon.

On July 26, 1769 Aubry announced to the residents of New Orleans that Don Alexandro O'Reilly had arrived at La Balise, and warned that the King of Spain must be very irritated to have sent a General of such distinction with so many troops. It was time, he said, for the people to open their eyes, realize the seriousness of their actions and prevent their destruction by prompt and absolute submission.

Lafrénière, Marquis (the principal proponent of a republic) and Joseph Milhet—all leaders of the revolution—received Aubry's permission to accompany Francisco Bouligny, O'Reilly's officer-messenger, back to the ship to forestall, if possible, any forthcoming retaliation for their actions. Listening intently and politely, O'Reilly promised to consider what they told him, do all the good in his power and desist from unnecessary punishment. Their fears allayed, the delegation returned to New Orleans where Lafrénière urged the populace to accept the new government. Despite these reassurances, it is doubtful that many in the town slept the night of August 17, 1769 as the frigate of O'Reilly and twenty three other vessels made fast to the shore near the Plaza de Armas. The following day the official and ecclesiastical ceremonies took place by which French Louisiane became Spanish Luisiana, after which O'Reilly immediately got down to the business at hand. Receiving the names of the chief revolutionaries from Aubry, he invited all the leaders of the colony to a reception, at which the fingered ones were quickly arrested and imprisoned. Joseph Roy Villeré was killed (some say he died of natural causes) at the time of his arrest.

After a trial, sentence was imposed on October 26, 1769. Lafrénière, Noyan, Caresse, Marquis and Joseph Milhet were condemned to be hanged, but finding no one willing to execute the hangings, the men were led to a small square in front of the barracks of the saddened city and shot—a tragedy that twisted the hopes and fears of the silent citizenry, who in their respective homes pondered the perplexities of the era through which they had come and the one they were about to enter. For the capricious cutting of the cable that loosed Ulloa's vessel, Joseph Petit was sentenced to life imprisonment. For their complicity in the disaster, Mazan and Doucet received ten years, and Jean Milhet, Boisblanc and Poupet six years of hard labor at Moro Fortress. The property of all was confiscated, extending the sentences of the perpetrators to their families.

A note of relief was sounded in the grim symphony when the son of Mazan traveled to Madrid to plead for his father's release, which would result in the freeing of all the prisoners at Havana after they had served only a year. Braud, the printer, was released because his work had been done on the order of Commissary Foucault, who on the basis of being a French Civil servant, refused to answer any questions or sign any statements when Aubry, Don Domingo Salcedo, Brigadier of the Spanish Army, and Chief Clerk of the Council Garic went to the home of Francisco Héry (Duplanty) where Foucault was being detained as a prisoner of state. Returned to France, the Commissary was consigned to the Bastille where he had plenty time to contemplate his duplicity. His case was revived later, however, and the bumptious bureaucrat continued his interrupted career.

Huchet de Kernion, who with Piot de Launay had served as a special committee to report on the petition of the colonists to expell Ulloa, didn't share the fate of the other revolutionary leaders. He had died June 13, 1769 at his Bayou St. Jean plantation, five weeks before the arrival of O'Reilly.

A peculiar postscript to this tragedy was the awarding by the French King of ten thousand livres to the widows of Lafrénière and his son-in-law Noyan.

O'Reilly, who has been described as courtly, intellectual, hard, vindictive and just, acknowledged most of these qualities when he said "all the world recognizes the necessity, the justice and the clemency of a judgment that has made an example, the memory of which will never be forgotten."

After the burial of the revolutionaries, O'Reilly—Captain-General and Governor of the province—immediately turned his attention to improving the circumstances of their former bailiwick, and history attests to his careful administration and "unSpanish" consideration for French feelings.[18]

And what of those who had labored so lengthily in the service of the colony? After writing a meticulous last dispatch to the commandants of the various posts in Louisiane, urging them to keep close watch to prevent dogs from entering the churches, Charles Philippe Aubry—the ever affected and afflicted middleman of Louisiane—left New Orleans on November 23, 1769, having turned down a pension and position with the Spanish. On February 17, 1770 the ship carrying him home to France split in half near Bordeaux, and he went to the bottom with the voluminous records of the colony he was taking back to Paris, as well as the 12,000 ecus he is said to have received from Spain for worthy and honorable service in the most trying of positions.

Commissary Bobé Desclosseaux remained in Louisiane to purchase as much of the outstanding French money as possible and to close colonial accounts. He wouldn't leave until August of 1773, when it was his fate, too, to be claimed by the briny deep, along with all the accounting records of the colony.[19]

During the orphan years of Louisiane—from 1762 to 1769—the livres of the colony had gradually been replaced with piastres, and the Charles Jeans and Josephs of French times were being called Carlos, Juan and Jose. And 'though the colony had legally belonged to Spain for over six years, it was not until after the reprisals for the uprising that Louisiane really became Spanish, and Grand Bayou de St. Jean was labeled Gran Bayu del San Juan on the maps and charts of the new masters of the province.

GRAN BAYU SAN JUAN IN SPANISH LUISIANA 1769 - 1803

(A minor exception to Spanish rule during this period, Spain had retroceded Luisiana to France by the secret Treaty of Ildefonso on October 1, 1800; but it was only from November 30th to December 20th, 1803, that Louisiane was again under French rule for twenty days.)

Chapter XVIII

LAWS, LAND AND COMMERCE UNDER O'REILLY AND UNZAGA—1769-1772

The economy of Luisiana began to look up after O'Reilly's arrival. Forming a citizens' militia, he appointed Don Gilberto Antonio de St. Maxent to head it. St. Maxent who already owned vast tracts of land at Chef Menteur and in Gentilly and who was to acquire several plantations on Bayu San Juan and in Gentilly during the 1770s, had represented Spain in the delivery of Luisiana to His Catholic Majesty and had saved the new ruler a considerable sum in the handling of inventories during the transition.*

With currency coming from Vera Cruz to pay the troops, more money began to circulate. But more money didn't increase supplies. Those ordered from Spain hadn't as yet arrived, and with extra troops to feed food was at a premium. Flour was selling as high as thirty dollars per barrel. The new governor was lucky, because Oliver Pollock—an adventuring Irish merchant, who during the 1760s had begun trading from Philadelphia to Cuba to New Orleans, and whom O'Reilly, then governor of Cuba, had come to know— tied up his ship in New Orleans; and the cargo was flour—the only supply in sight. Pollock could have sold his treasure for any price he named; but refusing to profit from the plight of the province, he offered the entire shipload to his old friend. For the flour Pollock received a nominal fifteen dollars a barrel, but for his good will and business sense he was given freedom of trade in all Spanish Luisiana, and recognition besides—a report of his exemplary conduct to the King of Spain. Having transferred his base of operations from Cuba to New Orleans in 1768, Pollock would, during the next few years, build a considerable reputation and fortune; and championing the cause of the American colonies during the following decade, he would ask for and receive the financial support of many outstanding citizens of Gran Bayu San Juan and New Orleans.[1]

On November 3, 1769 O'Reilly proclaimed that evidence presented in the trial of the revolutionaires proved that the Superior Council had encouraged revolt rather than loyalty to the new sovereign which neces-

*The complete story and detailed information about St. Maxent can be found in James Julian Coleman, Jr.'s excellent book — GILBERT ANTOINE DE ST. MAXENT — published by Pelican Publishing Company, New Orleans, Louisiana.

sitated abolishment of that tribunal. On November 26, 1769 the Spanish Cabildo was established to govern New Orleans. Carrying the King's commission as governor, Don Luis Unzaga y Amezaga, Colonel of the Regiment of Havana, had accompanied O'Reilly to Luisiana, but he couldn't assume the duties of that office until O'Reilly left or authorized him to fill the position. At the first sitting of the Cabildo on December 1, 1769 the Governor-General administered the oath and yielded the chair to Unzaga, and O'Reilly's remaining official acts in Luisiana were performed as Captain-General, which title, under Spanish rule in the Americas, was superior to that of governor; all successive Spanish governors of Luisiana would be subordinate to the Captain-General of Cuba.[2]

In addition to the municipal government, a governing body was established to rule Luisiana which under the Spanish was called a province, whereas the French had referred to it as a colony, although strictly speaking it had become a province in 1731 after the French King took over from John Law and his predecessor Crozat.

O'Reilly ordered that a set of instructions, regarding the institution and proceedings of civil and criminal actions according to the laws of Castille and the Indies, be prepared and published, so the people of the province—particularly judges and officers—might learn the law. Proceeding from the same Roman code as did French law, there were similarities as to matrimonial rights, testaments and successions; so it is believed that little inconvenience resulted from the change.[3]

The Spanish language was to be used by all public officers in their minutes, but French was tolerated in judicial and notarial acts. Indeed, except for a few high officials in the government and the military, and an insignificant number of troops and a handful of colonists who were to arrive later, Luisiana would remain French.

The December 12, 1769 ordinance of Unzaga, regarding the laying of "banquettes" (sidewalks)—the first use of the word in Spanish records—indicates that Frenchifying the Spaniard began almost immediately.[4]

The day before—December 11th—French Francois Héry (Duplanty), resident of Bayu San Juan, contracted with Don Alexandro O'Reilly to erect the first Cabildo on the site of the old French corps de garde (where the present Cabildo now stands). "Cabildo" referred not only to the building that housed the local officialdom, but was also what the municipal government itself was called. The contract called for completion and delivery of the townhall by the end of April, 1770; but the work wasn't finished until August 17, 1770, and that august body met for the first time in its new quarters on September 7, 1770. Héry had agreed to do the job for eighteen hundred piastres, but instead of money he received two squares of ground—from Decatur to Royal, between Iberville and Bienville—the site of former French Governor Vaudreuil's government house. Since this property was worth twenty five hundred piastres, Héry agreed to pay the difference over a four year period.[5]

Seemingly unaware of the fateful events of the summer of 1769 Contractor Héry had continued buying and selling real estate as he'd done during the late French regime. On August 2, 1769 he'd purchased two and a half lots, 150′ front by the usual depth, on St. Philippe and St. Ursule, bounded on either side by the residences of one Champion and free Negress Jumon. For the land and the old house—a wooden front with brick uprights—he paid two thousand livres in piastres to bayou residents Jose Chalon and his wife Isabel DesRuisseaux. Mrs. Chalon had inherited the lots from her father, but since she was still a minor, her husband signed for her, stating that she'd ratify the sale at the proper time.

Perhaps the Chalons had sold this asset to invest in something else, for on September 30, 1769 they and Mrs. Chalon's mother, Widow DesRuisseaux, had purchased from Francisco Dussau de la Croix Mazelliere, Captain of the Battalion of Luisiana, a plantation away from the city which measured eighteen arpents front by eighty deep. On the plantation was a small house, other buildings, twenty slaves, twenty head of cattle, four horses and farm implements—all valued at thirty thousand livres, which amount Widow DesRuisseaux guaranteed would be paid with 2,000 weight of good indigo, a third to be delivered at the end of each harvest in 1769, 1770 and 1771.[6]

An early Cabildo appointee was Don Juan Bautista Garic. Having served in the same position under the French, Garic purchased the office of Escribano (Clerk) and Notary of the Cabildo, which paid him twenty five pesos per month, and he continued in that job for several years.[7]

Don Henriques Despres (Desprez) was appointed Public Attorney by the Cabildo on December 23, 1769. Assisting many of the bayou people with their legal problems, Desprez would within the next few years marry and become a resident of Bayu San Juan.

Another attorney popular with bayou folk at this time was Leonardo Mazange who also represented the interests of Marguerita Wiltz, widow of executed Joseph Milhet, and Louise Cheval, wife of Jean Milhet, who had been sentenced to imprisonment at the Havana Fortress.[8]

O'Reilly's nephew, twenty seven year old Irish Maurice Conway (Marquis d'Auconis) from Demerique, had arrived in Luisiana ahead of his uncle, and on June 5, 1769 purchased a house on St. Louis Street for 660 livres. In addition to serving O'Reilly as private secretary, he went into partnership with Bartolomo MacNamara in May of 1770, running a tannery on St. Louis Street, the assets of which were mills, large earthen jars, Negroes and three horses, valued at 1,455 pesos. Maurice Conway, who lived at the tannery, was to figure largely in future affairs of the bayou and the province.[9]

The Luisiana Census of 1769, which included 307 citizens at Bayu San Juan and Gentilly, listed only sixty Indian slaves.

On December 1, 1769 O'Reilly announced there would be no future selling or trading of Indian slaves.The only change owners could make in their status was to set them free. O'Reilly also stipulated that the Indians in the upper part of the province were to be treated justly, given fair prices for their hides and furs, and that goods bartered for Indian products be fairly priced. After considerable consultation with those he trusted, the Captain-General decided that the best way to maintain the good will of the Redmen was to continue the French habit of giving presents—the first of which were distributed to forty nations in 1770 by Gilberto St. Maxent who had been appointed Commissioner of Indian Affairs. Although St. Maxent's fur-trading monopoly had terminated in 1767, this new Spanish appointment gave him more control than ever over that industry, because everything given to the Indians in the entire province had to be purchased through the firm of St. Maxent and Ranson, a company established for that specific purpose. The arrangement worked well for everybody. St. Maxent became richer, the Indians received the goods they wanted—a variety of things St. Maxent could procure because of his contacts and financial standing in Europe— and Spain realized her goals at a reduced cost.

However, where a considerable figure had shown up on the red side of Spain's ledger for a long time, the Indians had to pull in their reins. On January 23, 1770 O'Reilly notified the Commandant of Natchitoches not to buy any more horses or mules from the Indians. Penalties for transgression were steep and were devised to stop the thieving of livestock from Spanish settlements in the New Philippines (Texas) and to close the market for stolen animals that had been operating profitably during the entire French regime.[10]

To cover the cost of maintaining the levee, an anchorage duty of $6.00 on vessels of two thousand tons and up, and half that sum on smaller ones, was imposed; and O'Reilly accepted an offered annual contribution of $370.00 from the butchers, providing their liberality would not result in higher meat prices. A tax of twenty dollars was fixed on every boarding house; and every tavern, billiard table and coffee house in New Orleans had to pay an annual forty dollars. Learning that Luisiana citizens consumed fifteen hundred casks of distilled spirits every year, O'Reilly assessed a tax of a dollar per cask. The rivermen and Indians of this period drank rum made from the molasses of Martinique and Cuba which the Spaniards called tafia or aguardiente (firewater). French traders called it eau-de-vie (water of life), and later the Americans would call it taffy. It sold for four reales or fifty cents a gallon. New Orleanians of French descent drank red and white wine and brandy of two qualities from Bordeaux and the Provence. The cheaper brandy was also called aguardiente and eau-de-vie and sold for seventy five cents a gallon.[11]

To attract new settlers and promote self-sustenance, O'Reilly enacted liberal regulations regarding land grants on February 18, 1770. (Historian Gayarré's date is January 8, 1770.) Every family coming to settle in Luisiana was given extensive acreage with water frontage which allowed them to take the produce they raised and the wood they cut on their property to market and to bring in needed supplies by boat. All grants were made in the name of the King by the governor, who appointed a surveyor to establish side boundaries as well as front and depth measurements in the presence of the ordinary judge of the district and two neighbors from adjoining properties. The four signed the proces verbal of which three copies were made—one for the Escribano of the Cabildo, one for the governor, and the third copy was for the new proprietor to attach to the title of his grant.

The new concessionaire was obligated to build a levee to protect his land, and ditches to drain it. He also had to build a road forty feet wide along the front of his property and maintain it in good condition, as well as twelve foot wide bridges over any draining ditches that crossed the road. Grantees had to clear the entire front of their land to a depth of two arpents within three years of receiving their grants and enclose the cleared area, or the land would revert to the King. It was forbidden to sell a concession for three years, and then only with written permission from the governor who would only consent to the sale if the original grant conditions had been fulfilled.[12]

In 1770 the Spanish government conceded to Alexandro Latil of Bayou Road a small grant of land on Bayu San Juan, and the following excerpts are from one of the very few documents found in the archives confirming a land grant and bearing an official wax seal:

3/2/1770—a certificate declaring that among the edifices Spain had accepted from France was a naval arsenal situated on the banks of Bayu San Juan, adjoined on one side by the other bayou and on the opposite side by Mr. Brazillier's land. The edifice had been estimated for price.

3/10/1770—Alexandro Latil petitions Governor Unzaga, declaring that among the benefits he had received from His Excellency Governor O'Reilly, was a concession of a small lot of ground on Bayu San Juan. He prays that the necessary titles be executed to confirm him in possession thereof.

3/21/1770—The concession of land on Bayu San Juan is confirmed to Mr. Latil.

3/22/1770—Governor Unzaga orders Latil to present the title to the land given him by O'Reilly.

4/9/1770—Mr. Latil presents his decree for the concession and Unzaga orders a skilled engineer to survey the land and define its boundaries.

4/23/1770—Engineer Luis Andry presents his report on the survey —a trapezoid twenty toises front on Bayu San Juan by forty five toises deep, narrowing to twelve toises at the rear, situated by Mr. Brazillier's plantation, bounded on the north by a small estuary flowing into Bayu San Juan and on the south by the levee of the Brazillier plantation. Mr. Andry stakes off the ground in the presence of Mr. and Mrs. Brazillier and Mr. Maigrot who lives in the naval arsenal.

4/30/1770—Governor Unzaga confirms Mr. Latil's concession and grants the necessary title, which is signed and sealed with his arms.

The Luis Andry Survey Map of Kernion's property, dated September 26, 1771 shows the location of this grant between the small bayou running into Bayu San Juan and the boundary line separating the Brazillier and Kernion plantations, as well as the arsenal in which Jacques Maigrot lived.

Evidently Latil held this property for only a short time, as the Acts of Notary Garic disclose a sale of property by Latil to Juan Brazillier on August 26, 1771. Since this small concession was surrounded by Juan Bautista Brazillier's arpents it is logical that he wished to re-incorporate into his small plantation the property his father had transferred to the French government after 1729.[13] Conveyance records in later Spanish times show that this small plantation, including the site of the arsenal, belonged to Santiago Lorreins (Tarascon)—who inherited the property from his sister Pellagia Lorreins, Widow Brazillier—and Tarascon's heirs.

Since destruction of growing things by roaming cattle deprived the settlement of food, O'Reilly passed an ordinance establishing June 1, 1771 as the latest date on which stray cattle could be reclaimed by their owners. After that, any livestock running loose would be considered wild and could be legally killed by anyone—except between November 15th and March 15th when nothing was growing. From March 16th to November 14th the owner would be responsible for any damage done by his roving livestock.[14]

An entry in the Cabildo Records of March 19, 1770 discloses a familiar name—Francois Rivard. This could well be the son of the bayou resident of the same name, who in 1737 was trading to Illinois country. The case is noteworthy because it reveals items that were being brought into New Orleans in early Spanish times. Rivard and three other voyagers were petitioning the Cabildo for wages owed them by Juan Bautista Boyer, for whom they'd gone on a hunting expedition—probably to that 108 mile strip on the west bank of the Mississippi, 494 miles upriver in Illinois country, where New Orleans hunters wintered to collect salt meat, suet and bear oil for sale in New Orleans.

One of the hunters, having received only four pots of oil, informed the Cabildo that Boyer still owed him a hundred pounds of meat and 375 livres. He prayed for immediate justice, because if he had to stay in New Orleans he'd have further expense for food and lodging. He was paid that very day, and his petition attracted other creditors of Boyer, whose two boatloads of forty salted animals, fourteen hundred pounds of tallow mixed with meat, four hundred pots of bear oil, a hundred pounds of beaver, twenty three deer skins, twenty untanned roebuck skins, twenty three small and large bearskins and eighteen salted otter skins were seized by the authorities to pay Boyer's debts.[15]

Huchet de Kernion of Bayu San Juan had died before the arrival of O'Reilly, and early 1770 found Madame Jeanne Antoinette de Villemont, Widow Kernion and her son Jean René Huchet de Kernion requesting partition of his estate. On March 26, 1770 René turned over funds and an estate in lower Brittainy, France, to one Augustin Chantalou for seven thousand livres; and on May 7, 1770 arbitrators Jean Trudeau (Captain of the Infantry), Charles Fleuriau (Captain of the Infantry and Sheriff of the Cabildo) and Gentilly neighbor Mathurin Dreux went to the Kernion home on the bayou to make an amicable separation of the community property. Attorney Leonardo Mazange represented the son, Henriques

Desprez acted as attorney for Widow Kernion, and distribution was effected to the entire satisfaction of all concerned.

Young Kernion, along with other citizens of the community, had become reconciled to Spanish rule, and he had been appointed Alcalde Ordinaire of the Cabildo, a position of importance and dignity similar to that of judge.[16]

Fort Real Catolica (New Balize), built in 1766 by Ulloa on Isle Verd (Green Island) opposite French Balize, had been badly damaged during a storm of 1770, so O'Reilly ordered that it be abandoned. Establishing a small garrison at Old Balize, and having accomplished what he could for the betterment of Luisiana, O'Reilly left the province in the summer of 1770 taking with him all except 1,200 of the Spanish troops who'd come with him.

Governor Luis Unzaga, now in full charge, contracted with four butchers in the fall to supply the city, as well as the regidors, judges and their retainers, with beef (and mutton when it was available) for the following year. Agreeing to supply various kinds of clean meat for the city at 365 pesos annually, it was stipulated that the officials pay four sueldos per pounds for their protein, whereas Charity Hospital would have to pay only three for what was needed there.[17]

On the west bank of Bayu San Juan Maria Francisca Girardy, Widow DesRuisseaux was busy handling her affairs. In July she sold a twenty one year old Congolese slave who was free of debt, of good character and sound health, with no particular talents, for two hundred pesos, Mexican coin—the going price for a slave; and in December of 1770 she carried out her late husband's wishes by renting her fourteen arpent plantation on the west bank of the bayou to Francisco Héry Duplanty, (on Moss Street between Carrollton and Dumaine today). Houses, kitchen, grange, warehouse and other outbuildings were included in the contract as well as twenty slaves and all the animals of the stockfarm. The yearly rental was five hundred pesos, a fourth of which was to be paid every three months. The lease was to run for five years, and a marginal note on the record indicates that it was cancelled May 2, 1775.

Since Duplanty, in 1770, owned the eight arpent property sold him by Carlos Lorreins (Tarascon) to the immediate north of the large DesRuisseaux plantation, he now controlled the entire former Girardy-DesRuisseaux holdings on the bayou's west bank, except the six arpent grant (north of the Carlos Tarascon arpents) which Widow DesRuisseaux had sold her brother-in-law Luis Duvernay. Today the Duvernay place would be located in lower City Park in the vicinity of Taylor Avenue.

Charles Lorreins (Tarascon) was again looking out for Juana Héry, Widow Joseph Girardy, and in the spring of 1770 received nine hundred livres for his mother-in-law from Maurice Milon, guardian of the DesRuisseaux estate. Lorreins didn't have the responsibility for long, because Maria Juana Héry died December 8th of that year. Widow of one of the earliest settlers on Bayu San Juan, her death marked the end of a vital era on the stream. On February 26, 1771 her small estate was distributed to: Rose Girardy (Mrs. Luis Duvernay), Francisca Girardy (Widow DesRuisseaux) and Marie Louise Girardy (Mrs. Charles Lorreins Tarascon), her three daughters by Joseph Girardy. Her grand-children, minors Juan Bautista and Honorato, as well as Louisa and Carlos Barré who weren't present, were represented by Charles Lorreins (Tarascon), and Cecilia and Carlotta Barré were represented by Andres Reynaud.[18]

Unzaga's governorship was for the most part an agreeable surprise to the people of Luisiana. Mild as his mandates, he ruled with understanding and clemency, and he strengthened community ties by marrying Marie Elizabeth St. Maxent. Born on February 3, 1752 she was the eldest child of Antonio St. Maxent and Elizabeth La Roche.

In a village of seven to eight hundred wooden houses, it isn't surprising that the Governor's Ordinance of 1770 compelled New Orleans carpenters, joiners and mechanics to assist at fires or be fined a peso; and all citizens were required to have buckets, axes and gaffs in their homes for fighting fires or risk a fine of four pesos.

The local citizenry was most grateful, however, for Unzaga's lenient attitude toward their illegal trade with the English. Ulloa's regulation of 1766, limiting Luisiana's trade to six Spanish port cities, as well as other restrictions, had resulted in a severe food shortage discussed by the Cabildo on October 5, 1770. Realizing that it would take time for commercial connections to become established between local merchants and those in Spanish cities, Unzaga decided not to enforce O'Reilly's prohibition against illegal trade with the British, which carried a fine of a hundred dollars. Holding to the letter of the law would not only have been injurious to the general welfare, but was impossible to effect, since Lake Pontchartrain lapped the southern shores of British West Florida; and English goods, smuggled in through the Port of Bayu San Juan, were on the shelves of many New Orleans merchants.

The only butter, eggs and vegetables to be had were supplied by the German community (Les Allemands) twenty five miles upriver. Imported olive oil was very expensive, so the usual shortening was bear oil brought to New Orleans by hunters. Recognizing this as a source of extra revenue, the Cabildo—a year later—was considering raising the tax on it from 2½ to 3 reales.

In January of 1771, Unzaga announced that the Governor-General of Cuba had received Royal orders to free those confined at Morro Castle, Havana, for their complicity in the revolution of 1768. The released prisoners were sent to French St. Domingue by the first available Spanish boat, with the understanding they would never again set foot on Spanish soil, which, of course, precluded their return to Luisiana as long as Spain ruled the province. The response of the local populace to this divided blessing was a solemn mass at the Church of San Luis, where according to Unzaga, "they directed their clamors to the heavens."[19]

Francisco Héry, called Duplanty, one of the most active colonists of French and early Spanish times, died in 1771 and was buried in the Parish Church of San Luis* next door to the Cabildo he'd built for the Spanish government. On April 18, 1771 Magdalena Brazillier, Widow Duplanty, bestowed upon Henriques Desprez her general power-of-attorney, and on April 25, 1771 the Duplanty estate, left to the widow and four minor co-heirs (children of deceased brother Louis Héry) was inventoried, evaluated and notarized by Jean Garic. Three plantations were listed: (1) the principal plantation on Bayu San Juan, eight arpents front by twenty two arpents deep (the rear arpents had been sold by Mrs. Duplanty's father), bordered on the east by the public road leading to the bayou (Bayou Road) and on the west by the forks of the bayou (the vicinity of Orleans Street today). This, of course, was the old Langlois plantation Magdalena Brazillier had inherited from her father; (2) a plantation on the other side of the bayou which Héry had bought from Carlos Tarascon, eight arpents front by forty arpents deep, bordered on both sides by the land of Joseph DesRuisseaux. On this land was a small house, thirty feet long by twenty two feet wide, and the entire property was valued at thirteen hundred pesos. (This was the lower City Park plantation Louis Turpin had donated to Marie Girardy, Tarascon's wife, in 1734); (3) a plantation, granted originally to Maria Elizabeth de Mouléon on May 10, 1758 by the French government, bordered on the rear by the land of Pradel and on the other side by the land of Joseph DesRuisseaux. (Mrs. de Mouléon had sold this property to the Duplantys on June 28, 1768.)

---

*Anyone who donated a hundred pesos to the church could be buried there. Only a few of the hierarchy, such as the governor, the priest, or city treasurer seem to have been exempted from this charge. Those who could not afford the price were buried at no cost—except preparing the grave—in the walled cemetery located in front of Charity Hospital on the ramparts of the city.

As is often the case when women lose their husbands, Widow Duplanty was immediately confronted with a suit on May 23, 1771, in which Santiago Lamothe, resident of Bayu San Juan, alleged he had some time before purchased a house from Widow Maria Theresa Bunel for the account of Francisco Héry (Duplanty), but which for special reasons had been put in Lamothe's name. Now the note was due, and the plaintiff requested that Duplanty's estate pay the seven thousand livres due on the house, plus court costs. Widow Duplanty declared she knew nothing of the matter—that all she possessed were some doors, windows and three painted planks, remains of the Bunel house, which legal investigation revealed had been destroyed by order of either O'Reilly or Unzaga. Lamothe had previously sued Mrs. Bunel to annul the sale of the house, and now witnesses, including bayou resident Jose Chalon, were called; and after thorough consideration all parties interested effected a notarial agreement to rescind the original sale of the house, but it cost them assessor's fees of a hundred reales, and court costs of over ninety five pesos plus attorneys' fees—a costly introduction to meticulous, detailed lengthy Spanish litigation.

Santiago Lamothe of this case lived on Bayu San Juan with his wife and his brother Juan, a carpenter, who also worked and owned property in Opelousas during the 1770s. By early 1778 both brothers would have died, leaving Santiago's widow to straighten out the intestate succession of her brother-in-law, as well as details of her husband's estate.[20]

The records of Notary Public Juan Garic disclose an inordinate number of legal doings concerning bayou property during 1771 and the following several years—particularly transactions of Magdalena Brazillier (Widow Duplanty) Desprez, for she had soon married her attorney, whereupon they immediately proceeded to radically alter the Duplanty portfolio.

In addition to marital and professional pursuits, Desprez had become involved in a tragedy that shook the area in the late spring of 1771. At midnight, on May 31st, Juan Bautista Cezaire LeBreton, who lived about five miles upriver from New Orleans, was killed by two of his slaves, after they'd set fire to some of the plantation outbuildings to divert attention from their deed. Although slave-owners lived with the possibility of a black attack, it was extremely rare for a slave to murder his master, and the emergency put the creeping, nit-picking Spanish legal machinery into high gear.

After hasty interrogation of all involved, suspects were reduced to five; and on the rack, LeBreton's hunter Temba confessed to the killing and involved another slave Mirliton as well.

Leonardo Mazange accepted the difficult task of representing the accused, and the forty year old bachelor-hunter stated he'd killed his master because he didn't get enough time off. Temba—like many slaves of that day—was in the habit of sleeping with Negresses on neighboring plantations, and had been called on the carpet by LeBreton on various occasions for spending too many successive nights away from the place.

After trying to hang himself in his cell, Mirliton confessed that under pressure from Temba (who was feared by both blacks and whites on the plantation) he had carried coals from his cabin to set the fire, and that he and Temba had fired their guns simultaneously at their master.

Hanged on June 20th, the criminals were nailed up on the public road, with the warning that nobody—under pain of death—take their bodies down. Marianna, Temba's sleeping partner on the neighboring plantation, and a male slave, who had covered for the murderers, were lashed at the foot of the gallows and their ears were cut off close to their heads as a permanent reminder of their transgressions. The least involved third slave was mounted on a beast, tarred and feathered.

In twenty days—record time for such an important case—the Spanish legal system had disposed of the tragedy, and for the first and last time in Spanish legal archives no court costs were recorded.

Henriques Desprez was appointed curator ad lites of Francisco and Juana, minor children of the murdered LeBreton; and after a proper length of time, Maria Juana Francisca McCarty, Widow LeBreton, would marry Maurice Conway, nephew of O'Reilly, in 1777.[21]

Meantime, quite a community was developing at the mouth of Bayu San Juan. Besides the military personnel of the fort, people were beginning to settle there permanently. Born in New Orleans, J. P. Blaise (called Bellegard) had been living on the west bank of the bayou, south of the fort and north of Bayou Noir, since the late 1760s. In 1771 he fathered a daughter, and on April 20, 1771 Governor Unzaga granted him the two arpents (by forty arpents deep) fronting the bayou, on which he'd been living. This property represented the extreme lakeside segment of a larger grant Bartholomew Robert had received from the French government in 1766. Apparently desiring to occupy only the bayou frontage, he turned the thirty seven rear arpents of his concession back to Robert on May 14, 1771, but continued to live on the stream for the rest of his life; his daughter, Widow Severe, was living there in the 1820s. In later American times, this property, located in the vicinity of today's Robert E. Lee Boulevard, would be a part of Genois-Soniat property.

A few months later, on August 27, 1771, Governor Unzaga reaffirmed the balance of the 1766 grant—15 arpents, 29 toises front,—to original grantee Bartholomew Robert—land that in the early 1800s would become a part of Alexander Milne's bayou holdings, but not before others had been attracted to Robert's bayou frontage.

In 1770 brothers Charles and Pierre Labo (Labeau) settled on the stream, on modest lots to the immediate south of J. P. Blaise, where they were destined to live for almost forty years. Pierre's son Honori would occupy the land after them in 1809.

The Castillon and Rochon families were other newcomers. Andre Castillon was born at the mouth of Bayu San Juan in 1770, and eight year old Alexis Rochon, born in Mobile, came to the site in 1770.

Bartholomew Robert was also interested in the land on the east side of the bayou, and in 1771 purchased from Jean Lavergne the 1766 concession of Andres Jung, today located roughly from Fillmore Avenue north to a point between Prentiss and Burbank Streets. When Lavergne acquired the land is uncertain, and in 1771 Jung's original ten arpents had expanded to thirteen arpents, 28 toises. Leaving the property to his son, young Robert's wife—Marguerite, Widow Durocher, alias Castillon—would eventually sell this land called the Castillon Tract, to Alexander Milne on June 24, 1805.[22]

On August 21, 1771 Ships Carpenter Jean Lavergne was officially granted possession of a plot of land to the immediate north of the Blaise concession—property on which he'd been living since 1765. Contiguous to, and back of the fort which fronted on the bayou, Lavergne's triangular possession contained thirty seven arpents more or less. Measuring three arpents, ten toises and two lines on the bayou, the boundary line on the north ran on an angle parallel to Lake Pontchartrain as far west as the Orleans Canal of today; thence on a line measuring 13 arpents, 11 toises and 3 lines back to the bayou, which was the boundary separating Lavergne's property from that of Blaise. Lavergne's concession included all land within the triangle except Fuerte de San Juan del Bayu—the site of the fort, which fronted on the bayou for one hundred and twenty feet and had a depth of from seventy to eighty feet.

Jean Lavergne was twice married, having had two children—Nicholas and Barthelmy—by his first wife Jeanne LaClef; in 1765 he had married Louise Roquigny, by whom he had three children.[23] A simple man, whose main interest was to provide for a sizable family, it is doubtful he ever dreamed that this concession would set in motion a series of events resulting in lawsuits covering a period of more than a hundred years—a situation that wouldn't be resolved until the 1930s when the Orleans Levee Board would purchase and develop the present residential area of Lake Vista on Lake Pontchartrain. And that wouldn't be the end of it. In 1978 Levee Board ownership of the land would again be challenged.

In November, 1771, the largest plantation on the east bank of Bayu San Juan—some of the first land settled in this region by Antoine Rivard de LaVigne and others—again changed hands. This time Jean René Huchet de Kernion (son of deceased Huchet de Kernion, second husband of Widow Rivard, Jr.) who had lived on the bayou since 1739, sold the plantation to Santiago Lorreins, called Tarascon, brother of bayou residents Charles Lorreins (Tarascon) and Mrs. Juan Bautista Brazillier (Pelagia Lorrreins). In September the twenty two arpent front Kernion holdings had been surveyed and mapped by Luis Andry; and on November 15, 1771 the transaction was recorded. Three days later Kernion bestowed upon Leonardo Mazange his special power of attorney, and a month later sold Lorreins a slave.[24]

From the very beginning the pleasures of life weren't neglected on Bayu San Juan. The 1771 map of Kernion's property refers to Brazillier's Grog Shop, indicating that the versatile Juan Bautista dispensed intoxicating liquors from his home, conveniently located for the sailing element.

On the west bank of the bayou, across from the original Langlois plantation (owned by Widow Duplanty) on the rear of the DesRuisseaux arpents on the bayou, was located "a public house where people go to drink and dance."

While arpents were changing hands and grants were being conceded on Bayu San Juan, British Engineer Thomas Hutchins was eyeing the stream for an entirely different reason. Anxious about deteriorating relations between his country and Spain, which could lead to preclusion of British shipping rights on the Mississippi, British General Thomas Gage considered his country's alternatives: (1) seizing New Orleans, or (2) developing the alternative Manchac route through the lakes to the Gulf. To help him decide what to do, Gage dispatched Hutchins from Fort Chartres down the Mississippi to inspect all Spanish settlements, details of their fortifications (particularly those of New Orleans), and how they might be breached. Ordered to commit his instructions to memory and destroy his notes, Hutchins carried out his mission in late 1771 and early 1772 and reported to his superior that communication with British West Florida was very easy via Bayu San Juan, which was navigable for vessels drawing about four feet of water for a distance of six miles up from Lake

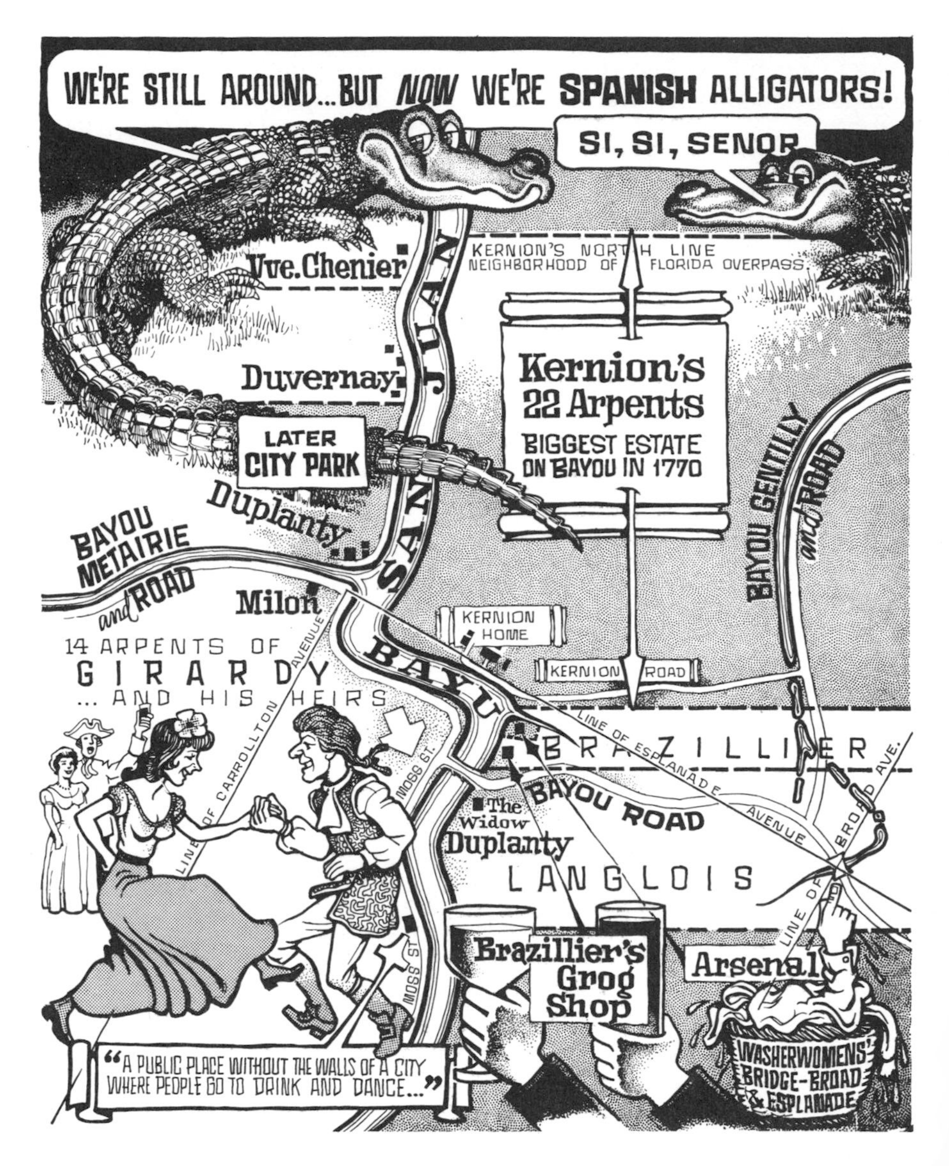

In 1771 Kernion sold his plantation to Santiago Lorreins (Tarascon); and Magdalena Brazillier (Widow Duplanty) owned and lived on the old Langlois Plantation she'd inherited from her father about 1763. Maurice Milon, Guardian of the DesRuisseaux estate, was living in the old Girardy home cityside of Bayou Metairie.

Pontchartrain to a landing place at which vessels loaded and unloaded (Port of Bayu San Juan). From this landing, he went on to say, it was two miles to the town. The entrance of the bayou at the lake, he reported, was defended by a battery of five or six cannon, and there were plantations along the stream as well as the road leading to town (Bayou Road). However, he didn't recommend a British approach to New Orleans via the lakes, Manchac or Bayu San Juan, nor did he advise an attack through the mouth of the Mississippi River.

The surest line of attack, he suggested, would be down the Ohio and Mississippi Rivers. However, he was even more enthusiastic about another route—into Lake Borgne, and up Bayou Mazant, from which point the way to New Orleans was clear. Nothing, he predicted, could prevent a British victory except an all-out defeat in the field. Sensitive to more than fortifications in 1771, Hutchins picked up the anti-Spanish vibes of New Orleans. O'Reilly's massacre still sorely rubbed the sentiments of families and friends of the "martyred."[25]

Some of the older French residents of Bayu San Juan had died. Among them was Francisco Caüe (Keeper of the King's Store in French times, and husband of Francoise de Villemont, stepdaughter of original bayou settler Antoine Rivard de LaVigne) who had involved himself with the LaVigne family and other bayou doings for the greater part of his life. After his death, Juan René Kernion was appointed tutor of the Caüe children, in which capacity he rented out the estate slaves and other property to the interest of the minors.

In 1771 a Mr. Hinard took over the lease on the entire Caüe estate, and rented mulatto Francisco, who had been Caüe's hunter, to another bayou resident, Carlos Lorreins (Tarascon), who in addition to his many local activities also traded to Pointe Coupée and Rapides.

In 1772 Gabriel Peyroux married one of the Caüe daughters; and Hinard—probably as a wedding present—gave the newlyweds the lease on Francisco. But since Tarascon was making his payments regularly and was satisfied with the Mulatto's services, the Peyrouxs decided not to change the working status of their new property, so Francisco continued to work for Tarascon.[26]

The Chalon-DesRuisseaux indigo project wasn't working out. From the time they'd purchased the de Mazelliere plantation in 1769 nothing had gone right. In the presence of her son Jacques Milon and neighbor Jacques Maigros, who then lived in the Naval Arsenal across the bayou, Widow DesRuisseaux was dunned at her Bayu San Juan plantation on January 29, 1770 for 5,078 livres they owed, on which occasion she asked for an additional five, six months to meet her bills. The situation hadn't changed on May 11, 1770 when creditor de Mazelliere registered an official complaint of non-payment; but on November 3rd he informed the court that he and Widow DesRuisseaux had come to an understanding about the unpaid note. But apparently nothing had really changed, because Chalon—in charge of the plantation—was cited three times in early 1771, and when Deputy Sheriff Santiago Hallays confronted him on October 9th, Chalon refused to produce collateral to satisfy what he owed, so the Sheriff seized 785 pounds of indigo and placed it in the hands of the receiver.

By early 1772, Chalon and his mother-in-law had no doubt had it with the venture, for on February 25th Widow DesRuisseaux petitioned the court for return of the original bill of sale. De Mazelliere had obviously had enough, too, because the bill of sale was returned, and Chalon forked over forty six pesos in court costs.[27]

A little closer to town, the DeMorands of Bayou Road were having their problems too; and the interminable legalese that had postponed settlement of their estate for two years didn't help. In most Spanish provinces legal documents were recorded on expensive, stamped paper, taxed by the sheet, but in Luisiana legal instruments were written on ordinary paper. Lusiana's poorness may explain this exemption, which resulted in the undue length of official records, for which the Historian is grateful because of the voluminous detail exposed; but for those who had to live through the litigation, the experience must have been extremely frustrating.

When Marie Rene de Lachaise, Charles DeMorand's second wife, had died in 1760, their four children had been consigned to the care of her second husband Alexandro Latil of Bayou Road. DeMorand's daughter Maria Felicidad had married in 1763, and in late 1767 her husband Joseph Dauterive de Valiere had become curator to his wife's three minor brothers—Carlos, Vincent and Luis Docmeny DeMorand. However, on August 30, 1770—apparently unable to handle the responsibility—de Valiere asked that another curator be appointed to receive his accounts. (The administration record he presented to the court disclosed an interesting item of expense denoting that Luis Docmeny had attended school for two months in 1768 and five months in 1769 at a cost of only ten livres per month.)

Carlos DeMorand, the eldest boy, was emancipated on October 17, 1771 after Captain of the Battalion of Luisiana Francisco Dusseau de la Croix Mazelliere, Guido Dufossat and Luis Dessale testified that although he was only twenty two years old, young DeMorand was able to handle his own affairs. A curator ad lites, representing the two younger boys, and a bondsman to guarantee the curator's performance were appointed and approved by the court. Having examined the records, the curator informed the court that de Valiere owed the DeMorand boys 9,216 livres, 126 sols and 6 deniers, but since he was their brother-in-law and insolvent, no recourse was available against him. The curator did request, however, that de Valiere relinquish the lease he held on the Chapitoulas plantation which belonged to the estate, and that he be replaced as administrator.

De Valiere responded by delivering the Chapitoulas property and requesting division of the estate; and on January 27, 1773 Alexandro Latil (already acting as appraiser in the case) was asked to be curator for the two younger DeMorands as the one previously appointed was not in town. At Latil's request, and in the presence of the various heirs, curators, appraisers, attorneys and Assessor General Odoardo of the Cabildo (in charge of the succession) an inventory of the DeMorand estate, consisting of land, houses, livestock, farm implements, carts, slaves, carpenters' tools and iron, was accomplished.

The principal properties were: (1) an eight arpent by forty deep plantation at the Chapitoulas, (2) a plantation on the west side of Bayou Road,* and (3) a house and lot at St. Philip and Dauphine. After thirty one of the negro slaves were adjudicated to de Valiere at inventory price, and nine to Carlos DeMorand, the property to be sold was called out by Public Crier Nicolas Jurdin (Jourdan) on three separate occasions, nine days apart, and Governor Unzaga set the auction for April 4, 1772.

Carlos DeMorand bought the Bayou Road plantation with improvements, livestock and furnishings for 2,370 pesos—payable in three years—agreeing to give his minor brother Luis Docmeny five percent of his share. The Chapitoulas plantation was sold to Antonio Barnabe for 160 pesos cash. There were no takers for the St. Philip Street house, because it had deteriorated from standing empty for so long; so after a third unsuccessful attempt to sell it, Unzaga ruled on June 1, 1772 that the estate be divided into four equal parts and distributed to the heirs. By September 25, 1772, after more than fifty consultations between the DeMorands, the legal luminaries and the Governor, the DeMorand estate had been distributed; and one may rest assured that everyone received precisely what was coming to him. Indeed, a postscript revealed that they received a little lagniappe, for on October 19, 1772 careful Alexandro Latil delivered to the court a note payable to the DeMorand heirs in the amount of 1,155 livres—an asset that hadn't been included in the estate. It helped pay the court costs of 265 pesos, which 'though a modest sum today, at that time amounted to almost twice what the Chapitoulas plantation had sold for.[28]

*The plantation on the east side of Bayou Road, granted Carlos DeMorand shortly before his death, had been sold to Claudio Treme.

A criminal prosecution of July 23, 1772, involving several bayou residents, charged Vincent Rillieux, of Pearl River in English territory, with attempted murder. Visiting his sister Mrs. Marianna Rillieux Clermont, Rillieux was accused of entering the home of Mrs. Joseph Maison and attacking her as she lay abed. Marianna Peche, who was occupying the same bed, testified she'd heard a noise that frightened her, but Mrs. Maison had assured her that the little negro girl sleeping in the room with them had no doubt stirred. Then Miss Peche's feet were seized, and Mrs. Maison screamed that someone had grabbed her about the neck and struck her in the stomach with his knees. It was too dark to see the aggressor who quickly made his exit along with the little girl who was thought to be an accomplice, but who was caught in the courtyard by Carlos Tarascon after the women screamed for help.

Evidence to establish a motive was pursued by the opposition whose witnesses testified that Rillieux's brother-in-law had some time before prosecuted an unsuccessful case against Joseph Maison; and past history was rehashed to establish Rillieux as a dangerous character. Maison maintained Rillieux had killed his own brother back in 1759, but that accusation was quickly put to rest with a certified copy of the proces verbal which had cleared Vincent of the accidental killing.

Then Maison testified that Rillieux had also threatened his Uncle Alexandro Chenet of the German Coast with a gun, which was quickly denied by Rillieux's faithful relative. However, the situation looked bad for the defendant who was imprisoned for a short time while his attorney Leonardo Mazange appealed the case, at which trial Juan Bautista Brazillier, Charles Tarascon and others appeared as witnesses. Establishing a complete alibi, Vincent Rillieux was finally acquitted on October 4, 1772 at a cost of 29 pesos, 5 reales—not to mention attorneys' fees.

Interesting evidence alluded to by Rillieux, but not allowed in the record because it had no bearing on the litigation, was the choice morsel that Maison was not married to his wife, but had stolen her—as well as other possessions—from a soldier in Canada. You may be sure this was one case that wouldn't be forgotten for a long time, nor would colorful Vincent Rillieux, who was to figure in many a future facet of bayou history.[29]

Gilberto St. Maxent's service to the Spanish was really paying off. On October 9, 1772 he received two grants of land. One was a trapezium-shaped acreage of 121¾ superficial arpents on the east bank of Bayu San Juan. Today this narrow property would extend approximately from the north end of Wisner Overpass down to the middle of the eastern bank of

Park Island. The other concession was a six arpent frontage on the Gentilly High Road, with a depth of twenty arpents. The Bermudez and Darcantel tracts on the Charles Zimpel map of 1834 are the properties conceded to St. Maxent in 1772.[30]

St. Maxent no doubt acquired his west bank plantation about the same time, for a year later he was in possession of an eight arpent frontage north of Duvernay's land (the DesRuisseaux six arpent grant of 1750), and south of Carlos Tarascon's concession of 1766. St. Maxent's west bank plantation approximated the Alpuente and some of the DeMorant west bank bayou properties of American times—land north of today's Taylor Avenue.

Not to be outdone by the puny efforts of mortal man, nature visited a horrible hurricane on New Orleans in 1772—the same year Spain made its first attempt to establish a public school in Luisiana. Don Andres Lopez de Armesto and three other dons were sent by King Charles III to teach elementary education, Latin, grammar, syntax, Spanish language, religion and obedience to the King. Up to that time about the only education available was that provided by tutors—often harsh and unsatisfactory—who lived in at outlying plantations. For those who couldn't afford tutors, there was the apprenticeship system, where trades ranging from locksmith and blacksmith to barber and frizzler could be learned under supervision. This type of schooling was not looked down upon, but the records reveal that contracts were often cancelled because the youngsters failed to learn.

Even some of the slaves profited from apprenticeships. On December 28, 1770 Juana—negress slave of Don Andres Jung—contracted with shoemaker Nicolas Lauve, who for fifty pesos promised to teach his trade to Juana's minor mulatto son. Juana agreed to feed and clothe her child, and to nurse him when he was sick.[31]

Chapter XIX

SLAVERY, VOUDOU AND THE THREAT OF BRITISH INVASION 1773-1777

1773 saw a shift in religious authority when Luisiana became a part of the diocese of Cuba, instead of Quebec, as it had been during French rule. And the cypress swamps of Bayu San Juan, as well as other undeveloped parts of this area, became hideouts for run-away slaves. In an effort to ease the situation, Unzaga offered pardon, with no punishment, to any slave who returned to his master of his own free will.

Slaves weren't the only ones running away. Jean Roubier, a French soldier serving under the Spanish, had deserted, and on April 29, 1773 he was found on a small English merchant vessel in Bayu del San Juan near the fort at Lake Pontchartrain, guarded by a sergeant, a corporal and ten men of Roubier's battalion. His capture was hindered by the paymaster, who objected to the breaking into of his vessel by arresting officers. Justice moved even slower. Three years later, Roubier was sent by schooner to serve seven years in the fixed regiment of Puerto Rico for his crime.[1]

With hunter-traders operating all over the province, it was sometimes impossible to get a debtor to stand still long enough to pay his bills. Bayu San Juan planatation owner Gilberto St. Maxent had become involved back in 1766 when one of his pirogues had been fitted out under the supervision of Alexander Clouet and rented to Antonio Lepine of St. Genevieve who promised to return the pirogue after he was through with it. When Lepine didn't bring the boat back, St. Maxent sued Lepine to get his money back. But Lepine was an elusive debtor. Whenever Clouet thought he had him pinned down, the hunter was somewhere else. After years of sleuthing, Clouet, in March of 1773, discovered that Lepine had a pirogue loaded with game coming to New Orleans under another name to avoid paying his bills, but his wily creditor petitioned the Cabildo to retain the goods Lepine was to receive in exchange for his game and turn it all over to him to cover the old debt.

Governor Unzaga's court ruled that the pirogue be detained until justice could be effected. However, by then Lepine was way off in Arkansas, whereupon Clouet asked that court proceedings be transferred to the commander of that post, authorizing him to seize Lepine's property to cover what he owed. Governor Unzaga complied, specifying that if justice didn't prevail in Arkansas, the case was to be returned to the Cabildo for continuing action.[2]

The same spring another boat deal brought bayou plantation owner Andres Jung into court to defend his reputation. Having repaired a sloop to the tune of 237 pesos for one Diego de Alba, he asked the court to allow him to hold the boat as collateral until the debt was paid. Then an alert principal accountant of the army—to whom the matter had been referred—advised Unzaga's court that de Alba had a bad reputation and Jung was probably colluding with his debtor to acquire the sloop "by means of their own debts." Jung protested that he was an honest man, that an accusation of this kind didn't do him any good, and requested that the court summon de Alba to swear that the debt was a just one. Doubts may have simmered for a while, but Jung's action closed the case on May 8, 1773.[3]

A trial that was not so cut and dried opened a month later. Although the African earth religion Vodun (Voudon, Voudou) —with West Indian variations — had existed in Luisiana since the first slaves arrived in the early 1700s, 1773 marks the first mention of it in colonial records. This primitive religion wouldn't pose a major problem for citizens of New Orleans until blacks arrived from the West Indies in great numbers and congregated in New Orleans during the first decade of the 1800's. However, this case reveals that as early as 1773 "gri-gri"—meaning to put an evil spell on a person or enterprise through charms, incantations, etc.—was a familiar term. In his limited Mandingo language, thirty year old Carlos, native of Guinea, who was accused of making the magic concoction, associated it with a charm for working one's will on another, and official records labeled this strange litigation "The Gri-Gri Case."

Other religions came into play during the trial. The ordinary testifying Catholic layman took the oath on the cross; the man of the cloth on his word as a priest; a gentlemen, knight or military officer pledged to tell the truth by kissing the cross on the hilt of his sword or "I affirm on my word of honor." Protestant witnesses swore on the Bible (King James or Calvinist?), and it isn't stated whether the Bible was in the courtroom or if the Protestants had to bring their own.

The criminal prosecution opened in Unzaga's court on June 12, 1773 when Captain Don Francisco Bellile, Commander and resident of the German Coast, arrived with three of his own slaves and one from a neighboring plantation, all of whom he had charged with conspiracy to poison his overseer Augustin. Preliminary investigation having been conducted on the plantation, Unzaga ordered the imprisonment of the

Negroes and examination of the gri-gri by Doctors Francisco Labeau and Juan Ruby. French, Spanish and African interpreters were appointed by the court, and deposition of witnesses began immediately, from which point the story evolves.

It had all begun the previous autumn when bullying first-overseer Augustin had beaten up second-overseer Francisco, a Creole Negro of Illinois; and although Captain Bellile had reprimanded Augustin, Francisco continued to seethe underneath and finally approached Cipion— a Negro from Guinea—and asked him to look into ways of doing away with Augustin and Master Bellile. Cipion replied he didn't know how to make a gri-gri—that only the "lately imported Negroes knew these arts," so the two of them summoned Carlos, recently arrived from Africa, to assist them in their cause. Carlos didn't take to the idea, protesting that he was content with his lot, whereupon the plotters tried to bribe him with pants and shirts, which the young slave turned down. But Francisco finally made a dent in Carlos' resistance when he offered to get him some alligator meat. Finding a dead one floating in the river, they cut it up and divided it, whereupon Francisco casually remarked that the heart could be used to kill the overseer who had treated him so badly. Immediately, Carlos refused to eat any of the beast, fearing it might harm him. Despite his reluctance, the simple slave was finally inveigled (probably by threats that his master would be informed of Carlos' dark abilities) into making the gri-gri.

The preparation took several months, as Carlos informed the collaborators that the charm wouldn't work until warm weather arrived. The gri-gri, made of alligator heart and gall, mixed with vegetable herbs, was carefully assembled and placed in the henhouse to develop the necessary power. After a time, another slave, doing chicken chores, was attracted to the stench, discovered the missile and reported the matter to his master. Under questioning Carlos admitted that at the urging of Francisco he'd made the gri-gri in order to kill Augustin and Master Bellile so Francisco could be overseer, but he said the charm wasn't ready yet— that when it dried up, it could be made into powder, which put into water would kill anyone who drank it.

As news of the discovery spread, tension mounted, and the gri-gri was blamed for other plantation happenings. Within the past several months twenty of Bellile's twenty one dogs had died; and overseer Augustin had been languishing for eight weeks.

Having heard none of the testimony, the doctors who had been assigned to investigate the gri-gri were called before the court to report their findings on the half-rod-long rotten mass, crawling with worms, the center of which resembled blood red dough and contained a little stick to stir it. Having examined the animal-vegetable concoction, they hadn't been able to decide if it was poisonous, so they had given sizable segments of it, mixed with good meat, to a dog on two different occasions; after several days they now reported to the court that the health of the animal hadn't suffered in the least from his unusual diet, and opined that the gri-gri, though nauseating, hadn't as yet arrived at the point of being poisonous, and therefore would not harm a human being.

The trial also put to rest the other gri-gri related fears. Bellile's dogs had been killed by a Negro who subsequently had been deported to Santo Domingo; and Augustin's prolonged illness was reliably proved to be due to other causes. Since no poison had been established, the case against three of the accused was probably dropped. But in early 1774 Attorney Francisco Broutin presented to the court a burial certificate stating that his client Carlos, who had been detained in prison, had died on November 28, 1773.

It isn't surprising that this child of the open air of Africa and the plantation had been killed by confinement and his fear of the unknown. Unable to speak anything but Mandingo, this ignorant soul was no doubt completely befogged about the entire proceeding, even though Bayu San Juan plantation owner Desprez's slave Thomas—who spoke Mandingo—interpreted everything that went on during the trial. The involved Blacks on the Bellile plantation, who had received at least the rudiments of Luisiana culture, might have helped Carlos adapt to his new environment. Instead, this gentle, obedient, seemingly content victim was used by them as a tool to their own ends. Undoubtedly baptized when he received his name, the death certificate indicated that he'd been administered the sacrament of penance, but no mention is made of the Eucharist (he was no doubt considered too slow mentally), nor did he receive the sacrament of extreme unction, for which those in charge probably felt he had no need.

Voudou cures may elicit a shudder, but when one considers that roasted toad powder, oil of turkey buzzards and hair from a virgin's head were potions regularly dispensed by physicians for the cure of America's ailing colonial forefathers, the Voudou methods weren't that far-fetched for the time.[4]

Conditions of colonial slavery are revealed in other court cases of the period. It was customary for some masters to allow their slaves to work at other plantations on feast days and on Sundays (except during divine services), cutting moss, gathering crops or performing other duties, in order to make a little extra income for themselves. No questions were asked as long as the slave showed up at his master's plantation for work on Monday morning. Other owners objected to the practice, insisting that it instigated robbery, deprived the master of his slave's services in an emergency, gave Negroes the notion they could work where they pleased to supply their wives and children with extras; and they charged that only those who didn't properly clothe and take care of their slaves allowed them to work away.

Cornbread was a favorite of the Blacks, and masters were obligated to give each slave a barrel of corn per year and a patch of ground on which to grow whatever he wanted. The slave was also allowed a plot of thirty, forty yards on which to raise chickens and hogs, the profits of which would buy him a woolen coat, a pair of long breeches, two, three shirts and enough bear grease for cooking. Winter working hours of slaves (who reporter Bouligny observed were as happy as European laborers) were from 7:00 or 8:00 A.M. 'til 12:00 and from 2:00 P.M. 'til dusk. In the summer the workday stretched from sunrise to 11:00 A.M. and from 3:00 P.M. until dark.[5]

In addition to local pursuits, many bayou residents engaged in trade away from New Orleans. Carlos Lorreins (Tarascon) not only had business partners in Pointe Coupée and Rapides Parish, he also spent a lot of time across the lake in English territory. Being away so much, his New Orleans affairs sometimes suffered.

On December 18, 1773 he was being sued by Francisco DesMazelliere, Captain of the Battalion of Luisiana. Tarascon, as curator ad bono to the Barré minors (grandchildren of his deceased mother-in-law), had leased DesMazelliere a plantation and mill which were supposed to be in good condition. However, the transaction had taken place in January when the waters were high, so it was impossible to ascertain the condition of the equipment; when the waters receded, it became apparent that the wooden foundation, galleries and body-work were rotten and wouldn't function. In response to the complaint Mrs. Lorreins asked DesMazelliere to do nothing until her husband returned from English territory; but the distraught lessee protested that something had to be done quickly, as the Mississippi was again on the rise, and unless repairs were made immediately he'd lose his entire crop. In desperation he appointed two experts to confirm his charges and petitioned the court to require Tarascon or his attorney to do the same. Demanding immediate repairs, DesMazelliere agreed to pay for them and charge the cost against the rental he paid for the property—the repairs to be appraised by experts for later settlement of the matter. The court ordered a search into Tarascon's whereabouts, and a few days later he was back in town. On January 19, 1774 he asked that the case be dropped as he and DesMazelliere had come to an agreement.[6]

That same summer Carlos Tarascon decided to sell the bayou plantation he'd been conceded by Aubry in 1766 when that French official was keeping things together until the Spanish could take over. On July 3, 1773 he sold Don Andres Jung the eight-arpent plantation fronting the west bank of Bayu San Juan—property that today would begin at a point across from the middle of Park Island, extend southerly for 1,536 feet and stretch westerly to the vicinity of Milne Boulevard. The official act, notarized by Don Almonester, noted that the plantation was bordered by the habitation of Don Antonio St. Maxent on one side, on the lakeside by the property of C. Bartholome, and was sold for sixty pesos.

Jung didn't hold the land for long. Eight months later he sold it to Mariana, free woman of color, which probably marks the first time that Bayu San Juan property of any extent was owned by Blacks. This situation no doubt came about because of Jung's relations with his slaves; three illegitimate childen of these liaisons were raised in Jung's home.

Although concubinage was illegal, Andres Jung—an independent, rich, politically influential man—evidently wrote his own rules, ignoring public opinion and got away with it because of unquestioning acceptance of different rights for the powerful.

Jung sold the plantation to Mariana for the same price he'd paid for it, and the place was described as in the previous Act of Sale, except that a house was included in the transaction. Notarized by Almonester on March 8, 1774, Jung maintained timber rights, specifying that he, as well as the purchaser, could cut cypress on the land at will.

This property—referred to in legal records as the Tarascon Grant—would be owned in entirety by free people of color until 1788, when the plantation began to be sold off piecemeal. The last two arpents of the original grant were owned by Blacks until 1829 when Alexander Milne, millionaire land owner on the bayou, purchased this last lot, reuniting in his portfolio the eight arpents of the Tarascon grant of 1766.

A few months after selling his land Andres Jung petitioned for a license to construct a schooner at the dockyard of Bayu San Juan, near 1300 Moss Street today. Jung requested that the boat, when completed, be registered with the Escribano of Registries and that a certified copy be delivered to him. It didn't take too long once Unzaga approved the license; on April 1, 1775 Escribano Andres Almonester registered *The Luisa*, a schooner of 42′ keel, 16′ breadth of beam, French measure, fifty ton, as free of all mortgages, and a certified copy was given Jung on April 25, 1775 to serve him as title of ownership.[7]

East bank bayou property was changing hands too. On December 27, 1773 Jean Tuon, who'd been granted ten arpents front by the French government on July 21, 1766, sold the plantation to Maurice Milon (son of Maria Francisca Girardy DesRuisseaux, by her first husband Joseph Milon). This property would today extend approximately from Mirabeau Avenue to Fillmore Avenue on the bayou and reach easterly to the vicinity of Paris Avenue.

The busiest people on Bayu San Juan in the 1770's were Magdalena Brazillier and her husband Henriques Desprez. In addition to buying and selling land and property, Desprez was up to his eyeballs in curator problems. On November 12, 1773 he renounced his position as curator ad lites to Francisco and Juana, minor children of Juan Bautista LeBreton, who'd been murdered in 1771, on the grounds that he couldn't devote enough time to their interests. And as curator to Santiago Roman, the attorney was being pressed on February 21, 1774 for 1,823 pesos, representing the minor's share of his maternal-paternal estate, plus a salary of a hundred pesos he claimed Desprez owed him. After several delays Desprez confirmed the inheritance, but said the salary should be sixty pesos, whereupon Roman petitioned that four of Desprez's slaves be seized and placed with the General Receiver to cover the debt; but when Deputy Sheriff Nicolas Fromentin went to the Desprez plantation on Bayu San Juan, the attorney refused to produce the Blacks, instructing the sheriff to "fulfill his duties and go look for the slaves in the mountains." After an extended search, the Sheriff acknowledged defeat; but in April the parties at conflict requested discontinuation of the suit, as the affair had been settled.

While her husband was straightening out his affairs, Magdalena Brazillier Desprez was busy selling. In 1773 she disposed of three houses—one to Francisco Bouligny, the Spanish officer who in 1769 had come to New Orleans to announce O'Reilly's arrival at Balize, and who in 1770 had married Marie Louise Dauberville.

Mrs. Desprez sold a schooner, livestock, wrought silver; and on April 25, 1774 she sold the eight-arpent-frontage on the west bank of Bayu San Juan, which her deceased husband had purchased from Carlos Lorreins (Tarascon). The new buyer was a brother of Carlos Tarascon—Magdalena Brazillier Desprez's neighbor, Santiago Lorreins (Tarascon).

Lorreins, who paid 1,300 pesos (the Duplanty inventory evaluation) for the west bank property, purchased the plantation so his daughter Francisca and her husband Juan Luis Allard would live and raise their children right across the bayou from him.

Mrs. Desprez was also collecting notes owed the estate, including six hundred pesos from Jose Chalon, all of which was too much for the four other young Duplanty heirs (nieces and nephews) who saw their inheritance of 3,321 pesos each slipping away transaction by transaction. In 1774 they sued, charging that ever since her marriage to Desprez, Magdalena Brazillier had been dissipating their property—that several executory suits had attacked the estate, that thirteen slaves had died and ten had run away. Of the original estate, valued at 26,606 pesos, property worth 20,104 pesos had been wasted or disposed of; and attorney Leonardo Mazange, representing some of the heirs, requested that Magdalena Brazillier either give bond for what was due them or turn their inheritance over to them immediately.

Mrs. Desprez refused to comply, stating that her marriage contract with Duplanty, her deceased husband, had stipulated that the survivor could enjoy the entire estate in full ownership without giving bond to anyone.

Francisco Broutin, curator ad lites to Maria Juana Héry (a niece of Duplanty and no doubt a relative of deceased Maria Juana Héry, Widow Girardy) petitioned that the court disallow further execution of notarial acts for the sale of Duplanty houses, lands or slaves, and alleged that "though Mrs. Desprez had use of the property as long as she lived," her second marriage had changed her status, requiring her to give bond in order that her first husband's heirs wouldn't suffer injustice. Broutin pointed out that she had no right to dispose of the estate when she only had the use of it; and considering that she'd sold or wasted more than half of it in three years, and that many who owed the estate money were insolvent, he asked the court's permission to unite with Attorney Mazange, representing the other heirs, to save court costs, and requested that all of the heirs be given bond if their inheritance was not immediately paid in full. Alcade Forstall ordered Desprez to give bond within three days.

Knowledgable in the law, Henriques Desprez contested giving bond, but agreed to give juratory security, claiming that money received from the sale of Duplanty property had been used to buy other—more valuable—properties, such as fields and a mill to make boxes for sugar.

Broutin refused juratory security, since Magdalena Brazillier Desprez had disposed of so much, and the new purchases changed the estate valuations outlined in the inventory-appraisement at the time of Duplanty's death. Broutin wanted nothing for his minors except hard cash, and pressed for another inventory, pointing out that Mrs.Desprez, not the minors, must stand the loss of the dead and run-away slaves. However, Henriques Desprez won that battle. Alcade Forstall ordered him to give juratory security, which Broutin and Mazange accepted on August 31, 1774.

On top of other claims, on July 2, 1774 Negro Juan Bautista (no doubt the favorite slave of Mrs. Desprez's brother) presented a bill to the Duplanty estate for work done back in 1766-7, explaining he hadn't asked to be paid before because he'd been sick and out of town. Since the slip of paper didn't have Duplanty's signature of acknowledgment, it is questionable that Juan Bautista collected anything.

The court case didn't deter Mrs. Desprez. On October 15, 1774 she sold the eight-arpent-front plantation she'd inherited from her father to bayou neighbors Maria Isabel DesRuisseaux and her husband Jose Chalon. All the buildings on the plantation (which was located to the immediate west of Bayou Road and extended to the forks of the bayou—between Orleans and Lafitte Streets today) were included in the sale, except the mill, fence, building material and lumber lying on the bayou bank, which she promised to move at a convenient time.

This was a big day for the Chalons, who also purchased from Magdalena Desprez the de Mouléon grant which fanned out in a modified triangle west-southwesterly from the rear of the west bank DesRuisseaux plantation, back toward Canal Street of the future. From October 15, 1774 to the time of Maria Isabel DesRuisseaux Chalon Roquigny's death (about 1815) the de Mouléon grant would be an integral part of her plantation on the west bank of Bayu San Juan.

With the fourteen arpent DesRuisseaux plantation she and her mother owned on the bayou's west bank, the de Mouléon grant and the eight-arpent (Langlois) plantation across the bayou, Maria Isabel Chalon in 1774 was giving Santiago Lorreins (Tarascon), with his twenty-two arpent front plantation on the bayou's east bank, and the eight arpent west bank plantation he'd purchased for his daughter and her family, good competition for the title of largest property owner on Bayu San Juan.

The younger Duplanty heirs were destined to wait for their inheritance. Four years later Francisco Blache, husband of Luisa Héry (Duplanty), would ask the court for a copy of Desprez's juratory security, as well as certified copies of the acts of sale covering Duplanty property sold by Mrs. Desprez. He would also request that witnesses be called to testify to the eight thousand pesos worth of his wife's property Desprez had lost in the last four months (in 1778). But the attorney managed to get things his way again, maintaining that as a Captain he was not required to answer the suit Blache had filed in the court of Alcalde Guido Dufossat —that he could be sued only in the court of the Governor General. The record of 1778 ends with Blache's agreement to carry his case to the other tribunal.[8]

Madame de Mouléon, whose 1758 grant had been purchased by the Chalons, invested in large holdings on the east bank of Bayu San Juan. Jacques de LaChaise, owner of the old DuBreuil plantation immediately below New Orleans, that stretched from the banks of the Mississippi back to Gentilly and Bayu San Juan, had died in 1768, and in 1774 Madame de Mouléon became the new owner.[9]

Alexandro Latil of Bayou Road was also expanding his portfolio. On November 1, 1774 Governor Unzaga granted him and Maurice Conway a huge tract of land upriver from New Orleans. The land had in French times been granted to one Brompere, but was sold by the French colonial government because of crimes Brompere committed. The land was then purchased by Titon, who eventually abandoned it. After being vacant for a time, the French Governor permitted Calazava, lawful chief of the Bayougoula and Houma Indians, to take possession of it for the use of the Indian tribes. They occupied the plot until October 5, 1774 when Calazava moved the Indians under his command to the other side of the Mississippi and relinquished the land to Latil and Conway for $150.00. Approved by Unzaga on November 1st, his patent to them described the land as a tract measuring upwards of half a league in front with the common depth of forty arpents.

Latil sold his moiety in the tract to Conway on January 4, 1776, and on September 9th of the same year Conway petitioned Governor Galvez for extra land in the rear of the original forty arpents, which patent was granted to Conway by Governor Galvez on July 21, 1777. These grants covered a valuable plot of land which came to be known as *The Houmas*. The rear building of *Houmas House*, on River Road, near Burnside, Louisiana, was built by Latil and Conway in 1780, and is still in existence.[10]

Jean Lavergne, who in 1771 had received a concession covering a triangle of land contiguous to the fort at the mouth of the bayou, died on December 1, 1774, and partition of his estate was made on February 18,

1775 in St. Jean Baptiste des Allemands, where land, Negroes, livestock and improvements were divided 'mongst Lavergne's two sons by his first marriage and the minor offspring of his widow Luisa Roquigny. Partition took place before Robert Robin de Logny, Captain-Judge of the Parish; and the widow's sister Charlotte (Mrs. Baptiste Seza) stood bond for her.

In September of the following year the bondsman for the Lavergne heirs petitioned the court to prohibit Widow Lavergne from selling a Negro; the widow proved that the slave was her own property, but offered the house she was living in as security for what she still owed the first and second set of Lavergne heirs. The court accepted the mortgage as security and allowed her to sell the slave.

Nowhere in these records is there mention of Lavergne's small Bayu San Juan plantation at Lake Pontchartrain. Apparently he had gone to the German Coast soon after receiving the grant in 1771; and his family had either forgotten the small acreage, considered it too inconsequential to be included in the inventory, or possibly believed the deceased Lavergne had disposed of the land. Being thus left in limbo may account for the difficulty the Lavergne heirs were to encounter some sixty years later when in 1837 they would finally claim the long neglected arpents at the mouth of the bayou.

It is also noteworthy that no family meeting was called at this time to consider the best interests of the Lavergne minors. The family meeting, which had played such an important role during French rule, was eliminated from Spanish proceedings, the Cabildo authorizing the curator of any minor to handle any and all problems according to his best judgment.[11]

Juan Bautista Brazillier was dead. Son of deceased Luis Brazillier and Juana Feran (Jeanne Tremant), he had lived for the most of his life on the small Bayu San Juan plantation to the immediate east of Bayou Road, which he'd inherited from his father. In his will dated April 18, 1775, Juan Bautista stated that he and Pelagia Lorreins (Tarascon), sister of Charles and Santiago Lorreins, who also lived on Bayu San Juan, had been married for over twenty six years, and that they had no children. Juan Bautista's only close relative was his sister Magdalena Brazillier Desprez, who until the year before had owned the old Langlois plantation directly across Bayou Road from his land. Naming his wife his sole and universal heir—since they had secured the property together—he specified that his brother-in-law Santiago Lorreins, who lived to the immediate lakeside of his plantation, be testamentary executor of his estate.

Santiago Lorreins could on occasion be a tough creditor, which no doubt accounted for the considerable estate he'd accrued. On April 25,

1775 he claimed that Philip Jacquelin Durey owed him 3,207 pesos, 5 reales on a note and petitioned the Cabildo to verify this and prevent the debtor from leaving the city until the amount was paid. His request was granted.

Durey responded that he'd already paid half the debt, agreed to pay half of the remainder immediately, and guaranteed payment of the balance with Santiago Beauregard's bond. Under these circumstances he asked the court to revoke its former decree.

Lorreins wasn't convinced, insisting that the court seize all of Durey's property, particularly the deerskins Lorreins had sold him, which were now in Luis Ranson's boat—enough to cover the debt plus court costs.

The court didn't go along with Lorreins' request, since Durey had given bond for the balance of his debt.

Another wealthy landowner was having difficulty collecting what was due him. A lot of levee work was being done in 1775 for which Andres Jung had the contract, and on March 3rd he petitioned the government for five hundred pesos covering a job he'd finished. On October 7th he requested an advance of three hundred pesos for similar work, but like most government contractors he had to wait for his money. On December 1st he was petitioning again—this time for four hundred pesos—but received only three hundred.[12]

Francisco, the mulatto hunter Gabriel Peyroux and his bride had received as a wedding gift in 1772, died in August of 1775; and the circumstances surrounding his demise caused confusion that wouldn't be resolved for five years. Francisco had been leased to Charles Lorreins (Tarascon) who had him working at Pointe Coupée and Rapides. Returning to Pointe Coupée on July 17, 1775 from a trip on which he'd done no work because he wasn't feeling well, Francisco's trouble was diagnosed as a tumor "as large as two fists, located in the umbilicus below the oquedad of the stomach," for which the doctor prescribed a malvas poultice and ordered that he be given whey and chicken broth. Surgeon Bertonville prognosticated that the slave would die if the tumor wasn't removed, whereupon Francisco begged to go to New Orleans. But after three doctors consulted together, they agreed the hunter would never reach New Orleans in his condition, and he died on August 2nd.

Owner Peyroux learned of Francisco's death when he was summoned to Pointe Coupée by the Commander-Judge of that parish, to pay Juan B. Tounoir—Tarascon's business partner at Pointe Coupée—146 livres, 17 sols, 6 deniers—money expended for the hunter's illness and funeral. Peyroux objected to paying this amount until he could investigate the circumstances of his slave's death—whether he'd been treated well and given the right medicine—and he maintained that Carlos Lorreins, to whom Francisco had been leased at the time of his death, was responsible for these bills. Peyroux also requested that Francisco's gun and whistle (for decoying birds) be turned over to him, since the dead Mulatto had been much loved by his former master, bayou resident Francisco Caüe, Peyroux's deceased father-in-law, for whom mulatto Francisco had been a hunter for a long time. Tounoir gave the items to Peyroux, but later found out they belonged to Tarascon, and had to go to no end of trouble, through an alcalde in New Orleans, to retrieve the articles for their rightful owner.

The case was held up until the court could establish responsibility, and the matter would not be revived until May 17, 1779, by which time governors had changed, and a new court had jurisdiction.

Despite Gabriel Peyroux de la Rochemolive's lengthy plea, the Governor ordered him—as owner of the slave—to pay Juan B. Tounoir 29 pesos, 3 reales to cover the expense of illness, death and burial, as well as court costs which were taxed at 27 pesos, 2 reales. Additionally Peyroux paid Goyon V. Garic, widow of the notary, 12 piastres, 7 escalins for professional services the notary had performed before his death.[13]

Concerned about local defense, Unzaga received thirty one cannons from Spain—twenty 18″ and five 6″ of iron and six 4″ of bronze; and in his despatch to the Governor-General of Cuba on September 17, 1775, the Governor reported that he'd placed sixteen of the eighteen-inchers in three batteries along the Mississippi, directly in front of the settlement and had installed the remaining four 18″ cannon, as well as two of the six-inchers in Bayu del San Juan, which flowed into Lago Pontchartrain, two leagues from the settlement. Protected by rotten stakes, he felt the latter could be of some use defensively at Fort San Juan. But having reviewed the situation carefully Unzaga stated he wasn't sure he'd made the right decision, because New Orleans "situated on an island, surrounded by lakes in the rear and in the front by the Mississippi River, could be invaded by many paths and bayous, and could be attacked from its sides and back, making useless all the defense in front of the village."

Don Francisco Bouligny, Colonel of the Regiment of Luisiana, had his own ideas about the state of defense. In an August, 1776 report to the Spanish government, he expressed concern about the firm relations England had established with Indians who had formerly been friendly to the French and Spanish. Capable of putting sixteen thousand Choctaws on the warpath, the English could easily reach the Mississippi through the lakes and the Iberville River (Bayou Manchac) without Spain's knowledge, because there was no one to watch their movement except those posted at the fort on Bayu San Juan and a detachment of two, three men on the Tigouyou. With only fifteen hundred regular troops, a hundred of them divided between the stations at Balize, Bayu San Juan, Manchac, Arkansas and the Illinois, and the remainder in New Orleans, not much of a defense could be staged against an attack. Bouligny stated that England had various avenues of approach to New Orleans: 1) through the mouth of the Mississippi, 2) from the north via the Ohio and the Mississippi, or 3) from Mobile and Pensacola through the lakes, from whence they could continue up Bayu San Juan; taking that settlement, they could, after a short trek on Bayou Road, capture New Orleans itself.

Another possibility, the Colonel added, was an attack by the local citizenry (not weaned to Spain) and the Indians. The situation was dubious, and Bouligny suggested that Spain: 1) fortify the two batteries at English Turn, established earlier by the French, 2) construct frigates armed with thirty or forty thirty-six-pound guns—vessels with such strong sides no enemy could pierce them—and position them in the river as floating batteries, and 3) rebuild and strengthen Fort San Juan at Lake Pontchartrain. Bouligny's perceptive eye noted that during a storm, south winds carried lake waters as far as the bank of the Mississippi, for which reason (as well as the lack of fresh water) the land bordering Lake Pontchartrain was generally uninhabitable. However, in the few places that could be cultivated, he suggested that families be established to watch the English on the lakes; the settlers could gather rainwater in tree trunks for daily use, game and fish were plentiful, and the soil was fertile for planting.

Bouligny was particularly worried about Manchac. Ninety percent of the trade of the province was being illegally conducted with the British; and plantation owners, fearing they might be prosecuted for these illegal doings, were moving to Manchac, where their demand for property—together with that of English citizens coming in from the East—had raised prices so much that untilled, forested acreage in that location was selling higher than improved property near New Orleans. Bouligny feared Manchac would absorb New Orleans and menace Spain's Mexican holdings. He urged that English commerce on the river be destroyed and that the fort at Spanish Manchac—a pistol shot away from British Manchac—be rebuilt.[14]

Despite Bouligny's pessimism New Orleans was expanding; five lots, between Toulouse and St. Louis, facing the garden of Charity Hospital on the outskirts of town, were offered for sale. And life on Bayu San Juan hummed along as usual, with Francisca DesRuisseaux, the Jose Chalons, Mr. and Mrs. Henriques Desprez, Santiago Lorreins (Tarascon) and

Maurice Milon filling the legal records of the time with their buying and selling.

In 1776 Francisca Girardy, Widow DesRuisseaux, by act under private signature, purchased the ten arpents fronting Bayu San Juan on its east bank, which Jean Tuon—the original grantee—had sold her son Maurice Milon on December 27, 1773. The oft-sold piece of land would remain in the DesRuisseaux family for the next thirty three years. Francisca Girardy would leave the land to her daughter Maria Isabel DesRuisseaux, who would then be married to her second husband Estevan (Etienne) Roquigny; and on January 28, 1806 she (represented by her son-in-law Jean Laurent Alpuente) would sell the land to Alexander Milne.

On February 8, 1776 Andres Jung bought a 160-ton brigantine, *The Amiable Jenny*, from Francois Pousset, for sixteen hundred piastres. Pousset had a little trouble collecting, however, for when Jung got around to examining the vessel moored in front of the Livaudais plantation on the Mississippi, he discovered that its capacity was only half that stated by the vendor, who soon hauled him before the bench to force him to pay the contract price. Jung claimed he didn't owe the entire amount because of misrepresentation, and although the record is incomplete, the two no doubt came to an understanding in or out of court.[15]

There were happy events too. On March 19, 1776 Jose Jacinto Chalon, son of Maria Isabel DesRuisseaux and Jose Chalon, was baptized in the Parish Church of San Luis. Born on April 30, 1774, he wasn't baptized until he was almost two years old. The God-parents of Widow DesRuisseaux's grandchild were Jacinto Panis, Aide-Major of the garrison of New Orleans and Margarita Wiltz. Margarita Wiltz was the widow of Joseph Milhet, wealthy merchant of New Orleans, who'd been executed for his part in the insurrection against Spain.

A month before the christening Margarita Wiltz had petitioned the court for "testimony regarding her legitimacy and purity of blood." The fourth question asked Nicolas Forstall and two other witnesses during this procedure was whether they knew if "Margarita Wiltz, her parents, grandparents and the rest of her antecedents, paternal and maternal, were old Christians, pure of all bad races such as Moors, Jews, Mulattoes and Indians, if they were converted, or had been prosecuted for infamy or crimes, if they had been made to do penance, or whether they had always enjoyed a good reputation for their habits and purity of blood."

This procedure was effected when a woman was considering marriage with a man to whom "purity" was important. From a practical standpoint, it also provided an official record of the exact extent of a woman's estate before entering matrimony. Both reasons may have applied in this instance, for in 1777 Margarita Wiltz married Jacinto Panis, who died about ten years later. The names of this couple would live in the history of Faubourg Lafayette (today's Garden District) because Panis purchased a parcel of land constituting a sizable segment of that future suburb.

On June 25, 1776 Francisca Dreux of Gentilly, widow of Maturino Dreux, asked that her son Guido (grandchild of original settler Mathurin Dreux) be emancipated and put in possession of his property.

On the same side of Bayu San Juan Madame de Mouléon decided not to hold her east bank property. On October 4, 1776 she sold the plantation (ceded to Villars DuBreuil in 1719) to Don Gilberto St. Maxent. This plantation, which fronted on the Mississippi River, angled all the way back to Bayu San Juan, having access to the bayou from a point south of today's DeSaix Boulevard to a point under Wisner Overpass. This was the third property St. Maxent owned on the east bank of the bayou. An official inventory of St. Maxent's estate—eight years later—would include a fourteen-arpent-front plantation and an adjoining twenty-eight-arpent front, extending his east bank holdings in 1776 from the vicinity of DeSaix Boulevard (today) up to the middle of Park Island.

The inventory valued two of his plantations at ten thousand pesos; and on one of them was a house seventy feet long by nineteen feet wide, with seven foot galleries, which, together with a forty six foot by eighteen foot kitchen in the rear, was appraised at thirty eight hundred pesos. On his small plantation (possibly the narrow acreage near today's Park Island) he kept a thousand pesos worth of cattle "to keep his slaves busy." St. Maxent owned two hundred and nine Negroes, some of which were Creole slaves, born in Luisiana, and others were imported from Mina, Senegal, Guinea and Mandingo, with an average worth of seven hundred pesos each.

He lived in the magnificent de LaChaise mansion just below New Orleans—a home adorned with columns, two dormers and chimneys and a lightening rod—just recently invented. All of this, in addition to the 33,000 acres at Chef Menteur, conceded to him in 1763, and the Gentilly land transferred to him in 1765 by the Capuchins, made Gilberto St. Maxent a very rich man—probably the richest in the province.[16]

But good times weren't limited to St.Maxent. Local business overall was looking up. In 1776 an agreement was drawn up between France and Spain, permitting trade between Luisiana and the West Indies, and two French Commissioners were assigned to New Orleans to supervise and handle any disputes arising from the new arrangement. Galvez asked that ships coming to New Orleans from France and Santo Domingo not sell their papers to English merchants, and the French paid for whatever they bought in specie, bills of exchange or Guinea (African) Negroes, since importation of those born or living in the West Indies had been prohibited by the colonial government since before the arrival of Ulloa. The economy continued to improve during the following years, with additional concessions on the part of Spain; in 1782 the King would allow direct importations from France, and Negroes would be obtainable from colonies of neutral or allied powers.

If Unzaga's governing lacked lustre, the coin flipped when his successor took office on February 1, 1777. Twenty one year old Bernardo de Galvez, of distinguished Spanish lineage, had been Colonel-Commander of the Luisiana Infantry Regiment and second in rank to Unzaga when he came to the province. Completely different from his predecessor in most ways, he followed his example by marrying a daughter of Don Gilberto St. Maxent. Marie Felicité had been the wife of Jean Baptiste Honore d'Estrehan (a locally prominent, wealthy family) who died on October 20, 1773, leaving her a rich young widow.

The bride's father wasn't standing still either. In 1777 he sold his home below New Orleans to Laurent Sigur, and built himself an even more impressive mansion on his Gentilly holdings—a house that on today's market would be worth $390,000.00.[17]

But there was much more than romance on the new governor's mind. Relations between the Spanish and English were tense. After the Seven Years' War, England had extended the western borders of her Atlantic colonies to the Mississippi River. The American colonies, further north on the Atlantic seaboard, who were fighting the British for their independence, extended westerly only to the Allegheny Mountains; and while they were absorbed in their battle for freedom, shrewd British military leaders established themselves to their rear—between the Allegheny Mountains and the Mississippi River. Expending vast sums to buy the cooperation of the Indians, the English encouraged the Redmen to raid, burn and slaughter the enemy while Britain fortified the occupied expanse in order to attack the Americans from behind.

England controlled most of the Mississippi's east bank—almost down to New Orleans; but Spain had New Orleans—the Mississippi Valley's seaport outlet to the rest of the world—and Galvez was acutely aware of Britain's designs on her property.

Sympathetic to the American colonies, the Spanish governor was nevertheless reluctant to openly take sides lest his attitude encourage revolution in other Spanish colonies. However, undercover he supported New Orleans merchant-trader Oliver Pollock, all-out champion of the American cause, not only with cash, but allowed shipment of arms, gunpowder and provisions to ascend the Mississippi under Spanish colors, to the American bottom in Illinois (near the confluence of the Mississippi and Ohio Rivers) from whence they could be transported to Virginia and Pennsylvania to help the Americans fight the British and the Indians.[18]

In March of 1777 Galvez was carefully considering the best way of meeting the threat on the local level. New Orleans had no fortress or surrounding walls to protect it, but he decided that rebuilding the city palisades or those of the Port of Bayu San Juan would be a useless expenditure, since both places could easily be taken without artillery. Besides, the season wasn't right for cutting the timber that would be needed for this project.

Giving the situation additional attention, he recommended in June that three or four lanchones (small light river craft) with eighteen or twenty four caliber cannon in the prow, be built. Not only would they be more maneuverable in the river than the frigates Bouligny had recommended the year before, six of the light craft could be built for a third of the cost of the frigates. Galvez decided to establish posts away from the city—at points from which the British might make their attack.[19]

The following month the rear arpents of the old Langlois-Brazillier plantation (the bayou frontage of which was now owned by the Jose Chalons) again changed hands when Arnoul sold them to Gabriel Peyroux on July 23, 1777. Peyroux would live there for the rest of his life, and his widow would own the land as late as 1799.

A few months later Peyroux's bayou neighbors were asking the court to enlarge their holdings by half a road. Joseph Chalon petitioned that Bayou Road be moved easterly by twenty feet. His property met that of his neighbor, Widow Juan Bautista Brazillier, at the very foot of the great bridge over Bayu San Juan (a point between DeSoto and Bell Streets today), and it was customary for each to contribute half of the land needed for the public road. However, up to this time the road had been on his land exclusively, and he asked that a survey be made prior to the departure of the King's Surveyor, Captain Luis Andry, to correct the situation. Despite Mrs. Brazillier's protests, the survey and change were made, and Jose Chalon received legal notification to that effect at his bayou plantation on December 1, 1777.

Bayou Road of early times began somewhat west of today's DeSoto Street, possibly halfway between that street and today's Bell Street, on the eastern boundary of Chalon's eight arpent property which extended westerly to the vicinity of Orleans Street.

Lakeside of Bayou Road Santiago Lorreins (Tarascon) increased his stature immeasurably when his daughter Francisca, who lived across Bayu San Juan, gave birth to Luis Allard in 1777. Named for his father Juan Luis Allard, young Luis was destined to be an active citizen of the bayou for the next seventy years, living on the same plantation his mother would inherit from her father—land that in 1850 would become New Orleans' first City Park. Today it is lower City Park.[20]

Chapter XX

BAYU SAN JUAN INVOLVEMENT IN THE WAR AGAINST GREAT BRITAIN 1777-1781

Because of the small garrison in New Orleans, Galvez established posts away from the town, at points where he anticipated attack. Things weren't going so well for the British either. Kaskaskia was captured by George Rogers Clark in late 1777, and American agent James Willing's flotilla, led by the armed *Rattletrap*, was coming down the Mississippi terrorizing English settlers along the way and seizing their possessions. The situation was so touchy Galvez gave the English and Americans in the province the choice of taking an oath of neutrality or leaving Luisiana.

England was aware of Spain's clandestine support of the Americans, but the British vessel *West Florida* had been operating on the lakes back of New Orleans for some time with Spanish permission to pass and re-pass Fort San Juan at the bayou's mouth. However, new instructions were issued by Galvez on April 21, 1778; the officer at the fort signaled the *West Florida* to stop, and Captain Burdon was forbidden to proceed. Reacting to this presumption by refusing any other boat the use of the lakes, or anywhere he happened to be cruising, the Captain had, within a week, taken two vessels on Lake Pontchartrain to which Galvez protested with little effect.

Mankind having failed to create enough complexity, the elements added their contribution to the predicament. From October 7th to the 10th, 1778, a fierce hurricane raged over the area. In addition to partially demolishing Charity Hospital, the sea rose higher than it had ever been known to do before, destroying nearly all the establishments at the Balize, Bayu San Juan and Tigouyou.* This eliminated one of the four locations from which the Spanish were able to watch British activity on Lake Pontchartrain, for British Engineer Hutchins, publishing in 1778, states that the small redoubt on the Tigouyou was in ruins. Plan du Lac Ponchartrain prepared by order of Governor Galvez (in the National

* Bayou Tigouyou, derived from the Indian tiak (pine) and ahoyo (where a search was made), entered Lake Pontchartrain from its southern shore, a considerable distance west and slightly to the north of Bayu San Juan. V. M. Scramuzza, refers to the "Tiguyu, the stream uniting Pontchartrain and Maurepas," which location I have found on no map.

Archives, Washington, D. C.) shows both Point Tigouyou, and further west and north on the south shore of the lake, Bayou Tigouyou "et corps de garde," in 1778.

Fort San Juan was another matter. Instructions of December 1, 1778, signed by Engineer Luis Andry, addressed to Captain Alvarez of the Royal Artillery Corps, refer to "the work which is to be done in the first place," indicating that some of the fort was rebuilt at this time, in addition to the repair work that had to be done.

Despite his anxiety in 1775 about the effectiveness of his artillery placement, Governor Unzaga had evidently followed through on his initial thoughts in the matter, for the instructions of 1778 reveal there were four eighteen-inch and two six-inch cannon, mounted on marine gun carriages at Fuerte del San Juan.

Prior to the construction done at this time, the fort must have been at its nadir, because in early American times, Francois Dutillet, an officer who had served under Spain at that time, testified that the fort was in bad condition, with only three pieces of cannon. Leveled with shells, it was shaped like a half moon, built of posts driven down into the earth, boarded about with planks, and with embrasures on Lake Pontchartrain and Bayu San Juan, whose waters washed the fort. Another court witness in this case—Pierre Duverges—testified that at that time there were no houses on Lake Pontchartrain or between the fort and Lake Pontchartrain—that there were only some fishermen living on the city side of the fort, on the bayou's east bank.[2]

In 1778 Engineer Thomas Hutchins urged his superiors to allow him to construct forts at Manchac and Natchez. Reversing his earlier judgment about the impossibility of a successful cut from the Mississippi into River Iberville (Bayou Manchac), he promised to effect a desirable all-water route between the Mississippi and the Gulf for a mere twenty five hundred pounds, which no doubt persuaded the English to reconstruct Manchac Fort, but without Hutchins' assistance. He was arrested in 1779 because of suspected American leanings.

Since the Continental Congress had refused to go along with the terms Spain demanded as a price for alliance, the Catholic King contented himself with declaring war on England on May 8, 1779; and a thousand British troops at Manchac stimulated Galvez to summon local military leaders for a Council of War on July 13, 1779 to discuss an attack on the English before they could come downstream to capture New Orleans. Because British ships, maneuvering on the lakes, could come up Bayu San Juan and take New Orleans, Galvez called up a part of the militia to protect the homefront while he and his men went on the attack. However, just as the Spanish had gotten things together and assembled their ships in the river, a ravaging hurricane hit on August 18, 1779, sinking most of the vessels and causing tremendous havoc. Needless to say the march on Manchac was delayed.

Galvez reported there wasn't a canoe or vessel left in the river, scarcely a house standing, and crops, cattle and stores were all lost. Oliver Pollock—in New Orleans at the time—said "It's too distressing to put on paper. . .books and papers I saved. . .the only articles in my house I could keep dry."

St. John's Charity Hospital, located on the square bounded by Rampart, Basin, St. Peter and Toulouse, which had been badly damaged in the hurricane of the previous year, was practically reduced to rubble. All that was left was the kitchen and a storehouse which were quickly converted into a provisional hospital with six beds.[3]

In an amazing recoup, which can be mustered only by determined youth, Galvez quickly prepared again, and set forth from New Orleans on August 27, 1779, adding to his forces at the German Coast with soldiers from Opelousas, Attacapas and Point Coupée, as he marched north—1427 men in all. Reaching Manchac on September 7, 1779, a third of his men had collapsed along the way from fatigue. Don Gilberto Antonio St. Maxent, Colonel of the New Orleans Militia and son of merchant-plantation owner St. Maxent, was the first to enter Fort Bute through a gunport.

Going on to capture Baton Rouge on September 21st, the terms of surrender also guaranteed Galvez control of Fort Panmure at Natchez.

As Galvez gathered victories, Spanish gunboats from the Navy Yard at the bend of Bayu San Juan (near Grand Route St. John on Moss Street today) proceeded down the stream, past Fort San Juan, and advanced through Lakes Pontchartrain and Maurepas into the Iberville Route (Bayou Manchac). Galveztown,* on the right bank of the Amite River, immediately below its confluence with Bayou Manchac (where Ascension, East Baton Rouge and Livingston Parishes meet) was in the thick of the conflict. Of the eight English ships captured at the time, only one was taken on the Mississippi, the rest were taken on the Iberville route.

Some of the British fighting force—a part of Waldeck's regiment, lately arrived at Pensacola from the British West Indian fleet,—had been delivered to Manchac and Baton Rouge. The two ships which had trans-

*It was to Galveztown, and today's St. Bernard Parish, that several Canary Island families had been sent in 1778 as colonists.

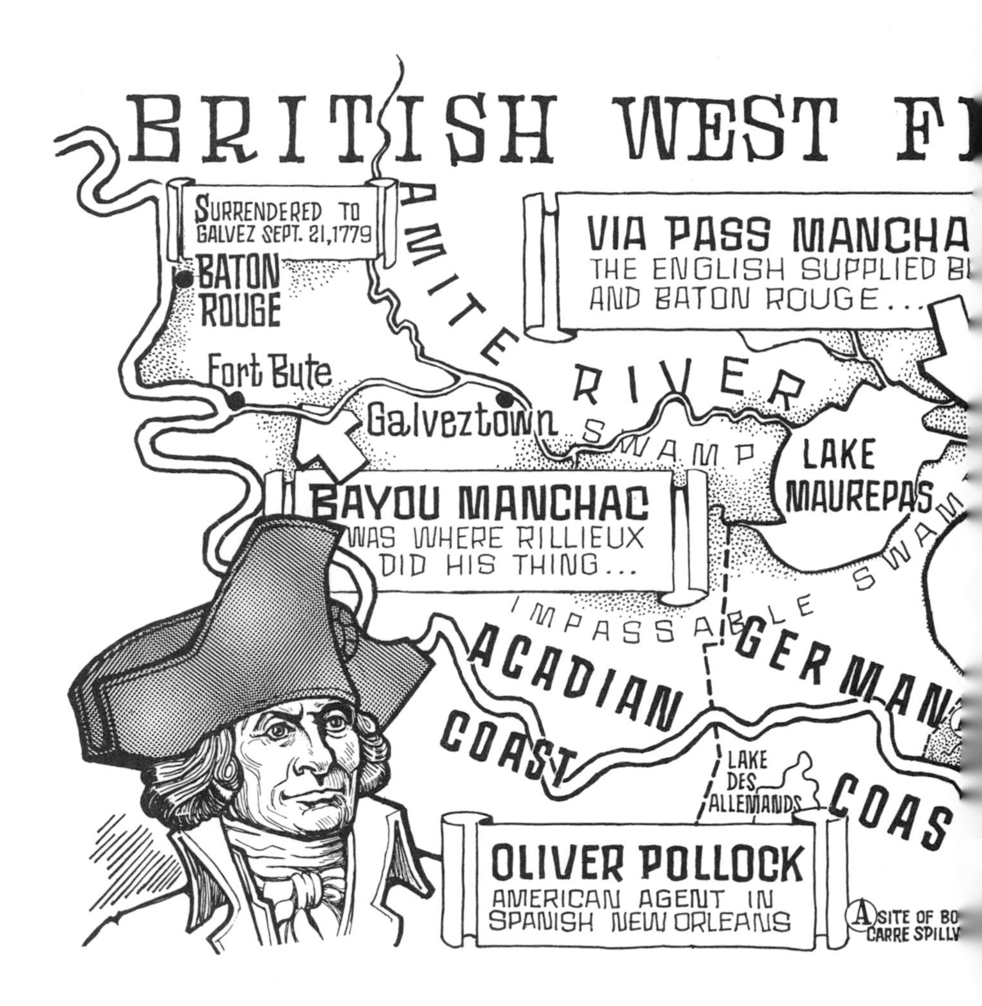

The British and the Spanish waged war 1779-1781.

ported them were due to return to Pensacola, and Galvez ordered them seized. To allay suspicion of his objective, Collel—in charge of the operation—loosed the rumor along the coast that one Sergeant Mondola had deserted from Spanish service—that along with other miscreants he'd stolen a boat at Bayu San Juan and was hiding out on Lake Maurepas. Pretending to go after these outlaws, Collel armed eight Spaniards, four Americans and four other soldiers and sent them under the command of Engineer LeBlanc to lie in ambush, capture the unsuspecting

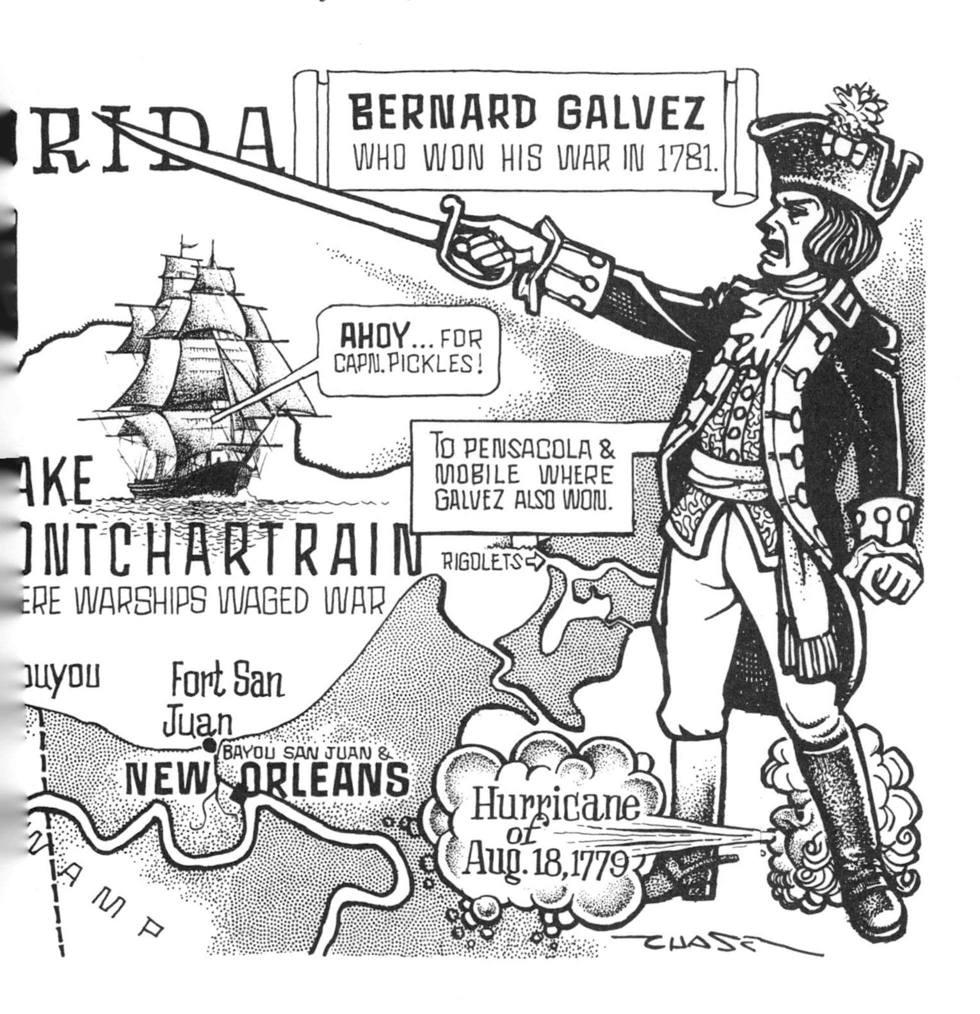

British vessels and take them directly to Bayu San Juan. Since the English had a ship's crew of only twelve men, Collel knew they'd offer little resistance. The two British ships passed Galveztown the evening of August 28th, on their way back to Pensacola, and LeBlanc's contingent left the same night. However, somewhere in the chain of events was a loose link, for news of the Spanish plot had reached the British who protested to Galvez. The governor had no alternative but to order Collel to desist, but the command was issued too late. On August 30th Collel informed

Galvez that the stroke had been delivered with the capture of two ships and nineteen prisoners; and that they were watching for an enemy brigantine, a flatboat lurking a half league from Galveztown, and for a schooner moored at Lafourche. The two captured vessels weren't sent to Bayu San Juan as planned because an English corsair on the lakes was on the lookout for Spanish ships. For the time being they hid them in one of the many bayous leading from the Amite River into the swamps.

September 7, 1779 was a lucky day for Spain. Manchac had fallen to Galvez, and fortune smiled sweetly on the forces of His Catholic Majesty on the Amite. Two English ships, carrying soldiers and provisions, had been captured, and credit for this feat went to Vincent Rillieux of New Orleans, who'd been placed in command of a small sloop which had sallied out of Bayu San Juan with a crew of fourteen determined men to intercept British supplies and reinforcements about which Rillieux had learned from the fishermen who lived in the little village at the mouth of Bayu San Juan. Deciding to surprise the English in the narrows of Bayou Manchac, Rillieux fortified a camp in the forest swamp, set up his guns, and maintained complete silence. As the English barques wound their way through the bends of the bayou, Rillieux and his men sprang up, shrieking an Indian war cry as they fired their whole battery at the British. In shock and stricken with terror the grenadiers of Waldeck, fearing they were at the mercy of a huge force of savages, remained below deck while Rillieux and his fourteen Creoles took fifty six prisoners. An English ensign was killed during the struggle, and ammunition, goods and a large supply of commissary stores were seized.

Rillieux was one of those hardies who never gave up on anything; Bayu San Juan was to be his bailiwick for years to come, and his son's after him.

Two other vessels, loaded with supplies, were taken by the Spanish, and on September 8th a Spanish Sergeant captured a whole detachment of eighteen English soldiers. On September 9th Collel sent sixty seven prisoners to New Orleans, on the 10th six more, as well as thirty guns, thirty bayonets and sixty cases of cartridges, and he informed his superiors he was holding forty three men in Galveztown.

The English frigate *West Florida,* carrying five guns and a crew of thirty, had had its way on Lakes Pontchartrain and Maurepas for two years, but finally got its comeuppance when American privateer William Pickles, having outfitted *The Morris,* a small sloop mounted with two and a half pounders and carrying a small crew, overhauled the English vessel on Lake Pontchartrain and ordered her to surrender. English Captain Paine laughed derisively as shots were exchanged, but Pickles ran in close, boarded the vessel and subdued her in hand to hand combat, in which four of the British were killed, including the arrogant Captain. On September 21, 1779, the day Baton Rouge surrendered to Galvez, Pickles raised the American flag on the north shore of Lake Pontchartrain, and the white settlers in the pine country between Bayou Lacombe and the Tangipahoa River took an oath of allegiance to the United States; but 122 Choctaws, whose ancestral land it was, asked to be transferred across the lake to Bayu San Juan, and Pickles obliged them. The Spanish could hardly believe that Pickles had brought in the *West Florida* without damaging her. Turned over to Pollock, he agreed with Galvez that the vessel should stay on the lakes as a cruiser for the common cause.

In March, 1780 Galvez took Fort Charlotte at Mobile, and surrender of Florida was complete with the taking of Fort George, Pensacola on May 9, 1781. The victory at Baton Rouge had made Galvez a Brigadier General; after Mobile, he advanced to Major General. With Pensacola under his belt, he became a Lieutenant General, and received the title of Count as well. In later years he would become Captain-General of Cuba, Luisiana and Florida; and following his father's death would assume the position of Viceroy of Mexico, the highest political office in the Americas the Spanish Crown could bestow. Dying at thirty eight years of age, he had achieved more—with honor—than most men twice his age.[4]

The continuing preoccupation with defense and offense makes it difficult to believe that a civil front existed at all; but for the folk of Bayu San Juan, life continued as usual.

On January 1, 1777 Henriques Desprez was confirmed by the Cabildo as Attorney General. That same month the daughter of a former prominent bayou family married. On January 14th Jeanne Antoinette de Glapion (daughter of Jeanne Antoinette Mirbaise de Villemont and Chevalier Christophe de Glapion) married Edmé Joseph de L'Homme. Their marriage contract was drawn up and witnessed in St. Charles Parish before the Commandant of Côte des Allemands. Of this union four boys and four girls would be born.

On May 4, 1777 the Tarascon grant changed hands again. Mariana, free woman of color, who had purchased the property from Jung in 1774, sold the eight arpents fronting the bayou's west bank to Naneta, another free woman of color. The sale was notarized by Don Almonester and the property was described as in the previous document, except that this transaction also covered two cows and four calves which increased the price to ninety eight pesos. The same month found Andres Jung collecting another hundred and fifty pesos from the City Treasurer for carting earth used to repair the levees.

On April 8, 1778 the records of Notary Juan Garic indicate that Pellagia Lorreins, Widow Juan Bautista Brazillier sold some property to Gilberto St. Maxent. This sale no doubt covered the rear portion of the original LaVigne plantation which fronted Bayou St. John for seventeen arpents and extended back toward Gentilly forty arpents, the usual depth of concessions. There is no record as to when Widow Brazillier had acquired this property.

The following month Vincent Rillieux petitioned the court to advise his mother Margarita Chenet that she must deliver to him his share of his father's estate located at Les Allemands. Galvez ordered that the inventory be made.

On October 19, 1778 Bayu San Juan plantation owner Santiago Lorreins (Tarascon) was fined court costs and ordered to pay thirty six pesos for luring Francisco Blache's thirty five year old slave Luis away to work for him. Good help was as hard to find in those days as it is today, and Luis was a combination brick mason, roofer and gardener. Returned to his master with a bubo (inflamatory swelling in the groin and armpit) and a venereal syphilitic canker, Luis declared he'd gotten the disease going up to Pointe Coupée. Since it was illegal to hire a slave without his master's consent, Lorreins had no defense.[5]

Lands, as usual, were changing hands. In 1778 Charles de LaChaise purchased from one Juin, a tract of land on Lake Pontchartrain (part of the Aubert Concession of 1765) beginning six arpents east of the mouth of Bayu San Juan and extending east. The land had a depth to the lands of Gentilly. On September 27, 1804 de LaChaise would sell this land to John H. Hudson, who in turn would sell half of it (nearest Bayou St. John) to Alexander Milne on November 25, 1805. Included in this sale to Milne was also a lot and house in the place where the fishermen lived on the east bank of Bayu San Juan.

And in 1778 Soniat de Fossat, husband of Francoise Claudine Dreux of Gentilly (to whom nine children would be born) bought a plantation from the Ursuline nuns—land that in 1815 would be owned by Villeré and would mark the site of the beginning of the battle of New Orleans.

In March, 1779 one of the most unlikely couplings in bayou history took place when Pelagia Lorreins, widow of Juan Bautista Brazillier, who had died in 1775, married perennial bachelor Andres Jung. The bride's brothers, Santiago and Carlos Lorreins (Tarascon), who probably knew the groom much better than his wife-to-be, must have viewed this union with deep skepticism, which may have contributed to the uncertain quality of this short marriage.

Mrs. Jung, who in her twenty six years of marriage to Juan Bautista Brazillier had always lived on Bayu San Juan, now evidently spent a great deal of her time at her husband's mansion on the Mississippi, where the routine was more sophisticated and on a materially grander scale than had been her wont. Juan Luis Allard, married to her niece, no doubt watched out for her bayou home, which the Jungs probably used for weekends or short vacations.[6]

In 1779, Chemin Chapitoulas (Metairie Road) which ran from a point near the Mississippi River above New Orleans to Bayu San Juan, was closed, and all the plantation owners, whose arpents extended from the Mississippi River back to Lake Pontchartrain, were in a dither, because they could no longer travel this back road to town. The situation verged on the desperate, because the Royal Road along the Mississippi was also closed due to a crevasse that flooded the entire area, and there was no way for the folk upriver to bring their produce to New Orleans and buy their supplies. Everybody blamed Francisco Pascalis de la Barre, Regidor Perpetuo and Sheriff of New Orleans, for the inconvenience, because he was the one who refused right-of-way where the road crossed his plantation.

It seemed that de la Barre had recently changed his mind about the road, because in the recent past he'd dug a canal in the vicinity, and Francisco Seimars de Bellile, Commander of the German Coast above New Orleans, with permission of Governor Galvez, had built a bridge over it, so travel on the back road could go on as usual. But de la Barre had destroyed the bridge, and Commander Bellile appeared before the Cabildo on June 14, 1779 to request that it be put back.

The defendant said he didn't see why he should allow travelers on his land just because there had been a crevasse, for which he wasn't to blame. He'd lived up to all his responsibilities, having gotten his arpents from the King in the proper manner and had built a good strong levee on the bank of the Mississippi according to rules. Acknowledging that he'd formerly permitted right-of-way on his land, he now prayed that Governor Galvez forbid anyone from traversing his property. Disapproving of de la Barre's action, the other property owners of the area presented petitions supporting Commander Bellile. Mr. Baure (Boré) stated that for the thirty years he'd lived on his plantation there had always been a road, on the rear of his land, that ran from the Chapitoulas to Bayu San Juan, and that he'd often used it, passing over the properties of Mr. de LaChaise, Messrs. LaFrénière (father and son)—former owners of some of the de la Barre acreage—and Mr. LeBreton.

A second petition, signed by the Beaulieu brothers, declared that Mr. Verret, who operated a dairy farm on the high land back of Mr. Cartier, had opened a route on the Metairie Ridge that went to the house of de LaChaise and up to Bayu San Juan—a road on which people drove their carriages to New Orleans.

Commander Bellile testified that many old inhabitants of the colony had their dairies on this high ridge (Metairie Ridge) and that the road had been used for a number of years by both horses and carriages. Indeed, de la Barre himself had often been seen traveling the route. The Commander argued that since de la Barre owned but fifteen arpents on Chemin Chapitoulas the road would deprive him of very little of his property, and would be to his advantage as well as that of other inhabitants in the rear of the city. Summing up, he petitioned the Governor to permit no one to obstruct Chemin Chapitoulas that led to Bayou Road and thence to New Orleans and asked that the bridge destroyed by the defendant be re-established.

Reviewing the evidence, Governor Galvez ruled that since the road through the land of de la Barre and many other owners had existed for the past thirty years, the Deputy Sheriff must notify Sheriff de la Barre to restore the bridge over the canal within fifteen days for the use of the public and the service of the King.[7]

Juan Garic, who had written and notarized legal instruments for bayou folk during French and Spanish times, died in 1779, possibly from smallpox, as that dreaded scourge was particularly virulent that year. His first marriage having been childless, his second marriage of ten years had produced four heirs, and during his busy life he'd acquired a house on Conti, situated on a lot seventy by two hundred forty feet deep, slaves, carts and horses, all of which were inventoried at the time of his death.

Estefania Goyon suffered the usual widow's estate problems. During their marriage the Garics had for three years owned a five arpent plantation fronting on the Mississippi a half league upriver from New Orleans and extending back to Bayu San Juan, on which was a house, a kitchen, storehouse, two pavilions with chimneys, two brick dovecotes, a little house for the overseer and other improvements. Garic had purchased the plantation—bounded by the properties of Santiago Livaudais and Pedro Aragon—from Pedro de Villemont on June 6, 1774, and had sold it—together with twelve slaves and four pair of oxen—to Francisco Enoul

Livaudais in November of 1777 for fifty five hundred pesos, terms extending through 1779. But November of 1780 arrived, and Widow Garic hadn't received a peso, whereupon she petitioned the court for justice. On November 14, 1780 a legal writ was issued ordering Livaudais to pay Estefania Goyon, Widow Garic what he owed her.

Any historian views the passing of Juan Garic with regret. His revealing records ceased in July, 1779 when he resigned as Secretary of the Cabildo in favor of Don Leonardo Mazange, Prosecuting Attorney, who was commissioned to replace him on November 26, 1779 at a monthly wage of twenty five pesos.[8]

In November, 1779 Pollock directed an official request to Governor Galvez asking that a Negro named Guy be turned over to him, as the slave had been lawfully captured by American agent James Willing during his raids on the English inhabitants in West Florida. Having been brought to New Orleans as a captive, the slave had been enticed away by Mr. Shakespeare, his former English owner, and Pollock wanted him back. Galvez informed his friend he'd have to produce proof before the case could be legally resolved.

In April, 1780 Pollock was again before the court with witnesses to verify his story, including protestant Guy, who testified he'd been captured above Natchez and had been brought to New Orleans, where his former master had asked if he wished to go with him to Pensacola, and that he'd willingly gone aboard the English frigate. The court ruled, however, that Guy was a fair captive of war and therefore Shakespeare not only had to turn his former property over to Pollock, but also had to pay court costs of twenty pesos, five reales for maliciously seizing his former slave and taking him away.

The next year Pollock was before the courts again, petitioning for the right to sell a thirteen arpent front by forty deep plantation at *The Houmas,* twenty two leagues upriver from New Orleans. He also requested permission to sell thirty slaves belonging to Jacques Willing and Philippe Morris of Philadelphia whom Pollock had represented since February 17, 1776. The slaves were sold, but the record doesn't specify sale of the plantation.

George Rogers Clark, who'd been fighting the British and Indians in the north, had drawn $25,000.00 worth of orders on Pollock, which were now under protest in New Orleans. The desperate debtor mortgaged his property, put his slaves to work on public lands to cover his loans, and borrowed money from the Spanish treasury at ten percent interest, as he continued to buy and ship supplies to the American colonies, despite the fact that the British had issued orders for his arrest on sight. The pressure of Pollock's creditors was so great he had to borrow from friends. Governor Galvez advanced him forty thousand dollars. New Orleans merchant Daniel Clark (whose nephew-namesake was destined to become a famous resident of Bayu San Juan in early American times) placed his entire substantial capital at Pollock's disposal. Andres Jung and Jose Chalon, both of whom traded to Philadelphia, lent him pesos, as did Maurice Conway and other New Orleanians. In late 1781 Pollock stayed out of debtors' prison only because of these loans, which permitted him to pay his most pressing creditors, and as yet he had received no relief from the Congress of the United States.[9]

In addition to having delayed the march on Manchac, the hurricane of August 18, 1779 was causing belated repercussions in New Orleans, because Galvez had declared that those suffering storm losses would not be held strictly to the due date of their debts.

Before the storm, Daniel Clark (the elder) had sold Juan B. Desilet (Juan René Kernion had married a Desilet girl) fifteen slaves for 5,300 pesos, which debt Desilet and his wife secured by pledging their present and future estates.

On May 8, 1780 the time had come and gone when a part of the contract was due, and Clark complained to the court that Desilet had not paid what he owed, had sold one of the mortgaged slaves, that one had run away and the two others were sick. The careful creditor feared the property he'd sold would slowly be dissipated, and that he'd never realize a peso from the transaction. A part of the trouble, Clark complained, was that Desilet was taking undue advantage of the governor's tolerance about debts due to hurricane damage; since Desilet owned neither plantation nor real property, he hadn't suffered at all from the storm. Clark asked the court to seize the debtor's belongings to the tune of 3,650 pesos—the amount past due—and that a bond, to be satisfied in December of 1780, be issued for the remainder of the bill.

The court denied Clark's petition, stating that the mortgage on the Negroes and the rest of Desilet's estate protected the creditor who waited until October 8th before petitioning again for a writ against Desilet for the outstanding 1,650 pesos. The court ordered the defendant to pay up within eight days or executory proceedings would follow. Desilet ignored the order, whereupon Clark petitioned for a writ of citation which was served by Francisco Langlois (son or grandson of 1720 Bayu San Juan plantation owner Etienne Langlois). Clark followed up with a request for writ of execution resulting in the seizure of seven of Desilet's

Negroes who were placed in custody of the General Receiver, arranged for three public calls, which took place on January 9, 13 and 17, 1781; and the auction was set for January 28th.

At the eleventh hour an agreement, signed by Daniel and Jane Clark, their attorney Oliver Pollock, and Juan B. Desilet requested cancellation of the litigation because the debtor had promised to pay. The suit was broken, but this futile court operation cost 115 pesos not to mention lawyers' fees.[10]

Hurricanes continued to hit New Orleans, and assistance from, Europe—requested by the Governor—was slow in reaching the province. Those who suffered damage in the storm of August, 1780 received no relief from Spain until June of 1781—nearly a year after the catastrophe.

A lawcase of 1780, wherein Negress Elena attempted to purchase her son's freedom from a politically powerful attorney, and a former Bayu San Juan plantation owner, is one of the most touching cases of colonial history. In order to realize her objective, Elena had to publicly debase and ridicule her offspring, which ploy—'though recognized as necessary—must have been a very trying task for a mother. The attorney, on the other hand, tried every trick in the book, including political pressure from his influential colleagues, to get a price far beyond the slave's worth, because he knew he held the upper hand in this emotionally charged situation.

The mother of slave Magloir appointed Bayu San Juan plantation owner Antonio Gilberto St. Maxent as her appraiser, but, for reasons personal or political, he asked to be recused, whereupon he was replaced with Basilio Ximenes, who placed a value of six hundred pesos on Magloir.

Slave owner Henriques Desprez, husband of Magdalena Brazillier, appointed as his appraiser Francisco Bellile, who immediately estimated Magloir's worth to be eight hundred pesos, whereupon it was necessary for the court to appoint a third appraiser to settle the matter.

Antonio Astier, third appraiser in discord, agreed with Ximines on the six hundred peso price, and Elena presented the money for her son's freedom. Then—with no previous precedent in the records—Alcalde Pedro Piernas, in charge of the case (and no doubt a friend of Henriques Desprez) referred Elena's petition to Assessor Postigo for review, the outcome of which was a new ruling, signed by alcalde and assessor, which stated that valuations didn't conform, that a fourth appraiser had to be appointed. Predictably the fourth appraiser agreed that the slave was worth eight hundred pesos, whereupon Elena challenged "the fourth appraiser as being contrary to law which spoke only of a third in discord." Describing her son as a poor miserable drunkard and thief with an arrest record, who possessed no trade, she charged that Desprez was claiming Magloir had talents and abilities he didn't possess. Five years before Desprez had purchased him for five hundred pesos, on terms—the equivalent of four hundred pesos cash, the going price for a slave without a trade.

Elena cited examples of slaves who'd been freed after a third appraiser decided the difference in evaluation, and went on to contrast the cost at which talented slaves had been freed as compared with the price being asked for her untalented son. A twenty five year old mulatto master carpenter-joiner had been freed for seven hundred and fifty pesos; an expert blacksmith had been valuated by a third in discord at eight hundred pesos. Surely, by comparison, her poor wretched son was worth only six hundred pesos.

The court denied her petition, ruling that the parties at variance must now appoint new appraisers; failing to do so the court would fill the positions. Louis Allard of Bayu San Juan was one of the new appointees, who valuated Magloir at eight hundred pesos, whereupon Andres Almonester, escribano in the suit, asked to be recused. When Secretary of the Cabildo, Leonardo Mazange, took his place, Almonester asked him to give Elena a receipt for the six hundred pesos she'd deposited with the court. The record ended without disclosing the outcome of the case. If Magloir's price was raised, was Elena able to scrape together more than the six hundred pesos she'd already paid?[11]

Young Antonio de St. Maxent—in his early twenties—was made Commander of Galveztown in July of 1781, while his father was doing his best to promote Spain's interests under very trying circumstances. Expelling the English from the Gulf had rid Spain of a troublesome element, but it had also almost ruined Luisiana's commerce, which—to a large extent—had been kept alive by illegal trade with the British.

With his superior trade connections, Gilberto St. Maxent operated in and out of Spanish trading restrictions, to his own interest as well as that of Spain; he could obtain what the country needed to placate the Indians and could dispose of the province's pelts where they were in demand; furs were not popular in Spain.

During Galvez's absence on military campaigns, the ranking military officer of the province had taken charge of things. Although he wouldn't officially fill the top slot until 1785, Don Esteban Rodriguez Miró, Colonel of the Luisiana Regiment, became acting governor during a tense time when many troops, free Negroes, slaves and crew from the ships in port had the run of New Orleans. During Carnival, 1781, they went to dance-halls masked, which resulted in much disturbing of the peace and robbery of homes at night. Responding to complaints, the Cabildo on January 1, 1781 prohibited masking during carnival and closed down the nightly dances where a lot of gambling was going on.[12]

In the spring of 1781 the old Langlois plantation on the east bank of Bayu San Juan (approximately between 1222 Moss Street on the east and west of Orleans Street) again changed hands. Sold to Luis Brazillier in 1737 by D'Hauterive, who'd acquired the arpents from original concessionaire Langlois about 1730, Brazillier had willed the plantation to his daughter Madeline (Magdalena) who had lived there with her two husbands—Francois Héry (Duplanty) and Henriques Desprez—until she sold the place to Mr. and Mrs. Jose Chalon on October 15, 1774. Now—in a sale notarized by Leonardo Mazange on May 7, 1781—Don Almonester Y Roxas became the new owner.

Born in 1725 at Mayrene, in Andalusia, Spain, forty four year old Almonester had come to New Orleans with O'Reilly.Apparently well connected, O'Reilly bestowed upon him the honorary office of Alferez Real (he carried the royal standard in public ceremonies) which entitled him to a seat in the Cabildo. In March, 1770 he became a notary public which brought him profit as well as honor. A colonel in the colonial militia ('though he'd never seemed to have done any fighting), Almonester had ambitions of becoming a brigadier, probably—according to local gossip—to satisfy his considerable vanity.

How he acquired his first city property has not been firmly established, but as was not uncommon with Spanish officials, he "knew how to make one hand wash the other." The land on St. Peter and St. Ann Streets, flanking the Place d'Armes, had originally belonged to the crown, but had been transferred to the municipality by O'Reilly in 1770. Almonester acquired this property, began building on it almost immediately, and soon accumulated other arpents along Bayou Road and in the vicinity of the town until he became a very rich man.[13]

The eastern portion of the rear arpents of Almonester's newly acquired bayou plantation—which had been purchased by Gabriel Peyroux in 1777—was the site of considerable controversy in 1781. For travel and drainage purposes there were two little bridges over the small bayous (one of them Petit Bayou) where the Gentilly high road branched east from Bayou Road. It was to these bridges that the negro washerwomen came to do their laundry. For some reason, Peyroux had torn down one of the bridges which stopped up the ditches alongside the road, and he was demanding a half reale from every washerwoman who came to wash her clothes on the remaining bridge. On May 25, 1781 he was hauled before Miro's court where he was ordered to clean up the ditches on his land so they'd drain properly, and to replace the bridge he'd destroyed, as his actions were contrary to all laws and ordinances.

Apparently he behaved for several years, but in 1787 he would again be brought before the authorities on the charge of stopping the current in a bayou on his property and impeding drainage.[14]

On May 26, 1781 the court was looking into a situation that had been developing since early French times. Although the case involved only theft of a cow, the case soon expanded into a full scale investigation of the habits and methods of runaway Negroes. These marooners, called fugitives by the Spanish, hid out in the swamps on both sides of the river and lived from hand to mouth, chiefly by stealing from nearby property owners. They built huts in the swamps and on the edges of lakes and bayous, living in squalor and constant dread of being captured and punished. As there are always those who will profit from the needs of others, the case revealed that some of the fugitives had been cutting timber in the swamps and delivering the squared logs to a sawmill operator, who no doubt got his raw material for next to nothing considering the limited bargaining power of his suppliers. Fifteen males and females—sixteen to twenty five year old slaves—had been living that way for a long time, and might never have been apprehended if one of them hadn't stolen a cow from Bienvenu, Captain of the urban militia of New Orleans, who was missing many fugitive slaves.

The case continued into 1783, as fugitives, who'd robbed the warehouse of the Barataria settlers, and a large group who'd been loitering near Lake Borgne, were apprehended. The return of the latter was a rough trip for both captives and those in charge of the expedition. Some of the captured fugitives in a pirogue behind that of the arresting Commandant fired into the official boat and tried to overturn it. To protect themselves, the expedition leader's slaves layed into the attacking fugitives with paddles, drowning one and forcing the others to swim for shore where they had to be again hunted down and captured.

By October of 1784 over fifty run-aways, including slaves of St. Maxent, Bienvenue, Kernion and Rillieux, were before the courts. The one responsible for the Barataria robbery, and those associated with St. Malo, notarious arch thief, received the most stringent sentences—four of them being sentenced to hang. Other punishments ran the gamut from lashings and wearing irons to exile from the province. Five of Bienvenue's slaves were extremely involved, but because hanging would have imposed economic ruin on their owner, they escaped with having their cheeks branded at the foot of the gallows before being returned to their master.

Despite the extreme price they paid, the slaves' desperate pursuit of freedom slowed only temporarily. Marooning was to go on and on.[15]

Fugitives weren't the only ones who were making things hot for the authorities. The goings-on of the gamblers, drunkards and thieves of New Orleans' underworld held a fearsome fascination for the law-abiding citizens of the town. In early 1781 Joseph Pivoto, a young rower, working his last voyage from Pensacola and Mobile to the Port of Bayu San Juan, became involved in a poker game with Joseph Lion, a notorious New Orleans gambler, and had to ante up twelve pesos he could ill afford to lose. Leaving the schooner at the Port of Bayu San Juan, Lion asked Pivoto what he'd do, now that he wasn't working, to which Pivoto—with the studied casualness of youth—replied that he'd steal for a living, which offhand remark eventually led him to six years of imprisonment and exile from New Orleans.

Events leading up to his arrest began the evening of February 14, 1781 at Clarisen's Tavern where Joseph Lion was drinking with a dragoon from Havana called Manuel. During the conversation the dragoon mentioned that his Captain, Antonio Fernandez, was staying at Salvador Cunille's boarding house, where Lion—a shoemaker by trade—also rented a room and took his meals. The dragoon had learned that the Captain kept three hundred pesos in a locked trunk in his room, and suggested it would be easy for Lion to slip into his room during his absence, lift the latch on the street door; and since the Captain was in the habit of drinking heavily with his evening meal, the trunk could easily be lifted out while Fernandez slept. Since Lion had gambled away a goodly sum, he went along with the plot, rendezvoused with Manuel at 3:00 A.M. the next morning, quietly opened the street door and lifted the trunk out while the Captain snored. Carrying the trunk around the corner, the two hacked it open with an axe Manuel had brought, removed the bag of pesos, and left the trunk and axe near the back wall of the boarding house.

Enroute to Juachin's house—another place Lion often went to drink and gamble—he spied young Pivoto (who rented a room at Juachin's when he was in town) in a doorway, whistled at him, waved him over, and asked him to take the bag of pesos to Juachin's and to wait for him and the dragoon there. Yaca, Robert Avart's slave, who worked at Juachin's, had apparently been tipped off, for she instructed Pivoto to put the bag in an inner room and slipped a half reale to a slave who accidently happened by—telling him to go get himself a drink and forget what he'd seen.

Lion and Manuel soon arrived, divided the money, and gambled and drank for a couple of hours. At first Lion was lucky, but wound up losing fifteen pesos to the dragoon, after which they left. Lion gave Pivoto twelve and a half pesos for having done his bidding and Yaca received a couple of pesos from the dragoon's money-belt.

Going on to the house of Galego Joseph Basques, Lion attempted to regain his losses, but ended up losing 217 pesos—the rest of his spoils. Sauntering over to Marianna Godeau's house, to relax and smoke a cigar, the Ave Maria began to ring in the parish church, and he walked back to Cunille's where he dutifully reported to the Captain's servant that a trunk, similar to that of his master's, had been found outside on the street corner.

Informed of the situation, Captain Fernandez ordered his servant to call his sergeant, his barber and his wigmaker; and while the servant left to do his duties, the Captain reported the robbery to Alcalde Mayor Jacinto Panis. Everyone in the vicinity of the crime was rounded up, and several suspects were arrested and interrogated as the wheels of justice began to grind. Jasmin, slave of Almonester, was immediately released when he proved he'd just come to the city from Lake Pontchartrain where, for a whole year, he had been making lime for his master at the mouth of the bayou. (Lime cement was made from the small shells along the margin of Lake Pontchartrain and along the banks of Bayu San Juan, where the finest and best river sand was also excavated.) And Maria, slave of Mrs. Chalon, could supply no significant information.

The protracted unraveling of the case was largely due to the evasiveness of those, who—uninvolved—colluded with those who might be, to protect their kind from more privileged accusers. Nonetheless, the real culprits were finally ferreted out and brought to trial.

On the witness stand nineteen year old Joseph Pivoto, born at the post of the Alibamons, and a member of the fixed regiment of that place, explained he was on leave of absence during the time he'd worked as a voyager, rower and hunter, for which he was paid eight and a half pesos per month, plus rations from the King. He admitted that even after his job was finished, he'd collected his ration of meat and rice from the

King's Store and taken it to Juachin's house. Outlining his activities on that fateful night, Pivoto said he'd left a party at Mrs. Chalon's to go to the home of Mrs. de la Barre to find her quadroon slave Theresa and take her back to the ball; but Mrs. de la Barre had heard him, and asking what he was doing there, he replied he was looking for a lantern, whereupon she warned him to get along or she'd have him arrested.

Protesting to the court that his youth and innocence had propelled him into the situation, he acknowledged he hadn't reported the robbery, because knowing Lion to be a gambler, he thought the sack of pesos represented his winnings in a game.

Joseph Lion confessed, saying the Demon and passion had blinded him—that it had been easy for him to commit the crime because he had no fear of God, had no religion nor respect for the laws of the Sovereign, and admitted that he did it to recover previous losses and to make money.

On November 21, 1781 Joseph Lion was condemned to six years imprisonment at the Fortress of San Carlos in Havana. Joseph Pivoto was exiled from New Orleans for six years, which time was to be spent within some fortress. And for her complicity, Yaca was sentenced to two hundred lashes. No mention is made of the dragoon's sentence, which was no doubt meted out to him by a military court. And though the guilty were ordered to repay the three hundred pesos they'd stolen, it is doubtful that the Captain of the Dragoons of Havana ever saw a reale of it.[16]

Chapter XXI

DEATH, EMANCIPATION AND INHERITANCE ON BAYU SAN JUAN 1781 - 1783

Things were finally looking up for Oliver Pollock. The legislature of Virginia had authorized a certificate of indebtedness, guaranteeing payments to him over the next four years. With this official commitment Pollock accepted the job of Consul to Havana, which—though carrying no salary—permitted him to trade; and he planned to repay his creditors as Virginia repaid him; but then, inexplicably, Virginia cancelled the certificate and stopped payment on vouchers already issued. When his New Orleans creditors learned of this, they asked the Cabildo to detain Pollock until their bills were paid off.

Pollock's family was allowed to leave, but his attorney was held prisoner in New Orleans. All seemed hopeless. Not even his friend Robert Morris, influential in the American colonial government, could speed up relief. It was Galvez—by then Governor of Cuba—who backed Pollock to the tune of $132,765.00, which permitted him to return to New Orleans, and enabled him to resume trading in order to liquidate some of what he owed. [1] During the 1780's and into the 1790's it was not unusual for successions and official transfers of bayou and New Orleans property to contain a declaration stating that Pollock owed the buyer nothing.

Though not as overwhelming as Pollock's troubles, bayou residents were having their difficulties too. Francisca DesRuisseaux's son, by her first husband, was before the court in 1781. Relations between those who build and those who buy homes have always been touchy, and when the folk involved are neighbor-friends, the quarrel can become keen. In August, Gabriel Peyroux de Rochemolive, who had owned the rear arpents of the old Langlois (now Almonester) plantation since 1777, hauled Mauricio Milon before the authorities because of the bad job he'd done taking down a house on Peyroux's arpents and rebuilding the structure on a city lot. Milon, then living at the Dreux's Gentilly plantation, promised to finish the work and put the house in good shape by the end of October. However July of 1782 rolled around and nothing had yet been done, so Peyroux again brought the matter to the attention of the authorities, asking that they put pressure on Milon to either finish the house satisfactorily or be made to pay a minimum monthly rental of thirty pesos until the house was habitable.

Citations were served and disregarded, and experts were appointed to examine the work and report to the court as to whether the contract had been fulfilled. The decision was problematical, because the contract had been verbal and the contractor had been paid in advance, none of which augured well for Peyroux, even though the experts reported to the court that the house was unfinished—some of the boards weren't nailed, two locks, two hooks and a bolt were missing, one side of the house was higher than the other, and it was neither firm nor solid on its foundation because the beams hadn't been nailed to the uprights. Additionally, the chimney was badly made, and they estimated it would cost two hundred pesos to make things right.

Milon responded that Peyroux had accepted the house with no complaints, and the matter dragged on into 1783 when other experts examined the house; but the matter remained unresolved in August of 1784 when the Alcalde ruled that the case must be brought to trial within nine days. Unfortunately, the record ended on this note, so home-builders will never know if Peyroux received justice or not.[2]

As if personal problems were not enough, August 24, 1781 marked the fourth consecutive year in which a fierce hurricane struck the New Orleans area. On August 30th Alexo Reaux appealed to the court for assistance; the roof had blown off his house, and since it had continued to rain hard for six days afterwards, he hadn't been able to examine his losses. A part of his habitation served as a warehouse wherein he kept various business papers for his brother, a merchant of Bordeaux, as well as a great many "styles" (coiffures) for hair dressing, from two merchants at Cap Francais, Santo Domingo; upon investigation, he found that the papers and styles were ruined, but requested the court's permission to sell the damaged hairpieces at public aution in order that he would at least realize a small amount from his losses.

Rainsoaked as they were, there was spirited bidding for the coiffures the morning of September 20th; and among the many bidders were Mr. Boré, who took six of them at one and a half pesos each, and five at one peso each; and Mr. Langlois who bought four at one peso, one reale per hairpiece.[3]

Pelagia Lorreins Brazillier and Mr. Andres Jung, had been married only two and a half years when she died on September 3, 1781 at the home of her brother Santiago Lorreins (Tarascon) who lived to the immediate lakeside of her Bayu San Juan plantation. The unusual circumstances surrounding her death made more bayou relatives unhappy with each other than any other happening of Spanish times and would be taken to court before everything was settled.

Born in Mobile, Pelagia was the daughter of Santiago Lorreins, called Tarascon, native of the City of Tarascon, Parish of San Didier in the county of Avignon, France, and Maria Avril (Abril) of Mobile, from the province of Burgundy, France, both of whom were dead.*

Like so many before and since, Mrs. Jung had put off writing her will until she became gravely ill, and on September 2nd her husband went to fetch a notary to perform this service. Returning to the plantation of his brother-in-law next morning Jung had to pass his wife's plantation just east of Bayou Road, and noticed Carlos (Tarascon), his wife's brother, and Juan Luis Allard, husband of Mrs. Jung's niece, leaving her house carrying things. Pulling up short he asked if they'd come to his house to rob him while he was gone. The situation deteriorated quickly, Jung shouting to some sailors and the owner of a schooner in Port San Juan (on the bayou side of the house) to witness the fact that Tarascon had insulted and injured him. After his wife's death the next day, Jung swore out proceedings requesting the arrest and punishment of his brother-in-law and seizure of Tarascon's property to satisfy any claims he, Jung, might have against him.

In a later, saner moment, the facts were established, but they didn't help Jung too much, as the dying woman had apparently been very worried that her last wishes might not be carried out by Jung—certainly not if he didn't get back with a notary in time for her to make a will. And considering it took Jung, seven, eight hours to return to the plantation, her misgivings may have been well-founded.

During her husband's absence the dying Pelagia had given her brother Carlos the keys for the armoire on her neighboring plantation, asking him to deliver to her niece Francisca (Mrs. Juan Luis Allard) whatever he found there. With the assistance of four slaves, Carlos had taken six to eight bags of money (2,000 pesos) from the armoire, put them in a pirogue and delivered them to Luis Allard who lived across the bayou in today's lower City Park. Then Tarascon and Allard had walked up the bayou, crossed the estuary and entered the Jung home again where they found two more bags of money. Gathering these up, together with various covers, wrought silver and papers and documents pertaining to the plantation, which Pellagia Jung wished her niece to have, they were about to leave and Allard was already paddling away with the articles in question, when Jung returned and accosted them.

*The records refer to the Lorreins as (Tarascon), or "called Tarascon," because of their place of origin in France. Many other residents of the bayou and New Orleans also had an additional name, denoting their home in the old world.

Mrs. Jung's succession was opened on September 7, 1781 when her husband petitioned the court for the right to administer her estate. Allowed to proceed, Escribano Leonardo Mazange went to the home of Santiago Lorreins (Tarascon) where Pelagia had died, and requested the keys for her place. Lorreins replied he'd sent them by his Negro Colas the day before to Juan Luis Allard who was staying at Mrs. Jung's plantation. Mazange went on to her place, collected the keys and applied seals on everything.

In her will Pelagia Lorreins Brazillier Jung stated that there were no children by either of her marriages, and since Jung had brought nothing to their marriage, there was no community property to divide, and he had no claim on what she left. Her estate consisted of twenty four slaves and a small plantation, two arpents front by thirty deep, on Bayu San Juan, near the King's Naval Arsenal. She owed nothing, but had lent her husband four hundred pesos two years before to buy a slave from bayou resident Mrs. Duvernet (Rose Girardy) which he hadn't repaid; although she had no note for it, it was her wish that the money be collected. Her niece, Mrs. Francisca Allard, must have been Pelagia's surrogate daughter, for to her she left her clothes, jewelry, wrought silver and furniture, as well as everything in the armoire and boxes in her house on the bayou. The remainder of her estate she left to her brother Santiago Lorreins, in whose home she died, and whom she designated as her sole and universal heir, with the specification that he help their brother Carlos in the event the latter ever lost his fortune. (In a codicil this was changed to an outright gift of five hundred pesos to Carlos Lorreins whom she named as her Testamentary Executor.)

Her will freed sixty year old slave Alexis, twenty five year old Luis, forty year old Opal, twenty year old Catalina, thirty one year old Maria Luisa, twenty year old Congo and her three year old child Francisco, because of their services to her, and the Testamentary Executor was instructed to give each of the freed slaves a cow and a calf.

To the will was attached a certified copy of an agreement stating that the heirs and Andres Jung had settled their differences out of court and declaring null and void any legal proceedings resulting from Mrs. Jung's death. The thirty one pesos court cost of Jung's legal accusation was shared by him and the heirs who no doubt felt a little guilty about the way they'd handled things.

Soon Carlotta, Pelagia Lorreins' slave, who'd observed and reported Carlos Tarascon's actions on that fateful night, complained to the court that because of the circumstances she'd been mistreated by him on several occasions and asked that she be turned over to Andres Jung. The court ruled that she stay with Jung until final disposition was made of her, whereupon the six slaves emancipated in Mrs. Jung's will petitioned for their immediate freedom, protesting that Carlos Lorreins had continued to hold them and had ordered them to work until after the harvest. The court declared that Lorreins must draw up the acts of emancipation within a day or face the consequences.

Carlos Lorreins then requested that an inventory of his sister's property be made in order that her estate might be settled promptly, and responsive legal wheels were set in motion. However, his brother Santiago Lorreins, Pelagia's universal heir, objected on the grounds that an inventory wasn't necessary since there were no absent or minor heirs. Carlos Lorreins, by then probably up to his impatient neck in the whole affair, asked to be relieved of the guardianship of his late sister's estate, and since he owed court costs, asked that the five hundred pesos left him in the codicil to her will, be paid him at once. The court instructed Luis Allard to pay Lorreins this sum, but Tarascon found it necessary to go before the bench once more in order to collect his due.

No doubt unable to use all of the slaves he'd inherited from his sister on his own plantation, Santiago Lorreins petitioned the Cabildo on October 27, 1781 for the right to sell ten of them, presenting as title of ownership a certified copy of Pelagia Jung's will of September 3, 1781. Alcalde Duffossat granted the necessary permit, and three public calls for the sale were made October 30th, November 2nd, and November 5th. Among other bidders and buyers at the auction held November 6th, Vincent Rillieux bought Esteban for four hundred pesos, bayou resident Luis Allard purchased Magdalena for three hundred pesos, and Henriques Desprez bought sixty three year old Lucia for sixty three pesos.

A couple of years later Santiago Lorreins sold eight more slaves from his sister's estate on July 16, 1783, for a total of 2,843 pesos, 4 reales, which sum was spent on repairs to his house, doctor bills and other expenses.[4]

In addition to legal complications affecting their immediate lives, Tarascon's obligations to others also had to be dealt with. In April of 1782, during the absence of her husband, Maria Luisa Baudin, Mrs. Santiago Lorreins, was asked to sell a house in New Orleans that belonged to Agata Pensde, Widow David (of age) and Luis Pensde (minor), heirs of Luis Pensde, both of whom lived at the Attacapas Post (St. Martinsville, La.), in order that they might invest the proceeds in livestock for their country farm.

Having received power-of-attorney for the Pensde heirs from Alexandre de Clouet, Commander at Attacapas, Maria Luisa Baudin Lorreins advised the court that it would be to the interest of the heirs if the house they owned in New Orleans was sold, since it was standing empty, uncared for and subject to ruin; but she asked the court to call witnesses to verify the situation.

After three witnesses had approved her decision, Mrs. Lorreins then requested that appraisers be appointed to evaluate the house on Royal Street, adjoined on one side by Mrs. Dreux's property and on the other by that of free mulattress Maria Theresa. Adrien de la Place and Francisco Bijon (popular appraisers of that period) were appointed and qualified before the court, and agreed on a value of three hundred pesos for the house and lot. The auction was held May 20th, and of the three bidding for the house, Philiberti Farche purchased it for four hundred pesos cash.

Legal involvements concerning Pelagia Jung's will were far from over. On April 29, 1782 Henriques Desprez filed suit to force Santiago Lorreins to deliver to Desprez's wife, Magdalena Brazillier, what was coming to her from the estate of her brother, the late Juan Bautista Brazillier, first husband of deceased Pelagia Lorreins Brazillier Jung. Attorney Desprez contended that Juan Brazillier's will on April 18, 1775, in which he had named his wife as his universal heir, was illegal, because it violated the community property contract drawn up before their marriage, which had to be handled according to the laws and customs of Paris even though the province was now under the rule of Spain. Since Juan Brazillier had received his plantation and some slaves from his parents, his sister now was due some of what he'd inherited from them. Desprez petitioned the court to have Juan Bautista's will declared null and void, and that half the property left to his son by the elder Brazillier, as well as produce of that half since the death of Pelagia Jung, be delivered to Magdalena Brazillier Desprez.

Then pressing his case a bit too far (as hard-nosed Desprez was inclined to do) he requested that since there was no doctor or master of the science of law in the province who could instruct and direct on points of law in the case, that the proceedings be referred to the Havana Tribunal for their decision. His petition was denied "because it was not the proceeding that was under consideration," but the court requested that the marriage contract be translated into Spanish for further study.

In order to establish values, since no inventory had been made, the former sensitive situation was again rehashed. Juan Luis Allard, officer in the Company of Carbineers of the Militia, was questioned as to the money he'd allegedly received from Carlos Lorreins the night of Pelagia Jung's death. Surprisingly, he denied knowing anything about any amount or having ever received it. Perhaps the whole matter had unsettled him, or he was trying very hard not to cooperate with Desprez, for he also denied knowing his own age, "because it was a long time since he'd seen his baptismal certificate."

Carlos Lorreins again recited in detail his activities during the seven, eight hours of the night of September 2nd and early September 3rd, 1781, when he had removed the bags of money,etc. from his deceased sister's home, brought them to Allard's house, and his confrontation with Jung at the end of the second trip.[5]

The record ended at this point, so the exact outcome of the case isn't known. However, since conveyance records at the end of the eighteenth century indicate that the wife and son of Santiago Lorreins (Tarascon) owned the east bank Bayu San Juan land up to Bayou Road (between Desoto and Bell Streets today) which included the small Brazillier plantation, it can be concluded that Lorreins either won the case or made a settlement out of court with Henriques Desprez and his wife.

Although slaves were a profitable investment and did the work the white man didn't want to do, the institution and everything connected with it must have been an onerous responsibility for slave owners, made even more exasperating by the lack of communication between the races.

On June 3, 1782 Vincent Rillieux, Brevet Lieutenant of the Infantry, was before the court charging his own slave Juan with taking a pirogue from Rillieux's plantation across Lake Pontchartrain, stealing turkeys and hens from neighbor Charles de LaChaise and bringing them to the city to sell.

Juan didn't seem to or didn't want to understand official interrogation, and it was with patient diligence that the whole story was finally extracted with the help of negro and white victims and witnesses. When the questioning was finished, it appeared that Juan had broken into various places and stolen a gun, powder flask, sweet potatoes, a couple of shirts (filched from a clothesline he passed) liquor, and eleven hens from the coop of a free Negress which he sold to folk along the levee.

Eventually admitting all, Juan blamed his delinquency on liquor; however, in the light of today's psychological perception, the answer probably lay for the most part in his mangled past. Twenty six year old Juan had quite a history. Having been taken from Guinea as a slave and sold in Santo Domingo, his master had brought him to Luisiana where he was sold to a merchant from Illinois. There he ran away three times, being returned on each occasion by the Indians, until his master finally put him on a boat as a rower to New Orleans where he had again been auctioned off. Vincent Rillieux no doubt rued the day he had ever set eyes on Juan, and since the record is incomplete, we will never know how the slave or his master coped with the uncertain future that lay ahead.

A note on this case, by the Louisiana Historical Quarterly Editor of 1935, that "this case is interesting for its reflection on Negro character, which appears to have changed little during the century and a half since 1782," is revealing of the general feeling on the subject during the thirties, which contrasts so sharply with the civil rights atmosphere of today.[6]

An interesting case before the Cabildo on September 4, 1782 involved the procedure of black emancipation, and the trouble an intelligent slave encountered when her owner refused to give her up. The case also reveals the rights Blacks had before the Spanish Court in Luisiana, and how persistence—even in extremely sensitive situations—paid off. In this instance, two worthwhile stubborn women—black and white—battled it out to the legal end.

The case began with Maria Theresa petitioning for her emancipation from the Royal Prison where she was being held as a runaway. Asking the court to place a value on her in order that she might buy her freedom, plus her day wages while the suit was pending, she appointed Adrien de la Place as her appraiser, and asked that Mrs. DesRuisseaux be notified to name her own appraiser or that the court do it for her.

Francisca DesRuisseaux didn't reply, and it was necessary for Maria Theresa to again petition the court for her release from arrest, and that her owner—who lived way out on Bayu San Juan—be cited again. The court ruled that the writ be issued, ordering Mrs. DesRuisseaux to appear within twenty four hours, and that Maria Theresa be released from jail. Since Mrs. DesRuisseaux could hardly disregard the second notice, she sent her son, Mr. Milon, for official instructions and to get first-hand information on her rights in the matter. Since she had named no appraiser, the court appointed Francisco Bijon in order that justice might proceed. He and Adrien de la Place agreed that despite her age the slave was worth five hundred pesos, because she was a good seamstress, washer and ironer, whereupon Maria Theresa petitioned that her owner draw up the act of emancipation so she could promptly pay all just and due fees.

Mrs. DesRuisseaux then got around to objecting that the court had proceeded to her prejudice and without her participation; and although the court ruled against her—citing the records to disprove her allegations—it was necessary for Maria Theresa to again ask her owner—through the courts—to come to the city to authorize the act of emancipation.

Procrastinating as long as she could, Mrs. DesRuisseaux finally acknowledged notification of a decree ordering her to name an appraiser, and appointed Lorenzo Wiltz, who valued the Negress at nine hundred pesos. Insisting that the court take into consideration the fact that Maria Theresa was an embroiderer, as well as an excellent cook, all of which had been taught her over many painstaking years of patient effort, Francisca DesRuisseaux also demanded wages from May 1, 1781—the day Maria Theresa had run away—to the present.

It was then incumbent upon the slave to request that the court appoint a third appraiser to resolve the difference in valuation. She also claimed that Mrs. DesRuisseaux was demanding sixteen months' wages (in addition to her worth) to prevent her from gaining her liberty, and asked that this request be denied.

The court decided that in addition to six hundred pesos, the amount on which the appraisers compromised, the Negress had to settle with her owner for the sixteen months she'd been absent at the rate of seven pesos per month, so it cost her 749 pesos, 5 reales to become a free woman.[7] It is also worth noting that although Mrs. DesRuisseaux had used every gimmick in the book to prevent Maria Theresa from leaving her, she had also provided for her slave an environment in which the woman's spirit had remained strong, and circumstances under which she was able to earn and save enough to hire a good lawyer to buy her freedom in the courts.

In 1782 a slave's refusal to carry a package from New Orleans to Bayu San Juan cost him dearly in suffering, and the litigation resulting from the attack provided revealing insight into the class consciousness of the blacks of that day and doctoring practices of the time.

Attorney Broutin opened the case, stating that at 8:00 o'clock, the evening of September 5th, free mulatto Joseph Forstall, son of Margarita Touton, had encountered Broutin's Negro Francisco, who was walking home from work, on the street in front of the Cheval house. Forstall asked Francisco to deliver a package to his uncle on Bayu San Juan, for which he'd pay him two reales. The slave refused, saying he'd worked enough that day, whereupon the Mulatto struck Francisco in the stomach and chest with the butt of his gun, injuring him so he was now in danger of losing his life.

A certified statement by Dr. Roberto Dow of the Royal Hospital, who'd been called to examine the injured man, disclosed that he'd found Francisco with labored breathing due to a blow to his chest which had been laid open by the impact, so that even if he didn't die, it was possible he might never work again—especially if there was a reoccurence of blood vomiting. Broutin requested that Forstall be put in prison immediately before he could take off with his military detachment. To the discomfiture of the accused, other witnesses testified that Forstall had bragged he wouldn't be imprisoned because of being in the military.

The attorney also requested that Forstall's property be seized to cover Broutin's property loss and costs of court. The Mulatto owned little other than his slave Sali and her four year old son, whom he'd hidden; but at the attorney's request, the court ordered that the escribanos of the city be put on notice to pass no acts of sale covering Sali or any other property Forstall might try to sell.

In prison, twenty three year old bachelor Joseph Touton Forstall, born in New Orleans, and a dealer in provisions, told his side of the story. He explained his attack on the slave, saying Francisco had been snooping around trying to hear what was going on inside the house where several Mulattoes and free Negroes had gotten together before leaving on a military expedition. Telling Francisco, in the parlance of the time, to butt out—that what was going on was none of his business—the slave had refused to leave and taunted Forstall, saying he had no authority to order him around. Irked beyond reason, Forstall had laid into him, striking him in the stomach with his gun butt and with his fists.

Empathizing with the defendant, witnesses testified to the same effect; and on October 4, 1782 another free brown resident went bond for Forstall who was released.

The case dragged on until Attorney Broutin got nervous about the whole thing, suggested that another doctor be called in to examine his slave, and assured the court he'd go along with whatever was decided, so there could be an end to the affair. Dr. Santiago Le Duc of Charity Hospital joined with Dr. Dow to pay Francisco a visit, and shades of current insurance cases—they found the slave wrapped up in blankets and a big coat made out of ship sails, sitting in front of a fire despite the unusually warm weather. Upon examination, Dr. Le Duc noted that Francisco's tongue looked all right, but that his pulse was disturbed, due—no doubt—to the fire and blankets heaped upon him. Although he still hurt when touched, Dr. Le Duc found no inflamation or abscess, nor were there other symptoms of illness.

Accepting the doctors' statement, Broutin requested that Forstall pay him for the twenty six days Francisco had not been able to work. (Broutin rented his Negro out by the day to work for others.) In addition to the nineteen pesos, four reales, Broutin also asked to be reimbursed for the special food and broth the slave had received during his illness, and for the four pesos he'd paid the three soldiers to arrest Forstall.

Doctor Dow presented his bill in the amount of nine pesos, covering six single visits at four reales each, and one in consultation with Dr. Le Duc. Dow had bled the Negro twice at four reales per time, and the balance of the bill represented camphor, balsamics, spermaceti and salts of nitre given the patient.

In addition to a fine of ten pesos, the costs of the extended court procedure amounted to over fifty eight pesos. Joseph Forstall had suffered an expensive bout of temper.[8]

On October 3, 1782 free Negress Naneta, owner of the eight arpent Tarascon grant on the west bank of Bayu San Juan, was drawing up her will; Notary Public Leonardo Mazange was at her home, because she was sick abed and wanted everything in order before she died.

A practicing, believing Roman Catholic, Magdalena Naneta, alias Lacled (Laclef) requested that three masses be said for her soul. Two reales were to be given to each of the forced bequests of the town; and in the custom of most estimable citizens of that time, she left $100.00 to Charity Hospital.

Declaring that she'd married Miguel, negro slave of bayou resident Widow DesRuisseaux, about 1775, her will specified that after her death the executor sell enough of her estate to purchase his freedom. She and Miguel had no children, but Naneta left her free mulatto daughter-in-law Nanita $100.00, six petticoats, all her jackets and two dozen handkerchiefs.

In addition to her plantation on the bayou, which she'd purchased from free Negress Mariana in 1777, her property included the curtains and furniture of her home, as well as some houses on St. Peter Street, bounded by the properties of Renato Brion and Cavalier Regidor Joseph Ducros. The latter was to be her universal executor with as much time as he needed, beyond the usual year, to settle her affairs.

She owned three slaves—Juanton, about fifty, Roseta about twenty five and Cipion, forty five years of age; after her death, the first two were to be emancipated. She also left fifty pesos to free Negress Veronica for good services, and asked that a two hundred and fifty pesos debt be collected from Pedro Mie Le Rioleta.

Since a part of one of her houses had been leased to Don Joseph Cultia, she requested that he be given the first opportunity to purchase the dwelling if the heirs decided to sell it. Naneta wanted the simplest of funerals—details to be decided by her executor—and left the remainder of her estate to her husband Miguel.

However, becoming emancipated wasn't quite as easy as the willing of it, especially since Miguel's owner happened to be Francisca DesRuisseaux, who wasn't too enthusiastic about the idea. After Naneta's death he broached the subject to his owner several times offering to pay a just price for his release, and finally appealed directly to the court to confirm Adrien de la Place as his appraiser, asking that his owner be notified to select her appraiser.

This time Mrs. DesRuisseaux responded promptly by appointing Francisco Roquigny; and after observing the necessary legalities he and de la Place set about their task. De la Place, who guessed Miguel was over sixty years old, "because his wool was perfectly white," estimated the slave's value to be five hundred pesos. Roquigny believed he was worth seven hundred pesos; so it was necessary that a third be appointed to settle the difference. Philipe Guinault, appointed by the court, reviewed the work of the other two, decided that the five hundred peso price was right, and on October 13, 1783 Alferez Francisco Maria de Reggio ordered Francisca DesRuisseaux to draw up the act of emancipation.

Miguel profited largely from his wife's generosity. Not only did he receive his freedom, he married again, had a son, and enjoyed Naneta's beneficence until his death in 1805.[9]

A lawcase of 1782 involved the family of Alpuente—a name that would be familiar along Bayou St. John in American times. In this particular court encounter, Mathias Alpuente, husband of Margarita Duplessis, figured in the sucession of Maria Saulier, wife of ship captain Francisco Duplessis. A major asset of Maria Saulier's estate was a seven arpent plantation fronting on the Mississippi, with a depth of fifty arpents extending back to Bayu San Juan. In early American times Jean Laurent Alpuente (husband of Isabel DesRuisseaux's daughter by her first husband Jose Chalon) would live on the west bank of Bayou St. John.

In early 1783 Bayou Road, leading from the Port of Bayu San Juan to the town, was full of holes, and the drainage ditches alongside it were in such bad shape the road was often flooded, which not only made travel difficult for the local citizenry, it also delayed the Pensacola-Mobile mail, arriving at the Port of Bayu San Juan, from reaching New Orleans on time.

On February 14, 1783 the Cabildo decided that within fifteen days the inhabitants who lived along the road must dig a three foot wide by two foot deep draining ditch where their lands abutted the road; bundles of wood having been placed in the road-holes, the dirt dug out of the ditches was to be placed on top of the wood to level off the surface. It was also decided that if water could not be made to drain directly into the bayou, it had to be funneled off through the back of the properties bordering Bayou Road to keep the road from flooding.

Apparently nothing was accomplished right away, for on August 1, 1783 the Commissioners were considering the matter again and reached the conclusion that the road had to be maintained in the same condition it had been when Messrs. DeMorand and Alexandro Latil staked it out originally. Since Latil had lived on Bayou Road since the 1750's, it is possible that the winding portage route of early French times had been straightened and improved that early. The commissioners again stressed that the road be put in good shape by the property owners and that the dirt dug out of the ditches be used to fill the holes in the road. They were given fifteen days to get the job done.[10]

In 1783 the records introduce Luis Antonio Blanc and his wife Luisa Gauvain, (Gauvin) important names along Bayu San Juan in Spanish and American times. Active, influential people, the Blancs owned an eight arpent plantation on the west bank of the bayou in the mid-1780's, and in 1793 would buy and occupy the old Langlois arpents on Bayu San Juan's east bank.

Luis Blanc had first married Henriqueta Gauvain, who died in 1782 at the age of twenty six. Blanc soon married her sister Luisa who was six years younger. Luisa and her brothers Pedro and Jeronimo were the remaining three of Juan Bautista Gauvain's six children by his third wife Maria Juana Cheval, whom he'd married in 1750; Gauvain's three marriages had resulted in a legal knot in which the heirs of Maria Juana Cheval were currently tied up.

Since early 1782, Blanc, on behalf of his wife (who was legally empowered to act for her absent brothers), had been petitioning the court to make Joseph Ducros, guardian of Maria Juana Cheval's estate, turn over to his wife, the 1,766 pesos, 3 reales she claimed was due her from the succession.

Complication in the person of Maria—Gauvain's spinster daughter by his first wife Suzana Santa Helena—was holding up the case. Maria, who was at present living in New Rochelle, France, had given her general and special power-of-attorney to Joseph Ducros to represent her interests in the Cheval succession.

The litigation revealed a great deal about the much-married Gauvain, whose philosophy apparently had been to live for today and forget about tomorrow; he'd given nary a thought to leaving anybody anything. Although he'd settled with Maria for what was coming to her from her maternal inheritance, he'd sold a considerable portion of his second wife's property and spent the proceeds, thus depriving his first daughter of a considerable inheritance, because Maria had become a favorite of Gauvain's second wife, Maria Luisa Soulard (widow of Bertrand Joffre), who in her will of July 2, 1740 had given Jean Baptiste Gauvain usufruct of her estate during his lifetime, but after his death the property was to go to Maria, child of his first marriage.

The kind of human who richly deserved an inheritance, Maria hadn't claimed her just due when her father died, because his third wife—Maria Juana Cheval (Mrs. Blanc's mother)—had a terminal illness, and the young woman allowed her stepmother to occupy the house at Bourbon Street and St. Ann until she died four years later. Since Maria hadn't been in New Orleans to look out for her interests at the time of death, the house had been sold to bayou resident Jose Chalon, who in turn sold it to Francisco Cheval (now deceased) for the same price he'd paid for it.

The lengthy litigation continued through 1784 and into 1785 when Don Esteban Miro, Colonel of the Fixed Regiment and Governor ad interim, finally decided the case on April 8th. Maria Gauvain received 1,111 pesos, proceeds from the will of her father's second wife Luisa Soulard; and to Luisa Blanc and her two brothers—heirs of the third Mrs. Gauvain —650 pesos, 3 reales were adjudicated. Since court costs alone, not including attorneys' fees, were taxed at 122 pesos, 4 reales, this exercise in frustration netted the wife of Luis Blanc little more than weariness with the Spanish judicial process.[11]

Strangely, it is ignorance, mischief, blunder, crime and the resulting official records that expose us to many circumstances of early times. A murder case of 1783 reveals a great deal about the sailing life of Spanish times— not too different from the way sailors operate today.

The afternoon of Holy Thursday, April 18, 1783, Thomas Guzman, thirty two year old native of the Canary Islands, went to the Port of Bayu San Juan with Skipper Manuel de los Santos, twenty six year old native of Soria, to examine a bark and arrange for its joint purchase. On the way back to New Orleans in the late afternoon, they joined up with a couple of other sailors; and after a lot of talk and argument, about everything from women to philosophy of life, they ended up at Tia Lorenza's Tavern, where the camaraderie degenerated into brawling and fighting.

During the late hours of the evening they were thrown out of the eating place of a German woman, and the scene quickly deteriorated. Santos, who had been walloped emotionally and physically by Guzman throughout the day, finally stabbed his tormentor in the side. Taken to the Main Guard Room by some soldiers, Guzman was transferred from there to the Royal Hospital on the riverfront about one o'clock in the morning where he was examined by Surgeon Major Joseph Montegut. The Doctor's preliminary report stated that the victim had suffered an inch-long wound transversely to the middle part and lateral to the breast on the left side. The sharp cutting instrument had penetrated to the full extent, but had not injured the vital organs of the area.

After Guzman's statement was taken at the Royal Hospital, a writ was issued for the arrest of Manuel de los Santos and for seizure of his property. Santos was nowhere to be found, but Alcalde Juan Ventura Morales, accompanied by the Assistant Minister and the Escribano, went to Bayu San Juan where they placed Santos' schooner, all its rigging and a small unlocked cedar chest in the official safekeeping of Mr. Paran— the remainder of the inventory to be accomplished later.

Santos finally turned up and was interrogated by Alcalde Morales at the public prison on April 30, 1783. The other sailors, who'd been with them that fateful evening, were also closely questioned; and although the testimony varied somewhat—always to the interest of the queried—there was no doubt that Santos had stabbed Guzman.

Santos' attorney then asked the court's permission to sell his client's schooner tied up at the Port of Bayu San Juan, as no one was guarding the boat, and it was subject to damage. The inventory of the boat, in which Guzman owned a half-interest, was completed, and it is worth a moment's consideration, chiefly because of the skipper's wardrobe. In addition to a consignment of flour which had been taken aboard, various trade memoranda and three guns, most of the boat's contents were clothes—lots of them; three white shirts, three blue-striped shirts, one vest of ordinary cotton, one blue-striped vest, one pair white trousers, one pair cotton trousers, one pair short white linen trousers, one pair blue satin trousers, one pair long striped trousers, six pair ordinary linen drawers, three pair thread stockings, one pair silk stockings, two pair of shoes—one new, one old—two jackets of Brabant linen, one short cloak of coarse cotton cloth, one thick red flannel coat and vest, six handkerchiefs and a black angora hat. There was also a wide leather pistol belt, a leather money pouch, two ells of printed calico, two gold buttons with green stones, two rings with precious stones (all broken) a fishing line, a bag, twenty five pounds of tobacco, a piece of sail cloth and a sailor's hammock.

When Thomas Guzman died on June 18th, the case was revived in the court of Alferez Real Francisco Maria de Reggio. Asked to certify as to the cause of death, Surgeon Major Joseph Montegut repeated his initial diagnosis of the evening Guzman was admitted, but went on to say that on his second visit to the patient he noticed pus had already formed, that the wound was pallid and the patient's energies were lax, which called for a further probing of the matter. On careful examination he discovered a filtration of acrid humor into the teguments, indicating general dropsy and trouble in the viscera, liver and spleen. This condition suggested that the patient had been sick for a long time, which was confirmed by Guzman who said he'd come down with a fever nine, ten months before and hadn't been able to throw it off. These complications required more attention than did the wound, which being simple, was of little consequence. Fever, exhaustion and copious suppuration followed, bringing on phthisis which ended Guzman's life on June 18th. Death, Surgeon Montegut asserted, was caused by corruption in the solid and fluid parts of the body—not as a result of the wound.

Santos' attorney again requested the court's permission to auction off his client's schooner, now tied up in Bayu San Juan at the lake, which had been stripped of sails, rigging and cordage and because of its deterioration was now worth only sixty pesos.

Concluding the case, Prosecuting Attorney Francisco Broutin convinced the court that although Santos had not intended to kill Guzman, the wound had been a contributing cause of death. On June 4, 1784 Manuel de los Santos was condemned to work in the galleys for six years. Unbelievably, since the case had gone on so long, court costs were only seven pesos.[12] Of course, attorneys' fees aren't mentioned.

Another miscreant of that era got his proper comeuppance, when in September of 1783 free Negress Fanchon threatened her boss Don Pedro Bonne with litigation if he didn't pay her the back wages he owed. Having worked for sixteen years as a housekeeper, Fanchon demanded 1,920 pesos (ten pesos per month) per an agreement they'd both signed at the beginning of her employment. Unfortunately for Fanchon, the written missile had been placed for safekeeping with another free Negress and had burned in a fire that destroyed the friend's home, so she no longer had proof of the contract. Bonne refused to settle with Fanchon, and after approaching him several times about the matter, Fanchon's only alternative was to bring him before the court where he could be questioned under oath and where her friend could witness for her cause.

The court granted Fanchon's petition, but the case never came to trial. Good housekeepers were as valuable in those days as in our time, and a certified statement attached to the record stated that the matter was settled out of court.

The following fall Pedro Bonne was again before the court, summoned this time by Carlos Lorreins (Tarascon)* who claimed the defendant owed him a hundred and twenty pesos for a Negro Lorreins had leased to him and Estevan Arlu. Bonne wasn't inclined to settle this debt either, so the Deputy Sheriff seized one of his Negroes to insure payment of the debt. This brought Bonne to attention, for that very day—November 29, 1784—Lorreins reported to the Escribano of the Court that Bonne and Arlu had paid him everything they owed.[13]

---

*This ebuillient character of colonial times (married to Marie Louise Girardy in 1752) would marry again in 1794. His wife would be Maria Delonde, Widow Boisdore.

Chapter XXII

THE DEATHS OF JOSE CHALON AND SANTIAGO LORREINS OF BAYU SAN JUAN 1783 - 1784

In June of 1783 three French residents of Philadelphia filed a marine protest with the Cabildo, claiming that their boat, the *Cobro*, coming down the Mississippi to New Orleans, had been attacked by an English Royalist pirate. In the fray one of their rowers had been wounded, and except for a few provisions they were allowed to keep, their entire boatload of merchandise had been seized. They filed their protest—as many times as the law required—in order that they might legally claim indemnity against whoever they could sue for the outrage.

The long list of confiscated articles included items they had planned to sell in New Orleans: a fifty one foot boat, two large canoes, two hundred and eighty six barrels of flour, one hundred and fifty four half-barrels of flour, seventy seven black velvet stocks, 4,427½ yards of lace, thirty four lace ruffles, twenty one and five-eighths yards of serge, twenty one yards of gingham, sixty and one-sixth yards of black and white brocade, seventy dozen gold and silver spangled buttons, forty-four swivel guns and seventy bullets for same, two hundred cartouches and a barrel of salt pork.

It is possible their protest received some attention after September 3, 1783—the day England, Spain, France and the United States signed a treaty ending the war that had been going on between Great Britain and her American colonies from the early 1770's. Spain now legally took possession of East and West Florida, the northern boundary of West Florida being fixed at the 31st parallel latitude and extending from the Mississippi to the Appalachicola River. This was not as extensive as the West Florida Britain had occupied, the northern boundary of which had been further north—latitude 32 degrees, 28 minutes—at the mouth of the Yazoo River.

This territorial difference, in which Natchez was located, would be the basis of continuing controversy during the next fifteen years of Spanish control in Luisiana—until Spain withdrew and the Americans occupied Natchez in the spring of 1798.[1]

DesRuisseaux difficulties were endless. Maria Isabel Chalon (Francisca DesRuisseaux's daughter) and her husband Jose Chalon had been separated for some time. When he died in Philadelphia in April of 1783, his widow didn't learn of it for four months, and she wasn't even mentioned in his will. Affairs surrounding his death strongly suggest that former bayou resident Jose Chalon had become deeply involved with Oliver Pollock in the American colonial cause, which may have contributed to their marital estrangement.

On October 16, 1783 Mrs. Chalon petitioned the court to acquire an accounting of everything connected with her husband's demise from his testamentary executor Oliver Pollock, resident of Havana. The case opened with her acknowledgment of a letter from Pollock, dated August 16, 1783 which contained a copy of Chalon's will, made in Philadelphia, a comprobation of same by proper Philadelphia authorities, and a note signed by Pollock for seven thousand pesos he'd borrowed from Chalon. The letter also conveyed to Widow Chalon Pollock's deepest sympathy, his offer of assistance, and the information that Jose Chalon had been buried with proper Catholic ceremonies in Philadelphia on April 9th.

Chalon's will, written March 1st, stated that he was a resident of Philadelphia and requested that his body be interred according to directions of his friends and executors Oliver Pollock, Guillermo Murray and Daniel Clark.

The total sum of his assets—amounts realized from the sale of his horse and calash, sums due him from the State of Virginia and other debtors —were to be delivered to his son Jose Jacinto Chalon when he reached the age of twenty one, excepting one thousand hard pesos— which were to be paid to his daughter Francisca Isabel at age eighteen or whenever she married. (His other daughter, also called Francisca, had died at an early age.)

In his will Chalon requested that his son be educated in Philadelphia, his schooling to be paid for with interest from his estate. His sword and a set of silver buckles were to be delivered to Jose Jacinto when he became old enough to use them.

Chalon's armchair and ebony walking stick he left to Guillermo Murray "to serve as a reminder of his deceased friend." And to Murray's son, Guillermo, he left his two best woolen coats—one black, the other trimmed with galloons—three pair of trousers, three white striped vests, eight new shirts with cuffs and six plain shirts with suitable stocks, nine pair of thread stockings and three pair of silk ones, as well as his dressing gown—all testifying to his friendship for the young man and his father.

The rest of his clothes he left to his servant Santiago Forest, because of his fidelity and the good care and assistance he'd given Chalon during his illness. Perhaps Forest had expected more, because a week later—on March 8, 1783—a codicil revealed that "as my last servant Santiago Forest, after the execution of my said will, has comported himself very badly, I annul the legacy that I made him...and it is my wish that the...legacy be sold and its products applied in conformity to the disposition of the rest of my personal estate." Two of the witnesses signing the will were Edmundo and Thomas Milne, a family name familiar along Bayu San Juan in Spanish and early American times.

Maria Isabel DesRuisseaux, widow Chalon, was asked by the court to submit copies of Pollock's letter and its contents, her marriage contract with Chalon, baptismal certificates of her three children, and the 1769 partition of her late father's estate between herself and her mother, Francisca Girardy, Widow DesRuisseaux, and that the documents written in English and French be translated into Spanish.

Widow Chalon requested that copies of everything be kept in the New Orleans office of the Escribano, while she appealed to Havana to force Pollock to account for his administration of her husband's estate, as well as to submit the original records of the inventory of her late husband's property. A marginal note stipulated that a copy of the suit was made on eighty four sheets of paper; and court costs up to November 26, 1783, were 53 pesos, 4 reales, with a lot more to be paid before the affair was finished.[2]

Late 1783 presented the unusual situation of a New Orleans debtor trying to convince his French creditor to take his money. In November, Antonio Jung—brother of bayou landowner Andres Jung—was explaining to the court that Merchant Lafitte had some time before accepted his bill of exchange in Bordeaux, which was to be redeemed in New Orleans a month after Lafitte's arrival. At the time and place agreed upon, Jung had offered to pay 150 pesos, plus 192 pesos for stowage of eight tons of freight, in treasury notes, which at that time were passing for hard money. Lafitte, however, was holding out for silver; and Jung asked the court to persuade his reluctant creditor to accept treasury notes in payment of his debt. The Judge ruled on November 5th that Lafitte must accept the treasury notes; but a couple of weeks later Jung had a change of heart (or possibly an acute vision of future business) for he settled out of court and paid costs besides.[3]

Financial difficulties seemed to dominate court activities of 1783. In December Francisco Durcy was attempting to raise enough money to pay off the balance he owed on property he'd purchased three years before. On September 18, 1780 he'd acquired an isla (island, square of ground), approximately twelve lots, which formed the corner of Burgundy and Hospital Streets, adjoining the guard room of Bayou Gate (which led from New Orleans onto Bayou Road), the rear of the square bordering on the rampart or stockade of New Orleans and other unappropriated lands.

Lazaro Estardy, from whom Durcy had purchased the property, had previously acquired it from Santiago Chapron on July 5, 1780; but the hurricane of August 24, 1780 damaged some of the buildings, and Estardy sold the lot, as it was, to Durcy for 2,400 pesos—1,400 pesos to be paid by the end of 1780 and the balance a year later.

On December 15, 1783 Estardy petitioned the court to make delinquent Durcy pay 1,000 pesos, plus a tenth and costs; and if payment wasn't forthcoming, he requested that the court seize enough of Durcy's property to pay what he owed. When the Sheriff went to the Bayou Gate house to deliver the decree, Durcy talked him out of serving the writ by promising to pay as soon as he could sell the house and lots, and then went before the court protesting Estardy's malice in the matter, asking that the auction of his property take place on condition that the entire sale net him three thousand pesos—enough to pay all his debts.

However, the law decided in favor of his creditor, and Estardy demanded that the Writ of Seizure, previously ordered by the court, be now executed and that the property be appraised. The house and lots were seized and valued by Adrien de la Place at 2,800 pesos. Three public calls were made on January 13, 22 and 31, 1784, and an auction was called for March 1, 1784. Disappointingly, it is not revealed if the unfortunate managed to escape his financial morass, for the unfinished record ran out with the ringing of the noonday bell—just after Durcy had offered 1,650 pesos for his own property.[4]

Failure to abide by the law—by none other than a knowledgeable attorney and former resident of Bayu San Juan—resulted in an interesting three-year legal twist which began in 1783, when Pedro Estoupan (who'd been living on the other side of the lake during British occupation of that territory) returned to New Orleans to find somebody living in his house located at the extreme end of Bourbon Street—where it formed a corner with the stockade surrounding the town.

Estoupan had purchased the house on June 15, 1769 from bayou resident Francois (Francisco) Héry, called Duplanty for 350 piastres gourdes, payable in eighteen months, with the understanding that if full payment was not forthcoming, the amount paid down would be considered rental and the property would be forfeited. Estoupan had paid five hundred livres down and had made a second payment of four hundred livres (a hundred and fifty pesos in all) on May 18, 1771, after Duplanty had died.

Eight years later, attorney Henriques Desprez, then married to Widow Duplanty, believing that Estoupan had abandoned the property since nothing had been heard from him, sold the half-lot measuring 30′ front by 120′ deep and house to Pedro Denis, called Panquinet. On June 3, 1780 Panquinet paid Desprez three hundred pesos in full payment for the place.

It took Estoupan three years after his return to New Orleans to realize he wasn't going to get his house back the easy way, and on March 28, 1786 Desprez was in court replying to a suit instituted by the plaintiff, who was demanding that Panquinet pay rental on his house from July, 1779 to the present and that Desprez pay court costs.

For once, the attorney's influence seemed to have run out; the court ruled that Estoupan could not be deprived of his property because of his absence from New Orleans nor for failure to make full payment—unless he'd been cited and a judgment had been rendered against him in a court of justice. Therefore, the plaintiff had a right to reclaim his house if he paid Desprez the 120 pesos he still owed him. Estoupan was also awarded rent on his house from July, 1779 to the time of the verdict, from which sum court costs had to be deducted. Panquinet, in turn, was given the right to reclaim his three hundred pesos from Desprez, but was ordered out of Estoupan's house within three days.

Notified of the decree, attorney Desprez threatened to appeal the case to the Superior Tribunal at Havana, but evidently changed his mind, for a marginal note of July 20, 1786 disclosed that he paid Pedro Panquinet three hundred pesos.[5]

The records of 1784 introduced Estevan (Etienne) Roquigny, who would soon become the second husband of bayou plantation owner Maria Isabel DesRuisseaux, Widow Chalon. The Roquignys would live on the old Girardy-DesRuisseaux plantation on the west bank of Bayu San Juan (on Moss Street, approximately from Carrollton Avenue to Orleans Avenue today) for the rest of his life and until Widow Roquigny's death about 1815.

Roquigny was a blacksmith by trade, and on April 23, 1784 testified in court that the late Pablo Lacour Dubourg had ordererd several mill parts from him, which he, Roquigny, had delivered, and for which he now wished the Dubourg estate to pay him a hundred and fifteen pesos. Producing several reliable witnesses, who testified to the legitimacy of the claim, the judge ruled on August 14, 1784 that the debt be listed, along with those of other creditors, who would be paid after the privileged debts had been liquidated. Two years later, Roquigny was still trying to collect his money, claiming that his charges represented personal labor which merited preference over certain other debts. On May 6, 1786 the alcalde issued an order to the guardian of the Dubourg estate to pay Roquigny what was due him.[6]

In some cases a man's death reveals as much about him as does his life. The will of Santiago Lorreins, called Tarascon, not only demonstrated a truly mature love for his wife of twenty seven years, it also showed his respect for her judgment and ability to handle his affairs after his death. The handling of this succession especially revealed the difference a good lawyer can make when the chips are down. In this instance, the lawyer-curator, representing the minor children—either through male chauvinism, envy or a desire to get what he could from an estimable estate—seemed to complicate the situation wherever he could. If it hadn't been for Widow Lorreins' compassionate, sensible attorney, whose wisdom was confirmed by the court, many lives on Bayu San Juan would have changed for the worse.

The last-minute-making of his sister's will and the unsettling confusion surrounding Pelagia Lorreins' death a couple of years before, had had its effect on her brother, for Santiago Lorreins (Tarascon) took care of that important task a year and a half before he died. But even careful anticipation, no doubt resulting in the state of peace in which the Escribano of the court found him the night of June 29, 1784—the day after he'd died—"laid out in one of his rooms with four lighted candles around his body," didn't eliminate the complication that always attends the transition of a man of substance and stature from his worldly abode to what lies beyond.

Santiago Lorreins, called Tarascon, was the son of Santiago Lorreins of Avignon, France and Maria Avril (Abril, Aubril), of Burgundy, France; both parents had died by the time Santiago Lorreins married Maria Luisa Baudin on October 13, 1757.

Following his death the legal machinery began to turn on June 30, 1784 when Escribano Rafael Perdomo collected one key to the decedent's wardrobe from Widow Lorreins, at which time he certified that death was from natural causes and noted that preparation for burial had begun.

The next item on the legal calendar was the search for the will and its reading. Declaring his Catholic religious faith, Lorreins asked to be buried simply (probably the only request that wasn't carried out by his widow), that three masses be said for the repose of his soul, and apparently believing that charity began and ended at home, he specified that alms of two reales be given once to each of the forced bequests of the town and only ten pesos to Charity Hospital.

Lorreins declared himself debtless, but if he had overlooked anything, this careful man wished to make it right, stating that his estate consisted of two houses in New Orleans, three plantations and some active debts recorded in his book of accounts and loose memoranda. He explained the debit-credit situation of an "extra judicial" (not covered by public or private documents) trading business into which he'd entered with Juan Bautista Tunoir.

To his four grandchildren—offspring of daughter Francisca and Juan Luis Allard—who lived across the bayou, he left eight hundred pesos, which were to be delivered to Allard immediately upon distribution of the estate.

Lorreins' will specified that after his death an act of emancipation be drawn up to free Margarita, a fifty eight year old Negress and her twenty three year old mulattress daughter Maria Adelaide, as a reward for their faithful services.

In addition to itemizing what his wife was to receive before partition of the estate (according to their marriage contract), he named her tutrix and curatrix ad bono to his minor children because of the great confidence he placed in her, and relieved her of giving the usual bond. To be sure everything was carried out according to his wishes, he also appointed her testamentary executrix and guardian of his estate.

As his sole and universal heirs, he named his children: Francisca, wife of Juan Luis Allard, Pelagia, unmarried and seventeen year old Santiago Lorreins.

When the court had ascertained there was no other will, the key to Lorreins' wardrobe and records of the succession were delivered to Widow Lorreins who then petitioned the court's permission to record the inventory. Joseph Adrien de la Place and Andres Wackernie were appointed and took the oath as public appraisers; and public attorney Francisco Broutin was appointed curator ad lites to represent the minor Lorreins children. Following through on legal formalities and having posted bond, he was placed in charge of the curatorship and received a copy of the records for his perusal.

The emancipation of Margarita and her daughter having been effected immediately, a certificate of freedom was promptly delivered to them.

And on July 10, 1784, Francisco Maria de Reggio, Regidor Alferez Real-Alcalde Ordinario (under whose jurisdiction the succession was being processed) Francisco Broutin, and Escribano Rafael Perdomo went to the dwelling of Widow Lorreins on Bayu San Juan where the appraisers awaited them, and His Honor ordered the beginning of the inventory and valuation of the Tarascon estate.

During the forenoon, the smaller furnishings—from groceries, dishes and sheets to furniture—were inventoried, among them eight large earthen water jars and four hundred pots of bear fat, the most available shortening of the time. Two promissory notes from Tounoir—covering another two hundred pots of bear lard—were also listed. (Bear oil no doubt constituted a large part of the business Lorreins had shared with Tounoir.) After the household items had been appraised at 746 pesos, the plantation bell rang for twelve o'clock prayers, the records were consigned to the care of Widow Lorreins, testamentary executrix, and His Honor called a halt to the proceedings, which were to be resumed at his convenience.

He found it convenient two days later when the same group again convened at Bayu San Juan to continue their work, beginning with inventory of the livestock. Forty six cows, thirty two calves, forty eight bulls and ten yokes of oxen were listed; and the appraising officials counted three long narrow carts, a small cart, a light gig for two horses, with all harnesses, a plough with all its equipment, eight axes, eight hoes, eight shovels, three sprinkling cans, ten large and small pots and a spit. Five hundred pesos of silver and paper money were listed, as well as a mounted copper bell which rang the Angelus at noon when work was suspended, total evaluations of 3,925 pesos having been accomplished.

After lunch, eleven plantation slaves, ranging from five to fifty years, were appraised at 4,950 pesos, the highest value—750 pesos—being placed on thirty year old negress Maria who washed, ironed and cooked.

The next inventory item was the large plantation itself fronting for twenty arpents on the east bank of Bayu San Juan, extending back to Bayou Gentilly, which Lorreins had purchased from René Kernion in 1771. (The 1771 Luis Andry Survey of the Kernion property gives the plantation twenty two arpents front, but measurements often varied, or Lorreins may have sold a small segment of the land.) Two years before his death, Lorreins had inherited the adjoining Dugué-Brazillier plantation of two to two and a half arpents front on the bayou; so his combined property on the east bank would today reach approximately from a point near DeSoto Street to the northern reaches of the National Guard installation—a large block south of DeSaix Boulevard.

The records denote that on the Lorreins plantation were fruit trees of various kinds and a new house, thirty four feet in front and the same in depth, containing four rooms and an eight foot gallery on three sides. There was also a kitchen, a storeroom, and six negro cabins nearby, built adjacent to another house and storeroom which were in bad condition. This large plantation, with all its improvements, was appraised at only 4,600 pesos. (It is possible that the new house in which Santiago Lorreins died, is the one, or part of the one, owned by Dr. Ignatius M. DeMatteo, that now stands at 1300 Moss Street.* Architect-Historian Samuel Wilson, Jr. believes that this residence may have been built about 1784. Of course, many changes and additions have been made to the original structure by subsequent owners of the place.)

The officials then moved across the bayou to record the assets of the plantation where Widow Lorreins' daughter Francisca, her husband and four children lived. Fronting eight arpents on the stream, by forty deep, a house had been built on this property which measured forty feet across the front, had back and front galleries and a new storeroom 30′ x 16′, all of which was valued at 2,200 pesos. (Today's lower City Park.)

When everything was completed at Bayu San Juan, Widow Lorreins gave a receipt for the real property and slaves and signed the necessary papers wtih the other officials and appraisers.

The next day two houses in New Orleans were inspected and appraised. A sixty by one hundred and twenty foot lot on Bourbon Street (bounded by the properties of Messrs. Blache and Masico), on which was located a three room house with kitchen, two galleries and a cabinet, was valued at

---

*The French-West-Indian plantation house at 1300 Moss Street—the oldest house on Bayou St. John today—had from the earliest times been referred to as the Custom House, although there is no record it was ever used as such. The original King's Warehouse-Receiving Station, was built in 1719-20, to the west of Bayou Road, which in French times began at Bayou St. Jean west of today's DeSoto Street. However, after Luis Brazillier purchased the Dugué plantation in 1729, he transferred a portion of that property on the bayou to the French government to be used as a Naval Arsenal. Maps of that time indicate that pirogues and ships were unloaded at that site, so the arsenal may have served as a warehousing area also, since the maps do not show the original warehouse west of Bayou Road during this period. The location of this arsenal, near the 1784 house, may account for the Custom House appellation.

When Spain took over Luisiana, the arsenal was ceded to that country, and Spanish officials ceded the site to Alexandro Latil in 1770, who—it is believed—sold the small plot back to Juan Bautista Brazillier who'd inherited the surrounding small plantation from his father. In 1777, at the request of Joseph Chalon, Bayou Road was moved easterly by twenty feet, bringing the location of the road closer to Grand Route St. John of today. At his death, Juan Bautista Brazillier's widow, Pelagia Lorreins, inherited the property and left it to her brother Santiago Lorreins, and it became an extension of his larger plantation on the east bank of Bayu San Juan.

2,500 pesos. The sixty by one hundred and fifty nine foot lot on the corner of St. Philip and Burgundy, (bounded by the properties of Messrs. Lacoste and Champion) on which was a house of three rooms, a kitchen-house and cabin, was listed at 3,200 pesos, and was the last item on the total inventory.

Francisco Broutin then requested the escribano to go to the home of Widow Lorreins on July 13th where she swore by God and the cross that she knew of no other property that had belonged to the deceased, whereupon Broutin asked that the court approve the inventory. He also requested that Maria Luisa Baudin Lorreins render an account of all properties and that an attorney be appointed to represent her. Approving Broutin's petition, the court named Pedro Bertonière, Procurator Publico del Numero (one of a special number of attorneys commissioned to practice in the courts)—a lucky choice for Widow Lorreins, as he immediately petitioned the court to adjudicate to the widow all the property at inventory valuation, to avoid further expense and privations she and her children would suffer if the estate were auctioned. He brought to the court's attention the fact that Mrs. Lorreins had to feed, clothe and educate her minor children, and promised that she would deliver to each of them his or her legitimate paternal inheritance as the children came of age. Alcalde de Reggio ordered a copy of the petition sent to the curator of the minors.

Francisco Broutin protested immediately, stating this would be prejudicial to the minors inasmuch as the present market would bring double the inventory valuation if the property was auctioned. Praying that the sale be permitted, copies of his petition were sent to the auditor and Widow Lorreins.

She replied to Broutin's proposal via her attorney, who again showed uncommon good sense. Bertonière pleaded before the court that the "pretensions of the curator" would in no way be favorable to Mrs. Lorreins nor the minors, as it was generally acknowledged that all property put up for sale at public auction immediately lost nearly two-thirds of its value. Additionally, because it was obligatory to grant buyers a year's credit (and from experience it usually took a half year beyond that), Mrs. Lorreins would have nothing with which to support her family if deprived of the use of her plantation, slaves and livestock. Furthermore, the attorney pointed out, Santiago Lorreins, her young son, had no other occupation than that of laborer on the plantation, and if it were sold he'd have no way of earning a living nor would the rest of the family be provided for.

The court decreed that the inventoried property be adjudicated to Widow Lorreins at valuation, and that she make herself responsible to her children for the paternal inheritance each was to receive.

Broutin immediately asked the court to have Maria Luisa Baudin prepare a sworn statement of the property, so the partiton schedule might be written; only a few days had elapsed after this request when Broutin complained to the court that the widow was in default, and the court notified Luisa Baudin Lorreins that she must produce the document within three days. Her lawyer then presented to the court a list of the estate inventory with valuations amounting to a total of 24,121 pesos, including a 2,000 peso note from Juan Bautista Tounoir's estate covering two hundred pots of bear fat.

Broutin responded immediately, accusing the widow of rendering a too-informal account in order to save the cost of writing an additional few pages, and complained that she'd omitted the debits of the account, such as funeral and burial expenses, doctor bills and other costs of the succession; he demanded that she immediately provide a complete account of debits and credits in better form. Hardly having made the request, he was again before the court pressing Widow Lorreins for the statement which hadn't materialized.

Having finally gotten her bills together, Luisa Baudin Lorreins wrote an account of expenses which she presented to the court. For comparison with contemporary funerals, the details of Lorreins' "simple burial" are worth noting:

	Pesos	Reales	
Burial	3	2	
Assistance of two priests	3		Paid to Father Antonio de
Three singers	4	4	Sedella for funeral
Three acolytes dressed in black	1		expenses.
Beadle and Sacristan	2		
Cope	2		
Bells	3		
Black covering on the altar	1		
Pall for deceased	1		
Vigil	4		
Thirty candles in church	7	4	It is not indicated that
Grave in church	1	4	Widow Lorreins had to
Twenty new candles for	7	4	pay a hundred pesos,

	Pesos	Reales	
distribution			formerly demanded, for burial within the church.
Three masses for the soul of the deceased	3		
	44	6	
For the mass	5		Paid to Father Antonio de Sedella for the Anniversary Mass on July 28, 1784 for the soul of her late husband.
Four singers	6		
Assistance of two priests	1	2	
Sacristan and two acolytes		4	
Cross and one censer		4	
Cope	2		
Bells	3		
Black palls	1		
Representation (Memorial Sermon)	1		
Nocturn	4		
Seven pounds of new wax	9	4	
	34	7	
7 ells crepe @ 4 reales	3	6	
4 pair gloves @ 4 reales	2		
3 candles @ 12 reales	4	4	
12 ells serge @ 3 reales	4	4	
3 pair black silk stockings @ 2 pesos	6		
	20	6	

There were additional charges of five pesos for making the coffin, six pesos for those who carried her husband's body to the cemetery, two hundred pesos, allowed by law, for mourning (for herself, her children and the servants) and thirty pesos for taxes and costs on this allowance.

It had cost his estate 341 pesos, 3 reales to bury Don Santiago Lorreins, called Tarascon.

Broutin was hard put to find anything wrong with the detailed account sent him by the court, but somehow he managed. He disapproved of the allowance for mourning, because Widow Lorreins lived on a plantation where expenses were low, in addition to which she'd been adjudicated all the property at inventory price. Reducing the mourning allowance by thirty pesos, he substituted his own bill of thirty pesos—covering his fee for contesting the account. Recapitulating the debits and credits, his record showed a balance of 23,879 pesos, 5 reales, half of which was to be distributed to the minors at the proper time. He also requested that Widow Lorreins account to the minors for one-half of two thousand pesos, a debt due the succession from the estate of Balthasar de Villiers' estate, when she received the money.

Three months after the death of Lorreins—a surprisingly short time considering the size of his estate—Francisco Maria de Reggio, Alcalde Ordinario, had on September 28, 1784 examined the records, approved them, and decreed that all parties should abide by them. However, Spanish officials were not about to give up so easily—not on so estimable an estate.

Francisco Broutin notified the court that since the case was nearly finished, he renounced his office as procurator in favor of Antonio Mendez, and asked the court to tax costs on the case so he could receive what was coming to him. He asked for thirty pesos—the same as the attorney of Mrs. Lorreins requested—to which de Reggio responded that the taxer, in accordance with justice, would decide all fees to be paid by Widow Lorreins.

After court acceptance of Antonio Mendez to represent the minors, the new curator ad lites petitioned the court for partition of the estate; and Luis Lioteaud, being legally sworn, prepared taxation of the costs of the case, which—in addition to various special fees which had been paid along the way—amounted to 141 pesos, of which Attorney Broutin received 206 reales, four reales less than he'd asked for.

After thorough re-examination and consideration of all legal documents involved in the estate, legal re-working back and forth of the credits and debits of the succession, more special fees, plus 42 pesos, 6 reales court courts, Luis Lioteaud, on April 15, 1785 presented to the court a final account of the partition of Santiago Lorreins' estate, the net total of which amounted to 21,545 pesos, 7 reales. In addition to what Luisa Baudin Lorreins had received before partition, half of this amount belonged to her; from the other half, 3,590 pesos, 28 reales were to be delivered to each of her three children as they came of age.

At considerable cost it had taken the Spanish courts nearly a year to legally confirm what Santiago Lorreins (Tarascon) had so carefully arranged before his death, to protect and sustain his widow and children.[7]

Chapter XXIII

DEATH, FIRE AND PHILANTHROPY UNDER GOVERNOR MIRO 1784 - 1789

Savage Negroes, running away and hiding out, presented a problem that concerned everybody in 1784. It had been going on for some time. On March 21, 1783 Renato Huchet de Kernion had received from the fund provided for that purpose two hundred pesos in payment for his runaway slave who had drowned trying to avoid a musket blow from a free Mulatto who was attempting to arrest him. In August of 1783 a woman petitioned the Cabildo for two hundred pesos her slave had been promised to point out the hiding place of some fugitives. The situation had gone downhill so rapidly that on April 30, 1784 the Cabildo passed an ordinance stipulating that any slave walking the street without his master's permit on his person would receive twenty five lashes. Saloon and hotel keepers were severely warned not to sell liquor to a slave without his master's permission; and people in general were asked to search their houses and property and send to jail any unauthorized person they found taking refuge on their land.

The predicament reached a climax of sorts in the summer of 1784 with an excitable discussion at the Cabildo. The Alcaldes believed the province was threatened with a general uprising of the Blacks, and argued that masters would soon find themselves catering to the slightest whims of their slaves—especially at harvest time—when they threatened to run away on the slightest pretext. Responding to the general alarm, the Governor issued strict orders that fugitives be diligently pursued by expeditions for which local residents would have to pay.

So many were requesting money for the capture of runaways; and owners so frequently demanded compensation for slaves killed in the course of capture that the fund providing for these contingencies was depleted. It was suggested that slave buyers be charged an additional dollar per head to replenish the fund.

A related clamour arose when four fugitive leaders were executed on July 19, 1784 without having a priest present. On October 4th, the local Capuchin Fathers received a scathing letter of reprimand from the Bishop of Cuba because of their spiritual failure to assist the criminals at the time of execution.[1]

Others were having problems of a business nature. In August, 1784 Ignacio Valderas, sublieutenant of the Fixed Regiment of the Infantry of Luisiana and Commander at Bayu San Juan, was seeking justice before the court of Governor Miro. The year before he'd entrusted Guillermo Dubuisson of Mobile with two hundred and fifty hard pesos to invest in merchandise, which he, Valderas, could sell for a little extra income. Dubuisson, however, had bought goods Valderas didn't much like, and he refused to accept it, whereupon Dubuisson offered to keep his purchases and reimburse Valderas when he'd disposed of them. But Valderas wasn't willing to wait for his capital, and petitioned the court for immediate return of his pesos. "Immediate" in Spanish court proceedings meant six months later, at which time Valderas requested a Writ of Execution to seize enough of Dubuisson's property to cover the debt. However, the record of February 16, 1785 indicates that the writ wasn't executed. Canny Dubuisson no doubt decided that it was to his future business interest to settle the matter out of court.[2]

Don Andres Almonester Y Roxas was increasing his suburban holdings. On August 2, 1784, before notary Raphael Perdomo, he purchased a huge tract of land to the immediate west of the Allard and DesRuisseaux plantations on the west bank of Bayu San Juan. Some of this land would in the 1830's be owned by the New Orleans Canal and Banking Company, and the New Basin Canal would be constructed through it. Known as *La Metairie* (the site of the old Village of the Colapissas), Almonester purchased these forty five to fifty arpents on both sides of Metairie Bayou, extending north as far as Lake Pontchartrain, from the Capuchin monks, thus accounting for Bayou Metairie being called the Bayou of the Chapter in the records of the time. The arpents had originally been conceded to Louis Cezaire LeBreton in French times, and he had sold the tract to Gilberto St. Maxent, who—together with his wife—had on January 27, 1765 exchanged *La Metairie* for land on the other side of Bayu San Juan—an eighteen arpent tract fronting on Bayou Gentilly and extending to Lake Pontchartrain.[3]

The 1780's saw the demise of many Bayou familiars—folk who from French times had been involved with the settlement and development of Bayu San Juan and vicinity. Three years after the death of his wife, and ten days after making his will, Andres Jung (Juen), widower of deceased Pellagia Lorreins Brazillier, died between eight and nine o'clock on September 4, 1784.

In his will Jung professed his Catholic faith, asked that he be shrouded in a white sheet and be given a humble burial in the Parish Church, requested that three masses be said for the repose of his soul, and specified that three reales be given to each of the forced bequests and a hundred pesos to Charity Hospital.

Jung declared his assets to be a dwelling-house in the city, a plantation on Bayu San Juan, a plantation in the process of being sold on the other side of the lake, forty negro slaves (for three of whom he willed emancipation), two thousand pesos in his coffers, furniture, wrought silver, gold and silver jewelry and wearing apparel. A considerable portion of his assets consisted of debts owed him by many in the province, which he ordered his executor to collect and apply to his estate.

His will confirmed that his deceased wife had managed the capital she brought to their marriage and at her death had disposed of her estate as she saw fit.

A soul-baring aspect of this last document was his acknowledgment that before contracting a late marriage, he had had three living illegitimate mulatto children, who since their birth had been fed, educated and maintained in his home as his own family. Going on to explain that he had no legitimate descendants or ascendents to fall heir to his fortune, he requested that his two brothers—Antonio and August Jung—be given two thousand pesos each, because of the great affection he felt for them.

In the interest of his illegitimate children, he requested that his executor (1) invest two thousand pesos so his son Juan Luis (child of free Negress Isabel) might live on the income during his life; in the event Juan Luis should marry, the amount should eventually be given to his children; if he remained single, at his death, the principal was to be returned to the estate, (2) Jung's twenty five year old daughter Roseta (by free Negress Goton) was to receive two thousand pesos outright so that she might manage for herself. This gift was in remuneration for her special care of him, and the paternal love he felt for her, (3) his twenty three year old daughter Goton (by deceased negress slave Luizon) was to be given a thousand pesos outright.

To Brixida de Reggio, unmarried, Jung left four thousand pesos, which she was to receive when she came of age, from her father Francisco Maria de Reggio, Alferez Real—Regidor Perpetuo—Alcalde Ordinario of New Orleans, who Jung named as his sole and universal heir, testamentary executor and guardian of his estate.

It is worth noting that his universal heir was a friend—a very important, influential man in the Spanish government—rather than one of his brothers for whom he expressed great affection. Under French rule, whites—and even manumitted or free born blacks—were prohibited from living in a state of concubinage with slaves; and there is no reason to believe the Spanish were more lenient in their treatment of black illegitimates than were the French. It is possible Jung reasoned that the only way he could insure posthumous assistance to his mulatto offspring was to appoint a man of governmental influence and reward him handsomely for his services. It would be interesting to know how these illegitimates actually fared after Jung's death, for their future depended on the loyalty, whims and good will of their dead father's friend, de Reggio, who immediately appointed public attorney Pedro Bertonière to represent him in the succession.

The court stipulated September 28, 1784 as inventory day; and after appointment and confirmation of appraisers Joseph Adrian de la Place and Guillermo Guinan (in the absence of Andres Waukernie), these two gentlemen, together with legatees Antonio and August Jung, Public Attorney Bertonière, Escribano Rafael Perdomo and Alcalde Esteban Boré (in charge of the succession) proceeded to Jung's dwelling house which was built on brick columns in front of the Mississippi levee, bounded by the properties of Sergeant Major Francisco de Bouligny and Estevan Plauche.

In this splendid house (which with lot was valued at four thousand and five hundred pesos), two thousand pesos in hard silver and notes found in an iron box were inventoried, as well as elaborate furnishings and wrought silver. A silver platter weighing thirty six ounces was listed at thirty six pesos; and the silver candlesticks, soup tureen, coffee pot, spoons, forks, etc. were estimated at one peso per silver ounce. There were other items too, attesting to Jung's way of life, such as crystal celery dishes, one hundred and one German damask table napkins and a hundred and sixty bottles in the wine cellar.

Jung must have been quite the cock-of-the-walk, for some of his wearing apparel was valuable enough to be included in the inventory—a blue cape, overcoat and trousers trimmed with gold braid, a gold embroidered rough silk vest, an apron with crimson velvet pockets, and many other articles of clothing worth a considerable sum.

All these luxuries had been administered to Mr. Jung, who loved the good things of life, by sixteen negro servants who had worked in his town house.

The decedent's involvement in multi-activities had necessitated meticulous record-keeping, and his inventory listed more notes, certifications, receipts and miscellaneous business documents than any other succession of colonial times. Having dealt heavily in pitch and tar, many of these items were inventoried on his bayou plantation, and notes and receipts indicated that he'd delivered them in quantity to the King's Store.

There was official documentation of houses which former bayou resident Jose Chalon had built in Barataria, and of Jung's dealings with Juan Ventura Morales of the Cabildo in supplying rations and repairing cabins for the families who had settled there. Other notes covered monies involved in various aspects of shipping and sales of landed property and slaves. Jung had been a materially successful, influential, industrious man of many parts.

The custom of pausing for prayer on the first toll of the Angelus at noon and at five o'clock was scrupulously observed throughout the entire inventory procedure.

At seven o'clock on October 1, 1784 the succession officials left New Orleans, and arriving at Jung's plantation on the west bank of Bayu San Juan, began their duties at 8:00 A.M. The plantation which measured eight arpents on the bayou, in the vicinity of today's Taylor Avenue, stretched westerly for eighty arpents, was bounded on the cityside by the lands of Allard and on the lakeside by those of Gilberto St. Maxent.*

On the plantation was a brick dwelling house, a frame kitchen, three cabins for Negroes, a storeroom that served as a cooperage and another for utensils, a few farm implements and simple house furnishings. The bayou plantation, with all improvements, was valued at only 1,100 pesos. Farm animals included two heifers, five bulls, two mules, two calves, a cow and calf, a saddlehorse and a horse for pulling the cart. Near the bayou was a schooner with three sails (no masts and spars), cordage, anchor, an old bark with tackle and rigging, the ribs of a ship and a fourteen foot pirogue.

On March 11, 1781 Jung had sold this plantation to Maurice Conway, nephew of O'Reilly, but a couple of months later Conway had sold it back

*Records covering early conveyances of Bayou St. John properties are so confused and incorrect that is is difficult to spot-cite them by today's landmarks. In early times it was almost impossible to accurately measure the bayou swamps. Since much of the unfenced land was used for hunting, cutting of timber and cattle grazing, most of the early settlers paid little attention to boundaries. It was only after that area was drained during the 1800's and became valuable that these matters were explored and resulted in ownership lawsuits —most of which would not be resolved until the early 1920's when the location was being purchased to establish City Park. An official map drawn up as a consequence of these lawcases would indicate that the middle line of the Jung plantation was located approximately where the railroad traverses the park, near the Wisner Overpass, half of the plantation fronting on Bayou St. John on either side of the tracks—land that in early American times would be owned by Beugnot plus the four lakeside arpents of the Allard Plantation, #116, purchased by Luis Allard, the younger.

to him on May 10th. The seventeen Negroes on the bayou plantation had worked with liquid pitch; the inventory included fifty one barrels of it, eighty partially filled and a hundred and fifty empty containers.

Later that day, the inventory-takers listed seven more slaves who apparently cared for nine oxen, nineteen dry cows and calves and five sheep on the lake plantation, after which the officers left the bayou at 5:00 P.M. They must have flown over Bayou Road on the return trip, for they arrived back in town at 5:30.

Though there were no newspapers in those days, word got around very quickly about proceedings of this kind, because in late September free Negro Valentin petitioned the court to purchase the freedom of his fifty year old brother Silvestre who was listed on the Jung inventory as being worth three hundred pesos. Of course, Francisco Maria de Reggio, universal heir to the estate, refused to accept that price, explaining that an inventory was nothing more than a legal formality which had to be effected in order to eliminate confusion at the auction sale—that a Negro valued at three hundred to five hundred pesos on the inventory would bring eight hundred to a thousand pesos at public auction, depending upon his particular talents which appraisers never took into consideration.

Offering no objection to de Reggio's request for a new appraisement, Valentin—through public attorney Antonio Mendez—requested that Dr. Joseph Montegut, surgeon of the local Regiment of Infantry, examine Silvestre and certify as to his physical condition, before he, Valentin, appointed an appraiser.

De Reggio agreed, but asked that the court permit examination of the slave by surgeon Juan Senac as well. Predictably, there was disagreement. Montegut reported a dislocation of the right knee which prevented Silvestre from making the proper movements. Senac, though admitting the slave was unable to work due to a possible rupture of the articular ligament, opined that the slave was not totally crippled and outlined various methods of alleviating the injury.

After Adrien de la Place was confirmed by the court as Valentin's appraiser, de Reggio named Estevan Plauche to represent him in the matter. De la Place placed a value of five hundred pesos on Silvestre vs. Plauche's one thousand, whereupon it became incumbent upon the court to appoint a third appraiser to settle the difference. On November 4th Antonio de Jan accepted the job, was confirmed by the court and compromised the matter at eight hundred pesos. The very next day Valentin brought the money to court and bought his brother's freedom for that amount plus court costs of thirty seven pesos, six reales.

Executor de Reggio continued to receive charges of various kinds against the Jung estate. On October 8, 1784 Francisco Bojard presented a bill of sixty pesos covering costs of court previously incurred at Pensacola Bay for examination of damages sustained by Jung's schooner, the *San Andrus*, of which Bojard had been the skipper.

Records of the succession are incomplete, so it is not revealed how much de Reggio actually inherited from Jung. Various lawcases of the early 1920's reveal that very soon after Jung's death de Reggio sold the bayou plantation to Augustin Jung, who quickly sold it to Luis Antonio Blanc on October 29, 1785, who in turn sold the eight arpents to the Gilberto St. Maxents who owned the contiguous lakeside property. Widow St. Maxent would eventually sell the eight arpents to a free woman of color called Fanchon Montreuil on December 11, 1797, which should have made Andres Jung—wherever he was—a very happy man.[4]

On November 24, 1784 Luis Antonio Blanc was before the court requesting a valid title to an eighty by one hundred twenty foot lot on Hospital Street (Governor Nicholls Street today), which during his absence in 1781 had been sold by his first wife who needed the money. Representing Mrs. Blanc, Francisco Cheval, had, by means of some simple document, transferred the lot to free Negro Jean Louis Meunie on November 8, 1781 for two hundred piastres; and now the purchaser was demanding a clear title to his land.

Other circumstances clouded the issue, for on April 25, 1778 Blanc had mortgaged his real property in favor of the Royal Treasury, which mortgage, he now admitted, had not included the lot sold by Henriqueta Gauvin, his deceased first wife. He therefore prayed for execution of a public instrument giving him belated title to the lot and requested that a proper act of sale be passed before the notary and clerk of court so a copy could be delivered to Jean Louis Meunie. Blanc's petition was referred to the fiscal of the Royal Treasury.[5]

While Governor Galvez was pursuing his military campaign against the English, Don Estevan Rodriguez Miro, Colonel of the Luisiana Regiment and ranking military officer of the province, had become acting governor; and in December of 1785, Miro, after playing a conspicuous role in the conquest of the Floridas, assumed the first position.

Following the example of previous governors Unzaga and Galvez, who had meshed romance with ruling, Miro—a man possessed of judgment, heart and honor—also married a local girl, one of the Macarty daughters.

Having received his formal appointment, he followed the Spanish colonial custom of issuing a "Bando de buen gobierno," in which he outlined his policies, recommended remedies for certain shortcomings, and expressed his intent as to observation of new regulations.

His concern about the moral climate of the community zeroed in particularly on the sexual relations of white male inhabitants with the black beauties of the province—a situation generally taken for granted by the community at that time. In an effort to eliminate these liaisons, by decreasing the attractiveness of the softer sex, Miro forbad females of color to wear plumes or jewelry in their tresses and directed them to bind up their hair in a kerchief, which marked the beginning of the well-known tignon ever after associated with negro women of Luisiana. However, artists that women are in arranging their assets, especially when the stakes are appeal to the opposite sex, the tignon—in its varying styles—became more of a resource than a liability. Miro was not the first, nor would he be the last, to learn that emotions cannot be legislated.[6]

Meanwhile, some of the local people were profiting from government work. In an official statement of March 20, 1785, of monies paid to local officials by the Spanish, is an item of 360 pesos, paid to Director of Works without military rank, Don Alexandro Latil, of Bayou Road.

Henriques Desprez, Captain of the Urban Militia, was litigiously involved as usual. Hauling Juan Bautista de Gruis before the Governor's court in March of 1785, he accused him of non-fulfillment of contract, whereby Desprez had suffered considerable financial loss. A year before —on May 29, 1784—he and de Gruis had entered into a contract by which the latter obligated himself to deliver to the plaintiff's mill twelve hundred feet of lumber in a single delivery when the river was high, so it could be cut into twelve and fourteen foot lengths for a customer who was willing to pay six hundred pesos for the job. De Gruis failed to deliver the wood when the river was high enough to power the mill, so Desprez was left hanging, and he was now asking compensation to cover his loss. The record ended with the calling of witnesses to support the plaintiff's claim, so it isn't known whether or not Desprez recouped his losses.[7]

Trouble ran up and down the social scale. A month later fugitive Felipe was up to his eyeballs in females and agitation. On June 25, 1785 he was interrogated by Senior Alcalde Nicholas Forstall in prison, where he'd landed on the charge of robbery. A bachelor-woodchopper by trade, he'd run away from his master in LaFourche, had taken a pirogue to Attacapas where he'd herded cattle for three weeks, from whence he went to Metairie, and via Bayu San Juan came to New Orleans where he met up with Modesta, a griffe slave of Mr. Morales. He had, however, left his chest, containing thirty seven and a half pesos, in the cabin of free Negress Margarita Vouis for safekeeping. Fearing apprehension, Felipe was constantly on the move, and in his absence Modesta had gone to the cabin of the free Negress with the key to the chest, saying she wished to collect twenty pesos. Knowing Felipe had slept with her, Margarita allowed her to take the money.

Confronted by Felipe, Modesta swore he'd given her the key to get the money, whereupon the fugitive seized a bundle of Modesta's clothing and gave them to another free Negress, Luisa, who lived at the Port of Bayu San Juan, to hold for him until Modesta returned his money. Since the entire proceeding is not disclosed, it is probable that after settling with all his women, Felipe was eventually returned to his master at LaFourche with no money at all.[8]

The steadier citizens of the province were also having their difficulties. Right after purchasing Andres Jung's eight-arpent plantation on Bayu San Juan on October 29, 1785, Luis Antonio Blanc was fired from his job by his older brother Antonio Blanc, Sr. This was but one of the many ramifications arising out of a legal instrument signed March 9, 1784 by Antonio Blanc, Sr. and Pedro Miravel, who on that day contracted to go into partnership in a tannery located on the square bounded by St. Louis Street, Burgundy, Conti and Rampart—the same business in which Maurice Conway and Bartolomo Macnamara had been partners back in May of 1770. However, ownership had changed hands several times since then. Macnamara's original half had been sold successively to Leonardo Mazange, F. Cheval, Luis Antonio Blanc and finally to Pedro Miravel, whereas Maurice Conway's moiety had been sold directly to Antonio Blanc, Sr.

The operation, situated on six and a half arpents (lots) had apparently evolved into a considerable business, consisting of a tanyard, tannery with nineteen vats, four small houses and several sheds, as well as a shoemaker shop and a couple of dwelling houses located on the premises. The age of the nine Negroes employed ranged from the middle twenties to the early thirties, and all of them received a reale per day for regular hours and overtime for Sundays and Feast Days. Various materials used in the tanning process were stored there, including 308 pounds of copperas, 142 pots of bear grease, forty pots of fish oil, 605 pounds of logwood and twenty eight cords of oak tanbark which was procured at five pesos a cord from one Edward who lived across Lake Pontchartrain. The cost of transporting the bark from the other side of the lake to the bayou was four piastres a cord, with an additional charge of six piastres for carting three cords over Bayou Road to the tannery.

In 1784 younger brother Luis Antonio Blanc (former owner of half the property) had been hired as Administrator-Manager. His duties included the fixing of prices, supervising the tanning of hides (deer, bull, calf, cow, roebuck, sheep, goats,—dry, salted or fresh—) received from the slaughterhouse or purchased from others. He also managed the shoemaker shop, kept figures on all receipts and expenditures, and was obliged to submit all information regarding the business to both partners on a monthly basis.

But it seemed that one of the partners had a good many debts, and as soon as his creditors realized that Miravel owned something of value, they began pressing him for payment. Demanding the sale of the business, so their bills could be paid, Junior Alcalde Renato Huchet de Kernion (who had lived on Bayu San Juan from 1739 to 1771) ordered seizure and sale of the property on September 30, 1785. This was only the beginning of a lengthy litigation that would remain before the Spanish court for four years.

Whatever the real reason for his dismissal, by the middle of November, 1785 Luis Antonio Blanc was suing his older brother (half owner of the business) for breach of contract, back salary, indemnity and remuneration for other losses sustained because of his forcible removal from his position. The forced sale of the property included a house on St. Louis Street, occupied by Luis Antonio Blanc, which meant he had to find somewhere else to live—quickly—for the court ordered that the premises be vacated within three days.[9]

All of these difficulties were no doubt a part of the impetus which in the 1790's propelled Luis Antonio Blanc in the direction of Bayu San Juan, where he would buy extensive property and settle down to work for the remainder of his days.

The destructive hurricanes of 1778 and 1779 had for practical purposes destroyed Charity Hospital on the ramparts of New Orleans, and in 1782 Bayu San Juan plantation owner Don Andres Almonester had begun rebuilding it. Finished in 1786, it was renamed Charity Hospital of San Carlos, in honor of the Spanish King. Built of brick and lime, it contained four wards with twenty four beds, a room for the hospital attendant, an apothecary shop, and a large chapel—all of which cost 114,000 pesos. Almonester took a great deal of personal interest in the day-to-day running of the place, writing the menus himself and going into considerable detail as to what constituted a ration of meat and the ounces to be contained in a serving of bread.

Patients who were able to pay apparently did, and some complained about the cost. On January 12, 1787 one of them presented a memorandum to the Cabildo protesting that Don Almonester was about to evict him if he didn't pay fifteen pesos a month. The memo was referred to the governor for justice.

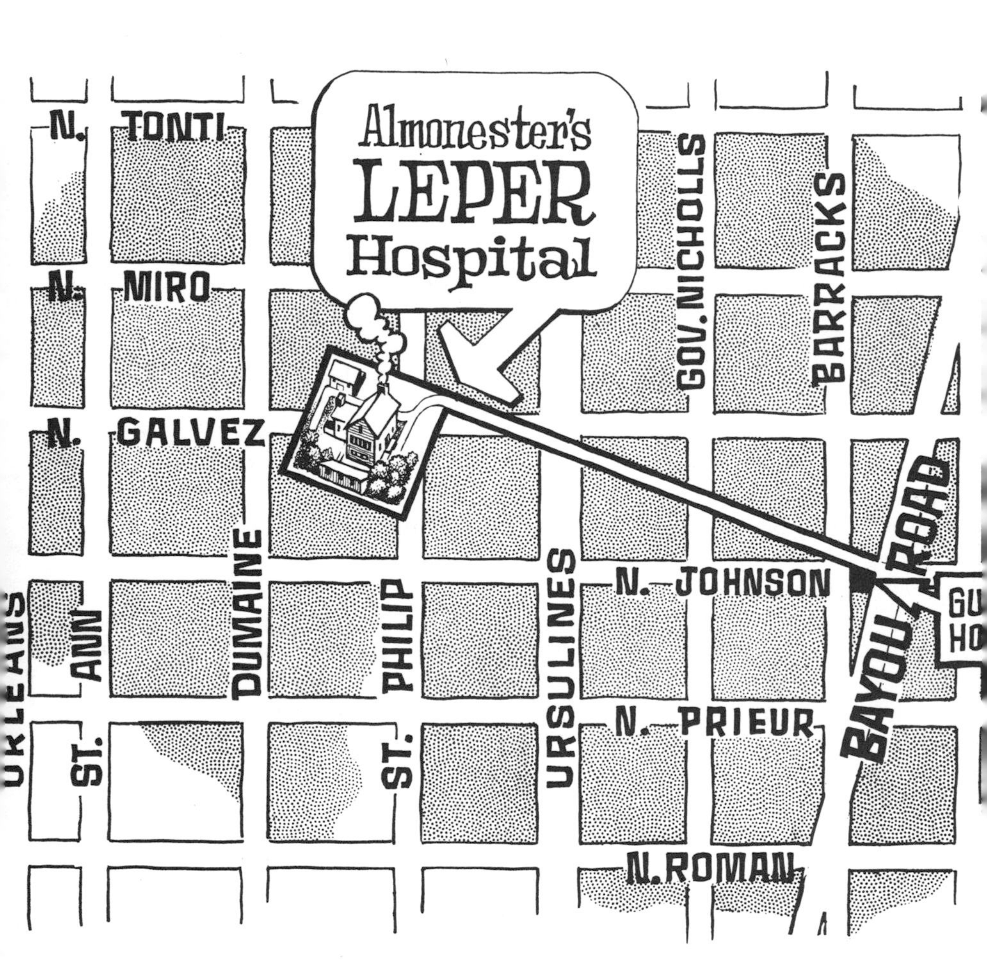

In 1785 this area back of today's French Quarter was all swamp. American Streets are overlaid on the map to give the reader a more precise location of the Leper Hospital.

But a grimmer problem begged solution. The exact how and when of the appearance of leprosy in the province is not known, 'though various sources attribute it to the arrival of the slave ships or the coming of the Acadians.* The histories first mention it in the accusations levelled against Governor Ulloa in 1766 when the Creoles charged him with "removing leprous children from the town to the inhospitable settlement at the mouth of the river (Balize)." In 1780 a Dr. Robert Dow had informed the Attorney General that a slave in the home of a lady, recently arrived from Mobile, seemed to be afflicted with the disease, and the Royal Physician and Surgeon were ordered to examine the patient; if he was found to be leprous he was to be isolated.

By 1785 about forty cases had developed, and the victims became a civic liability, because they gathered in town where begging was more profitable. On April 20th of that year, Almonester—then engaged in building San Carlos Hospital—notified the Cabildo that he had built, at his own expense, a hospital for lepers on his farm located a couple of gunshots from New Orleans. Divided into four sections, the hospital was large enough to accommodate many white families; and there were separate quarters for people of color. La Terre des Lepreux (Lepers' Land) was a narrow strip of land, which angled southwesterly from Bayou Road, for a distance of seven and two-thirds arpents—in the direction of the future site of the Carondelet Canal, but not quite reaching it. Bordered on one side by the land of Joseph Curtis, a canal for bathing the sick was constructed on the other. A small guardhouse was located on Chemin des Lepreux, where it branched off from Bayou Road, adjacent to and crossing today's Galvez Street. The hospital stood at an angle on the land, which an 1833 map indicates was bordered by Johnson, Galvez, Ursulines and St. Philip Streets.[10]

Almonester no doubt believed that separate care for the lepers was a logical extension of his concern for the sick, for the horror and fear of leprosy would have kept all needy patients away from San Carlos Hospital, so the special facility was placed in operation shortly after Almonester donated it to the Cabildo.

At that time ailments such as elephantiasis and a certain stage of syphilis were sometimes mistaken for leprosy. On November 11, 1785

---

*Dr. Gerald P. Walsh stated on January 29, 1976 that leprosy exists naturally in the marsh soil or in the insects of the Louisiana Gulf Coast, between Lake Charles and New Orleans, because wild armadillos wandering in the area have been found to carry the disease.

Doña Francisca Zecilia Roquigny declared before the Cabildo that certain doctors, from malice or ignorance, had wrongfully diagnosed the condition of her son Antonio, who had now been confined for five months to the Hospital for Lepers by order of the court. In support of her accusation she presented a certificate from Physician Don Estevan Fouignet de Pellegrue, which stated that Roquigny was not and never had been afflicted with leprosy—that the sores from which he suffered were the result of an improper application of mercury.

The court ordered Dr. Joseph Montegut and the others involved in the case to review the situation and report their findings to the court. Their professional reputations on the line, they came up with the same answers they'd originally given, stating that Antonio Roquigny suffered from leprosy in the second stage. However, in view of Dr. Pellegrue's convincing testimony that he could cure the patient, the court ordered Senior Alcalde Don Nicolas Forstall, permanent alderman in charge of the hospital's funds, to provide the doctor with two cows and any other assistance he required.

Regretably, the records are silent on the outcome of this case, but Pellegrue must have demonstrated some beneficial results, for a number of years later—in 1798—Pellegrue would be granted a lot in New Orleans on which a two story brick house was erected, but there is no evidence it was ever used as a hospital. History reveals that the only leper hospital of early times was the one located off Bayou Road in the vicinity of today's Galvez Street that was built and donated to the city by Don Almonester.[11]

While important public buildings were being erected, worthwhile citizens were receiving valuable concessions of land. On April 26, 1785 Governor Miro granted to Etienne (Estevan) Boré a vast tract of land—now occupied by Audubon Park and Tulane and Loyola Universities—land that ten years later would be the site of the first commercial production of sugar in our area.[12] Civic-minded Boré, who would serve as mayor under the French in 1803, would also send his slaves five miles daily in 1795 to assist in the digging of the Carondelet Canal—a water link connecting Bayu San Juan with the ramparts of New Orleans—to improve the drainage and transportation facilities of the colonial settlement.

1786 marked the arrival in New Orleans of another man who was to play an important role in the history of Bayu San Juan as well as the intricate power-play of politics that was to decide the future of the United States, Spain and France in Luisiana at the close of the eighteenth century. Daniel Clark was born in Ireland about 1766, attended Eton

College in England and moved to Germantown, Pennsylvania (just outside Philadelphia) with his parents. His uncle, also named Daniel Clark, had some years before settled in New Orleans where he had gained prominence and accumulated considerable wealth as a merchant. (The ledgers of Notary Juan B. Garic of the 1770's contain many records of sales and purchases by the elder Daniel Clark.) In 1786 Clark invited his nephew to come to New Orleans where he immediately displayed great talent in handling his uncle's business affairs and gained political favor with the Spanish authorities of the province. As the years passed, Uncle Clark was to spend more time on his Mississippi Territory plantation, and management of mercantile affairs would devolve largely upon the younger man. When the uncle died in 1799, he would leave the bulk of his large estate to his nephew-namesake. Thus Daniel Clark would become, before the Louisiana Purchase, one of the wealthiest and most influential English-speaking residents of New Orleans, and in the early 1800's one of the largest-ever landowners in the Bayou St. John-New Orleans area.[13]

The French and Spanish continued to feel each other out politically and economically. The French government permitted trade with the French West Indies in French ships only, whereupon the Spanish retaliated with a Royal Order of March 20, 1786 forbidding Luisiana and the Floridas from accepting imports of sugar, rum, molasses or coffee from non-Spanish colonies. Cuba and Puerto Rico managed to supply the molasses New Orleans needed to distill its tafia and rum.[14]

Happy as the authorities were in December of 1785 to welcome an additional 1,604 enthusiastic, industrious, loyal Acadians from France—the best kind of colonists—the Spanish had very mixed feelings about the "Kaintucks"who were thorns in their ambition to acquire all the land between the Mississippi River and the Appalachian mountains, from the Gulf to the Great Lakes. Spain wanted Spanish Luisiana to be what French Louisiane had been before the war of 1755-63; but the east coast Americans kept pushing west, trading and settling between the Allegheny and Blue Mountains and the Mississippi River. Since the barrier mountains cut them off from east-coast markets for their fur and produce, the easiest trade route open to them was to come down the branches of the Ohio River into the Mississippi, and down to New Orleans, from whence their products could be transported to the world.

Feeling abandoned by the loose government of the thirteen American colonies, which gave them no protection they could count on, these "westerners" felt they had to look out for their own interests, as the John

Jay Treaty—then being considered by the American Colonial government—which would give the Spanish exclusive right to the Mississippi for twenty five years—hardly appeared to be in their interest.

Spain was under acute pressure. If she permitted use of the lower Mississippi as an outlet for their products, these Kaintucks would continue to increase in number. If the river was closed to them, they might try to open it by force. Lucky for Spain various factions of these "westerners," who had petitioned the American colonial government without effect, couldn't agree on what the solution should be. One group felt that a show of force would make Congress pay attention to them; some felt they'd be better off independent of the United States; one segment wished to become a part of Luisiana under Spanish rule; others wanted to declare war on Spain and seize New Orleans. Some even wanted to solicit France to take Luisiana back and extend her protection to Kentucky.

Governor Miro, by intrigue and judicious bribery of some of the westerners (including Wilkinson), managed to avoid a crisis; but this was no more than a delaying action that would finally demand solution in 1795.[15]

Much to the despair of Spain, Luisiana was growing very slowly. The census of 1785 had listed a population of only 4,980 in New Orleans and 678 citizens at Bayu San Juan and Gentilly.

One threat to the expansion of the province, however, was handled with immediate dispatch. In 1779 a young Capuchin, the thirty two year old Reverend Antonio de Sedella, had come to New Orleans and had subsequently been appointed Commissary of the Inquisition—a practice accepted and followed in Spain and her colonies at that time. Writing Governor Miro in 1787 about his new position, Sedella requested future assistance of military guards in carrying out his duties, if after making secret and cautious investigation he should find it necessary to proceed against wrong-doers. The letter struck terror to the heart of the governor. Considering that his King had ordered him to increase the population of the province, with the implied promise that new colonists would not be molested in matters of religion as long as the only public mode of worship was Catholic, Miro knew that mere mention of the inquisition would jeopardize his colonization plans.

A few hours after sending his letter, Sedella was awakened by heavy knocking at his door, and was amazed to admit an officer and a file of grenadiers. Puzzled, he thanked them for their immediate compliance with his request, but assured them he didn't need their help at the moment—perhaps in the future. Stupefied, he was seized, arrested and hastily hustled aboard a vessel which sailed next day for Spain. On May 6, 1791 he would petition the King for the title of His Majesty's Preacher, and would return to New Orleans as a Priest. Pere Antoine, as he came to be affectionately called, lived, labored and was beloved in New Orleans until his death in 1829. No further hint of the inquisition was ever again heard in Luisiana.[16]

Business on the bayou proceeded at a regular pace. On June 19, 1787 Vincent Rillieux sold a brigantine, for hauling pitch and tar, to Pedro Joseph Pedesclaux. And the next month Francisco Riano, merchant and resident of New Orleans, bought a share in the brigantine *La Cometa.* Riano had served as appraiser the previous year when on January 17, 1786 Negress Carlotta had appointed him to assist her in securing her freedom. Francisco Riano had also purchased a plot of ground fronting on Gentilly Road from Lorenzo Sigur (a part of the old DuBreuil plantation) which in the following years would be purchased by Don Luis Declouet, Antonio de St. Maxent, and Don Francisco de Rocheblave. On January 20, 1802 Riano would become a property owner on the west bank of Bayu San Juan when he would purchase a small tract of land from Matteo Oxtein—arpents that would in early American times be a part of the Beugnot tract, in the immediate vicinity of today's Taylor Avenue.[17]

Controversial James Wilkinson was undoubtedly the best known American trader on the Mississippi during this period. Forbear of the present-day Wilkinson family, twentieth century residents of Bayou St. John, he had pioneered to Kentucky after a military career in the American colonial war, and came down the Mississippi in 1787 with a test-boatload of hams, butter, flour, lard and tobacco to see if he could establish warehouses in New Orleans for the sale and/or reshipment of these products. Retained in Natchez and again in New Orleans, his tobacco was confiscated—not to be paid for by the Spanish until years later when he would again reassume his U. S. military connections.

A fascinating interplay of intrigue evolved between the trader and the governor of Spanish Luisiana. Wilkinson inferred that Kentucky was on the verge of severing connections with both Virginia and the confederation, but insisted that good faith must be shown by the Spanish before the westerners would think of becoming a part of the province. He also pointed out that it would be easy for England, Canada and the westerners of Kentucky and Tennessee to invade and take possession of Luisiana. Settling sparsely populated areas of the province with Americans, Wilkinson took the oath of allegiance to Spain with his fingers crossed.

Accused by many of being a self-interested spy and double-crosser, Wilkinson usually managed negotiations that favored the westerners. Nor was Miro naive about this relationship. In his letter to Valdez of June 15, 1788, he wrote: "I'm aware that it is his (Wilkinson's) intention to enrich himself by means of flattering our hopes and afterwards knowing they will be in vain."

But neither caution, intrigue nor political sparring seemed to add much to the population of the province. The Census of 1788 showed an inappreciable increase over that of 1785. New Orleans was larger by only 358 persons (5,338), and Bayu San Juan and Gentilly could claim only 94 new citizens, making a total of 772.[18]

The disastrous fire of March 21, 1788, which destroyed a large part of New Orleans, eclipsed anything else on the local scene. That day a lighted candle on the chapel altar of Military Treasurer Don Vincente José Nunez fell against the lace curtains in his home on Chartres Street near St. Louis Street. The flames quickly spread, burning 856 buildings, including the Cathedral, the Capuchin Convent (and most of its books), the Cabildo, the watchhouse, the arsenal (only 750 muskets were saved), the public prison, several stores of merchants, and many dwellings of the principal inhabitants of the town. Losses of $2,595,561.00 were reported to the Spanish court, and seven hundred persons were given rice and housed in tents until more permanent housing could be established.

Collections of funds and emergency rations proceeded apace. Three ships were dispatched to Pennsylvania with 24,000 pesos to purchase three thousand barrels of flour. Thus continued that mutually lucrative connection, begun in 1770 between Oliver Pollock and Governor O'Reilly, which if not encouraged by Governor Miro and his successor, was none the less countenanced because of necessity; and American commercial houses were established in New Orleans in defiance of Spanish law.[19]

One of the losses of this fire was the school established in 1772 under Don Andres de Armesto, although only thirty or forty pupils from the poorer families had ever come for the reading and writing classes, despite the efforts of the Spanish to stimulate interest in higher disciplines of the mind, such as geography, philosophy and languages. Not one pupil had ever presented himself for the Latin class.

Before the fire there had also been the Ursuline Convent School and eight small private commercial schools with approximately four hundred children of both sexes enrolled.

Bayu San Juan plantation owner Don Andres Almonester (his sixtyish spirits no doubt ennobled by his marriage to the beautiful Creole Louise de Laronde in 1787) offered the use of a building thirteen by twelve feet, to serve as temporary quarters for the public school until a better one could be built. But since so many had retired to the country after the fire, the little building adequately housed the twelve pupils who presented themselves for classes; and Don Almonester's offer to rebuild the school at a cost of six thousand pesos was apparently never acted upon.[20]

The ubiquitous Henriques Desprez had died in early 1788, but his widow Magdalena Brazillier, despite her advanced age, was as active as ever. On March 12, 1788 she petitioned the court for the right to sell a parcel of land in Opelousas, and on March 15th of the same year, her runaway slave Isodore petitioned her for his freedom for which he was willing to pay three hundred pesos. Before the court, the slave claimed that some years before Desprez had bought him for that amount from Francisco Devillier with the understanding that Isodore would be freed after serving his new master for six years. Having served his time, the slave petitioned the court to order Widow Desprez to issue him a letter of freedom. Notified of the petition Widow Desprez agreed to grant him his freedom for three hundred pesos plus payment of his wages for the period during which he'd been a fugitive.

Presenting a letter to the court from his former master Devillier, stating that Isodore had served additional years which would more than cover the wages demanded, the court, nevertheless, decided that Isodore's contentions were not "in good faith" and ordered him returned to Widow Desprez to work out the amount due her. On top of that, there were court charges of twenty three pesos, two reales.

Later that year Widow Desprez was before the court on November 19th to establish her ownership of a lot on Ursuline Street which she had inherited—among other properties—from her former husband Francisco Héry (Duplanty). Claiming that her husband's title to the land had been lost during the hurricanes of 1779-80, the court confirmed her ownership.[21]

Pierre Philippe de Marigny de Mandeville, having married a d'Estrehan—thus becoming a brother-in-law of Governor Galvez—was accumulating property. Buying up deserted plantations above the town, he received large concessions from the Spanish government, and in 1788 purchased a wooded tract on the north shore of Lake Pontchartrain, opposite Bayu San Juan, where he built Fontainebleau, a low, rambling wooden mansion, as a summer residence. The site is now known as Mandeville.

The next year, land—a part of which ten years later would become the Marigny Plantantion below New Orleans—was sold on August 12, 1789. Colonel Gilberto de St. Maxent sold the old DuBreuil property to Laurent Sigur for $72,000.00, establishing Sigur as the new occupant of the beautiful old mansion on the Mississippi near Esplanade, which in times past had housed the French governors of the province.

The sale, before Notary Public O. de Armas, included a silk mill, a store, a kitchen, several negro cabins and all the other buildings St. Maxent had purchased from Madame de Mouléon on October 4, 1776. Additionally—it included the sale of the canal of the mill from the Mississippi to Bayu San Juan. This canal (which extended down today's Elysian Fields Avenue, then cut across the cypress swamps in the rear of the city, to the bayou near today's Florida Avenue) had not been mentioned in the earlier transfers of this plantation, indicating that during St. Maxent's ownership he had completed the millrace (later called the Marigny Canal) which would continue to flow into Bayou St. John until the 1890's when levees would be built along that part of the bayou.

Sigur's occupation of the beautiful old place wouldn't always be idyllic. In 1791, when the city was afflicted with incendiarism, fires were set on his fences and once in his home; and patrols of the city, including merchants and traders of the city and their friends, had to be increased. Three prison deserters were suspected of the crimes, and the surrounding woods were searched on horseback and foot; and from the Fort of Bayu San Juan an officer and six soldiers came every night to post themselves at the entrance of the two roads that led to the city.[22]

On October 12, 1789, Doña Luisa Baudin, Widow Santiago Lorreins (Tarascon) instituted court proceedings against Mateo Austin (Oxtein) and Andres Mercenario to compel them to remove two houses from her land on Bayu San Juan. They had apparently settled in on the small two and a half arpent front Dugué plantation owned by Widow Lorreins, and were a nuisance not only to her, but to everyone traveling the royal highway along the bayou; instead of the usual forty-foot-wide road along the stream, the passageway had been narrowed to twenty four feet by their buildings. Governor Miro ordered that Surveyor Carlos Trudeau inspect the site, and on the basis of his report, ordered on November 7, 1789 that the defendants remove the houses within fifteen days. Despite Matteo Oxtein's documents of 1787 and 1788, by which he claimed legal occupancy, the court decree held; Andres Mercenario presented no opposition, because he had died in the interim.[23]

Chapter XXIV

BLACK AND WHITE REVOLUTIONS AND THE BUILDING OF THE CARONDELET CANAL - 1788-1795

Civil and church authorities in 1788 were concerned about the old cemetery, in use since 1725, located in front of the Charity Hospital on the ramparts of New Orleans (bounded by St. Peter, Burgundy and Toulouse Streets). So many were buried there it was almost impossible to find a place for a new grave. Fearing that the bad odors emanating from the site might result in epidemic illness, it was decided that another cemetery should be established further away from the town. The old graveyard, consisting of twelve lots of land, sixty-foot-front by one hundred and twenty feet in depth, was to be used until the new one was established. After appropriate resolutions were passed by the Cabildo, the Governor on November 12, 1788 made the proper presentation to His Majesty on May 2, 1789, who approved the new project.

Although construction of St. Louis #1 (in the 400 block of Basin Street today) was approved in 1789, the old cemetery site would not be sold to individuals for private development for another fourteen years, because the new site was to constantly flood, compelling the priest to wade through pools of water and the mourners to remain at the gate. Besides, the new graveyard was too small—only half the size of the old one—and by 1801 more than half of it would already be filled.[1]

Names of future Bayou St. John residents appeared in the records of 1788. Captain of the Militia Carlos de Morant had sold a barrel of indigo and a canoe to Pedro Chavert, and when Chavert died, De Morant on November 27, 1788 requested that his bill be paid. However, two of Chavert's Negroes said he'd already been paid with a horse and two reales worth of fish every day for a year; but since a couple of other Negroes witnessed to the contrary, the money was paid.

The DeMorant family (no doubt relatives of the DeMorands of Bayou Road), would own property near today's Wisner Overpass on the west bank of Bayou St. John in mid-nineteenth century American times.

The following year Don Mathias de Alpuente instituted proceedings to purchase the position of Attorney General; and on March 2, 1789 orders were issued to give him the title. A couple of years before, when Juana Francisca Macarty, wife of Mauricio Conway, had died, Pedro Bertonière had been appointed on May 29, 1787 to serve the minor heirs as their curator; and when he resigned the position, Mathias Alpuente had taken over the post.

In American times the Alpuente family would own property on the west bank of Bayou St. John, cityside of the DeMorants.[2]

An interesting court case of 1789 harked back to French times when Jean Baptiste Prevost had been Agent of the Company of The Indies, supplying slaves to the citizens of Louisiane. In 1764 Doña Luisa Plasant, Widow Prevost, had petitioned the Superior Council to free her faithful negro slaves Marie, Cupidon (her husband), and their children. Promising that she'd keep the freed family in her employ for ten more years, paying them wages at the rate of one hundred livres each per year, Widow Prevost also promised to give them a thousand livres each in the event she dispensed with their services prior to the expiration of their contract, so they could take care of themselves. The council approved.

For several years thereafter, Marie and her family took care of a plantation belonging to the Prevosts until it was rented to somebody else, and the slaves were dismissed before their period of employment was up. Unfortunately, the widow also failed to give the slaves either the thousand livres or the certificate attesting to their freedom and the wage agreement. After Doña Luisa Plasant died the heirs kept the document hidden, and the Blacks didn't know where to apply for a duplicate. The notaries couldn't or wouldn't tell until Marie finally learned that the information might be located in the government archives where it was found. Twenty five years after receiving her freedom, Marie instituted proceedings against Solomon Prevost, nephew of her former master who had inherited the estate, claiming she was entitled to four hundred pesos plus three hundred pesos, representing interest on that amount over fifteen yars. Don Adrian J. de la Place and Don Santiago Bellair testified that Marie and her husband had been faithful servants and that they'd been dismissed because Mrs. Prevost had retired from the plantation business. After being branded "ungrateful" by the defendant, Marie finally was awarded four hundred pesos, plus six percent on the amount during the twelve months and six days of the court proceedings, but she didn't receive interest on the principal for the fifteen years she'd requested.[3]

Oliver Pollock, champion of the American colonial cause, was fighting it out financially in 1789. When he had left Havana in 1788, it seems the Captain General of that City, at the request of Pollock's New Orleans creditors, had seized 9,574 pesos from people in Cuba who owed

Pollock money, to guarantee payment of his New Orleans bills. On January 10, 1789 Pollock filed proceedings in New Orleans to prove—in the records —that all of his New Orleans lenders had been paid off; thus the court could inform the Havana authorities to lift the seizure on the sums owed him in that city, so the money could be paid to his General Agent Thomas Planke in Cuba. The New Orleans court so advised the Havana authorities.

The next month, however, Pollock was suing the agent of Mauricio Conway, who had been one of many local people to guarantee Pollock's debts. Seven hundred and fifty pesos worth of Conway's properties were seized to satisfy the claim, and a few months later Joseph Xavier de Pontalba, agent of Conway, instituted proceedings on July 17, 1789 against a debtor of Conway's deceased wife for 484 pesos; a writ of seizure followed.[4]

Alcalde Renato Huchet de Kernion was busy in 1789 defending his wife's interests in the succession of Chauvin de LaFrénière and the disposition of the eighteen-arpent-front Desillest plantation *Capitular,* located four leagues from New Orleans on Lake Pontchartrain. Francois Joseph LeBreton D'Oregenois was administrator-executor of LaFrénière's succession, and in July of the same year Kernion petitioned the court for the right to sell a lot of land to a mulatto woman. The property on Ursuline Street had been owned by his mother-in-law Mrs. Desillest, and the court approved the sale.[5]

The records of August 20, 1789 reveal that Maria Isabel DesRuisseaux, Widow Chalon, had remarried. Her second husband was Master Blacksmith Estevan (Etienne) Roquigny (Rocquigny). The Roquignys would continue to live on the DesRuisseaux plantation on the west bank of Bayou St. John into American times, during which time he would often repair the ballance bridge that was to be built over the bayou near their plantation in 1796.

On August 7, 1790 the Roquignys were petitioning the court to obtain possession of certain papers belonging to the succession of deceased Jose Chalon, papers which had been left with Don Guillermo Murray, among which were a number of American letters of exchange the Roquignys wished to have turned over to them for their own use.

On May 11, 1789, before Notary Pedro Pedesclaux, Don Almonester Y Roxas sold a goodly portion of the land he owned on both sides of Metairie Road—property he'd purchased from the Capuchin monks in 1784. Maurice Conway purchased from him sixteen to twenty one arpents of the original LeBreton grant called *La Metairie.* And the following December Almonester sold to Matthew Debo two arpents contiguous to and west of the land he'd sold Conway.

The following year Governor Miro petitioned his superior regarding the request of Almonester, Major and Senior Magistrate of the City, who wished the appointment of Colonel of the Militia of the Garrison—the position being vacated by Don Gilberto Antonio St. Maxent who was retiring. Miro considered Almonester to be worthy and meritorious in the eyes of the public, and since the captains of the battalion had no particular qualities to recommend them for the job, Miro felt they wouldn't resent the appointment, even though Almonester's credits extended only to charity, lepers and the charity hospital.

This appointment was undoubtedly a sop extended to Almonester, who in 1789 had promised to rebuild the St. Louis Church burned in the fire of 1788, because there were no funds in the treasury for the work. The philanthropist was supposed to begin work in January of 1790, and recognition of his good intentions came in the form of a commission as Royal Ensign and Perpetual Commissioner on March 16, 1790.

On February 16, 1791 Almonester was disposing of more of his property, when Royal Surveyor of the Province, Carlos Trudeau, was requested to survey several portions of the Metairie Tract which Almonester was selling to various individuals—twenty arpents on the extreme west to griffe Pedro Langlich, alias Canaway, Pedro de Mouey and free Negress Agnes Mattheu. As a guide for the survey, the owners presented to Trudeau a copy of the 1760's deed of sale of the forty five to fifty-arpent front of *La Metairie* from Mr. Louis Cesaire LeBreton, Auditor of Public Moneys of the Treasury of Paris, to Mr. Gilberto St. Maxent.[6]

With George Washington inaugurated as President of the United States on April 30, 1789, and James Wilkinson commissioned as Colonel in the United States Army in December, 1791, the lack of Spanish troops and defense became increasingly worrisome to Miro. He wrote his superiors he'd received reports of Americans assembling in Georgia and the Carolinas for the purpose of invading Luisiana, and suggested establishing a battery at Plaquemines to impede entry to the river, the installation of four cannon at the Rigolets, and as many at St. Maxent's cattle farm (New Orleans East today) to cut off enemy entry through Lake Pontchartrain and into Bayu San Juan. Luckily for the Governor, his administration came to an end on the last day of 1791.[7]

It was during the Spanish regime that one of the best known legends about the fort on Bayu San Juan originated. It is the story of Sancho Pablo, commandant of the fort, who is said to have died for love of a beautiful Indian maiden, and whose alleged grave is today marked by an iron fence on the fort site near Lake Pontchartrain.

On an island in the middle of Bayu San Juan, near the fort—so the legend goes—lived the Indian Chief Waw-He-Wawa (White Goose), whose daughter Owaissee (Bluebird) was tall and beautiful. While calling on Waw-He-Wawa to smoke a peacepipe in front of the campfire, Commandant Pablo spied the Chief's daughter and immediately fell in love with her. But Owaissee, in the best Indian tradition, held aloof from the paleface officer. Ignoring his attentions, she continued weaving baskets in her quiet way, hunting herbs and paddling her canoe almost every day on the waters of Lake Pontchartrain.

One day, as she was about to return home, a squall came up, and the lake became so choppy she could hardly manage her canoe. Just as it began to fall apart, she was rescued by the commandant who had been watching her from a large boat. Praises were showered on the officer by Chief Waw-He-Wawa when his daughter was safely returned to camp; and Owaissee, seeing him so warmly regarded, discarded her aloofness and returned his affection. Soon they were meeting every evening at a lonely spot on the banks of Bayu San Juan. But her observant father, noticing his daughter's increasing listlessness in her daily tasks, secretly followed her one evening to the trysting site. Enraged at seeing the two of them together without his permission, he hid the next evening near the meeting place; and when Sancho Pablo appeared, Owaissee's father attacked and mortally wounded him.

What happened to the Indian maid the legend doesn't reveal; but Sancho Pablo was buried by his men on the grounds of the fort between four trees.

Searching for the tomb between two magnolia trees in 1934, W.P.A. workers discovered a mass of brick and cement, which they believed to be the long-lost grave; unfortunately, it turned out to be a wall partition of the early American fortifications. Their work, however didn't go entirely unrewarded. In an area that had never been filled, they found an old Spanish coin and a pistol of the kind manufactured in Spain between 1735-1750. The articles had been dropped in the swamp and had sunk from sight until struck by the W.P.A. spade nearly a hundred and fifty years later.[8]

It was into a nervously tender situation that forty four year old Don Francisco Luis Hector, Baron de Carondelet de Noyelles was introduced as the sixth governor of Luisiana on the last day of 1791. A year and a half before—on July 14, 1789—in an act as symbolic as the signing of the

Declaration of Independence by the Americans on July 4, 1776—the citizens of France had seized the fortress-prison Bastille. Housing only a detachment of aging French soldiers and a dozen or so political prisoners at odds with the King, the Bastille was no tactical prize; but politically it was a rallying point for the revolutionaries. In full sympathy with the rank and file of their brethren across the sea, excitement ran high in New Orleans. Mass meetings were held, street crowds assembled, the martial strains of the Marseillaise were heard, and patriotic songs were sung in cafes—to all of which Carondelet called a halt.

Revolution was impinging upon Luisiane from various directions. Whether knowledge of the French uprising had reached the Blacks of St. Domingue, or whether the timing of their crushing savage bid for freedom was coincidental, the latter part of August, 1791 saw them rising against their French masters in a violent orgy of hate. Luisianians in government and those with trading-business interests in St. Domingue had been aware of the swelling disturbance since the late French period, when the Superior Council had issued two decrees forbidding importation of negro marrons (run-away Negroes) from St. Domingue and la Martinique on account of their "increasing ferocity and habits of theft and arson."

Discovered by Columbus in 1492, the small western end of Hispaniola —Santo Domingo it was called by the Spanish—was ceded by Spain to France in 1697; and during the days of the French Bourbons this small West Indian area had been considered their most valuable possession, with two-thirds of the commercial interest of France centered there before the French Revolution. Of its six hundred thousand people, five-sixths of them were full Negroes. About half the remaining population of one hundred thousand were Mulattoes (disqualified from holding office because of their negro blood). Between the Mulattoes and the forty, fifty-thousand Creoles (who held all the political and social privileges) a lot of jealousy existed.

The ferocity of this outburst had been growing for a long time. The first slave shipment to the island was in 1510, and the first slave revolt was recorded in 1522. The protest against enslavement, known in French as "marronage"—running away into the hills—had existed from the beginning, until by 1751 the surrounding hills held 3,500 belligerent Blacks. Raging against the brutality of displacement and enslavement, the gentle, protective, classic Rada religious rites of Vodun (Voudun)—the earth religion the slaves had brought with them from Dahomey, Africa—didn't work for them in their new desperate situation.

Earth religions—animistic, ancestor and spirit-worshipping—had existed in varying forms throughout the world prior to the rise of Judaism and Christianity; and the Indians of St. Domingue, whose religion resembled in some respects that of the Africans, and who had also escaped Spanish brutishness, shared with the Blacks a hatred of the white man. Between these two elements—from 1750 to 1790—the marrons had developed a New World aggressive religious approach—the violent Congo-Caribbean Petro version of Vodun, which inspired the slaves in their bid for freedom in the early 1790's.

The revolution began with a cult ceremony held on August 14, 1791 under Houngan (Priest Leader) Boukman. During this ceremony a great storm arose and there suddenly appeared an old Negress whose body trembled violently as she danced wildly and held a large knife over her head. Sacrifice of a black pig climaxed the ceremony, and all participants drank of the blood, swearing to follow Boukman. According to historians of Vodun, this was clearly a Petro ceremony, characterized by the pig sacrifice and the violent female Marinette, a Petro spirit; and one of the inducements to revolt, proposed by several of the Petro Houngans, was that the souls of the dead would return to Africa and their old way of life for which they yearned.

A week later—on August 23rd—the Blacks rose up against their masters, and in less than sixty days two hundred sugar plantations had been devastated and two thousand whites massacred.

The revolution, continuing sporadically until 1806, would result in the establishment of Haiti in 1804, as that black island republic is known to this day.

The white settlers, fortunate enough to escape with their lives, hastily departed the Island with the few belongings they could quickly gather up. Many of them—a refined aristocratic class who contributed largely to the culture of Luisiana—came to make their homes in New Orleans. Among them was a company of French Comedians from the Cap Francais Theater, who after several setbacks finally established themselves on the second floor of a small wooden building on St. Peter, between Royal and Bourbon Streets in 1792. This first theater in New Orleans cost $9,000.00.

The influx of these people, many of whom brought with them their faithful slaves, also marked the effective beginning of Vodun (Voudun, Voudou, Voodoo, Hoodoo) in this area, for although the Vodun religion had existed in Luisiana since the arrival of the first Africans, the Blacks had been, for the most part, dispersed on the various plantations, giving them little opportunity to socialize in numbers. During the late 1790's and the first decade of the 1800's, with a large concentration of slaves and free people of color in New Orleans, Vodun became better organized—a force Orleanians began to fear, and one with which they would have to reckon throughout the nineteenth century.

To this day Voudou, in varying forms, is practiced in New Orleans and surrounding areas; and although it is rarely mentioned most of the year, it usually receives some recognition on St. John's Eve, June 23rd, the most important date on the ritual calendar of Louisiana Voodoos. On October 15, 1817, fearful of the revolutionary possibilities of these gatherings, the City Council would forbid congregation of the Negroes, except in places and at times specified by the authorities. The Voodoos then moved out along Bayou St. John and Lake Pontchartrain to carry on their secret rituals. The author's home, called *The Wishing Spot* is located on Bayou St. John, not far from the site of the voodoo rites of the nineteenth century; and every year, since 1966, a party has been held on this date, exploring some of the beliefs and aspects of this old earth religion—a fascinating aspect of New Orleans history.[9]

1792 saw the end of Mauricio Conway, nephew of O'Reilly, who had established himself as an influential and active citizen of Spanish Luisiana. In his will of May 28th, recorded before Notary Francisco Broutin, he stated he was a widower, having been married in 1777 to Mrs. Jane Frances Macarty, widow of Cezaire LeBreton, from which marriage there had been no issue.

Declaring that he owned a plantation on the Metairie, thirty eight slaves, and that he was currently in account with Oliver Pollock, he bequeathed $12,000.00 to four of his sisters and the daughter of one who had died. The will named nephew William Conway as executor and universal legatee, with instructions for him to go to Ireland to deliver the legacy to his aunts.

Two years later William Conway sold ten of the *La Metairie* arpents to Alexander Baudin; and in 1798 Baudin would enlarge his Metairie holdings by an additional six arpents front, by fourteen deep, closer to Bayu San Juan, which he would purchase from Maria Isabel DesRuisseaux Roquigny—land bounding that of Widow Juan Luis Allard.[10]

Upon taking office, Carondelet's Bando de Buen Gobierno ordained that New Orleans be divided into four wards, with an Alcalde de Barrio in charge of each. This official functioned as a combined criminal judge, commissioner of police and chief of the fire department of his ward. It was his duty to register everybody within the limits of his jurisdiction, as well as to receive reports on the arrival of all travelers and strangers in his area of control. No amount of precaution was excessive during this intrigue-saturated time. Wilkinson, who had re-entered the U. S. Army in December, 1791 as a colonel had been promoted to brigadier-general on April 21, 1792, and President Washington continued to negotiate with the Spanish for new Mississippi River trade concessions.

The revolutionary government of France, at war in Europe, sought aid from the new American republic. Although Washington was sympathetic to their cause, he withheld assistance of a practical nature, whereupon "Citizen Genet," representative of revolutionary France, declared himself the adversary of the American president, and attempted to organize a body of volunteers in Kentucky for the purpose of invading Luisiana and Florida. August de LaChaise, descendant of an old New Orleans family, supported by Americans who demanded complete freedom of navigation on the Mississippi, came to his aid.

Writing his superiors on March 22, 1792 Governor Carondelet mentioned eighteen thousand men who might conceivably be headed Luisiana way; however, he leaned toward the opinion that their objective was to protect the area between the Yazoo, Pearl and Alabama Rivers to the east, against the Indians who resented usurpation of their land. The governor picked up on Miro's earlier suggestion of establishing batteries at Plaquemines, at the Rigolets and at St. Maxent's Cattle Ranch, and stated he would place galleys in Lake Pontchartrain to defend the Rigolets against revengeful Indians, Negroes or discontented persons who might try to set wooden roofs afire with incendiary arrows.

If Washington hadn't intervened to prevent this violation of neutrality on the part of the United States, by effecting the recall of Genet, it is possible that an invasion of Luisiana might have taken place at this time; and the reception given Genet in Kentucky convinced Carondelet that the Western Americans were more interested in conquering than joining with Spanish Lusiana.[11]

At the behest of members of the Cabildo, who were mightily concerned with the possibility of a slave insurrection because of the uprising in St. Domingue and the rampant local French revolutionary activity, Governor Carondelet on July 23, 1792 informed his government of his reasons for prohibiting the importation of Negroes from Jamaica and the French Islands. The Spanish King approved the governor's action, but granted special privileges to those engaged in slave trade from Africa, which would improve the agricultural situation of the province. Meantime, suffering from loss of trade with the West Indies, a thousand barrels of flour were imported from Philadelphia in August of 1792 to avert famine.

With the beheading of King Louis XVI on January 21, 1793, Spain, fearing the spread of revolutionary ideas to her colonies, declared war against France, with concomitant cessation of trade between Luisiana and that country. In addition to suppressing public gatherings of an inflamatory nature, Carondelet encouraged emigration to Luisiana of French nobility who were fleeing the guillotine. The introduction of these Royalists, ever-mindful of the responsibilities of birth and tradition, did much to reduce the local revolutionary spirit.

To add to the confusion, the Indian slaves of Luisiana, who until this time had been seemingly content, began importuning the governor en masse for their freedom in 1793. The Census of 1769 had disclosed but sixty of these slaves, and O'Reilly's proclamation of that year had prohibited their further exploitation, warning their owners to prepare for their emancipation. Now, blaming their sudden action on dissension-exciting agents, Carondelet recommended that their application for freedom be denied, and to this day the final fate of the group is unknown.[12]

On July 12, 1793 Gabriel Peyroux was taking judicial action to prevent the butchers of the city from establishing a slaughter house on his Bayou Road property. Since the butchers had taken action with the consent of the City Council, the attorney general was protecting the city's interests in the case.

The next month a hurricane on August 18th blew away some of the market roof near the Mississippi and damaged other parts of the structure, as well as wrecking a part of the levee. A year later, on August 10-11, 1794, another severe hurricane inflicted practically the same damage, and the New Orleans market and levee had to be repaired again.

On January 2, 1793 the old Langlois plantation on Bayu San Juan was sold. Andres Almonester Y Roxas, who had bought the east bank Bayou plantation from Isabel and Joseph Chalon on May 7, 1781, sold the property to Don Luis Antonio Blanc, the deed of conveyance being dated September 3, 1793 according to the American State Papers of January 9, 1812.

Described as fronting on Bayu San Juan, for eight arpents, (by twenty two arpents in depth), the plantation was bounded on the lakeside by land of Widow Santiago Lorreins, on the other side by Serion Seignora and in the rear by lands belonging to Gabriel Peyroux, who had purchased the entire rear portion of the original forty-arpent-deep Langlois plantation from Arnoul on July 23, 1777. (These rear arpents had originally been sold to others by Luis Brazillier in 1756, 1757 and 1760.)

This sale to Blanc, in the amount of $4,800.00, included all mortgage-free buildings on the property and all means of ingress and egress to the land in question.[13]

Luis Antonio Blanc no doubt built the house, or added to one that was already there when he purchased the property; but since there are no records as to the date of construction of the beautiful old home at 924 Moss Street, it can only be deduced that the house dates from the late Spanish period—one of three houses on historic Bayou Bend that does—the others being the DeMatteo residence at 1300 Moss Street and the Pitot House at 1440 Moss Street (originally located at 1370 Moss Street).

What the original Blanc residence and outbuildings consisted of cannot be ascertained, because so many changes have been made by those who have lived in the house after the Blancs.

Walter Parker, active in improvement of Bayou St. John and the contiguous residential area in the 1930's and 1940's, added the stair and slave quarter in the back of *Casa Solariega* (the house that keeps the sun away) and did extensive restoration inside the residence.

The present owners, Mr. and Mrs. Benjamin F. Erlanger, who purchased the property in the early 1970's, have labored long, with the assistance of Architect Bill Bergman, to restore *Sanctuary Plantation*—rundown after many years of sad neglect—to its pristine authenticity and beauty.

Carondelet himself was up at dawn superintending on horseback work on the forts of the city which had begun soon after his arrival; this work, together with the improvement and strengthening of Fort San Juan at the mouth of the bayou, and the rebuilding and repair of the fort at Plaquemines, continued into 1796.

The first attempt to protect the city by means of a surrounding moat and pickets had been made in 1730 after the Natchez massacre, and from time to time other efforts had been attempted. Pittman's 1770 Plan of New Orleans shows stockades and a ditch surrounding the town, but Carondelet's was the most elaborate endeavor to date.

The city forts were St. Charles (between today's Barracks and Esplanade Streets on the riverfront), Fort St. Louis (near Canal Street on the Mississippi) and three smaller forts on the rear of the town, located on today's Rampart Street. Fort Bourgogne or Burgundy was located near Canal Street, Fort St. Ferdinand occupied a central position on the rampart end of Orleans Street, near Charity Hospital; and Fort St. John, was situated between Governor Nicholls (then Hospital Street) and Esplanade, near the entrance to Bayou Road which led from New Orleans to Bayu San Juan.

The forts were surrounded by picket revetments and deep ditches; these water-filled protective moats connected with the draining channel of the town; but none of the forts could contain more than one hundred and fifty men, and it was suggested in a report of the time that their main purpose was to keep the town's insubordinate subjects under control.[14]

In a statement of the condition of the city's forts and posts, Baron Carondelet wrote on April 18, 1793 that Fuerte San Juan del Bayou needed eight pieces of artillery and was four short. He stated that this fort, defending the entrance of Bayu San Juan to Lake Pontchartrain, from which schooners and sloops would be forced to withdraw within less than a half league from the city, made this fort most essential. He felt the minimum protection there should be four caliber-eight cannon, and four caliber-four, extra long, and that it was necessary to repair the outer works at a cost of not more than three thousand pesos.

He also recommended building a post at the Maxent Cow Ranch, in the event of war—a redoubt of dirt and sticks with four extra-long cannon of caliber-six to cut communication between Lake Pontchartrain and Lake Borgne which had an outlet to the Gulf by which corsair sloops could enter. This, he estimated, could be done for six thousand pesos.

Three months later, in a confidential letter of July 5, 1793, Carondelet recommended arresting and sending to Havana anyone voicing opinions against keeping the peace. He stated that the government was storing flour in the isolated house of St. Maxent because there was a lack of warehouses near the San Carlos redoubt. He went on to say that retreat by the lakes, in the event of insurrection, would be impracticable because of the lack of small vessels suitable for going through Bayu San Juan, and the danger of the enemy taking possession of the woods on both sides of the bayou, thus preventing anyone from reaching the Fort of San Juan at the entrance to Lake Pontchartrain.[15]

On July 4, 1793 Governor Carondelet wrote his Excellency Don Luis de la Casas, General Secretary of State, a most interesting letter concerning a project that was very much on his mind. In it he suggested that the prisoners who'd been sent to New Orleans from Havana the year before be kept in the city, so he could use them to build a canal from Bayu San Juan to the ramparts of New Orleans. He explained that every time the Mississippi broke its levees the outskirts of the city flooded, and when the water subsided, the mud that remained raised the land level around the town, making it impossible for the water to drain from the streets after heavy rains. The resultant stagnant pools of water in the suburbs polluted the atmosphere and were conducive to disease. If the conditions were not promptly remedied, by means of a canal that would receive the waters on the outskirts of the town and carry them to the bayou, the governor predicted that New Orleans would have to be abandoned within a few years. If the canal was built, the governor promised a healthy, clean, beautiful city, as well as a considerable saving to the Spanish treasury, since all cargo being sent to Mobile, Pensacola and Apalache at that time had to be hauled by wagon to Bayu San Juan. To reinforce his argument he enclosed a statement of expenses, covering a period of one year, for 737 such trips to the Port of Bayu San Juan and to Fort San Juan at Lake Pontchartrain, itemizing the cost of cart-hire and wages paid to laborers, amounting to 7,148 silver reales. He felt that the canal would save the Spanish government a thousand pesos a year.

Pressing his argument further, he suggested that further savings would be made because the cost of maintaining prisoners in New Orleans was very low—only nineteen cents per capita per day. He assured his superior that the local inhabitants had promised the assistance of their slaves, which would enable him to finish the project in less time than the three years it would normally take to do such a job. It would be necessary to cut through ten thousand feet of densely wooded forests—work that could be done only during the summer, because the lands were covered with water the rest of the year. All he'd have to pay the borrowed Negroes was their daily ration of food.[16]

Governor Carondelet was very concerned about the many possible routes from which the city could be taken. Fortifying English Turn on the Mississippi below New Orleans wasn't sufficient, as the enemy could enter through Bayu San Juan, by Chef Menteur, Lake Borgne and Bayou Gentilly or Bayou Road, from Barataria Bay and the Bouligny Canal one league above the city, or via the Amite and Iberville Rivers entering the Mississippi four leagues below the Fort of Baton Rouge. He deplored the fact that five or six frigates could leave Havana, secretly anchor at Ship Island—since nobody frequented that part of the coast—and disembark barged troops at the deserted, tree-covered Chef Menteur only seven leagues from New Orleans. With three days' provisions the men could reach St. Maxent's Cattle Ranch within one day— where they wouldn't be seen because nobody lived there—and from whence they could march down Gentilly Road (detouring three or four houses), reaching the city by eleven o'clock the next day. Attacking Fort San Carlos and the passage to Bayu San Juan, New Orleans would be lost before the strike could be repelled.

Carondelet was also concerned about Fort San Juan on the bayou at the Lake, because it was still four cannon short, and had not been constructed with the attention its importance required. "It's precinct irregular form consists of nothing more than boards on the side of the sea, elevated upon strong pillars of lumber on the inside and on the out, the space between these boards having been filled in with small shells and dirt, which forms a parapet about one and a half feet high. On the land side its precinct consists of a strong stockade with an embrasure for a battery. The fort was sufficiently strong to impede with its artillery the passage of small boats from the lake to the river, but it would be easy to disembark above or below and attack it from the rear." The rebuilt and improved fort at the mouth of Bayu San Juan was of the same dimensions as the former one, the three buildings being within the surrounding walls of the fort which faced on the lake and bayou.

The Spanish King at that time was of the opinion that the Rigolets should be fortified with a good redoubt, mounted with four cannon of twelve-caliber which would impede the entrance of enemy ships to the lakes. This, of course, would have reduced the importance of Fort San Juan, so its garrison and artillery could have been transported elsewhere to prevent attacks from the rear.[17]

The year 1794—twenty seven years after French rule had ceased—marked the beginning of Luisiana's first French newspaper, *Le Moniteur de la Louisiane*. Louis Duclot, a French printer who had fled the negro uprising in Santo Domingo, landed in New Orleans and started the weekly paper which made its initial appearance on March 3, 1794. In 1801 Duclot would be succeeded by another Santo Domingan refugee— Jean Baptiste Lesseur Fontaine. The publication, which later became a semi-weekly, never had more than eighty paid subscriptions, so it was in the beginning no doubt subsidized by the Spanish government and served as its political instrument. It would be published for twenty years, the latest copy being dated July 2, 1814.[18]

Not so fortunate an event was the devastating fire of December 8, 1794, which destroyed 213 houses in the area from Orleans Street to today's Canal Street and back as far as Bourbon Street. Fortunately, the parish church, in the process of rebuilding since 1791 through the beneficence of Don Almonester Y Roxas (and in which the brick of the old St. Peter Cemetery wall had been used), was spared. Gilberto St. Maxent, who had an indirect hand in this triumph through the efforts of his architect nephew, Don Guilberto Guillemard, was not to see the new church which was dedicated on Christmas Eve, 1794. Having become ill, he and his wife had gone to live with their friend Lorenzo Sigur to whom they'd sold the house outside the French gate near Fort St. Charles. Dying insolvent on August 8, 1791, at the age of seventy, St. Maxent was buried in St. Louis Cemetery #1, but the tomb is not to be found, having been swallowed by the soft New Orleans earth long ago.

Shortly after, Doña Elizabeth La Roche, Widow St. Maxent, petitioned Governor Carondelet for a pension from the Military Pension Fund. Her husband had retired from the position of Colonel of the Militia of the Garrison in 1790, and the governor recommended that she receive the income. Widow St. Maxent died about 1796, and of the nine St. Maxent children, seven would still be living in 1817; Antoine, Etienne and MacMillan St. Maxent, and Mmes. Riano, Unzaga, Osorno and Madame Fessiet (Ferrier).

1794 also saw the demise of one of Luisiana's earliest historians—Chevalier Guy Soniat du Fossat, who having arrived in 1751 soon married Madeline Francoise Claudine Dreux, daughter of one of Gentilly's first settlers, Mathurin Dreux.[19]

Until 1794 New Orleans had never been lighted at night. Those venturing forth after dark carried their own lanterns. On May 2, 1794 eighty-seven lamps, costing seventeen pesos each, were received from Philadelphia. At the suggestion of a blacksmith, the new lighting system consisted of a lantern suspended from a rope stretched across the street at every corner, attached to buildings diagonally opposite each other. Lighted for the first time on August 24, 1794, ladders were included in the equipment, so the lamps could be filled regularly with bear oil.[20]

As originally laid out, New Orleans extended up and down the Mississippi River for a distance of something less than a mile and reached back from the river about a half-mile. The town was about six miles from Lake Pontchartrain and separated from it by a cypress swamp. Bayou St. Jean—then non-navigable except for skiffs and pirogues—flowed through this swamp; beginning one and a half miles northwest of the city ramparts, it ran in the direction of the lake.

In a February 24, 1794 communique to Spain, Carondelet again recommended that a canal, for drainage and sanitary purposes, be constructed from the city to Bayu San Juan. A half league long, he estimated it would cost between $25,000.00 and $30,000.00 (the estimated cost had increased), and he warned again that if it weren't done, the flooding that occurred whenever a levee or dike broke—raising the adjacent land by its deposits—would make of the town a kind of sink-hole with no drainage outlet.

Le Moniteur de la Louisiane of May 4, 1794 announced the project of the canal which would carry the waters of the city and its environs into one of the branches of Bayu San Juan, thus ridding New Orleans of the stagnating waters which contributed to its unhealthfulness as well as the vast quantity of "musquitoes" that made it so unpleasant in the summer. Since Spain was at war, the Royal Treasury couldn't be expected to contribute much to the project, but Carondelet requested that the Crown convicts who were about to be sent to Pensacola remain in New Orleans to assist in cutting the drain which in later years would be changed into a canal of navigation for schooners. Having secured His Majesty's permission, Carondelet announced in the article that during the month of June the local inhabitants would be asked to contribute the use of as many of their Negroes as they could spare to cut down trees. To further enlist local enthusiasm the paper spoke glowingly of two large banquettes, one on either side of the canal, which when planted with trees would afford agreeable promenades. (Nine years later—when Luisiana became a part of the United States—work on these promenades hadn't even started.)

A certain Bretonnier was employed by Baron Carondelet to solicit his neighbors to send their Negroes to work on the canal which was begun with sixty Blacks. The Baron's original intention was to build a canal thirty feet wide and four feet deep through a one hundred and fifty foot wide strip of public land, which would have allowed sixty feet on either side of the canal for the promenades. However, the first year's effort fell far short, producing only a shallow, curving ditch, six feet wide and not over three feet deep, which according to Bretonnier and Tanesse, the City Surveyor, wound around the massed roots of trees in a natural declivity toward which waters naturally converged during a heavy rainfall. The canal ran from Bayu San Juan (near today's intersection of North Jefferson Davis Parkway and Lafitte Avenue), along the approximate site of Lafitte Avenue to the vicinity of the rear central gate of the city a short distance lakeside of St. Peter and Rampart Streets, about fifty yards from Charity Hospital of those days.

The government-controlled press didn't hesitate to promote the incomplete project. A circular of September 15, 1795 noted the advantages the city had already derived from the flat-boating of firewood up to the city, as well as the marked decrease in mortality due to the draining of water from the back of the city during the preceding season. Pressing civil officers to solicit from inhabitants the additional labor of their slaves, the Moniteur of October 19, 1795 stressed the advantages to be realized by city commerce from the canal, through the opening of communication via the lakes to the sea.

On November 6, 1795 the commissioners discussed the benefits the inhabitants and farmers, living at a distance from the capitol, would derive from the canal the governor had opened to Bayu San Juan, but they suggested it would be necessary to build a drawbridge over the bayou, so the schooners and other small craft coming from Mobile, Pensacola and other ports could reach the city to load and unload.

The Moniteur of November 19, 1795 again urged local citizens to send their slaves to work on the project, stating that only six days of labor from the Negroes of the city and fifteen miles around would enable the government to complete the canal, so that schooners might come up as far as the city. However, they evidently miscalculated, for less than a week later, the Moniteur of November 23, 1795 asked for an extra eight days' work by the slaves of the inhabitants, which would be all that would be required because then the chain Negroes (prisoners) could finish the job. This article marked the completion of the enlarging of the canal to fifteen feet in width as far as Bayu San Juan, and mentions the projected deepening of the canal by one foot from the highlands of the Lepers (near Galvez Street today) up to the city ramparts to enable schooners to come up to the city, and to complete the half-moon-shaped basin (port) already begun at that point. (In 1907, after more than one hundred years of improvement and development by three American Navigation Companies, the Carondelet Canal would be sixty feet wide and nine feet deep.)[21]

Thus by the end of 1795, there was a navigable water route from the ramparts of New Orleans through the Canal, through Bayu San Juan to Lake Pontchartain, to the Gulf and the rest of the world. And the following inscription, engraved on marble in French, English and Spanish, was hung on the San Fernando door of Charity Hospital that faced the city. "The Baron de Carondelet, Governor General, planned, executed and perfected this canal in a manner almost without cost. In testimony of the public gratitude, and in the name of the residents, this most illustrious Cabildo decrees that it shall be named for all time the Carondelet Canal - 1796."[22]

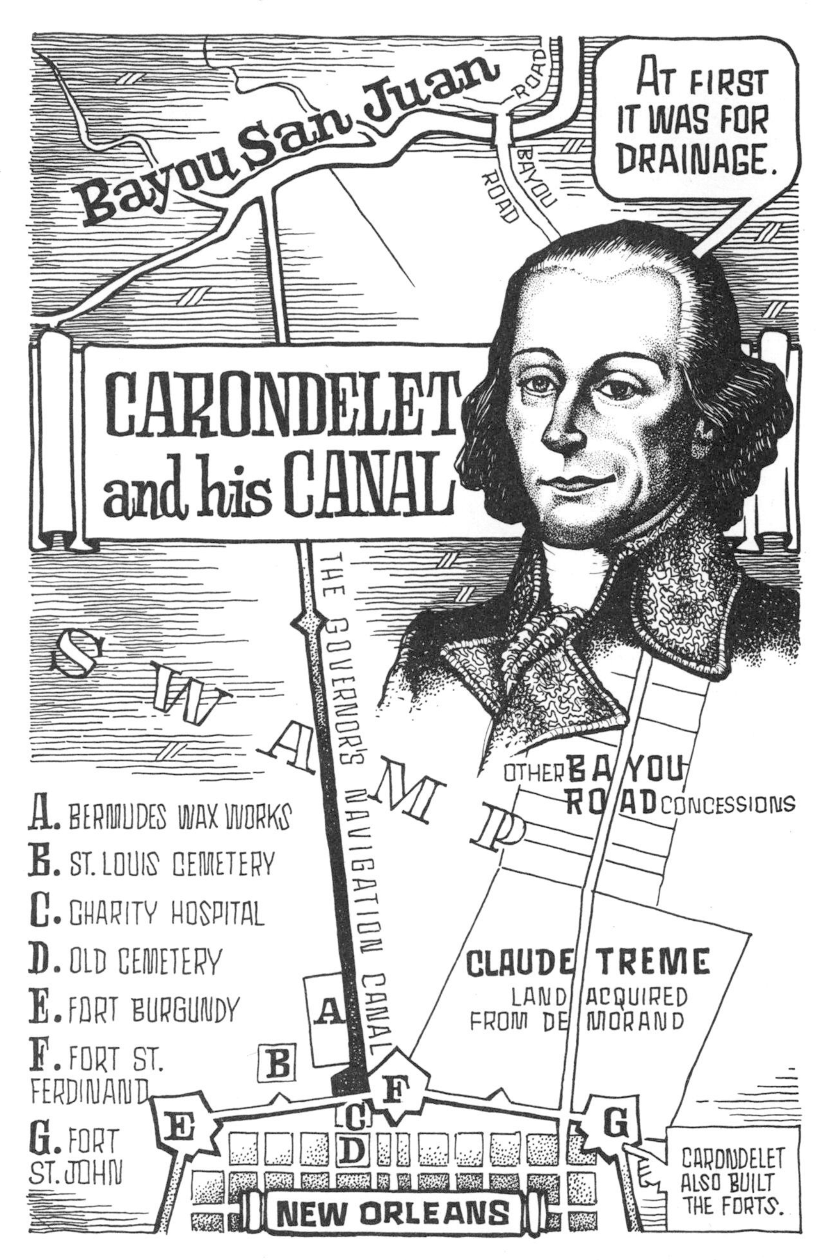

Construction of the Carondelet Canal in 1795 (along the approximate site of today's Lafitte Avenue, from the bayou to the Municipal Auditorium) allowed small ships to reach the ramparts of the city, resulting in the development of the area between Bayu San Juan and New Orleans.

Chapter XXV

DETERIORATION OF BAYU SAN JUAN AND THE CARONDELET CANAL IN THE LATE SPANISH PERIOD—1795-1799

The general atmosphere of revolution, plus hair-raising tales told by blacks and whites coming to Luisiana from rebellious Santo Domingo, no doubt contributed to the Negroes' hope of revolt on the plantation of Julien Poydras—plantation owner at Pointe Coupée—about a hundred fifty miles from New Orleans. Poydras' extensive traveling had given the conspirators time and opportunity to plot the outrage during his absence. All whites, with the exception of white adult females, were to have been slaughtered on April 15, 1795. However, disagreement as to timing of the attack led to quarreling 'mongst the leaders, and the wife of one of them exposed the plot to the parish commandant who immediately imprisoned the ringleaders, including three renegade whites.

The Blacks rose to the rescue of their incarcerated leaders, resulting in a conflict in which twenty five Negroes were slain and several wounded. A trial was held immediately, and twenty five of the guilty were hanged along the banks of the Mississippi between Pointe Coupée and New Orleans. Their corpses remained dangling from the gibbets for several days as a grisly reminder of what happened to those who threatened established order. Nine received lengthy prison sentences and thirty one were severely flogged, while the three whites—in a miserable miscarriage of justice—were simply sentenced to leave the colony. Anxiety stimulated by this uprising induced the Cabildo in February of the following year to petition the king, through Carondelet, to prohibit all slave importation into Luisiana.

To restore order and promote general ease of mind, Carondelet issued a decree on June 1, 1795, calling for the establishment of syndics at the distance of every nine miles. These officials were chosen from among the notable, respectable inhabitants of the district—people of property, who had the most to lose. Each syndic had to report weekly any and all occurrences of importance in his area of responsibility. Subordinate to the commandant, this position was renewed each year in the event the official didn't wish to continue in his job.[1]

The Church of San Luis, facing the Plaza de Armas, became the San Luis Cathedral when the Church in Luisiana became independent of the

Bishopric of Havana in 1793. Its first bishop, Luis Peñalver y Cárdenas arrived in New Orleans in July of 1795, but his report of that year hardly indicated that he was favorably impressed with his new see. Realizing that, in order to promote immigration, His Majesty tolerated Protestants in the colony ('though they weren't allowed public worship), the Bishop noted the large number of "bad Christians in the colony who think they are authorized to live without any religion at all." Approving the methods of the Ursuline Convent, he stated that the education the girls received there resulted in their being less vicious than the other sex. He further lamented the fact that upon leaving Spanish School at a very young age, the boys didn't go on to college where they would have been confirmed in religious principles, but that they usually retired to their parents' homes in the country where they heard neither the name of God nor King and were exposed daily to the corrupt morals of their elders. Hardly three or four hundred in New Orleans, he complained, attended the Lord's Supper once a year; and fathers even went so far as to procure courtesans for their sons, thus intentionally preventing them from marrying.

A short-lived coup of October 13th contributed briefly to the electric atmosphere of late 1795. Manned by forty four men, the French corsair *La Parisienne*, under command of Alexander Bolchoz, captured Fort La Balise at the mouth of the Mississippi, the garrison of which had been cut to twenty men. The adventurers, no doubt having had time to consider further deeds of derring-do, took off after a week's occupation, leaving nothing more memorable than an increased sense of vulnerability.

Since French planter DuBreuil's attempt in 1758, continuing efforts to make sugar had met with failure until 1785 when Sr. Solis, a Spanish Jew from Santo Domingo, imported a wooden mill from Havana and became the first in Luisiana to successfully convert cane juice into molasses at a plantation in Terre Aux Boeuf (St. Bernard Parish). In 1790 he was making tafia from the cane juice, but failed to make sugar. The following year, his plantation ten miles below New Orleans (a part of which would become the Olivier Plantation), was purchased by Antonio Mendez, another Spanish Jew from the West Indies. Mendez brought M. Morin, an experienced sugar-maker from Santo Domingo, who finally succeeded in making a few barrels of sugar, some of which was refined to the point where a few loaves of it were exhibited as a product of Luisiana at a banquet for public authorities given by Spanish Intendant Rendon. However, Mendez pursued the project no further, finding it more profitable to sell cane for seed.

It was Jean Étienne de Boré, living a few miles above New Orleans, who finally effected the hitherto impossible. Desperation over the continuing failure of his indigo (the ravages of insects had practically destroyed the 1793-4 crops), the hurricanes, competition of the East Indies, and the deleterious effect of indigo manufacture on his slaves, led him to this new venture despite the pessimism of everyone he knew, including his wife, whose father had failed in a previous attempt to make sugar.

Purchasing cane from Solis and Mendez, as well as hiring the sugar-maker, de Boré planted a hundred arpents of cane in 1795, to be harvested in 1796. Building a grinding shed, sugar mill, drying house and other sheds, with the help of thirty Negroes he made a hundred thousand pounds of raw sugar. It was further discovered that if the canes were cut, piled up and covered with straw they would keep for quite a while without becoming sour. In 1796 his granulating experiment proved successful, and his first commercial venture into sugar netted him $12,000.00. De Boré's courage and persistence laid the groundwork for a new industry which would yield large and fairly safe returns, and ten refineries are said to have been established in Luisiana the following year.[2]

A breath of relief in the succession of momentous events of 1795 was the signing on October 27th (in effect since August 2nd) of the Treaty of San Lorenzo—also called the Pinckney Treaty. This treaty established a new boundary line between southern United States and the Spanish Colonies of the Floridas, resulting in Spain's relinquishment of the sliver of West Florida which lay north of the 31st degree. This part of the treaty was to be ignored by the Spanish until armed Americans arrived at Natchez February 24, 1799, forcing Spain to evacuate. The most important part of the agreement allowed free navigation of the Mississippi River to the United States as well as to Spain. The treaty also gave the new republic use of the port of New Orleans, where produce and merchandise could be deposited while awaiting reloading to ocean-going vessels. This right, free from all charges and duties, except for storage and other expenses, was guaranteed for three years, subject to renewal.[3]

Cabildo Records of November 6, 1795 revealed a discussion on the necessity of building a drawbridge over Bayu San Juan, to allow schooners and small craft to reach the city. Agreeing to pay for it from city funds, the Councillors decided to advertise the work through the Public Crier and auction it to the person making the lowest bid, for which Don Nicolas Forstall was to be responsible.

On November 27, 1795 Commissioner Forstall informed the Council that no one had bid on the work and that the only carpenter capable of building the bridge was the man who'd done the drawbridges in the forts of the city. However, being a poor man, he would proceed only if materials were furnished and if he was paid for his labor. It was agreed that Pedro Guiot, alias "Lafeunesse" do the work under Forstall's supervision, and the work was completed by the middle of the following year; for on June 6, 1796 Louis Blanc (Luis Antonio Blanc) was appointed Syndic of the Bayou "charged with the police and supervision of the bridge." And at a meeting of the Cabildo on November 11, 1796 a bill in the amount of 1,697 pesos, 2½ reales, for construction of the bridge was presented and approved.

Spanning Bayu San Juan from the west bank to a point near today's DeSoto Street (east bank), the balance drawbridge was built in the middle of a dormant bridge which had been located there for over forty years, and which had been the means of communication between New Orleans (by way of Bayou Road), Grand Bayou, Metairie, Chapitoulas and Cannes Brulée. In 1810 a new bridge would be built two-hundred yards lakeside of this bridge, closer to today's Grand Route St. John at 1300 Moss Street.[4]

1795 ended on a happy note when the son of a former Bayu San Juan plantation owner remarried. On December 16, 1795 Juan Renato Huchet de Kernion, former French Officer and Spanish Alcalde (son of Jean Francois Ecuyer, Sr. de Kernion, former French Officer and Titulary Councilor of the Superior Council—Bayou St. Jean resident—and Jeanne Antoinette de Mirbaise de Villemont, widow of Francois Rivard de LaVigne, Jr.), married Marie Joseph Modeste de Verges. The sister of the bride, Marguerite Constance, was married to the groom's son, Jacques Huchet de Kernion, resulting in the unusual circumstance that the bride became both sister-in-law and step-mother of her sister's husband.

A year later Chrispin Charles le Bedoyère Huchet de Kernion was born. In American times he'd become a planter, and in 1815, when it seemed the British were about to overwhelm New Orleans, he was living at the old place on Bayou St. John. Shouldering his musket he marched out to the fields of Chalmette, but being physically weak, it was reported that his older brother had to carry his musket-loader for him. In 1822 he would marry Euphémie Arnill Lambert.

1795 found Guy Dreux, Mathurin Dreux's youngest son, maintaining the family brick business in Gentilly. One of his customers was the illustrious de Pontalba, who not only purchased five thousand bricks at eleven dollars per thousand, but who also hugely enjoyed the gay social excursions to the Dreux plantation. In his letters, de Pontalba complimented "Widow Guy Dreux" as being the most beautiful, charming and agreeable lady in the city. Charles and Pierre Dreux, sons of Guy Dreux, were both destined to die in the War between the States; but the lineage of the Dreuxs today runs in the families of Beauregard, Dugué, Verrett, de la Vergne, Livaudais, Jumonville, Destrehan, Fazende, Villeré, LeBreton, Delery and Soniat du Fossat.

At the end of the eighteenth century, visitors to New Orleans were always driven by carriage on Bayou Road out to Bayu San Juan to see the "handsome villas and gardens." The houses along Bayu San Juan had been the first "different" structures of New Orleans, most of the city's buildings being absolutely plain. Bayou homes were built with two stories of the "briquette entré poteau" structure (brick laid between an inner structure of heavy posts and plastered on the outside). During the summer the bayou was a favorite haunt for seekers of fresh air and bathing, the waters at that time being much clearer and cleaner than they were to be in later years when factory waste and debris from the streets of New Orleans drained into the stream.

Some four to five hundred people lived along the short stretch of Bayu San Juan but opposite its mouth, on the north shore of Lake Pontchartrain, little could be found except Indian settlements and a few scattered huts of hunters and would-be hermits.[5]

New Orleans had never been policed at night until 1796. On March 30th of that year, the Baron Carondelet reported to his government that due to frequent robberies "by vagabonds of every nation" in a city of six thousand souls, he'd installed street lamps, and had formed a body of thirteen watchmen. Since the cost of these innovations ran $3,898.00 annually, the Governor proposed a tax of nine reales ($1.12½) per year on each chimney, thereby distributing the tax burden according to the means of each citizen. However, so many houses had burned in the fires of 1788 and 1794, there weren't enough chimneys to carry the cost, so the amount was supplemented by a tax on wheat bread and meat. Apparently there were also other means of supplementing a personal income, for Historian Robertson states that watchmen of slight appointment were paid secretly by the bakers. These watchmen, called Serenos, were also the first weather-broadcasters of New Orleans, for from time to time on their rounds they announced the state of the weather in a loud voice—frequently calling out "sereno"—fair weather.

To further ease the tax burden, Carondelet suggested in a communication of March, 1796 that eighteen hundred feet of the commons (land immediately adjoining the city proper and belonging to the municipality) in the rear of New Orleans be divided into sixty by one hundred and fifty foot lots, to be conceded to citizens who would cultivate them, and for the privilege pay a sum toward the lighting of the city. These commons were near Charity Hospital, the basin of the Carondelet Canal and St. Louis #1 Graveyard—land usually under water six months of the year from heavy rainfall and flooding. Royal schedules of 1797 and 1801 continued to promote the scheme, and as late as 1804 American Governor Claiborne would still be urging the drainage and reclamation of this area.

The idea appealed immediately to one Francisco Bermudez who established on the west bank of the Carondelet Canal a manufactory for whitening wax, and with support from the Cabildo applied to the King of Spain for a concession. To encourage this type of industry, Bermudez was on May 3, 1799 granted three square arpents of pasture and meadow on the commons, on condition that the ground be used strictly for the manufacture of wax; if it was used for anything else, the grant would be voided, and the land returned to the city.

Finding that the square of land encroached on St. Louis #1, the shape of the grant was altered to an oblong, two arpents fronting on the fortifications and the basin of the Carondelet Canal, and four and a half arpents bordering the west bank of the Carondelet Canal. On this property Bermudez established a house for himself, cabins for Negroes, beehives and sheds for the manufacture of wax, and worked there until 1802 when he left, and his brother Ibanez took over the business. A few years later, Ibanez would attempt to establish a ropewalk on the property, for which he was hauled into court, where he had to prove that he was still making wax; but in order to keep the land he had to get out of the rope business. At that time (1806-1810) several of Charity Hospital's outbuildings were also located on the Bermudez arpents.[6]

In August of 1796 New Orleans suffered its first epidemic of yellow fever—the same type that had proved so fatal in Philadelphia in 1794, —and from whence many thought the disease had been transmitted to New Orleans. It would be over one hundred years before it was determined that the direct source of this scourge was the Aedes Aegypti mosquito which was attracted to the stagnant pools of water around New Orleans.[7]

But Philadelphia had a great deal more to offer the Crescent City than yellow fever. At the height of the onslaught there came to New Orleans from that city one James Pitot, aged thirty four, who was to figure largely in New Orleans and Bayu San Juan history for many years to come.* For ten years—from 1781-'91—French Jacques Francois Pitot had been a representative of several French mercantile firms at Cap Francais, St. Domingue, until fleeing the slave uprising, he returned to Paris. Conditions in revolutionary France didn't appeal to him either, so he applied for a passport to St. Domingue on July 6, 1793 to inspect his clients' interests, but on reaching Cap Francais he found a ruined desolate city and embarked immediately for the United States, arriving on the east coast about October 25, 1793. Learning there of the decree passed by the Convention of Paris on February 4, 1794, which liberated the slaves in the West Indies, he gave up the idea of returning to that colony, and on June 24, 1796 Jacques Francois became James Pitot, a naturalized citizen of the United States. His French background no doubt figured in his choice of New Orleans as his future home. Perhaps he shared the prevalent expectation that Luisiana would be retroceded to France, and surely the 1795 Treaty of San Lorenzo made New Orleans a likely place to succeed in business. However, the journey to his new home wasn't easy. Shipwrecked in the Gulf of Mexico, he went ashore at Pensacola and came to New Orleans in August of 1796 where he was detained at the mouth of Bayu San Juan because the shallow water on the sandbar at the bayou's entrance didn't permit his ship to enter.

Apparently some effort had been made by the Spanish to improve navigation on the bayou proper, for a Sevilla, Spain File discloses a letter from Intendant Francisco Rendon dated April 1, 1796 including a statement of expenses for "facilitating navigation on Bayu San Juan which had been blocked."

During Carondelet's administration planters from the north shore of Lake Pontchartrain had supplied wooden pickets (poles) which the Governor caused to be planted in the shape of a half moon, starting from each side of the bayou's mouth and extending out into the Lake—about two-thirds of the way to the site of the lighthouse which would be erected there in 1810. (The lighthouse would remain in that location for over a hundred years.) These pickets were placed close together in an effort to prevent the lake bottom sand from shifting unto the bars that formed naturally in this spot. Whenever a bayou comes in contact with tidal water—as in Lake Pontchartrain—a bar forms naturally. There is no evidence that the pickets increased the depth of the water, nor is there any record that the Spanish ever tried to deepen the fifteen-foot-wide pass or channel through the middle of the bar which was kept open only

*An interesting, detailed work on Pitot is: JAMES PITOT (1761-1831), A Documentary Study by Henry Clement Pitot, Bocage Books, New Orleans, 1968.

by the ploughing of vessels through it. At low tide, the bar, including the channel, had only eight to eighteen inches of water over it, and on a rare occasion was even dry. It would take American ingenuity—many years later—to make a working shipping-route out of Bayou St. John and the Carondelet Canal.

Rather than spend the night aboard the schooner that August night in 1796, Pitot accompanied the Captain in a pirogue up to the Port of Bayu San Juan, and returned the next day for his family and belongings. That first trip up the bayou—with other sandbars, floating logs and tree trunks jamming ten or twelve different sections of the stream—making it impossible for a schooner to pass without lightening its cargo and throwing out its ballast—no doubt motivated Pitot to do something about this potentially important trade artery. In 1805 he would become the first President of the Orleans Navigation Company—a company formed for the purpose of improving navigation on Bayou St. John and the connecting Carondelet Canal. Not one to be easily daunted, he immediately went into business with Jean Lanthois, a compatriot and former merchant at Port-au-Prince, St. Domingue, who had also become naturalized, in April, 1796, and they established the mercantile firm of Lanthois and Pitot.[8]

Problems with the Carondelet Canal had begun immediately after its completion when it was noted that heavy rains caused so much dirt to wash into the canal that it was feared it would soon fill up and be useless for navigation. Metzinger reported this condition to Carondelet, who replied that the canal was dug not only for navigation but also for the drainage of city waters; but he had three large wooden gutters installed on each side of the canal, which were closed by floodgates in times of rain and opened only after the water had deposited its sediment so it could run clear into the canal. The dirt deposited in the gutters was supposed to be used to fill in the low lots near the basin of the canal, so the land could be used for growing things. However, human affairs being what they are, attention to these gutters soon ceased, and scarcely two years after construction of the canal had begun, navigation had for all practical purposes ceased except in times of very high water. In 1796, according to James Pitot, only two or three small schooners were tied up in the basin, and had to remain there for two years before they could get out again. The cattle, roaming the area at will, crossing and recrossing the canal, trod down the soft mud banks, which were already caving in, and had filled it up so that hardly a pirogue could enter most of the time, according to Jose Pycharaca, a pilot, who operated vessels on Bayu San Juan and the lakes for the Spanish King. Another skipper of the time complained that the canal wasn't navigable for a loaded vessel except immediately after a gale from the northeast, which raised the waters on the south shore of Lake Pontchartrain, and in Bayu San Juan and the connecting Carondelet Canal.

In fact, navigation on Bayu San Juan itself was difficult at this time because of the sandbar at the mouth of the bayou. During times of low water, it was usual for those living across the lake to wait there for winds favoring the depth of water at the bayou's entrance; and those coming from farther away had to wait in the lake outside the bar for entry. Loaded craft, ready to leave New Orleans, would usually hold up at the Port of Bayu San Juan for easy egress, rather than venturing lakeward. Thus entry and departure of craft could be held up for days or weeks at a time awaiting a change in the weather.

In the 1790's a large schooner was built on the bayou near St. Maxent's Mill Race (vicinity of east bank Wisner Overpass today), but it was with great difficulty that she got out of the bayou because of the shallowness of the water, and she was never brought in again.

About this same time, Jose Pycharaca, at the instigation of Carondelet, attempted to bring in a gunboat drawing five feet of water; but the water on the bar was so shallow the boat had to remain in Lake Pontchartrain for a year until a hurricane raised the lake waters enough to allow the boat to enter, and it never got out again. Pycharaca often remained in the lake for four, five days—even with pirogues—for want of water on the bar. And he—as well as other shippers of the time—expected to have to unload to their cables and anchors in order to lighten their vessels enough to make it into Bayu San Juan at any time.

Many owners of vessels operating on the bayou and lakes (Rillieux, Luis Blanc and Juan Luis Allard of Bayu San Juan) had chalans or flat-boats (small, flat-bottomed boats with square sides and ends) at the bayou's mouth into which they'd unload the cargo from their schooners. These flats, which never drew more than fifteen to eighteen inches loaded, would carry the cargo over the bar, whereupon the lightened schooners could follow them into the bayou.

For those without chalans of their own, several were kept at Fort San Juan for rental. Commandant Periquet at the Fort and Mr. Miguel who owned property on the east bank of the bayou near the lake, rented flats. Renting wasn't cheap. The flat itself cost $2.50, plus the labor involved, the total of which might amount to $20.00 to $30.00 for a twenty-ton vessel loaded with barrels of pitch or tar. For vessels loaded with lime, the cost was even higher, according to Juan Luis Allard who owned a chalan drawing twelve to fourteen inches of water, which he used for transporting Lake Pontchartrain shells from which he made lime. On one occasion his flat was abandoned on the bar for eight days for lack of water, and at such times even hunters' pirogues would touch when going over the bar.[9]

Meantime, other parts of the world weren't standing still. In 1796 James Wilkinson became Commander of the U. S. Army as then constituted, and Spain declared war against Great Britain on October 7, 1796.[10]

It didn't take long for those who used the new bayou drawbridge to become careless. On March 17, 1797, members of the Cabildo decided to employ a watchman to see that the masters of schooners raised the bridge carefully; and at the next meeting of the Councillors, the expenses of bridge repair were discussed. The benefits accruing to those navigating from Bayu San Juan to Pensacola, Mobile and other places on the Gulf were stressed. Being able to come up as far as Charity Hospital on the City's ramparts to load and unload, shippers were saved the cost of land transportation which they'd formerly had to pay from either Fort San Juan at Lake Pontchartrain or from the Port of Bayu San Juan on Bayou Road to New Orleans. The members again talked about constructing at Bayu San Juan a hut to lodge the soldier, who at the wage of one reale per day, took care of the bridge. The contract for the building, it was agreed, would be auctioned to master carpenters by the same Commissioners who auctioned the bridge repairs.

It was to be a shingled house, built of pickets, sixteen feet long by ten feet wide, with a brick chimney, and its cost was to be paid from the City Treasury. The initial cost of the bridge, as well as all subsequent repairs to it, had been paid from the City Treasury, and the Commissioners resolved that each boat entering the bayou must pay a toll of one peso to reimburse the treasury for the money it had advanced. The fee would be collected by the Syndic of the Bayou Luis Blanc, who once a week would deliver the amount collected to the City Treasurer. No doubt as a check on the Syndic, the soldier-watchman, who by resolution had been installed to take care of the bridge, was also assigned the duty of making a weekly report to the City Treasurer of the boats that entered Bayu San Juan, with the names of their owners; and Governor Carondelet ordered the Commander of Fort San Juan at Lake Pontchartrain to permit no boat to pass out of the bayou without a receipt showing the toll had been paid. Further instructions were given by the Governor on March 28, 1797, supplementing the regulation, for the proper policing, protection and surveillance of the bridge spanning Bayu San Juan under which the bridge tender was to be appointed subject to the orders and supervision of the Syndic. Don Jose Castenado, merchant of New Orleans, finished building the watchman's hut on April 21, 1797, for which he was paid a hundred pesos.

A few months later, Master Blacksmith Estevan Roquigny, husband of Isabel DesRuisseaux, Widow Chalon, at the request of the Governor, placed an iron square hinge with the proper nails and a chain with hooks and a padlock to close the bridge, for which he received five pesos on July 21, 1797. Five months later the padlock was broken and was replaced by the City Treasurer. It was decided that an iron plate had to be placed on the drawbridge so carriages wouldn't carry the lead away with them.

At the same meeting the Council voted to supply two pesos a month, November 15th through March 15th, for firewood for the keeper of the bridge.

In July, Pedro Herrera, watchman of the Canal Carondelet, asked the Council for some tax relief. He had established a tavern for which his license cost forty pesos per year—same as in the City—but since business had been reduced to little or nothing, he asked to be relieved of paying the entire sum. Recognizing that since he'd established himself there had been no thefts on board the anchored boats—because the petitioner watched and took care of them—Herrera's license fee was reduced to ten pesos annually. In 1812 Alexander Milne would own the site of Herrera's tavern.

In town, the inhabitants were complaining on September 30, 1797 that animals were invading the old cemetery where burials were still taking place because the new one (St. Louis # 1) was flooded. Since Almonester had received the King's consent to use the bricks of the old cemetery wall to build the cathedral, it was decided to put a picket fence around the old cemetery to protect the graves.[11]

During this period another Bayu San Juan-New Orleans connection was being considered. Bertrand Gravier had owned the plantation immediately above New Orleans which measured seventeen arpents on the Mississippi River (originally Bienville's concession), a part of which had been mapped by Trudeau in 1778, and which was called Faubourg St. Marie. This faubourg, originally extended from Chapitoulas Street back to St. Charles, and was further enlarged back to Phillipa (Dryades) in 1796.

Bertrand Gravier died in 1797, and his brother Jean, who inherited the plantation, moved the property line back to Circus Street (now Rampart), and eventually eight squares further back than that. At the same time he reserved a strip of land forty feet wide in the center of today's Poydras

Street for a canal which was to connect with a branch of Bayu San Juan which flowed in the vicinity of Poydras Street on Hagan Avenue. Jean Gravier also reserved a hundred and eighty foot square towards Canal Street—a vacant portion of ground which was to be used as a public park and called "Place Gravier."

Governor Carondelet's interesting, accomplishing administration came to an end when he was appointed to the presidency of the Royal Audience of Quito; on August 5, 1797 he swore in Brigadier General Manuel Luis Gayoso de Lemos y Amorin, former Governor of the Natchez District, who succeeded him.

On January 19, 1798 Gayoso appointed young Louis Allard, who had recently returned to his father's bayou plantation from European schooling, as Syndic of Bayu San Juan; Louis Blanc, however, was to "retain his functions as Syndic charged with the policing and supervision of the bridge at the bayou."[12]

In 1798 New Orleans merchant James Pitot took a business trip to Philadelphia, going by way of the Natchez trace. One of his enthusiams on this trip was not the Indians for whom he seemed to have little respect, remarking that they were all pretty much alike—little more rational than animals of the forest, less modest and generally filthier, but as ferocious. Conceding that there might be some examples of sensibility and courage, he stated that others who had dealt with them found that same "ridiculousness of morals, futility of religious ceremonies, barbarism of politics, and a veneer of bestiality which hardly distinguished an Indian between civilized man and a tiger."

He returned with cargo and goods via Fort Pitt, floating twelve hundred miles down the Ohio and the Mississippi Rivers, returning to New Orleans from his ten-month trip on May 18, 1799.[13]

On April 5, 1797 the Spanish tribunal had finally rendered a judgement in the case of Laurent Sigur vs. the Spanish government and the estate of Gilberto St. Maxent, about the plantation Sigur had purchased from St. Maxent in 1789 for $72,000.00. Sigur had commenced action against St. Maxent in 1791 and had gotten a judgment of $25,557.75 as indemnity for land he'd paid for near the esplanade, but of which he'd later been deprived by the government when they built fortifications on the arpents in 1794. (This was the same controversial strip of land to which de LaChaise had signed away his rights when he purchased the plantation below the city from DuBreuil back in 1758.) The Spanish government had denied Sigur indemnity for the land it took on the grounds that St. Maxent had no right to sell this particular strip which wasn't his to dispose of.

Meantime, St. Maxent had died in 1794, and Sigur continued his suit against the syndics of the estate. The case of 1795 established that Sigur had already paid St. Maxent $41,986.00 for the plantation and five slaves, leaving a balance of $36,105.00, and that he had received a permit from St. Maxent's widow and nine children to sell the plantation to Pierre de Marigny, which he did on February 10, 1798.

The plantation house would today be located near Esplanade and the Mississippi River; and Marigny improved the sawmill on the site and the canal, built by St. Maxent, which ran along today's Elysian Fields Avenue. Then known as the Champs Elysees, the canal had originally been intended to connect Lake Pontchartrain (at the end of the avenue) with the Mississippi River. However, this idea, like so many before it, had been abandoned. Remnants of the St. Maxent-Marigny Canal, which was eventually filled up as the area developed in the late 1800's, existed as late as 1911.

It was no doubt in this plantation home that de Marigny, once a page at Versailles, entertained the three great great-grandsons of Regent Philippe d'Orléans (for whom New Orleans was named) who came to visit New Orleans in 1798. Louis Philippe, Duc d'Orléans, who after the fall of Napoleon would become King of France, and his two brothers Duc de Montpensier and Comte de Beaujolais, were sons of Philippe Egalité, a member of the convention, who had voted the death of his royal cousin Louis XVI. Difficult times for these nobles in exile, they were delighted to accept the hospitality of Julien Poydras and M. de Boré who in his youth had been a mousquetaire noir in the court of their grandfather.

Pedro Philippe de Marigny was not to enjoy his new home for long. In his succession of May 24, 1800, his worldly possessions went to his daughter Marie Celeste, wife of Jacques Enoult de Livaudais, daughter Antoinette, and his two sons Juan and Bernardo.

Later on—in American times—Bernardo, who by then was experiencing embarrassing financial difficulties himself—would go to France seeking reciprocity for his father's former beneficence to their royalty. Bernard's son Mandeville was offered free education at St. Cyr, and became a lieutenant in the cavalry corps d'elite. However, the role and the country didn't quite dovetail with Mandeville's American-Republican view of things. Fighting a duel with a brother-officer, who had slurred Americans, he would resign his commission and return to America.

On February 25, 1801 Sigur was finally allowed a deduction of $25,000.00 by the Spanish court, as well as a further exemption of

$3,194.00 for amounts he'd paid benefiting the widow and heirs at the time of St. Maxent's death. The case, however, was to drag on through the Territorial Superior Court in 1810 and wouldn't be settled until May 23, 1814 when the Louisiana Supreme Court finished the matter, at which time Sigur paid $1,892.87-½ in court costs.[13]

Spanish colonial philanthropist Almonester y Roxas died April 4, 1798 at the age of seventy three—only two years after the birth of his first and only child Micaela. Buried in front of the St. Louis Cathedral altar, which structure he'd built and donated to the city at a cost of $98,988.00, Almonester's busy, productive career had earned him a rightful resting spot in the center of early New Orleans. He had also rebuilt the Casa Capitular, now known as the Cabildo, but after his death, on December 3, 1798, his widow requested that someone else finish the job as only the ceiling and staircase were incomplete; and she and her daughter were refunded $28,500.00 by the city for the work Almonester had done.

Micaela would marry Joseph Xavier Celestin Delfau de Pontalba in 1811, and having inherited her father's determined civic-mindedness, she would in 1849-50 re-landscape Jackson Square and build the Pontalba Apartments flanking that site.[14]

As a result of the increased commerce of Spanish Luisiana with the young United States after the Treaty of 1795, 1798 saw a forward step in the political career of young Daniel Clark when he was recognized by the Spanish government as Temporary Consul of the United States.

The following year he would receive official recognition as U. S. Consul at New Orleans when American forces came down to occupy Natchez.

Clark was at this time handling most of his Uncle Daniel Clark's mercantile affairs in New Orleans, and he, (as well as Oliver Pollock) engaged in private banking and made advances to planters. During these years, silver money was brought from Mexico by the Spanish Governors, and whenever small change became scarce, these coins were cut into "bits.". A half dollar was four bits, quarters were two bits and this coin was further subdivided into four picayunes.[15]

It was also in 1799 that the Cabinet of Madrid, responding to an earlier petition of landed proprietors, permitted the introduction into New Orleans of 5,000 Negroes duty free. The embargo against slave importation had worked an immense hardship on plantation owners. It will be remembered that during the earlier years of Spanish rule, Luisiana had been severely depressed economically due to their own limiting trade restrictions, illegal trade competition by the English, fires, floods and hurricanes. The Treaty of 1795, the introduction of sugar production and importation of negro workers for the plantations brought prosperity to the planter-merchant-official class; however, this class domination of the city's economic resources may well explain the continued popularity of French Revolutionary propaganda during Spain's last years in Luisiana.[16]

A detailed description of the Leper Hospital operations was recorded in 1799. The San Lazaro Hospital (built and donated to the city by Almonester in 1785) was in that year administered by Juan de Castanedo, alderman and city treasurer. Hospital income was derived from two five-percent mortgage loans, and the proceeds of an alms box placed by order of the Governor before the guard quarters. To keep the patients isolated a number of guards under Corporal Christoval Rodrigues were stationed beside the building. The Corporal had the additional duty of disbursing money for food and other necessities to the five interned lepers. In 1799 one white man, one Negro, one Mulatto and two Negresses were patients in the hospital. Each inmate was allowed a reale (approximately 12½ cents) per day for food and was provided with individual cooking utensils. In return for his services, the administrator was granted one and a half percent of all revenues collected for the hospital. It is evident that no provision was made for any type of care or medical attention. The prime purpose seems to have been to shut the inmates off from society.

A year later—in September of 1800—Dr. Luis Giovellina, variously described as the surgeon of the Charity Hospital and of the Royal Hospital, reported that he found conditions at San Lazaro deplorable. The lepers were without servants and didn't even have partitions to separate the sexes. They were, he said, very uncomfortably lodged, as much by the narrowness and bad conditions of the building as by the lack of someone to take care of them, cook, and clean the place. The crowded conditions made it impossible to lodge several other persons afflicted by the malady, and the doctor recommended that the building be repaired, enlarged, and that an attendant be provided to care for the sick. He offered to provide medical attention and medicines if other physicians in town would cooperate. It is questionable that any major change took place, however, as the city continued to spend the very minimum for operating expenses. The records of the City Treasurer indicated that only 252 pesos, 7 reales were spent on San Lazaro in 1802.[17]

On January 4, 1799 Santiago Lorreins (Tarascon) was appointed Justice of the Peace for the area from Bayu San Juan to Metairie, and Le Chevalier Morand to the same position for Gentilly.

In August of 1799 the bridge at the bayou needed repair again, which was done by Rafael Barnabe, a free Negro, for forty seven pesos, 2 reales. The following year bayou resident Estevan Roquigny reconstructed the ironwork on the drawbridge, for which he collected 51 pesos, 1 reale on August 1, 1800. On August 14, 1801 the commissioners were sounding out the opinions of the residents to determine who would be willing to contribute to further repairs of the bridge which was in bad shape.

1799 also marked the formation of a lodge of Freemasons in the suburbs of New Orleans. (Today the location would be 1433 North Rampart Street.) Masonry, which had been introduced to the area about 1794, aroused a great deal of suspicion as to its objectives and there were questions as to possible criminal connections, because of its mixed membership, secret meetings and various functions which were not understood.

Out on Bayu San Juan, eight arpents fronting the east bank—to the immediate lakeside of Widow St. Maxent's property, and extending back to Gentilly—were conceded to Pierre Palao in 1799. A few years later—on February 13, 1805—he would sell his concession to Alexander Milne, early American millionaire, who at the time was busy amassing bayou and lakefront properties. The records do not indicate that this tract had been conceded during French times, so it may have been the last major plot of ground on Bayu San Juan to be granted to anybody.

Interestingly enough this bayou frontage, today called Bancroft Park, extending from Park Island Drive up to Mirabeau Avenue (in which the author's home was built in 1965) was the last large stretch of land on Bayou St. John to be filled and developed as a residential section during the early 1960's.

This concession was made under the new Spanish land policy effective October 22, 1798. When Don Francisco de Rendon had arrived in Luisiana in 1794, the Crown had misgivings about inviting Americans to migrate freely to Luisiana; and the tendency of the Governors to make huge concessions of land prompted the King to remove the land-granting power from them and give it to the Intendant. On July 17, 1799 Intendant Morales implemented Royal policy by issuing a complete new set of land laws.

Closer to New Orleans, the old LaVigne plantation on the east bank of Bayu San Juan, some of which dated back to 1708, again changed hands when Maria Luisa Baudin, widow of Santiago Lorreins (former owner of the plantation who had died in 1784) sold the arpents to her son Santiago Lorreins (Tarascon) in an act before Notary Public Pedro Pedesclaux on August 16, 1799.

A couple of months later—on October 9, 1799—before the same Notary, young Lorreins sold a portion of his newly acquired acreage (with no buildings of any kind) to Bartholome Bosque, merchant and resident of New Orleans, for $1,222.00. This property, which was located where the Cabrini High School of the Missionary Sisters of the Sacred Heart stands today near the Magnolia Bridge on Bayou St. John, fronted for two hundred feet on the bayou with a depth of five hundred and forty feet (three arpents), and was bounded by the property then owned by Surveyor Carlos Trudeau and by the remaining arpents of young Lorreins.[18]

Gayoso's administration was a short one. He died on July 18, 1799 at the age of fifty two—some say of fever, others from an over-indulgence in eating and drinking—and was buried in St. Louis Cathedral.

On July 19, 1799 Lieutenant-Governor Dr. Nicolás María Vidal, assumed the political and religious command ad-interim of Luisiana, while Colonel Francisco Bouligny, Commander of the Luisiana Infantry Regiment assumed the military functions of the Governor-General. Juan Manuel de Salcedo, a native of Bilvao in northern Spain, was named the last Governor-General of Luisiana November 18, 1799, but would not be sworn in until July 15, 1801.[19]

Chapter XXVI

NEW PROPERTY OWNERS ON THE BAYOU AS LUISIANA BECAME LOUISIANE 1800-1803

Apparently Dr. Nicolás María Vidal had confidence in the potential of the province for which he'd assumed certain interim governmental responsibility in 1799, for he began accumulating property on Bayu San Juan. On March 31, 1800 (American State Papers give the date as April 18, 1800) he received from the Spanish King one hundred and thirty superficial arpents on the east bank of that stream—land located to the immediate west of Luis Blanc's property, which on June 2, 1756 had been conceded to Ms. LeBreton by the French government.

The adjacent Blanc property angled easterly-westerly to a point on the bayou near today's Orleans Avenue; and the Vidal concession, bordered the stream from that point west to the Carondelet Canal, and fanned south-easterly in a trapezoid to the land of Joseph Suarez in the rear. The register of this concession described the land as inundated and so swampy that one was unable to enter the woods without getting into mire above the knees.

About the same time—apparently to acquire ingress to his new concession—Vidal purchased from Louis Blanc an adjoining neck of land which connected his grant with Bayou Road. Slightly more than seven and a half arpents in size, this tract (which today would cover a sizeable plot of ground between Broad and Dorgenois Streets) extended to "el puente de les lavanderes" (the bridge of the washerwomen) at the confluence of Petit Bayou and Camino Gentilly.

On July 24, 1804, Vidal would sell his concession and the smaller parcel of connecting land to Daniel Clark, who during the first decade of the 1800's would develop Faubourg St. John and lay out streets in the new suburb. But the property was destined to return to the Blancs. On October 30, 1821 the executors of Clark's estate would sell to Evariste Blanc (son of Louis Blanc) a part of the land Clark had purchased from Vidal; and without delineating several subsequent smaller land sales in this area, Evariste Blanc would on September 26, 1834 sell to the city of New Orleans a plot of ground measuring twelve arpents on Bayou St.

John, bounded by the Girod Canal (Orleans Street) Bayou Road and Dorgenois Street.[1]

Although the granting of concessions by Spanish Intendants had slowed down the giving away of land, those who owned property on or near the bayou couldn't seem to sell it fast enough. Bartholome Bosque, a Spaniard from Majorca (father-in-law of the first American Governor W. C. C. Claiborne) didn't hold the property he'd purchased from Santiago Lorreins in 1799 for long. Half a year after buying it, and having started to build a house on the land—in the same style as his imposing dwelling at 619 Chartres Street—he sold the property to Joseph Reynes (Renne), who on May 28, 1800 bought the two-hundred-foot front by three arpents deep property for $1,525.00 and finished the house Bosque had begun.

A few months later—on August 6, 1800—Merchant Reynes bought from Santiago Bautista Lorreins twelve arpents, twenty fathoms to the immediate rear of this property, giving him proprietorship from the bayou up to the boundary of St. Maxent's plantation on the north (vicinity of today's National Guard facility on the bayou).

The house on this land—one of the oldest on Bayou St. John today—was destined to have many interesting owners. On June 22, 1805 Reynes would sell the two-hundred-foot frontage (by sixteen arpents deep) to Marie Tronquet, widow of Vincent Rillieux, (one of the bayou's more colorful characters who had distinguished himself in the war against the British in 1779,) for $8,500.00. Five years later—on April 3, 1810—she would sell the same arpents to James Pitot, first democratically elected mayor of the incorporated city of New Orleans, for a hundred dollars less than she'd paid for it. Widow Rillieux was the great-grandmother of the French artist Degas, and her former Bayou home would be one of the houses to be sketched by French naturalist and artist Charles Alexander Lesueur of La Havre in 1828-30.

Owned by many over the succeeding years, the *Pitot House* was saved from demolition in 1964 by the Landmarks Society of New Orleans and moved from its original site at 1370 Moss Street (where the Cabrini High School now stands near the bridge) to the adjoining Desmare City Playground at 1440 Moss Street.

To those unfamiliar with bayou property, an interesting postscript was the building of a replica of the Pitot house prior to World War II in the eight hundred block of Moss street, some five blocks from the original structure, by Mrs. Carlotta Pollatsek-Reynolds, who had been compelled to move from the Pitot dwelling when the landlord missionary Sisters under Mother Cabrini needed it for a convent.[2]

Reynes' property was bounded on the immediate lakeside by a strip of land similar in size to his own, which extended from the bayou to St. Maxent's plantation on the north. Fronting the stream for one arpent, it had a depth of fifteen arpents, six toises and four feet, and was sold on August 20, 1800 by Santiago Bautista Lorreins to Andres Fernandez for 1380 Mexican pesos. The Fernandez property would in the nineteenth century become the Tissot House at 1400 Moss Street.

Just prior to August 6, 1800 Lorreins had sold to Jacques Bernardo Coquet a plot of land immediately lakeside of the land Fernandez bought on August 20, 1800. Measuring an arpent on Bayu San Juan, it extended north for fourteen to sixteen arpents to the St. Maxent land. In 1804-5 an irregular piece of this land (which would today be located on the lake-bayou side of Desmare Playground near the Pitot House) was opened as a place of public entertainment called *Tivoli*, where a ball was given once a week. John F. Watson, a visitor from Philadelphia in 1804, mentioned how most people going to dance at *Tivoli* "walk out in the dust and walk home after ten o'clock at night." Watson also observed ladies of the best families riding in an ox cart . . . fully dressed. Being perhaps one of the first discotheques on Bayou St. John, Watson was impressed by the "simplicity and humility of the times, marked with a complete lack of vainglorious pride. A lady never refuses any decent stranger who asks her to dance, although he is without introduction. I have seen a very genteel Tinman waltzing with the Spanish Intendant's daughter."

Proprietor Bernard Coquet had rented his first ballroom on St. Philip Street (where from 1799 he had held dances for colored people) to M. Auguste Tessier, who in November of 1805 operated the first on-record "Quadroon Ball" for free colored women and white gentlemen.

Subsequent owners (in the 1820s) of the amusement-park-turned-plantation were Pierre Morel and Samuel Kohn; when the latter sold the property to Frederick Frey, the pleasant country seat was described as having a large two-story house, a new building in the back yard divided into a store-house, kitchen, washing, ironing and servants' rooms, and in the garret a granary, also a privy, a deep well with a pump, and two large water cisterns. The adjoining yard contained a spacious stable with coach-house, pigeon house and shed. The excellent vegetable garden was newly-fenced, and there was an orchard of about three hundred fruit trees. Fronting the house was a parterre, laid out with tasteful arbors, shrubbery and plants from Europe and the West Indies; and fronting on the bayou was a convenient bathing house, with a pump and catching-tub. The auction-advertisement concluded: "Situated so the house is continually protected from the rays of the sun, this place is so well-known that further description is unnecessary." During the 1870's, the Fernandez and Coquet properties of 1800 would both belong to the Tissot family.[3]

As properties changed hands so quickly, descriptions in the Acts-of-Sale were often so vague that purchasers could well wonder what they'd bought—and where. Such was the case when a trapezoid-shaped-plot, fronting on Gentilly Road to the immediate cityside of the Marigny Canal, was sold by Laurent Sigur to Regidor (alderman) Francisco de Riano, with a notation which described the property as "a cypress swamp behind the land of the Mesdames Deverges." To settle the doubts of those whose land bounded the trapezoid, Royal Surveyor Carlos Trudeau measured and mapped the east bank of Bayu San Juan-Gentilly and wrote a detailed report on it July 16, 1800. The map accompanying Trudeau's report showed that Santiago Lorreins owned the seventeen arpents, three fathoms fronting Bayu San Juan (except the small plot he'd sold Bartholome Bosque), bordered on the north by the land of St. Maxent and on the south by the land of Widow Lorreins. Fifteen arpents in depth, Lorreins' land reached easterly to Bayou Gentilly. All the land in back of Lorreins' arpents—from Bayou Gentilly east—belonged to the Mesdames Deverges, who explained that their property constituted the rear portions of the Bayou San Juan concessions of the early 1700's. This land had at some time in the past become the property of Madame Juan Bautista Brazillier (Pelagia Lorreins), who had sold the arpents to Colonel de St. Maxent (an unreadable record in Notary Garic's files of April 8, 1778 p. 161, stipulates a sale of property by Pelagia Brazillier to Gilberto A. St. Maxent) from whom the Deverges ladies had no doubt acquired their property.

The Trudeau Survey Map accompanying this report showed that Widow Santiago Lorreins (mother of Santiago Bautista Lorreins) still owned the small plantation originally conceded to Francois Dugué in the early 1720's, which—through inheritance—had become a part of the Lorreins holdings. However, another map of 1800, shows the Dugué plantation belonging to Madame Juzan, a relative of the Lorreins, so it was undoubtedly sold about that time. This plan of the Marigny Plantation confirmed the other ownerships outlined by Trudeau, located the Riano purchase in Gentilly, and also showed various portions of the original DuBreuil Plantation, which in 1719 extended to Bayu San Juan, but parts of which were in 1800 retained by the estate of St. Maxent and others (DeClouet, Riano, Rocheblave) to whom some of the land had been sold.

A year later, another Trudeau map and survey report of May 5, 1801 showed the Dugué plantation belonging to Don Juan Juzan—brother-in-law of Jacques Lorreins (another name for Santiago Bautista Lorreins)—who at that time was selling another small plot of his plantation to Regidor Cayetano Baldes. Baldes' purchase, fronting the public road on the bayou for one arpent, was angularly positioned between Bayou Laurier and Bayou Road.

Juzan continued selling off the old plantation, for this survey map discloses that Negress Fanchon Carriére was in possession of a long narrow strip of land on the extreme west of the Dugué plantation; her home bordered Bayou Road a short distance north of the Baldes property. Fanchon Carriére, at this time, also owned a smaller piece of land next to the bridge over Gran Bayu San Juan, immediately west of Bayou Road, on the plantation of Don Luis Blanc.[4]

On May 18, 1801 Surveyor Trudeau measured and bounded a small tract of land of one arpent and six hundred and eighty superficial fathoms, located sixteen and a half arpents east of the big bridge over the bayou, in favor of Governor Nicolás Mariá Vidal, who bought this small piece of property cityside of Bayou Gentilly, located between the properties of Mme. Peyroux and Negress Fanchon Carriére from Juan Juzan.

Santiago Lorreins kept subdividing his east bank plantation. On November 26, 1800 he sold an additional twenty four superficial arpents to Joseph Reynes, bounded on two sides by Bayu San Juan, on the north by St. Maxent's land and on the east by Coquet's plantation.

The next spring Lorreins sold Manuel Lopez one and a half arpents fronting the bayou with a depth to St. Maxent on the north. Lopez's land, purchased April 10, 1801, was located immediately cityside of the first land Joseph Reynes had purchased the previous year.[5]

A Carlos Trudeau map of March 1, 1802 clearly depicts these five properties, extending in long narrow strips from Gran Bayu San Juan to the plantation of Antonio St. Maxent on the north. Today these plantations would be located approximately between east bank Moss Street, the National Guard property on the north, and between 1432 Moss Street on the east and Bayou St. John and Moss Street on the west.

Across the bayou several bayou-front plots of the old Girardy-DesRuisseaux plantation, between the big bridge and Metairie Road on the west bank, had been sold. Having retained a sizeable plot of land on the water, the Roquignys now had neighbors by the names of Danos, Mills, Fondvergne, Malford, Allard, Bonabel, Maroteau and Zamora.

Subdivision of the large Roquigny (formerly Girardy-DesRuisseaux) and the Lorreins (formerly LaVigne-Kernıon) plantations by 1802 was the beginning of the change from a plantation to an urban environment on Bayu San Juan.

Most of the old familiar names of French times were disappearing from the maps of 1800-1802. The rear arpents of the Luis Blanc plantation (old Langlois place) had been sold by Widow Gabriel Peyroux to Joseph Castenado and Manuel Ximines; and along both sides of Bayou Road, from the ramparts of New Orleans to Petit Bayou and "el puente de les lavanderes" (Washerwomen's bridge), all the names of the land-owners had changed, including DeMorand and Peyroux, whose plantations had been sold to Claudio Tremé and others.

On March 8, 1800 Tremé had the Royal Surveyor measure, bound and map seventeen superficial arpents northeast of Bayou Road, which he sold to Mr. Mills. The Mills purchase (the city-side portion of the French 1718 Hubert concession) was located to the immediate south of the eight and a quarter arpents Widow Peyroux had sold Juan Lugar March 1, 1800 (the bayou-side of the Hubert concession), both of which properties were bordered on the east by the Marigny plantation.

To the immediate southwest of these larger pieces of land, and bordering the Lugar property on Bayou Road, was a narrower strip of land owned by Don Antonio Ramis.

Gabriel Peyroux had bought this land in 1777, and since 1795 (the time of his death) controversy had been boiling about the boundaries in the area. In early 1799 the whole situation erupted into a full-fledged court investigation involving Widow Peyroux, Ramis and Tremé as to the extent of the concessions of Langlois and Dugué in the 1720's, the rear portions of which were now in question. Testimony established that these early concessions ran east and west, and that the Langlois-Provenche plantation had an original bayou frontage of only six and a half arpents. Mistakes in measuring early land grants in swampland had been more usual than not; but subsequent owner, Luis Brazillier's estate inventory of 1752 had firmly established the correct frontage as eight arpents.

During the court hearings reference was made to "the house Langlois built, now owned by Mr. Clark," but the exact location wasn't given; and since Luis Blanc had owned the Langlois plantaton since 1793, it is assumed that the house referred to was not the one situated at 924 Moss Street, today's location of the former Blanc residence. The Langlois-D'-Hauterive dwelling was undoubtedly located closer to Bayou Road.

Don Nicholas de Feniel, Engineer of his Catholic Majesty, began measuring the controversial lands on February 12, 1799; and on April 27, 1799 Pedro Desilet (representing Widow Peyroux), Ramis, Tremé, Nicolás María Vidal, Lt. Governor and other interested parties, assembled before Manuel Gayoso de Lemos, Governor of the Province, in an effort to terminate the controversy by compromise. Feniel's Plan of March 1, 1800 indicated that as a result of this lengthy search, Pierre Desilet, whose tiny plot of land on Bayou Road (purchased from Tremé), bordering Ramis' land on the south, received an additional arpent of land. If other changes were effected, it is not indicated in these records.[6]

Lands between the west side of Bayou Road and the Carondelet Canal were also changing hands about the same time—some of them concessions by the Spanish government. On February 13, 1800 Joseph Suarez was ceded eleven and a half arpents on the Canal, extending the property he'd purchased from Widow Peyroux which reached to Bayou Road and Petit Bayou. Suarez's two properties cut across the original 1752 French LeBreton concession; and on the Bayu San Juan side of his earlier purchase, the heirs of Alexandro Latil had abandoned the 1764 concession of the man who had played such a long and important role in bayou history.

A year later—on May 9, 1801—Suarez got a neighbor to his immediate southwest—between the Carondelet Canal and Bayou Road—when Don Carlos Guardiola received a concession adjoining a smaller strip of land he'd purchased from Widow Peyroux. Together Guardiola's properties totaled forty-seven arpents, two-hundred and ninety superficial fathoms. To the southwest of his original purchase, Madame Bertran owned a small similar sized plot of land.

A couple of days before—on May 7, 1801—Surveyor Carlos Trudeau had measured and bounded two tracts of land—sixty five arpents, eight hundred and sixty four fathoms, which Manuel Ximines had purchased from Widow Peyroux. Located in the barrio of Bayu San Juan, the tracts were bounded on the west by Bayou and Gentilly Roads, on the north by land belonging to the Mesdames Deverges, on the south by land sold to Mr. Barran and Joseph Castanedo, and on the east by Bernard de Marigny's plantation.[7]

Meanwhile at the ballance drawbridge at the Port of Bayu San Juan, five or six vessels were being loaded with troops and provisions, to be joined on the lakes and off Pensacola by armed vessels. Louis Bronier de Clouet commanded the battalion of free Mulattoes and Negroes in the 1800 coastguard expedition against Indian Chieftain William Augustus Bowles of Florida.

Jose Pycharaca (a Catalonian pilot for the Spanish King on the waters of Bayu San Juan and the lakes from the time of Carondelet into early American years) took part in this sally; and the largest of the transports belonged to one LaCoste, a New Orleans resident of long standing.

Bowles, a native of Maryland, had entered the British army in 1776 at the age of fourteen as a foot soldier. A year later, as an ensign, he was found guilty of insubordination in Jamaica, whereupon he escaped to the Florida Creek Indians. Learning their language and customs, he married the daughter of a Creek Chief and became a chief himself. Regaining British favor by assisting General Campbell with a party of Creeks in 1781, he went with an English garrison to the Bahamas where he became interested in the trading firm of Miller and Bonamy who wished to break the trading monopoly held in Florida by the Scottish firm of Panton and Leslie, patronized by the Spanish.

William Panton was a Tory, driven out of Georgia and South Carolina, who traded with the Creek Indians in Spanish Florida after the revolution.

Raising a large band of Indians, Bowles captured Panton's principal store at St. Marks in 1791 with the idea of setting up an independent Indian state with himself as head, for the purpose of negotiating trade treaties with the Spaniards—treaties that would replace Panton's company with Miller and Bonamy as suppliers of trade goods. After attacking Alexander McGillivray, who had been chief of the Creek Indians in Florida between 1783 and 1793, and with whom George Washington and Thomas Jefferson had signed the Treaty of York (the first Indian treaty under the federal government) on August 7, 1790—the objective of which was to break Panton's Spanish-Creek connections—Bowles waged a piratical war on William Panton, one-time friend of McGillivray. Then to escape having his ears cut off because of the all-around wrath he'd aroused in the region, Bowles spent a short interlude in England, heading a delegation of Creeks, Seminoles and Cherokees, because the British were attempting to enlist the sympathies of the Indians.

Subsequently, under the pretext of negotiating a treaty, Governor Carondelet lured Bowles to New Orleans where he was captured, but offered his freedom if he'd assist Spain in her struggle against the Creek nationals. Confirmed anglophile he was, Bowles refused, and was shipped off to Manilla where he remained in prison until 1797; during his transfer to Spain that year, he jumped ship at Sierra Leone, Africa, and the English Governor gave him passage back to London.

Under British papers he then privateered in the Gulf of Mexico against the commerce of Spain—particularly shipments to and from William Panton, the wealthy Pensacola merchant. Shipwrecked on the Florida Coast in 1799, he renewed activities with the Creeks against the Americans and Spaniards, his name becoming a household word for terror in Alabama and Florida, where by 1800 he had seized the Fort of Apalache and set himself up as Chief of the Independent Indian state of Muskogee.

But it was not until 1803 that the problem of Bowles was resolved. Spanish Governor Folch of Pensacola blockaded the coast and prevented Bowles' trade-goods from getting through; and since the Americans had no desire to see a powerful Indian State under British auspices in the southeast, American Indian Agent Benjamin Hawkins engineered Bowles' capture by arranging with Spanish Governor Salcedo to offer the Indians a reward of four thousand piastres for turning Bowles over to the authorities.

Seized at a reputedly sacred spot—a festival to which he'd come unsuspectingly—a party of savages brought Bowles to New Orleans in June of 1803 to collect their prize. When Governor Salcedo expressed surprise about the betrayal of their friend, Chief Tastiki straightfacedly informed him that should six thousand piastres be offered for the kidnapping of the Spanish governor, it could also be arranged under the collective noses of his garrison.

Sent to Havana, Bowles died in Moro Castle three years later, thus ending the adventuring life of one of this continent's would-be monopolists, who for many years had cost Luisiana a lot of trouble and expense.[8]

A memento of exciting times past, a miniature replica of the Panton-Leslie Warehouse, dedicated in the early 1960's by one of Panton's descendants, now shelters one of the city's water-pumping-stations in Pensacola's historic section.

The saga of the cemeteries continued in 1801, when on May 29th the City Treasury paid for finishing and filling St. Louis #1, finally being used for burial. In accordance with the Royal edict of May 12, 1789, to build the new cemetery and sell the old one (St. Peter, Toulouse, Burgundy and the Ramparts), active consideration was now being given to the leasing of the twelve lots of the old graveyard, provided that a contribution of six pesos per lot be made to the City Treasury; anyone wishing to lease them had to immediately build sidewalks, but not until the month of November, in the event it was necessary to remove corpses which had not yet been entirely consumed. The conversation continued the following year when the Acting Bishop refused to consent to the removal of old cemetery remains until the King had decided who really owned the property—the city or the church. The problem was not to be resolved immediately.[9]

Meanwhile, Napoleon Bonaparte, having returned from his Egyptian campaign, and having come to the head of French affairs in 1799 with his elevation to First Consul, sought popularity with his subjects by reviving the possibility of a French empire. Exploiting Spanish eagerness for prestige, Napoleon promised to exert pressure in the proper places in order that the Spanish King's son-in-law, instead of being a lowly Duke, might become the King of Parma, Italy. The aggrandizement of territory and subjects necessary to this end was to be the price Napoleon would pay for Spain's return of Luisiana to France.

To bring his files up-to-date, Napoleon requested of Luisiana Creole de Pontalba a detailed report on the prospective reacquisition. Among other interesting items in this lengthy report of October 1, 1800, Pontalba suggested that only two points needed protection from attack by sea—Mobile, for which two hundred and fifty men could provide adequate protection, and New Orleans, which would need twenty five hundred men. He noted that a battery of four guns at the Rigolets could easily oppose gunboats that might try to pass through Bayu San Juan on their way to New Orleans, and he was of the opinion that the entrance to Lake Pontchartrain could be defended by the two boats already there. Against an enemy entering the mouth of the Mississippi he advocated a system of cross-firing batteries on both sides of the river at Plaquemines Bend; and if that point was forced, he was sure that English Turn, just below the city, would be an impregnable point of defense.

Apparently the report was to Napoleon's liking, for the initial Treaty of Ildefonso, returning Luisiana to France, was drawn up October 1, 1800, with Spain soliciting from France its solemn pledge that should she decide not to keep the province she would never give Luisiana to any other power. Considerable trading continued, netting little to anyone except the keen Lucian Bonaparte, Napoleon's brother and official expediter in the Spanish court. It is said he benefited to the tune of twenty costly works of art and diamonds worth a hundred thousand crowns, which in time made him the richest member of the Bonaparte family. The Duke of Parma was never to reign as King, although references to him in the final treaty signed March 21, 1803 address him as Prince rather than Duke; and despite France's subsequent abandonment of the province, Luisiana was not to be returned to Spain.[10]

Garbage disposal of the 1800's left much to be desired. In addition to dumping much of the trash and refuse on the streets and quays of New Orleans, much of it was thrown on the side of Bayou Road near the St. John gate leading from the rear of the city, and lay there putrefying. In a letter to the Cabildo of January 24, 1800 General Barran suggested that the garbage be carried further away into the fields and buried. And to further improve the health conditions of New Orleans he suggested that those "unfortunate enough to be of faiths other than the Catholic religion" be buried in an enclosed site at a distance from the city in a simple shroud with enough lime to consume the body quickly, rather than follow the prevailing habit of burial close to the city in shallow graves easily opened by carnivorous birds and beasts.[11]

Meanwhile, the Spanish weren't neglecting their fortifications. In the Sevilla, Spain files is a letter from the Intendant of Luisiana, Ramon Lopez de Angulo, dated January 20, 1801, sending Minutes of the Board of the Royal Treasury, in which approval is granted to repair the roof of the guard-room and the sentry boxes of the Bayu San Juan Fort, at the request of its Commander.[12]

In 1801 bayou resident Luis Blanc was having shipping problems. His large flat-bottomed schooner had been built near the bridge, and was one of the largest boats operating on the bayou, drawing three feet, three inches when loaded and fourteen or fifteen inches when empty. After loading at the bridge, he found it necessary to unload three times in the bayou because of sandbars; and after unloading the last time at the bayou's mouth, Blanc had to wait twenty six days to get his schooner into Lake Pontchartrain because there was only a foot of water on the bar. Finally they laid the vessel on her side and pushed her over. Luckily, foresighted Blanc had chalans of his own, because continued rental of flats would have offset any profit he could have realized from bayou shipping.[13]

Much further north Thomas Jefferson, President of the United States, was desperately trying to keep things together in his bailiwick. On October 6, 1802—after the Treaty of Ildefonso had become an open secret—Ordonnateur Morales found it convenient to strictly interpret the Pinckney Treaty of 1795 and suspended the Americans' right of deposit at New Orleans. This, in addition to a Spanish Ordinance of July 18, 1802, forbidding American ownership of land in Luisiana, and rumors of a strong France superceding a weak Spain in control of the Mississippi's mouth, roused the westerners. To appease them, and prevent their military invasion of Luisiana, Jefferson entered into negotiations for the purchase of New Orleans.

In a letter to Chevalier Robert R. Livingston, U. S. Minister to France, it is interesting to note Jefferson's evaluation of various locations then considered appropriate places of deposit in Luisiana. New Orleans was the prime desiderative, East and West Florida together were considered one-fourth the value of New Orleans; and East Florida was worth only half that of West Florida.[14]

An interested party in these negotiations was English-speaking Daniel Clark, who after his uncle's death in 1799, had become one of the wealthiest residents of New Orleans. The winter of 1801-2 found him in Washington where he discussed with high officials the threat to growing western commerce should Luisiana come into the possession of France, then the most powerful nation of Europe. He seems to have impressed Jefferson who, believing Clark could be of real service in an official capacity, sent to the U. S. Senate his nomination as Consul of the United States at New Orleans to succeed Evans Jones. The nomination was confirmed, but Clark remained in New Orleans for only a short time, taking off for Europe in the summer of 1802 where he remained until early 1803 visiting Livingston and gleaning information on the status of Luisiana in international circles. Many writers have credited Daniel Clark with having been more responsible than any other in persuading the President of the United States to purchase the Isle of Orleans and West Florida.

Some opinions to the contrary, Daniel Clark secretly married Julie Carrière, called Zulime, in the spring of 1802, setting into action a bizarre series of events, the results of which wouldn't reach their ultimate conclusion until the late 1800's.

Zulime's family, originally from Provence, France, had resided in Biloxi before coming to New Orleans. On December 2, 1794 the teenage beauty became the bride of Geronimo DesGrange, an older man from France (by whom she had two children), who was a wine-seller-confectioner on St. Anne between Royal and Conde Streets where the couple lived over the shop.

In 1801, when DesGrange returned to France to check on some property, a relationship developed between Zulime and Clark who frequented the shop; but in November of that year, Clark left for Philadelphia, where he had business interests, to visit his parents.

About the same time, having reason to believe her husband was a bigamist, Zulime and her sister sailed north to check on the matter in Philadelphia where her suspicions were confirmed. Shortly afterwards, she and Clark entered into a private marriage ceremony, which, because of Clark's political-commercial position, couldn't be revealed until DesGrange's bigamy became publicly exposed.

Meantime, on January 10, 1802 the U. S. Senate confirmed Clark as consular representative in Spanish Luisiana (stating he was a Spanish subject, although he'd become a U. S. citizen in 1798), and he maintained Zulime in her own New Orleans residence waiting for the proper time to reveal their marriage. Their daughter Myra, born in 1805, was from the time of her birth nursed and cared for by friends of Clark in another New Orleans location.

Committed to prison, DesGrange managed to escape and leave Luisiana—it is said with the assistance of Spanish officials.

The denouement of this complication—involving Judge James Pitot, Francois Dussau de la Croix and Joseph Bellechasse (friends and business associates of Clark), large land holdings along Bayou St. John, and the efforts of a courageous woman, trying to establish her legitimacy as Daniel Clark's daughter—would continue in the courts for sixty years —until 1891.[15]

Despite the trading that was going on in the high courts of Europe, Napoleon had managed to keep his schemes pretty much under cover. His plans needed firming up before his enemies learned what was going on. If the impulsive westerners of the new nation across the sea got wind of these changes, there was no telling what their rashness might lead to. Since 1795 American dealings with the Spanish had progressed satisfactorily, while French relations with the United States had deteriorated into an undeclared shipping war on the seas.

Then there was the St. Domingue situation which had to be resolved. It was to be the mask concealing Napoleon's real target—Luisiana. The preparations he was making, the forces he was assembling, had as their apparent objective St. Domingue, which was to be but a relay station for the French troops enroute to occupy New Orleans.

But there was a very black fly in Napoleon's ointment. Toussaint L'Overture, leader of St. Domingue's revolutionaries, had proved to be more than Napoleon had bargained for. French General LeClerc had administered a crushing first blow, captured "the gilded African" and sent him to France as a prisoner in 1802, but the Blacks, brave from the prospect of re-enslavement, had continued to carry on a desperate guerilla war, delaying French occupation of the island. Then another enemy—Yellow Jack—practically wiped out two French armies. Out of 28,300 men sent to the island, only 4,000 were fit for service.

On top of everything else, the weather had declared war on Napoleon's intentions. The troops and supplies waiting at Dutch and Belgian ports for the occupation of Luisiana under General Victor, were held up by icebound ports, and a hurricane inflicted damage to the ships which required at least fifteen days to repair. When they were about to set sail, a despatch from the Ministry arrived. "The expedition fitted out at Halvoet Sluys (Dutch Coast) is not to sail; and on receipt of this letter you are to stop all expenses occasioned by it and have all the troops put ashore." That simple message spelled abandonment of Luisiana by Napoleon after several years of wit-matching and negotiating. France's unsteady peace with England had lasted only a year. The despatch of French vessels and troops across the Atlantic in the face of imminent renewal of hostilities would have diverted strength from a more urgent theater. Accepting sacrifice of his colonial dreams, Napoleon decided it was better to give Luisiana to the United States for a few million dollars, which France would need in her war with England, rather than to have the province captured without compensation; and increasing the power of the American Republic, which would be on the side of France in a maritime war, would diminish the dominance of England.[16]

Meanwhile in France, much to U. S. Representative Livingston's surprise and confusion, he was offered not only a place of deposit in the province, but the whole of Luisiane. James Monroe, who had joined him to expedite the procedure, began reporting October 4, 1802 on a situation which would take several months to resolve.

An important businessman of New Orleans looked at Luisiana's situation a bit differently than did Pontalba and Clark. James Pitot, believing that retrocession was imminent, prepared a lengthy observation on the Luisiana Colony (1796-1802) and took it to France with him in May of 1802 to provide the government and French businessmen with information about the country. A firm believer in the potential of the province, the purpose of Pitot's report was to show that lack of growth and progress in Luisiana had been due to repressive policies of the Spanish government.

Pitot foretold the eventual ownership of Luisiana by the United States a year before negotiations began, and in his report outlined the advantages derived from trade with the westerners. In 1802 the waterways of the Mississippi had brought to New Orleans thirty thousand more barrels of flour than during the previous year, twelve to fifteen thousand bales of cotton, and at least three million pounds of raw sugar.

Minuses on the economic scale included the very low price of tobacco which had caused its export to be suspended; very few pelts were being received because of corrupt supervision, and the harvest of indigo had been insignificant for years due to Luisiana's damp weather and the ravages of insects; and rice—priced at two, three piastres a barrel—

offered little incentive for raising it. Rosin and tar had great potential, but the government didn't allow exports to other Spanish colonies where it could be sold at a profit.

Pitot noted the convenience and reduced cost of shipping from New Orleans to West Florida and other Gulf Coast points due to the opening of the Carondelet Canal. Before its construction the ships coming into Bayu San Juan had docked two miles from the city at the Port of Bayu San Juan. The canal had allowed them to come up to the fortifications back of New Orleans to unload their cargoes. However, due to culpable indifference and lack of maintenance the canal was rapidly filling up so that even a pirogue could scarcely enter it in 1802. Pitot recommended that Bayu San Juan, filled with debris and fallen trees, be cleaned out, and that a pass be maintained at its mouth, because at normal tides pirogues could hardly enter the stream from the lake.

Despite Pitot's pessimism about the condition of Bayu San Juan, Historian Martin reports that in 1802 about five hundred vessels, including thirteen galleys and four boats (many vessels made repeated trips) entered Bayu San Juan. Schooners and sloops—from eight to fifty ton—some of them half-decked, supplied New Orleans with ship timber, lime, charcoal, naval stores and cattle from Pensacola, Mobile and the rivers and creeks flowing into Lake Pontchartrain, Lake Maurepas and the neighboring coast. (Other sources of that period give the size of the largest vessel as thirty-ton.)[17]

An observant traveler by the name of Dr. John Sibley visited New Orleans in the Fall of 1802, and in his journal described his walk from the city to the "buyo" one and a half miles east of town. He noted that the back of the city had been dug up in ancient irregular fortifications, and had ditches to drain some rear lots. Nearby was the canal dug up to the back of the city, within fifty yards of the H-shaped hospital (Charity Hospital), through which boats and small schooners could come. Walking along Bayou Road he remarked that "it was all the way built on within fifty or a hundred yards" with handsome places with orange groves and gardens, and that the strong clay soil was covered with fine grass and clover.

Further along Bayou Road he saw six to eight acres of beautiful meadow grass being mowed for hay. At the Port and Village of Bayu San Juan he counted fifteen small skallops and schooners, about fifty houses, and remarked on the brick and tile yards, blacksmiths, and the well-built ballance drawbridge spanning Bayu San Juan—so constructed that two men could raise it in half a minute to allow vessels to pass.

Along the bayou, above and below the Port of Bayu San Juan, where the vessels lay, were several Gentlemen's Country Seats—handsome places—some with large cleared adjoining plantations. Dr. Sibley noted that the water in the bayou was on a level with the sea, the tide rising about a foot, and that the stream was the recipient of the water from New Orleans' streets which drained into it via the Carondelet Canal. The land around Bayu San Juan, he remarked, was dryer than that near the town, but nowhere higher than five, six feet above sea-level. An avid observer, he was impressed with the large oysters in Spiritu Santo Bayou (a name for Lake Pontchartrain) as well as the small cockleshells used for making lime.[18]

Le Moniteur de la Louisiane No. 319, of November 27, 1802 announced that Sieur Francois d'Hebecourt had just opened a school where Latin, French, English, Geography, History and Mathematics would be taught. The agreeable talents of music, drawing and dancing were also to be included in the curriculum if they were requested.

Mrs. Robert E. Barbee, a descendant of de Hebecourt (Hevecourt) informed the author in 1968 that her forebear had the Bayu San Juan Academy in his home on the bayou, north of the bridge (listed in the 1822 Directory of New Orleans), and that he had conducted the school for twenty years.

On March 26, 1803 Pierre Clément Laussat, his family and a small staff of officers and civilians arrived at New Orleans in a single ship. The French Colonial government was to be formed upon the arrival of General Victor who was to serve as Captain-General of the province, while Laussat was to be Colonial Prefect—an office similar to that of a Spanish Intendant.

Laussat's mission was of no limited nature. Commerce was to be enlarged in the interests of the mother country and the province, eliminating competition of the English. New immigrants were to be inspired to clear land and raise large families. Roads were to be built, as well as bridges over streams and bayous—the latter to be cleared of obstruction. Education on all levels was to be established, the region was to be mapped, and there would be prospecting for minerals and studies made of plants to enrich medicine, the arts and agriculture. Disciplined, informed, trained, and zealous to be useful, Laussat brought with him the largest library ever seen in this country, which was to be utilized in the diverse branches of administration and instruction.

Domiciled in the home of Bernard de Marigny, Laussat and his family were treated "as one of themselves" by a number of French Creoles in the city. However, the rank and file—divided in their loyalties to the Royalists and the Republicans of France—were not unmindful of the advantages they'd come to enjoy under Spanish rule. With improved economic conditions since 1795, the merchants were apprehensive of a change that might restrict their commerce and bring a return of bad French money. The revolution of St. Domingue within feeling distance, the planters feared liberation of their slaves. Even the Ursuline nuns (with the exception of nine), recalling the outrages of the French Revolution, sailed for Havana, and some of the populace were even explaining away O'Reilly's behaviour of 1769 on the fact that he was a "foreigner" (Irish)—not Spanish.

The day after his arrival, Laussat was invited to dinner by Governor Salcedo, after which they took a carriage ride out to Bayu San Juan, which he described as "the fashionable drive here, but nevertheless a mournful one." Perhaps the trees lining the road contributed to the air of loneliness. They also supplied the rare shade of New Orleans which was to be found only along the Mississippi and the road to Bayu San Juan.

Despite his lack of official power, Laussat lost no time in sizing up the local situation. In a letter he says, "I have for the six days past established pleasant relations with a Ms. Clark, doing this at the request of the American government. He is a Commissioner of Commerce for the United States, a merchant and a planter of great means, who knows the country well, having resided here for the past twenty years. He is full of zeal for the cause of cession, and his ability for intrigue and his sagacity have seldom been equalled."

Laussat wasn't as impressed with the westerners, considered by both the French and Spanish to be insolent and overbearing. He remarked: "There is nowhere else, as is well known, so many loud-barking politicians as in the United States of America. Every small body-politic has its own gazette, and a mere few people speaking in them give me the impression of voicing the general opinion."

Five weeks after Laussat's arrival, the Marquis of Casa Calvo arrived from Havana as official representative of the Governor General of Cuba, the Floridas and Luisiana to act with Salcedo in the transfer of the province to France. His anti-French disposition asserted itself in a round of parties and balls to impress upon Orleanians how much they were going to lose with the departure of Spain. Madrid's orders of 1802 to give back to the Americans the privileges guaranteed in the Treaty of 1795 didn't ease the difficult position of the French prefect who was allowed no part whatsoever in the local government. Even the charming social disposition of Mme. Laussat was hard-put to counter the animosity. This duel for the devotion of the local citizenry was to continue until the news of Luisiana's cession to the United States arrived in New Orleans on August 17, 1803. Difficult as it is to understand, Laussat—still officially in the dark about the status of political events—could hardly believe the message.[19]

Meanwhile local affairs proceeded as usual. On January 21, 1803 Don Juan de Castanedo was elected Commissioner for the District and Road of Bayu San Juan; on May 16th he received instructions from the Governor to immediately get the bridge at Bayu San Juan repaired, paying for it out of the tolls collected from ships entering the bayou. On July 8th Don Bartholome Lafon presented his bill and was paid two hundred pesos for doing the work.

In 1805 the structure would be in such bad shape it was decided that any repair would be a loss and that a new one should be constructed on the lakeside of the old bridge—opposite Bayou Road—and that the swipe of the old bridge be removed so the public could use it for limited purposes. Only the most urgent repairs were made, allowing time for the selection and cutting of timber necessary for the building of the new bridge, which wouldn't be constructed until 1810.[20]

Loth as the Spanish were to relinquish their political authority in Luisiana, apparently they weren't averse to having French assistance in certain areas of the military. Making use of the few Officers of the Artillery and Engineers who had come with him, Laussat named Vinache Commander at New Orleans and had the strategic points of lower Luisiana garrisoned. Oliver took command of La Balise, on June 13th Citizen Leonard, Captain of a French Frigate, took possession of the Fort of Plaquemines, and on June 14th Citizen Rives, Lt. de Vaisseau took charge of the Fort at Bayu San Juan on Lake Pontchartrain. In a letter of this time Forts Plaquemines and San Juan are referred to as "the keys to this country."

In a report on the public buildings of New Orleans, Laussat included a military memoir by his Engineer Vinache which stated that the five small forts surrounding the city—its only defense—were in a sad state, the palisades being ruined and the surrounding ditch dry in many places. The engineer recommended razing them and replacing them with defense at important points such as Bayu San Juan, since "one can come easily from Lake Pontchartrain to attack the city on its rear." Coming down the bayou to within a half league of the city, the attacker could proceed from there on an easy road (Bayou Road) with heavy artillery.

Laussat noted that there was already located at Bayu San Juan "a redoubt which has been made to defend the pass of this bayou at its mouth—in earth, dressed with wood and armed with eight iron cannon," but that it required repair.[21]

Meanwhile negotiations had been going on which resulted in the signing of an official treaty on May 2, 1803 whereby the United States paid France fifteen million dollars for Luisiana. The immediate reaction was a series of tempests—domestic and international. Spain was angry because France hadn't given Luisiana back to her, there were rumors from abroad that Napoleon might change his mind, and Republican Jefferson and his Secretary of State doubted their authority under the Constitution to acquire new territory; but repudiation of the treaty would alienate the testy westerners and deprive the country of its opportunity to rank as a top-flight power in the world. Plagued by his Federalist opposition, Jefferson finally took the problem to the Senate and Congress, both of which ratified the agreement on October 26th and 27th.[22]

A month later—on November 30, 1803—three years after France had received the province from Spain—the French Prefect Pierre Clément Laussat took formal possession of Luisiana.

The formal ceremony of transfer began at midday with Salcedo and Casa Calvo arriving at the Plaza d'Armas where they were joined by Laussat and an escort of fourteen, fifteen Frenchmen. The Luisiana Regiment, heavy with prestige from the time of Galvez, and a contingent of Mexican Cavalrymen and local militia did honor to the occasion as salvos of artillery signaled the start of the ceremony.

The three officials were seated on a raised platform in the Sala Capitular (on the second floor of the Cabildo today). Laussat arose presenting credentials, and after the reading of instructions from the King of Spain to the Captain-General of Cuba, the Floridas and Luisiana, delineating the transfer of the province to France, Salcedo pronounced the formal presentation and delivered the keys of Fort St. Louis and Fort St. Charles to Laussat.

The French Prefect took Salcedo's chair as the new head of government, and Casa Calvo formally declared all colonists not desiring to retain their Spanish nationality absolved from allegiance to Spain. The proceedings—officially drawn up, certified and signed by the three officials—were read aloud in both French and Spanish to those present. The three officiating members walked to the balcony overlooking the Plaza d'Armas, a signal was fired by the artillery, the Spanish flag was lowered from its staff, and the French flag was hoisted in its place. Louisiane was again French.[23]

Chapter XXVII

FRENCH LOUISIANE BECAME AMERICAN LOUISIANA—1803

Although Laussat knew his regime would be a short one, he proceeded as though French occupation was to be permanent. Since the Cabildo ceased to exist with the transfer of Luisiana to France, Laussat established municipal government in New Orleans on the day of his inauguration so order would not for a moment be jeopardized during the changeover. The new governing body was composed of a Mayor (Etienne de Boré was appointed), two deputy mayors, a council of twelve members and a secretary, all of whom were immediately allotted duties and functions.

Among the councilmen appointed was Villeré, son of the man executed under O'Reilly, and young Louis Allard of Bayou St. Jean (his father had died by 1798). Allard and John Watkins, were appointed to inspect Charity Hospital, and were also put in charge of the Board of Health, which included supervising all bakeries. The bakers of New Orleans were called to City Hall to make a statement as to the quality of flour in their warehouses and were advised to provide Watkins and Allard with a weekly list of flour bought and consumed. If, on inspection, it was found to be unwholesome or unfit, it was to be thrown in the river. Allard was also given supervision of the levees and roads of the districts of Bayou St. Jean, Metairie and Gentilly.[1]

The Black Code (Code Noir) was maintained by Laussat, and he accepted the services of a Company of Infantry of about a hundred and twenty American citizens, under the command of Daniel Clark, to preserve order in New Orleans.

Laussat will be remembered for his proclamations. During his twenty days in office, he issued nineteen of them, eighteen of which may today be seen in the Manuscript Department of the Howard Tilton Special Collections Division at Tulane University. The following is a translation of the one issued December 2, 1803 regarding the bridge over Bayou St. Jean:

"Considering the regulations, supplemented by instructions given by the Governor Baron de Carondelet, on March 28, 1797, for the proper policing, protection and surveillance of the bridge that spans Bayou St. Jean, and under which a bridge-tender is appointed subject to the orders and supervision of the Syndic,

"Considering the appointment of Mr. Louis Blanc, as Syndic of the Bayou, made under date of June 6, 1796, by the aforesaid governor and the letter of Governor Don Manuel Gayoso de Lemos, dated January 19, 1798, in which he states and decides that while he has appointed Mr. Allard Syndic of the district, Mr. Louis Blanc is to retain his functions as Syndic, charged with the police and supervision of the bridge and with the execution of the regulations aforementioned,

"Considering further that the policing of the bridge is one that requires daily attention and should not be interrupted a single moment and that Mr. Louis Blanc has acquitted this task to the complete satisfaction of the public and of the government,

ORDERS, that Mr. Louis Blanc shall be continued in and as far as required is again appointed Syndic charged with the policing of the bridge on Bayou St. Jean and with the entire execution of the regulations adopted for that purpose on March 28, 1797,

"Given at New Orleans, on the 10th of Frimaire in the twelfth year of the French Republic, December 2, 1803, (signed) Laussat, for the Colonial Prefect, Commissioner of the French Republic. The Secretary of the Commission, (signed) Daugerot.[2]

C. C. Robin, an unusually observant traveler, came to New Orleans from Pensacola in 1803. He came by the lake route, because it was only a hundred and twenty five miles long, and travel time was but two days, whereas the journey through the mouth of the Mississippi was over two hundred miles, and depending on the current and winds could take up to thirty days from the river's mouth to New Orleans. His fare was six piastres ($6.00) which didn't include food.

Proceeding along the Gulf Coast, the schooner entered Mobile Bay and turned into the channel separating Dauphin Island from the mainland. Running along the north coast of Horn and Ship Islands, they entered the many-islanded channel called the Rigolets, navigation of which required an experienced pilot as well as a mosquito net. Coming into the passably clear waters of Lake Pontchartrain, Robin noted seemingly well-built houses at long-spaced intervals along its shores—homes of those who'd become rich raising cattle and cutting timber to be sold in New Orleans. Lime was also made in this area from shells picked up on the lakeshore as well as along Bayou St. Jean—lime of a superior quality and whiter than that of France. The manufacture of pitch, Robin estimated, was the most lucrative industry of the region, requiring fewer men than did agriculture. Four men could produce an annual income of three to four thousand gourdes (dollars).

Past the primitive light near the mouth of Bayou St. Jean, the entrance from Lake Pontchartrain was guarded by Fort St. Jean—an effort that was not too difficult because the bayou was narrow; and the sandbar, where the bayou waters met those of the lake, had built up so much from the bottom there was hardly three feet of water over it. In reality there was a series of three sandbars, altogether some sixty feet in length, beginning at the corner of Fort St. Jean and extending out into the lake.

Navigators of the bayou had learned from experience that high tides or heavy winds and hurricanes from the north or northeast increased the depth of water on the bar, and winds from the south and southwest caused the waters to fall. Pierre Baam, commander of a schooner on Bayu San Juan during late Spanish times, noted that winds depressing the water usually blew during the summer at which time most skippers laid up their vessels. Winds from the east, northeast and southeast would push waters from the Gulf into Lake Borgne causing a high tide in that lake. Then the flow from Lake Borgne through Chef Menteur and the Rigolets would cause Lake Pontchartrain waters, as well as those of Bayou St. Jean, to rise. If there was further shift of wind to the north or northeast, the higher Pontchartrain waters would be pushed from the north side of the lake onto the south shore making for unusually high water on the cityside of the lake and in Bayou St. Jean.

Anywhere from thirty to fifty schooners and smaller craft operated into and out of Bayou St. Jean from Appalachicola, Pensacola, Mobile and the rivers and creeks flowing into Lakes Pontchartrain and Maurepas. The schooners were built with flat bottoms, so they drew very little water. (Historian Chambers called them flat-bottomed sailing scows dignified as schooners.) Anything above twenty tons was considered a large vessel and was rarely seen on the bayou, because that size vessel would draw three and a half feet of water fully-loaded, and fourteen, fifteen inches when light. Of the craft operating in Bayou St. Jean, perhaps five or six were oyster boats, and approximately ten vessels operated from the north shore of Lake Pontchartrain—from the Tchefuncta and Tangipahoa rivers, bayous Lacomb and Bonfonca, Pearl River and the Gulf Coast, bringing lumber, pitch, tar, turpentine, brick, charcoal, bark, lime, vegetables, fish and fowl for sale in New Orleans and taking back miscellaneous merchandise and freight. There were also several small hunters' pirogues and chalans which drew fifteen to eighteen inches of water when loaded; and some of the pirogues even had sails and decks and sailed across the open gulf rather than sticking close to shore.

Once over the sandbar at the bayou's entrance, Robin proceeded down the stream which curved southerly through a cypress swamp in so many channels it was easy to lose one's way. Swarming with reptiles and alligators, it was shaded all along with cypress trees. Covered from their tops to the ends of their branches with a greyish moss, trailing down in weird festoons which bent the branches with their weight, this hoar—concealing the leaves of the trees—gave a strange air of sadness to the watery wilds. The bayou waters, brown and thick with the sediment of decaying vegetation, had a barely noticeable current caused by the lake. When the lake rose, because of winds or tides, the bayou would fill to overflowing, and when the lake waters receded so did those of the stream. At present, the land on both sides of the bayou, through which the schooner sailed in ever constant narrow windings—some no wider than twenty five feet—was completely flooded with only an occasional spot of land showing above water.

The condition of the bayou in 1803 made it very hard for navigators of that stream to make a living. Once over the bar, if the cargo could be reloaded onto the lightered vessel for the rest of the journey up to the Port of Bayou St. Jean, the skipper was fortunate. But this was an unusual circumstance, happening only in times of high water. Menaced by large, overhanging trees, the bed of the bayou was also full of tree-trunks, logs, stumps, shrubs growing underwater (called chicot) and other sandbars which were constantly snagging and hanging up craft from the size of a pirogue to a schooner, which necessitated further unloadings of the cargo into chalans and reloading back into the transporting vessel. During the process, the goods might be damaged, spoiled or ruined by exposure to the elements.[3]

Alexander Milne, who at that time was busily buying up land along the lake and on both sides of Bayou St. Jean, as far south as today's Park Island, was ever-aware of the hazards of old trees overhanging the bayou banks and was one of many to get hung up on underwater treetrunks while surveying the area in his skiff.

Born in Fochabers, Scotland, Alexander Milne had for a time been a servant to the Duke of Richmond at Gordon Castle; but when His Grace ordered him to cut his queue and adopt a new hair-style, the young individualist sailed westward to seek his fortune in the new world. The initial going was tough. It is said he was a strolling musician at first; then he became a vendor of lamps, his entire stock-in-trade loaded on a wheelbarrow which he trundled through the streets. He came to the Spanish town of New Orleans in 1776 when Galvez was governor. Setting himself up selling hardware and making bricks, his Scotch business sense stood him in good stead when the city was rebuilding after the fire of 1788; most of the bricks needed were furnished by Milne.

Of small stature and unprepossessing in appearance, he ambled about with his head hanging down and his eyes on the ground, oblivious of his surroundings. Dressed in the seedy garments of a beggar, no one would have recognized him as a prosperous businessman.

After 1838 the orphans of New Orleans would be the main beneficiaries of the fortune of millionaire-bachelor Milne, whose legacy continues even today in the Milne Boys' Home, 5420 Franklin Avenue and Milne's Home School for Girls at 1913 Gentilly Boulevard.[4]

Robin's journey of 1803 progressed uneventfully until L'Isle Bienville hove into view. Today Bienville Island would be east and northerly of Park Island. These islands weren't the same parcel of ground. Park Island, as we know it today, didn't exist until just before the outbreak of the War Between The States, when the low point of land extending from the bayou's west bank (near City Park today) was cut through to make a deep channel for navigation and to bypass Bienville Island and the original bed of Bayou St. John east of today's Park Island. L'Isle Bienville, according to tradition, is where Bienville is supposed to have eaten his first meal on the bayou when in 1699 he initially explored the stream. The sharp eastward curve of original Bayou St. Jean at L'Isle Bienville would come to be known as Devil's Elbow, because of the debris and drift-matter that naturally collected on the narrow bend, together with the swamp sand and sediment brought in by Bayou Bienville which flowed into Bayou St. Jean from the east at that point.

A short distance south of L'Isle Bienville, one encountered a slighter sandbar—a reminder that trouble wasn't over. But the next really wicked spot was opposite St. Maxent's Mill Race, then being called the Marigny Canal, (near Florida Avenue under Wisner Overpass today). This connecting stream poured enough sediment into Bayou St. Jean to make the stream almost impassable at this point. Inexperienced skippers sometimes had to load and unload their vessels three times by the time they reached the Marigny Canal. Experienced pessimists didn't reload their schooners from the chalans until they'd passed this last hazard, or would follow the loaded chalans all the way up to the Port of Bayou St. Jean in their lightered vessels. Whatever course the ship's captain chose, navigation through Bayou St. Jean was a risky, expensive and laborious business.

M. V. Rillieux operated two vessels on the bayou, (and after his death by 1805, his son Vincent would work them for his mother). Sometimes

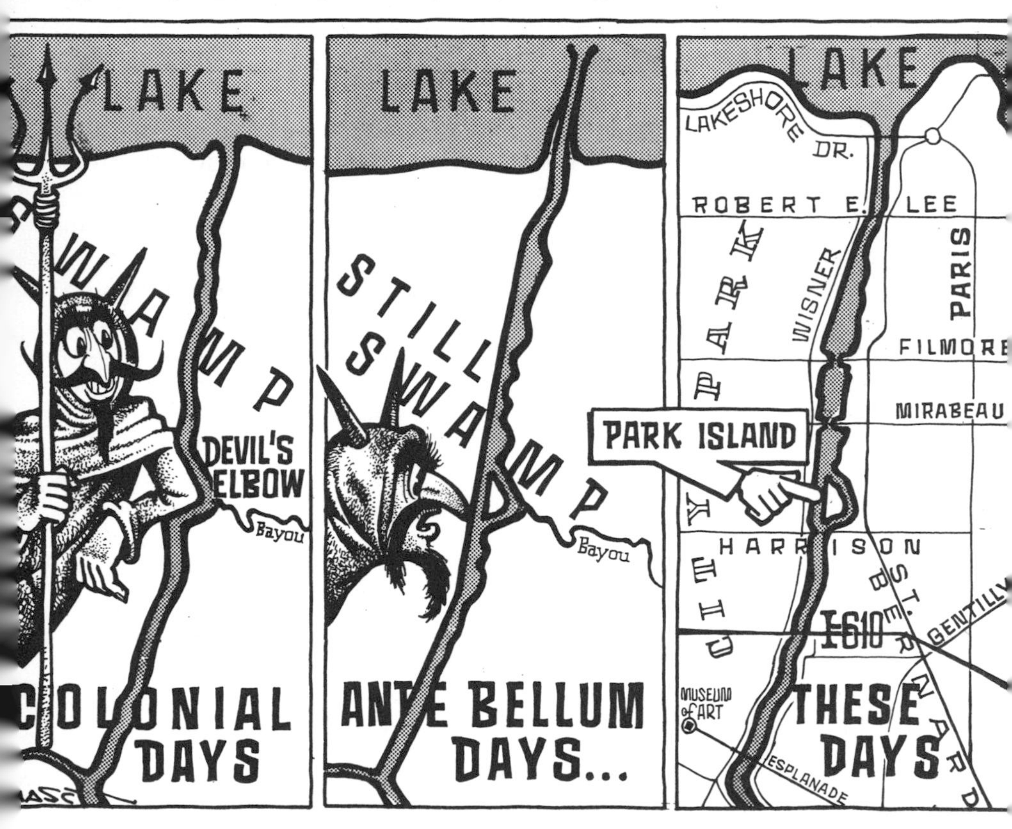

The Bayou St. John cut-off west of today's Park Island was planned as early as 1850. The work was begun in 1861-62. Interrupted by the War Between The States, the channel wasn't completed until many years after the war ended.

Rillieux sailed the schooners himself, most of his transport being lime from their kiln on the other side of Lake Pontchartrain. One of his schooners—the same size as Blanc's, carrying two hundred barrels—frequently went aground in the bayou; at its mouth there was seldom enough water two-thirds of the year for a vessel that size to get over the bar. Rillieux had his own chalans at Fort St. Jean, and not one to wait for somebody else to do the job, he was often seen in the water helping push his vessels to safety.

For one vessel that made it to the bridge at the Port of Bayou St. Jean without incident, three had to unload—at least once—during the journey up the bayou. And to this day one can find along the shores of Bayou St. John— especially around Park Island, where no slope-paving has been installed— large rocks of a nature foreign to this region. These were formerly used as ships' ballast, and had to be thrown overboard to lighter a vessel in the shallow waters of the bayou before its improvement by navigation companies in American times.[5]

Along the west bank of Bayou St. Jean—from Fort St. Jean at the lake to the bridge near the Port of Bayou St. Jean—was a trail, passable only during the dry season when the waters had evaporated. This swampy stretch, (with the possible exception of an isolated fisherman's or hunter's hut,) was without buildings of any kind—the shores of the bayou being habitable only on Metairie Ridge and in the immediate area of Fort St. Jean where workers connected with the fort lived and where a few fishermen's huts dotted the banks cityward of the Fort, not far from the dwelling of the commandant.

Unlike the stream of today, Bayou St. Jean in 1803 was the recipient of the waters of many connecting coolies, low spots, springs and other bayous and streams flowing into it from both banks along its entire course. The largest of these connecting streams was Bayou Metairie, flowing from the west along the approximate site of today's Metairie Road and City Park Avenue. Bayou Gentilly, to the east of Bayou St. Jean, flowed through Gentilly and connected with the lakes in the Chef Menteur area. A vast volume of rain and flood-water, draining into these connecting streams, from the valley extending from the Mississippi levee to Metairie Ridge and reaching from New Orleans up to what is now Kenner, poured into Bayou St. Jean. Being the only outlet to Lake Pontchartrain for these waters, this multiple inpouring tended to make the bayou, at certain times of the year, a naturally larger stream than it was to be later, with a clearer content and an often visible current.[6]

Visitor Robin now noticed land on either side of the stream that rose gradually to a habitable height at Metairie Ridge. Plots had been cleared, and handsome houses of various kinds were to be seen—some built of wood with Chinese-style galleries—others of brick with Italian-type galleries. Several had colonnades and were fine enough to do credit to a suburb of Paris. All of them had gardens in front, and several had avenues of sour orange trees. This strange fruit stayed on the tree all winter, becoming flabby and losing some acidity and juice; but in the spring the fruit filled out again to its usual shape and content.

On the west bank of the ridge, the Allard Plantation—land which had been occupied from the earliest French times—had been enlarged by six arpents on January 20, 1803, when young Luis Allard purchased the land from Widow Almonester. The other eight arpents (Carrollton Avenue and Lower City Park today), inherited by Allard, (and his two brothers and two sisters),had been purchased by his grandfather Santiago Lorreins, from Francisco Héry, who had bought the small plantation from Charles Lorreins (Tarascon) whose wife Marie Girardy had been given the acreage in 1734.

Coming to the drawbridge, several houses clustered into a village, and a minimal charge of $1.00 was charged the vessel for the raising, lowering and upkeep of the bascule bridge at the Port of Bayou St. Jean, where ships loaded and unloaded.

The next year, the contract for collecting this tax, having been properly advertised, would be awarded to Louis Blanc. Anything collected by him above $550.00 (which compensated him for his labor and hired assistance) would be paid to the city which maintained and repaired the bridge.[7]

Not far beyond the port, Bayou St. Jean lost itself in a cypress swamp, and Robin's schooner could proceed no further. A few years earlier he might have continued up to the ramparts of New Orleans by way of the canal Governor Carondelet had dug eight years before; but in 1803, the fifteen-foot-wide canal was so choked up with mud it could be used only by small pirogues.

Disembarking at the Port of Bayou St. Jean, Robin no doubt drove into town by carriage on Bayou Road, past the high-roofed houses of aristocratic Faubourg St. Jean, nestling 'mongst groves of evergreen. Because of the conditions of the Carondelet Canal, Bayou Road—when passable—was at this time being used extensively for the carting of merchandise from the Port to New Orleans. In very bad shape during the winter, the two wooden bridges on the road were also in wretched condition; and the entire area flooded in times of heavy rain from the overflowing of the Marigny Canal which cut across the cypress swamps to the north. This cartage represented a considerable additional expense to the businessmen of the time, as the prevailing fee for hauling a load from the bayou to New Orleans ran anywhere from ten bits ($1.25) to $1.50; in extremely bad weather as much as a dollar might be charged for transporting a single barrel, and vessels were often detained for long periods at the Port of Bayou St. Jean waiting to get their cargo hauled to town or to receive merchandise from New Orleans for their return trip.[8]

On the fourth day after leaving Pensacola, Robin reached New Orleans and found the streets of the city soaked. It had rained every day for three months. Located between the levee of the Mississippi and the cypress swamps in the rear, New Orleans spread out in the form of a parallelogram, extending approximately thirteen hundred yards along the riverfront, with a depth of about seven hundred yards. The levee, from English Turn below the city to some fifty miles above it, was ten to fifteen feet high and twice as broad on its leveled top which Orleanians used as a promenade, unpleasing as it must have been to the eye. The trees, planted along it during Carondelet's administration, had been ruined by those who had carelessly tied boats to them, and the quays were filthy with discarded ballast from ships and refuse thrown there by tavern keepers. The river water kept leaking through the levee, construction of which had begun in earliest French times, making the soil of New Orleans so soft and muddy that drainage was the citizenry's chief concern.

The streets, nearly forty feet wide, were in deplorable shape with chasms that could break a carriage to pieces. Pedestrians walked along banquettes (sidewalks) built close to the houses, which stopped at the end of each block, where a plank stretched across the drainage ditch to the street. Broken and slippery with mud, great agility was required to traverse these boards without falling down. The ditches surrounding the city blocks received the heavy rainfall and water that leaked through the levee, and intersected with larger canals designed to carry the excess water to the swamps in back of New Orleans, from whence they would drain into the Carondelet Canal, which in turn emptied into Bayou St. Jean. However, several of the drainage ditches were caved-in or filled with slop and garbage thrown into the street; and the main canal, into which all the others drained, was in such poor repair that many of the blocks, after a heavy rain, were completely surrounded by water and were called "islets," meaning small islands—a term introduced to New Orleans from the West Indies. The main reason for the deplorable drainage situation was caused by the extremely gradual descent from the Mississippi—the highest point in the region—to Bayou St. Jean. The downslope from the Mississippi River to the rear of the town was only six feet, and from there to Bayou St. Jean a negligible three feet.[9]

From a village of some 3,200 people, when transferred to Spain, New Orleans had grown to over eight thousand, and the districts of Bayou St. Jean and Gentilly to 489. Of New Orleans' population 1,335 were free Negroes, about two-thirds of whom were of mixed blood and who carried on small businesses, engaged in mechanical trades or were carpenters or tailors. Highly esteemed as soldiers, a large corps of people-of-color had been attached to the Spanish Services. Negro slaves numbered 2,773 in 1803, having increased from 1,128 in 1769. Negroes from the Caribbean were considered to be better mechanics and house-servants, with a value from one thousand to fourteen hundred piastres, whereas those from Africa, valued at five hundred piastres each, made better field workers, and were often rented out by their owners for twelve to fifteen piastres a month.

Several hundred Indians, living with their families in flimsy skin or leaf-covered huts on the outskirts of the city (many along Bayou and Gentilly Roads) had been protected by the Spanish government who gave them annual good-will gifts. The remainder of the population was white—half of them (about 2,500) being Creoles.

The houses of the average citizens were very "deer" according to a visitor of 1802, who remarked that a house selling for one hundred dollars in Carolina would cost two hundred and fifty dollars in New Orleans. And many of the homes were elegant, costing between forty and fifty thousand, built of brick or stone and covered with tile, plastered or painted white. A small cottage in an isolated neighborhood rented for from ten to twenty piastres a month; and a shop or store in a traveled neighborhood brought from twenty five to eighty piastres. Income from housing encouraged building, but Robin estimated it would take a long time for better structures to replace the poorer type of dwelling that predominated in the town.

New Orleans was a bourgeois city of business founded on petty trade and commercial enterprise, often conducted by "sordid speculation, and usury and informing were tolerated." The highest profession was that of merchant—one who bought and sold ships' cargoes, either outright or on a commission basis.

The products and exports of Louisiane were rice, sugar (on the increase) indigo (on the decrease), tobacco from Kentucky and Natchitoches, and cotton. (The invention of Whitney's seed-removing cotton gin in 1793 had made this a profitable crop.) The West Indies represented a continuing market for cedar, maple and cypress boards and shingles from Louisiane's plantation sawmills; and the demand was great for casks and boxes in which to ship West Indian sugar. Other Louisiane items of export were furs, pelts and salt meat from the wild cattle of Illinois.[10]

Education was at a low ebb, the oldest educational institution being the Ursuline Convent School with its abbess, eleven nuns, seventy boarding students and one hundred day pupils, who in 1803 paid according to their means. An academy for grammar had been opened by French refugees from St. Domingue in 1800, but it was too expensive except for a very few. For practical training of the moderate-meaned, there was the service of the trademasters to whom boys were apprenticed under specified conditions for a number of years to learn how to make a living. The rural areas had only the poorly trained pedagogue, who received from the planter room, board and a small fee for his limited services. Little wonder it is believed that in 1803 not more than two hundred of New Orleans' inhabitants were able to read or write well.

Science and the arts were without representation in New Orleans except for off-and-on theatre performances—dancing and gaming being the main diversions of the active bourgeois population.

Accounts of the time dismiss the Creole lady of the house as a creature of superficial talents, a quarrelsome nature, a sharp tongue and capable of physical cruelty to her slaves. Many of the white Creole men resorted to concubinage with mulatto women, setting them up in small houses on the city's ramparts—liaisons that lasted for many years. This may have explained the acid disposition of the women as well as their everyday attendance at religious services. It might also explain the absence at church (except for a few officers) of the gentlemen of New Orleans.

In 1803 there was only one church in New Orleans—St. Louis Cathedral—where five or six priests and friars, with long beards, big hats and robes tied around the middle, were in evidence.

James Pitot was a bit kinder in his assessment of the Creoles, especially the women, who, he said, had happy dispositions. He also observed that there was a considerable love of pleasure and dissipation—that the males liked to hunt, and that both sexes loved to dance. He did notice, however, that learning was hardly cultivated at all, because the colony had not prospered enough to attract teachers to settle there.[11]

In 1803 C. C. Robin noticed that vegetables were found only on the tables of the rich—that a picayune would purchase but three or four onions or turnips—the same price one paid for a pound or two of meat, which was eaten in great quantities. "Everywhere on the table one finds small pieces of bread and large pieces of meat," Robin commented, and remarked that a European would fear for his child's health because of this lopsided diet; surprisingly, however, he found that the youngsters grew tall, vigorous and were perfectly healthy. Vegetables were practically non-existent because plantation owners, concentrating on larger money-making crops, didn't want to bother growing gardens. The few available vegetables came from the German community of Les Allemands upriver, which also occasionally supplied eggs and butter. Even bear oil—a colonial shortening since earliest French occupation— was in such short supply in 1803 that its exportation was prohibited. A pound-loaf of bread cost as much as a pound or two of meat—cattle from Opelousas, Attakapas and Natchez costing only four dollars for a seven-hundred-pound carcass; and game, poultry, salt meat, fish, shrimp and crayfish were readily available. Okra gumbo was a popular staple dish of the time—for dinner or supper.[12]

Luisiana had been no bargain for the Spanish. Since 1768 nearly sixty million livres had been spent for no other reason than to maintain a protective barrier between the Anglo-American merchants on the east coast and Spain's Mexican possessions. In 1803, despite thirty three years of Spanish rule, New Orleans was still French in custom and manner, the few Spanish residents and occupiers having become, themselves, Frenchified.

Further north the U. S. colonies had been no bargain for Oliver Pollock either. Now sixty six weary years old, but without rancor because of the personal disaster he'd suffered from his complete confidence in and support of the United States from early Spanish times, he was still petitioning the Congress for recognition of his claims. He would die in 1823 at Pinckneyville, Wilkinson County, Mississippi, just north of the Louisiana line, where his body lies in an unmarked grave.[13]

Twenty days after Laussat had taken possession of Luisiana for France, a similar ceremony took place at the Place D'Armes on December 20, 1803 when William C. C. Claiborne, Governor of Mississippi, and General James Wilkinson, Commander of the Western Armies of the United States, received the province of Louisiane from Prefect-Commissioner Laussat.

Under the treaty of cession, Fort St. Jean at Lake Pontchartrain passed to the United States as a military reservation.

Fifty old soldiers formed themselves in a guard of honor to receive the tri-color as it descended; the sergeant at their head bore the flag as they silently marched past the American troops who presented arms. Carried to Sala Capitular, the flag was presented to Laussat. As the American flag was hoisted it stuck and was raised rather uncertainly—symbolic of the many difficulties that lay ahead for the new government. With the addition of this huge acreage west of the Mississippi, extending from the country's southern border to its most northern, the United States had doubled in size and had received its first real territorial thrust toward becoming the most powerful nation in the world.

A gracious loser, Laussat gave a ball for American and Spanish officials; and a reception was given by representatives of the municipality in honor of the popular Madame Laussat.

As a parting gesture, on leaving Louisiane, the French Prefect distributed a small quantity of gunpowder to those who in his estimation had shown great affection for France, the country of their ancestors. Among them were Rillieux, Captain of the Militia, and Louis Allard of the Municipal Council—both names of renown along the American stream now called Bayou St. John.[14]

PEOPLE ON BAYOU ST. JOHN DURING LOUISIANA'S COLONIAL PERIOD

ALLARD, Juan Luis
Married Francisca Lorreins, daughter of Santiago Lorreins (Tarascon), east bank bayou resident, who on April 25, 1774 purchased for the Allards an eight arpent front plantation, west bank Bayou St. John, (today's Carrollton Avenue and a segment of lower City Park). Son Luis (Louis) born to them in 1777. Juan Luis Allard died about 1798.
ALLARD, Louis (Luis)
Son of Juan Luis Allard and Francisca Lorreins, born in 1777 and lived on the west bank of Bayou St. John for the rest of his life. Schooled in France, he returned to Louisiana about 1798 and was appointed by French Prefect Laussat to the Municipal Council in 1803. Died 1847.
ALMONESTER Y ROXAS, Don Andres
Came to New Orleans with O'Reilly in 1769. Accumulating considerable real estate in New Orleans and its environs, he purchased from the Joseph Chalons the old Langlois plantation, east bank Bayou St. John (west of Bayou Road to the vicinity of Orleans Avenue) on May 7, 1781. Sold the plantation to Louis Blanc in 1793. Built and donated Charity Hospital to the City of New Orleans, as well as the Leper Hospital located off Bayou Road in the vicinity of Galvez Street in 1785.
AUBERT, Monsieur
On November 19, 1765 was granted a concession on the south shore of Lake Pontchartrain, beginning at Bayou Cochon (6 arpents east of mouth of Bayou St. John), extending easterly and southerly to lands of Gentilly.
BARRÉ, Paul (Pablo)
Married to Marie Jeanne Girardy, daughter of Joseph Girardy and Jeanne Héry, west bank Bayou St. John residents. Their children were: Eugene, Jean Baptiste, Honoré, Louise, Charles, Cecile and Carlotta. Died about 1761.
BAUDIN, Marie Louise (Maria Luisa)
Married Santiago (Jacques) Lorreins, called Tarascon, October 13, 1757. She and her husband purchased the old LaVigne plantation, east bank Bayou St. John (from today's Grand Route St. John to a point south of DeSaix Boulevard) in November, 1771. Widowed June 28, 1784, at which time they had three children: Francisca (married to Juan Luis Allard), Pellagia and Santiago Bautista. Maria Luisa sold the plantation to her son in 1799.
BEAUDREAU, (called Graveline), Jean Baptiste
Early colonist and inhabitant of Pascagoula. Purchased four arpent front

concession from St. Denis on the west bank of Bayou St. John (vicinity of today's Moss and Carrollton) in 1713. Owned Dugué plantation, east bank Bayou St. John, when it was sold to Brazillier in 1729. About 1730 claimed eight arpents in today's lower City Park, on which he established a dairy. Had son Jean Baptiste Beaudreau; and two children—Claude and Louise—by Marie Catherine Vincennes. Beaudreau died in 1762.

BEAUDREAU, Marie Catherine

Wife of Bayou St. John concessionaire Etienne Stephen Langlois in 1720's. Prior to this marriage she'd been wife to Noel Busson. After Langlois' death (about 1730) she married Urbain Gervais, who died about 1746. Had several children, most of them by Langlois, and died in 1747.

BLACHE, Francisco

Married to Luisa Héry (Duplanty), daughter of Luis Héry, and niece-heiress of Francois (Francisco) Héry, owner of Langlois plantation, east bank Bayou St. John, 1763-1771.

BLAISE, (Bellegard) John P.

Lived near the mouth of Bayou St. John from the late 1760's. Granted two arpents front by forty deep, west bank Bayou St. John, south of the Fort, on April 20, 1771; transferred 37 rear arpents to Bartholomew Robert, original concessionaire, May 14, 1771, and retained bayou frontage. Fathered a daughter in 1771, known in the 1820's as Widow Severe or Madame Bellegard.

BLANC, Luis (Louis) Antonio

Married to Henriqueta Gauvain, who died in 1782 at age 26; married her sister Luisa, age 20. Owned west bank Bayou plantation from October 29, 1785 until it was sold to Gilberto St. Maxent. Purchased Langlois plantation, east bank Bayou St. John, from Almonester September 3, 1793. Very active in bayou affairs in late Spanish and early American times.

BONNAUD, Arnaud

Appointed warehouse guard-storekeeper in 1717 by Company of the West. Worked at warehouse of the King, located to immediate west of Bayou Road on Bayou St. John, built 1719-20. Claimed property west bank Bayou St. John early 1720's.

BOSQUE, Bartholomew

Purchased two hundred foot frontage on east bank of Bayou St. John (by 540' deep) on October 9, 1799, and began to build what would later be the Pitot House.

BRAZILLIER (called Tourangeau), Louis (Luis)
Married to Jeanne Tremant, who died in 1727, by whom he had two children, Madeline and Jean Baptiste. Purchased the Dugué plantation east of Bayou Road in 1729. Purchased the Langlois plantation west of Bayou Road in 1737, owning 10½ arpents front on Bayou St. John (from today's Grand Route St. John to vicinity of Orleans Avenue). Sold off segments of rear arpents of Langlois plantation in 1756 and 1760. He had died by 1763.
BRAZILLIER, Jean Baptiste (Juan Bautista)
Son of Louis Brazillier and Jeanne Tremant, married Pelagia Lorreins August, 1748. Inherited the Dugué plantation from his father about 1763. He died, childless, in 1775.
BRAZILLIER, Madeline (Magdalena)
Daughter of Louis Brazillier and Jeanne Tremant. Signed wedding contract with Francois Héry (Duplanty) October 11, 1741. Inherited the Langlois plantation from her father about 1763. Purchased the de Mouléon grant (west of Bayou St. John) June 28, 1768. After Duplanty's death she married Henriques Desprez about 1771. Sold the eight arpent front, west bank Bayou St. John plantation (lower City Park today) to Santiago Lorreins April 25, 1774. Sold the Langlois plantation and the de Mouléon grant to the Joseph Chalons on October 15, 1774.
BRIAR (Briard, Driar), Marie
Came to Mobile from Canada in 1704. Married Antoine Rivard de LaVigne, one of the earliest concessionaires on the east bank of Bayou St. John. Had six children by him.
BRUENT (Bonnet, Bourbonnois), Jean
Co-owner with Jean Olivier of eight arpent front plantation, west bank Bayou St. John (lower City Park), prior to August 21, 1731, on which date the arpents were sold to Louis Turpin.
CASTILLON (Castillion), Andre
Born at the mouth of Bayou St. John in 1770. The Andres Jung grant of 1766, east bank of Bayou St. John (approximately from today's Fillmore Avenue to vicinity of Vista Shores Club), called the Castillion Tract in early 1800's.
CAÜE, Francois Louis Jean
Guardian of the King's Stores in the army marching against the Chickasaws in the 1730's. In the spring of 1739 married Francoise de Villemont, daughter of Antoinette Fourrier (widow of Bayou St. John resident Antoine Rivard de LaVigne) and her first husband Sr. Henry de Mirbaise de Villemont. Caüe died about 1771, and one of his daughters married Gabriel Peyroux in 1772.

CHALON, Joseph (Jose)
New Orleans merchant who married Marie Elizabeth (Maria Isabel) DesRuisseaux July 15, 1768, by whom he had three children: Francisca Isabel (who died at an early age), another Francisca Isabel, and Jose Jacinto. On October 15, 1774 the Chalons purchased the Langlois plantation and sold it to Sr. Almonester on May 7, 1781. Chalon died in April of 1783 in Philadelphia.

CONWAY, Maurice (Marquis d'Auconis)
Nephew of O'Reilly, he arrived in New Orleans June, 1769. Co-owner of tannery on St. Louis Street. On November 1, 1774 purchased (with Alexander Latil of Bayou Road) The Houmas. In 1777 married Maria Juana Francisca Macarty, widow of Juan Bautista Cezaire LeBreton. For two months in 1781 he owned a west bank Bayou St. John plantation which he purchased from Andres Jung. Died in 1792.

COUSTILLAS, Jacques
Acquired Gentilly plantation in 1723-4. Marine Captain with the Company of the Indies, he imported slaves on his own ship.Left for Arkansas to establish post in war against the Chickasaws August 26, 1738. Died there in early 1739.

D'AUBERVILLE, Monsieur
Purchased segment of rear arpents of the Langlois plantation from Louis Brazillier June 10, 1756; after D'Auberville's death, the land was sold to Alexander Latil on June 10, 1757.

D'AUBERVILLE, Marie Louise
Married Francisco Bouligny (Spanish officer who announced arrival of O'Reilly) in 1770.

DE BAULNE, (deBeame, deBaume, Beaune), Chartier
With title of King's Attorney he came to Bayou St. John in 1719, settled in Village of the Acolapissas. Lost his job in 1722 to Francois Fleuriau. In 1724 his plantation at the Chapitoulas was purchased by Louis Beaulieu and Nicolas de Lafrénière, the Chauvin brothers.

D'HEBECOURT (D'Hevecourt), Francois
Opened the Bayu San Juan Academy in his home on Bayou St. John November 27, 1802. The D'Hebecourt family lived on the west bank of Bayou St. John (near the bridge) for many years in American times.

DE LA CHAISE (de LaChaise or Delachaise), Charles
Son of Jacques de LaChaise and Marguerite Darensbourg. Married Marie Marguerite de Mouléon (daughter of Sr. Henry de Mouléon and Marie Elizabeth de Gauvrit) February 3, 1766. In 1778 purchased a segment of the 1765 Aubert grant on the south shore of Lake Pontchartrain, east of Bayou St. John.

DE LA CHAISE, Jacques
Keeper of the King's Store. On December 18, 1758 he purchased the 1719 DuBreuil concession below New Orleans, which extended from the Mississippi River back to Bayou St. John. Died in 1768.
DEMORAND (DeMorant), Charles (Carlos)
First married to Jeanne (Anne) Hay when he purchased plot of ground west of Bayou Road just outside New Orleans on May 12, 1731 and established a brickyard. After her death he married Marie Rene de LaChaise, by whom he had a son Charles, born December 27, 1749, a daughter Marie Felicité and two other sons, Vincent and Luis Docmeny. On June 19, 1756 he was granted a concession on the east side of Bayou Road and died shortly thereafter. Division of his estate in 1772.
DERBON, Maturino (Mathurin)
Early concessionaire on Bayou St. John. His land acquired by Antoine Rivard de LaVigne in 1720. It has been speculated that this name was a corruption of Mathurin Dreux.
DESPREZ (Despres), Henriques
Attorney for many Bayou St. John residents. Appointed Public Attorney by the Cabildo December 23, 1769. Married Magdalena Brazillier, Widow Duplanty, bayou resident, about 1771. Confirmed by Cabildo as Attorney General January 1, 1777. Captain of the Urban Militia in 1785. Had died by early 1788.
DESRUISSEAUX, Joseph (Jose) Lord of the Isle of Peraut, Canada
Married Marie Francoise Girardy, Widow Milon, November 24, 1744, by whom he had one daughter, Marie Elizabeth (Maria Isabel). Received a six arpent front grant of land on the west bank of Bayou St. John on August 10, 1750. Purchased the fourteen arpent front Girardy plantation, west bank Bayou St. John, September 1, 1750. Built road from Bayou St. John to the Chapitoulas 1765-6. Died in early 1767. Partition of his estate in January, 1769.
DESRUISSEAUX, Marie Elizabeth (Maria Isabel)
Only daughter of Marie Francoise Girardy and Joseph DesRuisseaux. Married Joseph (Jose) Chalon July 15, 1768, by whom she had two daughters, both of whom were named Francisca Isabel (one died early in life) and one son Jose Jacinto. With her husband she owned the old Langlois plantation, east bank of Bayou St. John, from October 15, 1774 to May 7, 1781. Purchased the DeMouléon grant, west of Bayou St. John, from Magdalena Brazillier October 15, 1774, which became a part of the Girardy-DesRuisseaux-Roquigny plantation, west bank Bayou St. John, until her death about 1815. Widowed in April, 1783, she married Etienne

(Estevan) Roquigny about 1789. Inherited the Tuon grant, east bank Bayou St. John, from her mother, and sold it to Alexander Milne in 1806.

D'HAUTERIVE (Dauterive de Valiere), Joseph

Married Marie Felicité DeMorand, daughter of Charles DeMorand and Rene de LaChaise November 11, 1763.

D'HAUTERIVE, Renaud

Owned the Langlois plantation, east bank Bayou St. John, from early 1730's until 1737. Married the widow of Sr. Francois Duval, Cashier of the Company of the Indies from 1731 to 1735.

DOUA, Sieur

Contractor for repair and refitting of schooners, he owned a plantation near the mouth of Bayou St. John in 1752.

DREUX, Mathurin

Emigrated to Louisiana in 1718. Received large concession of land in Gentilly. Married Claudine Francoise Hugot November 17, 1732. Lived in same house with brother Pierre. The two of them called "Sieurs of Gentilly." Had many children.

DREUX, Pierre

With brother Mathurin, emigrated to Louisiana in 1718. Married Anne Corbin Bachemin April 28, 1733. Had died by 1743.

DUBREUIL, Claude Joseph Villars (also called de Villars)

Arrived in Louisiana March, 1719. Received a concession at the Chapitoulas and also one just below New Orleans which extended from the Mississippi River to Bayou St. John. Died 1757.

DUFOSSAT, Chevalier Guy Soniat

Arriving in Louisiana after King George's War, he married Madeline Francoise Claudine Dreux, daughter of Mathurin Dreux of Gentilly, in 1753. Wrote a small History of Louisiana. Nine children born to this union. DuFossat was appointed Captain of the Military Forces in 1759 and until 1761 constructed and repaired forts in Illinois. Entered the service of Spain in 1769, and died in 1794.

DUGUÉ (Duguay), Francois

Concessionaire east bank Bayou St. John (to immediate west of today's Grand Route St. John) from 1720 to late 1720's. Claimed lower City Park in early 1720's. Also owned an eighteen arpent front plantation on the other side of the Mississippi River. Married Marie Bruslée, daughter of Philippe Antoine Bruslée and Marthe Fremont, on April 2, 1731. Died soon after.

DUPARC, Sieur

Purchased rear portions of old Langlois plantation (contiguous to land sold D'Auberville) from Luis Brazillier September 22, 1760. Undertook futile task of establishing sailing route from Manchac to Gulf in 1765.

DUPRATZ, Antoine Simon Le Page

Came to Bayou St. John in January of 1719. Received a concession on the east bank of Bayou St. John (later acquired by de LaVigne). Left for Natchez in 1721. Returned to New Orleans in 1726 to manage the slave plantation of the Company of the Indies across the river (Algiers). Wrote a History of Louisiana in 1758 after returning to France.

FERNANDEZ, Andres

Purchased property on the east bank of Bayou St. John August 20, 1800 from Santiago Bautista Lorreins, the bayou frontage of which would later become the site of the Tissot House at 1400 Moss Street.

FOURRIER, Antoinette

Came to Louisiana in 1719 with first husband Henri Martin de Mirbaize, Sieur de Villemont, by whom she had two daughters, Jeanne and Francoise. After de Villemont's death, she married Antoine Rivard de LaVigne (the elder), and lived on the east bank of Bayou St. John. Her daughter Jeanne, by de Villemont, married the son of her second husband, and her daughter Francoise married Francois Louis Jean Caüe. Antoinette Fourrier was widowed by LaVigne's death on February 11, 1729.

GARIC, Jean Baptiste (Juan Bautista)

Clerk-Notary Public in the French Superior Council and the Spanish Cabildo, he handled many legal documents for people on the Bayou. Childless by his first marriage, Garic had four children by his second wife Estefania Goyon. He died in 1779.

GIRARDY, Angelique

Daughter of bayou resident Joseph Girardy and the Indian Francoise. Angelique married Alain Dugué June 25, 1727, who was killed in the Natchez massacre. She then married Widower Jean Baptiste Rejas, called LaPrade on June 26, 1730. After his death she married Laurent Lerable. She had several children.

GIRARDY, Joseph

Early resident of west bank Bayou St. Jean in 1719, where by 1731 he had acquired a large plantation. Married to Jeanne Héry (Henry), by whom he had four daughters: Marie Francoise, Marie Jeanne, Marie Louise and Marie Rose. Prior to this marriage he had a daughter Angelique by the Indian Francoise. Girardy died in 1758.

GIRARDY, Marie Francoise (Maria Francisca)

Daughter of Joseph Girardy and Jeanne Héry, west bank Bayou St. John residents. First married Joseph Milon on June 20, 1734, by whom she had four sons: Jean, Jacques, Maurice and Henri. Married Joseph DesRuisseaux November 24, 1744 by whom she had one daughter — Marie Elizabeth (Maria Isabel). She and DesRuisseaux lived on the Girardy plantation (which her husband purchased in 1750) on the west bank of Bayou St. John.

GIRARDY, Marie Jeanne

Daughter of Joseph Girardy and Jeanne Héry, west bank Bayou St. John. Married to Paul (Pablo) Barré by whom she had five children: Eugene, Charles, Louise, Cecile (wife of Francois Roquigny) and Charlotte (wife of Bossier, named LeBrun). Marie Jeanne had died by 1759, and her husband had died by 1761.

GIRARDY, Marie Louise (Maria Luisa)

Daughter of Joseph Girardy and Jeanne Héry, west bank Bayou St. John. Married Louis Langlois on March 12, 1740, by whom she had one son. In 1734 Louis Turpin donated to her an eight arpent front plantation (today's lower City Park) on the west bank of Bayou St. John. Married for the second time in 1752, she and Charles Lorreins (Tarascon) lived on the west bank of Bayou St. John.

GIRARDY, Marie Rose

Daughter of Joseph Girardy and Jeanne Héry, west bank Bayou St. John residents. On April 6, 1740 she married Jean Baptiste Saucier (Saussier), by whom she had two children. She was married for the second time in 1747 to Louis Duvernay (Duvernet). Her daughter Marie Rose Saucier married Blaise Philipe Joseph Levos July 21, 1767.

GLAPION, Sr. Christophe de

Married Jeanne Antoinette Rivard de LaVigne (daughter of LaVigne, the younger, and Jeanne Antoinette Villemont) in 1757. Their daughter Jeanne Antoinette married Edme Joseph de l'Homme January 14, 1777, of which union eight children would be born.

HARANT, Hubert

First cousin of the Dreux brothers of Gentilly, Harant owned three lots on Bayou Road, which at the time of his death in 1739 were sold to baker Piquery.

HÉRY, (called Duplanty), Francois

Héry, the elder, lived on Bayou St. John and died in early 1746.

HÉRY, Francois (Francisco) called Duplanty

Son of Héry the elder, he married Madeline Brazillier, daughter of Luis Brazillier and deceased Jeanne Tremant, October 11, 1741. Lived on the old Langlois plantation, which his wife inherited about 1763, until his death in 1771. Built the Cabildo in 1770. Also owned the eight arpent front plantation on the west bank of Bayou St. John (today's lower City Park) at the time of his death.

HÉRY (Henry), Jeanne

Wife of Joseph Girardy, by whom she had four daughters (see Girardy). Lived on the west bank of Bayou St. John until her death December 8, 1770.

JUNG, Andres (Andre)

Son of Canadian Jean Jung and Rose Cousada of Bordeaux, France which for many years was his official residence. (His brother Jean Jung, Chandler of Bordeaux, operated in Louisiana from the earliest times, and a brother Augustin Jung is also mentioned in the records.) On June 22, 1766 he received a ten arpent grant on the east bank of Bayou St. John (between today's Fillmore Avenue and the Vista Shores Club). He owned the Tarascon Grant, west bank Bayou St. John 1773-4, and acquired another west bank bayou plantation, south of the Tarascon grant prior to 1781 which he owned until his death. In March of 1779 he married Pelagia Lorreins, Widow Juan Bautista Brazillier, who died in 1781. Jung died in 1784.

KERNION, Jean Francois Huchet, Ecuyer, Sieur de

Only child of Pierre Guillaume Huchet and second wife Thomase Renee Guesdan de Keravel. Born in Quimper, France in 1700, he came to Louisiana in 1720, and married Dame Jeanne Antoinette de Mirbaise de Villemont, Widow Rivard (the younger) on October 4, 1736. A son, Jean René, was born to them in 1739. Councillor Assessor on the Superior Council in 1748, he was active in the revolution of 1768. He lived on the old LaVigne plantation, east bank Bayou St. John, from 1736 to 1769, the year he died.

KERNION, Jean René (Renato), Huchet de

Son of Jean Francois Huchet Ecuyer Sieur de Kernion and Jeanne Antoinette de Villemont, Widow LaVigne (the younger), he lived on the LaVigne plantation, east bank Bayou St. John, from his birth in 1739 to November, 1771 when he sold the twenty-two arpent front plantation to Santiago Lorreins (Tarascon). On June 19, 1767 he married Louise Constance Chauvin de Lery des Islets (Desillest). In 1785 was Junior Alcalde in the Spanish Cabildo. On December 16, 1795 he married again—Marie Joseph Modeste de Verges.

LABEAU (Labo), Pierre

With his brother Charles, he settled near the mouth of Bayou St. John, west bank, in 1770. Pierre's son Honori would live there after 1809. The residences of both LaBeau brothers were the bayou frontage of Bartholomew Robert's 1766 grant.

LA CHEUVE, Sieur

Claimed concession, extending from vicinity of today's Park Island on Bayou St. John to Bayou Gentilly, in the early 1720's.

LAMOTHE, Santiago

Resident of Bayou St. John 1770-1778. His brother Juan, a carpenter, also lived on the bayou at the same time. In 1778, Santiago's widow was handling the estates of both brothers.

LANGLOIS, Etienne Stephen

Received a 3½ arpent front concession on the east bank of Bayou St. John (west of Bayou Road) on September 21, 1720. Purchased the adjoining Provenche three arpents in 1724. After 1752 these two grants would be listed as eight arpents front and extended from Bayou Road to the vicinity of today's Orleans Avenue. Married to Marie Catherine Beaudreau, by whom he had several children, he died about 1731.

LANGLOIS, Louis

Brother of Etienne Langlois. Involved in trade, he married Marie Louise Girardy of Bayou St. John on March 12, 1740, by whom he had one son. Died 1749.

LATIL, Alexander (Alexandro)

Married Marie Rene de LaChaise, Widow DeMorand (of Bayou Road) April 16, 1757. On June 19, 1757 he purchased a segment of the rear portion of the Langlois plantation near Washerwomen's Bridge on Bayou Road from D'Auberville. After the death of his wife on February 17, 1760 he married Jeanne Grondel. On April 30, 1770 he was granted the trapezoid site of the Spanish Naval Arsenal on the old Dugué plantation on the east bank of Bayou St. John. From 1774-1776 he owned (with Maurice Conway) the tract of land upriver called The Houmas. Died in late Spanish times.

LAVERGNE, Jean

He lived at the mouth of Bayou St. John in 1765. First married to Jeanne LaClef by whom he had two sons, Nicholas and Barthelmy. Married Louise Roquigny January 26, 1765, by whom he had three children. Prior to 1771, he owned the Jung grant, east bank Bayou St. John. On August 1, 1771 was granted a thirty-seven arpent grant of land contiguous to Fort St. John at the mouth of Bayou St. John. Died December 1, 1774.

LAVIGNE, Antoine Rivard de

Included in the Louisiana Census of August 1, 1706. Settled a small concession on the east bank of Bayou St. John in 1708. First married to Marie

Briard (Briar, Driar) of Mobile by whom he had six children. Owned the Village of the Acolapissas by 1718; and by 1721 had acquired seventeen arpents front on the east bank of Bayou St. John including his original concession. (His plantation extended from today's Grand Route St. John to a point south of DeSaix Boulevard.) After the death of his first wife, he married Antoinette Fourrier, widow of Henri Martin de Mirbaise, Sieur de Villemont. LaVigne died February 11, 1729.

LAVIGNE, Francois Antoine Rivard de

Son of Antoine Rivard de LaVigne (the elder) and Marie Briard. On February 20, 1730 he married Jeanne Antoinette de Villemont (his step-mother's daughter), by whom he had three children. One died early in life, Jeanne Antoinette was born in May, 1734 and Marie Francoise, a posthumous child, was born in 1735 or 1736. LaVigne died September 25, 1735.

LEBRETON, Monsieur

Received a small concession in the rear of the Langlois plantation on August 29, 1752. He was granted a concession fronting the east bank of Bayou St. John (west of the Langlois plantation) on June 2, 1756.

LORREINS (called Tarascon), Jacques (Santiago)

Left Chef de Baye on May 28, 1717 for Louisiana. Married to Maria Avril by whom he had three children: Charles, Santiago and Pellagia. After his wife's death, he married Marthe Coussine in 1742. Lorreins died in 1752.

LORREINS (called Tarascon), Charles (Carlos)

Son of Jacques (Santiago) Lorreins and Maria Avril. Married Marie Louise Girardy, Widow Langlois in 1752. They lived for several years on the eight arpent front plantation on the west bank of Bayou St. John (today's Carrollton Avenue and a segment of lower City Park) which his wife had been donated in 1734. Received a concession further north on the west bank of Bayou St. John called the Tarascon grant in 1766. Sold this plantation to Andres Jung in 1773.

LORREINS, Pelagia

Daughter of Jacques (Santiago) Lorreins and Maria Avril. Married Jean Baptiste Brazillier, Bayou resident, August 1748. Widowed in 1775. Married bachelor Andres Jung March, 1779. She died in 1781.

LORREINS (called Tarascon). Santiago (Jacques)

Son of Jacques (Santiago) Lorreins and Maria Avril. Married Maria Luisa Baudin October 13, 1757. They had three children: Francisca (married to Juan Luis Allard), Pellagia, and Santiago Bautista. Purchased the twenty-two arpent front LaVigne plantation from René Kernion in November, 1771. Grandson Louis Allard was born on the Bayou in 1777.

At Lorreins' death, on June 28, 1784, he owned the LaVigne plantation, east bank Bayou St. John, and a plantation on the west bank of the Bayou, which the Allards inherited from him.

LORREINS, Santiago Bautista (Jacques)

Son of Santiago (Jacques) Lorreins, called Tarascon and Maria Luisa Baudin. Lived on the old LaVigne plantation, east bank Bayou St. John, which his mother sold to him on August 16, 1799, at which time he began to subdivide.

MILNE, Alexander

Came to New Orleans in 1776. Sold hardware and bricks; purchased extensive property along Lake Pontchartrain and both banks of Bayou St. John (from the lake to today's Park Island) during the late Spanish and early American periods. Became a millionaire.

MILON, Joseph

Son of deceased Pierre Milon and Francoise Dominé, he married Marie Francoise Girardy of Bayou St. John on June 20, 1734, by whom he had four sons: Jean, Jacques, Maurice and Henri. A contractor, he worked for DuBreuil Villars on government projects. Died 1744.

MILON, Maurice

One of four sons of Joseph Milon and Marie Francoise Girardy. In 1766 the four brothers received an extensive land grant on the west bank of Bayou St. John, extending from Fort St. John toward the city for forty arpents front. As guardian of the estate of his mother's second husband (Joseph DesRuisseaux), in 1769 he was living on Bayou St. John at the old Girardy-DesRuisseaux house, with his wife Catherine Guedon and their two children. On December 27, 1773 he purchased the Tuon grant, east bank Bayou St. John (between Mirabeau and Fillmore Streets today), and sold it to his mother on December 26, 1776.

MONTBRUN, Jean Baptiste Bouché de

From Quebec, Canada. Trapper, trader and traveler in early Louisiana, he married Francoise Rivard, minor daughter of Antoine Rivard de LaVigne and Marie Briard, in February of 1736.

MOULÉON, Marie Elizabeth de Gauvrit de

Child of Sr. Joachim Gauvrit and Marianne Lesterie, and half sister of Madame Jean Baptiste Destrehan, she married Henri de Mouléon. Granted a concession west of Bayou St. John on May 10, 1758, she sold it to Madeline Brazillier on June 28, 1768. Her daughter, by Henri de Mouléon, Marie Marguerite, married Charles de LaChaise on February 3, 1766. Mme. de Mouléon owned the old DuBreuil plantation (extending from the Mississippi River to Bayou St. John) from March 22, 1774 to October 4, 1776 at which time she sold it to Gilberto St. Maxent.

NICOLAS (alias Delon)
Early concessionaire east bank Bayou St. John, near Antoine Rivard de LaVigne, 1708.
OLIVIER, Jean
Co-owner with Jean Bruent (Bonnet, Bourbonnois) of eight arpents front on the west bank of Bayou St. John (today's Carrollton Avenue and lower City Park), which they sold to Louis Turpin August 21-22, 1731. Sale recorded February 18, 1734 in Illinois.
PALAO, Pierre
Conceded eight arpents front, on the east bank of Bayou St. John (extending from today's Park Island north to Mirabeau Avenue) in 1799, today's Bancroft Park subdivision.
PELLERIN, Sieur
Lived on banks of Bayou St. John about 1719; then moved to Natchez.
PELLERIN, Girard
Guardian of the Company stores in 1728. Married to Francoise Ruellan, by whom he had two children: Francoise, who in 1748 became Mme. Barthelmy de Macarty, and Louis Gerard Pellerin, who married twice—Francoise Alexandre Ville and Marthe Hubert Bellair. Pellerin died in early 1736.
PEYROUX, Gabriel
Married the daughter of Francois Caüe in 1772. In 1777 he purchased a segment of the rear arpents of the Langlois plantation from Arnoul, the same arpents originally sold Duparc by Brazillier in 1760. Widow Gabriel Peyroux was still living there in 1799 at which time she was selling off the arpents to various buyers.
POLLOCK, Oliver
Irish merchant who traded from Philadelphia to Cuba to New Orleans during the 1760's. As champion of the cause of the American Revolution, he was assisted financially by many Bayou St. John and New Orleans citizens.
PORTIER, Baptiste
1708 concessionaire on east bank of Bayou St. John near Antoine Rivard de LaVigne.
PROVENCHE (Provanchez), Jean Baptiste
Received three arpents front on the east bank of Bayou St. John, located to the immediate west of Etienne Langlois, on April 21, 1721. On September 17, 1724 he sold his land to Langlois.
REYNES, (Renne) Joseph
Purchased two hundred feet front on the east bank of Bayou St. John from

Bartholome Bosque on May 28, 1800, and finished building what would later be known as the Pitot House. Purchased twelve arpents in the rear of former frontage on August 6, 1800.

RILLIEUX, Francois, Marie and Vincent, Sr. and Jr.

A family which visited Bayou St. John, where they had relatives and where they were active in shipping and trading. Originally from Pearl River near Biloxi, Vincent and his son of the same name operated on Bayou St. John during the late Spanish and early American periods. Widow Rillieux would live on the bayou in early American times.

ROBERT, Bartholomew

On June 12, 1766 he was conceded seventeen arpents, twenty toises front, on the west bank of Bayou St. John (approximately from Robert E. Lee Boulevard of today toward the city). His wife, Jeanne Bodmont, died in 1769 leaving six children. After 1766 Robert was at one time the owner of the Jung concession on the east bank of Bayou St. John (Fillmore Avenue north today). Marguerite Robert, Widow Durocher, alias Castillon (the second wife of Robert's son) lived on the Jung grant until she sold the property to Alexander Milne in early American times.

ROCHON, Alexis

Born in Mobile, he came to the mouth of Bayou St. John in 1770 at eight years of age. Still lived there in 1823.

ROQUIGNY, Etienne (Estevan)

Master Blacksmith, who married Maria Isabel DesRuisseaux, Widow Chalon, about 1789. The Roquignys lived on the Girardy-DesRuisseaux plantation, west bank of Bayou St. John, until her death about 1815. The plantation was subdivided by the end of the Spanish period. The DeMouléon grant, acquired by Maria Isabel DesRuisseaux on October 15, 1774, was a part of the Roquigny plantation until her death.

ST. DENIS (Denys), Louis Juchereau de

Received four arpents frontage on the west bank of Bayou St. John in 1708—land that would later become a part of the Girardy plantation. Selling these arpents in 1713 to finance his trade with the Spanish, he settled the post of Natchitoches by 1716, and lived there until his death on June 20, 1744.

ST. MAXENT, Gilbert Antoine de (Gilberto Antonio)

Owner of extensive property on Bayou St. John and in Gentilly during the Spanish period. On August 31, 1749 he married Elizabeth (Marie Anne) la Roche, by whom he had several children. On October 9, 1772 he received a concession on the east bank of Bayou St. John near today's Park Island. About the same time he owned a plantation on the west bank of Bayou St. John in the vicinity of today's Taylor Avenue. On October 4, 1776 he purchased from Mme. de Mouléon the old DuBreuil plantation, which extended from the Mississippi River below New Orleans, back to Gentilly and Bayou St. John. Owned it until 1789. On April 8, 1778 he purchased extensive Gentilly property from Widow Juan Bautista Brazillier. Died August 8, 1794.

SAUBAGNE (Soubagne, Soubaignie, Subanier), Jean

In early 1720's claimed a strip of property which extended from Bayou St. John (vicinity of Park Island today) back to Bayou Gentilly where he established his home.

SAUCIER (Saussier), Jean Baptiste

On April 6, 1740 he married Rose Girardy, daughter of Joseph Girardy and Jeanne Héry, bayou residents. Died about 1747. Their child Marie Rose Saucier married Blaise Philipe Joseph Levos on July 21, 1767.

TRUDEAU, Francois

Claimed property on the west bank of Bayou St. John, across the stream from the Langlois plantation in the early 1720's—land which would later become a part of the Girardy plantation.

TUON, Jean

Received a concession of ten arpents front on the east bank of Bayou St. John (approximately Mirabeau to Fillmore today) on July 21, 1766. On December 27, 1773 sold the land to Maurice Milon, who on December 26, 1776 sold it to his mother, Maria Francisca Girardy, Widow DesRuisseaux. Inherited by Maria Isabel DesRuisseaux Roquigny, this land was sold to Alexander Milne in the early 1800's.

VILLEMONT, Henri Martin de Mirbaize, Sieur de

Came to Louisiana in 1719 from Poitiers, France with his wife Antoinette Fourrier and two daughters. His widow married Antoine Rivard de LaVigne (the elder); his daughter Jeanne Antoinette married Francois Antoine Rivard de LaVigne (the younger), and in the spring of 1739 his daughter Francoise married Sieur Francois Louis Jean Caüe.

VINCENNES, Marie Catherine

Wife of Jean Baptiste Beaudreau (Graveline); widowed in 1762 at which time they had two children: Claude, 24 years of age, and Louise, 22 years old.

Bayou St. John in Colonial Louisiana

NOTES AND REFERENCES — The French Period

To conserve space, a reference will sometimes refer to an entire foregoing story or event, or a sequence of related events.

CHAPTER I

1) Louisiana Historical Quarterly (hereafter referred to as LHQ) 13, #2, 1930, p 253, footnote quoting Dr. William Read and Evelyn Soule.
2) Otvos, Professor Ervin, Earth Sciences Dept., LSU-NO, letters 7/22/69 to 4/3/74, to author.
3) Charlevoix, Father 1/25/1722, in Historical Collections of Louisiana III (hereafter referred to as HC-L), New York 1851, 179.
4) Kane, Harnett, Item-Tribune, 7/18/1937.
5) Martin, François-Xavier, History of Louisiana (hereafter referred to as Martin's), New Orleans, 1882, 402; Trudeau, Carlos, Map of New Orleans and Environment 12/24/1798; de Woiserie, J. L. Bouqueta, Plan of New Orleans, 1803, Cabildo, N. O.; Plan de la Nouvelle Orleans Ville Capitalle de la Province de Louissiane - commcd autrefois le Missisipy cette Ville est situe dans l'Amerique Septentridnale aua 32 degres de latitude Nord., Archives Paris Fix 68 - Circa 1730; Plan de la Nlle. Orleans Ville Capitalle de la Louissianne, Explication des Chiffres . . .Circa 1730, Map-LOC.
6) Dabney, Thomas Ewing, "And Broadmoor Had A Lake," and map of Bayou St. John and branches, in Times Picayune (hereafter referred to as T-P) Sunday Magazine 8/18/1935, 8; Dixon, Richard, "Broadmoor" New Orleans, 1975, 5.
7) Dabney, Thomas Ewing, "And Broadmoor Had A Lake," and map of Bayou St. John and branches, in Times Picayune, Sunday Magazine 8/18/1935, 8; Dixon, Richard, "Broadmoor" New Orleans, 1975, 5.

CHAPTER II

1) Robin, C. C., translation by Stuart O. Landry, Jr., Voyage to Louisiana 1803-5, New Orleans, 1966, 5 (hereafter referred to as Robin); DuPratz, LePage, History of Louisiana, Baton Rouge, 1972, 48 (hereafter referred to as DuPratz); Surrey-King, Commerce of Louisiana, LHQ 5 (Jan. 1922) 22.
2) DuPratz, History of Louisiana, 17, Chase, John, Frenchmen Desire Good Children, re "Okwata," p 14.
3) Thomas, Alfred B., Spanish Activities In The Lower Mississippi Valley 1513-1698, LHQ 22 (Oct. 1939) 933-942.
4) Humble, Sallie Lacy, Ouchita Valley Expedition, LHQ 25 (Jul. 1942) 638.
5) Dufour, Charles L., 250 Years in New Orleans, New Orleans, 1968, 12.
6) DuPratz, 3-4; Gayarré, History of Louisiana, Volume I, 26; Prichard, Walter, Romance of Research in Louisiana History, LHQ 20 (Jul. 1937) 557; Dufour, Pie, T-P 4/9/1967, 8.
7) Villiers Du Terrage, Marc De, "A History of the Foundation of New Orleans 1717-1722, translated by Warrington Dawson, LHQ 3 (Apr. 1920) 163-4 (hereafter referred to as Villiers' Foundation).
8) Thomas, Alfred B., Spanish Activities in The Lower Mississippi Valley 1513-1698, LHQ 22 (Oct. 1939) 933.
9) Penicaut, Andre, Fleur de Lys and Calumet, McWilliams Translation, Baton Rouge, 1953, fn p 1 (hereafter refered to as Penicaut.); Dufour, Pie, T-P, 1/5/1969; Villiers Du Terrage, Marc de, Last Years of French Louisiana, translation by Henri Delville de Sinclair, WPA, New Orleans, 1937-8, Special Collections Dept., Tulane University, N. O., quotes Godwin 1791-1797, III, 12, (hereafter referred to as Villier's Last Years . . .)
10) Villiers' Foundation, LHQ 3 (Apr. 1920) 163, fn 1; Penicaut, 60; Dufour, Pie, T-P 2/27/72, s3, p7; Quayle, Jennifer, Iberville Returns, T-P Magazine Section 3/31/74, 20.
11) Martin's, 96; Villere, Sidney, Translation of Unpublished Documents, National Archives, Paris, Vol I 1697-1721, Louisiana State Museum Library (hereafter referred to as LSML), 2. DuRu gives dates as 2/27/1699; King, Grace, Sieur de Bienville, New York 1892, 34; Dufour, Pie, T-P 2/18/68, s2, p7; Ibid, T-P 2/27/73, s3, p4.
12) Historical Collections of Louisiana, Vol. II, 14 (hereafter called HC-L); HC-L VII, New York 1875, 62-3, 84; Martin's 97; DuRu, Journal, New Orleans Public Libary, Louisiana Department, 26 fn. 32.
13) Villier's Foundation, LHQ 3 (Apr. 1920) 163.
14) King, Sieur de Bienville, 42; King, Creole Families of Louisiana, New York 1921, 59.
15) Private Claims, New Orleans, An Act of Congress 6/22/1860 //An Act for the final adjustment of private land claims in Florida, Louisiana and Missouri, Land Office, Baton Rouge, La. (Hereafter

referred to as Private Claims.) 399-400, Survey by Luis Andry of Brazillier-Chalon property boundaries 12/1/1777; Cable, George W., Creoles of Louisiana, Charles Scribner Sons, New York, 1910, p 138.
16) King, B. M., Map of Original New Orleans, CXXII 98, 1728, Map Division, Library of Congress, Alexandria, Va. (hereafter referred to as Map-LOC).
17) T-P 11/3/1968, 17.

CHAPTER III

1) Chambers, History of Louisiana, 54-5; Penicaut, fn 15; General Collot's Reconnoitering Trip, LHQ 1 (Apr. 1918) 312; King, Sieur de Bienville, 51; DuRu, Journal, 57; Martins's 98; King, Sieur de Bienville, 69-70; Dufour, Pie, Ten Flags In The Wind, New York 1967, 44 (hereafter referred to as Ten Flags); Villere, Translations, 5; HC-L, III, Benard de la Harpe, 24; Gayarré I, 98; Quayle, J, Iberville Returns, T-P Magazine Section 3/31/74, 20.
2) Penicaut, 12 and 13 fn 37, quoting Father DuPoisson, Jesuit in McDermott Glossary, 100.
3) Gayarré I, 50; De La Tour, Map of New Orleans Region and Lakes, 1720, #720/2 NOPL, La. Dept.
4) Giraud, Marcel, Historie De La Louisiane Francaise 1698-1715, Paris, 1953, (hereafter referred to as Giraud, History of La.) 35.
5) Giraud, History of La., 35; Martin's, 68.
6) McAlester, Bvt. Brig. General M.D., Major of Engrs., Map of Lake Pontchartrain and Mississippi Connection, 1/10/1868, Nat'l Archives, Washington, D. C. Map for locations of bayous on south shore of Lake Pontchartrain.
7) DuPratz, History of La., 235.
8) Penicaut, 13-17; HC-L III, 61.
9) For location of fort, Carlos Trudeau's Map of New Orleans and Environs, 12/24/1798, p 402, Martin's History of La., 1882 edition. Other maps also show Fort St. John and surrounding land on an island. Martin's History, p 68, gives the return date of Iberville as 12/7/1699; other sources, including Giraud, give the date of 1/8/1700.
10) For various growths on Metairie-Gentilly Ridge, Sauve Map, 1849, LSML.
11) Grandjean, Geo. H., Map of 2/14/1883, LSSC # 23518, Roussell vs. N. O. Ry. and Light Co., filed 1922; Zaccarie Map, 1885, LSML; Bell, S. C. Map, 6/16/1902, in Louisiana State Supreme Court (hereafter referred to as LSSC) #30718, N. O. Land vs. Levee Board Commissioners, filed 5/31/1930 — for location of Bayou Noir.
12) T-P, Flashback, 10/20/68, s2, p3 — for description of swamp dwellings.
13) Montigny, DuMont de, 1723 map #721/5, NOPL, La. Dept. — for location of island and stream running into Bayou St. John from the east.
14) Harrison, Maurice, map 3/10/1845, Nat'l Archives, Washington, D. C., shows two islands in this location; Harrison, Maurice, Map with report of 10/23/1849, Boston Library, shows island; Zaccarie Map, 1885; Pilie, Edgar, Map of 1/2/1895 "in accordance with L. Bringier Plan annexed to plan of Milne partition", NP A. Chiapella 8/29/1845, shows island at Vienna and Bayou and stream running from east between Vienna and Pressburg; Segher's Map 4/24/1905 shows two-pronged horse-shoe shape stream coming into Bayou St. John in vicinity of Vista Shores Club today. All maps for location of island and stream running into Bayou St. John at this point.
15) LSSC, State vs. Orleans Navigation Co., 11 Martin OS 38, 54; Lafon Map 1805, ACT 57 Michel de Armas, V. 18, 10/1/1819; U. S. Survey Map of Sulakowski, 1873, State Land Office, Baton Rouge, La. shows Bayou Bienville coming into middle of curve east of Park Island. Surveyor Pilie in Supreme Court case of mid-1800s testifies that correct name of "Devil's Elbow" is Isle de Bienville.
16) Map of Carondelet Canal and Bayou St. John, attached to report of 10/31/1853 in LSSC # 5094, Orleans Navigation Co. vs. Widow Wm. Bowman, 12/31/1857; Map accompanying report of Maurice Harrison, Engr., 10/23/1849 Boston Library, for location of "Devil's Elbow."
17) Map of Sauve's Crevasse 1849, LSML, for trees and growth along Metairie-Gentilly Ridge.
18) Trudeau, Carlos Map, 12/24/1798, Martin's History p 402, for trail from Lake Pontchartrain to Moss Street, which in early 1800s became Allard's Lake Road.
19) Andry, Luis, Survey Map of Kernion Properties, 1771, State Land Office, Baton Rouge, (Private Claims) for Cypress Bayou designation of Bayou Chapitoulas.
20) Bezou, Henry C., METAIRIE, Gretna, La. 1973, 15.
21) Trudeau, Carlos, Map of 12/24/1798, Martin's History, 1882 edition, p 402, for location of earliest concessions (1708) on east bank of Bayou St. Jean. These concessions extended lakeward to the approximate northern boundary of the National Guard property in that location today.
22) Castellanos, Henry C., New Orleans As It Was, 2nd Edition, New Orleans, 1905, 327.
23) Giraud, History of La., 35.

24) King, Creole Families of Louisiana, 59; King, New Orleans, The Place and the People, New York 1895, 44.
25) New Orleans City Guide, WPA Project, Cambridge, Mass, 1938, 383; Gayarré I, 60; Penicaut, 30; HC-L III, de la Harpe, 16; Martin;s, 100; Dufour, Ten Flags, 49; Dufour, Pie, T-P, 5/18/63, 6.
26) King, Sieur de Bienville, 82.

CHAPTER IV

1) Martin's, 68.
2) King, Sieur de Bienville, 84.
3) Villiers' Foundations..LHQ 3 (Apr. 1920) 163; Giraud, History of La., 35.
4) King, Sieur de Bienville, 84; DuRu, Journal, 57; Villiers, Foundations, LHQ 3 (Apr. 1920) 163.
5) Ries, Maurice, The Mississippi Fort Called de la Boulaye 1700-1715, LHQ 19 (Oct. 1936) 847.
6) HC-L III, Benard de la Harpe, written in France 1723, 17; Martin's 100.
7) DuRu, Journal, 5; Map #6, LHQ 19 (Oct. 1936) 879, for location of Fort de la Boulaye; Callendar, The Mississippi Fort called de la Boulaye, LHQ 19 (Oct. 1936) 847.
8) Ibid, 870; Giraud, History of La., 35.
9) DuRu, Journal, 16.
10) Villiers' Foundations . . . LHQ 3 (Apr. 1920) 164.
11) Giraud, History of La., 70.
12) Villiers' Foundations..LHQ 3 (Apr. 1920) 164; Hart, W. O., New Orleans, LHQ I (Apr. 1918) 353-4; Lafargue, André, Scrapbook I, NOPL, La. Dept. 12/11/27, 147.
13) DuRu Journal, 16.
14) Dabney, Thos. Ewing, T-P Magazine Section, 8/18/1935, 8; General Collot's Reconnoitering Trip, LHQ I, (Apr. 1918) 312; DuPratz, History of La., fn 113.
15) Waring, Geo. E., Jr. and Cable, Geo. W., Ancient New Orleans in Commercial, Social and Medical Statistics of New Orleans, 8/23/1881, 21.
16) Villiers' Foundations, LHQ 3 (Apr. 1920) 169; Gayarré I, 69-70.
17) Giraud, History of La. 70.
18) Villiers' Foundations, LHQ 3, (Apr. 1920) 166; Lafargue, André, Scrapbook I, 12/11/1927, NOPL-La. Dept., 147.
19) DuPratz, History of La. 296-7, 332.
20) Penicaut, 78.
21) DuPratz, History of La., 18; DuRu, Journal, fn 33 p 27; Giraud, History of La., 70.
22) Ibid, 70; Waring, Geo. E., Jr. and Cable, Geo. W., Ancient New Orleans, in Commercial, Social and Medical Statistics of New Orleans, 8/23/1881, 4. Giraud, History of La., 70.
23) Martin's, 110; Cable, Geo. Introduction, Historical Sketch Book and Guide to New Orleans, New Orleans Press, 1884, 6; Albrecht, Andrew C., The Origin and Settlement of Baton Rouge, LHQ 28 (Jan. 1945), 56; T-P Guide to New Orleans, 1908, 38.
24) Penicaut, fn. 17 p 27.
25) Map 6, LHQ 19 (Oct. 1936), showing Mississippi River, lakes and Gulf Coast; Chambers, History of La., 55; DuRu Journal, p7, fn 12; Martin, History of La., 98; Istrouma, LHQ 14 (Oct. 1931) quoting Margry's Penicaut p 503 and quoting Dr. William A. Read and Dr. William Scroggs p 509, on derivations; Penicaut, Fleur de Lys, 25-6, quoting Dr. Read, Louisiana Place Names, Baton Rouge, La. 1927, 32 on "iti humma."
26) DuRu, Journal, fn 36, p 28; Martin, History of La., 101.
27) Albrecht, Andrew C., Settlement of Baton Rouge, LHQ 28, (Jan. 1945) 52; T-P Guide to N. O., 1908, p 38 gives date as 1702. Historical Sketch Book and Guide to N. O. and Environs, edited and compiled by several leading writers of the N. O. Press (within last thirty years), Will H. Coleman, New York, 1885, page 8 states: "Tchoupchoumas (Oumas) Indians in 1702 built a village on the site of St. Louis #3 Cemetery. The village was there as late as 1720."
28) T-P Guide to N. O., 1908, 38.
29) Fischer, Dr. Ann, Anthropology Dept., Tulane University, T-P Magazine Section, 1/4/1970, 7-9; Albrecht, Andrew C., Settlement of Baton Rouge, LHQ 28, (Jan. 1945) 56-7.

CHAPTER V

1) Gayarré I, 102.
2) Penicaut, 106-113; DuPratz, History of La., 242
3) HC-L III, 116; Maduell, Chas. R., Jr. The Census Tables For The French Colony of La. from 1699 through 1732, Baltimore, Md. 1972, 8; Villiers' Foundations..LHQ 3 (Apr. 1920) 116; Gayarré I, 87; Chambers, 71.

4) Thompson, Sue, New Orleans Magazine, October 1972, 45-6.
5) Penicaut, 112.
6) Surrey-King, Commerce of La., LHQ 5 (Jan. 1922) 28.
7) Gayarré I, 98; T-P 1/28/68, s2, p11; Penicaut, fn 120.
8) Dunbar, Rowland and Albert G. Sanders, Mississippi Provincial Archives II, 1701-1729 (hereafter referred to as MPA), 53; Giraud, History of La., 327.
9) Ibid, 176; MPA II, 53, 59.
10) Giraud, History of La., 176; Superior Council Records (hereafter referred to as SCR) translations at LSML, #24 23/9, 5/25/1723.
11) Maduell, Census Tables of La. 1699-1732, 10.
12) Giraud, History of La., 326; Arthur, Stanley, Old Families of La., Baton Rouge, 1971, 303-6.
13) Giraud, History of La., 327, fn 3; Letter, Giraud to author 12/17/68; Trudeau, Carlos, Survey Map "Properties Santo Bautista Lawrence" (formerly LaVigne), State Land Office, Baton Rouge, La. 7/16/1800; Pintado Papers, Book I, No. 10, 152-4 for description of Trudeau Survey, LSML: Luis Andry Survey of Kernion (formerly LaVigne) properties, 1771, Private Claims, New Orleans, Land Office, Baton Rouge, La.
14) Giraud, History of La., 176.
15) T-P 7/18/76, s3, p8;
16) Bezou, METAIRIE, 15, 17, 76-77; Veach, Damon, T-P 9/4/77, s2, p6.
17) Villiers' Foundations, LHQ 3 (Apr. 1920) 168.
18) DuPratz, History of La. 5; Gayarré I, 102; Dufour, Pie, Ten Flags, 67.
19) Villiers' Foundations, LHQ 3 (Apr. 1920) 166-68.
20) Ibid.

CHAPTER VI

1) Villiers' Foundations..LHQ 3 (Apr. 1920) 170.
2) Ibid., 170; DuPratz, History of La., 10.
3) HC-L II, 85 - Folio IX from Archives; Villiers' Foundations..LHQ 3 (Apr. 1920) 176; Dufour, Pie, T-P 1/21/68, s3, p2; T-P 10/25/70, s3, p 15; T-P 11/13/77, p 27.
4) Villiers' Foundations..LHQ 3 (Apr. 1920) 175; Penicaut's fn 120;
5) HC-L III, 21; Penicaut's 24; Dufour, Pie, T-P 1/28/68, s2, p11.
6) Dart, Sally translator, Margry V, Chapter 6, p 599 "Instructions for Mr. Perrier, Chief Engr. of La., 4/14/1718," LHQ 15 (Jan. 1932) 41; Villiers' Foundations, LHQ 3 (Apr. 1920) 184.
7) Gayarré I, 253; Chambers I, 105; Dart, Sally, Translation, French Incertitude in 1718 As to Site of New Orleans, LHQ 15 (Jan. 1932) 37-43; Castellanos, N. O. As It Was, 330; King, Sieur de Bienville, 23.
8) Robin's Voyage to La. 5; DuPratz, History of La., 48.
9) Roberts, Lake Pontchartrain, 28; Cable, Geo., Introduction, Historical Sketch Book and Guide to N. O., 2; HC-L III, 178; DuPratz, History of La., 49; Dabney, Thos. Ewing, T-P Magazine Section, 8/18/1935, 8.
10) Fortier, History of Louisiana I, New York 1904, 68; T-P Editorial 2/29/68, s1, p12; Villiers' Foundations.., LHQ 3, (Apr. 1920) 179-80; T-P 11/3/1968, s4, p 17.
11) Dart, Sally, translation, French Incertitude in 1718 as to site of N. O., LHQ 15 (Jan. 1932) 37-43, (instuctions of 4/14/1718 to Chief Engr. Perrier.
12) Dart, Henry P., Politics in Louisiana 1724, LHQ 5 (Jul. 1922) 299; Penicaut's, 210; Trudeau, Carlos, Map of N. O. and Environs, 12/24/1798, in Martin's History, 402; Villiers' Foundations, LHQ 3, (Apr. 1920) l86, quoting DuPratz, History in La., 83.
13) Ibid, 179-80.
14) Ibid, 180; Giraud, History of La. being reviewed in T-P 6/3/68 s1, p 23.
15) Villiers' Foundations...LHQ 3 (Apr. 1920) 187-9.
16) Ibid., 190.
17) Ibid., 193.
18) Ibid., 193; Giraud, Marcel, letter to author 12/17/68.

CHAPTER VII

1) LHQ 15 (Jul. 1932) 463.
2) King, Creole Families of La., 62; Coleman, Will H., Historical Sketch Book and Guide to N. O. and Environs, New York, 1885, 3.
3) Villier's Foundations..LHQ 3 (Apr. 1920) 185-6, 193; Penicaut's fn 14 p 214; Dufour, Pie, T-P, 12-3-67, s3, p12; DuPratz, History of La., 16-18; Roberts, Lake Pontchartrain, 37-9; Trudeau map 12/24/1798, Martin's History, p 402; Map of Jacques Lorreins' properties, Trudeau, 1800, Land Office, Baton Rouge - for location of DuPratz concession; DuPratz, History of La., 19, 21, 23, 52, 272, 276.

4) Taylor, J. G., A Student's Guide to Localized History, Columbia University, N. Y. 1966, 17; Early Census Tables of Louisiana, LHQ 13 (Jan. 1930), 223-4; Dart, Henry P., The First Cargo of African Slaves, LHQ 14 (Apr. 1931) 163-177; Calendar of Original Documents Concerning History of Louisiana, La. Historical Publications IV, 1908, New York 1969, 19, 43, 61, (Letters Patent August 1717 Creating the Co. of the West,); Dart, Henry P., Slave Depot of the Co. of the Indies, LHQ 9 (Apr. 1926) 286; Cruzat, H. H., Documents Concerning Bienville's Land, LHQ 10 (Jan. 1927) 10; General information on slaves in: LHQ 19 (Jan. 1936) 29; HC-L III, 64; HC-L V, fn 119; Gayarré, C. Historical Notes on the Commerce and Agriculture of Louisiana 1720-1766, LHQ 2 (Jul. 1919) 286; Moody, V. Alton, Slavery on La. Sugar Plantations, LHQ 7 (Jan. 1924) 206-7; Surrey-King, Commerce of La., LHQ 5, (Jan. 1922) 32; SCR, 4/29/1737, LHQ 5 (Jul. 1922) 398.
5) Villiers' Foundations, 157-251; Sturgill, Claude C. and Price, Charles L., editors, of "On The Present State of the Province of Louisiana in the Year 1720 by Jean Baptiste Benard de la Harpe, LHQ LIV, (Summer Fall, 1971), 45; Bezou, METAIRIE, 7, 18; Fortier I, 63; Penicaut's fn 27 p 244; Map Nouvelle Orleans, LSML ca. 1723; LHQ 2 (Jul. 1919), 289; Penicaut's, 58; Map in LSSC # 1744, DuBreuil Villars Heirs vs. T. M. Kennedy et al, filed 1850; Faye, Stanley, Arkansas Post of Louisiana, French Domination, LHQ 26 (Jul. 1943) 661-3; Villier's Foundations..LHQ3 (Apr. 1920) 195; Dart, Henry P., The Career of DuBreuil in Louisiana, LHQ 18 (Apr. 1935) 269-70.
6) Penicaut's (B. F. French translation) NOPL, 146, 244-5; Census of 1721, LHQ 13 (Apr. 1930), 218 and fn,; Bezou, METAIRIE, 19-20, 76, 77; A Lawsuit Over the Sale of Office of Notary, LHQ 16 (Oct. 1933) 529, 587-95; Documents of Crozat Regime, LHQ 15 (Oct. 1932) 590; Dart, Henry P., Courts and Laws in Colonial La., LHQ 4 (Jul. 1921) 264; Fortier I, 68; Wilson, Sam, Ignace Broutin, Louisiana's First Architect, N. O. 1969, 239; Ledet, William P., History of Carrollton, LHQ 21 (Jan. 1938) 17, 22.
7) Bezou, METAIRIE, 76-77, quoting Dahlman-Junod Papers; Plan De La Nouvelle Orleans Ville Capitalle De La Louisiana Et Ses Environs, circa 1730 (Map-LOC).
8) Private Claims, Land Office, Baton Rouge, 270; Map Nouvelle Orleans, ca. 1723, LSML showing grants along Bayou St. Jean and the Mississippi.
9) Private Claims, Land Office, Baton Rouge, 259, 260, 272, 276, 279.
10) Map De La Nouvelle Orleans au Mississippi, ca. 1723 LSML; Maduell, Census Tables of Louisiana, 17, 18, 34, 37, 51, 65, 83, 108, 116, 125, 145; SCR, LHQ 6 (Oct. 1923) 669; Ibid, LHQ 1, (Jan. 1917) 110.
11) Villiers' Foundations, LHQ 3, (Apr. 1920) 215; New Orleans City Guide, Boston, 1938, 295-6, Gayarré I, New Orleans, 1885, 263-272.

CHAPTER VIII

1) Villiers' Foundations, LHQ 3 (Apr. 1920) 213-4.
2) Hart. W. O., New Orleans, LHQ 1 (Apr. 1918) 357; Villiers' Foundations, LHQ3 (Apr. 1920) 163, 192-3, 220-1, 229; HC-L III, 96; Elder, Mrs. S. B., Bienville's Difficulties in Founding of New Orleans, Louisiana Historical Society Publications, VIII, 1914-15, New York 1969, 40; Strugill and Price, State of La. in 1720, J. B. B. de la Harpe, LHQ LIV (Summer-Fall) 1971, 29.
3) Faye, Stanley, The Arkansas Post of La., French Domination, LHQ 26 (Jul. 1943) 661-3, fn. quoting from Daire, Economistes Financiers 427, 434, 440 and Harsin, John Law III, 425; T-P Dixie 11/13/77, p 27.
4) Villiers' Foundations, LHQ 3 (Apr. 1920) 220-1; LHQ 15, (Jul. 1932) 419.
5) Dart, Henry P., Documents Concerning Bienville's Land, LHQ 10 (Jan. 1927) 10, 16; Ledet, William P., History of Carrollton, LHQ 21, (Jan. 1938) 222; Map De La Nouvelle Orleans Au Mississippi, ca 1723, LSML, for location of Bienville's concessions.
6) Dufour, Pie, T-P 3/31/68, s3, p8; Faye, Stanley, The Arkansas Post of La., LHQ 26 (Jul. 1943) 879; Villiers' Foundations, LHQ 3 (Apr. 1920) 193; SCR 3/28/1725, 7/21/1725, LHQ 2 (Jul. 1919) 334-5; SCR # 25-913/28/1725; # 25-40 5/14/1725; # 25-212 5/5/1725; # 25-245 and # 148, 6/18/1725; # 25-248 6/21/1725, LSML.
7) D'Anville, Carte de la Louisiane, May 1732, LHQ 19 (Oct. 1936) 879; LHQ 19 (Oct. 1936) 25; Faye, Stanley, The Arkansas Post of La., LHQ 26 (Jul. 1943) 665.
8) Villiers' Foundations, LHQ 3 (Apr. 1920) 229-31.
9) HC-L V, 29, Dumont's Journal; Chambers I, 108; Surrey-King, Commerce of La., LHQ 5 (Jan. 1922) 21-22.
10) Census of 1721, Diron Dartaguette, Inspector General of the Troops in La., LHQ 13 (Jan. 1930) 220-1, 226; Surrey-King, Commerce of La., LHQ 5, (Jan. 1922) 30.
11) Early Census of 1721, LHQ 13 (Apr. 1930) 219-20; LHQ 16 (Oct. 1933) 575-7; Chambers I, 307.
12) LHQ 5 (Jan. 1922) 80.
13) Villiers' Foundations, LHQ 3 (Apr. 1920) 229, 235, date of June, 1721.
14) LHQ 19 (Jan. 1936) 29; Census of 1721, Diron Dartaguette, LHQ 13 (Jan. 1930) 226-7.

15) HC-L III, 119, Charlevoix in 1/26/1722; Kendall, John S., Old New Orleans Houses, LHQ 17 (Oct. 1934) 688.
16) Devron, Dr. Gustave, A Chapter of Colonial History 1717-1751, LHQ 6, (Oct. 1923) 543; Villiers' Foundations, LHQ 3 (Apr. 1920) 232-3.
17) Instructions of Chief Engr. Perrier, French Incertitude as to Site for New Orleans, 4/14/1718, LHQ 15 (Jan. 1932) 40; Villiers' Foundations, LHQ 3 (Apr. 1920) 224-8, quoting from archives; Plan of City filed by M. de Pauger in 1724; T-P 9/7/75, s3, p14.

CHAPTER IX

1) DeVille, Winston, The New Orleans French Period 1720-1733, Baltimore, Md. 1973, 57. (Hereafter referred to as DeVille, New Orleans French.)
2) Cruzat, H. H., New Orleans Under Bienville, LHQ 1 #3 (Jan. 1918) 78; Comeau, Brother Alfonso, A Study of the Trustee Problems St. Louis Cathedral, LHQ 31 (Oct. 1948) 899; Kendall, John S., Old New Orleans Houses, LHQ 17 (Oct. 1934) 688.
3) Villiers' Foundations, LHQ 3 (Apr. 1920) 235-6.
4) HC-L II - Folio IX, Dec. 1722 Archives and IX Archives, Jan. 1724; SCR, LHQ 1, #3 (Jan. 1918) 229; Baudier, Roger, The Catholic Church in La., New Orleans, 1939, 73; Villiers' Foundations, LHQ3 (Apr. 1920) 240; LHQ 15 (Jul. 1932) 376-7; HC-L V, Dumont, 41; Ditchy, Jay K., Early Census Tables of La., LHQ 13 (Jan. 1930) 227.
5) Villiers' Foundations, LHQ 3 (Apr. 1920) 239-248; Cruzat, H. H., Allotment of Bldg. Sites in N. O. 1722, LHQ 7 (Oct. 1924) 565; SCR # 24 - 97, 10/23/1724 LSML. Hart, W. O., New Orleans, LHQ I, (Apr. 1918) 358.
6) Statement of Companies of Infantry maintained by the Co. of the Indies In The Province of La. in the month of May, 1724, and the situation of the settlers in each post, LHQ 12 (Jan. 1929) 119-127.
7) Work of Indexing Louisiana's Black Boxes LHP VIII (1914-15) 10; Surrey-King, Commerce of La., LHQ 5 (Jan. 1922) 30; Banet's Report To The Company 1724, LHQ 12 (Jan. 1929) 119-127; SCR #24-97, 10/23/1724, LSML. Hart, W. O., New Orleans, LHQ I (Apr. 1918) 358.
8) HC-L V, fn. 121; Taylor, Joe Gray, A Student's Guide to Localized History, Columbia University, N. Y. 1966, 6; Dart, Henry P., 18th Century Louisiana, The Editor's Chair, LHQ 8 (Jul. 1925) 474-7.
9) Pilie, Louis H., Deputy Surveyor First Municipality, Plan showing the DuBreuil, the Brewery, Darby's and Coustillas' Concessions, 11/9/1847 (Map-LOC), (hereafter referred to as Gentilly Plantations, Pilie, 1847); SCR, May 1723, LHQ 1 (Jan. 1917) 109-110.
10) SCR # 23/9 No. 25, 5/25/1723 LSML; Maduell, Census Tables of La., 46-7; LHQ 2 (Jan. 1919) 114; Map Nouvelle Orleans.., ca 1723, LSML.
11) SCR 3/28/1725, 7/21/1725, LHQ 2 (Jul. 1919) 334-5; SCR #25-91 3/28/1725; #25-212 5/5/1725; #25-40 5/14/1725; #25-245 and #148 6/18/1725; #25-248 6/21/1725, LSML.
12) MPA III, 377, 516, Memoir on Louisiana, Bienville 1725; Giraud, Marcel, Letter to author 2/17/68.
13) SCR 9/3/1725, LHQ 2 (Oct. 1919) 469; SCR #25-337, 9/3/1725, LSML.
14) Surrey-King, Commerce of La., LHQ 5, (Jan. 1922) 26.
15) Bezou, METAIRIE, 41; Dart, H. P., Rev. Claude L. Vogel, Capuchins In French La. 1722-1766, LHQ 11, (Oct. 1928) 620-3; Riley, Martin Luther, Development of Education in La. Prior to Statehood, LHQ 19 (Jul. 1936) 600-7; SCR 7/25/1731, LHQ 5, (Apr. 1922) 243; Dufour, Pie, T-P 1/28/68, s2, p 11.

CHAPTER X

1) Villiers' Foundations, LHQ 3 (Apr. 1920) 243-6.
2) Hart, W. O., New Orleans, LHQ 1 (Apr. 1918) 360; SCR 2/3/1724, LHQ I (Jan. 1918) 229; T-P 1/13/74, s5, p 17; Soniat, Charles T., The Title To The Jesuits' Plantation, Louisiana Historical Society Publications V, 1911, New York, 1969, 12.
3) SCR 5/13/1726, LHQ 3 (Jul. 1920) 406.
4) SCR 6/2-4-6/1726, LHQ 3, (Jul. 1920) 407-8; SCR, #26/84, 6/6/1726, LSML; SCR 9/11/1726, LHQ 3 (Jul. 1920) 416.
5) SCR 3/31/1727, LHQ 3 (Jul. 1920) 443; SCR #27/97, 3/31/1727, LSML; SCR H. H. Cruzat translations, LHQ 8 (Jan.-Oct. 1925) 23-5; SCR #327 7/8/1728; #328 28/86, 7/10/1728, LSML.
6) SCR #30/12, 1/16/1730, found in Succession of Soubaigné 2/14/1731, LSML; SCR 2/14/1731, LHQ 5 (June 1922) 108.
7) Villiers' Foundations, LHQ 3, (Apr. 1920) 158-251. Letters of Marie Madeleine Hachard Ursuline of N. O. 1727-28, translated by Myldred Masson Costa, New Orleans, 1974, 54.

8) Private Claims, State Land Office, Baton Rouge, 272; SCR 5/1/1735 - 7/16/1737, LHQ 8 (Jan.Oct. 1925) 124-137; SCR #10815, 6/26/1735, 7/8/1735 through 10/19/1735; #10879, 12/20/1735; #10753, cattle auctioned; 3/20/1736, transfers of property; #10325, 7/22/1737, LSML; SCR #A 33 59/19, 7/4/1733, LSML.
9) CR, 3/21/1770, LHQ 7 (Jan.-Oct. 1924) 160-161.
10) SCR, LHQ 4 (Jul. 1921) 344; DeVille, N. O. French...88; Arthur, Stanley, Old Families of La., Baton Rouge, 1971, 305; SCR 1/27/1738, LSML; Plan de la Nouvelle Orleans Ville Capitalle de la Louisiane et ses Environs #360 187 27, Map-LOC; Plan de la Nouvelle Orleans Ville Capitalle de la Province de la Louissianne, both maps circa 1730-1732.
11) Gayarré I, 373.
12) Ibid., 381-2; Chambers I, 168.
13) Ibid., 382.
14) Gayarré I, 410-11; Hearsay, Clem G., The Vengeance of the Natchez, LHQ 12 (Apr. 1929) 266-287; Kernion, George C. H., The Chevalier de Pradel, LHQ 12 (Apr. 1929) 243; LHQ 16 (Oct. 1933) 558; Villiers, Last Years..39; DuPratz, History of La., 71-87.
15) MPA I, 65; Gayarré I, 381; Wilson, Sam, Ignace Broutin..256, 269; MPA III, 664; Taylor, Guide to La. History, 6.
16) DuPratz, History of La. 83-4; Green, John A., Governor Périer's Expedition Against the Natchez Indians, LHQ 19 (Jul. 1936) 549.
17) DeVille, N. O. French 1720-33, 38, 86; HC-L V, 99; King, N. O., The Place and the People, 75.
18) Hearsay, Clem, Vengeance of the Natchez, LHQ 12 (Apr. 1929) 286-7; Gayarré I, 438-9; LHQ 4 (Oct. 1921) 524; Maps: Embouchures du Mississippi, June 1718 (No. 3); D'Anville's Carte de la Louisiane, May 1732 (No. 6), LHQ 19 (Oct. 1936) 879, location of Chouachas; HC-L V, 101; Rev. John Delanglez, S. J., The Natchez Massacre and Governor Périer, LHQ 17, (Oct. 1934) 631-40.
19) King, Creole Families of La., 204.
20) DeVille, N. O. French, 86.
21) Private Claims, State Land Office, Baton Rouge, La. 272; SCR 5/1/1735 - 7/16/1737; LHQ 8 (Jan.Oct. 1925) 125-137; SCR #10815, 6/26/1735, 7/8/1735 through 10/19/1735; #10879, 12/20/1735; #10753, cattle auctioned; 3/20/1736, transfers of property; #10325, 7/22/1737, LSML; Plan de la Nouvelle Orleans, about 1730, MAP-LOC No. 30, with D'Auterive's (formerly Langlois) house.
22) Hutchins, Thomas, An Historical Narrative and Topographical Description of Louisiana and West Florida, Gainesville, Florida, 1968 (hereafter referred to as Hutchins') 51; Villiers, Last Years, 59; DuPratz, 86-7.
23) Noble, Stuart G. and Nuhrah, Arthur G., Education in Colonial La., LHQ 32 (Oct. 1949) 762-5.
24) Cruzat, H. H., The Concession at Natchez, LHQ 8 (Jul. 1925) 389; Wilson, Sam, Jr., An Architectural History of the Royal Hospital, LHQ 29, (Jul. 1946) 569, 572-3; DuPratz, History of La. 96-99.
25) Ibid., 85.

CHAPTER XI

1) SCR 9/7/1725, LHQ 2 (Oct. 1919) 470; SCR 4/13/1728, LHQ 4 (Oct. 1921) 482; DeVille, N. O. French, 38; Ibid., 30; Private Claims, Baton Rouge, La. 272.
2) SCR 4/4/1731, LHQ 5 (Jan. 1922) 116; SCR #31-36, 59/19 and 31-37, 3/4/1731, LSML; SCR, LHQ 18 (Oct. 1935) 987; CR 11/19/1781, LHQ 17 (Apr. 1934) 395.
3) Trudeau, Carlos, Map, 12/24/1798, Martin's p 402, for location; SCR 10/9/1731, LHQ 5 (Apr. 1922) 245.
4) DeVille, N. O. French, 29.
5) Ibid., 36; King, Creole Families of Louisiana, 63.
6) Penicaut's fn 6 p 252; SCR 6/4/1735, LHQ 5 (Apr. 1922) 250; SCR #5310 A-35-39 and #5311, 6/4/1735, LSML.
7) Ancient Map, Exhibit D-1, State vs. Carondelet Canal and Navigation Co., #89798 3/9/1910, for location of grant; Soniat, Charles T., The Title To the Jesuit Plantation, Louisiana Historical Society Publications, V, 1911, New York, 1969, 16; Sidelights of La. History from Papers of Bicentennial Celebration of N. O. La. Historical Society, LHQ I, (Jan. 1918) 120; LSSC #44, Mayor, Aldermen, et al vs. J. B. Bermudez, 5/18/1812.
8) Surrey-King, Commerce of Louisiana, LHQ 5 (Jan. 1922) 25.
9) SCR 2/18/1734, LHQ 5 (Apr. 1922) 252; SCR #52/168, 11/6/1752 LSML; SCR 5/11/1734, LHQ 7 (Oct. 1924) 696-701; SCR #A 33 59/19, 7/4/1733, LSML.
10) SCR 6/20/1734, LHQ 7 (Oct. 1924) 701-2; SCR #1594 pp 5088-92, 6/20/1734, LSML; SCR 7/6/1736, LHQ 8 (Apr. 1925) 298.
11) Devron, Gustave, A Chapter in Colonial History, LHQ 6 (Oct. 1923) 567; SCR #10202, 9/27/1735,

LSML; SCR, LHQ 5 (Apr. 1922) 272; SCR 9/3/ and 10/7/1735, LHQ 8 (Jan. 1925) 142-3; Documents Concerning Bienville's Land, LHQ 11 (Jul. 1928) 464.
12) SCR, LHQ 10 (Oct. 1927) 533-37; SCR #D 41/205A, 10/1/1741, LSML; Noble and Nuhrah, Yale University, Education in Colonial Louisiana, LHQ 32 (Oct. 1949) 767; Cruzat, H. H., French Political Procedures in La. for Appointment of Tutors to Minors 1735, LHQ 8 (Apr. 1925) 218-9.
13) Gayarré II, 62; LHQ 16 (Oct. 1933) 556; Abstracts from Old Papers, LHQ I (Jan. 1918) 241-4; Work of Indexing Louisiana's Little Black Boxes, La. Hist. Society Publications VIII 1914-15, N. Y. 1969, 10; SCR 12/14/1730, LHQ 6 (Apr. 1923) 282; SCR 5/28/1747, LHQ 18 (Apr. 1935) 455; LHQ 16 (Apr. 1933) 209; Post, Lauren C., The Domestic Animals and Plants of French La. as mentioned in Literature, with references to sources, varieties and uses..LHQ 16 (Oct. 1933) 556-7.
14) Gayarré I, 469-70.

CHAPTER XII

1) SCR 2/9/1736, LHQ 8 (Apr. 1925) 278; SCR 7/27/1736, LHQ 8 (Apr. 1925) 479; SCR #1837 (5918) 7/27/1736, LSML; SCR 1/28/1745, LHQ 13 (Jan.-Oct. 1930) 507.
2) HC-L V, 104-5; DuPratz, History of La., 88-9.
3) SCR 4/27/1737, LHQ 9 (Jan. 1926) 128-9; SCR 2/4/1736, LHQ 5 (Jul. 1922) 379; SCR #1751, 2/4/1736, LSML; Gayarré I, 470.
4) Gayarré I, 470-484; Waring, Geo. E. and Geo. Cable, Historical and Present Conditions of N. O., 1881, 218; Cable, Geo. W., Creoles of La., New York 1910, 34; Martin I, 173-5; HC-L V, 114; Hutchins, Journal 70-1; Carte De La Louisiane 1767, in Fortier II, 76 - locations mentioned in this chapter, including Chickasaw country; HC-L V, fn 104; Penicaut fn 18 215; HC-L II, 83, Folio Archives 5/26/1736.
5) HC-L II, 83, Folio XX Archives; Gayarré I, 487; HC-L V, 114.
6) Ibid., 484-88.
7) King, Creole Families of La., 204.
8) SCR, Documents 6110 through 6119, 9/15 through 10/4/1736, LSML; Luis Andry Survey of Kernion holdings 9/26/1771, Land Office, Baton Rouge, La.; Plano de la Habitacion de Dr. Pedro de Marigny, 1798, in #1744 LSSC Heirs of DuBreuil Villars vs. T. M. Kennedy et al, filed 1850, for Lorreins (formerly Kernion) frontage on Bayou St. John; Zacharie, James S., Map of 1885, New Orleans Guide of James S. Zacharie, Census 1880, LSML. See Treasure Street (later DeSaix Blvd.) marking approx. lake-end of Kernion property.
9) SCR #2016, 3/20/1737, LSML; SCR 8/14/1737, LHQ 9 (Apr. 1926) 315; SCR 6/10/1737, LHQ 9 (Apr. 1926) 291-2; SCR #8368-9 (2062), 6/10/1737, LSML; SCR LHQ 9 (Apr. 1926) 502; SCR 5/30/1745, LHQ 14 (Jan. 1931) 118; SCR 12/26/1744, LHQ 13 (Oct. 1930) 329.
10) SCR 4/29 to 5/4/1737, LHQ 5 (Jul. 1922) 398-9; Dart, H. P., Bienville's Claim Against the Co. of the Indies for back salary, etc. 1737, LHQ 9 (Apr. 1926) 210-22; Maduell, Census Tables of La., 106, Travelers from N. O. killed in Natchez massacre; O'Connor, Stella, First Charity Hospital for Poor of N. O., LHQ 31 (Jan. 1948) 9-12; SCR LHQ 4 (Oct. 1921) 361-2; SCR, LHQ 3 (Oct. 1920) 551-63; SCR 11/16/1735, LHQ 5 (Apr. 1922) 275; SCR 1/20/1736, LHQ 5 (Jul. 1922) 377-79; SCR 7/12/1737, LHQ 9 (Apr. 1926) 303-4; SCR 3/6/1744, LHQ 12 (Oct. 1929) 669; #5498 A 35/85, 11/16/1735, #5660, 5/5/1736, #1789 5/10/1736, SCR #1807 (5740) and #3785 (23780), 3/6/1744, LSML.
11) Private Claims, Baton Rouge, La. 272; SCR 7/23/1737, LHQ 9 (Apr. 1926) 307-10.
12)SCR 10/8/1738, LHQ 6, (Jan. 1923) 127; SCR 7/13 - 22/1737, LHQ 9, (Apr. 1926) 304-7; SCR 10/5/1744, LHQ 13 (Apr. 1930) 309.
13) Wilson, Sam, Jr., Ignace Francois Broutin, 265; SCR 11/2/1738, LHQ 6, (Jan. 1923) 138; SCR 1/5/1744, LHQ 12 (Oct. 1929) 649;SCR #23670, 1/5/1744 (Folio 25) LSML; Kendall, John S., The Huntsmen of Black Ivory, LHQ 24 (Oct. 1941) 9.
14) Pilie, Gentilly Concessions, 11/9/1847 (Map-LOC); SCR #2457, p 11125-32 8/26/1738, LSML; SCR 8/26/1738, LHQ 10 (Jan. 1927) 118; SCR 8/28/1738, LHQ 10 (Jan. 1927) 118-9; Plan de la Nouvelle Orleans Ville Capitalle de la Louisiana Et Ses Environs, 1730 (Map-LOC); SCR 9/3/1725, LHQ 2 (Oct. 1919) 469; SCR #25-337, 9/3/1725, LSML; Wilson, Sam, Ignace Broutin, Louisiana's First Architect, N. O. 1969, 239; Penicaut, 244-5.
15) SCR 3/29/1739, LHQ 6 (Apr. 1923) 301; SCR #39 19, 2/26/1739, LSML; SCR #38/100 (802) 9/25/1738, #39/35, 3/13/1739, LSML.
16) SCR 2/21/1737, LHQ 7 (Apr. 1924) 334-5; SCR #11293, 11/5/1739, LSML.
17) SCR 1/4/1744, LHQ 12 (Oct. 1929) 648; SCR 9/28/1744, LHQ 14 (Oct. 1931) 578; SCR #39 23 2/26/1739; #C 40 103a, 9/21-24/1740; #43 162, 7/24/1743; #3662, 23201, 7/25/1743; #23645, 1/11/1744; #D 45/2, 5/20/1745, LSML.

18) King, Creole Families of Louisiana, 207-8.
19) SCR 4/25/1739, LHQ 6 (Jul. 1923) 499.
20) Castellanos, Henry C., N. O. As It Was, 1905, 151-4; Dart, Henry P., The Career of DuBreuil in French La., LHQ 18 (Apr. 1935) 270-1.
21) SCR 3/29/1739, LHQ 6 (Jul. 1923) 483; SCR 11/20/1739, LHQ 6, (Jul. 1923) 676; SCR 8/20/1739, #91438, LSML.
22) SCR 9/29/1739, LHQ 7 (Jul. 1924) 485-6.
23) SCR 10/16/1739, LHQ 7 (Jul. 1924) 497; SCR #C 3925, 10/16/1739, LSML.
24) Favrot, H. M., Colonial Forts of Louisiana, LHQ 26 (Jul. 1943) 735; Hutchins' Journal, 57; Gayarré I, 507; HC-L III, 22; Martin's, 178; DuPratz, History of La., 93-4; HC-L V, 115; Kernion, G. C. H., Reminiscences of Deverges, LHQ 7 (Jan. 1924) 64-5.
25) SCR, LHQ 11 (Oct. 1928) 633.
26) SCR, LHQ 10 (Apr. 1927) 272; SCR #C 40 76, 4/6/1740, LSML.
27) SCR 10/11/1741, LHQ 18 (Apr. 1935).
28) SCR 4/25/1739, LHQ 6 (Jul. 1923) 499; SCR 9/1/1744, LHQ 13 (Jan. 1930) 156; SCR, 9/1/1746, LHQ 17 (Jan. 1934) 183; SCR 3/20-22/1748, LHQ 19 (Apr. 1936) 502-3; SCR 10/27/1740, LHQ 10 (Jul. 1927) 433; SCR 6/1/1748,LHQ 19 (Oct. 1936) 1079-80; SCR 3/20/1748, LHQ 19 (Oct. 1936) 502-4;SCR 8/20/1753, LHQ 20 (Jul. 1737) 500; SCR 8/28/1742, LHQ 11 (Apr. 1928) 304; SCR #52/131, 9/2/1752, LSML; SCR 7/1/1752, LHQ 20 (Apr. 1937) 580-1; SCR 8/5/1752, LHQ 31 (Jul. 1938) 886; SCR 8/5 and 9/2/1752, LHQ 20 (Oct. 1937) 886-900; SCR #D-52-132, 9/2/1752, LSML; SCR 9/22/1754, LHQ 21 (Jul. 1938) 903; SCR #52/177, 11/11/1752, LSML.
29) SCR 7/15/1743, LHQ 11 (Oct. 1928) 633.
30) SCR, LHQ 22 (Apr. 1939) 534, Madeline Brazillier's marriage.
31) SCR, LHQ 11 (Oct. 1928) 633; Villiers' Last Years..45; Gayarré II, 158; Chambers, 219.

CHAPTER XIII

1) Chambers, 229; SCR 11/21/1743, LHQ 12 (Jul. 1929) 471; SCR 2/15/1744, LHQ 12 (Oct. 1929) 661.
2) O'Connor, Stella, The First Charity Hospital of La., LHQ 31 (Jan. 1948) 9-12; SCR, LHQ 4 (Oct. 1921) 361-2; SCR, LHQ 3 (Oct. 1920) 551-63; SCR 11/16/1735 LHQ 5 (Apr. 1922) 275; SCR 1/20/1736, LHQ 5 (Jul. 1922) 377-79; SCR 7/12/1737, LHQ 9, (Apr. 1926) 303-4; SCR 3/6/1744, LHQ 12 (Oct. 1929) 669; #5498 A 35/85, 11/16/1735, #5660, 5/5/1736, #1789, 5/10/1736, SCR #1807 (5740) and #3785 (23780), 3/6/1744, LSML; Records and Deliberations of the Cabildo, Vol. 4 #4, 9/19/1800 - 7/17/1802, WPA Archives NOPL, 39; Map Toulouse Street Cemetery, #1480 Pintado Papers, Book III, LSML, 29; Dufour, Charles, T-P 11/26/1972, 8.
3) Cable, Geo. W., Creoles of Louisiana, New York 1910, 45; Gayarré I, 520.
4) King, Creole Families of Louisiana, 60; SCR 3/26/1738, LHQ 9, (Oct. 1926) 745; SCR 12/29/1749, LHQ 20, (Apr. 1937) 517.
5) SCR 10/19/1744, LHQ 13 (Oct. 1930) 309; SCR 7/29/1744, LHQ 13 (Jan. 1930) 143.
6) SCR 6/20/1744, LHQ 13 (Jan. 1930) 138.
7) SCR LHQ 12 (Oct. 1929) 657; Luis Andry Survey Map of Kernion properties, 11/26/1771, Private Claims, Land Office, Baton Rouge, La.; SCR 12/30/1744 LHQ 13 (Apr. 1930) 332; SCR 1/4/1745, LHQ 13 (Jul. 1930) 491; SCR 1/9/1745, LHQ 13 (Jul. 1930) 494-5; SCR #25395 (3944) LSML; SCR 2/22/1745, LHQ 13 (Oct. 1930) 675; SCR 7/1/1752, LHQ 21 (Apr. 1938) 581; SCR #D 52 69, 6/1/1752, #52-73, 6/6/1752, #1317, 7/1/1752, LSML; Coleman, Gilbert St. Maxent, 21.
8) SCR 1/22/1745, LHQ 13 (Oct. 1930) 503-5; SCR D 45/8, 1/23/1745, LSML.
9) SCR 8/9/1745, LHQ 13 (Jul. 1930) 456; Pilie, Gentilly Concessions, 11/9/1847, (Map-LOC).
10) Surrey-King, Commerce of La., LHQ 5 (Jan. 1922) 27; Chambers, 233; SCR 9/28/1745, LHQ 14 (Oct. 1931) 575-9.
11) SCR 1/28/1746 LHQ 15 (Jan. 1932) 128-9; SCR #27101, (Jan. May 1746), 1/28/1746, LSML.
12) SCR, LHQ 15 (Oct. 1932) 672; Surrey-King, Commerce of La., LHQ 5 (Jan. 1922) 22; Hutchins' Journal, 25; SCR 7/6/1749, LHQ 15 (Jul. 1932) 520-1, quoting letter of March 1746; Porteous, Laura, Inventory of Prevost Estate, LHQ 9 (Jul. 1926) 414; SCR 2/4/1746, LHQ 15 (Jan. 1932) 137; SCR 5/6/1749, including letter of 1746, LHQ 15, 1932, 520; SCR 4/29/1749, LHQ 19 (Jul. 1936) 757; SCR 12/2/1747, LHQ 18 (Oct. 1935) 987-993.
13) SCR 30833 12/9/1747, LSML; SCR 12/7-18/1747, LHQ 18 (Oct. 1935) 989-91; SCR 12/20/1747, LHQ 18 (Oct. 1935) 991; SCR D 48/4, 1/17/1748, (Jan.-Feb. 1948) LSML; SCR 1/22/1748, LHQ 19 (Jan. 1936) 231; SCR, LHQ 19 (Apr. 1936) 494; SCR, 3/13-19/1748, LHQ 19 (Jan.-Apr. 1936) 231, 480; SCR 3/2-22/1748, LHQ 19 (Apr. 1936) 503; SCR #30817, 3/20/1748, (Mch. 1748) LSML; SCR 6/1/1748, LHQ 19 (Oct. 1936) 1080-1; SCR D 48 89 5/27/1748, Mch-Apr. 1748, LSML; SCR 5/28/1748, LHQ 19 (Jul. 1936) 776; SCR 6/1-

6/1748, LHQ 19 (Oct. 1936) 1087; SCR #30909, 6/6/1748, LSML; SCR# D 49/41, 7/5/1749, LSML; SCR 10/5/1753, LHQ 22 (Oct. 1939) 1173-4.

14) SCR 1/9/1751, LHQ 20 (Oct. 1937) 1112; SCR, Feb.-Mch. 1752, LHQ 21 (Jan. 1938) 292; SCR # D 52-70, 6/3/1752, LSML; SCR 11/28/1748, LHQ 20 (Jan. 1937) 237; SCR 3/30/1752, LHQ 21 (Jan. 1938) 306-7; SCR 5/28/1752, LHQ 20 (Apr. 1937) 318; SCR 7/1-7/1752, LHQ 21 (Apr. 1938) 584-5;SCR 8/5/1752, LHQ 21 (Jul. 1938) 886-7.
15) SCR 2/17/1746, LHQ 15 (Jan. 1932) 142; SCR 3/6/1746, LHQ 15 (Jul. 1932) 514-5; SCR #4154 (27268) 3/6/1746, LSML; SCR, LHQ 18 (Jul. 1935) 713; SCR #4413 (30548), May-Aug. 1747, LSML; SCR 3/28 and 5/30/1746 (Jul.-Oct. 1932) 521, 673; SCR 6/11/1746, LHQ 16 (Jan. 1933) 140-1;SCR, LHQ 11 (Jan. 1928) 141; Dart, H. P., Career of DuBreuil Villars in Louisiana, LHQ 18 (Apr. 1935) 267-80; SCR 3/14/1746, LHQ 15 (Oct. 1932) 518; SCR 5/16/1749, LHQ 20 (Apr. 1937) 500; SCR 2/21/1749 to 3/9/1751, LHQ 20 (Apr. 1937) 494-5; SCR LHQ 18 (Jan. 1935) 177; SCR #4321 (29212) 4/11/1747, LSML; SCR 6/25 and 7/6/1748, LHQ 19 (Oct. 1936) 1100-1108; SCR 6/19/1748, LHQ 19 (Oct. 1936) 1098; SCR #31492, 6/19/1748, LSML; SCR 8/17/1748, LHQ 18 (Jul. 1935) 478.
16) SCR 1/10-14/1747, LHQ 17 (Apr. 1934) 365-7; Gayarré 2, 38, 51.
17) Villiers' Last Yrs...48; Gayarré II, 39-40; SCR #4200 (28628) 8/24/1746, LSML; Chambers, History of La., 236-7.
18) SCR 11/17/1747, LHQ 18 (Oct. 1935) 985; SCR #4451, 30755, 11/18/1747, LSML; SCR 1/22/1748, LHQ 19 (Jan. 1936) 230, 234-5; SCR 1/22/1748, LSML.
19) SCR #4396, 29290, 6/26/1747, LSML; SCR 12/30/1747, LHQ 18 (Oct. 1935) 1003.
20) SCR 3/20-22/1748, LHQ 19 (Apr. 1936) 502-3; SCR 10/27/1740, LHQ 10 (Jul. 1927) 433; SCR 6/1/1748, LHQ 19 (Oct. 1936) 1079-80; SCR 3/20/1748, LHQ 19 (Oct. 1936) 502-4; SCR 8/20/1753, LHQ 20 (Jul. 1937) 500.
21) SCR 3/9/1748, LHQ 19 (Apr. 1936) 493.
22) SCR 5/18-26/1748, LHQ 19 (Jul. 1936) 769-771.
23) SCR 9/1/1744, LHQ 13 (Jan. 1930) 156; SCR 3/22/1748, LHQ 19 (Apr. 1936) 503-4; SCR #4510, 31209, 3/22/1748, LSML.
24) SCR 2/22/1749, LHQ 20 (Apr. 1937) 494; SCR 2/25/1749 #1174 LSML.
25) Villiers' Last Yrs..51; Gayarré II, 46, 48-9.
26) LSSC #2529 Arrowsmith vs. City of New Orleans, 1872; SCR D 52-69, 6/1/1752, D 51/2, 9/4/1751 (June-Aug. 1752) and (1749-1751) LSML; Notarial Records Juan Garic, Roll 2 pps 95-179; SCR 7/1/1752, LHQ 21 (Apr. 1938) 581; SCR #D 52 69, 6/1/1752, #52-73, 6/6/1752, #1317, 7/1/1752, LSML; Coleman, Gilbert St. Maxent, 21.
27) Chambers, 22; Gayarré II, 48-9; SCR 4/23/1748, LHQ (Apr. 1921) 216; HC-L II, Portfolio V, 645.
28) Gayarré II, 64; HC-L V fn. 114.

CHAPTER XIV

1) Gayarré II, 62.
2) Gayarré I, 497; SCR 2/8/1748, LHQ 19 (Apr. 1936) 470.
3) Martin's I, 183, 190; Dart, Henry P., The Career of DuBreuil in French La., LHQ 18 (Apr. 1935) 279; Gayarré II, 286; Rand, Clayton, Articles on Famous People, Scrapbook 5 (NOPL) 118; Chambers, 234.
4) Gayarré II, 47; Villiers, Last Yrs..132; Historical Notes on the Commerce and Agriculture of La. 1720-1766, LHQ 2 (Jul. 1919) 289; Post, Lauren C., Domestic Plants and Animals in French La., LHQ 16 (Oct. 1933) 583-586.
5) Chambers, 234; Gayarré II, 62.
6) Private Claims, Baton Rouge, La. 273-6; SCR, LHQ 21 (Jul. 1938) 886; SCR 12/28/1752, 1/12/1753, LHQ 22 (Oct. 1939) 1208-9; SCR D 52/118, 7/20/1752; #52/202, 12/28/1752; #52/202, 1/12/1753, LSML; SCR 4/6/1753, LHQ 22 (Apr. 1939) 534; SCR, LHQ 22 (Oct. 1939) 1208-9.
7) SCR, LHQ 13 (Jan. 1930) 131; SCR 7/1/1752, LHQ 21 (Apr. 1938) 580; SCR 2/5/1752, LHQ 21 (Jan. 1938) 288-95; SCR 7/1/1752, LHQ 21 (Apr. 1938) 580; SCR # D 52 103, 7/1/1752, LSML.
8) Private Claims, Baton Rouge, La. 267, 269, 274, 276, 277-8, 402, 404; Carlos Trudeau Map 12/24/1798, Martin's p 402 - general location of these properties.
9) SCR LHQ 21 (Jul. 1938) 887-892; SCR #66940, 10/30/1754, LSML.
10) SCR 8/5/1752, LHQ 21 (Jul. 1938) 876.
11) SCR 8/5/1752, LHQ 21 (Jul. 1938) 884-5; SCR# D 53/143, 9/22/1753, LSML; CR 9/14/1784, LHQ 24 (Oct. 1941) 1258-1274.
12) SCR LHQ 22 (Oct. 1939) 1172; SCR 11/6/1752, LSML; SCR 10/28 - 11/27/1752, LHQ 21 (Oct. 1938) 1226-30; SCR #52/168, 11/6/1752; #52/187, 11/27/1752; #52/192, 12/2/1752, LSML; SCR #1331, 12/2/1752,

LSML; SCR #A 33 59/19, 7/4/1733, LSML; SCR 9/28/1753, LHQ 22 (Jul. 1939) 899; SCR, LHQ 22 (Oct.1939) 1174, 1176, 1183; SCR #D 53/158, 12/2/1752 and 10/5/1753, SCR #D 53/147, 9/28/1753 (Sept.-Dec. 1753) LSML; SCR, LHQ 5 (Apr. 1922) 252; SCR, LHQ 7 (Oct. 1924) 701; SCR, LHQ 21 (Oct. 1938) 1244.

13) SCR 10/6/1753, LHQ 22 (Jul. 1939) 899, 1174-5; SCR #D 63 163, 10/8/1753, LSML.
14) SCR, LHQ 21 (Oct. 1938) 1226.
15) SCR #52/199, 12/26/1752, LSML.
16) SCR 6/1/1753, LHQ 22 (Apr. 1939) 514-5.
17) Roberts, Lake Pontchartrain, 67-8.
18) Villiers' Last Yrs..79, 87, 90, 102-4, 118-120; Gayarré II, 75; Chambers, 240-1.
19) Villiers' Last Yrs..117-120.
20) SCR 10/19/1772, LHQ 8 (Jan.-Oct. 1925) 535; Seebold, Herman, Old Louisiana Plantations, Homes and Family Trees II, New Orleans, 1941; du Fossat, Soniat, Synopsis of History of La. (NOPL) 4.
21) Private Claims, Baton Rouge, La. 267, 269, 274, 276, 277-8, 402, 404; Carlos Trudeau map 12/24/1798, Martin's p 402 - location of properties.
22) SCR #65 A 107, 8/7/1765, Aug.-Sept. 1765, LSML; Plan of City of N. O., Carlos Trudeau 12/24/1798, Martin's 402, Jas. A. Gresham Publishers, N. O. 1882.
23) Penicaut, fn 27 p 244; SCR #54769-70, 1758, LSML; Pilie Concessions Plan 1847 (Map-LOC); Trudeau Map 1795, 1798, 1800 in LSSC #1744 Heirs of DuBreuil vs. T. M. Kennedy et als, filed 1850, showing sections of plantation sold at various times; SCR #7699, p 61305-6, SCR #7700, p 6137-8, 7/4/1760, LSML; Dart, H. P., Career of DuBreuil in La., LHQ 18 (Apr. 1935) 279-90.
24) SCR #7233, 6/21/1758, LSML; SCR 8/30/1760, LHQ 23 (Jan. 1940); CR 7/1/1780, LHQ 24 (Jan. 1941) 290.
25) SCR 9/22/1754, LHQ 21 (Jul. 1938) 903; SCR #52/177, 11/11/1752, LSML; SCR #7400, 2/23/1759, LSML; SCR #7372 (56540) 1/26/1759, #53362, 8/30/1760, LSML; SCR LHQ 21 (Oct. 1938) 1231-2; SCR 8/30/1760, LHQ 23 (Jan. 1940) 286; King, Creole Families of La., 204.
26) LSSC 3 Lou Ann 86, Pontalba et al vs. Copeland; Map of Louis C. LeBreton grants of 10/6/1757 and 2/15/1764, surveyed by Louis H. Pilie and Geo. R. Grandjean, 6/2-7/1884, under instructions of 3/24-4/7/1884, Office of the Surveyor General, District of La., N. O. (N. O. Levee Bd. files), see this map for Claim O.B. 308 (9th claim) of Jean Baptiste Castillon; LSSC #4241, and Third District Court #6030 John Arrowsmith vs. E. H. Durrell and N. O. Canal and Navigation Co., filed 11/7/1855; SCR 10/4/1763, LHQ 26 (Jan. 1943) 179-184, Claim 137 by Arrowsmith, based on Mouléon Grant, sketch, Private Claims, Baton Rouge, 53.
27) Martin's I, 190-1; Chambers, 243.
28) Villiers' Last Yrs..138-9; Chambers 241-2.
29) Villiers' Last Yrs..86, 138-9, 156, 232; Roberts, Lake Pontchartrain, 68.
30) SCR #7194, p 52183, 1758, LSML: SCR #7304, p 55153, 11/13/1758, LSML; SCR #7400, 2/23/1759, LSML; SCR #7441, p 57020, 5/12/1759; SCR #55155, 10/15/1759, LSML.
31) SCR #63/105, 8/17/1761, LSML; SCR #8443, p 70628, 8/16/1763, Aug-Sept. 1763, LSML.
32) SCR #7365, p 55494, 2/17/1759, LSML.
33) SCR #7385, LSML; SCR 9/28/1763, LHQ 25 (Oct. 1942) 1163; SCR #8694, 5/2/1764, LSML; SCR #8864, p 75286, 12/21/1764, LSML.
34) SCR 10/7/1763, LHQ 26 (Jan. 1943) 212.
35) SCR LHQ 8 (Jul. 1925) 523-4; SCR #7464, 6/29/1759, LSML.
36) Villiers' Last Yrs..138-9, 156, 188; Chambers, 243.
37) LSSC #1744 Heirs of DuBreuil Villars vs. T. M. Kennedy et als, filed 11/7/1850; Pilie, Gentilly Concessions, 11/9/1847; Gayarré II, 87; Villiers' Last Yrs..188.
38) Fortier I, 141; Villiers' Last Yrs..227-8, 235; Chambers, 259; HC-L II, 63, Folio V, Archives; Roberts, Lake Pontchartrain, 72.

CHAPTER XV

1) Villiers' Last Yrs...232, 254-5; Chambers, 264, for maps of territory exchanged 246, 255; Fortier I, 142-3; Gayarré II, 109; Roberts, Lake Pontchartrain, 70-1.
2) SCR #7150 (53001), 2/23/1758, LSML; SCR Jan.-June, 1762, LSML; SCR 4/7/1762, LHQ 23 (Apr. 1940) 630.
3) SCR 3/8/1762, LHQ 23 (Jul. 1940) 902; SCR #8113, p 66993, 3/8/1762, LSML; SCR #8296, p 68829-30, LSML; SCR LHQ 23 (Oct. 1940) 1278.
4) SCR #65 A 107, 8/7/1765, Aug.-Sept. 1765, LSML; Private Claims, Baton Rouge, La. 269; SCR 11/10/1762, LHQ 24 (Apr. 1941) 568-70; SCR #8286 11/10/1762, LSML; SCR 6/27/1763, LHQ 25, 1942, 254; SCR #8994, 5/14/1763, LSML; SCR #8545, p 81145-7, 11/11/1763, LSML; SCR #8901, p 77071, 4/27/1765, LSML; SCR #9162, p 79206, 11/25/1765, LSML; SCR #65 A 75, 5/7/1765, LSML.

5) SCR 2/4/1763, LHQ 24 (Jul. 1941) 804-5.
6) SCR #75189, 2/14/1765, LSML; SCR LHQ 24 (Apr. 1941) 572-6; SCR 69439, 7/16/1763, LSML; SCR 10/15/1763, LHQ 26 (Jan. 1943) 202; SCR #8527, p 71078, 10/31/1763, LSML; SCR 10/31/1763, LHQ 26, (Jan. 1943) 254-5; SCR #63 99, 11/2/1763, LSML; SCR #8805, p 75035-6, 10/6/1764, LSML; SCR #75202, 2/14/1765, LSML.
7) Chambers, for maps of territory exchanged, 246, 255; Fortier I, 142-4; Gayarré II, 91, 109; Roberts, Lake Pontchartrain, 70-1; Hutchins' Journal, 9, 23; Villiers' Last Yrs...254-7; T-P (Dixie) 2/2/1975, 11.
8) American State Papers, Duff-Green edition, Washington, 1834, Vol. II Claims #321 and 322, p 278. (Hereafter referred to as Duff-Green.)
9) Ibid.; Chambers 295-6; Villiers' Last Years..549; Coleman, Jr., James Julian, Gilbert Antoine de St. Maxent, 20-30.
10) Gayarré II, 99; Sketch of the Expulsion of the Society of Jesus from Colonial La., La. Historical Society Publications IX, 1916 (New York 1969) 18; Villiers' Last Yrs..274; SCR #63/12, 7/9/1763, #57/17, LSML; Fortier I, 146.
11) Chambers, 260; Villiers' Last Yrs...269, 280; Martin's, 194; SCR #76537-38, 1/4/1765, LSML.
12) Villiers' Last Yrs..280-6; Gayarré 96-7; Martin's, 194; Chambers, 264, 311; Howard, C. N., The Interval of Military Gov't in West Fla., LHQ 22, (Jan. 1939) 18-20.
13) Ibid., 22-23; Martin's 193; Hutchins' Journal, Intro ix; Villiers' Last Yrs..298, 302, 305-8; Gayarré II, 101-3.
14) Villiers' Last Yrs..,311, 315; Gayarré II, 105-6; HC-L II, 82, Archives IX.
15) Dart, Henry P., The Career of DuBreuil in French La., LHQ 18 (Apr. 1935) 276; HC-L V, 141; Gayarré II, 115, 124; Waring and Cable, Historical and Present Conditions of N. O., 1881, 241; N. O. City Guide (Boston 1938) 12; SCR 4/25 - 5/4/1763, LHQ 24 (Oct. 1941) 1196-7; SCR 6/10 - 7/13/1763, LHQ 24 (Apr. 1941) 22-25; SCR 6/21-23/1763, LHQ 25 (Jan. 1942) 249-53; Samuel, Martha Ann Brett, and Samuel, Ray, The Great Days of the Garden District and the Old City of Lafayette (New Orleans 1961) 12; Martin, 196.
16) SCR #D 68 89, 5/16 - 6/4/1769, LSML: Duff-Green II, 261, Claim #383; Gales and Seatons (American State Papers) I, 327.
17) Villiers' Last Yrs..259, 323, 337.
18) SCR #1823, 9/5/1764; #1843, 9/10/1764, LSML.
19) SCR #1850, 11/14/1764, LSML.
20) SCR 3/21/1770, LHQ 7 (Jan.-Oct. 1924) 160; SCR #73473, 73495, 6/16/1764; #73482-3, 6/17/1764; #73484-5, 6/18/1764; #73491-2, 6/20/1764, 7/30 - 8/6/1764, LSML.
21) SCR #75252-57, 12/12/1764, #8862, p 75250-1, 12/19/1764, LSML.
22) Villiers' Last Yrs..309, 4/18/1764; p 320, 7/3/1764, 330; Howard, C. N., The Interval of Military Gov't in West Fla., LHQ 22 (Jan. 1939) 24-5; HC-L II, 81, Folio IX; HC-L V, fn. 142.
23) SCR Oct.-Dec. 1764, 10/1/1764, LSML.
24) Villiers' Last Yrs..340.
25) Chambers I, 268; Gayarré II, 127-9; Villiers' Last Yrs..344; Roberts, Lake Pontchartrain, 73; Lafargue, André, LHQ 23 (Jan. 1940) 109; Howard, C. N., The Interval of Military Gov't in West Fla., LHQ 22 (Jan 1939) 28-9.

CHAPTER XVI

1) SCR 10/4/1763, LHQ 26 (Jan. 1943) 179-84; Pilie - Grandjean Map of LeBreton Concessions, 1884; Private Claims, Baton Rouge, La. 236; Note on Exhibit Plan C, Private Claims, Baton Rouge, La. for various owners of "La Metairie;" SCR #8895, p 75426, 1/27/1765, LSML.
2) SCR #1765, 4/24/1765, LSML.
3) SCR #1899, 11/14/1765, 11/19/1765, LSML; SCR #1913, 5/28/1766, LSML; SCR D 65, 6/22/1765; #9025, p 77218-19, 6/22/1765; #66 A 61, 6/28/1765; #65 A 45, 7/12/1765; #D 65 39, 8/2/1765; #D 65 42, 8/10/1765, 8/20/1765; #68 A 3, 7/8/1768, 8/10/1768, LSML; Private Claims, Baton Rouge, La., 52; Luis Andry Survey Map of Kernion Properties, 1771, Baton Rouge, La. for location of Duplanty purchase from Lorreins.
4) SCR #8893, p 75419, 1/26/1765, LSML; SCR #66 A 53A, 6/12/1766, LSML.
5) SCR #9048, 7/29/1765, LSML; Private Claims, Baton Rouge, La. 52.
6) SCR #9179, p 79302-3, 12/19/1765, LSML.
7) Chambers, 268; HCL-II, Folio VIII 3/12/1765 Archives, 78; Villiers' Last Yrs..351, 363-7
8) Ibid., 362; Gayarré II, 123.
9) Villiers' Last Yrs..362-7, 371; Gayarré II, 123-4; Roberts, Lake Pontchartrain, 76; Howard, C. N., The Interval of Military Gov't in West Fla., LHQ 22 (Jan. 1939) 30.

10) Cruzat, Heloise, translation, A Savage Law of the French Regime in Louisiana, LHQ 15 (Jul. 1932) 482; HC-L II, 46, 11/16/1765; Howard, C. N., The Interval of Military Gov't in West Fla., LHQ 22 (Jan. 1939) 30.
11) Document 73, "In Pursuance of an Act of Congress approved 7/4/1832 - An Act for the final adjustment of claims to lands in the southeastern Land District of Louisiana, Register of Lands Office, Baton Rouge, La. (Hereafter referred to as Document 73), Claim 33, p 14; Gales & Seaton, 305-6, "94 arpents front, 2,167 superficial arpents, confirmed to Alexander Milne, 1812;" SCR #9815, 2/3/1766, LSML; Duff-Green II, Claim #214, p 290, "Land Claims in Eastern District of Orleans Territory, communicated to the House of Representatives 1/9/1812;" CDC #91799 and 91800, Leader Realty Co., Ltd. vs. Lakeview Land Co. and N. O. Land Co., filed 5/13/1912; SCR #90893, 12/5/1768, LSML; Cabildo Records, 5/7/1771, Jan.-Dec. 1771, LSML, (hereafter referred to as CR.); Act of NP Caire, Pilie Gentilly Concessions Plan, 11/9/1847 (Map-LOC).
12) SCR #9851, 4/26/1766, LSML.
13) Bunner, History of Louisiana, from its first discovery and settlement to the present time. (New York 1842) 126, (hereafter referred to as Bunner's History of La.); Gayarré II, 133, 183, 185; Villiers' Last Yrs..,383-5, 390-7; Chambers, 275.
14) Duff-Green II, Session 1/9/1812, Claim #17, p 258; Gales & Seaton I, 301; SCR #2219, 8/3/1767, LSML; CR 9/18/1769, LHQ 6 (Jan. 1923) 146-50; CR #1-B, 1-C, File 10591, 9/19/1769, 10/18/1769, 11/5/1769; #2-A 10/10/1769, 12/12/1769, LSML.
15) Duff-Green II, Claim 164, 270; Gales Seaton I, 315, "confirmed to A. Milne, 1812."
16) Document 73, Claim 44, 17, Land Office, Baton Rouge, Louisiana.
17) Duff-Green II, Claim 48, 261, confirmed to Milne 1/9/1812; Gales & Seaton I, 304; Castillon Plot #5, Milne Inventory 5/18/1839, and Record of Land Office of Terr. of Orleans 2/12/1806, Book I, folios 289, 290, 292, 293, contained in LSSC #20818, Leader Realty Co. vs. Lakeview Land Co. and N. O. Land Co., 5/14/1914; LSSC #821, Milne vs. Labo, filed 4/7/1823.
18) CR #67 A 23, 7/1/1767, LSML; Duff-Green II, Claim 100, 265; Gales-Seaton I, 310; Roquigny Plot #4, Milne Inventory, 5/18/1839, and entered on record of Land Office for Territory of Orleans 2/28/1806, Book I, pages 414, 416, 418, contained in LSSC #20818 Leader Realty Co. vs. Lakeview Land Co. and N. O. Land Co., filed 5/14/1914; Martin's 208; Fortier, 229.
19) S. A. Calonge's Sons, Civil Engrs. and Surveyors, New Orleans map. Registered with State Land Office 1/12/1924, Baton Rouge, La., for location of tracts west bank of Bayou St. John, as decided by courts after a series of cases regarding this area. (Hereafter referred to as Calonge's Map, 1924.); Board of Directors of Public Schools, City of New Orleans vs. N. O. Land Co., CDC #92,795, filed 11/16/1914, Reasons for Judgment; Gayarré III, 6; LSSC #22740 and 143 La. Reports 858-874, State of La. vs. N. O. Land Co., filed 5/27/1918; LSSC #22950 and 151 La. Reports 134-142, Brott vs. N. O. Land Co. 2/27/1922, from CDC #85,758, 1908; LSSC #21069 and 138 La. Reports 320-59, Directors of Public Schools of Parish of Orleans vs. N. O. Land Co., 4/12/1915; LSSC #17,697, Castera Heirs vs. N. O. Land Co., 3/14/1910; LSSC #20818, Leader Realty Co. vs. Lakeview Land Co. 1/18/1921.
20) SCR #1908, 4/26/1766, #1909, 5/2/1766, #1910-1912, 5/21/1766, #1917, 6/4/1766, #1921, #1922, 6/7/1766, LSML.
21) Martin, 199; SCR #66 A 63, 7/4/1766, #1928, 7/13/1766, #1935, 7/14/1766, #1946, 7/30/1766, #66 A 99, 8/22/1766, #67 A 21, 5/31/1767, #2212, 7/29/1767, #4 67 40, 8/2/1767, #2299, 11/8/1767.LSML.
22) Gayarré II, 183; HC-L II, 61, Portfolio IV Archives; Villiers' Last Yrs..392, 399-400, 410; Hutchins' Journal, 33; Reconnoitering Chart of the South Frontier of the United States Of America, from the River Perdido towards the East, 1817 (Nat'l Archives, Washington, D. C.); Map of New Orleans and Adjacent Country, John Melish, 1815, (Map-LOC), for location of New Balise.
23) Captain Harry Gordon, Extract From Journal of an Expedition Along The Ohio and Mississippi, 1766, Archives at Ottawa, LHQ 6, (Jan. 1923), 15, with some corrections in spelling and punctuation by author.
24) Wood, Minter, Life in New Orleans In The Spanish Period (Ulloa) LHQ 22 #3 (Jul. 1939) 693.

CHAPTER XVII

1) SCR #2038, 2/9/1767, #67 A 17, 5/2/1767, LSML; SCR D 6826, 2/19/1767, LSML; SCR #9858, 5/13/1766, LSML; SCR #2014, 1/28/1767,LSML; SCR #2046, 2/27/1767, LSML; SCR #67 A 30, 7/11/1767, LSML.
2) Duff-Green II, Claim 509, p 227, communicated to the Senate 1/20/1817, 2nd specie of incomplete French or Spanish claims granted prior to 12/20/1803; SCR #2158, 2159, 6/10/1757; #2163, 6/15/1767; #2170, 6/27/1767; #2179, 7/4/1767; #2187, 7/11/1767; #67 A 35, 8/6/1767; #2233, 2234, 8/13/1767, LSML.
3) SCR #9977, 11/20/1766, LSML; SCR 9972, 11/15/1766, LSML.
4) SCR #2045, 5/27/1767 and SCR #3172, 6/23/1767, LSML.

5) SCR #66 A 63, 7/4/1766, #1928, 7/13/1766, #1935, 7/14/1766, #1946 7/30/1766, #66 A 99, 8/22/1766, #67 A 21, 5/31/1767, #2212, 7/29/1767, #4 67 40, 8/2/1767, #2299, 11/8/1767, LSML; T-P 5/10/68, s1, p5.
6) HC-L II, 73, 1/20/1767, Folio VII Archives; Villiers' Last Yrs..406-10, 413-16; Coleman, de St. Maxent, 32-37.
7) King, Creole Families of N. O. (Baton Rouge, La.) 1971, 208; SCR #2036, 2/14/1767, #2167, 6/19/1767, #2201, 7/21/1767, LSML.
8) SCR #2325, 12/2/1767, SCR #2319, 11/27/1767, SCR #D 68 14, 1/14/1768, LSML.
9) Villiers' Last Yrs..556-7.
10) Ibid., 455, 476; Chambers, 278.
11) SCR #2363-4, 5/16/1768; D 68 90, 5/17, 1768, #2367, 5/20/1768, D 68 117, 5/30/1768, D 68 123, 6/3/1768, LSML.
12) SCR, LHQ 22 (Jan. 1939) 287-297; SCR, LSML; SCR, 7/30/1768, LHQ 25 (Apr. 1942) 587.
13) Villiers' Last Yrs..428, 436, 447, 472-6; Coleman, St. Maxent, 38; Dufour, Pie, T-P 10/27/68, s3 p6; Gayarré II, 166-172, 202, 213-19; Fortier, 166-172, 179, 208; Chambers, 272-4, 280.
14) Villiers' Last Yrs..419, 466, 480-4, 486, 489, 491; Fortier, 207-8; Martin's, 202.
15) SCR #10497, 1769, LSML; SCR, LHQ 22 (Jan. 1939) 287-297.
16) Fortier, 235-7; SCR D 69 9, 1/14/1769, D 69 141, 4/17-22/1769, LSML.
17) SCR #7194, p 53183, 1758, LSML; Juan B. Garic, Notarial Records, Microfilmed New Orleans 7/12/1968, NOPL, Index Roll I, Act 9190, 2/28/1765, Index Roll I, Act 8962, Section 33, and Act 9132, 10/12/1765,; Private Claims, Baton Rouge, La., 52; SCR #D 68 13, 1/12/1768, SCR #D 68 10, 1/9-12/1768, SCR D 68 36, 3/14/1768, SCR #10394, 3/16/1769, CR #69 216, July, 1969, CR D 69 217, Jul. 1969, SCR #10430, 4/27/1769, D 69 209, 6/23/1769, LSML.
18) Villiers' Last Yrs..496-504, 510-12, 515-519, 532, 541; Chambers, 284-6; Fortier, 210-11; HC-L II, Folio IV 9/1/1769, 60; Fortier, 229; Martin's 208; CR #10515, P 93182-90, Doc. 1B Box 25, 10/5/1769, LSML; Arthur, Stanley Clisby, Old Families of Louisiana (Baton Rouge 1971) 200.
19) Villiers' Last Yrs..546, 548-555; Martin's 212-15; Devron, Dr. Gustavus paper, LHQ II, (Jan. 1919) 29; Fortier II, 17.

NOTES AND REFERENCES — The Spanish Period

CHAPTER XVIII

1) Favrot, H. Mortimer, Colonial Forts of La., LHQ 26, 1943, 740; Martins's 210-211; Chambers, 304-5; Thompson, Ray, Oliver Pollock, New Orleans, Magazine, Dec. 1972, 48; Coleman, Gilberto Antoine de St. Maxent, 40-41.
2) Chambers, 211, 304.
3) Ibid, 298; Martin's 211.
4) Ibid. 212; LHQ VI (Jan. 1923) 160.
5) LHQ 11 (Oct. 1928) 607; LHQ 6 (Jul. 1923) 521-2; Wilson, Sam, The Cabildo on Jackson Square, 13-15.
6) Cabildo Records 8/2/1769, No. 10509, Jul.-Dec. 1769, Doc. 34, 9/30/1769, Box 26, Louisiana State Museum Library, (hereafter referred to as CR and LSML); CR 5/11/1770 in LHQ VII (Jul. 1924) 528.
7) Dart, Sally, A Lawsuit Over The Office of Notary, LHQ 16, 1933, 588.
8) Records and Deliberations of the Cabildo, I, p 14, WPA Translations, 1934, New Orleans Public Library (hereafter referred to as NOPL); CR, LHQ VI (Jan. 1923) 154; CR, LHQ VI, (Jul. 1923) 514-5.
9) CR 6/5/1769, #10466 (92905), May-June, 1769, LSML; CR 5/28/1770 in LHQ VII (Jul. 1924) 536-7; CR #10725, p 9702 9032, 1770, Apr.-Jul., LSML.
10) Chambers I, 307 and fn; Gayarré III, 20-25; Wood, Minter, Life in N. O. In The Spanish Period, LHQ XXII (Jul. 1939) 654; Coleman, Maxent, 41-44.
11) Faye, Stanley, The Arkansas Post of Louisiana Spanish Domination, LHQ XXVII (Jul. 1944) 691; Martin's, 213-14; 2 Martin O. S., 258; Gayarré III, 34-5; Zacharie, James S., LHQ II (Jul. 1919) 58.
12) Duff-Green Edition V, gives 2/18/1770 date, p 290; Gayarré III, 99 gives 1/8/1770 date; Moody, Alton, M., Slavery on Sugar Plantations, LHQ VII (Apr. 1924), fn 191; Schmidt, Gustavus, Louisiana Law Journal I, part 2, p 61, August 1841.
13) CR 1770, LHQ VII (Jan. 1924) 160-1; CR. File 10634, Doc. 42, Box 26, Jan.-Mch. 1770, LSML; Luis Andry Survey Map Kernion's Property on Bayou San Juan, 9/26/1771, Land Office, Baton Rouge, La.; Garic, Juan B., Index to Roll 2, NOPL.
14) Martin's 213; Schmidt, Gustavus, O'Reilly's Ordinance of 1770 Concerning Grants of Land in Louisiana to New Settlers, Louisiana Law Journal I, part 2, 61 in LHQ XI (Apr. 1928) 238.
15) CR 3/19 and 4/5, 1770, LHQ VII (Jan. 1924) 154-5; Hutchins' Journal, 56, 95.

16) Garic, Notarial Records, LHQ VI (Apr. 1923) 33; LHQ VI (Apr. 1923) 33; CR, Doc. 670A, Box 25, Apr.-Jul.,1770, LSML; King, Creole Families of New Orleans, 209.
17) Padgett, James A., Boundaries of British West Florida, LHQ XXVI (Jan. 1943) 9; Favrot, H. Mortimer, Colonial Forts of La., LHQ XXVI (Jul. 1943) 740; Martin's, 215; CR 9/12/1770, LHQ VI (Jul. 1923) 525.
18) CR, LHQ VI (Jul. 1923) 533; CR 12/4/1770, LHQ VI (Jul. 1923) 536; CR, File 3997, Doc. 148, Box 26 1770, LSML; Luis Andry Map Kernion Properties of 9/26/1771, Land Office, Baton Rouge, La.; CR, LHQ VIII (Jan. 1925) 169-70.
19) Coleman, Maxent, 52; Wood, Life in Spanish La., LHQ XXII (Jul. 1939) 696; LHQ IV , 1921, 201; Chambers, 312-13, 316; Villiers' Last Yrs...601-4; Gayarré III, 28, 35, 44, 45, 314-15; Wood, Minter, Life in Spanish La., LHQ XXII (Jul. 1939) 664, 671; Gordon's Diary, 1766, LHQ VI (Jan. 1923) 17; CR 1/18/1771, 53; Despatches of Spanish Governors of La., Book I, Vol. 3, 1/15/1771, 1766-1774, LSML.
20) CR #1145, 111-3, LSML; Private Claims, Baton Rouge, La. 52; CR 5/23/1771, LHQ VIII, (Apr. 1925) 332-3; CR 3/15/1778, LHQ XIII (Apr. 1930) 336-7.
21) CR 6/1-20/1771, LHQ VIII (Jan. 1925) 6-22; CR, Jan.-Dec., 1771, LSML; CR, LHQ VIII (Jul. 1925) 512-16.
22) Castillion Plot #5, Milne Inventory 5/18/1839, and Record of Land Office of Territory of Orleans 2/12/1806, Book I, folios 289, 290, 292, 293, contained in LSSC #20818 Leader Realty Co. vs. Lakeview Land Co. and N. O. Land Co. 4/14/1914; LSSC #21,069, Board of Directors of Public Schools, Parish of Orleans vs. The N. O. Land Co., filed 4/12/1915; LSSC #821 Milne vs. H. Labo, filed 4/7/1823 and map of 6/17/1805 in case showing location of properties along Bayou St. John at bayou's mouth.
23) LSSC Lavergne Heirs vs. Elkin Heirs, March 1841, 17 La. 220, appeal from Court of First Judicial District; Civil District Court #19,265, 1909; LSSC #3278 Heirs of Lavergne vs. City of N. O. 9/18/1877; CDC #8630 Succession of Jean Lavergne and wife, filed 5/17/1883.
24) Garic, Notarial Records, Roll #2, p 328, 329, 343, microfilmed by Salt Lake City Geneological Society at N. O. 7/12/1968, NOPL.
25) Hutchins' Journal, intro xvi, xvii, xix, xx, xxi and pps 37, 38, reproduction of 1784 edition, University of Fla. Press, Gainesville, Fla. 1968. (Hutchins' Journal)
26) CR 5/15/1776, LHQ XI (Oct. 1928) 654-60.
27) CR 5/11/1770, LHQ VII (Jul. 1924) 528; CR, Doc. 34, Box 26, 9/30/1769, LSML; CR File 4004, Doc. 148, Box 26, 12/19/1770, LSML; CR 2/25/1772, LHQ VIII (Jan. 1925) 172-3.
28) CR 10/19/1772, LHQ 8, (Jul. 1925) 534-42; Plano de la Ciudad, de Nueva Orleans, 24 Diciembre 1798, Carlos Trudeau, LSML, for location of plantation on Bayou Road.
29) CR, 7/23/1772, LHQ 8 (Jul. 1925) 518-25; Private Claims, Baton Rouge, 278.
30) Bermudez Claim 6, Document 73, p 7, Land Office, Baton Rouge, La.
31) Wood, Minter, Life in N. O. In The Spanish Period, LHQ 22 (Oct. 1939) 685; Chambers I, 313; CR Doc 141, Box 26, File 108-18, LSML.

CHAPTER XIX

1) Bunner, E. History of La., Harper & Bros. N. Y. 1842, 144-5; Despatches of Spanish Governors, Book I, Vol. V, Vol. VI, 7/19/1776, LSML.
2) CR 3/4/1773, LHQ 9 (Apr. 1926) 322-3.
3) CR 5/8/1773, LHQ 9, (Apr. 1926) 344.
4) Porteous, Laura, translator of CR "The Gri-Gri Case," LHQ 17, (Jan. 1934) 48-63; Dr. Hugh F. Rankin and W. R. Irby, Tulane Educational Conference, T-P 3/14/1976, s1, p 48.
5) CR 1/23/1774, LHQ 12 (Jan. 1929) 84-113; Bouligny's Report of 1776, Fortier II, 20-52.
6) CR, LHQ 11 (Oct. 1928) 654-60; CR LHQ 10 (Jan. 1927) 153-4.
7) CR, LHQ 24 (Oct. 1941) 1260; LSSC #22950, Brott vs. N. O. Land Co., filed 2/27/1922, 151 La. Report, 134-142, same case in CDC #85,758, filed 1908; LSSC #22740, State of La. vs. N. O. Land Co., filed 5/27/1918, 143 La. Reports, 858-874; Map, S. S. Calogne and Sons, Civil Engrs. and Surveyors, N. O. showing location of Tarascon Grant and other tracts on the west bank of Bayou St. John, as decided by the courts after a series of law cases regarding these properties; LSSC #21,069 Board of Directors of Public Schools, Parish of Orleans vs. N. O. Land Co., Judgment 4/12/1915; LSSC #20818, Leader Realty Co. vs. Lakeview Land and N. O. Land Co., Judgment 6/30/1917, 142 La. 169; CR, LHQ 10, (Jul. 1927) 169, 454.
8) Duff-Green II, #100, 265; CR LHQ 8 (Jul. 1925) 512-7; CR 2/21/1774, (Apr. 1927) 298-9; CR 8/18/1775, LHQ 8 (Oct. 1925) 729; Acts of J. Garic, Vol. 4, 4/14/1773, 133; CR 3/17/1774 and 7/14/1778, LHQ 10 (Apr. 1927) 306-9, Acts of Garic #5, 4/25/1774, sale Brazillier to Lorreins; Private Claims, Land Office Baton Rouge, La. 52; Garic's Acts, Vol. 5, 10/15/1774, 192; #LSSC 4241, Arrowsmith vs. Durrell, 11/7/1855; Richardson vs. Liberty Oil Co., 143 La. Reports 138.

9) LSSC #1744, Heirs of DuBreuil vs. T. M. Kennedy et als, 1850, and Trudeau Map 1795, 1798, 1800 in case showing sections of DuBreuil Plantation sold at various times.
10) Senate Document 45, pp 32, 33; Historic Homes Houses (Pamphlet given tour groups) 1800-1840, published 1975, gives date of Latil construction as about 1790; Duff-Green Edition 2, #125, 287; Argument Against The Houmas in LSSC #34 A. A. Laforest vs. D. N. Downing, filed 1/31/1861; Houmas House: c 1780, T-P 7/4/76, s7, p 76.
11) CR 9/17/1776, LHQ 19, 1936, 533-4; CR 1771, LHQ 9 (Apr. 1926) 293.
12) CR, LHQ 18 (Apr. 1935) 479; CR 4/25/1775, LHQ 11 (Jan. 1928); Recs. and Delibs. of the Cabildo, Vol. I, 8/18/1769 - 8/25/1779, 209, 223-230, LSML.
13) CR 5/17/1776 - 8/7/1789, LHQ 11 (Oct. 1928) 654-60.
14) Despatches of Spanish Governors in Louisiana, Vol. II, Bundle 1146, No. 186, LSML; Scramuzza, V. M., GALVESTON, LHQ 13 (Oct. 1930) 558-9; Bouligny's Report, Fortier's II, 20-52; Plan du Lac Pontchartrain, 1778, made on order of Gov. Galvez, National Archives M2, P.F. #88, Washington, D.C.; Map of New Orleans and Adjacent Country, 1815, John Melish, #463521, G 19, 34, (Map-LOC).
15) CR 1/18/1776, LHQ 11 (Jan. 1928); LSSC #20818 Leader Realty Co. vs. Lakeview Land Co. and N. O. Land Co., filed 5/14/1914; Duff-Green Vol. II, Claim No. 100, 1/9/1812, 265; CR 1776-1785, LHQ 28 (Apr. 1945) 1245-6.
16) CR, LHQ 22 (Jan. 1939) 283; Briede, Kathryn C., A History of the City of Lafayette, LHQ 20 (Oct. 1937) 909; CR LHQ 11 (Apr. 1928) 330; CR, LHQ 18 (Jan. 1935) 200; CR LHQ 20 (Jan.-Oct. 1937) 909-10; CR, LHQ 11 (Oct. 1928) 667; LSSC #1744 Heirs of DuBreuil Villars vs. T. M. Kennedy et al, 11/7/1850; Coleman, Maxent, 49-52.
17) Villiers' Last Yrs..452-3, 602, 604-6, Gayarré III, 106-8, Chambers, 318-19; Records of the Cabildo, No. 2, 4/19/1782, 110-114; Coleman, Maxent, 49-53.
18) Chambers, 319-23; Gayarré III, 109-113; Fortier, II, 57; Villiers' Last Yrs., 607; Thompson, Ray, Oliver Pollock, N. O. Magazine, Dec. 1972, 48-62; Chase, John, The Centennial's Invisible Man, Dixie Roto, T-P 12/14/1775, 10-11.
19) Favrot, H. Mortimer, Colonial Forts of La., LHQ 26 (Jul. 1943) 722-754.
20) Private Claims, New Orleans, Land Office, Baton Rouge, 267, 269, 274, 276, 277-8, 400-4; Martin's, 1882 edition, 402, map of Bayu San Juan; Courrier 5/17/1847 (year of Allard's death) p1, c4.

CHAPTER XX

1) Favrot, H. Mortimer, Colonial Forts of La., LHQ 26 (Jul. 1943) 741; Caughey, John, Willing Expedition Down the Mississippi, LHQ 15 (Jan. 1932) 24, 25; Villiers' Last Yrs..607.
2) Gayarré III, 120; Fortier II, 51; Scramuzza, V. M., LHQ 13 (Oct. 1930) 558-9; Hutchins' Journal, 38; Papers from Cuba 112-Archives, Sevilla, Spain, 12/9/1968, letter from Rosario Parra, Director, to author; First District Court #13025, in CDC Case #110,666, N. Lavergne vs. S. Elkins, filed 10/14/1837; Read, Wm. A. Indian Place Names in La., in LHQ 11, 1928, 460; Plan du Lac Pontchartrain 1778, Nat'l Archives Washington, D. C.; Map of N. O. and Adjacent Country, 1815, John Melish, (Map-LOC); Scramuzza, V. M., LHQ 13 (Oct. 1930) 558-9.
3) Hutchins' Journal, intro xxiii xxiv; Prichard, Walter, Romance of Research in Louisiana, LHQ 20 (Jul. 1937) 560; Gayarré III, 121; Favrot, Forts of La., LHQ 26 (Jul. 1943) 741; Despatches of Spanish Governors of La., Book II, Vol. IX, ltr. 8/25/1799; Fortier II, 105; Villiers' Last Yrs..607; Wood, Minter, Life in N. O. Spanish Period, LHQ 22 (Jul. 1939) 642-703; O'Connor, Stella, Charity Hospital of Louisiana at N. O., LHQ 31 (Jan. 1948) 8-20.
4) Chambers, 326-7, 331-4; Villiers' Last Yrs..608, 611; Faye, Stanley, The Arkansas Post of La., Spanish Domination, LHQ 27 (Jul. 1944) 699; Robert Farmar's Journal, Bernard de Galvez' Seige of Pensacola, LHQ 26 (Apr. 1943) 311; Scramuzza, GALVEZTOWN, LHQ 13 (Oct. 1930) 554, 590-3; Roberts, Lake Pontchartrain, 97; Coleman, Maxent, 53-4; LHQ 13 (Jan.-Oct. 1930) 554; Waring and Cable, Ancient New Orleans, Commercial Social & Medical Statistics of New Orleans, 8/23/1881, p 21.
5) Recs. and Delibs. of the Cabildo I, 252; Arthur, Stanley, Old Families of La., 68; LSSC #22950 Brott vs. N. O. Land Co., filed 2/27/1922 from CDC #85,758; CR 5/29/1777, 1777-78 LSML; Garic, Roll 9, 161; Trudeau, Carlos, Map 1800, Land Office, Baton Rouge, La.; CR Doc. 514, Box 3660, LSML; LHQ 13 (Apr. 1930) 346; CR LHQ 13 (Jan. 1930) 361; CR, file 3633, Doc. 522. LSML.
6) LSSC #821, Alexander Milne vs. H. Labo et al, filed 4/7/1823; Arthur Stanley, Old Families of La., 261-2; CR, March 1799, LHQ 18 (Apr. 1935) 478-9.
7) CR 6/14/1779, LHQ 13 (Oct. 1930) 698-9; Map of Chapitoulas area, showing land-owners, Private Claims, Baton Rouge, La. 245.
8) Gayarré III, 120; CR 12/10/1779, LHQ 14 (Jan. 1931) 146; CR 11/14/1780, LHQ 15 (Jan. 1932) 168-9; Recs. and Delibs. of Cabildo, Vol. II, 9/8/1779, 6/25/1784.

9) Thompson, Ray, Oliver Pollock, New Orleans Magazine, Dec. 1972, 48-62; CR 4/22/1780, LHQ 14 (1931) 475-77; CR 2/22/1782, LHQ 17 (Jul. 1934) 598-9.
10) CR 5/8/1780, LHQ 14 (Jul. 1931) 478-9.
11) Recs. and Delibs. Cabildo, Vol. II 6/15/1781, 60; CR 8/12/1780, LHQ 14 (Oct. 1931) 620-1.
12) Villiers' Last Yrs..611; Coleman, Maxent, 83-90; Chambers, 341; Recs. and Delibs., Cabildo, Vol. II, 1/19/1781, 47.
13) Translation of Spanish Document attached to Notarial Act #508, passed before Felix de Armas, NP 9/24/1834, LSML; Kendall, John S., The Pontalba Bldgs., LHQ 19 (Jan. 1936) 124.
14) Recs. and Delibs., Cabildo, Vol. II, 5/25/1781, 56; Ibid., Vol. I, 3/9/1787, 159-199.
15) CR 5/26/1781, LHQ 16 (Jul. 1933) 516; CR 3/1/1783, LHQ 20 (Oct. 1937) 840.
16) Cable-Waring, Ancient New Orleans, History of Present Conditions in New Orleans, p 5; CR 2/16/1781 (Oct. 1932) 686-706.

CHAPTER XXI

1) Thompson, Ray, Oliver Pollock, New Orleans Magazine, Dec. 1972, 48-62.
2) CR 7/2/1782, LHQ 19 (Jan. 1936) 253-7.
3) CR 8/20/1781, LHQ 17 (Jan. 1934) 210-11.
4) CR, LHQ 17 (Jan. 1934) 212-18 and 389-90; LHQ 18 (Apr. 1935) 480-1; CR 9/3/1781, Doc. 656-7, Box 38, LSML; CR 10/27/1781, Doc. 670, Box 38, LSML; CR 7/1/1784, LHQ 24 (Jan 1941) 296-8.
5) LHQ 18 (Apr. 1935) 466-7 and 478-85; CR 4/12/1782, CR 10/29/1782, Doc. 713, Box 39, LSML.
6) CR 6/3/1782, LHQ 18 (Oct. 1935) 1004-1110; CR 6/3/1782, Doc. 721, File 46, LSML.
7) CR 9/4/1782, LHQ 19 (Apr. 1936) 512-15.
8) CR, LHQ 19 (Apr. 1936) 515-522.
9) CR, LHQ 22 (Jan. 1939) 269-71; CR Doc. 876, Box 41, File 3519, 10/9/1783, LSML; Will of Naneta 10/13/1782, NP L. Mazange, and Will of Miguel DesRuisseaux 1/25/1805, NP Pierre Pedesclaux, in LSSC #20818 (from CDC #91,799) Leader Realty Co. vs. Lakeview Land Co. filed 6/24/1914.
10) CR 8/18/1782, LHQ 19 (Jan. 1936) 263-7; Private Claims, Baton Rouge, La., 52; Recs. and Delibs. Cabildo, Vol. I, 164, 191, NOPL.
11) CR 10/15/1776, LHQ 11 (Apr. 1928) 678; CR 10/24/1782, LHQ 10 (Apr. 1927) 538; CR, Dec., 1783, LHQ 22 (Apr. 1939) 593-603; CR 4/14/1784, LHQ 23, (Apr. 1940) 636-659; CR 4/14/1784, Doc. 937, Box 42, File 116, LSML; CR 1/17/1786, Doc. 1197, Box 45, File 88, LSML.
12) CR, LHQ 20 (Oct. 1937) 1148-1166; LHQ 22 (Jan. 1939) 270-1; CR #69, 4/18/1783, LSML.
13) CR 11/24/1784, LHQ 26 (Apr. 1943) 596-98.

CHAPTER XXII

1) CR 6/2/1783, LHQ 21 (Jan. 1938) 325-7; Chambers, 339, 389; LHQ 26, (Apr. 1943) 311; Bunner, History of La., 152; Hutchins' Journal, 22.
2) LSSC #4241 Arrowsmith vs. Durrell and N. O. Canal and Navigation Co., filed 5/18/1855; CR 10/16/1783, 11/26/1783, LHQ 22 (Jan. 1939) 282-298.
3) CR 11/5/1783, LHQ 22 (Apr. 1939) 576-7.
4) CR 12/16/1783, LHQ 22 (Oct. 1939) 912-17.
5) CR 11/26/1783, LHQ 22 (Apr. 1939) 606-11.
6) CR 4/23/1784, LHQ 23 (Apr. 1940) 672-3.
7) Wilson, Sam, Guide to Architecture of New Orleans, 1699-1957, New York, 1959; CR 7/1/1784, LHQ 24 (Jan. 1941) 286-93; CR 6/30/1784, Doc. 959, Box 42, File 138, LSML.

CHAPTER XXIII

1) Recs. and Delibs. Cabildo, Vol. I, 169, 192, 215, NOPL; Ibid., Vol. III 7/2/1784 - 12/14/1787, 1-3, 7, 20, 153, NOPL.
2) CR 8/27/1784, LHQ 24 (Jul. 1941) 903-5.
3) Private Claims, Baton Rouge, 145 - maps, charts, same source.
4) Historical Sketch Book and Guide to N. O. and Environs, edited and compiled by several leading writers of the N. O. Press, New York, Will H. Coleman, 1885, 168; Locations of certain lands known as Terascon Grant and Property of Beugnot, F. Alpuente and DeMorant, N. O., La. 2nd District, by S. A. Calonge Sons, Baton Rouge, La. 1/12/1924; CR 9/14/1784, LHQ 24 (Oct. 1941) 1258-74; CDC #17,697, Castera Heirs vs. N. O. Land Co., 11/16/1909; CR LHQ 24 (Oct. 1941) 1274-80; CR 9/14/1784 Doc. 980, Box 42, File 141, LSML; CR 10/8/1784, LHQ 25 (Jan. 1942) 277; CR 10/8/1784, Doc. 973-A, Box

42, LSML

5) CR 11/24/1784, LHQ 25 (Apr. 1942) 596-7.
6) Chambers 341; Villiers' Last Yrs..611; Gayarré III p 179, says 1784-1791; King, N. O. The Place and The People, 128; Fortier II, 113.
7) LHQ 29, 1946; CR LHQ 26, (Oct. 1943) 1213.
8) CR, LHQ 29 (Apr. 1946) 548-50.
9) CR, LHQ 29 (Jan. 1946) 209-261.
10) O'Connor, Stella, Charity Hospital of N. O., LHQ 31 (Jan. 1948) 21-25; Recs. and Delibs. Cabildo, Vol. III, 7/2/1784 - 12/14/1787, 149; T-P 1/29/1976 s2, p3; 1833 map of Leper Hospital in LSSC #707 Mme. de Pontalba vs. Mayor of N. O., filed 12/20/1847 from 3rd District Court; Resolutions and Ordinances Conseil de Ville, Vol. I, 151, Session 4/14/1808; Recs. and Delibs. Cabildo Vol. III, 7/2/1784 - 12/14/1787, 4/22/1785, 49-50; Council Records of Municipality 4/20/1785 Spanish Documents 1770-1792, No. 101, Cabildo Folio 30 4/22/1785; N. O. City Guide 1938, 190; Map T125 R11E, S. E. District La., Exhibit D-2 in CDC #18211 State of La. vs. CC&NCo., filed 7/18/1911, map 1871-1872, Sulakowski Map shows Castillon (formerly Almonester) property.
11) Duffy, History of Medicine in La., Vol. I, Rudolph Matas Trust Fund, 259-65; Fortier II, 109; King, N. O., The Place and The People 128; Wood, Minter, Life in N. O. During the Spanish Period, LHQ 22 (Jul. 1939) 680; Gayarré III, 167; Villiers' Last Yrs..613; Recs. and Delibs. of Cabildo, Vol. 3, 7/2/1784 - 12/14/1787,. 79-80; CR, Sept-Dec. 1785, 11/11/1785, #3037, Doc. 1166, Box 44, LSML.
12) Dufour, Pie, T-P 2/19/1967, Kuntz Collection, Tulane University, N. O.
13) LHQ 31 (Apr. 1948) 310.
14) Faye, Stanley, The Arkansas Post of La., Spanish Domination, LHQ 27 (Jul. 1944) 691.
15) Chambers, 348.
16) Fortier, II, 110; Gayarré III, 170, 269; Martin's 239; LHQ 22 (Jan. 1939) 99; Gayarré III, 269; Villiers' Last Yrs..140-1, 615; Castellanos, N. O. As It Was, 284; Chambers I, 347; Burns, Francis P., Legislation and Litigation of St. Louis Cathedral, LHQ 18 (Apr. 1935) 364; Jackson, Wesley, Religion in La., A History, T-P 5/27/1973, s2 p7, gives 1787 date; Recs. and Delibs., Cabildo, Book III, 1/1/1788-5/18/1792, 63.
17) CR, Doc. 1560, Box 48, File 14 LSML; CR Doc. 1567, Box 48, 7/2/1787, LSML; CR Doc. 1375, Box 47, File 147, LSML; NP Pedro Pedesclaux, Notary 1/20/1802; Trudeau Map of the Habitation of Pedro Marigny composite map of 1796, 1798, 1800 in LSSC #1744, Heirs of DuBreuil Villars vs. T. M. Kennedy et als, 1850.
18) Dufour, Pie, Ten Flags..113-4; Chambers I, 348-361; Villiers' Last Yrs..613-4; LHQ 2, 9/14/1919, 103; Taylor, J. G., A Student's Guide to Localized History, 7; King, N. O. The Place and the People, 140; Martin's 251; Fortier II, 119; Gayarré III, 192, 215.
19) Ibid, 203; King, N. O. The Place and the People, 129; Chambers I, 347; Villiers' Last Yrs..614; LHQ 22 (Jul. 1939) 665-6.
20) LHQ 22 (Jul. 1939) 683-4; King, N. O. The Place and the People, 131; Gayarré III, 204.
21) Cabildo Records translated: Doc. 1753, Box 50, file 2400, 3/12/1788; Doc. 1758, Box 50, file 2628, 3/15/1788; Doc. 1896, Box 52, File 2394, 11/19/1788, LSML, N. O.
22) Roberts, Lake Pontchartrain, 101-3; LSSC #1744 Heirs of DuBreuil Villars vs. T. M. Kennedy et al, filed 1850, Trudeau Map in case showing sections of DuBreuil plantation sold at various times; Pilie Concessions, 11/9/1847, (Map-LOC); Despatches of Spanish Governors of La., Vol. XXI, 64, LSML.
23) Cabildo Records: File #2038, 10/12/1789, Doc. 2391, Box 56, LSML.

CHAPTER XXIV

1) Recs. and Delibs. Cabildo, Vol. 4, 9/19/1800 - 7/17/1802, WPA City Archives, NOPL, 39-41, 102-4, 202-202a; Dufour, Pie, T-P 11/26/1972, s2, p8; Pintado Papers, Book III, C No. 3, LSML, 99, map of old cemetery.
2) CR, Doc. 1542, Box 48, File 2745 5/9/1787, LSML; CR Doc 1900, Box 52, File 189 11/27/1788; CR File 2789, Doc. 2028, Box 53, 3/2/1789, LSML.
3) CR. Doc. 2204, Box 54, File 2075, 6/25/1789, 1 - 65, LSML.
4) CR. Doc. 2022, Box 53, 3/2/1789, LSML; CR. Doc. 2227, Box 55, File 2312, 7/17/1789, LSML.
5) CR Doc 2391, Box 57, file 1808, 1789; CR., Doc 2539, Box 59, File 1854, 7/1/1790, LSML.
6) Private Claims, Land Office, Baton Rouge, La., 145, 177, 236, 475; Recs. and Delibs. Cabildo, WPA Translations, 1934, Book III 1/1/1788 - 5/18/1792 - 11/6/1789, 81, 87 and 3/16/1790, 101; Despatches of Spanish Governors of La., Vol. XX, Box 4, 21, WPA TRanslations 1937, 384, LSML; CR. Doc. 2260, Box 55, File 2044 8/20/1789; Doc. 2577, Box 59, File 45, 8/7/1790, LSML; Recs. and Delibs. Cabildo, Vol. 4, No. 2 7/14/1797 - 12/20/1798, Jos. Barcenas Translation, NOPL 1937, 7/21/1797, 6.

7) Chambers I, 362-5; Despatches of Spanish Governors of La., Book VI 8/12/1790 - 4/29/1792, 380-82; WPA translations 1937, '38, '40 LSML.
8) Corbin, Carl, T-P 1/23/1938, s2, columns 1-8; T-P 7/6/1934 "Old Fort Proves Spanish Military Engrs. Skill", p3, cl; Despatches of Spanish Governors of La., Book I, 1/7 to 8/20/1792, 1939 translations, 163, LSML.
9) Chambers I, 368, 402; Fortier II, 146; The Last Yrs. of French Louisiana, Villiers, 452-3; Cardinal Goodwin, LHQ III, 12; Pitot, James, Henry Pitot, 23; Deren, Maya, Divine Horsemen; The Voodoo Gods of Haiti, Chelsea House Publishers, N. Y. 1970, 62-5; History of Santo Domingo, Daily Picayune 1/15/1871, c1, p2; Chambers I, 370; Gayarré III, 309-11; Fortier II, 146; King, N. O. The Place and the People, 1791, 147; Wood, Life in N. O., Spanish Period, LHQ 22 (Jul. 1939) 692; 250th Anniversary of New Orleans by Cabildo Friends, 26; Resolutions and Ordinances C de V, II, 1816-1821, 10/15/1817, 138.
10) Records of Notary Francisco Broutin, 176; Records of Pedro Pedesclaux, 3/31/1794 and 3/10/1798, p 154; Private Claims, Baton Rouge, La. 145, 179-184.
11) Gayarré III, 312; Chambers I, 363, 366-8; Fortier II, 158; Villiers' Last Yrs., 616-7; Despatches of Spanish Governors of La., Book I, 1/7/1792 - 8/20/1792, WPA Survey Archives of La. 1937-8, 163-7, NOPL.
12) Gayarré III, 314-25; Fortier II, 152; Chambers I, 368; Jacobinism in Spanish La., LHQ 22 (Jan. 1939) 48; Wood, Life in N. O. In The Spanish Period, LHQ 22 (Jul. 1939) 654-5.
13) Recs. and Delibs. Cabildo, Vol. III, 5/25/1792 - 4/17/1795, Barcenas trans. 1936, 75, 82, 149; Leonardo Mazange, NP, 5/7/1781; Private Claims, Baton Rouge, La. 267, 269, 278; Duff-Green Vol. 2, Claim 126 to Daniel Clark, p 267; Act of Felix de Armas, NP, 9/24/1834.
14) Favrot, Mortimer, Colonial Forts of La., LHQ 26 (Jul. 1943) 746-8; T-P Guide 1913, 51; Carlos Trudeau Map 12/24/1798 for location of forts; Fortier II, 152; Castellanos, N. O. As It Was..316, 17; Scrapbook I, La. and N. O., Meigs Frost 4/21/1940, 375, NOPL; Villiers' Last Yrs..616.
15) Despatches of Spanish Governors of La., Book VIII 4/20/1792 - 7/31/1793, WPA Translations 1937-8, and Statement of Expense Bundle 412-417, LSML.
16) Cabildo Records Translated, Bundle 1442, Letter #387, Book III Despatches of Spanish Governors of La., Carondelet, 3/11/1793 - 8/30/1793, WPA Survey 1937-8, and Statement of Expense Bundle 1442, Letter #389, pps 352-355, LSML.
17) Despatches of Spanish Governors of La., WPA translations 1937, 1938, 1940, Book XI, 8/6/1794-6/9/1796, Bundle 2354, No. 129, 11/24/1794, pps 283-5; First District Court #13025, N. Lavergne vs. S. Elkin, filed 10/14/1837, in CDC #110,666; Favrot, Colonial Forts of La., LHQ 26, (Jul. 1943) 749.
18) Tinker, Edward Larocque, Creole City Its Past and Its People, Longmans, Green & Co., N. Y. 1953, 158; Kendall, John S., Early N. O. Newspapers, LHQ 10 (Jul. 1927) 385; King, N. O. The Place and the People, 147; Sidelights on La. History from Papers of the La. Bicentennial Celebration of N. O., LHQ I (Jan. 1917) 215.
19) Villiers' Last Yrs..622; Wilson, St. Louis Cemeteries of N. O., St. Louis Cathedral, 1963, 9; Wilson, Sam, The Cabildo on Jackson Square, 21-22; Coleman, Maxent, 110-5; Despatches of Spanish Governors of La., Vol. XX, Book 4, 21, WPA translations 1937, 1938, 1940, Survey of Federal Archives in La. LSML; Ibid, Book V, Oct. 1794 - Nov. 1795, 413; LSSC #227 Heirs of Maxent vs. J. Morel Chappilon and Clotilde Celeste (wife) 6/16/1817; LSSC #2442, Execs. of I. Laroche St. Maxent vs. Laurent Sigur and J. B. Labatut, Syndics of Creditors of St. Maxent, Judgment 3/2/1811; Synopsis of History of La., Soniat du Fossat, small history at La. Dept., NOPL.
20) Recs. and Delibs. of Cabildo, Vol. III #3, 5/25/1792 - 4/17/1795, pps 152, 306, 1934 WPA translations.
21) LSSC #18211, State of La. vs. CC&N. Co., Judgment in rehearing, CDC 6/30/1911; Fortier II, 154; Gayarré III, 331; LSSC, Orleans Navigation Co. vs. Mayor, 2 Martin O. S., 10, Fall 1811; Recs. and Delibs. Cabildo, Vol. III 5/25/1792 - 4/17/1795, Barcenas translation 1936, 11/6/1795, 59; LSSC #18211, State of La. vs. Carondelet Canal & Navigation Co., Application for rehearing by defendants, filed 4/16/1919.
22) Chambers, 374; Gayarré III, 331, 351-2; Wood, Life in N. O., Spanish Period, LHQ 22 (Jul. 1939) 674-76; Rand, Clayton, Scrapbook 5, 144, NOPL; LSSC Orleans Nav. Co. vs. Mayor, OS, Spring 1811, 269; Orleans Nav. Co. vs. Mayor et al, 2 Martin OS, 10, Fall, 1811; Orleans Nav. Co. vs. Mayor, 2 Martin OS, 214; LSSC #2296 Appeal from Fifth District Court of N. O. and #3921 Fifth District Court of N. O., State of La. vs. Orleans Nav. Co. 5/2/1851; U. S. Circuit Court #13244 Geo. G. Wheelock et al vs. St. Louis and San Francisco R. R., filed 12/6/1909; LSSC #18211 (appeal from #89, 798 CDC) State of La. vs. CC&N Co. and Liquidators, filed 4/16/1910; Cabildo Book IV #1, 145.

CHAPTER XXV

1) Villiers' Last Yrs..622; Fortier II, 164, 173; Chambers, 370-2' A Decree for La. Issued By the Baron

Carondelet, 6/1/1795, LHQ 20 (Jul. 1937) 590; Wood, Life in N. O., Spanish Period, LHQ 22 (Jul. 1939) 697; Gayarré III, 350-1, 354-5.

2) Ibid, 347, 376; Fortier, II, 161, 165, 208; Dufour, Ten Flags..120; Chambers, 376-7; Villiers' Last Yrs..623; Moody, V. Alton, Slavery on La. Sugar Plantations, LHQ 7 (Jan. 1924) 198-9; Proctor, Samuel, Jewish Life in N. O. 1718-1860, LHQ 40 (Apr. 1957) 110-15; Wood, Life in N. O., Spanish Period, LHQ 22 (Jul. 1939) 668; Bunner History of La., 162; Fossier, Albert E., N. O. The Glamour Period, Pel. Pub. Co., N. O. 1957; Sugar Cane - Its Cultivation in La., The N. O. Times, 8/27/1865, p8 c1; Pitot, James, Observation Sur La Colonie de la Louisiane de 1796 - 1802, James Pitot trans. and edited by Henry C. Pitot, 76-78, N. O. Historic Collections, N. O., La.

3) Villier's Last Yrs..622-3; Chambers, 369, 378; Wood, Life in N. O. Spanish Period, LHQ 22 (Jul. 1939) 666-7; Prichard, The Romance of Research in La. History, LHQ 20 (Jul. 1937) 561; Taylor, Joe, La. A Student's Guide to Localized History, 7; King, N. O., The Place and the People, 369, 378.

4) Recs. and Delibs. of the Cabildo, Book 4, Vol. I, 4/24/1795-7/7/1797, Baume trans. 1936, 59, 71, 158; Louisiana Gazette 8/27/1810; Resolutions and Ordinances Conseil de Ville, Vol. I, 181-5; Meeting of the Council, Conseil de Ville Proceedings, Book II, #2, 80-2, Resolution 7/12/1809; Lafargue, André, Pierre Clement de Laussat, Colonial Prefect and High Commissioner of France in Louisiana, LHQ 20 (Jan. 1937), 176.

5) Kernion, Geo. C. H. Reminiscenses of the Chevalier Bernard de Verges, An Early Colonial Engineer of La., LHQ 7 (Jan. 1924) 75-76; King, Creole Families of N. O., The MacMillan Co., N. O., 1921, 61, 65; Chambers I, 395, Moody, V. Alton, Slavery on La. Sugar Plantations, LHQ 7 (Apr. 1924) 192.

6) LSSC #44 Mayor, Aldermen et al vs. J. B. Bermudez, Syndic of Frances Bermudez, filed 5/18/1812, Map for location of wax manufactory.

7) Chambers, 368, 394-5; Fortier II, 165; Gayarré III, 374-5; Fossier, History of Yellow Fever in N. O. LHQ 34 (Jul. 1951) 206; Waring, Cable, History and Present Conditions of N. O., 1881; New Orleans Book, Orleans School Board 1919, 20; Wood, N. O. During the Spanish Period, LHQ 22 (Jul. 1939) 679, 697; LSSC Orleans Navigation Co. vs. Mayor, 2 Martin OS, 214; Pitot, H. C., James Pitot, Observations on La., N. O. Historic Collections, 67; Hester, Helen E., If They Had Their Way We'd Be A Ghost Town, Dixie, T-P, 3/19/1978, 20.

8) Pitot, James, 1761-1831, A Documentary Study by Henry Clement Pitot, Bocage Books, N. O. 1968, 20-37; File Archives Santo Domingo 2643, Sevilla, Spain, quoted in letter to author by Archives Director Rosario Parra 12/9/1968; LSSC #3759, Sate of La. vs. N. O. Navigation Co., 11/13/1821, from book at Tulane, Rare Books Dept., State of La. vs. Carondelet Canal and Navigation Co. (976.31 (626) C293, pps 148-64, re bar formation, J. L. Gubernator, lessee of Bayou St. John and Carondelet Canal 1861; 4th Justice Court #4539, Parish of Orleans, testimony 5/11/1877, in Supreme Court Case #6668; Lighthouses and Lightships of the Northern Gulf of Mexico, Dept. of Transportation, U. S. Coast Guard, 26.

9) Orleans Nav. Co. vs. Mayor et al, 2 Martin OS, Fall 1811, p 10; U. S. Supreme Court #78, Carondelet Canal and Nav. Co. vs. State of La., Term 1913; #13025 First District Court (in CDC Case #110,666,) N. Lavergne vs. S. Elkin Heirs, filed 10/14/1837; 1st Judicial District Ct. #3759, State of La. vs. Orleans Navigation Co., 11/1/1821.

10) Chambers, 363; Fortier II, 165.

11) Recs. and Delibs. Cabildo, 4/24/1795 - 7/7/1797, 1936 Baume translations, Book 4, Vol. I, 199, 204-5, 207-8, 211; Pierre Clement de Laussat, Colonial Prefect and High Commissioner of France in La., His Memoirs, Proclamations, and Orders by André Lafargue, LHQ 20 (Jan. 1937) 176; Recs. and Delibs. Cabildo, Book 4, Vol. I, Baume translation 1936, 6, 62, 93, 97.

12) Soniat, Meloncy C., Faubourgs Forming the Upper Section of the City of N. O., LHQ 20 (Jan. 1937) 193; Holmes, Jack D. L., Louisiana, The Spanish Years, Lecture of Friends of the Cabildo, in Friends of the Cabildo News Letter, Dec. 1969; Fortier II, 170 gives date os 8/1/1797; LHQ 20 (Jan. 1937) 176.

13) Pitot, James, Observations on Louisiana, 1796-1802, translated by Henry C. Pitot, fn. 12, p 6, 55-6, N. O. Historic Collections, N. O.; Trudeau Map of N. O. and Environs, 1798, for location of Canal; LSSC #1744, Heirs of DuBreuil Villars vs. T. M. Kennedy, et al, 1850, for date of transaction; Cruzat, J. W., Biographical notes on Family of Phillipe de Mandeville compiled for Historical Society, LHS V, 1911, 445; Hart, W. O., New Orleans, LHQ I (Apr. 1918) 364; CR, File 99, Doc. 3906, 5/24/1800, LSML; LSSC #47, John B. Labatut, Syndic of St. Maxent's Estate vs. Laurent Sigur, 5/23/1814, case begun in Superior Court for Terr. of Orleans 6/3/1810; Chase, John information given EBF 7/14/79; King, Grace, Old Families of New Orleans, 19.

14) O'Connor, Stella, Charity Hospital of La. at N. O., LHQ 31 (Jan. 1948) 27; King, N. O. The Place and the People, 132; Fortier II, 188; Chambers I, 347; 250 Years in New Orleans, Friends of the Cabildo, 1968, 25; Records and Deliberations of the Cabildo, Vol. IV #2, 7/14/1797 - 12/20/1798, Jos. Barcenas trans. 1937, 183.

15) Gayarré II, 397; Fortier II, 172; Villiers' Last Yrs..625; Thompson, T. P., Early Financing in New Orleans being the story of the Canal Bank 1831-1915, LHSP VII, 1913-14, p 14-15; LHQ 31 (Apr. 1948) 310.
16) Wood, Minter, Life in N. O. Spanish Period, 172, LHQ 22 (Jul. 1939) 675.
17) History of Medicine in La., Vol. I, Duffy, Copyright 1958, Rudolph Matas Trust Fund, 259-65; Recs. and Delibs. Cabildo, Vol. 4, No. 4, 9/19/1800 - 7/17/1802, WPA trans. 1938, 2, NOPL.
18) Ibid., Vol. 4 #3, 1/1/1799-9/12/1800, barcenas trans. 1937, 4, 61, 128, 100; N. O. City Guide, 299; King, N. O. The Place and The People, 147; Notarial Act, NP Narcissus Broutin, 2/13/1805; Record of Land Office for Terr. of Orleans 2/28/1806, in Book I, folios 413, 421, 422, 423, 425, LSSC Library; Duff-Green Vol. 2 (1812), 103, 268; LSSC #20818, Leader Realty Co. vs. N. O. Land Co. and Lakeview Land Co., filed 5/14/1914, Inventory of Alexander Milne in this case - Plan A Milne No. 3; Record Book, Private Claims, Land Office, Baton Rouge, La. 249, 301; Arena, C. Richard, Landholding and Political Power, LHQ 38, 1955, 37.
19) Holmes, Jack D. L., Louisiana The Spanish Years 1762 - 1803, Lecture of Friends of the Cabildo, Cabildo News, December 1769.

CHAPTER XXVI

1) Pintado Papers, Book II, No. 10, Plan 1380 3/31/1800, 97-8; Ibid., Map and Act of Trudeau's Survey of Vidal Concession and purchase from Louis Blanc; Act Pierre Pedesclaux 7/24/1804, #2023, 10/30/1821. Sale Relf-Chew Executors of Daniel Clark to E. Blanc, with map, Notarial Archives, N. O.; Duff-Green II, 1/9/1812, Item 126 p 267; Felix de Armas, Act No. 58, Sale of land E. Blanc to Corporation of N. O., 9/26/1834.
2) Act, NP Pedro Pedesclaux 5/28/1800, 357, 8/18/1800, 508; Private Claims, Baton Rouge, La., 249, 301-3; Jacobs, Howard, Pitot House, Dixie T-P 6/14/1970, 12; Pintado Papers II, No. 10, Plan of Survey No. 1444, 8/6/1800, 163, LSML.
3) Act of NP Pedro Pedesclaux 8/20/1800, 509, file of Bayou St. John Properties, LSML; Plan of Carlos Trudeau 1800, showing Fernandez and Reynes Properties, attached to Act of Marc Lafitte 9/28/1819, 343; Pintado Papers, Book II. No. 10, Plan 1433, p 177, LSML; Kmen, Music in New Orleans, 8-9, 46-7; Dufour, T-P 3/23/1969, s2, p4; Advertisement, Le Courrier de la Louisiane, 3/8/1828, City Hall Archives, BSJ File, LSML; Record of Tissot House, LSML file on BSJ properties; COB 98/83, 7/30/1870, Conveyance Office, N. O.
4) NP Garic, 4/8/1778, 161, sale Pelagie Brazillier to Gilberto Maxent; Trudeau Map and Survey Report No. 1434, 7/16/1800, Pintado Papers II, No. 10, 152-4, LSML; Private Claims, Baton Rouge, La. 286-289; Plan of Marigny Plantation in LSSC #1744 Heirs of DuBreuil Villars vs. T. M. Kennedy, et als, 1850; Trudeau Plan and Survey 1469, 5/5/1801, Pintado Papers III, C, No. 3, p 16, LSML.
5) Pintado Papers, Book III, C No. 3, Register 6, Plan 1472 5/18/1801, Ibid, Trudeau Map and report, J. Laurent to M. Lopez 3/30/1801, p 11, LSML; Trudeau Survey Report #1435, 11/26/1800, Pintado Papers, Book II, No. 10, p 177, Jacques Laurent to J. Reynes, LSML; Act, NP P. Pedesclaux, 4/10/1801, James B. Lorreins to Manuel Lopez, Private Claims, Baton Rouge, La. 249.
6) Borrador - Del Plano, de la Ciudad de Nueva Orleans y de las - habitaciones del contorno formado de ord en de L. L. Don Juan Bentura Morales Intendente gri e la provincia de la Luisiana, 1 Marzo 1802, Carlos Trudeau, LSML; same properties shown on a map apparently copied by V. Pintado, Havana 23 de Noviembre 1819 (Map-LOC); Plan 1374, Register E No. 2, Pintado Papers, Book II, 91; Ibid., Plan 1375, 92; Ibid, Plan 1384, 1800, 102; Plan 1373, 3/1/1800, p 90, LSML; Private Claims, Baton Rouge, La. 259, 271, 273-80.
7) Pintado Papers, Book II, No. 10, Plan 1375, p 92; Ibid., Book III, C, No. 3, Plan 1470, p 17-18, Ibid., 5/7/1801, p 19-20, LSML.
8) Robin, C. C., Voyage to La. pps 12-19; Louis Declouet's Memorial to the Spanish Gov't 12/7/1814, edited by Stanley Faye, LHQ 22, 1939, p 795; Roane, Arthur, 1790 U. S. Indian Pact "Authentic", T-P 1/8/1976, s1 p1; Gayarré III, 315-322; Villiers' Last Yrs..694; Fortier II, 151, Martin's, 306.
9) Recs. and Delibs. Cabildo, Book IV, Vol. 4, Barcenas translation, 1938 WPA translation, 92, 99, 147, 158.
10) Prichard, Walter, The Romance of Research in La. History, LHQ 20 (Jul. 1937) 561; Villiers' Last Yrs..634-9; Chambers, 398-404; Fortier II, 206; Gayarrę III, 445.
11) Letter of General Barran to Cabildo of N. O. Complaining of Sanitary Conditions in 1800, 1/24/1800, translated by Laura Porteous, LHQ 15, (Oct. 1932) 612-15.
12) Santo Domingo File 2617, Archivo General de Indias, Sevilla, Spain, letter to author 12/9/1968 from Rosario Para, Director.
13) First Judicial Court #3759, State of La. vs. Orleans Navigation Co. 11/13/1821.

14) C. Richard Arena, Landholding and Political Power in Spanish Louisiana (Morales and Land Laws of 7/17/1799), LHQ 38, (Oct. 1955) 36 - 37; Prichard, Walter, The Romance of Research in Louisiana History, LHQ 20 (Jul. 1937) 561-2; Chambers 405-6.
15) Rader, Perry Cott, The Romance of American Courts Gaines vs. New Orleans, LHQ 27 (Jan. 1944) 8-315; Kendall, John S., The Strange Case of Myra Clark Gaines, LHQ 20 (Jan. 1937) 5-42; LSSC #5789 Rhoda E. White vs. Myra Clark Gaines, filed 5/4/1875; E. P. Gaines and Wife vs. Chew, Relf, et al, Term 1844, 2 Howard (43 U.S.) 619-641; C. Patterson vs. E. P. Gaines, Jan. Term, 1848, 6 Howard (47 U. S.) 55-603; Myra C. Gaines vs. Richard Relf and B. Chew, Dec. Term 1851, 12 Howard (53 U.S.) 472-545; Myra Clark Gaines vs. Duncan N. Hennen, Dec. Term 1860, 24 Howard (65 U.S.) 533-624; Gaines vs. New Orleans, December, 1867, 6 Wallace (73 U.S.) 642-684; N. O. vs. Gaines, Dec. 1872, 15 Wallace (82 U.S.) 624-627; N. O. vs. Gaines Administrator, Oct. Term, 1888, 131 (U. S. 191) argued 10/13-14/1887, decided 5/13/1889, 192-216; N. O. vs. Gaines Administrator - Gaines's Adminstrator vs. New Orleans, appeals from Circuit Court of U. S. for Eastern District of La., argued 1/15-16/1891, decided 3/2/1891. This suit commenced in 1879 to recover fruits and revenues of 135 arpents of land on Bayou St. John, from 1837.
16) Villiers' Last Yrs..540-651; Pitot, James, Observations on La., trans. H. C. Pitot, 53, Historic Collections, N. O.; Fortier II, 180; Chambers, 401-404.
17) Prichard, Walter, Selecting a Governor for Orleans, LHQ 31 (Apr. 1948) 310-11, Chambers, 406; Observations on La., 1796-1802, James Pitot, trans. Henry C. Pitot, Historic N. O. Collections, N. O., Preface ii 25, 35, 65, 73, 112-113; Martin's, 318; LHQ 16, 1933, 221.
18) The Journal of Dr. Sibley, Jul.-Oct. 1802, LHQ 10 (Oct. 1927) 478-481; Fortier II, 219; Telephone conversation, author with Mrs. Robert E. Barbee, 9/20/1968 (she died 12/26/1970); Arrowsmith Map 1831, and Zimpel Map 1834, for location of Hebecourt property, west bank, Bayou St. John; Chambers, 422-7; Villiers' Last Yrs..670, 677; Robin, Voyage to La., 35, 61; Chambers, 424-8; Villiers' Last Yrs..554, 695, 716.
19) Fortier II, 219; Telephone conversation with Mrs. Robert E. Barbee 9/20/1968 - she died 12/26/1970; Robin 35, 61; Chambers 422-8; Villiers' Last Years..554, 670, 677, 695, 716.
20) Recs. and Delibs. Cabildo, Book V 7/19/1802 - 11/18/1803, WPA trans. 1935, p 41, 73, 86; Council Meetings, Vol. I, Bk. I, 11/30/1803 - 3/29/1805, City Archives, 1936, NOPL, 84, 87-90, 93, 206, 267.
21) Villiers' Last Yrs..734; Favrot, H. Mortimer, Colonial Forts of La., LHQ 26 (Jul. 1943) 747.
22) Dufour, Ten Flags..130; U. S. Statutes at Large, 8 Congress, I Sessions 283-89, LSSC Library, N. O.; Chambers, 420-1; Villiers' Last Yrs..662-6.
23) Prichard, Walter, Romance of Research in La. History, LHQ 20, (Jul. 1937) 562; Chambers, 430-32; King, N. O., The Place and the People, 159.

CHAPTER XXVII

1) King, N. O., The Place and the People, 159; Chambers, 430-2; Conseil de Ville Proceedings of Council Meetings, WPA 1936 Book I, #1, Nov. 30-1803 to 3/29/1805, 11/30/1803, p 6-7, City Archives, NOPL.
2) Lafargue, André, Pierre Clement de Laussat, LHQ 20 (Jan. 1937) 176.
3) Waring, Cable, Ancient New Orleans, 5; re bar formation see testimony J. L. Gubernator, lessee of Bayou St. John and Carondelet Canal in 1861, from Fourth Justice Court #4539, Parish of Orleans, 5/11/1877, in LSSC #6668; information to author from A. L. Willoz, Chief Engr. and Secretary of the N. O. Levee Board, 1976; Chambers, 374, State vs. Orleans Navigation Co., 11 Martin O.S. 54, 1822. Robin, C. C., Voyage to Louisiana, 25-31; Lighthouses and Lightships of the Northern Gulf of Mexico, Dept. of Transportation, U. S. Coast Guard, 1976, 26.
4) Information in files at Milne Boys' Home, Franklin Avenue, N. O., 7/12/1971.
5) State of La. vs. Orleans Navigation Co., March 1822, Appeal from Court of First District, 11 Martin O.S. 54; information about L'Isle Bienville, Bayou Bienville and Devil's Elbow from witnesses: J. H. D'Hemecourt, Louis W. Pilie and John L. Gubernator in Fourth Justice Court #4539, Carondelet Canal and Navigation Co. vs. Narcisse Parker, May 1877, 29 A 430; Lafon Map 1805, Act 57, NP Michel de Armas V 18, 10/1/1819, and U. S. Survey Map of Sulakowski, 1873, State Land Office, Baton Rouge, La., shows Bayou Bienville coming into middle of curve east of Park Island. Surveyor Pilie in #4539 testifies that the correct name of "Devil's Elbow" is Isle de Bienville; map of Carondelet Canal and Bayou St. John, attached to report of 10/31/1853 in LSSC #5094, Orleans Navigation Co., vs. Widow Wm. Bowman 12/31/1857, and map accompanying report of Maurice Harrison, Engineer, 10/23/1849, Boston Library, for location of Devil's Elbow; Except for specific references, the status of the bayou in 1803 is from testimony in Law Case #3759, First Judicial District Court, State of La. vs. Orleans Navigation Co. 11/13/1821. The testimony of these witnesses is summarized and repeated in

brief form in Law Case #18211, State of La. vs. Carondelet Canal and Navigation Co., La. Supreme Court, 6/25/1910. Witnesses testifying in 1821 were: Jose Pycharaca, native Catalonian, and inhabitant of Louisiana for forty years, keeper of the bridge on Bayou St. John, 1821, and former pilot for Spanish King on bayou and lakes, and continuing into American times, as pilot. Vincent Rilleux and his father M. V. Rilleux, both operators of two vessels on Bayou St. John, son only in 1821; Alexis Rochou, free man of color, employed on Schooner Bonnabel for thirteen months during this period; Alexander Milne; Pierre Baam, commander of schooner on Bayou during Spanish times; Paul Lanusse, resident of Bayou St. John since 1796, in 1805 employee of Orleans Navigation Co. to sound Canal and bayou for depth; Louis Blanc, resident of country since 1788, resident of Bayou St. John and operator of schooner; Juan Luis Allard's son, Louis Allard, returned to Bayou from French schooling about 1798; Guillaume Benoit, resident for forty years (before 1821), commanded vessel on bayou during Spanish times for six years; Joseph Ravassa, in employ of Navigation Co. in 1821, native of Louisiana, and well acquainted with navigation of bayou for past twenty-three years; J. H. Holland, well acquainted with navigation of bayou and canal since 1802.

6) #13025 (In CDC CASE #110666) N. Lavergne vs. S. Elkin Heirs, filed 10/14/1837, testimony of witnesses; Witnesses D'Hemecourt, Pilie, Hardee, Civil Engrs. and Surveyors, Case #4539, Fourth Justice Court, 5/11/1877, in LSSC #6668, Carondelet Canal and Navigation Co vs. Narcisse Parker, May 1877 (29 A 430).

7) Robin, Voyage to La., 25-31; Act, Pedro Pedesclaux, NP; Property #73 (Almonester) confirmed to Allard 5/3/1835, Act of Congress 5/3/1835, American State Papers, Public Land Vol. 6, p 669; same page #82, Tarascon arpents; Maumsell White's Visit to New Orleans, August, 1801; History and Present Conditions of N. O., Waring, Cable 1881, 239; State vs. Orleans Nav. Co., March 1822, II, Martin O.S. 55, appeal from First District Court; Conseil de Ville, Proceedings of Council Meetings, City Archives, WPA 1936 trans., 1/28/1804, 29, City Archives, NOPL.

8) Robin, Voyage to La., 30; Maumsell White's Visit to N. O. 1801; History and Present Conditions of N. O. Waring, Cable, 1881, 239; Conseil de Ville Proceedings of Council, Vol. I, #1, Sessions 6/13 and 6/16/1804, 113, 116; Ibid, 113-116; First Judicial Court #3759, State of La. vs. Orleans Navigation Co., 11/13/1821.

9) Robin, Voyage to La., 31-32; The Political Situation in N. O. at the Close of the Last and Beginning of the present Year, LHQ 11 (Jan.-Oct. 1928) fn. p378; Wood, N. O. In Spanish Period LHQ 22 (Jul. 1939) 643, 645-6, 642; Pitot, James, Observations on La., N. O. Historic Collections, 105.

10) Robin, Voyage to La., 32, 36, 53, 97, 109-110; Wood, Minter, Life in N. O. Spanish Period, LHQ 22 (Jul. 1939), 655-58, 673, 667-8; Fortier II, 208, 301; Sibley's Journal, LHQ 10 (Oct. 1927) 478.

11) Wood, Minter, Life in N. O. Spanish Period, LHQ 22, (Jul. 1939) 650-2, 657, 684-5, 688-92; McCutcheon, Roger P., Books and Booksellers in N. O., LHQ 20 (Jul. 1937) 606; Robin, Voyage to La. 656-7; Sibley's Journal, LHQ 10 (Oct. 1927) 478; Kendall, Shadow Over The City, LHQ 22 (Jan. 1939) 142, Latrobe's remarks; Pitot, James, Observations on Louisiana, trans. by Henry C. Pitot, 36-37, N. O. Historic Collections.

12) Robin, Voyage to La., 27, 37, 54; Wood, Life in N. O. Spanish Period, LHQ 22 (Jul. 1939), 670-1; Sibley's Journal, LHQ 10 (Oct. 1927) 480.

13) Thompson, Ray, Oliver Pollock, N. O. Magazine, Dec, 1972, 48-62; Chambers, 304-5; John Chase, The Centennial's Invisible Man, Dixie T-P 12/14/1975, 10-11.

14) Norvell, Lillian S., Spanish Fort Retrospective, T-P 6/25/1911, s3, p14; King, N. O. The Place and the People, 159; Robin, Voyage to La., 65; Chambers, 401 shows territory gained, 433-4, 533; Fortier II, 288, 292.

SELECTED BIBLIOGRAPHY

ARTICLES

A Statement of Companies of Infantry Maintained by the Co. of the Indies in the Province of Louisiana in the month of May, 1724, and the situation of the settlers in each post., LHQ 12 (Jan. 1929) 119-127.

Albrecht, Andrew C., The Origin and Settlement of Baton Rouge, LHQ 28 (Jan. 1945) 5-68.

Arena, C. Richard, Landholding and Political Power in Spanish Louisiana, LHQ 38, (Oct. 1955) 23-29.

Banet's Report To The Co. of the Indies, 1724, LHQ 12 (Jan. 1929) 119-127.

Bienville's Will, LHQ 1 (Jan. 1918) 52-53.

Briede, Kathryn C., A History of the City of Lafayette, LHQ 20 (Oct. 1937), 895-964.

Bullard, Henry Adams, Discourse by President of Louisiana Historical Society 1/13/1836, LHQ 19 (Jan. 1936) 21-42.

Burns, Francis P., Notes on the Legislature and Litigation of St. Louis Cathedral, LHQ 18 (Apr. 1935) 363-376.

Calendar of Original Documents Concerning History in Louisiana, Louisiana Historical Society Publications, Vol. IV, 1908 (New York 1969) 6.

Caughey, John, Willing's Expedition Down the Mississippi, 1778, LHQ 15 (Jan. 1932), 5-36.

Collot, General, Reconnoitering Trip Down the Mississippi, and his Arrest in New Orleans in 1796 by order of the Baron de Carondelet, Governor of Louisiana, LHQ 1 (Jan. 1918) 303-329.

Comeau, Brother Alfonso, A Study of the Trustee Problem St. Louis Cathedral, LHQ 31, (Oct. 1948) 896-971.

Cruzat, Heloise Hulse, Allotment of Building Sites in New Orleans 1722, LHQ 7 (Oct. 1924) 564-566.

Cruzat, Heloise Hulse, A Savage Law of the French Regime in Louisiana 11/23/1765, LHQ 15 (July 1932) 482-485.

Cruzat, Heloise Hulse, Documents Concerning Bienville's Land, LHQ 10 (Jan. 1927) 5-24, LHQ 11 (Jul. 1928) 463-466.

Cruzat, Heloise Hulse, French Political Procedures in Louisiana for Appointment of Tutors to Minors 1735, LHQ 8 (April 1925) 218-220.

Cruzat, Heloise Hulse, The Concession at Natchez, LHQ 8 (July 1925) 389-397.

Cruzat, Heloise Hulse, New Orleans Under Bienville, LHQ 1 (Jan. 1918) 52-86.

Cruzat, J.W., Biographical and Genealogical Notes Concerning the Family of Philippe de Mandeville Ecuyer Sieur de Marigny, 1709-1910, Louisiana Historical Society Publication (LHSP) Vol. V, 1911, AMS Press, New York, N.Y., 1969, 42-53.

Dart, Albert LaPlace, Ship Lists of Passengers Leaving France for Louisiana 1718-1724, LHQ 15 (July 1932) 453-467.

Dart, William Kernan, The Edict of 12/15/1721 Providing for the Appointment of Dual Tutors to Minors in France and In Her Colonies, LHQ 10 (Oct. 1927) 533-538.

Dart, Henry P., A Criminal Trial Before the Superior Council, (translations by H.H. Cruzat), LHQ 13 (July 1930) 363-392.

Dart, Henry P., Bienville's Claim Against The Company of the Indies for Back Salary, etc. 1737, LHQ 9 (April 1926) 210-220.

Dart, Henry P., Courts and Laws in Colonial Louisiana, LHQ 4 (July 1921) 255-287.

Dart, Henry P., Imprisonment for Debt in Louisiana, LHQ 8 (Oct. 1925) 549-556.

Dart, Henry P., Politics in Louisiana in 1724, LHQ 5 (July 1922) 298-315.

Dart, Henry P., The Career of DuBreuil in Louisiana, LHQ 18 (April 1935) 267-331.

Dart, Henry P., The First Cargo of African Slaves, LHQ 14 (April 1931) 163-177.

Dart, Henry P., The Slave Depot of the Co. of the Indies at New Orleans, LHQ 9 (Apr. 1926) 286.

Dart, Sally, A Lawsuit Over the right to sell the Office of Notary in Louisiana During The French Regime, 1769, LHQ 16 (Oct. 1933) 587-595.

Dart, Sally, Instructions to Perrier, Chief engineer of Louisiana 4/14/1718 French Incertitude in 1718 As to the Site of New Orleans, LHQ 15 (Jan. 1932) 37-43.

Dart, Sally and Edith Dart Price, The Jamaica Pirates and Louisiana Commerce, 1739, LHQ 16, (April 1933) 209-220.

DeLanglez, Rev. John, S. J., The Natchez Massacre and Governor Périer, LHQ 17 (Oct. 1934) 631-641.

Devron, Dr. Gustave, A Chapter of Colonial History, LHQ 6 (Oct. 1923) 543-565.

Ditchy, Jay K., Translation of Diron D'Artaguette's Census of 1721, LHQ 13 (Jan. 1930) 203-222.

Elder, Mrs. S.B., Bienville's Difficulties in the Founding of New Orleans, Louisiana Historical Society Publications, Vol. VIII, 1914-15 (New York 1969) 40-47.

Favrot, H. M., Colonial Forts of Louisiana, LHQ 26 (July 1943) 722-754.
Faye, Stanley, Louis Declouet's Memorial to the Spanish Government 12/7/1814, LHQ 22, (Jul. 1939), 795-818.
Faye, Stanley, The Arkansas Post of Louisiana, French Domination, LHQ 26 (Jul. 1943) 633-721.
Faye, Stanley, The Arkansas Post of Louisiana, Spanish Domination, LHQ 27 (Jul. 1944), 629-716
Fischer, Dr. Ann., Anthropology Dept., Tulane University, The Houmas T-P Magazine Section, 1/4/1970, 7-9.
Fossier, A.E., M.D., History of Yellow Fever in New Orleans, LHQ 34 (Jul. 1951) 205-215.
Gayarré, Charles, Historical Notes On the Commerce and Agriculture of Louisiana, 1720-1766, LHQ 2 (July 1919) 286-291.
Green, John A., Governor Périer's Expedition Against the Natchez Indians LHQ 19, (July 1936) 547-577.
Hart, W.O., New Orleans, LHQ 1 (April 1918) 353-366.
Hearsay, Clem C., The Vengeance of the Natchez, LHQ 12 (April 1929) 266-287.
Howard, C.N., The Interval of Military Government in West Florida, LHQ 22 (Jan. 1939) 18-30.
Humble, Sallie Lacy, Ouachita Valley Expedition, LHQ 25 (July 1942) 607-643.
Jefferson Parish, Dixie (T-P) 2/2/1975, 11.
Kendall, John S., Early New Orleans Newspapers, LHQ 10 (Jul. 1927) 383-401.
Kendall, John S., Old New Orleans Houses, LHQ 17 (Oct. 1934) 680-705.
Kendall, John S., The Pontalba Buildings, LHQ 19 (Jan, 1936) 119-149.
Kendall, John S., New Orleans' Peculiar Institution, LHQ 23 (July 1940) 864-886.
Kendall, John S., Shadow Over The City, LHQ 22 (Jan. 1939) 142-165.
Kendall, John S., The Huntsmen of Black Ivory, LHQ 24 (Jan. 1941) 9-34.
Kernion, George H., The Chevalier de Pradel, LHQ 12 (Apr. 1929) 238-254.
Kernion, George C.H., Reminiscences of Chevalier Bernard de Verges, LHQ 7 (Jan. 1924) 56-86.
King, Grace, Notes on the Life and Services of Bienville, LHQ 1 (Jan. 1918) 39-49.
Lafargue, André, The Louisiana Purchase, LHQ 23 (Jan. 1940) 107-117.
Lafargue, André, Pierre Clement de Laussat, Colonial Prefect and High Commissioner of France in Louisiana, His Memoirs, Proclamations and Orders, LHQ 20 (Jan. 1937), 159-182.

Ledet, William P., History of Carrollton, LHQ 21 (Jan. 1938) 220-281.

Liljegren, Ernest R., Jacobinism in Spanish Louisiana, 1792-1797, LHQ 22 (Jan. 1939) 47-97.

Linn, Alan, The New World's Secret Weapon, The Smithsonian, (July, 1973) 60-61.

Loughlin, James J., The Black Code, Louisiana Historical Society Publications, Vol. VIII (New York 1969) 28-35.

McCutcheon, Roger P., Books and Booksellers in New Orleans, 1730-1830, LHQ 20 (Jul. 1937) 606-618.

Moody, V. Alton, Slavery on Louisiana Sugar Plantations, LHQ 7 (Jan. 1924) 191-301.

Noble, Stuart G. and Arthur G. Nuhrah, Yale University, Education in Colonial Louisiana, LHQ 32 (Oct. 1949) 759-776.

O'Brien, Rev. J.J., Expulsion of the Society of Jesus from Colonial Louisiana, Louisiana Historical Society Publications, Vol. IX, 1916 (New York 1969) 9-23.

O'Connor, Stella, The Charity Hospital of Louisiana, LHQ 4 (Oct. 1921) 361-368, LHQ 31 (Jan. 1948) 5-109.

Padgett, James A., Bernardo de Galvez's Seige of Pensacola in 1781, from the Journal of Robert Farmar, LHQ 26 (Apr. 1943) 307-329.

Padgett, James A., Governor Peter Chester's Observations on the Boundaries of British West Florida about 1775, LHQ 26 (Jan. 1943) 5-11.

Porteous, Laura, Inventory of the Prevost Estate, LHQ 9 (Jul. 1926) 411-498.

Porteous, Laura, Sanitary Conditions in New Orleans Under the Spanish Regime, 1799-1800, LHQ 15 (Oct. 1932) 610-617.

Porteous, Laura, The Gri-Gri Case, A Criminal Trial in Louisiana During The Spanish Regime, LHQ 17 (Jan. 1934) 48-63.

Post, Lauren C., The Domestic Animals and Plants of French Louisiana As Mentioned In The Literature With Reference to Sources, Varieties and Uses, LHQ 16 (Oct. 1933) 554-586.

Price, William, Indexing Louisiana's Black Boxes, Louisiana Historical Society Publications. VIII, 1914-1915 (New York 1969) 7-20.

Prichard, Walter, Romance of Research in Louisiana History, LHQ 20 (July 1937) 557-558.

Prichard, Walter, Selecting a Governor for the Territory of Orleans, LHQ 31 (April 1948) 269-393.

Proctor, Samuel, Jewish Life in New Orleans 1718-1860, LHQ 40 (April 1957) 110-132.

Read, William A., More Indian Place Names in Louisiana, LHQ 11 (July 1928) 445-460.

Read, William A., Istrouma, LHQ 14 (Oct.1931) 503-15.
Ries, The Mississippi Fort called Fort de la Boulaye 1700-1715, LHQ 19 (Oct. 1936) 829-889.
Riley, Martin Luther, The Development of Education in Louisiana prior to Statehood, LHQ 19 (July 1936) 595-634.
Sanders, Albert Godfrey, Documents Concerning the Crozat Regime in Louisiana 1712-1717, LHQ 15 (Oct. 1932) 589-609.
Schmidt, Gustavus (trans.) O'Reilly's Ordinance of 1770 Concerning Grants of Land in Louisiana to New Settlers, LHQ 11 (Apr. 1928) 237-240.
Scramuzza, V. M., Galveztown, A Spanish Settlement of Colonial Louisiana, LHQ 13 (Oct. 1930) 553-609.
Sibley, Dr. John (of Natchitoches), The Sibley Papers, Journals and Letters, LHQ 10, (Oct. 1927) 467-512.
Sidelights of Louisiana History from Papers of Bicentennial Celebration of New Orleans, LHQ 1 (Jan. 1918) 87-153.
Soniat, Charles T., The Title to the Jesuits' Plantation, Louisiana Historical Society Publications, Vol. V. 1911 (New York 1969) 5-30.
Soniat, Meloncy C., Faubourgs Forming the Upper Section of the City of New Orleans, LHQ 20 (Jan. 1937) 192-211.
Surrey, N.M. Miller, Ph.D., Columbia University, critique by Grace King, The Commerce of Louisiana During The French Regime 1699-1763 LHQ 5(Jan. 1922) 19-33.
Thomas, Alfred B., Spanish Activities in the Lower Mississippi Valley 1513-1698, LHQ 22 (Oct. 1939) 932-42.
Thompson, Sue, Article on Cooking, New Orleans Magazine (Oct. 1972) 71.
Thompson, T.P., Early Financing in New Orleans, being the Story of the Canal Bank, 1831-1915, Louisiana Historical Society Publication Vol. VII, 1913-14, AMS Press New York, N.Y., 1969, 11-61.
Vogel, Claude L. (Dart's Editor's Chair), Capuchins in French Louisiana 1722-1766, LHQ 11 (Oct. 1928) 620-23.
Wilson, Samuel, An Architectural History of the Royal Hospital and the Ursuline Convent of New Orleans, LHQ 29, (July 1946) 555-659.
Wood, Minter, Life In New Orleans in the Spanish Period, LHQ 22 (Jul. 1939) 642-709.

CORRESPONDENCE, MAGAZINES, NEWSPAPERS, PAMPHLETS, SCRAPBOOKS

Bezou, Henry C., Times Picayune 11/25/1973, s3, p7.

Chase, John, The Centennial's Invisible Man, Dixie, T-P 12/14/1975, 10-11.
Corbin, Carl, T-P 1/23/1938, s2, columns 1-8.
Courrier 5/17/1847, p1, c4.
Dabney, Thomas Ewing, Times Picayune Sunday Magazine "And Broadmoor Was A Lake", 8/18/1935, p8.
Dixon, Richard, Broadmoor, New Orleans, 1975, p5.
Dufour, Charles L., Kuntz Collection, Tulane University New Orleans, T-P 2/19/1967.
Dufour, Charles, Times Picayune, 4/9/1967, p8.
Dufour, Charles, Times Picayune, 12/3/1967, s3 p12.
Dufour, Charles, Times Picayune, 1/21/1968, s3 p2.
Dufour, Charles, Times Picayune, 1/28/1968, s3 p11.
Dufour, Charles, Times Picayune, 2/18/1968, s2 p7.
Dufour, Charles, Times Picayune, 3/31/1968, s3 p8.
Dufour, Charles, Times Picayune, 10/27/1968, s3 p6.
Dufour, Charles, Times Picayune, 1/5/1969.
Dufour, Charles, Times Picayune, 10/25/1970, s3 p15.
Dufour, Charles, Times Picayune, 2/27/1972, p4.
Dufour, Charles, Times Picayune, 11/26/1972, s2 p8.
Dufour, Charles, Times Picayune, 2/27/1973, s3 p4.
Dufour, Charles, 250 Years in New Orleans, New Orleans, La. 1968
Frost, Meigs, Scrapbook I, Louisiana and New Orleans, 4/21/1940, NOPL.
Giraud, Marcel, Paris, France, letter to Author 12/17/1968.
Giraud, Marcel, Times-Picayune, 6/3/1968, s1 p23.
Hester, Helen, E., If They Had Their Way We'd Be a Ghost Town, Dixie, T-P 3/19/1978, 20.
History of Santo Domingo, Daily Picayune 1/15/1871, cl, p2.
Houmas House, Historic Homes, Houses, 1800-1840, 1875.
Hyde, Gordon B., New Orleans Insurance Rates, New Orleans, 1965.
Jackson, Wesley, Religion in Louisiana, A History, T-P 5/27/1973, s2 p7.
Jacobs, Howard, Pitot House, Dixie T-P 6/14/1970, 11-14.
Kane, Harnett, Item Tribune 7/18/1937.
Lafargue, Andre, Scrapbook I, New Orleans Public Library, 12/11/1927, p147.
Life Magazine, 9/18/1970.
Norvell, Lillian S., Spanish Fort Retrospective, T-P 6/25/1911, s3, p14.
Old Fort Proves Spanish Military Engineers' Skill, T-P 7/6/1934, p3,c1.
Quayle, Jennifer, Iberville Returns, Times Picayune, Magazine Section 3/31/1974 p20.

Rand, Clayton, Scrapbook 5, New Orleans Public Library, pps 117-118, 144.
Rankin, Dr. Hugh F., and Irby, W.R., Tulane Educational Conference, T-P 3/14/1976, s1, p48.
Roane, Arthur, 1790 U.S. Indian Pact Authentic, T-P 1/8/1976, s1 p1.
Sugarcane—Its Cultivation in Louisiana, The New Orleans Times, 8/27/1865, p8, c1.
Thompson, Ray, Oliver Pollock, New Orleans Magazine, December 1972, 48-62.
Times Picayune Editorial, 2/29/1968, s1, p12.
Times Picayune Flashback, 10/20/1968, s2, p3.
Times Picayune 11/3/1968, s4, p17.
Times Picayune 11/21/1971.
Times Picayune 1/13/1974, s5, p17.

DIGESTS, DIRECTORIES, GUIDES AND CONTEMHORARY HISTORIES

Bezou, Henry C., Metairie, Gretna, Louisiana, 1973.
Bunner, E., History of Louisiana, New York 1842.
Cable, George W., The Creoles of Louisiana, New York 1910.
Chambers, Henry E., History of Louisiana, Chicago and New York, 1925.
Chase, John, Frenchmen, Desire, Good Children, New Orleans, 1960.
Coleman, James Julian, Gilbert Antoine de St. Maxent, New Orleans, Louisiana, 1968.
Coleman, Will H., Historical Sketch Book and Guide to New Orleans and Environs, New York, 1885.
Dufour, Charles, Ten Flags In The Wind, New York 1967.
DuPratz, M. LePage, The History of Louisiana, Baton Rouge, 1972.
Fortier, Alcée, Cyclopedic History, A-K, Vol. I, Madison, Wisconsin, 1914.
Fortier, Alcée, History of Louisiana, I & II, New York, 1904.
Fortier, Alcée, Louisiana Studies, New Orleans, 1894.
Fossier, Dr. Albert E., The Glamour Period 1800-1840, New Orleans, 1957.
Friends of the Cabildo, 250th Anniversary of New Orleans, 1968.
Gayarré, Charles Étienne, History of Louisiana, Volume I, New Orleans, 1885; Volumes I, II, III, New Orleans, 1903.
Giraud, Marcel, Histoire De La Louisiane Francaise 1698-1715, Paris,1953.
King, Grace, Creole Families of New Orleans, New York, 1921.

King, Grace, New Orleans, The Place and The People, New York, 1895.
King, Grace, Sieur de Bienville, New York, 1892.
Martin, Francois Xavier, History of Louisiana, New Orleans, 1882.
Orleans School Board, the New Orleans Book. 1919.
Penicaut, Andre, Annals of Louisiana From The Establishment of the First Colony Under M. d'Iberville to the Departure of the Author to France in 1722. (New York 1875), B.F. French translation.
Penicaut, Andre, Fleur de Lys and Calumet, McWilliams Translation, Baton Rouge, 1953.
Historical Sketch and Guide to New Orleans, New Orleans Press, 1884.
New Orleans City Guide, WPA Project, Cambridge, Mass., 1938.
Roberts, W. Adolphe, Lake Pontchartrain, Indianapolis, 1946.
Rowland, Dunbar, History of Mississippi II, Jackson, Mississippi 1912.
Rowland, Dunbar and Albert G. Sanders, Mississippi Provincial Archives, 3 volumes, Jackson, Mississippi, 1927-1932.
Times-Picayune Guide to New Orleans, 1908.
Tinker, Edward L., Creole City, Its Past and Its People, New York, 1953.
Villiers Du Terrage, Marc De, Last Years of French Louisiana, typewritten copy, translated by Henri Delville de Sinclair, WPA, New Orleans 1937-1938, Tulane University, New Orleans, La.
Villiers Du Terrage, Marc De, A History of the Foundation of New Orleans, translation by Warrington Dawson, Louisiana Historical Quarterly III, (Apr. 1920) 158-251.

LAW CASES

Arrowsmith, John vs. City of New Orleans, April 1867, October 1868, Louisiana State Supreme Court #2529, 24 Lou Ann 194-198.
Arrowsmith, John vs. E.H. Durrell and N.O. Canal and Navigation Co., filed 11/7/1855, Louisiana State Supreme Court #4241, Third District Court #6030.
Board of Directors Public Schools, City of New Orleans vs. N.O. Land Co., Reasons for Judgement, filed 11/16/1914, Civil District Court #92,795.
Brott vs. N.O. Land Co., La. Supreme Court #22950, 2/27/1922, 151 La. Reports 134-142 Civil District Court #85,758, 1908.
Canal Bank et al vs. Copeland, Louisiana Supreme Court, 6 La. Reports 543-554, May 1834
Carondelet Canal and Navigation Co. vs. Narcisse Parker, Fourth Justice Court #4539 and La. Supreme Ct. #6668, 29 A 430, May 1877.

Carondelet Canal and Navigation Co. vs. State of Louisiana, U.S. Supreme Court #78, Term 1913.

Castera Heirs vs. New Orleans Land Co., Civil District Court #17,697, 11/16/1909.

City of New Orleans vs. Carrollton Land Co., 131 La. Reports, 1091-1102.

Directors of Public Schools, Parish of Orleans vs. New Orleans Land Co., La. Sup. Ct. #21069 filed 4/12/1915, 138 La. Reports 32-59.

DuBreuil Villars, Heirs of, vs. T.M. Kennedy, et al, Louisiana Supreme Court #1744, filed 11/7/1850.

Gaines, E.P. and wife vs. Chew, Relf, et al, 2 Howard (43 U.S.) Term 1844, 619-641.

Gaines Myra Clark vs. Duncan N. Hennen, 24 Howard (65 U.S.), Dec. term 1860, 553-624.

Gaines vs. New Orleans, 6 Wallace (73 U.S.), December 1867, 642-684.

Gaines, Myra C. vs. Richard Relf and B. Chew, 12 Howard (53 U.S.), Dec. term 1851, 472-545.

Labatut, John B., Syndic of St. Maxent's estate, vs. Laurent Sigur, La. Sup. Ct. #47, 5/23/1814 (case begun in Superior Court for Terr. of Orleans 6/3/1810.)

Laforest, A.A. vs. D.N. Downing, La. Sup. Ct. #34, filed 1/31/1861.

Lavergne, N. vs. Elkins, S., Civil District Court #110,666, filed 10/14/1837, appeal from #13025 First District Court.

Lavergne, Heirs of, vs. City of New Orleans, La. Sup. Ct. #3278, filed 9/18/1977.

Lavergne Heirs vs. Elkin Heirs, 17 La. 220, March, 1841.

Lavergne, Jean, and wife, Succession of, Civil District Court #8630 filed 5/17/1883.

Leader Realty Co. vs. Lakeview Land Co. and N.O. Land Co., Louisiana Supreme Court #20818 filed 5/14/1914, 142 La. 169, from Civil District Court #91799 and #91800, filed 5/13/1912.

Louisiana, State of, vs. Carondelet Canal and Navigation Co., La. Sup. Ct. #18211, filed 4/16/1910, judgement in rehearing from Civil District Court #89,798, 6/30/1911; application for rehearing filed 4/16/1919.

Louisiana, State of, vs. New Orleans Land Co., La. Sup. Ct. #22740, 5/27/1918, 143 La. Reports, 858-874.

Louisiana, State of, vs. New Orleans Navigation Co., First Judicial Court #3759, filed 11/13/1821, 11 Martin OS 38, 54, March 1822.

Louisiana, State of, vs. Orleans Navigation Co., La. Sup. Ct. #2296, 5/2/1851.

Maxent, I. Laroche, executors of, vs. Laurent Sigur and J.B. Labatut, Syndics of Creditors of St. Maxent, La. Supreme Court #2442, judgement 3/2/1811.

Maxent, heirs of, vs. J. Morel Chappilon and Clotilde Celeste (wife), La. Sup. Ct. #227, 6/16/1817.

Mayor, Adermen, et al vs. J.B. Bermudez, Syndic of Frances Bermudez, La. Supreme Court #44, filed 5/18/1812.

Milne vs. Labo, Louisiana Supreme Court #821, filed 4/7/1823.

Milne, Alexander, Succession of, Civil District Court #35904, Box 113-13 of papers relating to case.

New Orleans vs. Gaines, 15 Wallace (82 U.S.), Dec. 1872, 624-27.

New Orleans vs. Gaines Administrator, 131 U.S. 191, October Term, 1888, argued 10/13-14/1887, decided 5/13/1889, 192-216.

New Orleans vs. Gaines Administrator; Gaines Administrator vs. New Orleans, appeals from Circuit Court of U.S. for Eastern District of La., argued 1/15-16/1891, decided 3/2/1891, (commenced in 1879).

Orleans Navigation Co. vs. Mayor, 2 Martin OS 10, Spring 1811.

Orleans Navigation Co. vs. Mayor, 2 Martin OS, Fall 1811.

Patterson, C. vs. E. P. Gaines, 6 Howard (47 U.S.), Jan. Term 1848, 55-603.

Pontalba, et al vs. Copeland, 3 Lou Ann 86, 1846.

Richardson vs. Liberty Oil Co., 143 La. Report 138, Jan.-Apr., 1918.

Wheelock, George G. et al vs. St. Louis and San Francisco Railroad, U.S. Circuit Court #13244 filed 12/6/1909.

White, Rhoda E., vs. Myra Clark Gaines, La. Sup. Court #5789, filed 5/4/1875.

MAPS

Ancient Map, Exhibit D-1, State Vs. Carondelet Canal & Navigation Co., filed 4/9/1910, CDC #89798.

Andry, Luis—Survey of Kernion Properties, 1771, Private Claims, New Orleans, (Baton Rouge, La.).

Bell, S.C., 6/16/1902, New Orleans Land Co. vs. Levee Board Commissioners, filed 5/31/1930, LSSC #23518.

Bermudez, Frances, wax-manufactory, Louisiana Supreme Court Case #44, Mayor, Aldermen, et al vs. J.B. Bermudez, filed 5/18/1812.

Calonge, S.A., Sons, Civil Engineers and Surveyors, New Orleans, Registered with State Land Office 1/12/1924, for location of tracts west bank Bayou St. John, as decided by courts after a series of cases regarding this area.

Carte De La Louisiane, 1767, in Fortier II, 76.

Carondelet and Bayou St. John Canal, property of N.O. Canal and Navigation Co., included with report dated 10/31/1853, in Orleans Navigation CO. vs. Widow William Bowman, 12/31/1857, LSSC #5094.

Chapitoulas Area Chart, showing land-owners, Private Claims. Baton Rouge, La., 245.

Course of the Mississippi from Bayougoulas to the Sea, (Map 4), early 1700s, LHQ 19 (Oct.1936) 879.

Dabney, Thomas Ewing, compilation map of branches of Bayou St. John, Times Picayune Magazine Section, 8/18/1935, 8.

D'Anville's Carte de la Louisiane, May 1732, Louisiana Historical Quarterly 19, (Oct. 1936) 879.

De La Nouvelle Orleans Ville Capitalle De Louisiane Et Ses Environs, ca 1730, Library of Congress Map Division, Alexandria, Virginia.

De La Nouvelle Orleans Au Mississippi, ca 1723, Louisiana State Museum Library, N.O.

De La Tour, 1720, New Orleans Public Library, Louisiana Department.

DuMont de Montigny, Map of Bayou St. Jean, 1723, MaM 721/5, New Orleans Public Library, Louisiana Dept.

De Woiserie, J.L. Bouqueta, Plan of New Orleans, 1803, 2nd Floor Cabildo, New Orleans.

Galvez, by order of, Plan du Lac Ponchartrain, 1778, National Archives, Washington, D.C.

Grandjean, Geo. H., 2/14/1883, Roussell vs. N.O. Railway and Light Co., 1922, LSSC #23518.

Harrison, Maurice, City Engineer, Map of City and environs of New Orleans, under Supervision of Commissioners of General Assembly of Louisiana, 3/10/1845, (National Archives, Washington, D.C.)

Harrison, Maurice, City Engineer, Map of Bayou St. John accompanying his report of 10/23/1849 (Map, Boston Library).

King, B.M., 1728—CXXII 98, Library of Congress Map division, Alexandria, Virginia.

Labo Residences, mouth of Bayou St. John 6/17/1805, La. Supreme Court, Milne vs. Labo #821, filed 4/7/1823.

Lafon, B., Map of Bayou St. John 6/17/1805, attached to Act 57, Vol. 18 NP Michel de Armas, 10/1/1819.

Leper Hospital, site of, 1833, La. Supreme Court #707, Mme. de Pontalba vs. Mayor of New Orleans, filed 12/20/1847.

Marigny, Pedro de, Plan de la plantacion, 1795, 1798, 1800, in La. Sup. Court #1744, Heirs of DuBreuil Villars vs. T.M. Kennedy, filed 11/7/1850.

Melish, John, Map of New Orleans and Adjacent Country, 1815, Library of Congress, Map Division, Alexandria, Virginia.

McAlester, Bvt. Brig. General M.D., Major of Engrs., Lake Pontchartrain and Mississippi Connections, 1/10/1868, National Archives, Washington, D.C.

Mouléon Grant, John Arrowsmith vs. E.H. Durrell and N.O. Canal and Navigation Co., filed 11/7/1855, LSSC #4241, from #6030 Third District Court.

Pilie, Louis H., Deputy Surveyor First Municipality, "Plan Showing the DuBreuil, The Brewery, Darby's and Coustillas Concessions, 11/9/1847," Library of Congress Map Division, Alexandria, Virginia. (Referred to as Gentilly Concessions Plan.)

Pilie, Louis H., and Grandjean, George H.—Map of Louis C. LeBreton Grants of 10/6/1757 and 2/15/1764, surveyed by above 6/2 to 7/5/1884, according to instructions of 3/24 and 4/17/1884, Office of Surveyor General, District of Louisiana, New Orleans. (Levee Board, New Orleans.)

Pilie, Edgar, 1/2/1895, Bayou St. John area, "in accordance with L. Bringier Plan annexed to plan of Milne partition," NP Chiapella 8/29/1845.

Pintado, V., New Orleans, map apparently copied from that of Carlos Trudeau 3/1/1802, 11/23/1819 Library of Congress, Alexandria, Va.

Sauve's Crevasse, 1849, Louisiana State Museum Library, New Orleans, La.

Segher's Map 4/24/1905, of lower Bayou St. John.

Sulakowski, U.S. Survey Map, Bayou St. John area, 1873, State Land Office, Baton Rouge, La.

Sulakowski, S.E. District, La., Exhibit D-2, 1871-2, Exhibit D-2 in Civil District Court, State of Louisiana vs. Carondelet Canal and Navigation Company, filed 7/18/1911.

Trudeau, Carlos, Borrador—Del Plano de la Ciudad de Nueve Orleans y de y de las habitaciones del contorno, formado de or den de L.L. Don Juan Bentura Morales Intendente gri de la provencia de la Luisiana, 1 Marzo 1802.

Trudeau, Carlos, Early properties on Bayou St. John, and Mrs. Brazillier's land east of Bayou Gentilly, 1800, Land Office, Baton Rouge, La.

Trudeau, Carlos, Plano de la Ciudad, de Nueve Orleans, 24 Diciembre, 1798, LSML.

Trudeau, Carlos, New Orleans and Environs 12/24/1798, reproduced in Martin's History of La., 1882 edition, p 402.

Trudeau, Carlos, Map #1480 of Toulouse Street-St. Peter Cemetery, Pintado Papers, III, 29, Louisiana State Museum Library.

Trudeau, Carlos, survey map of Properties of Santo Bautista Lawrence Properties, (State Land Office, Baton Rouge.) 7/16/1800.

U.S. Engineers Reconnoitering Chart of the South Frontier of the United States of America, 1817, (National Archives, Washington, D.C.)

Zacharie, James S., Map of New Orleans, in Guide of Zacharie, Census of 1880, 1885, Louisiana State Museum Library.

Zimpel, Charles, New Orleans, 1834, Library of Congress, Alexandria, Virginia.

MEMOIRS AND TRAVEL ACCOUNTS

Castellanos, Henry C., New Orleans As It Was (2nd Edition), New Orleans, La. 1905.

DuFossat, Guy Soniat, Synopsis of History of Louisiana From The Founding Of The Colony to 1791, translation from the French by Charles T. Soniat, Esq., New Orleans, La. 1903.

DuRu, Paul, Journal, February 1—May 8, 1700, Chicago, 1934.

Gordon, Harry, Extract From Journal of an Expedition Along the Ohio and Mississippi, 1766, Ottawa Archives, Louisiana Historical Quarterly 6, (Jan, 1923) 15.

Historical Collections of Louisiana, I—Memoirs of LaSalle, Tonty, Joutel and Father Hennepin, New York 1846.

Historical Collections of Louisiana, II, Memoirs of DeSoto, Coxe, Philadelphia 1850.

Historical Collections of Louisiana, III, Memoirs of de la Harpe and Charlevoix, New York, 1851.

Historical Collections of Louisiana, IV, Memoirs of Marquette, Allouez, Membré, Hennepin, Anastase Douay, New York 1852.

Historical Collections of Louisiana V, Memoirs of Dumont and Champigny, New York, 1853.

Historical Collections of Louisiana VII, New York, 1875.

Hutchins, Thomas, An Historical Narrative and Topographical Description of Louisiana and West Florida, Gainesville, Florida, 1968.

Robins, C.C. Voyage to Louisiana 1803-1805, translated by Stuart O. Landry, Jr., New Orleans, 1966.

MONOGRAPHS AND SPECIAL STUDIES

Arthur, Stanley Clisby, Old Families of Louisiana, Baton Rouge 1971.

Baudier, Roger, The Catholic Church in Louisiana, New Orleans, 1939.

Cable, George W. and George E. Waring, Jr., Ancient New Orleans, in Commercial Social and Medical Statistics of New Orleans, 8/23/1881, Washington, D.C. (Dept. of the Interior)

Costa, Myldred Masson, Translation of Letters of Marie-Madeleine Hachard Ursuline of New Orleans, New Orleans, 1974.

Deren, Maya, Divine Horsemen: The Voodoo Gods of Haiti, Chelsea House Publishers, New York, 1970.

DeVille, Winston, The New Orleans French Period 1720-1733, Baltimore, Maryland, 1973.

Duffy, John, The Rudolph Matas History of Medicine in Louisiana, Vol. I, edited by J. Duffy, published for the Rudolph Matas Trust Fund by LSU Press, 1958.

Kmen, Henry A., Music in New Orleans, The Formative Years, 1791-1841, LSU Press, Baton Rouge, La. 1966.

Lighthouses and Lightships of the Northern Gulf of Mexico, Dept. of Transportation, U.S. Coastguard, Photojournalist David L. Cipra, 1976.

Maduell, Charles R., Jr., The Census Tables For the French Colony of Louisiana, 1699-1732, Baltimore, Maryland, 1972.

Pitot, Henry Clement, James Pitot, 1761-1831, A Documentary Study, Bocage Books, New Orleans 1968.

Pitot, Henry C., James Pitot, Observation Sur La Colonie de la Louisiane de 1796-1802, translation, New Orleans Historic Collections, New Orleans, La.

Private Claims, New Orleans, An Act for the final adjustment of private claims in Florida, Louisiana and Missouri, Act of Congress 6/22/1860, Baton Rouge, La.

Samuel, Martha Ann Brett and Raymond Samuel, The Great Days of the Garden District and The Old City of Lafayette, New Orleans, 1961.

Seebold, Herman, Old Louisiana Plantations, Homes and Family Trees, II, New Orleans, 1941.

Some Data In Regard to Foundations In New Orleans and Vicinity, WPA 1937, New Orleans Public Library, Louisiana Department.

Taylor, J.G., A Students' Guide to Localized History, New York, 1966.

Villere, Sidney, Translation of Unpublished Documents, National Archives, Paris, Vol. I 1697-1721, Louisiana State Museum Library, New Orleans.

Wilson, Sam, Guide to Architecture of New Orleans, 1699-1957, New York, 1959.

Wilson, Sam, Ignace Broutin, Louisiana's First Architect, New Orleans 1969.

Wilson, Sam, St. Louis Cemeteries of New Orleans, St. Louis Cathedral, 1963.

Wilson, Sam, Spanish Fort Abandoned (unpublished), City Park Files, New Orleans, 1935.

Wilson, Sam, The Cabildo on Jackson Square, 1723-1803, Friends of the Cabildo, 1970.

SPECIAL

American State Papers, Duff-Green Edition, Vols. II, III and V, Washington, 1834, Louisiana Law Library, New Orleans, La.

American State Papers, Public Land Volume, VI, Washington, 1834, Louisiana Law Library, New Orleans, La.

American State Papers, Gales & Seaton, Volume I, Washington, 1834.

Armas, Felix de, Notary Public, Act #508, 9/24/1834, translation of Spanish Document, Notarial Archives, New Orleans, La.

Bayou St. John Properties, special file, Louisiana State Museum Library (LSML).

Cabildo Records (CR), 1769-1785, Louisiana State Museum Library, translations.

Conseil de Ville Proceedings, translations, Volumes I and II, 1803-1809, City Archives, New Orleans Public Library, Louisiana Section.

Council Records of the Municipality, translated Spanish documents 1770-1792, Cabildo Folio 30, Louisiana State Museum Library.

Despatches of Spanish Governors of Louisiana, 1766-1796, WPA translations 1937, 1938, 1939, Louisiana State Museum Library.

Document 73-An Act for the final adjustment of claims to lands in the southeastern Land District of Louisiana, Baton Rouge, La.

Garic, Juan B., Notarial Records, filmed at New Orleans by the Mormons 7/12/1968, New Orleans Public Library (NOPL).

Harrison, Maurice, Engineer, Report and Map, Bayou St. John, 10/23/1849, Boston Library, Boston, Massachusetts.

Holmes, Jack D.L., Louisiana The Spanish Years, Lecture to Friends of the Cabildo, reported in Newsletter, December, 1969.

Louisiana Historical Quarterly Publications (LHQ), Volumes I through XLIV, 1917-1961, New Orleans Public Library, Louisiana Section. Translations of Superior Council and Cabildo Records, 1723-1785 in these volumes.

Louisiana Historical Society Publications, Volumes I through IX, 1908-1916, AMS Press, New York, N.Y., 1969, New Orleans Public Library, Louisiana Section.

Milne, Alexander, will, 10/17/1836, Notary Public Carlile Pollock.

Milne Boy's Home, New Orleans, La., files as of 7/12/1971.

Papers from Cuba 112-Archives, Sevilla, Spain—in 12/9/1968 letter from Rosario Parra, Director to Edna B. Freiberg.

Pedesclaux, Pedro, Notary Public, records 3/31/1794—3/10/1798, Notarial Archives, New Orleans, La.

Pintado Papers, Books II and III, Louisiana State Museum Library, New Orleans, La.

Private Claims, Act of Congress 6/22/1860—An Act for the final adjustment of private land Claims in Florida, Louisiana and Missouri, Land Office, Baton Rouge, La.

Records and Deliberations of the Cabildo, Volumes I through V, 1769-1803,WPA translations, 1934-1938, New Orleans Public Library and Louisiana State Museum Library.

State of Louisiana vs. Carondelet Canal and Navigation Company, volume containing lawcases pertaining to Bayou St. John and Carondelet Canal, in Special Collections Department (formerly Rare Books Dept.), Tulane University, New Orleans, La.

Superior Council Records (SCR), 1723-1770, translated, Louisiana State Museum Library, New Orleans, La.

INDEX